Anatomy & Physiology
with Integrated Study Guide | Fifth Edition

Stanley E. Gunstream
Pasadena City College

Connect
Learn
Succeed™

ANATOMY & PHYSIOLOGY: WITH INTEGRATED STUDY GUIDE, FIFTH EDITION

Published by McGraw-Hill, a business unit of The McGraw-Hill Companies, Inc., 1221 Avenue of the Americas, New York, NY 10020. Copyright © 2013 by The McGraw-Hill Companies, Inc. All rights reserved. Printed in the United States of America. Previous editions © 2010, 2006, and 2000. No part of this publication may be reproduced or distributed in any form or by any means, or stored in a database or retrieval system, without the prior written consent of The McGraw-Hill Companies, Inc., including, but not limited to, in any network or other electronic storage or transmission, or broadcast for distance learning.

Some ancillaries, including electronic and print components, may not be available to customers outside the United States.

This book is printed on acid-free paper.

1 2 3 4 5 6 7 8 9 0 DOW/DOW 1 0 9 8 7 6 5 4 3 2

ISBN 978–0–07–337823–7
MHID 0–07–337823–2

Vice President & Editor-in-Chief: *Marty Lange*
Vice President, EDP: *Kimberly Meriwether David*
Senior Director of Development: *Kristine Tibbetts*
Publisher: *Michael S. Hackett*
Executive Editor: *Colin H. Wheatley*
Director of Digital Content Development: *Barbekka Hurtt, Ph.D.*
Developmental Editor: *Mandy C. Clark*
Marketing Manager: *Chris Loewenberg*
Senior Project Manager: *Jayne L. Klein*
Senior Buyer: *Sandy Ludovissy*
Lead Media Project Manager: *Judi David*
Manager, Creative Services: *Michelle D. Whitaker*
Cover Designer: *Studio Montage, St. Louis, Missouri*
Cover Image: *© John Lund/Drew Kelly/Blend Images LLC*
Senior Photo Research Coordinator: *John C. Leland*
Photo Research: *LouAnn K. Wilson*
Compositor: *S4Carlisle Publishing Services*
Typeface: *10/12 Melior*
Printer: *R. R. Donnelley*

Library of Congress Cataloging-in-Publication Data

Gunstream, Stanley E.
  Anatomy & physiology: with integrated study guide / Stanley E. Gunstream. — 5th ed.
    p. cm.
  Includes index.
  ISBN 978–0–07–337823–7 — ISBN 0–07–337823–2 (hard copy: alk. paper)
  1. Human physiology. 2. Human physiology—Study guides. 3. Human anatomy. 4. Human anatomy—Study guides. I. Title. II. Title: Anatomy and physiology.

QP34.5.G85   2013
612—dc23   2011030002

www.mhhe.com

CONTENTS

PART FOUR

Maintenance of the Body 223

■ CHAPTER ELEVEN

Blood 223

■ CHAPTER TWELVE

The Cardiovascular System 241

■ CHAPTER THIRTEEN

Lymphatic System and Defenses Against Disease 271

■ CHAPTER FOURTEEN

Respiratory System 289

PREFACE

Anatomy & Physiology with Integrated Study Guide, Fifth Edition, is designed for students who are enrolled in a one-semester course in human anatomy and physiology. The scope, organization, writing style, depth of presentation, and pedagogical aspects of the text have been tailored to meet the needs of students preparing for a career in one of the allied health professions.

These students usually have diverse backgrounds, including limited exposure to biology and chemistry, and this presents a formidable challenge to the instructor. To help meet this challenge, this text is written in clear, concise English and simplifies the complexities of anatomy and physiology in ways that enhance understanding without diluting the essential subject matter.

Themes

There are two unifying themes in this presentation of normal human anatomy and physiology: (1) the relationships between structure and function of body parts, and (2) the mechanisms of homeostasis. In addition, interrelationships of the organ systems are noted where appropriate and useful.

Organization

The sequence of chapters progresses from simple to complex. The simple-to-complex progression also is used within each chapter. Chapters covering an organ system begin with anatomy to ensure that students are well prepared to understand the physiology that follows. Each chapter concludes with a brief consideration of common disorders that the student may encounter in the clinical setting. An integrated study guide, unique among anatomy and physiology texts, is located between the text proper and the appendices.

Study Guide

The *Study Guide* is a proven mechanism for enhancing learning by students and features full-color line art. There is a study guide of four to eight pages for each chapter. Students demonstrate their understanding of the chapter by labeling diagrams and answering completion, matching, and true/false questions.

The completion questions "force" students to write and spell correctly the technical terms that they must know. Each chapter study guide concludes with a few critical-thinking, short-answer essay questions where students apply their knowledge to clinical situations.

Answers to the *Study Guide* are included in the *Instructor's Manual* to allow the instructor flexibility: (1) answers may be posted so students can check their own responses, or (2) they may be graded to assess student progress. Either way, prompt feedback to students is most effective in maximizing learning.

Other Learning Aids

A variety of additional learning aids are incorporated to facilitate the learning process and to stimulate interest in the subject.

Chapter Preview and Learning Objectives

Each chapter begins with a list of major topics discussed in the chapter, and under each topic the learning objectives are noted. This informs students of the major topics to be covered and their minimal learning responsibilities.

Key Terms

Several features have been incorporated to assist students in learning the necessary technical terms that often are troublesome for beginning students.

1. A list of *Selected Key Terms* with definitions, and including derivations where helpful, is provided at the beginning of the chapter to inform students of some of the key terms to watch for in the chapter.
2. Throughout the text, key terms are in bold or italic type for easy recognition, and they are defined at the time of first usage. A *phonetic pronunciation* follows where students need help in pronouncing the term. Experience has shown that students learn only terms that they can pronounce.
3. *Keys to Medical Terminology* in appendix A explains how technical terms are structured and provides a list of prefixes, suffixes, and root words to further aid an understanding of medical terminology.

4. At the end of each chapter, a section titled *Building My Vocabulary* provides a list of *Selected New Terms* that allows students to review their understanding of the new terms. Also, a few *Related Clinical Terms* are defined with phonetic pronunciations to help students to start building a clinical vocabulary.

Figures and Tables

Over 350 high quality, full-color illustrations are coordinated with the text to help students visualize anatomical features and physiological concepts. Tables are used throughout to summarize information in a way that is more easily learned by students.

Clinical Insight

Numerous boxes containing related clinical information are strategically placed throughout the text. They serve to provide interesting and useful information related to the topic at hand. The clinical boxes are identified by a *doctor's clipboard* for easy recognition.

Check My Understanding

Review questions at the end of major sections challenge students to assess their understanding before proceeding.

Chapter Summary

Each chapter summary consists of a numerical listing of key concepts for each major heading of the chapter. The summary provides a quick review of each chapter for the student.

Self-Review

A brief quiz, composed of completion questions, allows students to evaluate their understanding of chapter topics. Answers are provided in appendix B for immediate feedback.

Critical Thinking

Each chapter concludes with several critical thinking questions, which further challenge students to apply their understanding of key chapter topics.

Changes in the Fifth Edition

The fifth edition has been substantially improved to help beginning students understand the basics of human anatomy and physiology.

Chapter 1

New figure to replace old figure 1.4
New figure 1.12

Rewrite of A&P to emphasize structure/function relationships
Rewrite of Levels of Organization
Added umbilical region to table 1.2
Rewrite/organization of items 9-14 in Summary of Body Cavities
Study Guide: New text art with body regions to label; Answer changes for IM to match new figures

Chapter 2

Rewrite of Covalent Bonds
Rewrite of Hydrogen Bonds
Rewrite of Chemical Reactions
Rewrite of Enzymes
New figure to replace old figure 2.11
New Clinical Insight on prions

Chapter 3

Rewrite of Plasma Membrane
Rewrite of Protein Synthesis
New figure to replace old figure 3.19

Chapter 4

New introduction to include stem cells
Label addition to figure 4.13

Chapter 5

New coverage of hypothermia and hyperthermia
New figure to replace old figure 5.6

Chapter 6

Rewrite of Microscopic Structure
Rewrite of Endochondrial Ossification
Deleted ear ossicles from cranium bones in table 6.3 for simplicity
Rewrite to update osteoporosis
Proximal and distal articular cartilages labels added to figure 6.1
Epiphyseal disc replaced by epiphyseal plate in figure 6.4
Axial and appendicular skeletons distinguished by color in figure 6.5
Redrawn segments of figure 6.32 to correctly illustrate inversion/eversion and projection

Chapter 7

New table 7.2: Microscopic Anatomy of a Skeletal Muscle Fiber
Rewrite Mechanics of Contraction
Rewrite Energy for Contraction
New Clinical Insight (Curare)
New figure 7.3 showing T tubule system and sarcoplasmic reticulum

New Figure 7.6: Sliding filament model
New figure 7.7: Actin and myosin filaments in
  contraction
Study Guide: Rewrite items: 2(9), 2(10), and 3a

Chapter 8

New figure 8.1: Components of the nervous system
New figure 8.4: Structural types of neurons
New figure 8.6: Types of neuroglia cells (replaces "old"
  figure 8.4)
New table 8.1: Functional types of neurons
New paragraph on structural types of neurons
Rewrite of paragraph on Dendrites
Updated Study Guide for new material on structural
  types of neurons

Chapter 9

New table 9.1: Types of Sensory Receptors
New paragraph on Proprioceptors
New figure 9.10: Crista ampullaris
New figure 9.11: Dynamic equilibrium
New paragraph on neural pathway for taste sensations
Related changes in Study Guide and Instructor's Manual

Chapter 10

New figure 10.2: Action of a steroid hormone
New figure 10.3: Action of a nonsteroid hormone
New figure 10.5: Concentration of hormone in blood
New legend for figure 10.6 and label change to include
  release-inhibiting hormones
Label change for figure 10.11
Rewrite of intro to contrast endocrine and exocrine glands
Rewrite of Steroid and Nonsteroid Hormones
Rewrite of control of endocrine glands
Rewrite of Control of Posterior Lobe of Pituitary
Rewrite of Thyroxine and T_3 to include BMR
Rewrite of Calcitonin
New Clinical InSight on diabetes mellitus
Rewrite of Pineal Gland
Deleted box on melatonin
Rewrite of Thymus Gland

Chapter 11

New figure 11.1*a*
New figure 11.2: Erythrocytes
New figure 11.3: Negative-feedback loop corrects
  for a low O_2 concentration in blood
New figure 11.4: Formed elements development
New figures 11.5–11.9 Photomicrographs of white
  cells (with uniform coloring)
New Clinical Insight on sickle-cell disease with
  photograph
Rewrite of RBC production to emphasize role
  of O_2 concentration in blood

Rewrite of role of mast cells and histamine
Rewrite of role of monocytes/macrophages

Chapter 12

New figure 12.1: Cardiovascular system
New figure 12.3: The pericardium and heart wall
New figure 12.15: Fluid exchange
New figure 12.17: Pulse points
Rewrite of intro to included pulmonary and systemic
  circuits
Rewrite of Protective Coverings
New table 12.2: Heart valves
New Clinical Insight on mitral valve prolapsed (MVP)
Rewrite of Exchange of Materials

Chapter 13

New figure 13.7: The spleen
New Clinical Insight on edema
Rewrite of section on the spleen
New Clinical Insight on difference of bacterial and viral
  pathogens
Rewrite of paragraph on delayed immune reactions
Rewrite of section on autoimmune disease
Rewrite of paragraph on Hodgkin's lymphoma
New section on SCID

Chapter 14

New figure 14.8: Pleural membranes
New figure 14.12: Respiratory control centers
New figure 14.14: Gas exchange
Modification of figure 14.15 Transport of carbon dioxide
Rewrite of section on trachea
Rewrite of section on Control of Breathing
New intro to Factors Influencing Breathing
New inclusion of COPDs in Disorders of the
  Respiratory System
Rewrite in Study Guide of section on Control of Breathing

Chapter 15

New figure 15.10: Control of gastric secretion
New figure 15.11: Pancreas, liver, and duodenum
New figure 15.12: Control of pancreatic secretion
New figure 15.14: Control of bile secretion
Rewrite of swallowing reflex and peristalsis in esophagus
Rewrite of section on the pancreas
Rewrite to include IBDs and IBS in inflammatory
  disorders

Chapter 16

New figure 16.2: Internal kidney structure
New figure 16.5: Juxtaglomerular apparatus
New figure 16.8: Renin-angiotensin mechanism
Rewrite of Juxtaglomerular Apparatus

Rewrite of Glomerular Filtration
Rewrite of Renin-Angiotensin Mechanism

Chapter 17

New figure 17.3b: Spermatogenesis
New figure 17.4: Spermatogenesis
New figure 17.5a: Sperm structure
New figure 17.8: Oogenesis
New figure 17.14: Breast and mammary glands
New figure 17.15: Examples of birth control devices
   and chemicals
Rewrite of Spermatogenesis
Rewrite of Oogenesis
New section on Menopause

Chapter 18

New figure 18.2: Fertilization
New figure 18.6: Extraembryonic membranes
New figure 18.13: Postnatal circulation
Limited rewrite of Fertilization
Limited rewrite of Genes

Teaching and Learning Tools

McGraw-Hill ConnectPlus® Anatomy & Physiology

 www.mcgrawhillconnect.com

McGraw-Hill Connect® Anatomy & Physiology provides online presentation, assignment, and assessment solutions. It connects your students with the tools and resources they'll need to achieve success.

With Connect Anatomy & Physiology you can deliver assignments, quizzes, and tests online. A robust set of questions and activities are presented and aligned with the textbook's learning outcomes. As an instructor, you can edit existing questions and author entirely new problems. Track individual student performance—by question, assignment, or in relation to the class overall—with detailed grade reports. Integrate grade reports easily with Learning Management Systems (LMS), such as WebCT and Blackboard.

ConnectPlus Anatomy and Physiology provides students with all the advantages of Connect® Biology, plus 24/7 online access to an eBook. This media-rich version of the book is available through the McGraw-Hill Connect platform and allows seamless integration of text, media, and assessments.

McGraw-Hill LearnSmart™

 www.mhlearnsmart.com

McGraw-Hill LearnSmart™ is available as an integrated feature of McGraw-Hill Connect® Anatomy & Physiology and provides students with a GPS (**G**uided **P**ath to **S**uccess) for your course. Using artificial intelligence, LearnSmart intelligently assesses a student's knowledge of course content through a series of adaptive questions. It pinpoints concepts the student does not understand and maps out a personalized study plan for success. This innovative study tool also has features that allow instructors to see exactly what students have accomplished, and a built-in assessment tool for graded assignments. Visit the site below for a demonstration.

McGraw-Hill Anatomy & Physiology Revealed®

www.aprevealed.com

McGraw-Hill Anatomy & Physiology Revealed® is an interactive cadaver dissection tool to enhance lecture and lab, which students can use anytime, anywhere. Detailed cadaver photographs blended together with a state-of-the-art layering technique provide a uniquely interactive dissection experience. Anatomy & Physiology Revealed can now be customized to your course. Choose the specific structures that you require in your course and APR 3.0 does the rest. Once your list is generated, APR 3.0 highlights your selected structures for students.

McGraw-Hill Create™

www.mcgrawhillcreate.com

With McGraw-Hill Create™, **www.mcgrawhillcreate.com**, you can easily rearrange chapters, combine material from other content sources, and quickly upload content you have written like your course syllabus or teaching notes. Find the content you need in Create by searching through thousands of leading McGraw-Hill textbooks. Arrange your book to fit your teaching style. Create even allows you to personalize your book's appearance by selecting the cover and adding your name, school, and course information. Order a Create book and you'll receive a complimentary print review copy in 3–5 business days or a complimentary electronic review copy (eComp) via email in minutes. Go to **www.mcgrawhillcreate.com** today and register to experience how McGraw-Hill Create™ empowers you to teach your students your way.

My Lectures–McGraw-Hill Tegrity®

 www.tegrity.com

McGraw-Hill Tegrity® records and distributes your class lecture, with just a click of a button. Students can view anytime/anywhere via computer, iPod, or mobile device. It indexes as it records your PowerPoint®

presentations and anything shown on your computer so students can use keywords to find exactly what they want to study. Tegrity is available as an integrated feature of McGraw-Hill Connect® Anatomy and Physiology or as standalone.

Traditional Resources

As always, McGraw-Hill offers the following resources for instructors.

Laboratory Manual

Anatomy & Physiology Laboratory Textbook, Essentials Version, by Stanley E. Gunstream, Harold J. Benson, Arthur Talaro, and Kathleen Talaro, all of Pasadena City College. Kyla Ross of Georgia State University made significant contributions to the sixth edition of the laboratory manual. This excellent lab text presents the fundamentals of human anatomy and physiology in an easy-to-read manner that is appropriate for students in allied health programs. It is designed especially for the one-semester course; it features a simple, concise writing style, self directing exercises, full-color photomicrographs in the Histology Atlas, and numerous illustrations in each exercise.

Text Website

www.mhhe.com/gunstream5

The website for *Anatomy & Physiology,* Fifth Edition, offers a wealth of study aids for students, such as quizzes, study guides, web links, animations, etc., as well as teaching aids for instructors. Instructors will appreciate having password-protected access to all teaching resources online, such as lecture PowerPoints, instructor's manual, test banks for creating exams, illustrations/tables/art files for creating transparencies or handouts, and more.

Presentation Tools

Everything you need for outstanding presentations in one place!

- *Lecture PowerPoints with Animations*—animations illustrating important processes are embedded in the lecture material.
- *Animation PowerPoints*—animations only are provided in PowerPoint.
- *Labeled JPEG Images*—full-color digital files of all illustrations that can be readily incorporated into presentations, exams, or custom-made classroom materials.
- *Base Art Image Files*—unlabeled digital files of all illustrations.

Presentation Center

In addition to the images from your book, this online digital library contains photos, artwork, animations, and other media from an array of McGraw-Hill textbooks.

Computerized Test Bank

A comprehensive bank of test questions is provided within a computerized test bank powered by McGraw-Hill's flexible electronic testing program, EZ Test Online. A new tagging scheme allows you to sort questions by Bloom's difficulty level, learning outcome, topic, and section. With EZ Test Online, instructors can select questions from multiple McGraw-Hill test banks or author their own, and then either print the test for paper distribution or give it online.

Acknowledgments

The development and production of this fifth edition has been the result of a team effort. My dedicated and creative teammates at McGraw-Hill have contributed greatly to the finished product. I gratefully acknowledge and applaud their efforts. It has been a pleasure to work with these gifted professionals at each step of the process. I am especially appreciative of the support of Colin Wheatley, Executive Editor and Jayne Klein, Senior Project Manager.

The following instructors have served as critical reviewers:

Sharon Barnewall, *Columbus State Community College*
Patricia Bernard, *Erie Community College*
Karen Frederick, *Terra State Community College*
Eric Green, *Salt Lake Community College*
Greg Hartnett, *Sandford-Brown Institute*
Christopher Herzog, *Sandford-Brown Institute*
Dale Horeth, *Tidewater Community College*
Christopher Hubbard, *Northern Illinois University*
Karen Huffman-Kelly, *Eric Community College*
Beverly Kirk, *Northeast Mississippi Community College*
Alice Macomber, *Keiser University*
Erica Matthew, *Florida Career College*
Helen Mills, *Keiser University*
April Murphy, *Columbus Technical College*
Kerney Smoak, *Piedmont Technical College*
Frederick Eldon Stemple, Jr., *Tidewater Community College*
Mary Torrano, *American River College*
Benjamin Tran, *West Coast University*
Valencia Williams, *West Coast University*
Fadi Zaher, *Gateway Technical College*

Their suggestions have been very helpful, and I am grateful for their input.

I especially thank Margie for her patience and support.

S.E.G.

NOTE TO STUDENTS

You are starting a fascinating and challenging study of human anatomy and physiology. The course will be rigorous, but you can improve your chances of success by taking advantage of the learning aids found in this text. The suggestions noted below have been helpful to many students. Consider incorporating them into your study habits.

1. You can best profit from your instructor's lecture if you have prepared for it by studying the reading assignment *before* you attend the lecture. If you do this, you will know the new terms that will be encountered and at least the general aspects of the subject matter. This will enable you to better understand the lecture and take better lecture notes. It will save you study time later on.

2. Before you read a chapter, you need to do two things. First, examine the *Chapter Preview and Learning Objectives.* This will inform you of the sequence of major topics to be covered and your minimal learning responsibilities. Second, study the list of *Selected Key Terms* to learn their meanings. After you have done these two things, you will be prepared to learn effectively as you read the chapter.

3. As you read a chapter, watch for new terms and be sure to learn their pronunciation and meaning before going on. Use the *Glossary* and *Keys to Medical Terminology* (Appendix A) as necessary to assist you. Key terms are in bold or italic print so that you can easily recognize them. Where pronunciation help is needed, a *phonetic pronunciation* immediately follows in parentheses to help you pronounce the term correctly. Say the term out loud a few times to be sure that you know the correct pronunciation. This will help you remember the term.

   The phonetic pronunciation breaks terms into syllables and includes marks denoting long vowel sounds and major accents. Vowels marked with a line above the letter are pronounced with a long sound—the same sound as when saying the letter. Some examples follow:

   - ā as in take
   - ē as in be
   - ī as in time
   - ō as in hole

   Vowels without these marks are pronounced with short sounds as in the following examples:

   - a as in above
   - e as in pet
   - i as in hip
   - o as in pot
   - u as in mud

The accent mark indicates the major accent in the term, such as in terminology (ter-min-ol'-ō-jē) and anatomy (a-nat'-ō-mē).

You can best learn new terms and their meanings by preparing *flash cards* from 3 × 5 index cards. Place the term on one side and the definition on the other. *Place only one term on each card.*

4. Use a highlighter pen liberally to mark the key statements in each paragraph as you read. This will help you identify the key points to study later on. You may want to make flash cards to help you learn these key points.

5. Review questions are strategically located in the text to allow you to check your understanding of each major section. It is important to be able to answer these questions correctly before proceeding.

6. After reading the chapter, review the *Chapter Summary* to be sure that you understood the key points of the chapter. This section will give you a quick review of the chapter later on as well.

7. Learning new terms is one of the more difficult aspects of a course in anatomy and physiology. After reading a chapter, use *Building My Vocabulary* to help you master the terminology. Review the list of *Selected New Terms* to be sure that you know their meanings. If not, look them up in the chapter or in the glossary. Then learn the *Related Clinical Terms* to start building your clinical vocabulary.

8. After you think that you understand the topics pretty well, complete the *Study Guide* for the chapter you are studying (Study Guides appear in back of book starting on page 407.) It covers the major points of the chapter, and it includes a few critical thinking questions that apply your knowledge to clinical situations. Your instructor has the answer key so you can check your responses.

9. Complete the *Self-Review.* The answers to the questions are located in Appendix B for immediate feedback.

10. Finally, complete the *Critical Thinking* section, which will help you integrate and apply your understanding of the chapter topics.

If you have completed all of the above learning aids and have completely answered the questions correctly, you may be confident of your understanding.

CHAPTER 1

Introduction to the Human Body

Chapter Preview & Learning Objectives

Anatomy and Physiology
1. Define anatomy and physiology.

Levels of Organization
2. List and describe the levels of organization in the human body.
3. List the major organs and functions for each organ system.

Directional Terms
4. Use directional terms to describe the location of body parts.

Body Regions
5. Locate the major body regions on a chart or manikin.

Body Planes and Sections
6. Name and describe the four planes used in making sections of the body or body parts.

Body Cavities
7. Name the two major body cavities, their subdivisions and membranes, and locate them on a chart or manikin.
8. Name the organs located in each body cavity.

Abdominopelvic Subdivisions
9. Name the abdominopelvic quadrants and nine regions, locate them on a chart or manikin, and list the major internal organs found in each.

Maintenance of Life
10. Describe the general nature of metabolism.
11. List the five basic needs essential for human life.
12. Define homeostasis and explain its relationship to both normal body functions and disorders.
13. Describe the general mechanisms of negative feedback and positive feedback.

Chapter Summary
Building My Vocabulary
Self-Review
Critical Thinking

Anatomy & Physiology | **REVEALED®**
aprevealed.com

Module 1
Body Orientation

SELECTED KEY TERMS

Anatomy (ana = apart; tom = to cut) The study of the structure of living organisms.

Anterior (ante = before, in front of) The abdominal or ventral side of the body.

Appendicular (append = to hang) Pertaining to the extremities (arms and legs).

Axial (ax = axis) Pertaining to the longitudinal axis of the body.

Cephalic (cephal = head) Pertaining to the head.

Cervical (cervic = neck) Pertaining to the neck.

Homeostasis (homeo = same; sta = make stand or stop) Maintenance of a relatively stable internal environment.

Meninges (mening = membrane) Membranes covering the brain and spinal cord.

Metabolism (metabole = change) The sum of the chemical reactions in the body.

Parietal (paries = wall) Pertaining to the wall of a body cavity.

Pericardium (peri = around; cardi = heart) The membrane surrounding the heart.

Peritoneum (peri = around; ton = to stretch) The membrane lining the abdominal cavity and covering the abdominal organs.

Physiology (physio = nature; logy = study of) The study of the functioning of living organisms.

Pleura (pleura = rib) The membrane lining the thoracic cavity and covering the lungs.

Posterior (post = after, behind) The dorsal or backside of the body.

Visceral (viscus = internal organ) Pertaining to organs in a body cavity.

ou are beginning a fascinating and challenging study—the study of the human body. As you progress through this text, you will begin to understand the complexity of organization and function found in the human organism. Keep in mind that the goals of your study are to learn (1) how the body is structured and organized and (2) how the body functions.

This first chapter provides an overview of the human body to build a foundation of knowledge that is necessary for your continued study. Like the chapters that follow, this chapter introduces a number of new terms that must be learned. It is important that you start to build a vocabulary of technical terms and continue to develop it throughout your study.

1.1 Anatomy and Physiology

Knowledge of the human organism is obtained primarily from two scientific disciplines—anatomy and physiology—and each consists of a number of subdisciplines.

Human **anatomy** (ah-nat′-ō-mē) is the study of the structure and organization of the body and the study of the relationships of body parts to one another. There are two subdivisions of anatomy. *Gross anatomy* involves the dissection and examination of various parts of the body without magnifying lenses. *Microanatomy* consists of the microscopic examination of tissues and cells.

Human **physiology** (fiz-ē-ol′-ō-jē) is the study of the function of the body and its parts. Physiology involves observation and experimentation, and it usually requires the use of specialized equipment and materials.

In your study of the human body, you will see that there is always a definite relationship between the anatomy and physiology of the body and body parts. Just as the structure of a knife is well suited for cutting, the structure (anatomy) of a body part enables it to perform specific functions (physiology). For example, the arrangement of bones, muscles, and nerves in your hands enables the grasping of large objects with considerable force and also the delicate manipulation of small objects. Correlating the relationship between structure and function will make your study of the human body much easier.

1.2 Levels of Organization

The human body is complex, so it is not surprising that there are several levels of structural organization, as shown in figure 1.1. The levels of organization from simplest to most complex are chemical, cellular, tissue, organ, organ system, and organismic (the body as a whole).

Chemical Level

The *chemical level* consists of the *atom, molecule, macromolecule,* and *organelle* subdivisions. At the simplest level, the body is composed of chemical substances that are formed of atoms and molecules. *Atoms* are the fundamental building blocks of chemicals, and atoms combine in specific ways to form *molecules.* Some molecules are very small, such as water molecules, but others may be very large, such as the macromolecules of

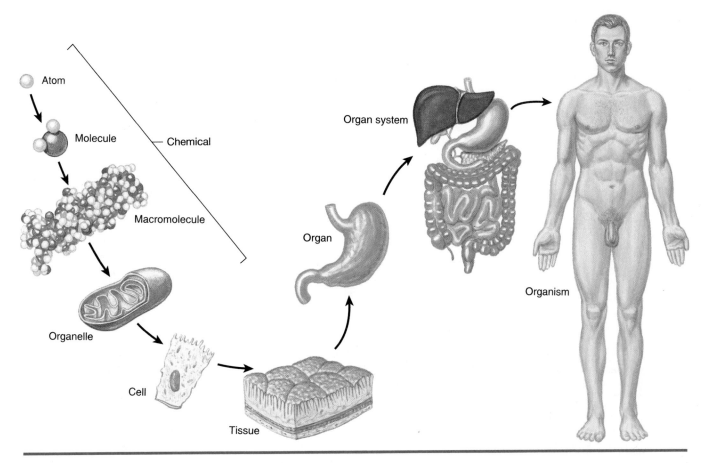

Figure 1.1   Six levels of organization in the human body range from chemical (simplest) to organismic (most complex).

proteins. Various small and large molecules are grouped together to form organelles. An **organelle** (or ″-ga-nel′) is a microscopic subunit of a cell, somewhat like a tiny organ, that carries out specific functions within a cell. Nuclei, mitochondria, and centrioles are examples.

Cellular Level

Cells are the basic structural and functional units of the body because all of the processes of life occur within cells. A cell is the smallest unit of life. Nothing smaller than a cell is alive. The human body is composed of trillions of cells and many different types of cells, such as muscle cells, blood cells, and nerve cells. Each type of specialized cell has a unique structure that enables it to perform specific functions.

Tissue Level

Similar types of cells are usually grouped together in the body to form a tissue. Each body **tissue** consists of an aggregation of similar cells that perform similar functions. There are several different types of tissues in the body. Muscle and nerve tissues are examples.

Organ Level

Each **organ** of the body is composed of two or more tissues that work together, enabling the organ to perform its specific functions. The body contains numerous organs, and each has a definite form and function. The stomach, heart, and brain are examples of organs.

Organ System Level

The organs of the body are arranged in functional groups so that their independent functions are coordinated to perform specific system functions. These coordinated, functional groups are called **organ systems**. The digestive and nervous systems are examples of organ systems. Most organs belong to a single organ system, but a few organs are assigned to more than one organ system. For example, the ovaries and testes belong to both the reproductive and endocrine systems.

Figure 1.2 illustrates the organ systems of the body and lists the major components and functions for each system. Although each organ system has its own unique functions, all organ systems are interdependent on one another. For example, all organ

Integumentary system

Components: skin, hair, nails, and associated glands
Functions: protects underlying tissues and helps regulate body temperature

Skeletal system

Components: bones, ligaments, and associated cartilages
Functions: supports the body, protects vital organs, stores minerals, and forms blood cells

Muscular system

Components: skeletal muscles, cardiac muscle of the heart, and smooth muscle in walls of internal organs
Functions: moves the body and body parts and produces heat

Figure 1.2 The organ systems of the body. AP|R

systems rely on the cardiovascular system to transport materials to and from their cells. Organ systems work together to enable the functioning of the human body.

Effective communication among health-care personnel depends upon the use of anatomical and physiological terms to provide precise meaning. These technical terms usually have Latin roots and endings. To change such terms from singular to plural requires a change in the ending but not the addition of an *s*. Instead, terms ending in *us* are changed to *i*, those ending in *a* are changed to *ae*, and those ending in *um* are converted to *a*.

Organismic Level

The highest organizational level is the *organismic level*, the human organism as a whole. It is composed of all of the interacting organ systems. All of the organizational levels from chemicals to organ systems contribute to the functioning of the entire body.

Respiratory system

Components: nasal cavity, pharynx, larynx, trachea, bronchi, and lungs
Functions: exchanges O_2 and CO_2 between air and blood in the lungs

Cardiovascular system

Components: blood, heart, arteries, veins, and capillaries
Functions: transports materials to and from the body cells

Lymphatic system

Components: lymph, lymphatic vessels, and lymphatic tissue
Functions: collects, cleanses, and returns interstitial fluid to the blood; provides immunity

Urinary system

Components: kidneys, ureters, urinary bladder, and urethra
Functions: regulates volume and composition of blood by forming and excreting urine

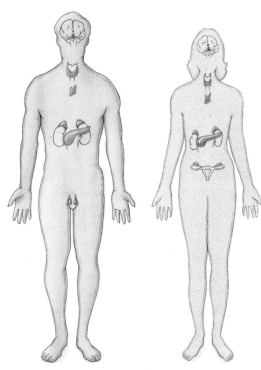

Endocrine system

Components: hormone-producing glands
Functions: secretes hormones that regulate body functions

Nervous system

Components: brain, spinal cord, nerves, and sensory receptors
Functions: rapidly coordinates body functions and enables learning and memory

Digestive system

Components: mouth, pharynx, esophagus, stomach, intestines, anus, liver, pancreas, and associated structures
Functions: digests food and absorbs nutrients

Male reproductive system

Components: testes, vasa deferentia, prostate gland, bulbourethral gland, and penis
Functions: produces sperm and transmits them into the female vagina during sexual intercourse

Female reproductive system

Components: ovaries, uterine tubes, uterus, vagina, and vulva
Functions: produces ova, receives sperm, provides intrauterine development of offspring, and enables birth of baby

1.3 Directional Terms

Directional terms are used to describe the relative position of a body part in relationship to another body part. The use of these terms conveys a precise meaning enabling the listener or reader to locate the body part of interest. It is always assumed that the body is in a standard position, the *anatomical position,* in which the body is standing upright with arms at the sides and palms of the hands facing forward, as in figure 1.3. Directional terms occur in pairs, and the members of each pair have opposite meanings, as noted in table 1.1.

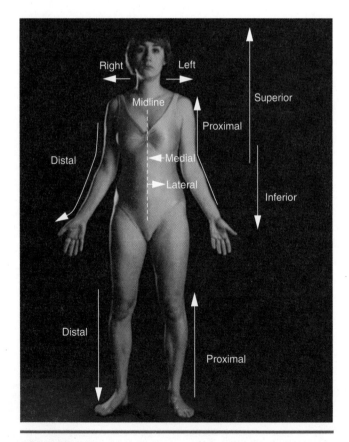

Figure 1.3 Anatomical position and directional terms. AP|R

Table 1.1	Directional Terms
Term	**Meaning**
Anterior (ventral)	Toward the front or abdominal surface of the body
Posterior (dorsal)	Toward the back of the body
Superior (cephalad)	Toward the head
Inferior (caudad)	Away from the head
Medial	Toward the midline of the body
Lateral	Away from the midline of the body
Parietal	Pertaining to the outer boundary of body cavities
Visceral	Pertaining to the internal organs
External (superficial)	Toward or on the body surface
Internal (deep)	Away from the body surface
Proximal	Part of an extremity that is nearer the point of attachment of the extremity to the trunk
Distal	Part of an extremity that is farther from the point of attachment of the extremity to the trunk
Central	At or near the center of the body or organ
Peripheral	External to or away from the center of the body or organ

1.4 Body Regions

The human body consists of an **axial** (ak'-sē-al) **portion**, the head, neck, and trunk, and an **appendicular** (ap-pen-dik'-ū-lar) **portion**, the upper and lower extremities (arms and legs). Each of these major portions of the body is divided into regions with special latinized names to facilitate communication and to aid in the location of body components.

The major body regions are listed in tables 1.2 and 1.3 to allow easy correlation with figure 1.4, which shows the locations of the major regions of the body. Take time to learn the names, pronunciations, and locations of the body regions.

1.5 Body Planes and Sections

In studying the body or organs, you often will be observing the flat surface of a section that has been produced by a cut through the body or a body part. Such sections are made along specific *planes.* These well-defined planes—transverse, sagittal, and frontal

Table 1.2   Major Regions of the Head, Neck, and Trunk

Region	Location
Head and Neck	
Cephalic (se-fal′-ik)	The head; composed of cranial and facial regions
Cervical (ser′-vi-kal)	The neck
Cranial (krā′-nē-al)	The part of the head containing the brain
Facial(fā′-shal)	The face
Anterior Trunk	
Abdominal (ab-dom′-i-nal)	The region between the lowest ribs and the pelvis (hip bones)
Abdominopelvic (ab-dom-i-nō-pel′-vik)	Composed of abdominal and pelvic regions
Inguinal (ing′-gwi-nal)	The groin; depressed regions at the junction of the thighs to the anterior trunk
Pectoral (pek′-tōr-al)	The chest
Pelvic (pel′-vik)	The region enclosed by the pelvic bones
Sternal (ster′-nal)	The region over the breastbone and between the two pectoral regions
Umbilical (um-bil′-i-kal)	The cental part of the abdomen
Posterior Trunk	
Dorsum (dor′-sum)	The posterior surface of the thorax
Gluteal (glu′-tē-al)	The buttocks
Lumbar (lum′-bar)	The lower back region between the lowest ribs and the pelvis
Sacral (sāk′-ral)	The region over the sacrum and between the buttocks
Vertebral (ver-tē′-bral)	The region over the vertebral column or backbone
Lateral Trunk	
Axillary (ak′-sil-lary)	The armpits
Coxal (kok′-sal)	The hips
Inferior Trunk	
Genital (jen′-i-tal)	The external reproductive organs
Perineal (per-i-nē′-al)	The small region between the anus and external reproductive organs

Table 1.3   Major Regions of the Extremities

Region	Location
Upper Extremity	
Antebrachial (an-tē-brā′-kē-al)	The forearm
Antecubital (an-tē-kū-bi-tal)	The anterior portion of the elbow joint
Brachial (brā′-kē-al)	The upper arm
Carpal (kar′-pal)	The wrist
Cubital (kū′-bi-tal)	The elbow joint
Digital (di′-ji-tal)	The fingers
Olecranal (ō-lēk′-ran-al)	Posterior surface of the elbow joint
Palmar (pal′-mar)	The palm of the hand
Lower Extremity	
Crural (krū′-ral)	The leg
Digital (di′-ji-tal)	The toes
Femoral (fem′-ōr-al)	The thigh
Patellar (pa-tel′-lar)	The anterior portion of the knee joint
Pedal (pe′-dal)	The foot
Plantar (plan′-tar)	The sole of the foot
Popliteal (pop-li-tē′-al)	The posterior portion of the knee joint
Sural (sū′-ral)	Calf of the leg

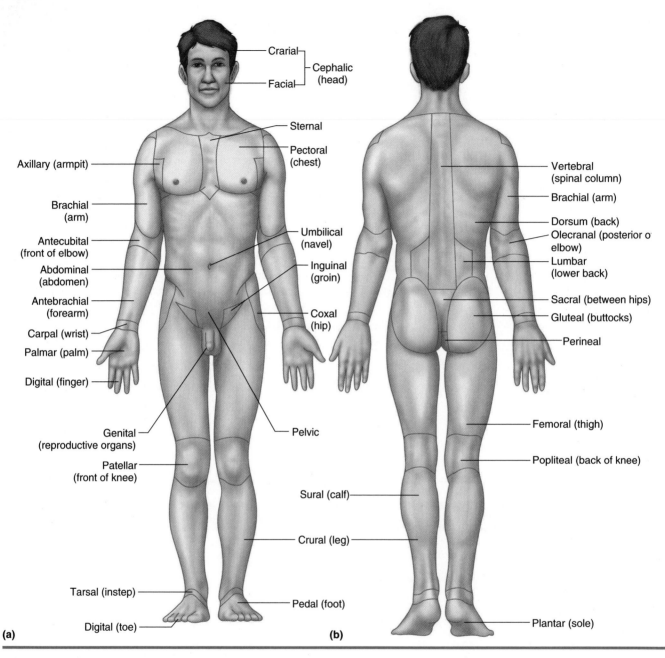

Figure 1.4   Major regions of the body. AP|R

planes—lie at right angles to each other as shown in figure 1.5. It is important to understand the nature of the plane along which a section was made in order to understand the three-dimensional structure of an object being observed.

Transverse, or horizontal, **planes** divide the body into superior and inferior portions, and they are perpendicular to sagittal planes and the longitudinal axis of the body. Sections made along transverse planes are often called *cross sections*.

Sagittal planes divide the body into right and left portions and are parallel to the longitudinal axis of the body. Sections made along sagittal planes are often called *longitudinal sections*. A **medial** (midsagittal) **plane** passes through the midline of the body and divides the body into equal left and right halves.

Frontal (coronal) **planes** divide the body into anterior and posterior portions. These planes are perpendicular to sagittal planes and parallel to the longitudinal axis of the body.

Check My Understanding

3. How do sagittal, transverse, and frontal planes differ from one another?

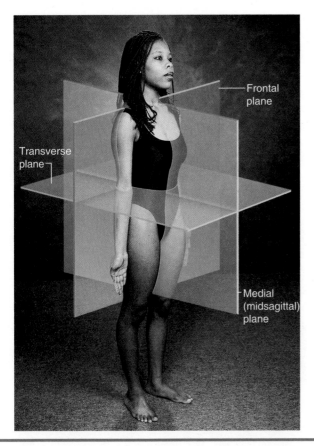

Figure 1.5 Anatomical planes of reference. AP|R

1.6 Body Cavities

There are two major cavities of the body that contain internal organs: the dorsal (posterior) and ventral (anterior) cavities. The body cavities protect and cushion the contained organs and permit changes in their size and shape without impacting surrounding tissues. Note the locations and subdivisions of these cavities in figure 1.6.

The **dorsal cavity** is subdivided into the **cranial cavity,** which houses the brain, and the **vertebral canal,** which contains the spinal cord. Note in figure 1.6 how the cranial bones and the vertebral column form the walls of the dorsal cavity and provide protection for these delicate organs.

The **ventral cavity** is divided by the *diaphragm*, a thin dome-shaped sheet of muscle, into a superior **thoracic cavity** and an inferior **abdominopelvic cavity.** The thoracic cavity is protected by the *rib cage* and contains the heart and lungs. The abdominopelvic cavity is subdivided into a superior **abdominal cavity** and an inferior **pelvic cavity,** but there is no structural separation between them. The abdominal cavity contains the stomach, intestines, liver, gallbladder, pancreas, spleen, and kidneys. The pelvic cavity contains the urinary bladder, sigmoid colon, rectum, and internal reproductive organs.

Check My Understanding

4. What organs are located in each subdivision of the dorsal cavity?
5. What organs are located in each subdivision of the ventral cavity?

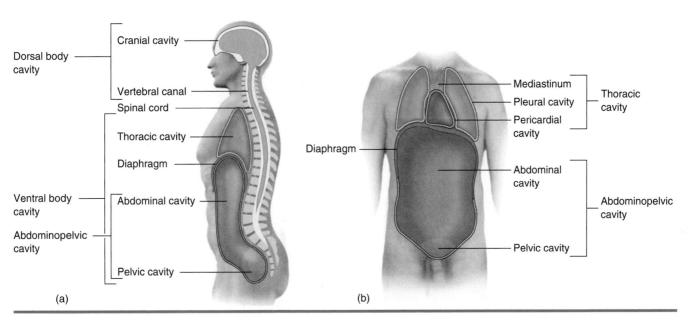

Figure 1.6 Body cavities and their subdivisions. (a) A midsagittal section. (b) A frontal section. AP|R

Clinical INSIGHT

Physicians use certain types of diagnostic imaging systems, for example, *computerized tomography (CT)* and *magnetic resonance imaging (MRI)*, to produce images of sections of the body to help them diagnose disorders. In computerized tomography, an X-ray emitter and an X-ray detector rotate around the patient so that the X-ray beam passes through the body from hundreds of different angles. X-rays collected by the detector are then processed by a computer to produce sectional images on a screen for viewing by a radiologist. A good understanding of sectional anatomy is required to interpret CT scans. What structures can you identify in the CT image shown? AP|R

Membranes of Body Cavities

The membranes lining body cavities support and protect the internal organs in the cavities.

Dorsal Cavity Membranes

The dorsal cavity is lined by three layers of protective membranes that are collectively called the **meninges** (me-nin′-jēz). The outermost membrane is attached to the wall of the dorsal cavity, and the innermost membrane tightly envelops the brain and spinal cord. The meninges will be covered in chapter 8.

Ventral Cavity Membranes

Serous membranes line the ventral cavity and the surfaces of the contained internal organs, and they secrete a watery lubricating fluid. As organs rub against one another or the ventral cavity wall, the fluid and serous membranes provide a smooth, friction-reducing surface.

The serous membranes lining the thoracic cavity are called **pleurae** and **pleural membranes.** The walls of the left and right portions of the thoracic cavity are lined by the *parietal* (pah-rī′-e-tal) *pleurae*. The outer surfaces of the lungs are covered by the *visceral*

(vis′-er-al) *pleurae*. The parietal and visceral pleurae are separated by a thin film of *serous fluid,* a watery fluid secreted by the pleurae. Serous fluid reduces friction as the pleurae rub against each other as the lungs expand and contract during breathing. The potential space (not an actual space) between the parietal and visceral pleurae is known as the **pleural cavity**.

The left and right portions of the thoracic cavity are divided by a membranous partition, the *mediastinum* (mē-dē-a-stī′-num). Organs located within the mediastinum include the heart, thymus gland, esophagus, and trachea.

The heart is enveloped by the **pericardium** (per-i-kar′-dē-um), which is formed of membranes of the mediastinum. The thin *visceral pericardium* is tightly adhered to the surface of the heart, but the thicker *parietal pericardium*, a double membrane, forms a loosely fitting sac around the heart. The potential space between the visceral and parietal pericardia is the **pericardial cavity,** and it contains serous fluid to reduce friction as the heart contracts and relaxes.

The walls of the abdominal cavity and the surfaces of abdominal organs are lined with the **peritoneum** (per-i-tō-nē′-um). The *parietal peritoneum* lines the walls of the abdominal cavity but not the pelvic cavity. It descends only to cover the upper portion of the urinary bladder. Because the kidneys are located posterior to the parietal peritoneum, only a portion of their surfaces are covered by it. The *visceral peritoneum*, an extension of the parietal peritoneum, covers the surface of the abdominal organs. Double-layered folds of the visceral peritoneum, the *mesenteries* (mes'-en-ter''-ēs), extend between the abdominal organs and provide support for them. The potential space between the parietal and visceral peritoneal membranes is called the **peritoneal cavity**.

Check My Understanding

6. What membranes line the dorsal and ventral cavities?
7. What is the function of serous fluid?

1.7 Abdominopelvic Subdivisions

The abdominopelvic surface is subdivided into either four quadrants or nine regions to aid physicians and nurses in locating underlying organs in the abdominopelvic cavity. By knowing the internal organs that are located within each quadrant or region, organs that may be responsible for a patient's complaint of abdominopelvic pain may be identified.

The four quadrants are formed by two planes that intersect at the umbilicus (navel), as shown in figure 1.7. Note the organs within each quadrant.

The nine regions are formed by the intersection of two sagittal and two transverse planes as shown in figure 1.8. The sagittal planes extend downward from the midpoints of the collarbones. The superior transverse plane lies just inferior to the lowest ribs, and the inferior transverse plane lies just below the hip bones.

Identify the organs located within each quadrant and region by comparing figure 1.7 to table 1.4, and figure 1.8 to table 1.5.

Study figures 1.9 and 1.10 to increase your understanding of the locations of the internal organs and associated membranes.

Now examine the colorplates that follow this chapter. They show an anterior view of the body in progressive stages of dissection that reveals major muscles, blood vessels, and internal organs. Study these plates to learn the normal locations of the organs of the ventral cavity. Also, check your understanding of the organs within each abdominal quadrant and region.

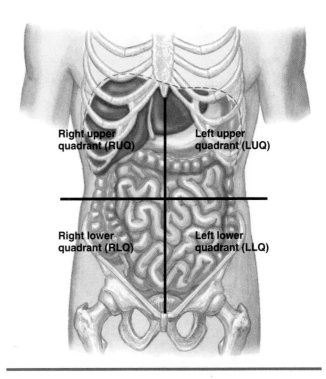

Right upper quadrant (RUQ)

Left upper quadrant (LUQ)

Right lower quadrant (RLQ)

Left lower quadrant (LLQ)

Figure 1.7 The four quadrants of the abdominopelvic area. AP|R

Table 1.4	Organs in Abdominopelvic Quadrants
Quadrant	**Organs**
Right upper	Gallbladder; most of liver and duodenum; right kidney; parts of right ureter; parts of pancreas, small intestine, ascending and transverse colon
Right lower	Appendix; cecum; parts of ascending colon, small intestine, right ureter, urinary bladder, rectum
Left upper	Stomach; spleen; parts of duodenum and pancreas; left kidney; parts of left ureter, small intestine, transverse and descending colon
Left lower	Parts of small intestine, descending and sigmoid colon, rectum, left ureter, urinary bladder

Check My Understanding

8. What are the four quadrants and nine regions of the abdominopelvic region?

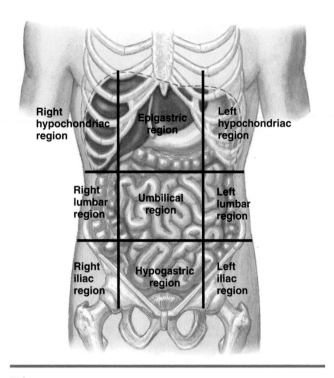

Figure 1.8 The abdominopelvic area is subdivided into nine regions. AP|R

Table 1.5	Organs in Abdominopelvic Regions
Region	**Organs**
Right hypochondriac	Gallbladder; parts of liver, transverse colon, and right kidney
Right lumbar	Ascending colon; parts of small intestine and right kidney
Right iliac	Appendix; cecum; parts of small intestine
Epigastric	Parts of liver, stomach, pancreas, duodenum, transverse colon
Umbilical	Parts of duodenum, small intestine, kidneys, ureters
Hypogastric	Urinary bladder; rectum; parts of ureters, small intestine, and sigmoid colon
Left hypochondriac	Spleen; parts of stomach, transverse colon, left kidney
Left lumbar	Descending colon; parts of left kidney and small intestine
Left iliac	Parts of small intestine, descending and sigmoid colon

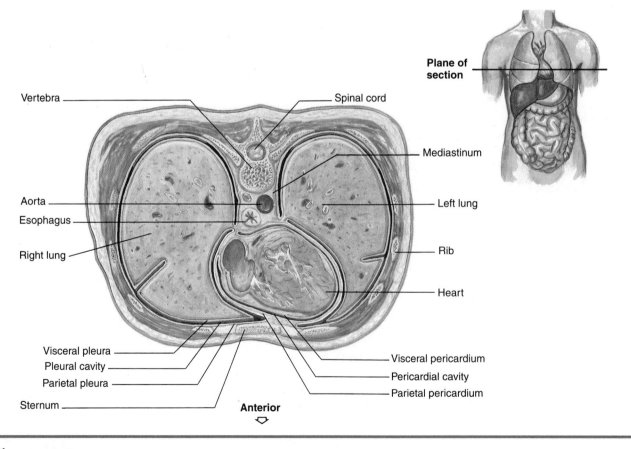

Figure 1.9 A transverse section through the thorax reveals the serous membranes associated with the heart and lungs (*superior view*). AP|R

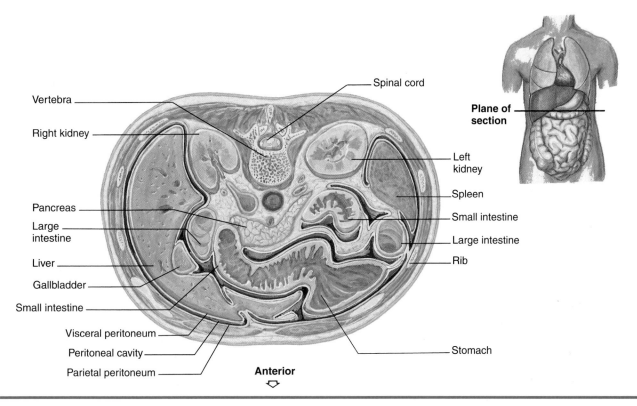

Spinal cord

Vertebra

Right kidney

Plane of section

Left kidney

Spleen

Pancreas

Small intestine

Large intestine

Large intestine

Liver

Rib

Gallbladder

Small intestine

Visceral peritoneum

Peritoneal cavity

Parietal peritoneum

Stomach

Anterior

Figure 1.10 Transverse section through the abdomen (*superior view*). AP|R

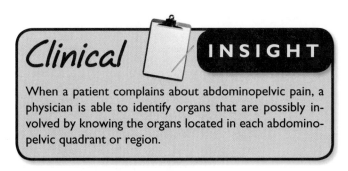

Clinical **INSIGHT**

When a patient complains about abdominopelvic pain, a physician is able to identify organs that are possibly involved by knowing the organs located in each abdominopelvic quadrant or region.

1.8 Maintenance of Life

Humans, like all living organisms, exhibit the fundamental processes of life. **Metabolism** (me-tab′ō-lizm) is the term that collectively refers to the sum of the life processes—that is, all of the chemical reactions that collectively are known as life.

There are two phases of metabolism: anabolism and catabolism. **Anabolism** (ah-nab′-ō-lizm) refers to processes that use energy and nutrients to build the complex organic molecules that compose the body. **Catabolism** (kah-tab′-ō-lizm) refers to processes that break down complex molecules into simpler molecules.

Life is fragile. It depends upon the normal functioning of trillions of body cells, which, in turn, depends upon factors needed for survival and the ability of the body to maintain relatively stable internal conditions.

Survival Needs

There are five basic needs that are essential to human life:

1. **Food** provides chemicals that serve as a source of energy and raw materials to maintain cells of the body.
2. **Water** provides the environment in which the chemical reactions of life occur.
3. **Oxygen** is required to convert organic nutrients into energy, which powers life processes.
4. **Body temperature** must be maintained close to 37°C (98.6°F) to allow the chemical reactions of human metabolism to occur.
5. **Atmospheric pressure** is required for breathing to occur.

Homeostasis

Homeostasis is the maintenance of a relatively stable internal environment by self-regulating physiological processes. Homeostasis keeps body temperature and the composition of blood and intercellular fluids within rather narrow limits. Note that the internal environment is kept in a dynamic, rather than static, balance. This relatively stable internal environment is maintained in spite of the fact that internal and external factors tend to alter body temperature, and materials are continuously entering and exiting the blood and intercellular fluid.

All of the organ systems are involved in homeostasis. A breakdown in homeostatic mechanisms leads to disorder and disease.

Homeostasis is maintained and most physiological processes are regulated by **negative-feedback mechanisms,** which minimize deviation from the norm. Negative-feedback mechanisms consist of three components: *sensor*, *control center*, and *effector*. A sensor detects deviation from the norm and "informs" the control center of the deviation. The control center activates an effector, whose action returns the internal environment to the norm (figure 1.11).

For example, body temperature is normally 98.6°F. When body temperature falls below the norm, sensors inform the temperature control center in the brain that body temperature has decreased. The temperature control center constricts blood vessels in the skin to reduce heat loss and, in extreme cases, stimulates involuntary muscle contractions (shivering) to generate heat to return body temperature to normal. If body temperature rises above the norm, sensors inform the temperature control center. The temperature control center dilates blood vessels in the skin, which increases heat loss and causes sweating to cool the body and return body temperature to normal (figure 1.12).

Positive-feedback mechanisms exist but they are rare. They stimulate and promote, rather than curtail, the change that is occurring. They continue to act until stopped by an event outside of the feedback mechanism. The formation of blood clots and uterine contractions in childbirth are examples of positive-feedback mechanisms. In childbirth, pressure of the baby's head on the cervix is detected by sensory receptors, which inform the brain of the event. The brain stimulates the

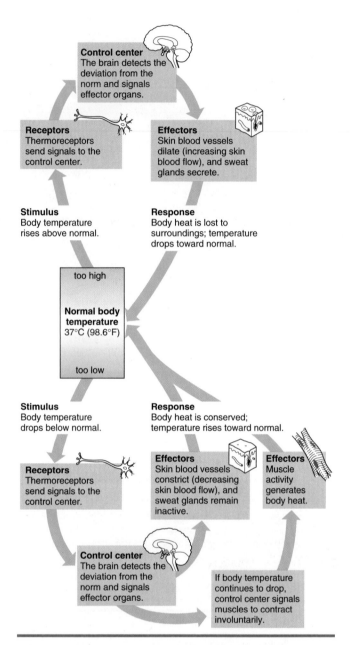

Figure 1.12 The negative-feedback homeostatic mechanism that regulates body temperature.

release of a hormone, which promotes ever stronger uterine contractions until the baby is born.

A positive-feedback mechanism can be harmful if it is not controlled. For example, an infection may cause metabolic changes that produce a fever. In extreme cases, the metabolic changes can raise body temperature so high that death may result.

Check My Understanding

9. What is homeostasis? How is homeostasis regulated?

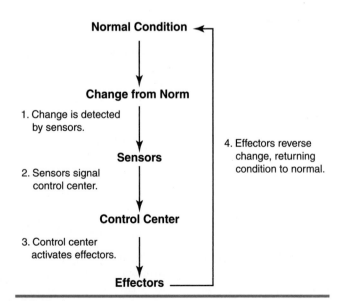

Figure 1.11 A negative-feedback mechanism controlling homeostasis.

CHAPTER SUMMARY

1.1 Anatomy and Physiology

- Human anatomy is the study of body structure and organization.
- Human physiology is the study of body functions.

1.2 Levels of Organization

- The body consists of several levels of organization of increasing complexity.
- From simple to complex, the organizational levels are chemical, cellular, tissue, organ, organ system, and organismic.
- The organs of the body are arranged in coordinated groups called organ systems.
- The organ systems of the body are

integumentary	cardiovascular
skeletal	lymphatic
muscular	respiratory
nervous	urinary
endocrine	reproductive
digestive	

1.3 Directional Terms

- Directional terms are used to describe the relative positions of body parts.
- Directional terms occur in pairs, with the members of a pair having opposite meanings.

anterior—posterior	proximal—distal
superior—inferior	external—internal
medial—lateral	parietal—visceral
central—peripheral	

1.4 Body Regions

- The body is divided into two major portions: the axial portion and the appendicular portion.
- The axial portion is subdivided into the head, neck, and trunk.
- The head and neck contain cervical, cranial, and facial regions. The cranial and facial regions combine to form the cephalic region.
- The trunk consists of anterior, posterior, lateral, and inferior areas.
- Anterior trunk regions include the abdominal, inguinal, pectoral, pelvic, and sternal regions. The abdominal and pelvic regions combine to form the abdominopelvic region.
- Posterior trunk regions include the dorsal, gluteal, lumbar, sacral, and vertebral regions.
- Lateral trunk regions are the axillary and coxal regions.
- Inferior trunk regions are the genital and perineal regions.
- The appendicular portion of the body consists of the upper and lower extremities.
- The upper extremity is attached to the trunk at the shoulder. Regions of the upper extremity are the antebrachial, antecubital, brachial, carpus, digital, olecranal, and palmar regions.
- The lower extremity is attached to the trunk at the hip. Regions of the lower extremity are the crural, digital, femoral, patellar, pedal, plantar, popliteal, sural, and tarsal regions.

1.5 Body Planes and Sections

- Well-defined planes are used to guide sectioning of the body or organs.
- The common planes are transverse, sagittal, and frontal.

1.6 Body Cavities

- There are two major body cavities: dorsal and ventral.
- The dorsal cavity consists of the cranial cavity and vertebral canal.
- The ventral cavity consists of the thoracic and abdominopelvic cavities.
- The thoracic cavity lies superior to the diaphragm. It consists of two lateral pleural cavities and the mediastinum, which contains the pericardial cavity.
- The abdominopelvic cavity lies inferior to the diaphragm. It consists of a superior abdominal cavity and an inferior pelvic cavity.
- The body cavities are lined with protective and supportive membranes.
- The meninges consist of three membranes that line the dorsal cavity and enclose the brain and spinal cord.
- The parietal pleurae line the inner walls of the pleural cavities, and the visceral pleurae cover the external surfaces of the lungs.
- The pleural cavity is the potential space between the parietal and visceral pleurae.
- The parietal pericardium is a saclike membrane in the mediastinum that surrounds the heart. The visceral pericardium is attached to the surface of the heart.
- The pericardial cavity is the potential space between the parietal and visceral pericardia.
- The parietal peritoneum lines the walls of the abdominal cavity but does not extend into the pelvic cavity. The visceral peritoneum covers the surface of internal abdominal organs.
- The peritoneal cavity is the potential space between the parietal and visceral peritoneal membranes.
- The mesenteries are double-layered folds of the visceral peritoneum that support internal organs.

1.7 Abdominopelvic Subdivisions

- The abdominopelvic region is subdivided into either four quadrants or nine regions as an aid in locating underlying organs.
- The four quadrants are
  right upper   left upper
  right lower   left lower
- The nine regions are
  epigastric   right lumbar
  left hypochondriac   hypogastric (pubic)
  right hypochondriac   left iliac (inguinal)
  umbilical   right iliac
  left lumbar

1.8 Maintenance of Life

- Metabolism is the sum of all life processes, and it consists of anabolism, the synthesis of body chemicals, and catabolism, the breakdown of body chemicals.
- The basic needs of the body are food, water, oxygen, body temperature, and atmospheric pressure.
- Homeostasis is the maintenance of a relatively stable internal environment.
- Homeostasis is regulated by negative-feedback control mechanisms.
- Negative-feedback mechanisms consist of three components: sensors, control center, and effectors.
- Positive feedback promotes an ever-increasing change from the norm.

BUILDING MY VOCABULARY

1. **Selected New Terms**
   abdominal cavity, p. 9
   cranial cavity, p. 9
   distal, p. 6
   dorsal cavity, p. 9
   frontal plane, p. 8
   inferior, p. 6
   lateral, p.6
   medial, p. 6
   medial plane, p. 8
   negative-feedback mechanism, p. 14
   organ, p. 3
   organ system, p. 3
   pelvic cavity, p. 9
   pericardial cavity, p. 10
   pleural cavity, p. 10
   positive-feedback mechanism, p. 14
   proximal, p. 6

   sagittal plane, p. 8
   superior, p. 6
   thoracic cavity, p. 9
   transverse plane, p. 8
   ventral cavity, p. 9
   vertebral canal, p. 9

2. **Related Clinical Terms**
   Meningitis (men-in-jī′-tis) Inflammation of the meninges.
   Pathology (path-ol′-ō-jē) Medical specialty studying anatomical and physiological changes caused by disease.
   Peritonitis (per-i-tō-nī′-tis) Inflammation of the peritoneum.
   Podiatry (pō-dī′-ah-tre) Medical specialty treating foot disorders.

SELF-REVIEW

Answers are located in Appendix B.

1. A study of body functions is called _____.
2. Blood, the heart, and blood vessels compose the _____ system.
3. Rapid coordination of body functions is the function of the _____ system.
4. The fingers are located _____ to the wrist.
5. The upper and lower extremities compose the _____ portion of the body.
6. The posterior surface of the knee is known as the _____ region.
7. The thigh is known as the _____ region.
8. The _____ body cavity is divided into the cranial cavity and _____ canal.
9. The gallbladder is located in the _____ quadrant and the _____ abdominopelvic region.
10. The _____ separates the left and right portions of the thoracic cavity.
11. The abdominal cavity is lined by the _____.
12. The maintenance of a relatively stable internal environment is called _____.

CRITICAL THINKING

1. Complete the learning objectives on the first page of this chapter.
2. A hypoglycemic (low blood sugar) patient is given orange juice to drink. Explain how this raises blood sugar and the organ systems involved.
3. Describe the location of the kneecap in as many ways as you can using directional terms.
4. Describe where serous membranes are located in the body and explain the function of serous fluid.
5. Explain how negative-feedback control mechanisms regulate homeostasis.

Visit this book's website at www.mhhe.com/ gunstream5 for practice quizzes, learning exercises, case studies, and other study tools.

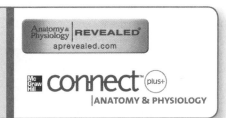

Anatomy & Physiology | REVEALED®
aprevealed.com

Mc Graw Hill **connect**™ (plus+)
|ANATOMY & PHYSIOLOGY

COLORPLATES OF THE HUMAN BODY

The seven colorplates that follow show the basic structure of the human body. The first plate shows the anterior body surface and the superficial anterior muscles of a female. Succeeding plates show the internal structure as revealed by progressively deeper dissections.

Refer to these plates often as you study this text in order to become familiar with the relative locations of the body organs.

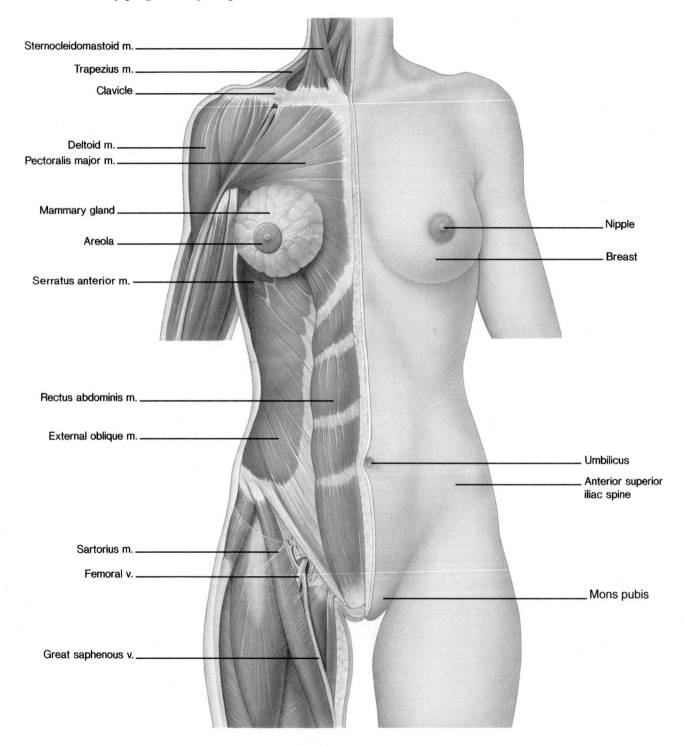

Sternocleidomastoid m.
Trapezius m.
Clavicle
Deltoid m.
Pectoralis major m.
Mammary gland
Areola
Serratus anterior m.
Rectus abdominis m.
External oblique m.
Sartorius m.
Femoral v.
Great saphenous v.

Nipple
Breast
Umbilicus
Anterior superior iliac spine
Mons pubis

Plate 1 Female torso with skin removed to expose superficial muscles. (m. = muscle, v. = vein)

Larynx

Common carotid a.

Internal jugular v.

Sternocleidomastoid m.

Thyroid gland

Clavicle

External intercostal m.

Deltoid m.

Coracobrachialis m.

Pectoralis major m.

Pectoralis minor m.

Latissimus dorsi m.

Biceps brachii m.

Rectus abdominis m.

Serratus anterior m.

External oblique m.

Transversus abdominis m.

Internal oblique m.

Linea alba

Transversus abdominis m.

Rectus abdominis m. (cut)

Tensor fasciae latae m.

Femoral n.

Femoral a.

Sartorius m.

Rectus femoris m.

Femoral v.

Great saphenous v.

Plate 2 Male torso with deeper muscles exposed. (m. = muscle, v. = vein, n. = nerve, a. = artery)

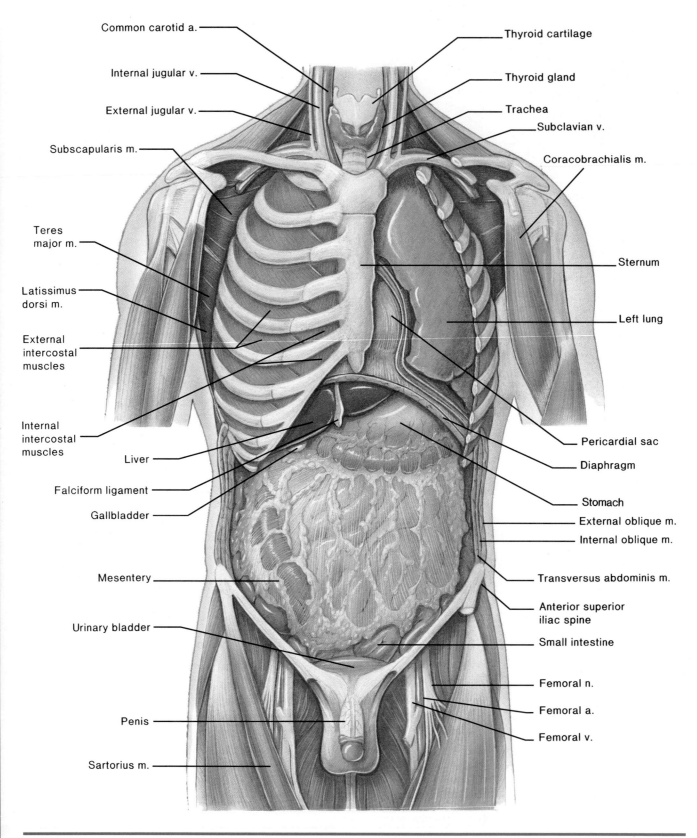

Common carotid a.

Internal jugular v.

External jugular v.

Subscapularis m.

Teres major m.

Latissimus dorsi m.

External intercostal muscles

Internal intercostal muscles

Liver

Falciform ligament

Gallbladder

Mesentery

Urinary bladder

Penis

Sartorius m.

Thyroid cartilage

Thyroid gland

Trachea

Subclavian v.

Coracobrachialis m.

Sternum

Left lung

Pericardial sac

Diaphragm

Stomach

External oblique m.

Internal oblique m.

Transversus abdominis m.

Anterior superior iliac spine

Small intestine

Femoral n.

Femoral a.

Femoral v.

Plate 3 Male torso with some internal organs exposed. (m. = muscle, v. = vein, a. = artery)

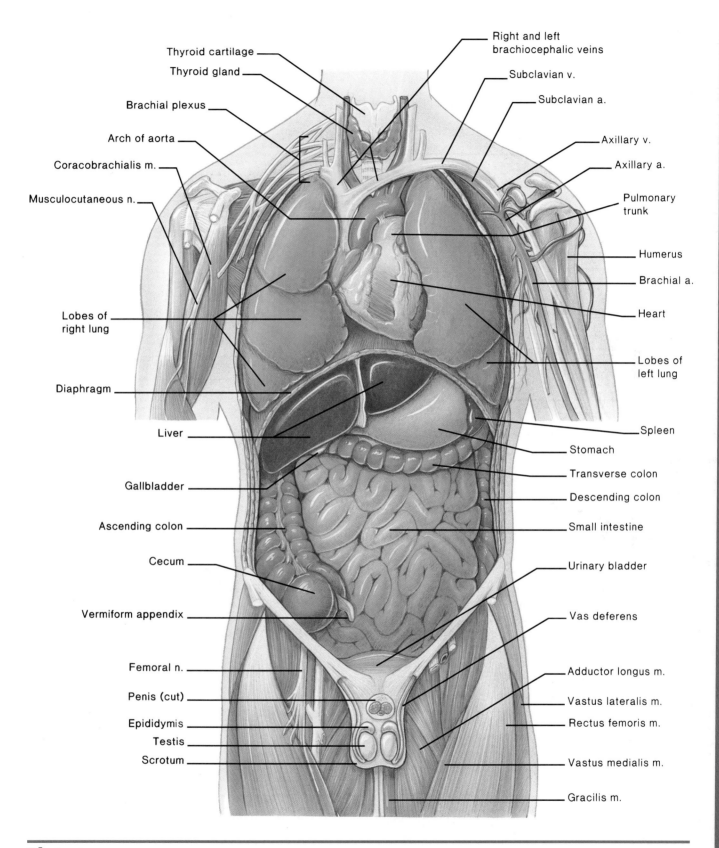

Plate 4 Male torso with thoracic and abdominopelvic organs exposed. (m. = muscle, v. = vein, a. = artery)

Larynx
Trachea
Right common carotid a.
Left subclavian a.

Right subclavian a.
Brachiocephalic a.
Superior vena cava
Arch of aorta
Pulmonary a.
Pulmonary trunk
Pulmonary v.
Right atrium
Left atrium
Right ventricle
Lung
Left ventricle
Lobes of liver
Diaphragm
Gallbladder
Spleen
Cystic duct
Stomach
Duodenum
Transverse colon
Ascending colon
Jejunum (cut)
Mesentery
Descending colon
Ileum (cut)
Ureter
Cecum
Sigmoid colon
Vermiform appendix
Rectum
Common iliac a.
Uterus
Ovary
Tensor fasciae latae m.
Uterine tube
Round ligament of uterus
Femoral a.
Urinary bladder
Femoral v.
Adductor longus m.
Great saphenous v.
Gracilis m.
Rectus femoris m.
Vastus lateralis m.
Vastus medialis m.
Sartorius m.

Plate 5 Female torso with lungs and heart in coronal section and small intestine removed. (v. = vein, a. = artery)

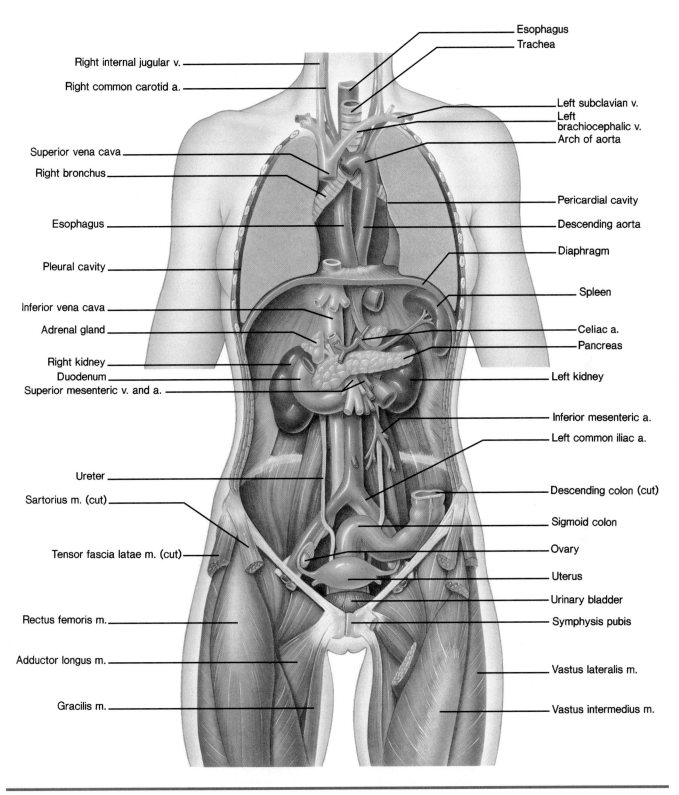

Right internal jugular v.

Right common carotid a.

Superior vena cava

Right bronchus

Esophagus

Pleural cavity

Inferior vena cava

Adrenal gland

Right kidney

Duodenum

Superior mesenteric v. and a.

Ureter

Sartorius m. (cut)

Tensor fascia latae m. (cut)

Rectus femoris m.

Adductor longus m.

Gracilis m.

Esophagus

Trachea

Left subclavian v.

Left brachiocephalic v.

Arch of aorta

Pericardial cavity

Descending aorta

Diaphragm

Spleen

Celiac a.

Pancreas

Left kidney

Inferior mesenteric a.

Left common iliac a.

Descending colon (cut)

Sigmoid colon

Ovary

Uterus

Urinary bladder

Symphysis pubis

Vastus lateralis m.

Vastus intermedius m.

Plate 6 Female torso with some organs removed to expose esophagus, deep vessels, kidneys, and ureters. (v. = vein, a. = artery)

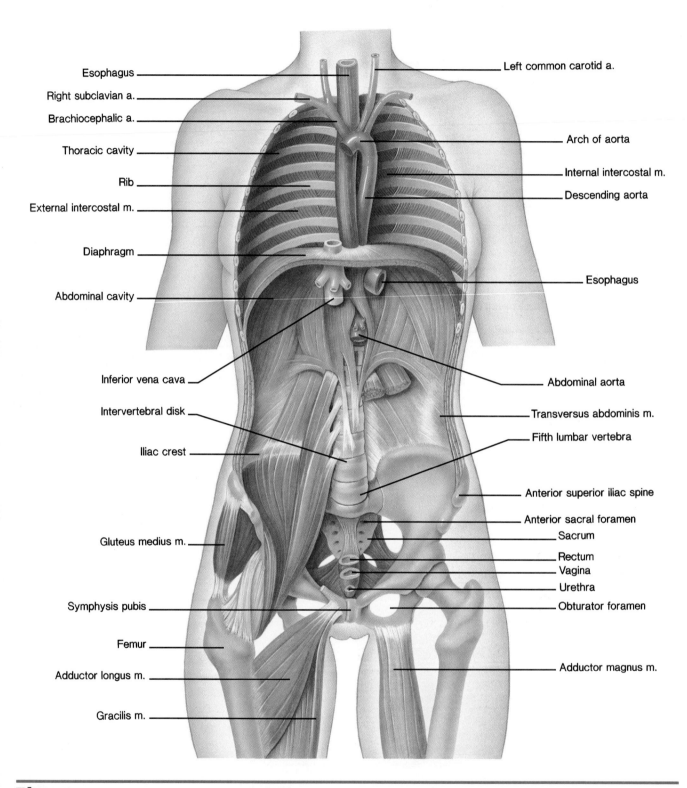

Plate 7 Female torso with viscera removed to expose posterior walls of thoracic and abdominopelvic cavities. (m. = muscle, v. = vein)

CHAPTER 2

Chemical Aspects of Life

Module 2
Cells & Chemistry

SELECTED KEY TERMS

Atom (atomos = indivisible) The smallest unit of an element.

Carbohydrate (carbo = carbon; hydr = water) A group of organic compounds composed of C, H, and O usually in a 1:2:1 ratio; mono-, di-, and polysaccharides.

Chemical compound (componere = to place together) A substance formed of two or more elements combined in a fixed ratio.

Chemical element A substance that cannot be broken down into simpler substances by chemical means.

Decomposition reaction (de = down from) The breakdown of complex molecules into simpler molecules.

Enzyme (en = in; zym = ferment) A protein that catalyzes chemical reactions.

Isotope (iso = equal) An atom of an element having the same number of protons and electrons but a different number of neutrons than most atoms of the element.

Lipid (lip = fat) A group of organic compounds containing fats.

Molecule (molecula = little mass) The smallest unit of a compound;

composed of two or more atoms chemically combined.

Monosaccharide (mono = one; sacchar = sugar) A simple sugar; a carbohydrate molecule composed of a single saccharide unit.

Nucleic acid (nucle = kernel) A complex organic molecule composed of nucleotides.

Protein A group of nitrogen-containing organic compounds formed of amino acids.

Synthesis reaction (syn = together; thesis = to put) Formation of a molecule by combining atoms or simpler molecules.

C hemistry is the scientific study of substances, especially the interaction of substances. A basic knowledge of chemistry is necessary for health-care professionals because the human body is composed of chemicals, and the processes of life are chemical interactions.

2.1 Atoms and Elements

Anything that has weight and occupies space is **matter.** The entire physical universe, both living and nonliving, is composed of matter. All matter is composed of **chemical elements,** substances that cannot be broken down by chemical means into simpler substances. Carbon, hydrogen, and nitrogen are examples of chemical elements.

There are 92 naturally occurring chemical elements, and 26 elements are found in the human body. About 96% of the body weight consists of only four elements: hydrogen, oxygen, carbon, and nitrogen. Many of the elements in the body are called *trace elements* because they occur in exceedingly small amounts. Table 2.1 lists the elements composing 99.9% of the human body.

Atomic Structure AP R

An **atom** (a'-tom) is the smallest unit of an element that participates in chemical reactions. Atoms of a given element are similar to each other, and they are different from atoms of all other elements. Atoms of different elements differ in size, weight, and how they interact with other atoms.

Table 2.1	The Most Abundant Elements Composing the Human Body		
Name	**Symbol**	**% by Weight**	**Importance**
Oxygen	O	65	Component of most organic molecules and water
Carbon	C	18.5	Forms "backbone" of all organic molecules
Hydrogen	H	9.5	Component of organic molecules, including all foods; part of water molecule
Nitrogen	N	3.2	Component of proteins and nucleic acids
Calcium	Ca	1.5	Component of teeth and bones; essential for blood clotting, muscle contraction, and nerve function
Phosphorus	P	1.0	Component of teeth, bones, nucleic acids, ATP, and many proteins
Potassium	K	0.4	Essential for nerve function and muscle contraction
Sulfur	S	0.3	Component of many proteins
Sodium	Na	0.2	Essential for nerve function; helps maintain water balance in body fluids
Chlorine	Cl	0.2	Helps maintain water balance in body fluids
Magnesium	Mg	0.1	Component of many proteins

Atoms are composed of three types of subatomic particles: protons, neutrons, and electrons. Each **proton** has a positive electrical charge. Each **electron** has a negative electrical charge. Each **neutron** has no electrical charge. Protons and neutrons are located in the centrally located **nucleus** of an atom. Electrons rotate, or orbit, at high speed around the nucleus. See the diagram of atomic structure in figure 2.1.

An atom is electrically neutral because it has the same number of protons as electrons, although the number of neutrons may vary. Table 2.2 summarizes the characteristics of subatomic particles.

The atoms of each element are characterized by a specific atomic number, symbol, and atomic weight. These characteristics are used to identify the element. The **atomic number** indicates the number of protons and also the number of electrons in each atom. The *symbol* is a shorthand way of referring to an element or to an atom of the element. The **atomic weight** is the sum of the number of protons and neutrons in each atom. For example, the element carbon has an atomic number of 6, a symbol of C, and an atomic weight of 12. From this information, you know that an atom of carbon has six protons, six electrons, and six neutrons. Examine table 2.3, which lists the atomic characteristics for some common elements in the human body.

Isotopes

All atoms of an element have the same number of protons and electrons, but some atoms may have a different number of neutrons. An atom of an element with a different number of neutrons is called an **isotope** (ĭ′-so-tōp). For example, carbon has three isotopes: ^{12}C, ^{13}C, ^{14}C. All isotopes of an element have the same chemical properties because they have the same number of protons and electrons.

Certain isotopes of some elements have an unstable nucleus that emits high-energy radiation as it breaks down to form a more stable nucleus. Such isotopes are called *radioisotopes*. Certain radioisotopes are used in the diagnosis of disorders and in the treatment of cancer. See the clinical insight box on page 29.

p = protons
n = neutrons
• = electrons

6p
6n

carbon

Figure 2.1 Diagram of a carbon atom. The number of protons and electrons are equal, which makes the atom electrically neutral.

Table 2.2 Characteristics of Subatomic Particles		
Particle	**Electrical Charge**	**Location**
Proton	Positive (+)	Nucleus
Neutron	0	Nucleus
Electron	Negative (−)	Electron shells

Table 2.3 Atomic Characteristics of the Common Elements in the Body					
Element	**Symbol**	**Protons***	**Neutrons**	**Atomic Weight****	**Electrons in Valence Shell**
Hydrogen	H	1	0	1	1
Carbon	C	6	6	12	4
Nitrogen	N	7	7	14	5
Oxygen	O	8	8	16	6
Sodium	Na	11	12	23	1
Magnesium	Mg	12	12	24	2
Phosphorus	P	15	16	31	5
Sulfur	S	16	16	32	6
Chlorine	Cl	17	18	35	7
Potassium	K	19	20	39	1
Calcium	Ca	20	20	40	2

*Number of protons = Number of electrons = Atomic number.
**Isotopes not included.

Check My Understanding

1. What is the relationship among matter, elements, and atoms?
2. What is the basic structure of an atom?

2.2 Molecules and Compounds

Atoms combine chemically in specific ways to form **molecules** (mol'-e-kūlz). For example, two atoms of oxygen may combine to form a molecule of gaseous oxygen (O_2), and an atom of sodium may combine with an atom of chlorine to form a molecule of sodium chloride (NaCl). Sodium chloride is a **chemical compound** because it is composed of two elements chemically combined in a *fixed ratio*. A molecule is the smallest unit of a compound that exhibits the properties of the compound. A compound can be broken down into its component elements by chemical means.

Chemical Formulas

A **chemical formula** expresses the chemical composition of a molecule. Chemical symbols indicate the elements of the atoms involved, and subscripts identify the number of atoms of each element in the molecule. A chemical formula expresses both the composition of a single molecule and the composition of a compound. For example, the chemical formula for water is H_2O, which indicates that two atoms of hydrogen combine with one atom of oxygen to form a water molecule.

Chemical Bonds AP|R

Electrons are involved in the formation of **chemical bonds,** which join atoms together to form a molecule. A chemical bond is a force of attraction between two atoms. It is not a structure. An atom combines with another atom in order to fill its **valence shell,** its outermost shell of electrons. A full valence shell makes an atom more stable. To do this, atoms either (1) donate or receive electrons or (2) share electrons.

The first shell of electrons, the shell closest to the nucleus, can hold a maximum of two electrons even if it is the only electron shell. An atom with two or more electron shells reacts with other atoms to fill its valence shell with eight electrons. Note the number of electrons in the valence shell of atoms of the elements in table 2.3.

Ionic Bonds

Atoms that form ionic bonds do so by donating or receiving electrons. Atoms with more than one electron shell and with one, two, or three electrons in the valence shell tend to donate electrons. Atoms with five, six, or seven electrons in the valence shell tend to receive electrons.

Consider the interaction of sodium and chlorine in the formation of sodium chloride (table salt), as shown in figure 2.2. Sodium has a single electron in its valence shell, and chlorine has seven electrons in its valence shell. The transfer of an electron from sodium to chlorine causes the sodium atom to have a net electrical charge of +1 and the chlorine atom to have a net electrical charge of −1.

Atoms with a net electrical charge, either positive or negative, are called **ions.** Thus, the transfer of

Figure 2.2 The synthesis of a molecule of sodium chloride by the formation of an ionic bond. The transfer of an electron from sodium to chlorine converts sodium to a positive ion and chlorine to a negative ion. The attraction between these oppositely charged ions is an ionic bond.

Clinical INSIGHT

Nuclear medicine is the medical specialty that uses radioisotopes in the diagnosis and treatment of disease. Very small amounts of weak radioisotopes may be used to tag biological molecules in order to trace the movement or metabolism of these molecules in the body. Special instruments can detect the radiation emitted by the radioisotopes and identify the location of the tagged molecules.

In *nuclear imaging,* the emitted radiation creates an image on a special photographic plate or computer screen. In this way, it is possible to obtain an image of various organs or parts of organs where the radioisotopes accumulate. Positron emission tomography (PET) uses certain radioisotopes that emit positrons (positively charged electrons), and it enables precise imaging similar to computerized tomography (CT) scans. PET can be used to measure processes, such as blood flow, rate of metabolism of selected substances, and effects of drugs on body functions. It is a promising technique for both the diagnosis of disease and the study of normal physiological processes.

Another form of nuclear medicine involves the use of radioisotopes to kill tumor cells. Certain radioisotopes may be attached to specific biological molecules and injected into the blood. When these molecules accumulate in cancerous tissue, the emitted radiation kills the cancerous cells. A similar effect is obtained by implanting pellets of radioactive isotopes directly in cancerous tissue.

Positron Emission Tomography (PET)
Transverse section through the skull. The highest level of brain activity is indicated in red, with successively lower levels represented by yellow, green, and blue.

---

an electron from sodium to chlorine has (1) resulted in the valence shell of each atom being filled with electrons and (2) produced a sodium ion (Na^+) and a chloride ion (Cl^-). The force of attraction that holds these ions together is an **ionic bond.** Ionic bonds always are formed between ions of opposite electrical charges. Positively charged ions, such as Na^+, are called *cations.* Negatively charged ions, such as Cl^-, are called *anions.*

When ionic compounds are dissolved in water, their molecules tend to **ionize** (dissociate), releasing ions. Such compounds are called **electrolytes** (ē-lek'-trō-lītz) because when dissolved they can conduct an electrical current. The composition and concentration of electrolytes in the body must be kept within narrow limits to maintain normal body functions. AP|R

Covalent Bonds

Atoms that form molecules by sharing electrons are joined by **covalent bonds.** The shared electrons orbit around each atom for part of the time so that they may be counted in the outer shell of each atom. Thus, the valence shell of each atom is filled.

A simple example of covalent bonding is found in a molecule of hydrogen gas. A hydrogen atom with a single electron requires one more electron to fill its valence shell. Two hydrogen atoms can form a molecule of hydrogen gas (H_2) by sharing their electrons. In this way, the valence shell of both atoms is complete and a single covalent bond is formed. The single covalent bond is shown in a structural formula as a single straight line between atomic symbols for hydrogen (H—H).

Double and triple covalent bonds can also form. A molecule of gaseous oxygen (O_2) is formed when two oxygen atoms share two pairs of electrons. Each oxygen atom requires two electrons to complete its valence shell, so by sharing two pairs of electrons the valence shell of both atoms is complete and a double covalent bond (O=O) is formed.

A water molecule (H_2O) is another example of covalent bonding. Each hydrogen atom shares its electron with the oxygen atom, and the oxygen atom shares one of its electrons with each hydrogen atom so that the valence shell of all three atoms is complete. Thus, a single covalent bond is formed between the oxygen atom and each hydrogen atom (H—O—H). See figure 2.3.

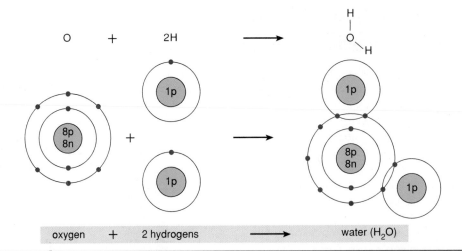

oxygen + 2 hydrogens ⟶ water (H_2O)

Figure 2.3 The synthesis of a water molecule by the formation of covalent bonds. Two hydrogen atoms and one oxygen atom share electrons to complete their outer electron shells. Two shared electrons compose one covalent bond.

Hydrogen Bonds

A third type of chemical bond does not form molecules but occurs within or between some molecules formed by covalent bonding because of the unequal distribution of electrons within the molecules. When a hydrogen atom is covalently bonded to an oxygen or nitrogen atom, the shared electrons spend less time in the hydrogen atom and more time in the oxygen or nitrogen atom. Therefore, the hydrogen atom is slightly positively charged, and the oxygen or nitrogen atom is slightly negatively charged. The bonds of such molecules are called *polar covalent bonds,* and the molecule is said to be a **polar molecule** because each "end" of the molecule has a different electrical charge. This sets the stage for the formation of a **hydrogen bond**—a weak attractive force between a slightly positive hydrogen atom and a slightly negative oxygen or nitrogen atom at a different site within the same molecule or in a different molecule.

For example, hydrogen bonds between water molecules cause water molecules to cling together in the liquid state (figure 2.4). Boiling water breaks the hydrogen bonds, and individual water molecules are released as steam. Hydrogen bonds play important roles in living organisms by maintaining the three-dimensional shape of proteins and nucleic acids.

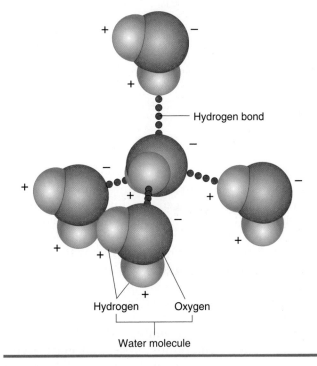

Figure 2.4 Hydrogen bonds form between adjacent water molecules. A hydrogen bond forms between a slightly positive hydrogen atom of one molecule and a slightly negative oxygen atom of an adjacent water molecule.

Chemical Reactions

In chemical reactions, bonds between atoms are formed or broken, and the result is a new combination of atoms. There are three basic types of chemical reactions: synthesis, exchange, and decomposition reactions. Such reactions occur continuously within the body.

> *Check My Understanding*
>
> 3. How do ionic and covalent bonds join atoms to form molecules?
> 4. What are hydrogen bonds?

Synthesis reactions form new chemical bonds and new products, and energy is required for the reactions to occur. Atoms or simple molecules combine to form a more complex product. The reaction of hydrogen and oxygen *(reactants)* to form water *(product)* is an example. Synthesis reactions produce complex molecules used in the growth and repair of body parts. Synthesis reactions may be generalized as

$$A + B \rightarrow AB$$

A **decomposition reaction** is just the reverse. Chemical bonds of a complex molecule are broken to form two or more simpler molecules, releasing energy in the process. For example, water can decompose to form hydrogen and oxygen. Decomposition reactions are used to break down food molecules to form nutrients usable by body cells. Decomposition reactions may be generalized as

$$AB \rightarrow A + B$$

Exchange reactions occur when two different reactants exchange components, resulting in the breakdown of the reactants and the formation of two new products. Thus, exchange reactions involve both decomposition of the reactants and synthesis of the new products. Exchange reactions may be generalized as

$$AB + CD \rightarrow AD + CB$$

Many chemical reactions are reversible, meaning that the product(s), on the right side of the arrow, can change back into the reactants, on the left side of the arrow. Several factors determine the reversibility of a reaction, such as energy available and relative abundance of reactants and products. Reversible reactions are indicated by a double arrow:

$$A + B \rightleftharpoons AB$$

Check My Understanding

5. How do synthesis, decomposition, and exchange reactions differ?

2.3 Compounds Composing the Human Body

Compounds composing the human body include both inorganic and organic substances. Molecules of **inorganic compounds** may contain either carbon or hydrogen in the same molecule, *but not both.* Bicarbonates, such as sodium bicarbonate ($NaHCO_3$), are the exception to this rule. Molecules of **organic compounds** always contain *both* carbon and hydrogen, and they usually also contain oxygen. The carbon atoms form the "backbone" of organic molecules. Table 2.4 compares the major characteristics of inorganic and organic compounds.

Major Inorganic Compounds

The major inorganic compounds in the body are water, most acids and bases, and inorganic salts. Acids, bases, and mineral salts **ionize** to release ions when dissolved in water, as you will see shortly.

Water

Water is a very important compound. It composes about two-thirds of the body weight, which makes it the most abundant compound in the body. Water is able to absorb or release large amounts of heat without much change in its own temperature. Thus, it helps to distribute heat throughout the body and prevents sudden fluctuations in body temperature.

Water is an excellent **solvent** and dissolves many substances **(solutes),** especially ionic compounds. Body fluids are aqueous (water) solutions in which numerous solutes are dissolved. Chemical reactions that occur in the body take place in an aqueous solution.

Water serves as a lubricant, reducing friction where internal body parts rub together, and it aids the movement of food through the digestive tract.

The specific locations where water is found in the body are called *water compartments.* They are

Intracellular fluid (ICF): water within cells; about 65% of the total body water.
Extracellular fluid (ECF): all water not in cells; about 35% of the total body water.

Table 2.4 Comparison of Inorganic and Organic Compounds

Inorganic Compounds	Organic Compounds
Molecules contain relatively few atoms.	Molecules usually contain many atoms.
Molecules do *not* contain both carbon and hydrogen.	Molecules *always* contain both carbon and hydrogen.
Molecules are usually formed by ionic bonding.	Molecules are always formed by covalent bonding.

Tissue fluid (interstitial fluid): water in tiny spaces between cells.
Plasma: fluid portion of blood.
Lymph: fluid in lymphatic vessels.
Specialized fluids: water in more limited locations, such as serous fluid (fluid secreted by membranes lining the ventral body cavity).

Acids and Bases

An **acid** increases the **hydrogen ion (H⁺)** concentration of a solution by dissociating to release H⁺.

The stronger the acid, the greater is the degree of dissociation, which results in a greater concentration of H⁺. Hydrochloric acid (HCl) is a strong acid. It dissociates into hydrogen and chloride ions (H⁺ and Cl⁻).

$$HCl \rightarrow H^+ + Cl^-$$

A **base** decreases the concentration of H⁺ in a solution by combining with the H⁺. The stronger the base, the greater is its ability to combine with H⁺. Some bases combine directly with H⁺. Other bases, such as sodium hydroxide (NaOH), dissociate to release hydroxide ions (OH⁻), which combine with H⁺ to form water.

$$NaOH \rightarrow Na^+ + OH^-$$

$$H^+ + OH^- \rightarrow HOH$$

The symbol **pH** is a measure of the hydrogen ion concentration in a solution.

pH: Acid–Base Balance   Chemists have developed a pH scale that is used to indicate the measure of acidity or alkalinity of a solution, that is, the relative concentrations of hydrogen ions (H⁺) and hydroxide ions (OH⁻) in a solution. The **pH scale** ranges from 0 to 14. Figure 2.5 shows the pH scale and the relative concentration of H⁺ and OH⁻ at each pH value. The concentration of H⁺ decreases and the concentration of OH⁻ increases as the pH values increase. These ions are equal in concentration at pH 7, so a solution with a pH of 7 is neither an acid nor a base. For example, pure water has a pH of 7.

Solutions with a pH less than 7 are acids, and those with a pH greater than 7 are bases. The lower the pH value below 7, the more acidic is the solution, and the higher the pH value above 7, the more basic is the solution. There is a 10-fold difference in the concentrations of H⁺ and OH⁻ when the pH changes by one unit. For example, an acid with a pH of 4 has a concentration of H⁺ that is 10 times greater than that of an acid with a pH of 5.

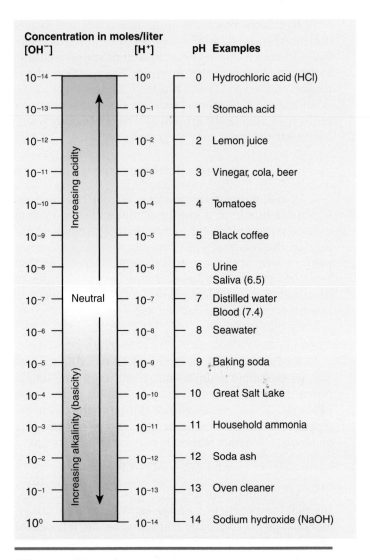

Figure 2.5   The pH scale. A pH of 7 is neutral because the concentrations of OH⁻ and H⁺ are equal. Solutions with a pH less than 7 are acidic, and those with a pH more than 7 are basic. Note that the concentration of OH⁻ increases and the concentration of H⁺ decreases as the pH values increase.

Buffers   Cells of the body are especially sensitive to pH changes. Even slight changes can be harmful. The hydrogen ion concentration (pH) of blood and other body fluids is maintained within narrow limits by the lungs, kidneys, and buffers in body fluids. A **buffer** is a chemical or a combination of chemicals that either picks up excess H⁺ or releases H⁺ to keep the pH of a solution rather constant.

Buffers are extremely important in maintaining the normal pH of body fluids, but they can be overwhelmed by a disruption of homeostasis. The normal pH of the blood is 7.35 to 7.45. In *acidosis,* the pH is less than 7.35, and the patient feels tired and disoriented. In *alkalosis,* the pH range is greater than 7.45, and the patient feels agitated and dizzy. Extreme variations may be fatal.

Salts

Like inorganic acids and bases, *inorganic salts* are ionic compounds that dissociate in an aqueous solution, but they do not produce hydrogen and hydroxide ions. The most important salts in the body are sodium, potassium, and calcium salts. Calcium phosphate is the most abundant salt because it is a main component of bones and teeth. For example, sodium chloride (NaCl), a common salt in body fluids, dissociates into sodium and chloride ions (Na^+ and Cl^-).

$$NaCl \rightarrow Na^+ + Cl^-$$

Inorganic salts provide ions that are essential for normal body functioning. Physiological processes in which ions play an essential role include blood clotting, muscle and nerve functions, and pH and water balance (table 2.5).

Check My Understanding

6. Where is water located in the body, and why is it so important?
7. What is the relationship among acids, bases, and pH?
8. What are inorganic salts, and why are they important?

Major Organic Compounds

The major organic compounds of the body are carbohydrates, lipids, proteins, and nucleic acids (table 2.6). Another compound, adenosine triphosphate, is also considered here because it plays such a vital role in the transfer of energy within cells.

Table 2.5 Important Inorganic Ions

Ion	Symbol	Functions
Bicarbonate	HCO_3^-	Helps maintain acid–base balance
Calcium	Ca^{++}	Major component of bones and teeth; required for muscle contraction and blood clotting
Carbonate	CO_3^{-2}	Major component of bones and teeth; helps maintain acid–base balance
Chloride	Cl^-	Helps maintain water balance
Hydrogen	H^+	Helps maintain acid–base balance
Hydroxide	OH^-	Helps maintain acid–base balance
Phosphate	PO_4^{-3}	Major component of bones and teeth; required for energy transfer
Potassium	K^+	Required for muscle and nerve function
Sodium	Na^+	Required for muscle and nerve function; helps maintain water balance

Table 2.6 Important Organic Compounds

Compound	Building Units	Examples	Functions
Carbohydrates	Monosaccharides (simple sugars)	Glucose	Primary energy source for cells
		Starch	Storage form in plants; common in plant foods
		Glycogen	Storage form in animals; stored in liver and muscles
Lipids	Glycerol, fatty acids, phosphate	Triglycerides (fats)	Energy source and storage
		Phospholipids	Cell structure
		Steroids	A variety of functions (e.g., sex hormones promote sexual development)
Proteins	Amino acids	Structural proteins	Cell structure
		Functional proteins	Nonstructural functions (e.g., enzymes catalyze chemical reactions)
Nucleic acids	Nucleotides	DNA	Directs cell functions by controlling protein synthesis
		RNA	Helps in protein synthesis

Carbohydrates

Carbohydrates (kar″-bo-hī′-drātz) are formed of carbon, hydrogen, and oxygen. In each carbohydrate molecule, there are two hydrogen atoms for every oxygen atom. Carbohydrates are the primary source of nutrient energy for cells of the body. Carbohydrates are classified according to molecular size as monosaccharides, disaccharides, or polysaccharides (figure 2.6).

The simplest carbohydrates are **monosaccharides** (mon-ō-sak′-ah-rīds), or simple sugars. For example, **glucose** ($C_6H_{12}O_6$) is a six-carbon simple sugar that is the major carbohydrate fuel for cells. It is often called blood sugar because it is the form in which carbohydrates are transported to body cells. Fructose and galactose are other six-carbon simple sugars found in foods. Six-carbon monosaccharides are chemically combined to produce more complex carbohydrates.

The chemical combination of two monosaccharides forms a **disaccharide** (dī-sak′-ah-rīd), a double sugar. The common disaccharides in foods are *maltose,* or malt sugar (glucose + glucose), *sucrose,* or table sugar (glucose + fructose) and *lactose,* or milk sugar (glucose + galactose).

A **polysaccharide** (pol-ē-sak′-ah-rīd) is formed by the chemical combination of many monosaccharide units. Two polysaccharides are important to our study: glycogen and starch. Both are formed of many glucose units.

Glycogen is the storage form of carbohydrates in the body. Some of the excess glucose in blood is converted into glycogen and stored primarily in the liver, but small amounts are stored in muscle cells. Glycogen serves as a reserve energy supply that can be quickly converted into glucose. For example, whenever the level of blood glucose declines, the liver converts glycogen into glucose to raise the blood glucose level.

Starch is the storage form of carbohydrates in plants, so it is present in many foods derived from plants.

Lipids

Lipids are a large, diverse group of organic compounds that consist of carbon, hydrogen, and oxygen atoms. Carbon atoms form the backbone of the molecules, and there are many times more hydrogen atoms than oxygen atoms. The most abundant lipids in the body are triglycerides (fats), phospholipids, and steroids.

Molecules of **triglycerides** (trī-glys′-er-īds), or **fats,** consist of one **glycerol** (glys′-er-ol) molecule and three **fatty acid** molecules joined together (figure 2.7). Triglycerides are the most concentrated energy source found in the body. Excess nutrients (energy reserves) are stored as triglycerides in the fat cells of the body, primarily around internal organs and under the skin. Fats are not soluble in water—that is, they are *hydrophobic.*

Triglycerides may be classified as either saturated or unsaturated fats. In **saturated fats** (animal fats), the bonds of the carbon atoms in the fatty acids are saturated (filled) by hydrogen atoms so that the carbon–carbon bonds are all single bonds. Saturated fats, such as butter and lard, are solid at room temperature. Excessive saturated fats in the diet are associated with an increased risk of heart disease (coronary artery disease).

In **unsaturated fats** (plant fats), not all carbon bonds in the fatty acids are filled with hydrogen atoms, and one or more double carbon–carbon bonds are present. Fatty acids of monounsaturated fats (e.g., olive, peanut, and canola oils) have one carbon–carbon double bond; those of polyunsaturated fats (e.g., corn, safflower, and soy oils) have two or more carbon–carbon double bonds. Unsaturated fats occur as oils at room temperature.

Hydrogenation, the process of adding hydrogen atoms to unsaturated fats, converts most

(a) Monosaccharide   (b) Disaccharide

(c) Polysaccharide

Figure 2.6 (*a*) The building units of carbohydrates are monosaccharides. (*b*) Two monosaccharides combine to form a disaccharide. (*c*) The combination of many monosaccharide units forms a polysaccharide.

Figure 2.7 A triglyceride molecule consists of three fatty acids joined to a glycerol molecule.

carbon–carbon double bonds to carbon–carbon single bonds and changes vegetable oil to a solid (e.g., margarine) at room temperature. This process also changes the bonding pattern of some fatty acids to form *trans fats,* which increase the risk of coronary artery disease even more than do saturated fats. It is better to cook with oils than with lard or margarine because saturated and trans fats are more easily converted into the "bad" cholesterol associated with heart disease. In figure 2.7, two fatty acids are saturated and one is monounsaturated.

Phospholipids (fos′-fō-lip′-idz) have molecules similar to triglycerides. The basic difference is that one of the fatty acids is replaced with a phosphate-containing group. Unlike fats, phospholipids are partially soluble in water. The end of the molecule with the phosphate group is soluble in water but not in lipids, and the end with the two fatty acids is fat soluble but insoluble in water. Thus, phospholipids can join—or serve as an interface between—a water environment on one side and a lipid environment on the other. They are major components of cell membranes. Figure 2.8 shows the basic structure of a phospholipid molecule.

Steroids constitute another group of lipids, and their molecules characteristically contain four carbon rings. Cholesterol and sex hormones are examples of steroids. Figure 2.9 shows the structure of cholesterol and testosterone. Cholesterol (kō-les′-ter-ol) is an essential component of body cells and serves as the raw material for the synthesis of other steroid molecules. But cholesterol can be hazardous when present in the diet in excessive amounts. See the clinical box on the next page.

Proteins

Proteins (pro′-te-ins or pro′-tēns) are large, complex molecules composed of smaller molecules (building units) called **amino acids.** There are 20 different kinds of amino acids, and each is composed of carbon, hydrogen, oxygen, and nitrogen. As the name implies, each amino acid consists of an *amine group* (—NH₂) and an *acid*

Figure 2.8 Comparison of triglyceride (fat) and phospholipid molecules. (*a*) A triglyceride consists of three fatty acids attached to a glycerol. (*b*) In a phospholipid, one fatty acid is replaced by a phosphate-containing group.

Figure 2.9 Steroids include cholesterol and testosterone (male sex hormone). Note the four carbon rings, which are characteristic of steroids.

group (—COOH), but it is the *R group,* the remainder of the molecule, that distinguishes the different kinds of amino acids. Figure 2.10 depicts the basic structure of an amino acid.

Amino acids are joined by **peptide bonds.** Two amino acids bonded together form a **dipeptide.** A chain up to 50 amino acids long forms a **polypeptide.** A chain of 50 to thousands of amino acids forms a protein. Hydrogen bonds between various parts of a polypeptide or protein molecule cause the molecule to twist and fold. The result is that each specific polypeptide or protein has a unique three-dimensional shape. Therefore, it is the sequence of amino acids and the hydrogen bonding between the amino acids that determine

a protein's shape, which, in turn, determines its function.

Proteins may be classified as either structural or functional proteins. *Structural proteins* compose parts of body cells and tissues, where they provide support and strength in binding parts together. Ligaments, tendons, and contractile fibers in muscles are composed of structural proteins. *Functional proteins* perform a variety of different functions in the body. *Antibodies,* which provide immunity, and *enzymes,* which speed up chemical reactions, are examples of functional proteins.

Enzymes   Without **enzymes,** the body's chemical reactions would occur too slowly to maintain life. Body cells contain thousands of enzymes, and each enzyme *catalyzes* (speeds up) a particular chemical reaction. An enzyme may catalyze synthesis, decomposition, or exchange reactions. Figure 2.11 illustrates enzyme action in synthesis and decomposition reactions.

The enzyme must have just the right shape so the **substrate** molecule(s) can fit onto the active site of the enzyme, somewhat like a piece of a puzzle. The enzyme binds to the substrate to form an *enzyme–substrate complex* where chemical bonds are formed between substrate molecules in synthesis reactions, or chemical bonds of the substrate molecule are broken in decomposition reactions. Once the reaction has occurred, the product separates from the enzyme. The enzyme is not altered in the reaction and may be recycled and used again and again. A single enzyme may catalyze thousands of reactions. An enzymatic reaction may be generalized as

$$E + S \rightarrow ES \rightarrow E + P$$

Clinical INSIGHT

High levels of cholesterol are associated with an increased risk of heart disease. Cholesterol occurs in the blood in combination with triglycerides and proteins. These lipid–protein complexes are called *lipoproteins.* Considerable evidence links a high concentration of low-density lipoprotein (LDL), the so-called "bad" cholesterol, with heart disease. In contrast, high levels of high-density lipoprotein (HDL), the "good" cholesterol, reduce the risk of heart disease. Cholesterol levels result from a combination of heredity, diet, and exercise.

A total cholesterol level of less than 200 mg/dl (milligrams per deciliter) is a desirable goal. An LDL

concentration of 100 to 130 mg/dl is near optimal. Persons at risk of coronary artery disease, such as smokers and the elderly, should strive for an LDL level of less than 100. Reducing the amount of saturated fats (red meat, milk products, and egg yolks) and trans fats (present in hydrogenated oils) in the diet can lower the LDL level.

HDL levels average 40 to 50 mg/dl in men and 50 to 60 mg/dl in women. HDL levels may be increased by exercise and maintaining a healthy weight.

Figure 2.10 Amino acids. (*a*) The basic structure of an amino acid. (*b*) Representative amino acids. Note that the amino group and carboxyl (acid) group are the same in all amino acids. It is only the R group that is different among different amino acids.

Like other proteins, the three-dimensional shape of an enzyme is determined by hydrogen bonds. And hydrogen bonds are easily broken by several factors, such as temperature and pH changes, poisons, and radiation. If an enzyme's hydrogen bonds are altered, its shape is changed, and the enzyme is inactivated (denatured). Because it cannot bind to the substrate, the reaction it catalyzes will not occur. If the reaction is vital, the result can be fatal.

Nucleic Acids

Nucleic (nū-klā′-ic) **acids** are composed of very large molecules. Two types of nucleic acids occur in cells: DNA and RNA. **Deoxyribonucleic** (dē-ok″-se-rī″-bō-nū-

klā′-ic) **acid (DNA)** composes the hereditary portion of chromosomes in the cell nucleus. DNA contains the *genetic code,* encoded information that determines hereditary traits and cellular functions. The genetic code does this by determining the structure of proteins. The portions of DNA that encode for specific proteins are called **genes** (jēns). **Ribonucleic acid (RNA)** carries the coded instructions from DNA to the cellular machinery involved in protein synthesis.

Both DNA and RNA consist of repeating units called **nucleotides** (nū′-klē-ō-tīds). Each nucleotide consists of three parts: a five-carbon sugar, a phosphate group, and an organic base. Figure 2.12 shows four nucleotides that form part of a strand of a nucleic acid. Note that the five-carbon sugars and phosphate

(a) Synthesis

(b) Degradation/decomposition

Figure 2.11 A model of enzyme action. (*a*) A synthesis reaction. (*b*) A decomposition reaction. The substrate binds to the active site of the enzyme where the reaction occurs. Then the product is released, and the enzyme is recycled. **AP|R**

We often think that infectious diseases are caused only by viruses and microorganisms, but surprisingly that is not the case. *Prions* (prē-ahns) are unusual proteins because they can assume more than one shape, and when in an abnormal shape, they are actually infectious. Abnormal prions can bind to normal prions and convert them into the abnormal infectious shape. Mammals are susceptible to these abnormal prions and are infected via their food. These prions are the infectious agents causing "mad cow" disease in cattle and Creutzfeldt–Jakob disease in humans. These diseases cause the destruction of brain cells, loss of brain function, and death. There is no cure.

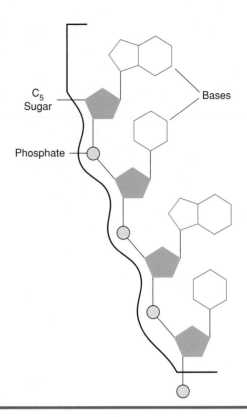

Figure 2.12 Four nucleotides of a nucleic acid molecule. Each nucleotide consists of a five-carbon sugar, a phosphate group, and an organic base. The phosphate groups join the sugars of the nucleotides together to form the strand, and the organic bases project from the sugar molecules.

groups form the backbone of the strand and that the organic (nitrogen-containing) bases project from the sugar molecules.

DNA consists of two strands of nucleotides joined together by hydrogen bonds that form between the complementary pairing nitrogenous bases. It superficially resembles a "twisted ladder." See figure 2.13. The "sides of the ladder" are formed of deoxyribose sugar and phosphate. The "rungs of the ladder" are composed of the paired nitrogenous bases: **adenine** (A) pairs with **thymine** (T), and **cytosine** (C) pairs with **guanine** (G). In contrast, RNA consists of a single strand of nucleotides. The backbone is formed of ribose sugar and phosphate, and the nitrogenous bases are adenine, uracil, cytosine, and guanine. Note that **uracil** is present in RNA instead of thymine, which occurs in DNA.

Adenosine Triphosphate (ATP)

ATP, or **adenosine** (ah-den′-ō-sēn) **triphosphate** (trī-fos′-fāt), is a modified nucleotide that consists of adenosine and three phosphate groups. The last two phosphate groups are joined to the molecule by special bonds called *high-energy phosphate bonds*. In figure 2.14, these bonds are represented by wavy lines. Energy in these bonds is released to power chemical reactions within a cell. In this way, ATP provides immediate energy to keep cellular processes operating. It is the *only* molecule that performs this role.

Energy extracted from nutrients by cells is temporarily held in ATP and then released to power chemical reactions. When the terminal high-energy

phosphate bond of ATP is broken and energy is transferred, ATP is broken down into **adenosine diphosphate (ADP)** and a low-energy phosphate group (—P). The addition of a high-energy phosphate group to ADP re-forms ATP. ATP is continuously broken down into ADP to release energy, and it is re-formed as energy is made available from nutrients.

Check My Understanding

9. What distinguishes the chemical structure and functions of carbohydrates, lipids, proteins, and nucleic acids?
10. What is the role of enzymes in body cells?
11. What is ATP, and what is its role in body cells?

(a) (b) (c)

Figure 2.13 The structure of DNA. (*a*) A model showing the double helix or "twisted ladder" structure of DNA. The complementary pairing of the nitrogenous bases forming the rungs of the ladder holds the sugar–phosphate strands together. (*b*) A small segment of DNA showing sugar–phosphate molecules forming the backbone of each strand, and the strands joined together by hydrogen bonds formed between the paired nitrogenous bases. (*c*) A more complex molecular model. **AP|R**

Figure 2.14 The breakdown of ATP forms ADP and a phosphate group and releases energy to power cellular reactions. ATP is synthesized from ADP, phosphate, and energy extracted from nutrients.

CHAPTER SUMMARY

2.1 Atoms and Elements

- Matter is composed of elements, substances that cannot be broken down into simpler substances by chemical means.
- Oxygen, carbon, hydrogen, and nitrogen form 96% of the human body by weight.
- An atom is the smallest unit of an element.
- An atom consists of a nucleus formed of protons (+1) and neutrons (0) and electrons (−1) that orbit around the nucleus.
- Elements are characterized by their atomic numbers, symbols, and atomic weights.
- Isotopes of an element have differing numbers of neutrons.
- Radioisotopes emit radiation.

2.2 Molecules and Compounds

- A molecule is formed of two or more atoms joined by chemical bonds; it is the smallest unit of a compound.
- A compound is formed of two or more elements combined in a fixed ratio.
- A chemical formula indicates the number of atoms of each element in the molecule.
- Chemical bonds join atoms to form molecules.
- An ionic bond is the force of attraction between two ions with opposite electrical charges. It results from one atom donating one or more electrons to another atom.
- A covalent bond is formed between two atoms by the sharing of electrons in the valence shell.
- A hydrogen bond is a weak force of attraction between a slightly positive H atom and a slightly negative atom either in the same molecule or in different molecules.
- Synthesis reactions combine simpler substances to produce more complex substances.
- Decomposition reactions break down complex substances into simpler substances.
- Exchange reactions involve both decomposition of the reactants and synthesis of new products.

2.3 Compounds Composing the Human Body

- Inorganic compounds do *not* contain both carbon and hydrogen. Organic compounds contain *both* carbon and hydrogen.
- Water (H_2O) is the most abundant inorganic compound in the body, and it is the solvent of living systems.
- There are two major water compartments: intracellular fluid (65% of body water) and extracellular fluid (35% of body water).
- An acid releases H^+ in an aqueous solution, and a base releases OH^- in an aqueous solution.
- A salt releases positively and negatively charged ions in an aqueous solution, but they are neither H^+ nor OH^-.

- pH is a measure of the relative concentrations of H^+ and OH^- in a solution.
- A buffer keeps the pH of a solution relatively constant by picking up or releasing H^+.
- Carbohydrates are composed of C, H, and O with a 2:1 ratio between H and O.
- Monosaccharides, or simple sugars, are the building units of carbohydrates. Disaccharides consist of two simple sugars. Polysaccharides are formed of many simple sugars.
- Lipids are a diverse group of organic compounds that include triglycerides, phospholipids, and steroids.
- Triglycerides (fats) consist of three fatty acids bonded to glycerol. Unsaturated fats differ from saturated fats by having one or more double carbon–carbon bonds in their fatty acids. Excess nutrients are stored as fats.
- Phospholipids consist of two fatty acids and a phosphate-containing group bonded to glycerol.
- Steroids are an important group of lipids that includes sex hormones and cholesterol.
- Proteins are large molecules formed of many amino acids. The 20 different kinds of amino acids are distinguished by their R groups.
- Amino acids are joined by dipeptide bonds.
- Structural proteins form parts of cells and tissues. Functional proteins include enzymes and antibodies.
- Enzymes catalyze chemical reactions.
- Nucleic acids are very large molecules formed of many nucleotides.
- A nucleotide consists of a five-carbon sugar (ribose in RNA and deoxyribose in DNA), a phosphate group, and an organic base.
- There are two types of nucleic acids: deoxyribonucleic acid (DNA) and ribonucleic acid (RNA). DNA determines hereditary traits and controls cellular functions. RNA works with DNA in the synthesis of proteins.
- Adenosine triphosphate (ATP) is a modified nucleotide that temporarily holds energy in high-energy phosphate bonds and releases that energy to power chemical reactions in a cell.

BUILDING MY VOCABULARY

1. **Selected New Terms**
   acid, p. 32
   amino acid, p. 36
   ATP, p. 38
   base, p. 32
   buffer, p. 32
   covalent bond, p. 29
   dipeptide, p. 36
   disaccharide, p. 34
   DNA, p. 38
   electrolyte, p. 29
   electron, p. 27
   hydrogen bond, p. 30

   ionic bond, p. 29
   neutron, p. 27
   nucleotide, p. 38
   pH, p. 32
   phospholipid, p. 35
   polypeptide, p. 36
   polysaccharide, p. 34
   proton, p. 27
   RNA, p. 38
   solute, p. 31
   solvent, p. 31
   steroid, p. 35
   triglyceride, p. 34

2. **Related Clinical Terms**
   Acidosis (as″-id-ō′-sis) Abnormally low blood
   pH (< 7.3).
   Alkalosis (al″-kah-lō′-sis) Abnormally high blood
   pH (> 7.5).

Dehydration (dē-hī-drā′-shun) A significant decrease
in the water content of the body.
Hypovolemia (hī-pō-vol-ēm′-ia) Abnormally low
volume of blood plasma.

SELF-REVIEW

Answers are located in Appendix B.

1. An atom contains the same number of electrons as
   _____.
2. An _____ is an atom with a net electrical charge.
3. A _____ is the smallest unit of a compound.
4. When atoms share electrons, a _____ bond is formed.
5. The most abundant compound in the body is _____.
6. An acid has a pH _____ than 7.

7. In a _____ reaction, smaller molecules are combined
   to form a larger molecule.
8. The building units of a carbohydrate are _____.
9. The building units of proteins are _____.
10. The building units of nucleic acids are _____.
11. Glycerol and fatty acids combine to form _____.
12. _____ is the energy carrier that releases energy to
    power cellular processes.

CRITICAL THINKING

1. Complete the learning objectives on the first page of this chapter.
2. Explain the meaning of the letters and numbers in this chemical formula: $6C_6H_{12}O_6$. What is the chemical?
3. Potassium (K) has an atomic number of 19. How many electrons are in its valence shell? What type of chemical bond is
   it likely to form?
4. The pH of an aqueous solution is 6.0. Explain how the addition of the following substances would alter (or not alter)
   the pH of the solution.
   a. HCl   b. NaOH   c. HOH
5. What determines the shape of an enzyme? In what ways may an enzyme's shape be altered?

**Visit this book's website at www.mhhe.com/
gunstream5 for practice quizzes, learning exercises,
case studies, and other study tools.**

CHAPTER 3

Cell

Anatomy & Physiology REVEALED®
aprevealed.com

Module 2
Cells & Chemistry

SELECTED KEY TERMS

Active transport Movement of substances through a plasma membrane requiring the expenditure of energy by the cell.

Cell (cella = room, cell) The simplest structural and functional unit of living organisms.

Cellular respiration Breakdown of organic nutrients, which releases energy to form ATP.

Centrioles (centr = center) Paired cylindrical organelles adjacent to the nucleus that form the spindle during cell division.

Chromosome (chrom = color; soma = body) A threadlike or rodlike structure in cell nuclei that is composed of DNA and protein.

Cytoplasm (cyt = cell; plasma = molded) The semifluid substance located between the cell nucleus and the plasma membrane.

Diffusion Passive movement of molecules from an area of higher concentration to an area of lower concentration.

Endocytosis (end = inside; cyt = cell; sis = condition) Engulfing substances by invagination of the plasma membrane.

Endoplasmic reticulum System of membranes extending throughout the cytoplasm.

Exocytosis (exo = outside) Extrusion of substances by evagination of the plasma membrane.

Filtration The forcing of small molecules through a membrane by hydrostatic pressure.

Mitochondrion Organelle where aerobic cellular respiration occurs.

Mitosis (mit = thread; sis = condition) Separation and distribution of chromosomes to daughter cells during mitotic cell division.

Nucleus (nucle = kernel) Spherical organelle containing chromosomes and controlling cellular functions.

Organelle (elle = little) A specific part of a cell that performs a specific function.

Osmosis The diffusion of water through a selectively permeable membrane.

Passive transport Movement of substances through a plasma membrane without expenditure of energy by the cell.

Ribosome (ribo = ribose; soma = body) Tiny cytoplasmic organelle, composed of RNA and protein, that is the site of protein synthesis.

Selectively permeable membrane A membrane that allows some, but not all, substances to pass through it.

Like all living organisms, humans are composed of **cells**. In fact, there are about 75 trillion cells in the human body. Many different kinds of cells compose the body, and each type is specialized to perform specific functions. Just like organs of the body, the structure of a cell determines its function. Although these cells vary in size, shape, and function, they exhibit many structural and functional similarities.

Human cells are very small and are visible only with a microscope. Knowledge of cell structure is based largely on the examination of cells with an electron microscope, a type of microscope that provides magnifications up to 200,000× or more.

3.1 Cell Structure

Although human cells are small, they are amazingly complex with many specialized parts. The composite cell in figure 3.1 illustrates the major structures known to compose human cells. These structures are shown as they appear in electron microscope images. Most, but not all, of these structures are found in each human cell. As each part of a cell is discussed, note its structure and relationship to other structures in figure 3.1.

The Plasma Membrane

The **plasma membrane** forms the outer boundary of a cell. It maintains the integrity of the cell and separates the intracellular fluid from the extracellular fluid surrounding the cell. The plasma membrane consists of two layers of phospholipid molecules, aligned back-to-back, with their fatty acid tails forming the interior of the membrane (figure 3.2). Cholesterol molecules are scattered among the phospholipids where they serve to increase the stability of the plasma membrane. The fatty acid interior of the plasma membrane enables lipid-soluble substances to pass through the membrane but prevents the passage of water-soluble substances. Thus, the plasma membrane serves as a barrier between water-soluble substances in the aqueous intracellular and extracellular fluids.

Many different types of protein molecules are embedded in the plasma membrane, and each type has specific functions. Some proteins form channels or pores through which water and water-soluble substances move through the membrane. Some of these proteins allow a variety of substances to pass through; others permit only specific molecules or ions to enter or exit a cell. Some proteins serve as receptors for substances, such as hormones, that influence the function of a cell. Other proteins are enzymes that catalyze

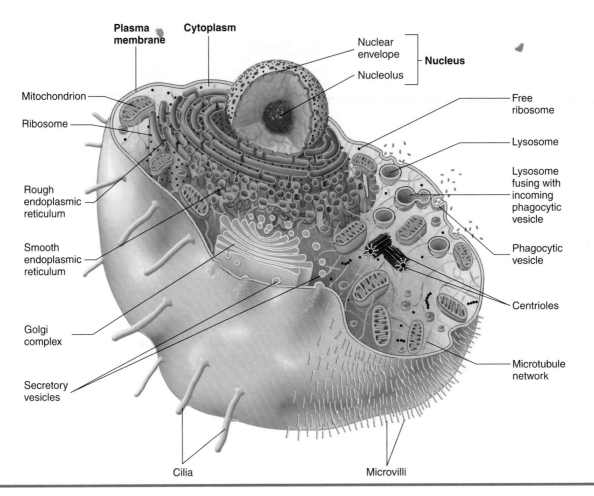

Figure 3.1   A composite human cell showing the major organelles. No cell contains all of the organelles shown. AP|R

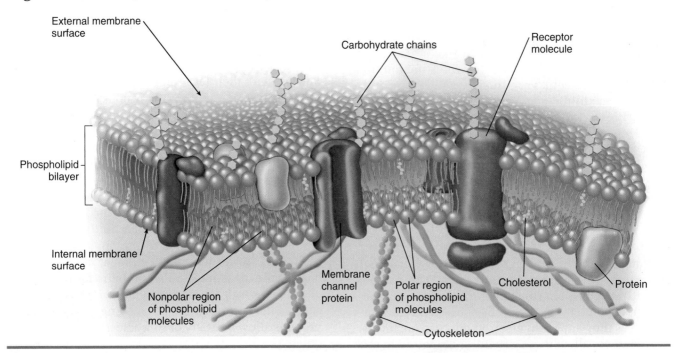

Figure 3.2   The plasma membrane is composed of two layers of phospholipid molecules with scattered embedded proteins. The hydrophilic polar heads of the phospholipids face outward, and the hydrophobic nonpolar, fatty acid tails form the interior of the membrane. AP|R

metabolic reactions. Certain proteins, in combination with carbohydrate molecules, serve as identification markers allowing cells to recognize each other, which may lead to similar cells binding together to form a tissue. And these identification markers allow the immune system to recognize "self" cells from "non-self" (foreign) cells, a distinction essential in fighting disease-causing pathogens.

All materials that enter or exit a cell must pass through the plasma membrane. The plasma membrane is a **selectively permeable membrane** because it allows only certain molecules to enter or exit the cell. Whether or not molecules can pass through the membrane is determined by a number of factors that include molecular size, solubility, ionic charges, and attachment to carrier molecules.

Cytoplasm

The interior of the cell is filled with the fluid or gel-like **cytoplasm** (sī'-tō-plazm). It contains 75% to 90% water plus an assortment of organic and inorganic compounds. It is semitransparent and usually slightly thicker than water, but at times it may have almost a gel-like consistency. It is supported by (1) intracellular membranes and (2) the cytoskeleton.

Organelles

A variety of **organelles** (or-gah-nel'z), or tiny organs, are surrounded by the cytoplasmic fluid. Each type of organelle performs a specific role in the cell. Organelles are distinguished by size, shape, structure, and function. Table 3.1 summarizes the structure and functions of the major parts of a cell.

Nucleus

The largest organelle is the **nucleus** (nū'klē-us), a spherical or egg-shaped structure that is slightly more dense than the surrounding cytoplasm. It is separated from the cytoplasm by a double-layered **nuclear envelope** containing numerous pores that aid the movement of materials between the nucleus and cytoplasm.

Table 3.1	Summary of Cell Parts	
Component	**Structure**	**Function**
Plasma membrane	Phospholipid bilayer with proteins and cholesterol molecules embedded in it	Selectively controls movement of materials into and out of the cell; maintains integrity of the cell; has receptors for hormones
Cytoplasm	Gel-like fluid surrounding organelles	Site of numerous chemical reactions
Organelles		
Nucleus	Largest organelle; contains chromosomes and nucleoli	Controls cellular functions
Endoplasmic reticulum (ER)	System of membranes extending through the cytoplasm; RER has ribosomes on the membrane; SER does not	Serves as sites of chemical reactions; channels for material transport within cell
Ribosomes	Tiny granules of rRNA and protein either associated with RER or free in cytoplasm	Sites of protein synthesis
Golgi complex	Series of stacked membranes near nucleus; associated with ER	Sorts and packages substances in vesicles for export from cell or use within cell; forms lysosomes
Mitochondria	Contain a folded membrane within a smaller exterior membrane	Sites of aerobic cellular respiration that form ATP from breakdown of nutrients
Lysosomes	Small vesicles containing strong digestive enzymes	Digest foreign substances or worn-out parts of cells
Microfilaments	Thin rods of protein dispersed in cytoplasm	Provide support for cell; contraction gives cell movement
Microtubules	Thin tubules dispersed in cytoplasm	Provide support for cell, cilia, and flagella; form spindle during cell division
Microvilli	Numerous, tiny extensions of the plasma membrane on certain cells	Increase the surface area, which aids absorption
Centrioles	Two short cylinders formed of microtubules; located near nucleus	Form spindle fibers during cell division
Cilia	Numerous short, hairlike projections from certain cells	Move materials along cell surface
Flagella	Long whiplike projections from sperm cells	Enable movement of sperm
Vesicles	Tiny membranous sacs containing substances	Transport or store substances

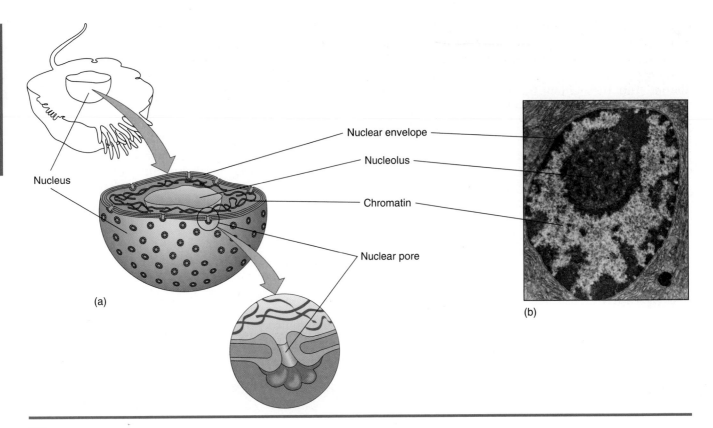

Nucleus

Nuclear envelope

Nucleolus

Chromatin

Nuclear pore

(a)

(b)

Figure 3.3   (a) The nuclear envelope is selectively permeable and allows certain substances to pass between the nucleus and the cytoplasm. (b) Transmission electron micrograph of a cell nucleus (8,000×). It contains a nucleolus and masses of chromatin. AP|R

Chromosomes (krō′-mō-sōms), the most important structures within the nucleus, consist of DNA and protein. The DNA of chromosomes contains coded instructions that determine the functions of the cell. When a cell is not dividing, chromosomes are extended to form thin threads that appear as *chromatin* (krō′-mah-tin) *granules* when viewed microscopically, as in figure 3.3. During cell division, the chromosomes coil and shorten and become rod-shaped. Each human body cell contains 23 pairs of chromosomes, with a total of 46 in all.

One or more dense spherical bodies, the **nucleoli** (nū-klē-ō-lē), are also present in the nucleus. A nucleolus consists of RNA and protein and is the site of ribosome production.

Ribosomes

Ribosomes are tiny organelles that appear as granules within the cytoplasm even in electron photomicrographs. They are composed of ribosomal RNA (rRNA) and protein, which are preformed in a nucleolus before migrating from the nucleus into the cytoplasm. Ribosomes are the sites of protein synthesis in cells. They may occur singly or in small clusters and are located either on the endoplasmic reticulum or as free ribosomes in the cytoplasm.

Endoplasmic Reticulum

The numerous membranes that extend from the nucleus throughout the cytoplasm are collectively called the **endoplasmic reticulum** (en″-dō-plas′-mik rē-tik′-ū-lum), or **ER** for short. These membranes provide some support for the cytoplasm and form a network of channels that facilitate the movement of materials within the cell.

There are two types of ER: rough ER and smooth ER. *Rough endoplasmic reticulum (RER)* is characterized by the presence of numerous ribosomes located on the outer surface of the membranes. *Smooth endoplasmic reticulum (SER)* lacks ribosomes and serves as a site for the synthesis of lipids (figure 3.4).

Golgi Complex

This organelle appears as a stack of flattened membranous sacs that are usually located near the nucleus and in close association with the nucleus and ER. The **Golgi** (Gol′-jē) **complex** processes and sorts synthesized substances, such as proteins,

(a)

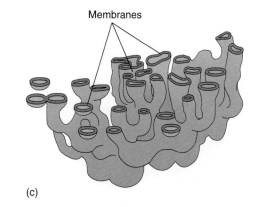

Figure 3.4 (a) Transmission electron micrograph of rough endoplasmic reticulum (ER) (100,000×). (b) Rough ER is dotted with ribosomes, and (c) smooth ER lacks ribosomes. AP|R

(b)

(c)

into vesicles. **Vesicles** are tiny membranous sacs that carry substances from place to place within a cell. *Secretory vesicles* transport substances to the plasma membrane and release them outside the cell (figure 3.5).

Mitochondria

The **mitochondria** (mī″-to-kon′-drē-ah) are relatively large organelles that are characterized by having an inner folded membrane surrounded by an outer smooth membrane. The inner membranous folds are called *cristae,* and on their surfaces are the enzymes involved in aerobic cellular respiration.

The release of energy from nutrients and the formation of ATP by aerobic cellular respiration occur within mitochondria. For this reason, mitochondria are sometimes called the "powerhouses" of the cell. Mitochondria can replicate themselves if the need for additional ATP production increases (figure 3.6).

Lysosomes AP|R

Lysosomes (lī′-sō-sōms) are formed by the Golgi complex. They are small vesicles that contain powerful digestive enzymes. These enzymes are used to digest (1) bacteria that may have entered the cell, (2) cell parts that need replacement, and (3) entire

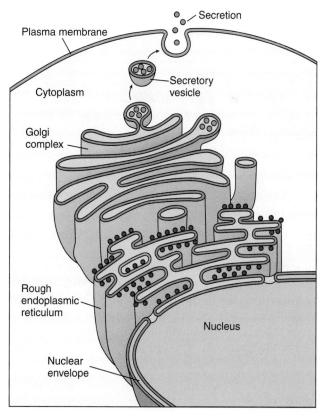

Figure 3.5 The Golgi complex packages substances in vesicles that may move to the plasma membrane to release the substances outside the cell.

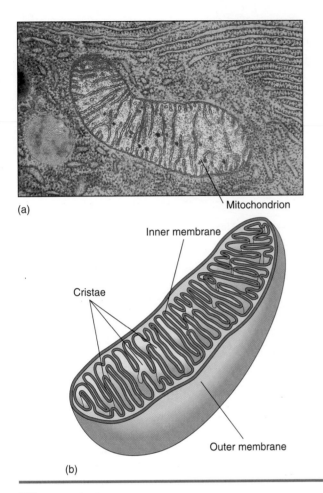

(a) Mitochondrion

Inner membrane

Cristae

Outer membrane

(b)

Figure 3.6 A mitochondrion. (a) A transmission electron photomicrograph (40,000×) and (b) a drawing of a mitochondrion show the cristae formed by the inner membrane. AP|R

Figure 3.7 A false-color electron photomicrograph (750×) shows the microtubules and microfilaments of the cytoskeleton in green. AP|R

cells that have become damaged or worn out. Thus, they play an important role in cleaning up the cellular environment.

The Cytoskeleton

Microtubules and microfilaments (not shown in figure 3.1) compose the cytoskeleton. **Microtubules** are long, thin protein tubules that provide support for the cell and are involved in movement of organelles. The thinner **microfilaments** are tiny rods of contractile protein that not only support the cell but also enable cell movement (figure 3.7).

Centrioles

The **centrioles** (sen′-trē-olz) are two short cylinders that are located near the nucleus and are oriented at right angles to each other. Nine triplets of microtubules

are arranged in a circular pattern to form the wall of each cylinder. Centrioles form and organize the spindle fibers during cell division, and they are involved in the formation of microtubules found in cilia and flagella.

Cilia, Flagella, and Microvilli

Cilia and flagella are small, hairlike projections from cells that are capable of wavelike movement. **Cilia** (sil′-ē-ah) are numerous, short, hairlike projections from cells that, in humans, are used to move substances along the cell surface (figure 3.8). **Flagella** (flah-jel′-ah) are long, whiplike projections from cells. In humans, only sperm cells possess flagella, and each sperm has a single flagellum that enables movement. Both cilia and flagella contain microtubules that originate from centrioles positioned at the base of these flexible structures (figure 3.9).

Microvilli are extensions of the plasma membrane that are smaller and more numerous than cilia. They do not move like cilia or flagella, but they

---

Check My Understanding

1. What are the distinguishing features and functions of a mitochondrion, a nucleus, the Golgi complex, and rough endoplasmic reticulum?
2. What organelles enable cell movement or move substances across a cell surface?

(a)

(b)

Figure 3.8 (a) Cilia are located on the free surface of certain cells, such as those lining the respiratory tract. Because the cells are stationary, beating cilia move substances across the surfaces of the cells. (b) An electron photomicrograph of cilia (10,000×).

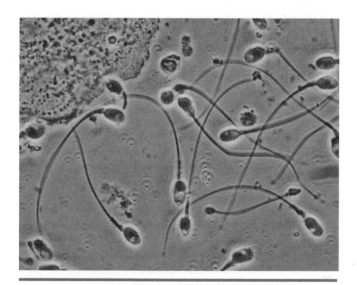

Figure 3.9 A light photomicrograph of human sperm cells (1,000×). Sperm cells are the only human cells that have a flagellum. Each sperm is propelled by the beating of its whiplike flagellum.

increase the surface area of the plasma membrane and, therefore, aid absorption of substances. Microvilli are abundant on cells lining the intestines.

3.2 Transport Through Plasma Membranes

Substances move through a plasma membrane by either passive or active processes. In **passive transport,** substances move across the membrane without assistance by the cell. **Active transport** requires the expenditure of energy (ATP) as the cell assists in the transport process.

Passive Transport

There are three major types of passive transport: diffusion, osmosis, and filtration.

Diffusion

Diffusion (di-fū′-zhun) is the net movement of molecules from an area of their higher concentration to an area of their lower concentration. Thus, the movement of molecules is along a **concentration gradient,** the difference between the concentration of the specific molecules in the two areas.

Diffusion occurs in both gases and liquids and results from the constant, random motion of molecules. Diffusion is not a living process; it occurs in both living and nonliving systems. For example, if a pellet of a water-soluble dye is placed in a beaker of water, the dye molecules will slowly diffuse from the pellet (the area of higher concentration) throughout the water (the area of lower concentration) until the dye molecules are equally distributed, that is, at equilibrium. Figure 3.10 shows diffusion in a liquid environment.

In a similar way, molecules of some substances are able to diffuse through a plasma membrane along a concentration gradient due to differences between the concentrations of the substance inside and outside the cell. For example, the exchange of respiratory gases occurs by diffusion. Air in the lungs has a greater concentration of oxygen and a lower concentration of carbon dioxide than in the blood. Therefore, oxygen diffuses from air in the lungs into the blood, and carbon dioxide diffuses from the blood into the air in the lungs.

Osmosis

The diffusion of water through a selectively permeable membrane is called **osmosis** (os-mo′-sis). Water molecules move through the membrane from an area of higher water concentration (lower solute concentration)

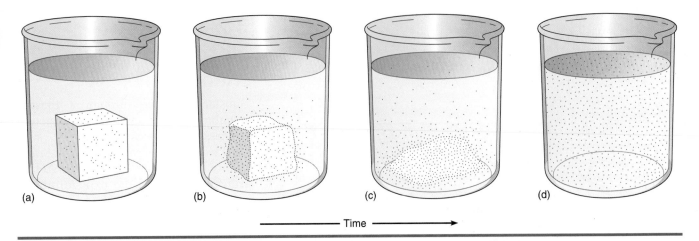

Time →

Figure 3.10 An example of diffusion. As a sugar cube gradually dissolves in a beaker of water—(a), (b), and (c), the sugar molecules diffuse from the region of their higher concentration to a region of their lower concentration. In time (d), diffusion causes the sugar molecules to be equally distributed throughout the water. AP|R

into an area of lower water concentration (higher solute concentration).

Figure 3.11 illustrates the concept of osmosis. The beaker is divided into two compartments (A and B) by a selectively permeable membrane that allows water molecules but not sugar molecules to pass through it. Because the higher concentration of water is in compartment B, water diffuses from compartment B into compartment A. Sugar molecules cannot pass through the membrane, so water molecules from compartment B continue to diffuse into compartment A, causing the volume of its solution to increase as the volume of water in compartment B decreases.

When aqueous solutions of unequal solute concentrations are separated by a selectively permeable membrane, water *always* diffuses from a **hypotonic solution,** a solution with a lower concentration of solutes and therefore a higher concentration of water, into a **hypertonic solution,** a solution with a higher concentration of solutes and a lower concentration of water. The greater the difference in water (or solute) concentration between hypotonic and hypertonic solutions, the faster osmosis occurs. Solutions that have the same concentration of solutes are **isotonic solutions.** There is no net movement of water between isotonic solutions separated by a selectively permeable membrane. The ability of a solution to affect the tone or shape of living cells by altering the cells' water content is called *tonicity* (figure 3.12).

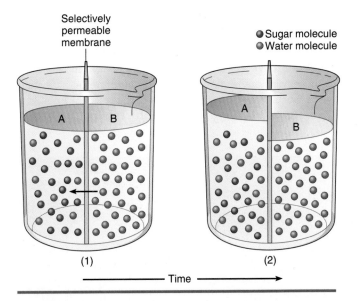

Selectively permeable membrane

● Sugar molecule
● Water molecule

(1)   (2)

Time →

Figure 3.11 Osmosis (1) A selectively permeable membrane separates the container into two compartments. At first, compartment A contains water and sugar molecules, and compartment B contains only water. As a result of molecular motions, water diffuses by osmosis from compartment B into compartment A. Sugar molecules remain in compartment A because they are too large to pass through the pores of the membrane. (2) Because more water enters compartment A than leaves it, water accumulates in this compartment. The level of liquid in compartment A rises above that of compartment B. AP|R

Filtration

Recall that a solution consists of a *solvent,* such as water, and one or more dissolved substances, collectively called *solutes,* whose molecules may vary in size. **Filtration** is the forcing of smaller molecules in a

solution through a membrane due to greater *hydrostatic pressure* on one side of the membrane. Hydrostatic pressure is the pressure exerted by a fluid against a wall or membrane. In the body, filtration is powered by blood pressure. For example, smaller molecules

(a) In a hypotonic solution, there is a net gain of water by the cell causing it to swell. Ultimately, the cell may burst.

(b) In an isotonic solution, there is no gain or loss of water by the cell.

(c) In a hypertonic solution, there is a net loss of water from the cell.

Figure 3.12   The effect of tonicity on human cells. (a) When a cell is in a hypotonic solution, water diffuses into the cell, causing it to swell and burst. (b) When a cell is placed in an isotonic solution, there is no net movement of water into or out of the cell. (c) When a cell is in a hypertonic solution, water diffuses out of the cell and the cell crumples. **AP|R**

are forced out of a capillary and into the tissue fluid (extracellular fluid) surrounding cells because blood pressure in the capillary is greater than the hydrostatic pressure of the tissue fluid. Larger molecules are too big to pass through the capillary wall (figure 3.13).

Active Transport

Unlike passive transport, active transport requires the cell to expend energy (ATP) to move molecules across a plasma membrane. There are three basic active transport mechanisms: carrier proteins, endocytosis, and exocytosis.

Carrier Proteins

Carrier proteins are embedded in the plasma membrane and have receptors that allow certain molecules or ions to bind with them. When this happens, energy is used to change the shape of the carrier protein, which releases the molecule or ion on the other side of the membrane. In this way, carrier proteins may move substances across a plasma membrane either with or against a concentration gradient. Figure 3.14 illustrates how a carrier protein moves a molecule across a plasma membrane against a concentration gradient (i.e., from an area of lower concentration to an area of higher concentration) of the molecule. There is a different carrier protein for each type of molecule or ion moved by active transport.

For example, the pumping of sodium ions (Na^+) out of a cell occurs via carrier proteins. Because Na^+ is pumped out faster than it can diffuse in, there is a greater concentration of Na^+ outside of cells than inside cells.

Dialysis involves the application of diffusion to remove small solute molecules through a selectively permeable membrane from a solution containing both small and large molecules. Dialysis is the process that is used in artificial kidney machines. As blood is passed through a chamber with a selectively permeable membrane, small waste molecules diffuse from the blood across the membrane into an aqueous solution that has a low concentration of these waste molecules. In this way, waste products in the blood are reduced to normal levels.

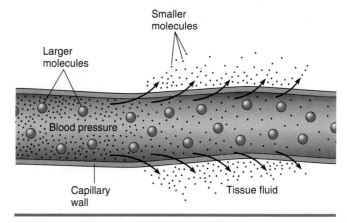

Figure 3.13   In this example of filtration, blood pressure forces smaller molecules through tiny openings in the capillary wall. Larger molecules remain inside.

Figure 3.14 Transport of a molecule across a plasma membrane against a concentration gradient. (a) The transported molecule combines with a carrier protein causing it to change shape. (b) With the expenditure of cellular energy, the carrier protein releases the transported molecule on the other side of the membrane. AP|R

Endocytosis and Exocytosis AP|R

Materials that are too large to be actively transported by carrier proteins enter and exit a cell by totally different mechanisms. **Endocytosis** (en″-dō-sī-tō′-sis) is the engulfment of particles and droplets of liquid. **Exocytosis** is a reverse process in which substances are expelled (secreted) from the cell.

Figure 3.15 illustrates how substances are engulfed during endocytosis. The plasma membrane flows around the substance to be engulfed, forms an enveloping vesicle around the substance, and re-forms the plasma membrane exterior to the vesicle so that the vesicle and substance are brought inside the cell. There are two types of endocytosis: pinocytosis and phagocytosis. **Pinocytosis** (pī″-nō-sī-tō′-sis) is the engulfment of small droplets of fluid. **Phagocytosis** (fag″-ō-sī-tō′-sis) is the engulfment of small particles. Many types of cells use these processes, but phagocytosis is especially important for certain white blood cells that engulf and destroy bacteria as a defense against disease.

Exocytosis is the reverse of endocytosis, and it is used to remove substances from cells. A vesicle containing the substance forms within the cell. It then moves to the plasma membrane and empties its contents outside of the cell. The secretion of enzymes and hormones by cells involves exocytosis.

Figure 3.15 Endocytosis. A particle or liquid droplet is engulfed in a vesicle and is brought inside the cell.

Table 3.2 Summary of How Materials Enter and Leave Cells	
Type	**Process**
Passive transport	Diffusion (solutes)
	Osmosis (water)
	Filtration (water and solutes)
Active transport	Transport by carrier proteins (solutes)
	Endocytosis
	Phagocytosis (particles)
	Pinocytosis (liquids)
	Exocytosis (solutes, liquids)

Table 3.2 summarizes transport through plasma membranes.

Check My Understanding

3. By what means do substances enter and exit living cells?

3.3 Cellular Respiration

Cells require a constant supply of energy to power the chemical reactions of life. This energy is directly supplied by ATP molecules, as noted in chapter 2. Because cells have a limited supply, ATP molecules must constantly be produced by cellular respiration in order to sustain life.

Cellular respiration is the process that breaks down nutrients to release energy held in their chemical bonds and transfers some of this energy into the high-energy phosphate bonds of ATP. About 40% of the energy in a nutrient molecule is "captured" in this way; the remainder is lost as heat energy. The building units of carbohydrates, proteins, and lipids may be used as nutrients in cellular respiration, but glucose is the most common nutrient.

The summary equation for the cellular respiration of glucose is shown in figure 3.16. Note that the reaction requires oxygen and yields carbon dioxide and water in addition to energy (ATP). The actual process is complex, and each step requires a special enzyme. But it may be simplified as shown in figure 3.17.

Cellular respiration involves two sequential processes: anaerobic respiration and aerobic respiration. **Anaerobic** (an-a-rō'-bik) **respiration** (1) does not require oxygen and (2) occurs in the cytoplasm. As shown in figure 3.17, it breaks down a six-carbon glucose molecule into two three-carbon pyruvic acid molecules to yield a net of two ATP molecules. As you recall from chapter 2, energy, ADP, and a low-energy phosphate group (—P) are required to synthesize ATP. The low level of ATP production by anaerobic respiration is insufficient to keep a person alive.

Aerobic respiration, the second part of cellular respiration, (1) requires oxygen, (2) occurs only within mitochondria, and (3) is essential for human life. Aerobic respiration breaks down the two pyruvic acid molecules produced by anaerobic respiration into carbon dioxide and water and yields a net of 34 ATP molecules. Thus, the respiration of a molecule of glucose yields a net total of 36 ATP.

Clinical INSIGHT

A person deprived of oxygen or of the ability to use oxygen in cellular respiration (as in cyanide poisoning) quickly dies because anaerobic respiration does not provide sufficient ATP to sustain life.

Check My Understanding

4. What is cellular respiration, and why is it important?

$$C_6H_{12}O_6 \quad + \quad 6\,O_2 \quad \xrightarrow{\quad 36\,ADP \atop 36\,P \rightarrow 36\,ATP \quad} \quad 6\,CO_2 \quad + \quad 6\,H_2O \quad + \quad Energy$$

Glucose + Oxygen ⟶ Carbon dioxide + Water + Energy

Figure 3.16 Cellular respiration of glucose. Glucose is broken down to release energy that is used to form ATP from ADP and —P. Oxygen is an essential reactant, and the reaction produces carbon dioxide and water.

Figure 3.17 Cellular respiration of a glucose molecule occurs in two steps. Anaerobic respiration occurs in the cytoplasm, does not require oxygen, and yields a net of 2 ATP. Aerobic respiration occurs in mitochondria, requires oxygen, and yields a net of 34 ATP. About 40% of the energy in the chemical bonds of glucose is captured to form ATP molecules.

3.4 Protein Synthesis

Proteins play a vital role in the body. Structural proteins compose significant portions of all cells, and functional proteins, such as enzymes and hormones, directly regulate cellular activities. Remember that a protein is formed of a long chain of amino acids joined together by peptide bonds. Protein synthesis involves placing a specific amino acid in the correct position in the amino acid chain.

DNA and RNA are intimately involved in the synthesis of proteins.

The Role of DNA

Recall the structure of DNA described in chapter 2. The two coiled strands of nucleotides are joined by hydrogen bonds between the nucleotide bases in each strand by *complementary base pairing*. Adenine (A) pairs with thymine (T), and cytosine (C) pairs with guanine (G) (figure 3.18).

The sequence of bases in a DNA molecule encodes information that determines the sequence of amino acids in a protein. More specifically, a sequence of three nucleotide bases (a triplet) in DNA encodes for a specific amino acid. For example, a sequence of ACA encodes for the amino acid cysteine, and AGG encodes for serine. In this way, inherited information that determines the structure of proteins is encoded in DNA.

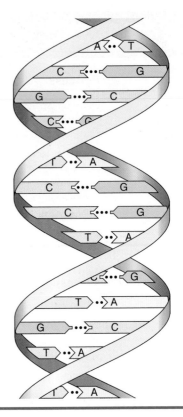

Figure 3.18 A portion of a DNA molecule. The two strands of nucleotides are held together by hydrogen bonds formed between the organic bases. The helical shape resembles a twisted ladder. Note that adenine bonds only with thymine and that cytosine bonds only with guanine. `AP|R`

The Role of RNA

In contrast to DNA, RNA consists of a single strand of nucleotides. Each nucleotide contains one of four organic bases: adenine, cytosine, guanine, or *uracil* (U). Note that uracil is present in RNA instead of thymine, which occurs in DNA. RNA is synthesized in a cell's nucleus by using a strand of DNA as a template. Complementary pairing of RNA bases with DNA bases produces a strand of RNA nucleotides whose bases are complementary to those in the DNA molecule. Uracil (U) in RNA pairs with adenine (A) in DNA; adenine (A) in RNA pairs with thymine (T) in DNA.

There are three types of RNA, and each plays a vital role in protein synthesis.

Messenger RNA (mRNA) carries the genetic information from DNA into the cytoplasm to the ribosomes, the sites of protein synthesis. This information is carried by the sequence of bases in mRNA, which is complementary to the sequence of bases in the DNA template.

Ribosomal RNA (rRNA) and protein compose ribosomes, the sites of protein synthesis. Ribosomes contain the enzymes required for protein synthesis.

Transfer RNA (tRNA) carries amino acids to the ribosomes, where the amino acids are joined like a string of beads to form a protein. There is a different tRNA for transporting each of the 20 kinds of amino acids used to build proteins.

Table 3.3 summarizes the characteristics of DNA and RNA.

Transcription and Translation

The process of protein synthesis involves two successive events: **transcription,** which occurs in the nucleus, and **translation,** which takes place in the cytoplasm.

In *transcription,* the sequence of bases in DNA determines the sequence of bases in mRNA due to complementary base pairing. Thus, transcription transfers the encoded information of DNA into the sequence of bases in mRNA. For example, if a triplet of DNA bases is AGG, which encodes for the amino acid serine, the complementary paired triplet of bases in mRNA is UCC. A triplet of bases in mRNA is known as a **codon,** and there is a codon for each of the 20 amino acids composing proteins. Messenger RNA consists of a chain of codons. Once it is synthesized, mRNA moves out of the nucleus into the cytoplasm where it combines with a ribosome, the site of protein synthesis. AP|R

In *translation,* the encoded information in mRNA is used to produce a specific sequence of amino acids to form the protein. As the ribosome moves along the mRNA strand, tRNA molecules bring amino acids to the ribosome and place them in the correct sequence in the forming polypeptide chain (protein) as specified by the mRNA codons. AP|R

Each tRNA molecule has a triplet of RNA bases called an **anticodon** at one end of the molecule. Because there are 20 different kinds of amino acids composing proteins, there are at least 20 kinds of tRNA whose anticodons can bind with codons of mRNA. A tRNA molecule can only transport the specific amino acid that is encoded by the codon to which its anticodon can bond. For example, a tRNA transporting the amino acid serine has the anticodon AGG that can bond with the mRNA codon UCC to place serine in the correct position in the forming amino acid chain. See figure 3.19.

By transcription and translation, DNA determines the structure of proteins, which, in turn, determines the functions of proteins. Transcription and translation may be summarized as follows:

$$DNA \xrightarrow{\text{Transcription}} mRNA \xrightarrow{\text{Translation}} Protein$$

Check My Understanding

5. How does chromosomal DNA determine the structure of proteins?

3.5 Cell Division

Two types of cell division occur in the body: mitotic cell division and meiotic cell division. **Mitotic** (mī-tot′-ik) **cell division** is the replication of a parent cell so that the two new daughter cells have the same number of chromosomes (46) and composition of chromosomes as the parent cell. It enables growth and the repair of tissues. **Meiotic** (mī-ot′-ik) **cell division** occurs only in the production of ova and sperm. It produces four daughter cells that contain only half the number of chromosomes (23) as found in the parent cell. In this chapter, we consider mitotic cell division only. Meiotic cell division is studied in chapter 17.

Mitotic Cell Division

Starting with the first division of the fertilized egg, mitotic cell division is the process that produces new cells for growth of the new individual and the replacement of worn or damaged cells. Mitotic division occurs at different rates in different kinds of cells. For example, epithelial cells undergo almost continuous division but muscle cells lose the ability to divide as they mature. Three processes are involved in mitotic cell division: (1) replication (production of exact copies) of chromosomes, (2) mitosis, and (3) division of the cytoplasm.

Table 3.3 Distinguishing Characteristics of DNA and RNA		
	DNA	**RNA**
Strands	Two strands joined by the complementary pairing of their organic bases	One strand
Sugar	Deoxyribose	Ribose
Bases	Adenine	Adenine
	Thymine	Uracil
	Cytosine	Cytosine
	Guanine	Guanine
Shape	Helix	Straight

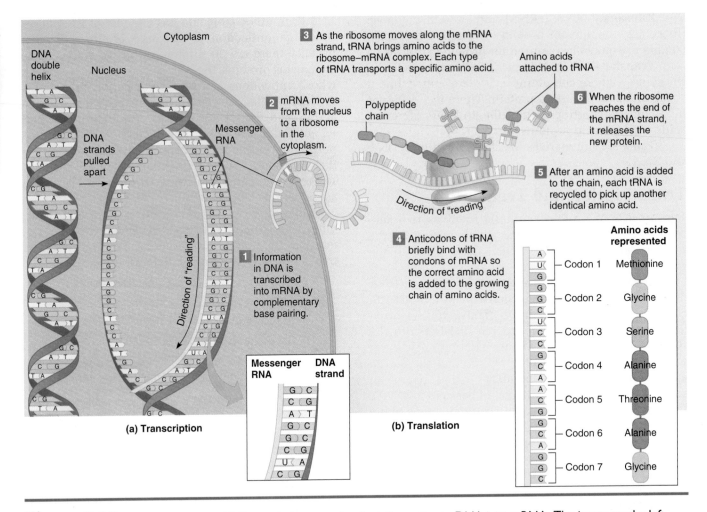

Figure 3.19 Protein synthesis. (a) Transcription encodes the information in DNA into mRNA. The insert on the left shows how this occurs by complementary base pairing. (b) Translation of encoded information in mRNA determines the equences of amino acids in a protein. The insert on the right shows a few mRNA codons and the amino acids that they encode.

In dividing cells, the time period from the separation of daughter cells of one division to the separation of daughter cells of the next division is called the **cell cycle. Mitosis** constitutes only 5% to 10% of the cell cycle. Most of the time, a cell is not dividing but is carrying out its normal functions (figure 3.20).

Interphase is defined as the phase when the cell is not involved in mitosis. When viewed with a microscope, a cell in interphase is identified by its intact nucleus containing chromatin granules. In cells that are destined to divide, both the centrioles and chromosomes replicate during interphase, and other organelles are synthesized and assembled. There is a growth period before and after replication of the 46 chromosomes.

A chromosome consists of a very long DNA molecule coated with proteins. During interphase, chromosomes are uncoiled and resemble very thin

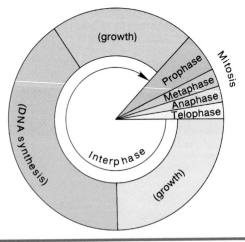

Figure 3.20 The cell cycle. Interphase occupies most of the cell cycle. Only 5% to 10% of the time is used in mitotic division. DNA and chromosome replication occur during interphase. AP|R

threads within the cell nucleus. Chromosomes replicate during interphase in order to provide one copy of each chromosome for each of the two daughter cells that will be formed by mitotic cell division. Chromosome replication is dependent upon the replication of the DNA molecule in each chromosome. Figure 3.21 illustrates the process of DNA replication.

The two DNA strands "unzip," and new nucleotides are joined in a complementary manner by their bases to the bases of each DNA strand. When the new nucleotides are in place and joined together, each new DNA molecule consists of one "new" strand of nucleotides joined to one "old"

strand of nucleotides. In this way, a DNA molecule is precisely replicated so that both new DNA molecules are identical.

Mitotic Phases

Once it begins, mitosis is a continuous process that is arbitrarily divided into four sequential phases: prophase, metaphase, anaphase, and telophase. Each phase is characterized by specific events that occur.

Prophase During **prophase,** the replicated chromosomes coil, appearing first as threadlike structures and finally shortening sufficiently to become rod-shaped. Each replicated chromosome consists

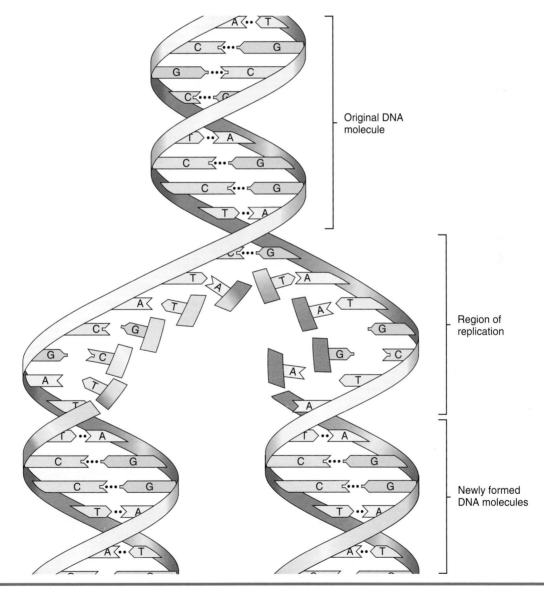

Figure 3.21 When a DNA molecule replicates, the two strands unzip. Then a new complementary strand of nucleotides forms along each "old" strand to produce two new DNA molecules. AP|R

of two **chromatids** joined at their **centromeres.** Simultaneously, the nuclear envelope gradually disappears, and each pair of centrioles migrate toward opposite ends of the cell. A **spindle** is formed between the migrating centrioles. The spindle consists of *spindle fibers* that are formed of microtubules (figure 3.22).

Metaphase   During the brief **metaphase,** the replicated chromosomes line up at the equator of the spindle. Each replicated chromosome consists of a pair of chromatids joined at the centromere. The centromeres are attached to spindle fibers (figure 3.23).

Anaphase   During **anaphase,** separation of the centromeres results in the separation of the paired chromatids. The members of each pair then migrate toward opposite ends of the spindle. They appear to be pulled along by the spindle fibers attached to their centromeres. The separated chromatids are now called chromosomes, and each new set of chromosomes is identical (figure 3.24).

Telophase   During **telophase,** the spindle fibers disassemble and a new nuclear envelope starts forming around each set of chromosomes as the new nuclei begin to take shape. The chromosomes start to uncoil, and they will ultimately become visible only

(a)   (b)

Figure 3.22   Prophase. (a) The replicated chromosomes first appear as threadlike strands and then shorten further to appear rod-shaped; the two pairs of centrioles move toward opposite sides of the cell, forming a spindle of microtubules between them; and the nuclear membrane disintegrates. (b) A photomicrograph of a cell in prophase (1,000×).

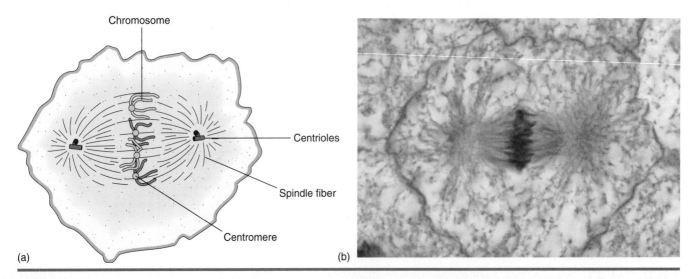

(a)   (b)

Figure 3.23   Metaphase. (a) The replicated chromosomes line up at the equator (midline) of the spindle. Note that each replicated chromosome consists of a pair of chromatids joined by a centromere. (b) A photomicrograph of a cell in metaphase (1,000×).

as chromatin granules. The new daughter nuclei are completely formed by the end of telophase.

During this time, the most obvious change is the division of the cytoplasm, which is called **cytokinesis** (si″-to-ki-nē′-sis). It is characterized by a furrow that forms in the plasma membrane across the equator of the spindle and deepens until the parent cell is separated into two daughter cells. The formation of two daughter cells, each having identical chromosomes in the nuclei, marks the end of mitotic cell division (figure 3.25).

Table 3.4 summarizes the cell cycle.

Check My Understanding

6. What are the phases of mitosis, and how is each phase distinguished?

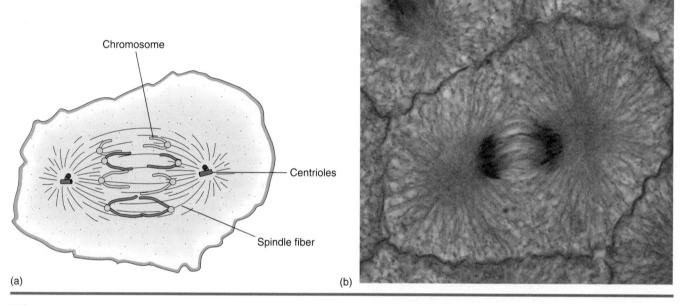

(a)

(b)

Figure 3.24   Anaphase. (a) The centromeres divide, and spindle fibers pull members of each pair of chromatids, now called chromosomes, to opposite ends of the spindle. The two sets of chromosomes are identical. (b) A photomicrograph of a cell in anaphase (1,000×).

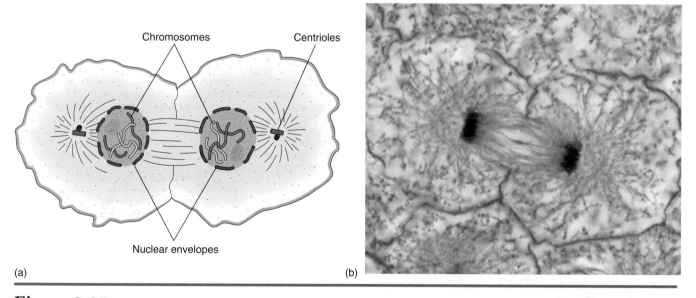

(a)

(b)

Figure 3.25   Telophase. (a) The chromosomes in each set uncoil, first appearing threadlike and ultimately as chromatin granules; a nuclear envelope forms around each set of chromosomes; and cytokinesis begins leading to the formation of two daughter cells. (b) A photomicrograph of a cell in telophase (1,000×).

Table 3.4 Summary of the Cell Cycle

Phase	Events
Interphase	A nondividing cell carries on its normal functions. A cell that is destined to divide also undergoes replication of the centrioles and chromosomes.
Mitosis	
Prophase	Replicated chromosomes coil and shorten; nuclear envelope disappears; centriole pairs start migration toward opposite ends of the cell, forming the spindle between them.
Metaphase	Chromosomes line up at equator of spindle.
Anaphase	Chromatids separate; members of each chromatid pair migrate toward opposite ends of the spindle.
Telophase	Nuclear envelopes form around each set of chromosomes; spindle fibers disappear; chromosomes uncoil and extend; cytokinesis produces two daughter cells.

Clinical INSIGHT

Mitotic cell division is normally a controlled process that ceases when it is not necessary to produce additional cells. Occasionally, control is lost and cells undergo continuous division, which leads to the formation of tumors. Tumors may be benign or malignant. *Benign tumors* do not spread to other parts of the body and may be surgically removed if they cause health or cosmetic problems. *Malignant tumors,* or *cancers,* may spread to other parts of the body by a process called metastasis (me-tas′-ta-sis). Cells break away from the primary tumor and are often carried by blood or lymph to other areas, where continued cell divisions form secondary tumors.

Treatment of malignant tumors involves surgical removal of the tumor, if possible, and subsequent chemotherapy and/or radiation therapy. Both chemotherapy and radiation therapy tend to kill malignant cells because dividing cells are more sensitive to treatment, and malignant cells are constantly dividing.

CHAPTER SUMMARY

3.1 Cell Structure

- The plasma membrane is composed of a double layer of phospholipid molecules along with associated cholesterol and protein molecules. It is selectively permeable and controls the movement of the materials into and out of cells.
- The cytoplasm lies external to the nucleus and is enveloped by the plasma membrane.
- The nucleus is a large, spherical organelle surrounded by the nuclear envelope.
- Chromosomes, composed of DNA and protein, are found in the cell nucleus. The uncoiled chromosomes appear as chromatin granules in nondividing cells.
- The nucleolus is the site of rRNA synthesis.
- Ribosomes are tiny organelles formed of rRNA and protein. They are sites of protein synthesis.
- The endoplasmic reticulum (ER) consists of membranes that form channels for transport of materials within the cell. RER is studded with ribosomes that synthesize proteins for export from the cell. SER lacks ribosomes and is involved in lipid synthesis.
- The Golgi complex packages materials into vesicles for secretion from the cell.
- Mitochondria are large, double-membraned organelles within which aerobic cellular respiration occurs.
- Lysosomes are small vesicles of digestive enzymes used to digest foreign particles, worn-out parts of a cell, or an entire damaged cell.
- The cytoskeleton is formed by microtubules and microfilaments.
- A pair of centrioles is present near the cell's nucleus. The wall of each centriole is composed of microtubules arranged in groups of three.
- Cilia are short, hairlike projections on certain cells. The beating of cilia moves materials along the cell surface.
- Each sperm cell swims by the beating of a flagellum, a long whiplike organelle.

3.2 Transport Through Plasma Membranes

- Passive transport does not require the expenditure of energy by the cell.
- Diffusion is the movement of molecules from an area of higher concentration to an area of lower concentration. It results from the constant motion of molecules in gases and liquids.
- Osmosis is the diffusion of water through a selectively permeable membrane.
- Hypotonic solutions have a greater water concentration than hypertonic solutions. Isotonic solutions have the same water concentration.
- Water always diffuses from hypotonic solutions into hypertonic solutions when they are separated by selectively permeable membranes. There is no net movement of water between isotonic solutions.
- Filtration is the forcing of small molecules through a membrane by hydrostatic pressure when the pressure is greater on one side of the membrane.
- Active transport requires the cell to expend energy.
- Molecules are transported through the plasma membrane by carrier proteins in one form of active transport.
- The engulfment of particles and liquid droplets by endocytosis and the expulsion of cell products by exocytosis are specialized forms of active transport.

3.3 Cellular Respiration

- Cellular respiration is the breakdown of nutrients to release energy and form ATP molecules, which power cellular processes.

- Cellular respiration involves two phases: anaerobic and aerobic.
- Anaerobic respiration occurs in the cytoplasm and yields 2 ATP; aerobic respiration occurs in mitochondria and yields 34 ATP.

3.4 Protein Synthesis

- Protein synthesis involves the interaction of DNA, mRNA, rRNA, and tRNA.
- The sequence of bases in DNA determines the sequence of codons in mRNA, which, in turn, determines the sequence of amino acids in a protein.

DNA $\xrightarrow[\text{Transcription}]{}$ mRNA $\xrightarrow[\text{Translation}]{}$ Protein

3.5 Cell Division

- Mitotic cell division produces two daughter cells that have the same number and composition of chromosomes. It enables growth and tissue repair.
- Meiotic cell division occurs in production of ova and sperm. Four daughter cells are formed that have half the number of chromosomes as the parent cell.
- Most of a cell cycle is spent in interphase, where cells carry out normal metabolic functions. In cells destined to divide, chromosomes and centrioles are replicated in interphase.
- After chromosome replication, mitosis is the orderly process of separating and distributing chromosomes equally to the daughter cells.
- Mitosis consists of four phases: prophase, metaphase, anaphase, and telophase.

BUILDING MY VOCABULARY

1. **Selected New Terms**
   anaphase, p. 58
   cilia, p. 48
   cytokinesis, p. 59
   flagella, p. 48
   Golgi complex, p. 46
   hypertonic solution, p. 50
   hypotonic solution, p. 50
   interphase, p. 56
   isotonic solution, p. 50
   lysosome, p. 47
   messenger RNA, p. 55
   metaphase, p. 58
   microfilament, p. 48
   microtubule, p. 48
   phagocytosis, p. 52
   pinocytosis, p. 52
   prophase, p. 57
   ribosomal RNA, p. 55

   telophase, p. 58
   transcription, p. 55
   transfer RNA, p. 55
   translation, p. 55

2. **Related Clinical Terms**
   Benign (be-nīn′) tumor (too-mer) A noninvasive growth of tissue caused by uncontrolled cell division.
   Dialysis (dī-al′-i-sis) The process separating small molecules from larger molecules in a solution by diffusion through a selectively permeable membrane.
   Dysplasia (dis-plās′-ia) Abnormal change in cell shape or size.
   Hypertrophy (hī′-per-trōph-ē) Abnormal enlargement of a cell, tissue, or organ.
   Malignant (mah-lig′-nint) tumor An invasive, metastasizing tumor caused by uncontrolled cell division; a cancer.
   Necrosis (ne-krō′-sis) Death of a group of cells.

SELF-REVIEW

Answers are located in Appendix B.

1. Movement of materials in and out of cells is controlled by the _____.
2. Molecules of _____ located in chromosomes control the activities of cells.
3. Aerobic cellular respiration occurs within _____.
4. The sites of protein synthesis are _____.
5. The _____ assembles protein and RNA to form ribosomes.
6. The _____ consists of intracellular membranous channels for material transport.
7. Movement of molecules from an area of their higher concentration to an area of their lower concentration is known as _____.
8. The forcing of small molecules through a membrane by blood pressure is _____.
9. Movement of molecules through a membrane by carrier proteins is a form of _____.
10. Breakdown of organic nutrients to release energy and form ATP is called _____.
11. Instructions for synthesizing a protein are carried from DNA to ribosomes by _____.
12. The equal distribution of chromosomes to daughter nuclei occurs by _____.

CRITICAL THINKING

1. Complete the learning objectives on the first page of this chapter.
2. Describe the various ways materials can enter or leave a cell.
3. How is the correct sequence of amino acids in proteins determined?
4. How are glucose, pyruvic acid, mitochondria, oxygen, ADP, and ATP involved in cellular respiration?
5. How does mitosis yield daughter cells with the same DNA content?

Visit this book's website at www.mhhe.com/ gunstream5 for practice quizzes, learning exercises, case studies and other study tools.

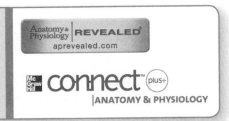

CHAPTER 4

Tissues and Membranes

Chapter Preview & Learning Objectives

Epithelial Tissues
1. Describe the distinguishing characteristics of each type of epithelial tissue.
2. Indicate the common locations and general functions of epithelial tissues.

Connective Tissues
3. Describe the distinguishing characteristics of each type of connective tissue.
4. Indicate the common locations and general functions of connective tissues.

Muscle Tissues
5. Describe the distinguishing characteristics and locations of each type of muscle tissue.
6. Indicate the general function of muscle tissues.

Nerve Tissue
7. Describe the distinguishing characteristics and general functions of nerve tissue.
8. Indicate the common locations of nerve tissue.

Body Membranes
9. Compare epithelial and connective tissue membranes.
10. Give examples of each type of membrane.

Chapter Summary
Building My Vocabulary
Self-Review
Critical Thinking

Module 3
Tissues

Adipose tissue (adip = fat) A connective tissue that stores fat.

Cartilage A connective tissue with a relatively rigid, semisolid matrix.

Chondrocyte (chondro = cartilage; cyt = cell) A cartilage cell.

Connective tissue (connect = to join) A tissue that binds other tissues together.

Epithelial tissue (epi = upon, over; thel = delicate) A thin tissue that covers body and organ surfaces and lines body cavities.

Fibroblast (fibro = fiber; blast = germ) A cell that produces fibers in connective tissue.

Matrix The intercellular substance in connective tissue.

Muscle tissue (mus = mouse) A tissue whose cells are specialized for contraction.

Nerve tissue A tissue that forms the brain, spinal cord, and nerves.

Neuron (neur = nerve) A nerve cell.

Osseous tissue A hard connective tissue with a rigid matrix of calcium salts; bone.

Osteocyte (oss = bone; cyt = cell) A bone cell.

Pseudostratified (pseudo = false; stratum = layer) Cells appear to be arranged in layers, but they are not.

Tissue (tissu = woven) A group of similar cells performing similar functions.

The different kinds of cells composing the human body result from the specialization of cells during embryonic development. **Embryonic stem cells** of an early embryo are unspecialized cells containing encoded information in their DNA that enables them to form all types of specialized cells. As these cells divide repeatedly producing many generations of cells, the daughter cells become partially specialized. Such cells can produce daughter cells for only certain related types of specialized cells. This trend of decreasing potential (increasing specialization) continues through many generations of cells, ultimately producing the highly specialized cells in the human body plus a few partially specialized cells known as **adult stem cells**. Once fully specialized, cells may or may not divide, but if they do, they can only form specialized cells like themselves; for example, skin cells divide to produce only skin cells. Because all of a person's cells (except red blood cells, which lack nuclei) contain the same set of inherited instructions, the transition from unspecialized embryonic stem cells to fully specialized body cells results from cellular mechanisms that turn off specific portions of the encoded information in DNA.

A **tissue** is a group of fully specialized similar cells that perform similar functions. Most tissues seem to contain a few adult stem cells, as well, which play an important role in tissue repair. Each type of tissue is distinguished by the structure of its cells, intercellular substance, and the function it performs. The structure of a tissue is a reflection of its function.

The different tissues of the body are classified into four basic types: epithelial, connective, muscle, and nerve tissues.

1. **Epithelial** (ep ″-i-thē′-lē-al) **tissue** covers the surfaces of the body, lines body cavities and cavities of organs, and forms the secretory portions of glands.

Clinical INSIGHT

Adult stem cells from a variety of tissues are used in medical therapies. For example, stem cells in bone marrow are used to treat leukemia. Medical scientists think that, with more research, stem cells may be used to treat cancer, brain and spinal cord injuries, multiple sclerosis, Parkinson's disease, and other injuries and disorders.

2. **Connective tissue** binds organs together and provides protection and support for organs and the entire body.
3. **Muscle tissue** contracts to enable movement of the body and body parts.
4. **Nerve tissue** coordinates body functions via the transmission of nerve impulses.

4.1 Epithelial Tissues AP|R

Epithelial tissues may be composed of one or more layers of cells. The number of cell layers and the shape of the cells provide the basis for classifying epithelial tissues. Epithelial tissues are distinguished by the following five characteristics:

1. Epithelial cells are packed closely together with very little intercellular material between them.
2. The sheetlike tissue is firmly attached to the underlying connective tissue by a thin, noncellular **basement membrane.**
3. The surface of the tissue opposite the basement membrane is always free and exposed, that is, not attached to other tissues.

4. Blood vessels are absent, so epithelial cells must receive nourishment from blood vessels in the underlying connective tissue.
5. Epithelial tissues regenerate rapidly by mitotic division of the cells. Large numbers of epithelial cells are destroyed and replaced each day.

The functions of epithelial tissues vary with the specific location and type of tissue, but they include *protection, absorption, filtration,* and *secretion.* Certain epithelial cells form *glandular epithelium,* the cells in glands that produce the gland's secretions. Two basic types of glands are contained in the body: exocrine and endocrine glands. **Exocrine glands** have ducts (small tubes) that carry their secretions to specific areas; sweat glands and salivary glands are examples. **Endocrine glands** lack ducts. Instead, their secretions are released into the blood, which carries them to target tissues. The thyroid gland and adrenal glands are examples of endocrine glands.

Simple Epithelium

Simple epithelium consists of a single layer of cells that may be flat, cubelike, or columnlike in shape. These tissues are located where diffusion, secretion, or filtration occur in the body.

Simple squamous (skwă′-mus) *epithelium* consists of thin, flat cells that have an irregular outline and a centrally located nucleus. In a surface view, the cells somewhat resemble tiles arranged in a mosaic pattern. Simple squamous epithelium functions to aid diffusion, osmosis, and filtration. Its location in the body includes (1) the air sacs of the lungs, where O_2 and CO_2 diffuse into and out of the blood, respectively; (2) parts of the kidneys, where blood is filtered in urine production; and (3) the serous membranes that line the ventral cavity. The squamous epithelium that lines the interior of the heart, blood vessels, and lymphatic vessels is called **endothelium** because of its interior location (figure 4.1).

Simple cuboidal epithelium consists of a single layer of cube-shaped cells. The cells have a single, centrally located nucleus. Its basic functions are absorption and secretion. Simple cuboidal epithelium forms the (1) secretory portion of glands, such as the thyroid and salivary glands; (2) kidney tubules where secretion and reabsorption of materials occur; and (3) the surface layer of the ovaries (figure 4.2).

Simple columnar epithelium consists of a single layer of elongated, column-shaped cells. Scattered among these cells are **goblet cells,** specialized mucus-secreting cells whose shape resembles a goblet or

Figure 4.1 Simple squamous epithelium (250×). **AP|R**
Structure: A single layer of flattened cells.
Location: Inner lining of the heart, blood vessels, and the ventral body cavity; forms air sacs of the lungs and glomeruli of the kidneys.
Function: Absorption, secretion, and filtration.

wine glass. Goblet cells secrete a protective layer of mucus on the free surface of the cells. Secretion and absorption are the chief functions of this tissue. Cells lining the uterine tubes possess cilia that propel the egg toward the uterus. Cells lining the stomach and intestines possess numerous microvilli, often collectively called a "brush border," that greatly increase the cell's absorptive surface area (figure 4.3).

Pseudostratified ciliated columnar epithelium consists of a single layer of cells. It is said to be **pseudostratified** because it appears to be formed of more than one layer of cells, but it is not. The layered effect results from the nuclei being located at various levels within the cells. All cells are joined

Figure 4.2 Simple cuboidal epithelium (250×). AP|R
Structure: A single layer of cube-shaped cells.
Location: Forms kidney tubules, ducts of some glands, and the surface layer of the ovaries.
Function: Absorption and secretion.

Figure 4.3 Simple columnar epithelium (400×). AP|R
Structure: A single layer of column-shaped cells; contains scattered goblet cells.
Location: Lines the interior of the stomach and intestines and the ducts of many glands.
Function: Absorption and secretion.

Stratified Epithelium

Stratified epithelium consists of more than one layer of cells, which makes them more durable to abrasion. Only the innermost layer of cells produces new cells by mitotic cell division. The cells are pushed toward the surface of the tissue as more new cells are formed below them. Cells in the surface layer are continuously lost as they die and are rubbed off by abrasion. Protection of underlying tissues is an important function of stratified epithelia. These tissues are named according to the shape of cells on their free surfaces.

to the basement membrane, but all of them do not reach the surface of the tissue. Mucus-secreting goblet cells are scattered throughout the tissue. This epithelium lines the interior of the upper respiratory passageways, where it collects and removes airborne particles. The particles are trapped in the secreted mucus, which are moved by the beating cilia to the throat, where they are either swallowed or expectorated (figure 4.4).

Cilia
Surface of tissue
Nuclei
Goblet cell
Basement membrane
Connective tissue

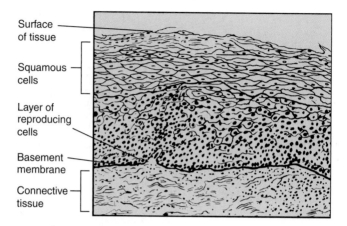

Surface of tissue
Squamous cells
Layer of reproducing cells
Basement membrane
Connective tissue

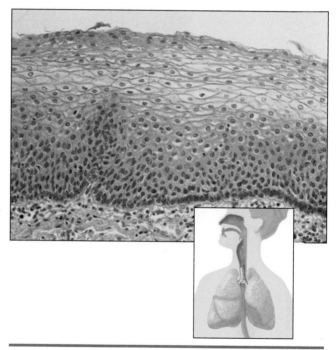

Figure 4.4 Pseudostratified ciliated columnar epithelium (500×). AP|R

Structure: A single layer of ciliated columnar cells that appears to be more than one layer of cells; contains scattered goblet cells.

Location: Lines most of the upper respiratory tract.

Function: Secretion of mucus; beating cilia remove secreted mucus and entrapped particles.

Figure 4.5 Stratified squamous epithelium (70×). AP|R

Structure: Several cell layers; cells in the innermost layer are cuboidal in shape but gradually become flattened as they migrate to the surface of the tissue.

Location: The keratinized type forms the epidermis of the skin; nonkeratinized type lines the mouth, esophagus, and vagina.

Function: Protection.

Stratified squamous epithelium occurs in two distinct forms: keratinized and nonkeratinized. The keratinized type forms the outer layer (epidermis) of the skin. Its cells become impregnated with a water proofing substance, **keratin** (ker′-ah-tin), as they migrate to the surface of the tissue. The nonkeratinized version lines the mouth, esophagus, and vagina. Both types provide resistance to abrasion (figure 4.5).

Transitional epithelium lines the interior of the urinary bladder and stretches as the bladder fills with urine. It consists of multiple layers of cells, and the surface cells of the unstretched tissue are large and rounded. When stretched as the bladder fills with urine, the surface cells become thin, flat cells resembling squamous epithelial cells (figure 4.6).

(a)

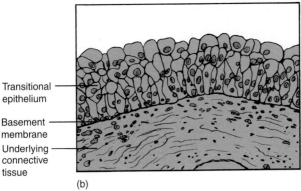

Transitional epithelium

Basement membrane

Underlying connective tissue

(b)

(c)

Figure 4.6 Transitional epithelium. (a) A photomicrograph (250×) and (b) drawing showing several layers of rounded cells when the urinary bladder wall is contracted. (c) When the bladder wall is stretched, the tissue and cells become flattened. AP|R

Structure: Several layers of large, rounded cells that become flattened when stretched. *Location*: Lines the interior of the urinary bladder.

Function: Protection; permits stretching of the bladder wall.

Check My Understanding

1. What are the characteristics and general functions of epithelial tissues?
2. How do the types of epithelial tissues differ as to structure, location, and function?

Table 4.1 summarizes the major types of epithelial tissues. Two relatively rare types of stratified epithelial tissues are not included. *Stratified cuboidal epithelium* lines larger ducts of certain glands (e.g., mammary and salivary glands). *Stratified columnar epithelium* lines parts of the pharynx and male urethra.

4.2 Connective Tissues AP|R

These widely distributed tissues are the most abundant tissues in the body. As the name implies, **connective tissues** support and bind together other tissues so they are never found on exposed surfaces. Like epithelial cells, connective tissue cells have retained the ability to reproduce by mitotic cell division.

Connective tissues consist of a diverse group of tissues subdivided into two broad categories: (1) connective tissue proper consists of the common connective tissues that bind other tissues and organs together and (2) connective tissues with more specialized functions—cartilage, bone, and blood.

All connective tissues consist of relatively few, loosely arranged cells and a large amount of intercellular substance called **matrix** (mă′-triks). Matrix is produced by the cells and may be liquid, gel-like, or solid; and it contains fibers formed of protein. The type of matrix is used to classify connective tissues.

Connective Tissue Proper

These connective tissues are the "ordinary" connective tissues in the body that bind together other tissues and form the basic supporting framework of organs. They are characterized by a matrix that consists of a semifluid or jellylike *ground substance* in which fibers and cells are embedded. Most of the cells are **fibroblasts** that produce the ground substance and the protein fibers in the matrix.

Three types of protein fibers are found in the matrix of connective tissues. **Collagenous** (white) **fibers** are relatively large fibers formed of collagen. They provide strength, nonelasticity, and flexibility. *Reticular fibers* are very thin and highly branching

Table 4.1 Epithelial Tissues

Tissue	Structure	Location and Function
Simple Epithelia		
Squamous	Single layer of flat cells	Walls of capillaries, air sacs in lungs; diffusion, osmosis, filtration
Cuboidal	Single layer of cubelike cells	Glands, surface of ovaries, kidney tubules; secretion, absorption
Columnar	Single layer of columnlike cells	Lining of digestive tract; secretion, absorption, protection
Pseudostratified ciliated columnar	Single layer of ciliated columnlike cells that appears as multiple layers	Lining of upper air passages; sweeps away mucus and foreign particles, secretion, protection
Stratified Epithelia		
Squamous	Multiple layers of flat cells	Outer portion of the skin; protection
Transitional	Multiple layers of oval cells that flatten when the tissue is stretched	Lining of urinary bladder; protection

collagenous fibers that provide a delicate supporting framework for the tissue. **Elastic** (yellow) **fibers** may be slightly stretched but recoil to their original length, providing elasticity for tissues that contain them.

Loose Connective Tissue

Loose, or *areolar* (ah-rē′-ō-lar), *connective tissue* derives its name from the loose arrangement of the collagenous and elastic fibers within the matrix. It is the most abundant connective tissue in the body. Fibroblasts are the most numerous cells, but certain white blood cells migrate into the tissue to attack invading pathogens. A semifluid ground substance fills the spaces between the cells and fibers. Loose connective tissue (1) attaches the skin to underlying muscles; (2) provides a supporting framework for internal organs, nerves, and blood vessels; and (3) is a site for many immune reactions (figure 4.7).

Adipose Tissue

Large accumulations of fat cells form **adipose** (ad′-i-pōs) **tissue,** a special type of loose connective tissue. It occurs throughout the body but is more common beneath the skin and around internal organs. The fat cells, or adipocytes, are filled with fat droplets that push the nucleus and cytoplasm to the edge of the cells. In addition to fat storage, adipose tissue serves as a protective cushion for internal organs, especially around the kidneys and behind the eyeballs, and it helps to insulate the body from abrupt temperature changes (figure 4.8).

Fibrous Connective Tissue

Fibrous connective tissue (sometimes called *dense fibrous connective tissue*) is characterized by an abundance of tightly packed collagenous fibers and relatively few cells. Nearly all of the cells are fibroblasts that are arranged in rows between the bundles of fibers. Fibrous connective tissue has great strength, but it is also flexible. It is the main component of ligaments, which attach bones to bones; tendons, which attach muscles to bones; and the inner layer (dermis) of the skin. This tissue has a poor blood supply, which results in slow healing of injuries to tendons and ligaments (figure 4.9).

Clinical INSIGHT

Because epithelial and connective tissue cells are active in cell division, they are prone to the formation of tumors when normal control of cell division is lost. The most common types of cancer arise from epithelial cells, possibly because these cells are often in contact with *carcinogens,* cancer-causing agents, in the environment. A cancer derived from epithelial cells is called a *carcinoma.* Malignant tumors that originate in connective tissue are also common types of cancer. A cancer of connective tissue is called a *sarcoma.*

Matrix

Fibroblast

Elastic fiber

Collagenous fiber

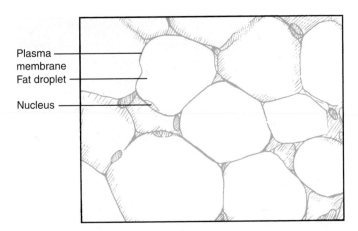

Plasma membrane

Fat droplet

Nucleus

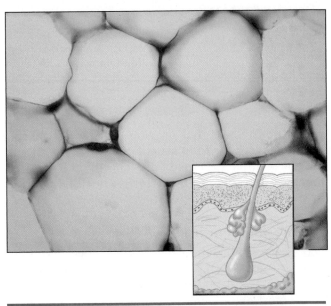

Figure 4.7 Loose connective tissue (250×). AP|R
Structure: Formed of scattered fibroblasts and a loose network of collagenous and elastic fibers embedded in a gel-like ground substance.
Function: Attaches the skin to underlying muscles; supports internal organs, blood vessels, and nerves.

Figure 4.8 Adipose tissue (250×). AP|R
Structure: Formed of closely packed fat cells with little intercellular material. Large fat-containing vacuole pushes the cytoplasm and nucleus to the edge of the cell.
Function: Storage of excess nutrients as fat; occurs primarily under the skin and around internal organs.

Elastic Connective Tissue AP|R

An abundance of elastic fibers in the matrix distinguishes *elastic connective tissue.* Collagenous fibers are also present, and fibroblasts are scattered between the fibers. Elastic connective tissue occurs where elasticity is advantageous, such as in the lungs, air passages, and arterial walls. For example, elastic connective tissue enables the expansion of the lungs as air is inhaled and the contraction of the lungs as air is exhaled.

Cartilage

Cartilage consists of a semisolid matrix in which cartilage cells, or **chondrocytes** (kon′-drŏ-sītz), are embedded. The spaces in the matrix that contain the chondrocytes are called **lacunae** (lah-kū′-nē). The major functions of cartilage are support and protection. All types of cartilage act as a cushion to absorb shock, and their resiliency allows them to be deformed by pressure and return to their original shape when the pressure is removed. Three types of cartilage are present in the body: hyaline cartilage, elastic cartilage, and fibrocartilage.

Figure 4.9 Fibrous connective tissue (100×). AP|R

Structure: Consists of tightly packed collagenous fibers that are separated by scattered rows of fibroblasts.

Function: Strong attachment; forms ligaments attaching bones to bones at joints, tendons attaching muscles to bones, fibrous capsules around organs, and the dermis of the skin.

Figure 4.10 Hyaline cartilage (250×). AP|R

Structure: Smooth glassy matrix with many chondrocytes in lacunae.

Function: Forms protective covering of bones at joints; attaches ribs to breastbone, and supports walls of air passages.

Hyaline Cartilage

The matrix of *hyaline* (hī′-a-lin) *cartilage* has a smooth, glassy, bluish white appearance. It contains collagenous fibers, but they are not easily visible. Numerous chondrocytes in lacunae are present. Hyaline cartilage is the most abundant cartilage in the body. It provides (1) a protective covering on bone surfaces forming joints, (2) forms part of the nose, and (3) supports the walls of air passages. During embryonic development, most bones of the body are initially formed of hyaline cartilage. Subsequently, the cartilage is gradually replaced by bone tissue (figure 4.10).

Elastic Cartilage

This tissue is similar to hyaline cartilage, but *elastic cartilage* contains an abundance of elastic fibers that impart greater resiliency and flexibility to the tissue. The distribution in the body is rather limited. Elastic cartilage forms part of the larynx (voice box), and it forms the supportive framework for the external ear (figure 4.11).

Fibrocartilage

The matrix of *fibrocartilage* contains many tightly packed collagenous fibers that lie between short rows or clumps of chondrocytes. This cartilage forms (1) the intervertebral disks that are located

Elastic fibers

Matrix

Chondrocyte
Nucleus

Lacuna

Figure 4.11 Elastic cartilage (100×). AP|R
Structure: Consists of numerous cartilage cells occupying lacunae in a gel-like matrix containing numerous elastic fibers.
Function: Provides the supporting framework for the external ears.

between vertebrae, (2) the cartilaginous pads in the knee joints, and (3) the protective cushion of the symphysis pubis (anterior union of the pelvic bones). Fibrocartilage is especially tough, and the dense collagenous fibers enable it to absorb greater shocks and pressures without permanent damage (figure 4.12).

Bone

Of all the supportive connective tissues, **bone,** or **osseous tissue,** is the hardest and most rigid. This results from the minerals, mostly calcium salts, that compose the matrix along with some collagenous fibers. Bone tissue provides the rigidity and strength necessary for the skeletal system to support the body.

The bone matrix is deposited in concentric rings, or **lamellae** (lah-mel'-ē), around microscopic tubes, the **osteonic** or **central, canals.** These canals contain blood vessels and nerves. The bone cells, or **osteocytes** (os'-tē-ō-sītz), are located in lacunae that are arranged in concentric rings around osteonic canals between the lamellae. The tiny canals extending from the lacunae are called **canaliculi** (kan"-ah-lik'-ū-li), and they contain cell processes that extend from the osteocytes. Canaliculi serve as passageways for the movement of materials between the blood vessels in the **osteonic canals** and the osteocytes. An osteonic canal and the lamellae and osteocytes around it form an **osteon,** the structural unit of compact bone (figure 4.13).

Blood

Blood is a specialized type of connective tissue. It consists of numerous formed elements that are suspended in the plasma, the liquid matrix of the blood. There

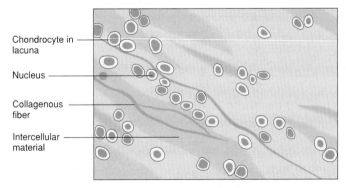

Chondrocyte in
lacuna

Nucleus

Collagenous
fiber

Intercellular
material

Figure 4.12 Fibrocartilage (250×). AP|R
Structure: Consists of rows or clusters of cartilage cells occupying lacunae in a matrix containing tightly packed collagenous fibers.
Function: Composes the intervertebral disks between vertebrae and cartilaginous pads in the knee joint where it serves as a protective shock absorber.

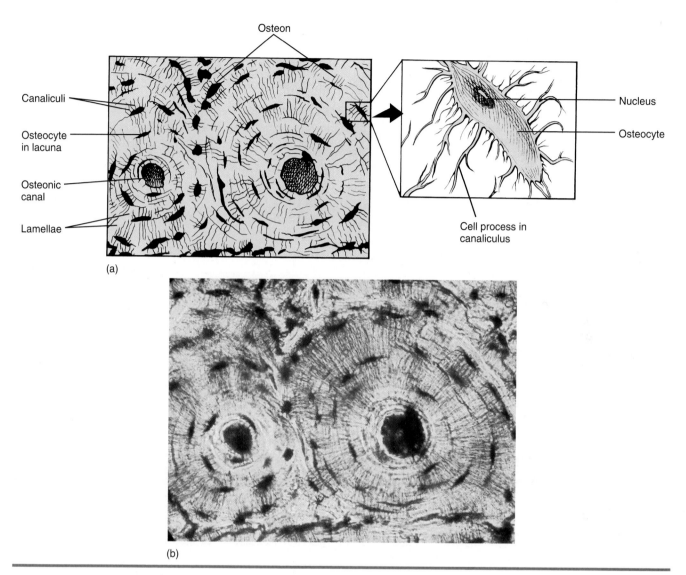

Osteon

Canaliculi

Osteocyte
in lacuna

Osteonic
canal

Lamellae

(a)

Nucleus

Osteocyte

Cell process in
canaliculus

(b)

Figure 4.13   (a) (b) Compact bone (160×). AP|R
Structure: Consists of rings of bone cells located in lacunae within a hard matrix of calcium salts. The matrix is arranged in concentric layers around osteonic (central) canals. Canaliculi, minute channels between lacunae, enable movement of materials between bone cells.
Function: Forms bones of the skeleton that provide support for the body and protection for vital organs.

are three basic types of formed elements: red blood cells, white blood cells, and platelets. Blood plays a vital role in carrying materials throughout the body (figure 4.14).

Table 4.2 summarizes the characteristics of connective tissue.

Check My Understanding

3. What are the general characteristics and functions of connective tissue?
4. What are the characteristics, locations, and functions of the different connective tissues?

4.3 Muscle Tissues AP|R

Muscle tissue consists of muscle cells. Muscle cells have lost the ability to divide, so destroyed muscle cells cannot be replaced. Because muscle cells are long, thin cells, they are called **muscle fibers** in anatomical terms. Muscle cells are specialized for contraction (shortening). Contraction is enabled by the interaction of specialized protein fibers. The contraction of muscle cells enables the movement of the body and body parts and also produces heat energy.

Three types of muscle tissue—skeletal, cardiac, and smooth muscle tissue—are classified according to their (1) location in the body, (2) structural features, and (3) functional characteristics.

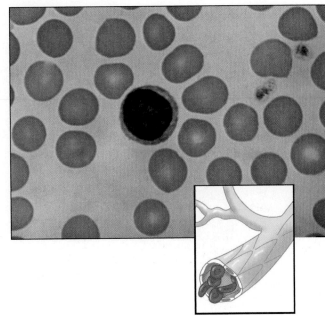

Red blood cells

Intercellular fluid (plasma)

Platelet

White blood cell

Figure 4.14 Blood (1,000×). AP|R

Structure: Consists of red blood cells, white blood cells, and platelets that are carried in a liquid matrix, the plasma.
Function: Transports materials throughout the body and provides a defense against disease.

Table 4.2 Connective Tissues

Tissue	Structure	Location and Function
Connective Tissue Proper		
Loose connective tissue	Matrix with loose arrangement of collagenous and elastic fibers in semifluid ground substance; fibroblasts scattered	Attaches skin to underlying muscles; forms supporting framework for organs
Adipose tissue	Closely packed fat cells	Forms protective cushion around organs; insulates body; energy storage
Fibrous connective tissue	Matrix contains densely packed collagenous fibers; fibroblasts arranged in rows	Covers skeletal muscles; forms tendons binding muscles to bones and ligaments binding bones to bones
Elastic connective tissue	Matrix with many elastic fibers; scattered fibroblasts	Walls of blood vessels, air passages, and lungs; allows expansion and contraction; imparts flexibility
Specialized Connective Tissue		
Cartilage		
Hyaline	Matrix glassy and smooth; few collagenous fibers	Covers ends of bones at joints; forms walls of air passages; supports part of nose; protection and support
Elastic	Matrix with many elastic fibers	Supports external ear; forms part of larynx (voice box); support, flexibility
Fibrocartilage	Matrix with densely packed collagenous fibers	Forms intervertebral disks and pads in the knee joint; absorbs shocks
Bone	Matrix is hard and solid; osteocytes arranged in concentric circles around osteonic canals	Forms bones of the skeleton; provides support and protection
Blood	Matrix is liquid with suspended blood cells	Transports materials

Skeletal Muscle Tissue

Named for its location, **skeletal muscle tissue** is attached to bones. Its contractions enable movement of the head, trunk, and extremities. The cells are elongated and cylindrical, with many nuclei located at the periphery of the cells. *Striations,* alternating light and dark bands, extend across the width of the fibers. Functionally, skeletal muscle tissue is considered to be **voluntary** muscle because its rapid contractions are under conscious control (figure 4.15).

Cardiac Muscle Tissue

The muscle tissue that occurs in the walls of the heart is **cardiac** (kar′-dē-ak) **muscle tissue.** It consists of branching cells or muscle fibers that interconnect in a netlike arrangement. **Intercalated** (in-ter-kah′-lā-ted) **disks** are present where the cells join together, and a single, centrally located nucleus is present in each cell. Like skeletal muscle, cardiac muscle cells are striated. The rhythmic contractions of cardiac muscle are **involuntary** because they are not consciously controlled (figure 4.16).

Smooth Muscle Tissue

Smooth muscle tissue derives its name from the absence of striations in its cells. It occurs in the walls of hollow internal organs, such as the digestive tract and blood vessels. The cells are long and spindle-shaped with a single, centrally located nucleus. The slow contractions of smooth muscle tissue are *involuntary* (figure 4.17).

Table 4.3 summarizes the characteristics of muscle tissues.

4.4 Nerve Tissue

The brain, spinal cord, and nerves are composed of **nerve tissue,** which consists of **neurons** (nū′-ronz), or nerve cells, and numerous supporting cells that are collectively called **neuroglia** (nū-rog′-lē-ah). Neurons are the functional units of nerve tissue. They are specialized to detect and respond to environmental changes by forming and transmitting nerve impulses. Neuroglial cells nourish, insulate, and protect the neurons.

Figure 4.15 Skeletal muscle tissue (250×). AP|R
Structure: Consists of cylindrical muscle cells (fibers) that have striations and multiple, peripherally located nuclei. *Function*: Voluntary, rapid contractions; composes skeletal muscles.

Labels on figure: Striations, Muscle fiber, Nuclei

Clinical INSIGHT

Following minor injuries, tissues repair themselves by *regeneration*—the division of the remaining intact cells. The capacity to regenerate varies among different tissues. For example, epithelial tissues, loose connective tissue, and bone readily regenerate, but cartilage and skeletal muscle have little capacity for regeneration. Cardiac muscle never regenerates, and nerve tissue in the brain and spinal cord usually does not regenerate.

After severe injuries, repair involves **fibrosis,** the formation of scar tissue. Scar tissue is formed by an excess production of collagenous fibers by fibroblasts. Scar tissues that join together tissues or organs abnormally are called *adhesions,* which sometimes form following abdominal surgery.

A neuron consists of a **cell body,** the portion of the cell containing the nucleus, and one or more *neuron processes,* or nerve fibers that extend from the cell body (figure 4.18). There are two types of neuron

Striations

Nucleus

Intercalated
disk

Figure 4.16 Cardiac muscle tissue (400×). AP|R

Structure: Consists of striated cells that are arranged in an interwoven network. Intercalated disks are present at the junctions between cells. A single, centrally located nucleus is present in each cell.
Function: Involuntary, rhythmic contractions; forms the muscular walls of the heart.

Plasma
membrane

Cytoplasm

Nucleus

Figure 4.17 Smooth muscle tissue (250×). AP|R

Structure: Consists of elongate, tapered cells that lack striations and have a single, centrally located nucleus.
Function: Involuntary, slow contractions; forms muscle layers in the walls of hollow internal organs.

processes. **Dendrites** respond to stimuli by forming nerve impulses and transmitting them toward the neuron cell body and axon. An **axon** transmits nerve impulses away from the cell body and dendrites.

A neuron may have many dendrites but only one axon. The complex interconnecting network of neurons enables the nervous system to coordinate body functions.

Table 4.3   Muscle Tissues

Tissue	Structure	Location and Function
Skeletal muscle	Striated; long fibers with many peripherally located nuclei	Attached to bones; moves body and appendages; rapid voluntary contractions
Cardiac muscle	Striated; interwoven fibers joined by intercalated disks; single nucleus in each cell	Muscle of heart wall; involuntary rhythmic contractions
Smooth muscle	Nonstriated; single nucleus in each cell; slow contractions	Muscle in walls of hollow internal organs; involuntary

Check My Understanding

5. What are the distinguishing characteristics of the three types of muscle tissue?
6. What types of cells form nerve tissue, and what are their functions?

4.5 Body Membranes

Membranes of the body are thin sheets of tissue that line cavities, cover surfaces, or separate tissues or organs. Some are composed of both epithelial and connective tissues; others consist of connective tissue only.

Epithelial Membranes

Sheets of epithelial tissue overlying a thin supporting framework of loose connective tissue form the epithelial membranes in the body. Blood vessels in the connective tissue serve both connective and epithelial tissues. There are three types of epithelial membranes: serous, mucous, and cutaneous membranes.

Serous membranes line the ventral body cavity and cover most of the internal organs. They secrete **serous fluid,** a watery fluid, which reduces friction between the membranes. The pleurae, pericardium, and peritoneum are serous membranes.

Mucous membranes line tubes or cavities of organ systems, which have openings to the exterior. Their goblet cells secrete **mucus,** which coats the surface of the membranes, keeping the cells moist and lubricating their surfaces. The digestive, respiratory, reproductive, and urinary tracts are lined with mucous membranes.

The **cutaneous membrane** is the skin that covers the body. Unlike other membranes, its free surface

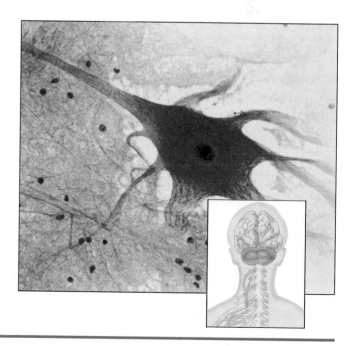

Figure 4.18 Nerve tissue (50×). **AP|R**

Structure: Consists of neurons and supportive neuroglial cells. Each neuron consists of a cell body, which houses the nucleus, and one or more nerve fibers.

Function: Impulse formation and transmission; forms the brain, spinal cord, and nerves.

is dry, composed of nonliving cells, and exposed to the environment. The skin is discussed in detail in chapter 5.

Connective Tissue Membranes

Some specialized membranes are formed only of connective tissue, usually fibrous tissue. These are considered with their respective organ systems, but here are four examples:

1. The **meninges** are three fibrous membranes that envelop the brain and spinal cord.
2. The **perichondrium** is a fibrous membrane covering the surfaces of cartilage. It contains blood vessels, which are the only blood supply for cartilage.

3. The **periosteum** is a fibrous membrane that covers the surfaces of bones. It contains blood vessels that also serve the bone.
4. **Synovial membranes** line the cavities of freely movable joints, such as the knee. They secrete watery synovial fluid, which reduces friction in the joint.

Check My Understanding

7. What are the two kinds of body membranes?
8. How do the types of epithelial membranes differ?

CHAPTER SUMMARY

- As cells specialize during embryonic development, they form groups of similar cells called tissues.
- The body is formed of four basic types of tissues: epithelial, connective, muscle, and nerve tissues.

4.1 Epithelial Tissues

- Epithelial tissue covers surfaces of organs and of the body and lines the body cavities.
- Epithelial tissue is composed of closely packed cells with little intercellular material.
- The cells are attached to underlying connective tissue by a noncellular basement membrane.
- Epithelial tissue lacks blood vessels.
- Epithelial tissues function in absorption, secretion, filtration, and protection.
- Epithelial tissues are classified according to the number of cell layers and the shape of the surface cells. The epithelial tissues are
  Simple
  - squamous
  - cuboidal
  - columnar
  - pseudostratified ciliated columnar
  Stratified
  - stratified squamous
  - transitional

4.2 Connective Tissues

- Connective tissue is composed of relatively few cells located within a large amount of matrix.
- All but cartilage are supplied with blood vessels.
- Connective tissue binds other tissues together and provides support and protection for organs and the body.
- Connective tissue is classified according to the nature of the matrix. The connective tissues are
  Connective tissue proper
  - loose connective tissue
  - adipose tissue

  - fibrous connective tissue
  - elastic connective tissue
  Cartilage
  - hyaline
  - elastic
  - fibrocartilage
  Bone, or osseous, tissue
  Blood

4.3 Muscle Tissues

- Muscle tissue is composed of muscle cells that are specialized for contraction.
- Contraction of muscle cells enables movement of the body and body parts.
- Muscle tissue is classified according to its location in the body, the characteristics of the muscle cells, and the type of contractions (voluntary or involuntary).
- Three types of muscle tissue are skeletal, cardiac, and smooth muscle tissue.

4.4 Nerve Tissue

- Nerve tissue consists of neurons and supporting neuroglial cells.
- Neurons consist of a cell body and long, thin cell processes, and they are adapted to form and conduct impulses.
- Nerve tissue forms the brain, spinal cord, and nerves.

4.5 Body Membranes

- Membranes in the body are either epithelial membranes or connective tissue membranes.
- There are three types of epithelial membranes: serous, mucous, and cutaneous.
- Examples of connective tissue membranes are meninges, perichondrium, periosteum, and synovial membranes.

BUILDING MY VOCABULARY

1. Selected New Terms
canaliculi, p. 72
cutaneous membrane, p. 77
endocrine gland, p. 65
endothelium, p. 65
exocrine gland, p. 65
keratin, p. 66
lamellae, p. 72
mucous membrane, p. 77
neuroglia, p. 75
osteonic (central) canal, p. 72
serous membrane, p. 77

2. Related Clinical Terms
Adhesions (ad-hē′-shuns) Excessive scar tissue binding organs together abnormally.
Carcinoma (kar-si-nō′-mah) Cancer arising from epithelial cells.
Keloid (kē′loid) Mass of scar tissue at skin surface due to excessive formation of connective tissue during healing of a wound.
Sarcoma (sar-kō′-mah) Cancer arising from connective tissue cells.

SELF-REVIEW

Answers are located in Appendix B.
1. Simple epithelial tissues consist of _____ layer(s) of cells.
2. Epithelial tissue contains _____ (little/much) intercellular material.
3. The upper air passages of the respiratory system are lined with _____ epithelium.
4. The digestive tract is lined with _____ epithelium.
5. Filtration, secretion, and absorption are functions of _____ tissue.
6. The intercellular substance in connective tissues is called _____.
7. The supporting framework of internal organs is provided by _____ connective tissue.
8. Cushioning pads in the knee joint are composed of _____.
9. Muscle tissue in the wall of the heart is _____ muscle tissue.
10. Muscle tissue lacking striations and found in walls of the digestive tract is _____ muscle tissue.
11. Nerve tissue consists of neurons and supporting _____ cells.
12. Membranes lining digestive, respiratory, and urinary tracts are classified as _____ membranes.

CRITICAL THINKING

1. Complete the learning objectives on the first page of this chapter.
2. Substances are exchanged between body cells and blood in capillaries, which are composed of a single layer of epithelial cells. What type of epithelium do you think composes capillaries? Explain.
3. How are connective tissues classified?
4. How are skeletal muscle tissue, fibrous connective tissue, and bone involved in movement of appendages?

Visit this book's website at www.mhhe.com/ gunstream5 for practice quizzes, learning exercises, case studies and other study tools.

CHAPTER 5

Integumentary System

Anatomy & Physiology **REVEALED®**
aprevealed.com

Module 4
Integumentary System

SELECTED KEY TERMS

Apocrine gland (apo = detached; crin = separate off) A sweat gland opening into a hair follicle.

Cutaneous (cutane = skin) Pertaining to the skin.

Dermis (derm = skin) The inner layer of the skin.

Eccrine gland (ec = out from) A sweat gland opening on the skin surface.

Epidermis (epi = upon) The outer layer of the skin.

Hair follicle (folli = bag) A saclike epidermal ingrowth in which a hair develops.

Hypodermis (hypo = under) The loose connective tissue under the skin.

Integument (integere = to cover) The skin.

Keratin (kerat = horny, hard) Waterproofing, abrasion-resistant protein in epidermal cells.

Melanin (melan = black) The brown-black pigment formed by melanocytes.

Sebaceous gland (seb = grease, oil) A sebum-producing gland associated with a hair follicle.

Subcutaneous (sub = under, beneath) Pertaining to the hypodermis.

Sudoriferous gland (sudori = sweat) A sweat gland.

he skin and the structures that develop from it—hair, nails, and glands—form the *integumentary* (in-teg-ū-men′-tar-ē) *system*. The skin, or **integument,** is also known as the **cutaneous membrane,** one of the three types of membranes as noted in chapter 4. The skin is pliable and tough, and it provides a water-proof, self-repairing barrier separating underlying tissues and organs from the external environment. Although it often gets little respect, the skin is vital to our existence.

5.1 Functions of the Skin

The skin performs five important functions:

1. **Protection**. The skin provides a physical barrier between underlying tissues and the external environment. It provides protection from abrasion, dehydration, ultraviolet radiation, and bacterial invasion.

2. **Excretion**. The production of perspiration by sweat glands removes small amounts of organic wastes, salts, and water.

3. **Temperature regulation**. During periods of excessive heat production by the body, the secretion of perspiration and its evaporation from the body surface help to lower body temperature. During periods of excessive heat loss, blood vessels near the body surface constrict to reduce heat loss.

4. **Sensory perception**. The skin contains nerve endings and receptors that detect stimuli associated with touch, pressure, temperature, and pain.

5. **Synthesis of vitamin D**. Exposure to ultraviolet radiation converts precursor molecules in the skin into vitamin D.

Clinical **INSIGHT**

Physicians often find the condition of the skin helpful in making diagnoses, even of diseases that do not directly affect the skin. For example, dry, coarse skin may indicate dietary or glandular disorders. Of course, certain child-hood diseases (e.g., measles and chicken pox), allergies, and local infections produce characteristic skin *lesions* (lē′-zhuns), that is, localized tissue damage.

5.2 Structure of the Skin and Hypodermis

The skin is thickest in areas subjected to wear and abrasion, such as the soles of the feet, where it may be 6 mm in thickness. It is thinnest on the eyelids, eardrums, and external genitalia, where it averages about 0.5 mm in depth.

The skin consists of two major layers: the epidermis and the dermis. The *epidermis* is the thinner outer layer, which is composed of stratified squamous epithelium. The *dermis* is the thicker inner layer, and it is composed of fibrous connective tissue. Beneath the dermis is the *hypodermis*, which is not part of the skin but is considered here because of its close association with the skin. Figure 5.1 shows the arrangement of epidermis, dermis, and the hypodermis as well as accessory organs of the skin. Table 5.1 summarizes these three tissue layers.

Epidermis

The **epidermis** is formed of stratified squamous epithelium. Because it lacks blood vessels, epidermal tissue must obtain nutrients from blood vessels in

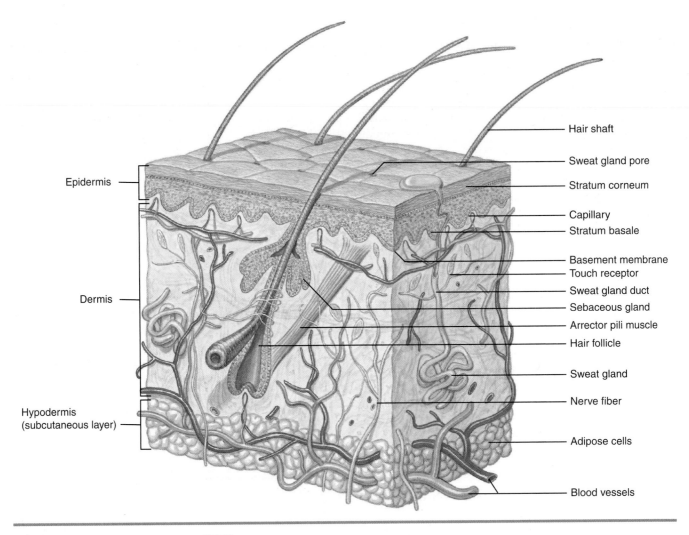

Figure 5.1 A section of skin. AP|R

Table 5.1	The Skin and Hypodermis	
Layer	**Structure**	**Function**
Epidermis	Stratified squamous epithelium; forms hair and hair follicles, sebaceous glands, and sweat glands that penetrate into the dermis or subcutaneous layers	Protects against abrasion, evaporative water loss, and bacterial or viral invasion
Dermis	Fibrous connective tissue containing blood vessels, nerves, and sensory receptors	Provides strength and elasticity; sensory receptors enable detection of touch, pressure, pain, cold, and heat; blood vessels supply nutrients to the epidermis
Hypodermis	Loose connective tissue and adipose tissue; contains abundant blood vessels and nerves	Provides insulation and fat storage; attaches skin to underlying organs

the underlying dermis. The epidermis is the boundary between the body and the environment. It protects the body against (1) the entrance of pathogenic organisms, (2) ultraviolet radiation, and (3) excessive water loss.

The innermost layer of cells, the **stratum basale** (ba-sah'-le), or basal layer, is composed of stem cells, which continuously produce new epidermal cells by mitotic cell division. The older cells are gradually pushed toward the surface, as new cells are formed beneath them. As the cells move toward the epidermal surface, they move farther from their nutrient-supplying blood vessels in the dermis and ultimately die. The constant division of cells in the stratum basale enables the epidermis to repair itself if it is injured. In this way, the epidermis maintains a protective barrier in spite of wear and tear and injuries.

As cells migrate to the surface, they change in composition so that several distinctive layers of cells are recognizable when sections of epidermis are viewed microscopically (figure 5.2). During this transition, the cells accumulate deposits of **keratin** (ker′-ah-tin), a waterproofing protein that is resistant to abrasion. The outermost layer, the **stratum corneum** (kor′nē-um), consists of numerous layers of dead, flat, keratinized cells. The superficial cells of the stratum corneum are constantly sloughed off and replaced by underlying cells moving to the surface. It takes about two to four weeks for a newly formed cell to migrate to the surface and be sloughed off.

Two types of specialized cells are also present in the epidermis. **Melanocytes** (mel-an′-ō-sitz) are associated with the stratum basale. They produce the brown-black pigment that is primarily responsible for skin color. **Dendritic (Langerhans) cells** are located in the intermediate layers of the epidermis. They are derived from monocytes, a type of white blood cell. These cells move into the epidermis where they detect and engulf pathogens trying to enter the body and alert the immune system to launch an attack.

Dermis

The **dermis** is composed of fibrous connective tissue, which provides strength, extensibility (ability to stretch), and elasticity (ability to return to its original shape) for the skin. Both collagen and elastic fibers are abundant in the dermis. Collagen provides the strength and toughness of the dermis, and elastic fibers provide the extensibility and elasticity.

Where the dermis and epidermis join are numerous **dermal papillae** (pah-pil′-ē), conelike projections of the dermis that fit into recesses in the epidermis. The dermal papillae anchor the epidermis to the dermis so both epidermis and dermis move as a unit. These dermal papillae contain blood vessels, and many contain touch receptors (see figure 5.1). Pressure, pain, heat, and cold receptors are located in the deeper portions of the dermis. The epidermal ridges and grooves that produce fingerprints and toe prints unique to each person result from the pattern of dermal papillae.

The dermis is well supplied with nerves and blood vessels. Blood vessels in the papillary layer supply nutrients to the adjacent epidermal cells. The dermal blood vessels play an important role in temperature regulation, which is considered later in this chapter.

Hypodermis

The **hypodermis,** also called the *subcutaneous layer* or superficial fascia (fash′ē-ah), attaches the skin to underlying tissues and organs. It consists primarily of loose connective tissue and adipose tissue. It is the site used for subcutaneous injections and where white

Figure 5.2 A photomicrograph of skin in cross section. Note the thick stratum corneum at the surface and the stratum basale next to the dermis. **AP|R**

blood cells attack pathogens that have penetrated the skin. Subcutaneous adipose tissue serves as a heat insulator and a storage site for fat. It conserves body heat and retards the penetration of external heat into the body. Blood vessels and nerves within the hypodermis give off branches that supply the dermis.

Check My Understanding

1. What are the general functions of the skin?
2. What changes occur in epidermal cells after they are formed?
3. What are the functions of the dermis and subcutaneous layers?

5.3 Skin Color

The color of the skin results from the interaction of three different pigments: hemoglobin, carotene, and melanin. **Hemoglobin** (he′mō-glō″-bin) is the red pigment in red blood cells that gives the red color to blood. **Carotene** (kair′-ō-tēn) is a yellowish pigment found in egg yolks and yellow and orange vegetables and fruits. It accumulates to varying degrees in the stratum corneum and dermis. **Melanin** (mel′-ah-nin) is the most important pigment determining skin color. It is the brown-black pigment that is formed by **melanocytes** (mel-an′-ō-sītz), special cells found in the deeper layers of the epidermis (figure 5.3).

When melanin is produced by melanocytes, it is picked up by adjacent epidermal cells. The amount of melanin that a person can produce is inherited. The greater the production of melanin, the darker is the skin color. Melanin protects the body from harmful ultraviolet radiation that is present in sunlight. Generally, melanocytes are equally distributed, but when they occur in small clumps, melanin is concentrated in small patches called *freckles*.

Exposure to ultraviolet light increases melanin production and produces a tanned appearance in light-skinned individuals. The increased production of melanin is a protective, homeostatic mechanism. When exposure to ultraviolet radiation decreases, melanin production also decreases and the tan is lost in a few weeks when the tanned cells migrate to the surface and are sloughed off.

The skin color that is characteristic of the various human races results primarily from varying amounts of carotene and melanin in the skin. The effect of hemoglobin is relatively constant, but it is often masked by high concentrations of melanin. Dark-skinned races produce abundant melanin and have a greater protection from ultraviolet radiation. Caucasians produce relatively little melanin and

Figure 5.3 A melanocyte with cellular extensions that transfer melanin granules to adjacent epidermal cells. AP|R

are susceptible to the harmful effects of ultraviolet radiation. The reduced amount of melanin in light-skinned Caucasians allows the hemoglobin of blood within dermal blood vessels to show through and give the skin a pinkish hue. Some people of Asian descent have a yellowish-tinged skin color due to the presence of a different form of melanin. These differences in skin color are inherited.

Check My Understanding

4. What relationship exists between skin color and protection against ultraviolet radiation?

5.4 Accessory Structures

The accessory structures of the skin—hair, nails, and glands—develop from the epidermis. These structures are located in either the dermis or subcutaneous layer because they originate from inward growths of the epidermis. Table 5.2 summarizes these accessory structures.

Table 5.2 Accessory Structures

Structure	Origin	Function
Hair	Fused keratinized epidermal cells formed at base of hair follicle	Scalp hair: protects scalp from excessive heat loss and mechanical injury Eyelashes and eyebrows: protect eyes from sunlight and dust Nasal hairs: keep dust and insects out of the nose
Nails	Fused keratinized epidermal cells formed within an ingrowth of the epidermis	Protect the dorsal tips of fingers and toes
Sebaceous glands	Formed as an epidermal outpocketing from a hair follicle	Sebum: prevents excessive dryness and keeps hair and skin pliable and soft; reduces evaporative water loss
Sudoriferous glands	Apocrine glands formed as an epidermal outpocketing from hair follicles in axillary and genital regions	Unknown in humans
	Eccrine glands formed as epidermal ingrowth	Evaporation of perspiration: cools body and eliminates excessive heat
Ceruminous glands	Modified sudoriferous glands	Waxy cerumen: keeps eardrum moist and captures dust entering ear canal

Hair

A *hair* is formed of keratinized cells and consists of two parts: a shaft and a root. The *shaft* is the portion that projects above the skin surface. The *root* lies below the skin surface in a **hair follicle,** an inward, tubular extension of the epidermis. The follicle penetrates into the dermis and usually into the hypodermis (see figure 5.1). The region of cell division, where the stratum basale forms new hair cells, is located in the *bulb* (base) of the follicle. The bulb is enlarged where it fits over a dermal papilla, which contains blood vessels that nourish the dividing epidermal cells. The hair cells become keratinized, die, and become part of the root as they move away from the source of nourishment. The continuing production of new cells causes growth of the hair.

Each hair follicle has an associated *arrector pili muscle* that is attached at one end to the lower portion of a hair follicle and to the papillary layer of the dermis at the other end (figure 5.4). Each muscle is formed of a small group of smooth muscle fibers. When a person is frightened or very cold, the arrector pili muscles contract and produce goose bumps. These muscles raise the hairs on end but have little value in humans. In many mammals, the erect hairs express rage to enemies or increase the thickness of the insulating layer of hair in cold weather.

Hair is present over most of the body, but it is absent on the soles, palms, nipples, lips, and portions of the external genitalia. Its primary function is protection, although the tiny hairs over much of the body have little function. Eyelashes and eyebrows shield the

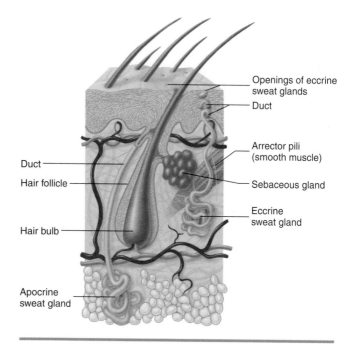

Figure 5.4 A section of skin showing the association of a hair follicle, arrector pili muscle, and sebaceous gland. A hair grows when cells at the base of the follicle divide, pushing older epidermal cells outward, where they become keratinized. **AP|R**

eyes from sunlight and foreign particles. Hair in the nostrils and ear canals protects against the entrance of foreign particles and insects. Hair protects the scalp from sunlight and mechanical injury.

Nails

The hard, hornlike *nails* cover the dorsal surface of the terminal portions of the fingers and toes. They are formed of keratinized epidermal cells (figure 5.5). A nail consists of a *body*, the portion that is visible, and a *root*, the proximal portion that is inserted into the dermis. Nails are colorless, but they normally appear pinkish due to the blood vessels in the underlying nail bed. The nails appear bluish in persons suffering from severe anemia or oxygen deficiency. Near the root is a whitish, crescent-shaped area that is called the *lunula*. The major function of nails is protection, but fingernails are also useful in manipulating small objects.

Glands

Exocrine glands associated with the skin are of three types: sebaceous (oil), sudoriferous (sweat), and ceruminous (wax) glands. Each type of gland is formed by an inward growth of the epidermis during embryonic development.

Sebaceous Glands   AP|R

Sebaceous (se-bā-shus) **glands** are oil-producing glands that empty their secretions into hair follicles (see figures 5.1 and 5.4). This oily secretion is called **sebum**, and it helps to keep the hair and skin pliable and soft. It also reduces evaporative water loss and inhibits the growth of some bacteria.

Sudoriferous Glands   AP|R

Sudoriferous (sū-dō-rif'-er-us) **glands** are sweat glands. Sweat glands are richly supplied with blood vessels, and they play an important role in regulating the body temperature.

The two types of sweat glands are *apocrine* and *eccrine glands*. Both types are tubular in shape with a coiled secretory portion located deep in the dermis or subcutaneous layer and a narrow duct that carries the secretion toward the surface.

Apocrine (ap'-ō-krin) **glands** have a duct that empties the secretion into a hair follicle (see figure 5.4).

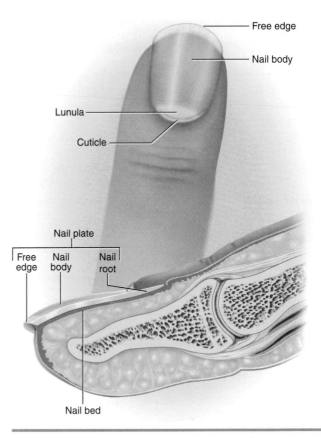

Figure 5.5   The structure of a fingernail. A fingernail is composed of heavily keratinized epidermal cells that are formed and undergo keratinization in the nail root.   AP|R

They occur primarily in the axillary and genital regions and become active at puberty under the influence of the sex hormones. These glands are active during times of stress and sexual excitement. The presence of proteins and fats gives their secretions a milky color. Although the secretions are essentially odorless, decomposition by bacteria produces waste products causing body odor. The precise function of apocrine glands is unknown, but studies suggest that they may be analogous to that of sexual scent glands in other mammals.

Eccrine (ek'-rin) **glands,** the most numerous sweat glands, occur over all of the body, and they produce a clear, watery perspiration lacking proteins. The perspiration consists of mostly water plus small amounts of salts and urea. Thus, sweating is a form of excretion. Eccrine glands are active throughout a person's lifetime. Production of perspiration is stimulated when body temperature starts to rise. Perspiration is released directly onto the surface of the skin where its evaporation cools the skin and body. (See figures 5.1 and 5.4 for the structural similarities and differences of apocrine and eccrine sweat glands.)

Ceruminous Glands

Ceruminous (se-rŭ′mi-nus) **glands** are modified sweat glands that produce a waxy secretion called *cerumen*. They are simple coiled, tubular glands that occur in the external auditory canal. The sticky, waxy nature of cerumen helps to keep foreign particles and insects out of the auditory canal.

Check My Understanding

5. How is a hair formed?
6. What is the function of sebaceous glands?

5.5 Temperature Regulation

Humans are able to maintain a normal body temperature of 37°C (98.6°F), although the surrounding environmental temperature may vary widely. Variations in body temperature of 0.5° to 1.5°F during a 24-hour activity cycle are normal, but variations of more than a few degrees can be life threatening. The brain controls the regulation of body temperature, and the skin plays a key role in conserving or dissipating heat. Of course, the source of body heat is cellular respiration, especially in metabolically active organs like the liver and muscles. Figure 5.6 illustrates the major aspects of temperature regulation.

Clinical **INSIGHT**

Occasionally, excessive production of cerumen causes a buildup of wax that becomes impacted in the auditory canal. This condition may cause a slight hearing loss as well as pain. Once the impacted wax is removed by irrigation and/or mechanical means, hearing returns to normal.

Clinical **INSIGHT**

Physicians have known for a long time that the ultraviolet (UV) radiation in sunlight produces damaging changes in the skin. The damage is cumulative, although a single day's exposure can produce noticeable changes. Short-term changes include sunburn and a tan as the body tries to protect itself from UV radiation by producing more melanin. Long-term UV damage ranges from increased wrinkling and loss of elasticity to liver spots and skin cancer.

Because the long-term effects of UV radiation do not appear for a number of years, the summer tans so important to many light-skinned teenagers and young adults will accelerate aging of the skin and may produce skin cancers in later life. The advent of tanning salons only increases potential problems for unwary users.

Skin cancer is by far the most common type of cancer. Fortunately, most skin cancers are *carcinomas* involving basal or squamous cells and are usually curable by surgical removal. However, *melanoma*, cancer of melanocytes, tends to spread rapidly to other organs and can be lethal if it is not detected and removed in an early stage. Melanoma is fatal in about 45% of the cases.

The undesirable effects of overexposure to UV radiation can easily be prevented by reducing the exposure of the skin to sunlight and by the liberal use of sunscreens. UV radiation is at its peak between 11:00 A.M. and 3:00 P.M., so avoiding exposure during these hours is especially helpful.

Sunscreens are available with different levels of protection, and they are labeled according to the sun protection factor (SPF) provided. This allows the selection of a sunscreen that is appropriate for a particular type of skin. For example, sunscreens with an SPF of 30 or higher are available for fair-skinned persons who burn easily. Sunscreens with an SPF of 15 may give adequate protection for olive-skinned persons who rarely burn.

A Cutaneous Malignant Melanoma.

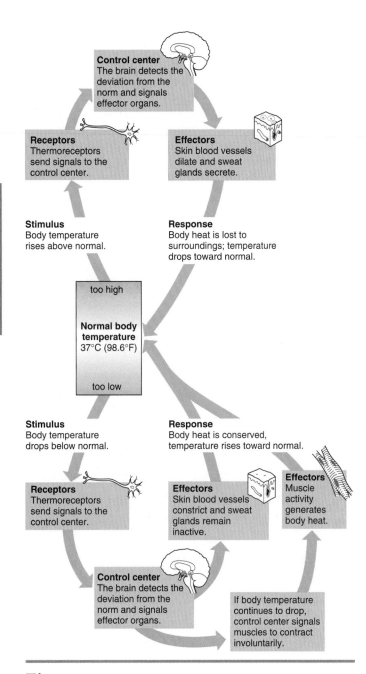

Figure 5.6 The negative feedback homeostatic mechanism that regulates body temperature. **AP|R**

When the body temperature is higher than normal, the brain increases the flow of blood to the skin. This increases heat loss by radiation from the body surface and causes the sweat glands to produce perspiration. As perspiration spills out on the surface of the skin and evaporates, heat loss is accelerated, which lowers the body temperature to normal levels.

When body temperature drops below normal, the brain reduces the flow of blood to the skin. The decreased blood flow to the skin reduces heat loss by radiation from the body surface and prevents sweat glands from secreting perspiration that would cool the body further. If heat loss becomes excessive, the nervous system stimulates small groups of skeletal muscles to produce involuntary, rapid, small contractions (shivering). This increases cellular respiration and generates additional heat to raise the body temperature.

Sometimes the temperature-regulating mechanism is insufficient to counter environmental extremes of temperature. *Hypothermia*, a body temperature below 35.0°C (95.0°F), can result from prolonged exposure to cold, which overwhelms the body's temperature-regulating mechanism. Without treatment, an initial feeling of coldness and shivering can progress to mental confusion, lethargy, loss of consciousness, and death. Persons with little subcutaneous fat (e.g., very old or thin persons) are more susceptible to hypothermia. In treating a person with hypothermia, the body temperature must be raised gradually to stabilize the cardiovascular and respiratory systems.

In *hyperthermia*, the temperature-regulating mechanism cannot prevent a dangerous increase in the body temperature. When exposed to both high temperature and high humidity, a person will perspire but perspiration will not evaporate to cool the body surface. The high temperature prevents heat loss by radiation, and if higher than body temperature, heat is gained from the surrounding air. In such an environment, excessive physical exertion is a common trigger. Persons who are dehydrated and overweight are especially susceptible. A person with hyperthermia has a body temperature over 40°C (104°F). It may be caused solely by environmental factors or a high fever due to infection. Either way, it can become a medical emergency. Without treatment, progressive symptoms may include nausea, headache, dizziness, confusion, loss of consciousness, and death. Lying in a tub of cool (not cold) water is an effective treatment except in severe cases.

Check My Understanding

7. How is the skin involved in the regulation of body temperature?

5.6 Aging of the Skin

A newborn baby's skin is very thin, and there is not a lot of **subcutaneous** fat present. During infancy a baby's skin thickens, and more subcutaneous fat is deposited, producing the soft, smooth skin typical of infants.

As a child grows into adulthood, the skin continues to become thicker, and it is subjected to numerous harmful conditions: sunlight, wind, abrasions, chemical irritants, and invasions of bacteria. The continued exposure of the skin through the adult years produces damaging effects. However, noticeable changes usually are not apparent until a person approaches 50 years of age. Thereafter, continued aging of the skin is more noticeable.

Typical changes in aging skin are as follows: (1) a breakdown of collagen and elastic fibers (hastened by exposure to sunlight) causes wrinkles and sagging skin; (2) a decrease in subcutaneous fat makes a person more sensitive to temperature changes; (3) a decrease in sebum production by sebaceous glands may cause dry, itchy skin; (4) a decrease in melanin production produces gray hair and sometimes a splotchy pattern of pigmentation; and (5) a decrease in hair replacement results in thinning hair or baldness, especially in males.

5.7 Disorders of the Skin

Because the skin is in contact with the environment, it is especially susceptible to injuries, such as abrasions (scraping), contusions (bruises), and cuts. Other common disorders of the skin may be subdivided into infectious and noninfectious disorders. Some inflammatory disorders may fall into either group, depending upon the specific cause of the disorder. Common childhood diseases, such as chicken pox and measles, are not listed here but produce skin lesions that characterize the particular disease.

Infectious Disorders

Acne (ak′-nē) is a chronic skin disorder characterized by plugged hair follicles that often form pimples (pustules) due to infection by certain bacteria. It often appears at puberty, when reproductive hormones stimulate increased sebum secretion.

Athlete's foot is a slightly contagious infection that is caused by a fungus growing on the skin. It produces reddish, flaky, and itchy patches of skin, especially between and under the toes, where moisture persists.

Boils are acute, painful *Staphylococcus* infections of hair follicles and their sebaceous glands as well as the surrounding dermis and subcutaneous tissue. The union of several boils forms a *carbuncle*.

Fever blisters, or cold sores, are clusters of fluid-filled vesicles that occur on the lips or oral membranes. They are caused by a *Herpes simplex* virus (type 1) and are transmitted by oral or respiratory exposure. *Genital herpes* is a similar disorder in which painful blisters form on the genitals as a result of infection transmitted by sexual intercourse.

Impetigo (im-pe-tī′-gō) is a highly contagious skin infection caused by bacteria. It typically occurs in children and is characterized by fluid-filled pustules that rupture, forming a yellow crust over the infected area.

Warts are small skin tumors that have a normal skin color. They are caused by a virus infection that stimulates excessive growth of epithelial cells.

Noninfectious Disorders

Alopecia (al-ō-pāy′-shē -ah) is the loss of hair. It is most common in males who have inherited male pattern baldness, but it may result from noninherited causes, such as poor nutrition, sensitivity to drugs, and eczema.

Bedsores (decubitis ulcers) result from a chronic deficiency of blood circulation in the dermis and subcutaneous layers. Bedsores form over bones that are subjected to prolonged pressure against a bed or cast. They are most common in bedridden patients. Frequent turning of bed patients helps to prevent bedsores.

Blisters, fluid-filled pockets, form when an abrasion, burn, or injury causes the epidermis to separate from the underlying dermis.

Burns are damage to the skin caused by heat, chemicals, or radiation. Burns are classified according to the degree of damage. A *first-degree burn* involves only the epidermis. Healing is usually rapid. A *second-degree burn* produces damage to the epidermis and the outer portion of the dermis. Blisters form within the epidermis, and there is usually no infection. Healing requires two to several weeks, and scarring may occur. A *third-degree burn* destroys the epidermis, dermis, glands, hair follicles, and nerve endings. Normal skin functions are lost, so care must be given in order to control fluid loss and bacterial infection. Skin grafting is often necessary, and scarring usually results.

Calluses and **corns** are thickened areas of skin that result from chronic pressure. Calluses are larger and often occur on the palms of the hands at the metacarpal joints and on the balls of the feet. Corns are smaller and usually occur on the upper surface of the toes. Improperly fitting shoes are frequent causes of corns on the feet.

Cancers result from excessive cell division by cells that have lost control of the process. Excessive exposure to sunlight is the primary cause of skin cancers. Cancers of the skin are usually *carcinomas* (basal cell carcinomas or squamous cell carcinomas) involving epidermal cells. Less frequently, skin cancers are *melanomas*, cancers of the melanocytes. Melanomas are especially dangerous because they tend to grow and metastasize (spread to other parts of the body) rapidly. Because of its deadly nature, the American Cancer Society has devised the "ABCD rule" for recognizing malignant melanoma from a mole: *A* for asymmetry (one side has a different shape than the other); *B* for border irregularity (the border is not uniform); *C* for color (color is not uniform, often a mixture of black, brown, tan, or red); *D* for diameter (more than ¼ inch).

Dandruff is the excessive shedding of dead epidermal cells from the scalp as a result of excessive cell production. It is usually caused by seborrheic eczema of the scalp, a noninfectious dermatitis.

Eczema (ek-zē′ -mah) is an inflammation producing redness, itching, scaling, and sometimes cracking of the skin. It is noninfectious and noncontagious, and it may result from exposure to irritants or from allergic reactions. *Seborrheic eczema* is characterized by hyperactivity of sebaceous glands and patches of red, scaling, and itching skin. It may occur at the corners of the mouth, in hairy areas, or in skin exposed to irritants.

Hives are red, itchy bumps or wheals that usually result from an allergic reaction to certain foods, drugs, or pollens.

Moles are slow-growing skin tumors that are usually brown or black in color.

Psoriasis (sŏ-rī′-ah-sis) is a chronic, noncontagious dermatitis that is characterized by reddish, raised patches of skin that are covered with whitish scales. It results from excessive cell production that may be triggered by emotional stress or poor health. The affected area may be slightly sore or may itch. Psoriasis occurs most often on the scalp, elbows, knees, buttocks, and lumbar areas.

CHAPTER SUMMARY

- The integumentary system is composed of the skin and its epidermal derivatives.
- The skin is also called the cutaneous membrane.

5.1 Functions of the Skin

- Protection
- Excretion
- Temperature regulation
- Sensory perception
- Synthesis of vitamin D

5.2 Structure of the Skin and Hypodermis

- The skin is composed of an outer epidermis that covers the inner dermis.
- The epidermis consists of stratified squamous epithelium, which lacks blood vessels and nerves.
- New epithelial cells are constantly formed by the basal layer. As the cells migrate toward the surface, they become keratinized, die, and finally are sloughed off.
- The dermis consists of fibrous connective tissue that contains both collagen and elastic fibers.
- The dermis contains blood vessels, nerves, and sensory receptors.
- The hypodermis attaches the skin to underlying tissues and organs.
- The hypodermis consists of loose connective tissue and adipose tissue. It contains blood vessels and nerves.

5.3 Skin Color

- The color of the skin is inherited and results from the presence of three pigments: hemoglobin in dermal blood vessels, carotene in the epidermis and dermis, and melanin in the epidermis.
- Melanin is a brown-black pigment produced by melanocytes in the deeper layers of the epidermis and is incorporated into the epidermal cells.
- Melanin protects the body from ultraviolet radiation.

5.4 Accessory Structures

- Accessory structures are formed from the epidermis.
- Hair consists of keratinized epidermal cells that are formed at the base of a hair follicle.

- An arrector pili muscle is attached to the side of each hair follicle at one end and to the papillary layer of the dermis at the other end. Its contraction pulls the hair into a more erect position.
- Hair occurs over most of the body.
- Nails protect the dorsal surface of the ends of fingers and toes.
- Nails are formed of layers of heavily keratinized epidermal cells.
- Glands associated with the skin are the sebaceous, sudoriferous, and ceruminous glands.
- Sebaceous glands produce sebum, an oily secretion that is emptied into hair follicles.
- Sudoriferous glands are sweat glands. Apocrine sweat glands occur in axillary and genital areas and secrete a relatively thick perspiration into hair follicles. Eccrine sweat glands occur all over the body and secrete a watery perspiration that is carried directly to the surface of the skin.
- Ceruminous glands are located in the external auditory canal and secrete a waxy substance called cerumen.

5.5 Temperature Regulation

- Normal human body temperature is 37°C (98.6°F).
- Body heat is produced as a by-product of cellular respiration.
- When heat loss is excessive, blood vessels in the dermis are constricted to reduce heat loss and arrector pili muscles contract. Under extreme heat loss, spontaneous weak muscle contractions (shivering) produce additional heat.
- When heat production is excessive, blood vessels in the dermis dilate to increase heat loss and perspiration is produced. The evaporation of perspiration increases heat loss.
- When temperature regulation is overwhelmed, hypothermia and hyperthermia become medical emergencies.

5.6 Aging of the Skin

- After 50 years of age, wrinkles and sagging skin become noticeable.
- The effects of aging are caused by a breakdown of collagen and elastic fibers, a decrease in sebum production, a decrease in melanin production, and a decrease in subcutaneous fat.

5.7 Disorders of the Skin

- Infectious disorders of the skin include acne, athlete's foot, boils, fever blisters, impetigo, and warts.
- Noninfectious disorders of the skin include alopecia, bedsores, blisters, burns, calluses and corns, cancers, dandruff, eczema, hives, moles, and psoriasis.

BUILDING MY VOCABULARY

1. **Selected New Terms**
   carotene, p. 84
   ceruminous gland, p. 87
   hemoglobin, p. 84
   melanocyte, p. 84
   sebum, p. 86

2. **Related Clinical Terms**
   Birthmark A tumor or localized discoloration of the skin that is visible at birth.

Cyst (sist) A fluid-filled sac in epithelial tissue.
Dermatology (der-mah-tol′-ō-jē) Medical specialty that treats diseases of the skin.
Melanoma (mel-a-nŏ′-mah) Cancer of melanocytes.
Pustule (pus′-tūl) A localized, raised, pus-filled area of skin.

SELF-REVIEW

Answers are located in Appendix B.

1. New epidermal cells are formed by the stratum _____.
2. Resistance to abrasion and waterproofing of the epidermis are due to the presence of _____.
3. The strength and elasticity of the skin are due to protein fibers within the _____.
4. The skin is attached to underlying tissues and organs by the _____.
5. Epidermal cells are nourished by blood vessels located in dermal _____.
6. The _____ glands produce an oily secretion that keeps the hair and skin moist, soft, and pliable.
7. Watery perspiration is produced by _____ sweat glands.
8. Goose bumps are produced when _____ muscles contract.
9. Constriction of dermal blood vessels _____ heat loss.
10. As the skin ages, a breakdown of collagen and elastic fibers leads to the formation of _____.
11. _____ is a common skin disorder caused by a fungus.
12. _____ and _____ are thickened areas of epidermis resulting from chronic pressure.

CRITICAL THINKING

1. Complete the learning objectives on the first page of this chapter.
2. The skin provides a protective barrier. What tissue is responsible for this barrier? What things are prevented from passing through the skin?
3. Skin cancers in dark-skinned people are relatively rare. Explain why.
4. Young people of Caucasian ancestry seem to enjoy sunbathing to get a "tan." Why is a "tan" a temporary state? What harm can come from excessive sunbathing?

Visit this book's website at www.mhhe.com/ gunstream5 for practice quizzes, learning exercises, case studies and other study tools.

CHAPTER 6

Skeletal System

Anatomy & Physiology REVEALED®
aprevealed.com

Module 05
Skeletal System

SELECTED KEY TERMS

Articular cartilage Cartilage covering the ends of bones forming a joint.

Articulation (articul = joint) A joint formed between two bones.

Compact bone Dense bone tissue formed of numerous tightly packed osteons.

Diaphysis (dia = through, apart; physis = to grow) The shaft of a long bone.

Endochondral ossification (endo = inside; chondr = cartilage; oss = bone) The formation of bone tissue within a cartilage.

Epiphysis (epi = upon) The enlarged ends of a long bone.

Intramembranous ossification (intra = inside) The formation of bone tissue within a fibrous membrane.

Ligament A band or cord of fibrous connective tissue that joins bones together at movable joints.

Medullary cavity (medulla = marrow) The cavity within the shaft of a long bone that is filled with yellow marrow.

Osteoblast (osteo = bone; blast = bud) A bone cell that deposits matrix.

Osteoclast (clast = break) A bone cell that breaks down bone matrix.

Osteocyte (cyt = cell) A bone cell occupying a lacuna.

Paranasal sinus (para = beside) An air-filled cavity in a bone located near the nasal cavity.

Periosteum (peri = around; os = bone) The fibrous membrane that covers bones.

Spongy bone Bone tissue that contains numerous spaces filled with red marrow.

---

he skeletal system serves as the supporting framework of the body, and it performs several other important functions as well. The body shape, mechanisms of movement, and erect posture observed in humans would be impossible without the skeletal system. Two very strong tissues, bones and cartilages, compose the skeletal system.

6.1 Functions of the Skeletal System

The skeletal system performs five major functions:

1. **Support.** The skeleton serves as a rigid supporting framework for the soft tissues of the body.
2. **Protection.** The arrangement of bones in the skeleton provides protection for many internal organs. The thoracic cage provides protection for the internal thoracic organs including the heart and lungs; the cranial bones form a protective case around the brain, ears, and all but the anterior portion of the eyes; vertebrae protect the spinal cord; and the pelvic girdle protects reproductive, urinary, and digestive organs.
3. **Attachment sites for skeletal muscles.** Skeletal muscles are attached to bones and span across joints between bones. Bones function as levers, enabling movement at joints when skeletal muscles contract.
4. **Blood cell production.** The red marrow in spongy bone forms red blood cells, white blood cells, and platelets.
5. **Mineral storage.** The matrix of bones serves as a storage area for large amounts of calcium phosphate, which may be removed for use in other parts of the body when needed.

6.2 Bone Structure

Each bone is an organ composed of a number of tissues. Bone tissue forms the bulk of each bone and consists of both living cells and a nonliving matrix formed primarily of calcium salts. Other tissues include cartilage, blood, nerve, and fibrous connective tissue.

There are four basic types of bones based on their shapes: *long bones* (e.g., thigh bone); *short bones* (e.g., wrist bones); *flat bones* (e.g., most skull bones); and *irregular bones* (e.g., bones of the spine).

Structure of a Long Bone

The femur, the bone of the thigh, will be used as an example in considering the structure of a long bone. Refer to figure 6.1 as you study the following section.

At each end of the bone, there is an enlarged portion called an **epiphysis** (ē-pif´-e-sis). The *epiphyses* (plural) articulate with adjacent bones to form joints. The articular surface of each epiphysis is covered by an **articular** (hyaline) **cartilage** that protects and cushions the end of the bone and provides a smooth surface for movement. The long shaft of bone that extends between the two epiphyses is the **diaphysis** (dĭ-af´-e-sis). Each epiphysis is joined to the diaphysis by an **epiphyseal plate** of hyaline cartilage in immature bones or by an **epiphyseal line,** a line of fusion, in mature bones.

Except for the region covered by articular cartilages, the entire bone is covered by the **periosteum**

Epiphyseal lines

Proximal articular cartilage

Spongy bone

Spaces containing red marrow

Compact bone

Medullary cavity

Yellow marrow

Periosteum

Distal articular cartilage

Proximal epiphysis

Diaphysis

Distal epiphysis

Femur

Figure 6.1 Major parts of a long bone. AP|R

(per-ē-os´-tē-um), a fibrous connective tissue membrane that is firmly attached to the underlying bone. The periosteum provides protection and also is involved in the formation and repair of bone tissue. Tiny blood vessels from the periosteum help to nourish the bone tissue.

The interior structure of a long bone is revealed by a longitudinal section. **Spongy** or **cancellous bone** forms the interior of small bones, skull bones, and the epiphyses in long bones. It consists of thin rods or plates called *trabeculae* (trah-bek´-u-lē) that form a meshlike framework containing numerous spaces. Spongy bone reduces the weight of a bone without reducing its supportive strength. The numerous spaces in spongy bone are filled with **red marrow.**

Compact bone forms the wall of the diaphysis and a thin surface layer over the epiphyses. As the name implies, compact bone is formed of tightly packed bone tissue that lacks the spaces found in spongy bone. Compact bone is very strong, and it provides the supportive strength of long bones. The cavity that extends the length of the diaphysis is the **medullary cavity.** It is lined by a thin membrane, the **endosteum** (en-dos´-tē-um), and it is filled with fatty **yellow marrow.**

Microscopic Structure

As noted earlier, there are two types of bone tissue: compact bone and spongy or cancellous bone. When viewed microscopically, compact bone is formed of a number of subunits called osteons. An **osteon** (os´-tē-on) is composed of an **osteonic** or **central canal** containing blood vessels and nerves, surrounded by the **lamellae** (lah-mel´-lē), concentric layers of bone matrix. Bone cells, the **osteocytes** (os´-tē-ō-sītz), are arranged in concentric rings between the lamellae and occupy tiny spaces in the bone matrix called **lacunae** (lah-kū´-nē). Extensions of the osteocytes extend into tiny channels, the **canaliculi** (kan-ah-lik´-ū-lī), that extend between lacunae and between the innermost lacunae and the osteonic canal.

Blood vessels and nerves enter a bone through a **foramen** (fō-rā´-men; plural, *foramina*), a channel entering or passing through a bone. The blood vessels form branches that pass through communicating canals and enter the osteonic canals to supply nutrients to the bone cells. Materials are exchanged between bone cells and the blood vessels via numerous canaliculi (figure 6.2).

The bony plates of spongy bone lack osteons, so bone cells receive nutrients by diffusion of materials through canaliculi from blood vessels in the red marrow surrounding the bony plates.

Check My Understanding

1. What are the general functions of the skeletal system?
2. What is the basic structure of a long bone?

6.3 Bone Formation

The process of bone formation is called **ossification** (os-i-fi-kā´-shun). It begins during the sixth or seventh week of embryonic life. Bones are formed by the replacement of existing connective tissues with bone tissue (figure 6.3). There are two types of bone formation: intramembranous ossification and endochondral ossification. Table 6.1 summarizes these processes.

Figure 6.2 Compact bone is composed of osteons cemented together.

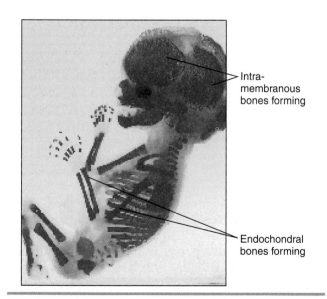

Figure 6.3 Note the stained, developing bones of this 14-week fetus.

In both types of ossification, some primitive connective tissue cells are changed to become bone-forming cells called **osteoblasts** (os´-tē-ō-blasts). Osteoblasts deposit bone matrix around themselves and soon become imprisoned in lacunae. Once this occurs, they are called osteocytes, or bone cells.

Intramembranous Ossification

Most skull bones are formed by **intramembranous ossification.** Connective tissue membranes form early in embryonic development at sites of future intramembranous bones. Later, some connective tissue cells become osteoblasts and deposit spongy bone within the membranes starting in the center of the bone. Osteoblasts from the covering membrane (periosteum) deposit a layer of compact bone over the spongy bone.

Some bone tissue must be removed and re-formed in order to produce the correct shape of the bone as it develops and grows. Cells that remove bone matrix are called **osteoclasts.** The opposing actions of osteoblasts

Table 6.1   Comparison of Intramembranous and Endochondral Ossification

Intramembranous	Endochondral
1. Membranes of embryonic connective tissue form at sites of future bones.	1. Bone is preformed in hyaline cartilage.
2. Some connective tissue cells become osteoblasts, which deposit spongy bone within the membrane.	2. Cartilage is calcified, and osteoblasts derived from the periosteum form spongy bone, which replaces cartilage in ossification centers.
3. Osteoblasts from the enclosing membrane, now called the periosteum, deposit a layer of compact bone over the spongy bone.	3. Osteoblasts of periosteum form a collar of compact bone that thickens and grows toward each end of the bone.

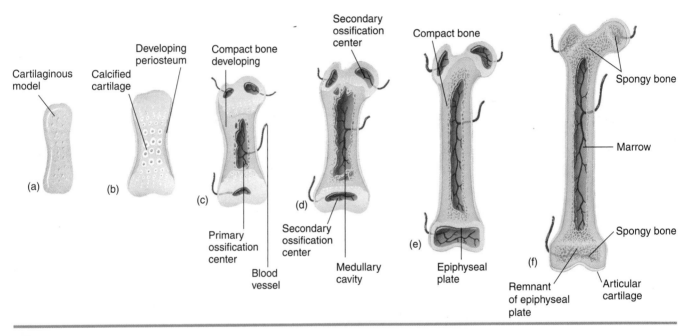

Figure 6.4 Major stages (a–f) in the development of an endochondral bone. (Bones are not shown to scale.)

and osteoclasts ultimately produce the shape of the mature bone.

Endochondral Ossification

Most bones of the body are formed by **endochondral** (en-dō-kon´-drul) **ossification.** Future endochondral bones are preformed in hyaline cartilage early in embryonic development. Figure 6.4 illustrates the ossification of a long bone.

In long bones, a *primary ossification center* forms in the middle of the bone, and osteoblasts from the periosteum form a collar of compact bone around the ossification center. Cartilage in the primary ossification center calcifies, and the chondrocytes die. Blood vessels and nerves penetrate into the primary ossification center carrying along osteoblasts from the periosteum, which form spongy bone. A *secondary ossification*

center forms in each epiphysis, and osteoclasts begin to remove spongy bone in the diaphysis to form the medullary cavity. The bone continues to grow as ossification progresses. As cartilage continues to be replaced, the cartilage between the primary and secondary ossification centers decreases until only a thin plate of cartilage, the *epiphyseal plate,* separates the epiphyses from the diaphysis.

Subsequent growth in diameter results from continued formation of compact bone by osteoblasts from the periosteum. Growth in length occurs as bone replaces cartilage on the diaphysis side of each epiphyseal plate while new cartilage is formed on the epiphysis side. The opposing actions of osteoblasts and osteoclasts continually reshape the bone as it grows.

Growth usually continues until about age 25, when the epiphyseal plates are completely replaced by bone tissue. After this, growth in the length of a bone is not possible. The visible lines of fusion between the epiphyses and the diaphysis are called *epiphyseal lines.*

Homeostasis of Bone

Bones are dynamic, living organs, and they are continually restructured throughout life. This occurs by the removal of calcium salts by osteoclasts and by the deposition of new bone matrix by osteoblasts. Physical activity causes the density and volume of bones to be maintained or increased, though inactivity results in a reduction in bone density and volume.

Calcium salts may be removed from bones to meet body needs when dietary calcium is inadequate. When dietary calcium salts return to a sufficient level, they are used to form new bone matrix.

Children have a relatively large amount of protein fibers in their bone matrix, which makes their bones somewhat flexible. But as people age, the amount of protein gradually decreases. This trend causes older people to have brittle bones that are prone to fractures. Older persons may also experience a gradual loss of calcium salts (osteoporosis), which reduces the strength of the bones.

Check My Understanding

3. How do intramembranous ossification and endochondral ossification differ?
4. How does physical activity affect the homeostasis of bones?

6.4 Divisions of the Skeleton

The human adult skeleton is composed of two distinct divisions: the axial skeleton and the appendicular skeleton. The **axial** (ak´-sē-al) **skeleton** consists of the bones along the longitudinal axis of the body that support the head, neck, and trunk. The **appendicular** (ap-en-dik´-ū-lar) **skeleton** consists of the bones of the upper extremities and pectoral girdle and of the lower extremities and pelvic girdle (figure 6.5).

A study of the skeleton includes the various surface features of bones, such as projections, depressions, ridges, grooves, and holes. Specific names are given to each type of surface feature. The names of the major surface features are listed in table 6.2 for easy reference as you study the bones of the skeleton.

6.5 Axial Skeleton

The major components of the axial skeleton are the skull, vertebral column, and thoracic cage. Bones of the axial skeleton are listed in table 6.3.

Skull AP|R

The **skull** is subdivided into the *cranium,* which is formed of eight fused bones encasing the brain, and the *facial bones,* which consist of 13 fused bones and the movable lower jaw. The fused bones are joined by immovable joints called **sutures** (sū´-churs) because they resemble stitches. Several bones in the skull contain air-filled spaces called **paranasal sinuses** that reduce the weight of the skull (table 6.4) and add resonance to a person's voice. The bones of the skull are shown in figures 6.6 to 6.10. Locate the bones on these figures as you study this section.

Cranium

The **cranium** is formed of the following bones: one frontal bone, two parietal bones, one sphenoid bone, two temporal bones, one occipital bone, and one ethmoid bone (figure 6.6).

The **frontal bone** forms the anterior part of the cranium, including the superior portion of the eye orbits (sockets), the forehead, and the roof of the nasal cavity. There are two large sinuses in the frontal bone, one located over each eye (figure 6.7).

The two **parietal** (pah-rī´-e-tal) **bones** form the sides and roof of the cranium. They are joined at the midline by the *sagittal suture* and to the frontal bone by the *coronal sutures* (figure 6.8).

The **occipital** (ok-sip´-i-tal) **bone** forms the posterior portion and floor of the cranium. It contains a large opening, the *foramen magnum,* through which the brain stem extends to join with the spinal cord. On each side of the foramen magnum are the *occipital condyles* (kon´-dīls), large knucklelike surfaces that articulate with the first vertebra of the vertebral column. The occipital bone is joined to the parietal bones by the *lambdoidal* (lam-doy´-dal) *sutures* (figures 6.9 and 6.10).

The **temporal bones** are located inferior to the parietal bones on each side of the cranium. They are joined to the parietal bones by *squamosal* (skwa-mō´-sal) *sutures* and to the occipital bone by the lambdoidal suture. In each temporal bone, an **external auditory canal** leads inward to the eardrum. Just anterior to the auditory canal is the *mandibular fossa,* a depression that receives the mandibular condyle to form the *temporomandibular joint.*

Three processes are located on each temporal bone. The *zygomatic* (zī-gō-mat´-ic) *process* projects

Axial Skeleton

Appendicular Skeleton

Axial Skeleton

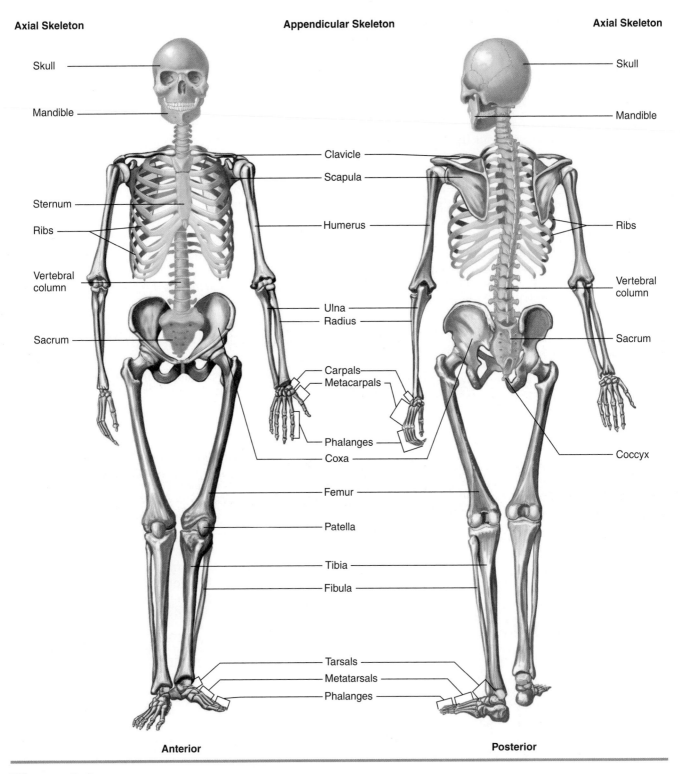

Skull

Mandible

Sternum

Ribs

Vertebral column

Sacrum

Clavicle

Scapula

Humerus

Ulna

Radius

Carpals

Metacarpals

Phalanges

Coxa

Femur

Patella

Tibia

Fibula

Tarsals

Metatarsals

Phalanges

Skull

Mandible

Ribs

Vertebral column

Sacrum

Coccyx

Anterior

Posterior

Figure 6.5   The human skeleton. Bones of the axial skeleton are colored ■. Bones of the appendicular skeleton are colored gold. AP|R

anteriorly to join with the zygomatic bone. The *mastoid* (mas´-toyd) *process* is a large, rounded projection that is located inferior to the auditory canal. It contains small spaces called air cells and serves as

an attachment site for some neck muscles. The *styloid process* lies just medial to the mastoid process. It is a long, spikelike process to which muscles and ligaments of the tongue and neck are attached.

Table 6.2 Surface Features of Bones

Feature	Description
Processes Forming Joints	
Condyle	A rounded or knucklelike process
Head	An enlarged, rounded end of a bone supported by a constricted neck
Facet	A smooth, nearly flat articulating surface
Processes for Attachment of Ligaments and Tendons	
Crest	A prominent ridge or border
Epicondyle	A prominence above a condyle
Trochanter	A very large process found only on the femur
Tubercle	A small, rounded process
Tuberosity	A large, roughened process
Depressions and Openings	
Alveolus	A deep pit or socket
Canal	A tubelike passageway into a bone
Foramen	An opening or passageway into or through a bone through which blood vessels or nerves pass
Fossa	A small depression
Groove	A furrowlike depression
Sinus	An air-filled cavity within a bone

Table 6.3 Bones of the Axial Skeleton

Region and Bones	Number of Bones	Region and Bones	Number of Bones
Skull		*Hyoid*	1
Cranium			1
Ethmoid	1	**Vertebral Column**	
Frontal	1	Cervical	7
Occipital	1	Thoracic	12
Parietal	2	Lumbar	5
Sphenoid	1	Sacrum	1
Temporal	2	Coccyx	1
	8		26
Face		**Thoracic Cage**	
Inferior nasal concha	2	Ribs	24
Lacrimal	2	Sternum	1
Mandible	1		25
Maxilla	2		Total = 80
Nasal	2		
Palatine	2		
Vomer	1		
Zygomatic	2		
	14		

Table 6.4   Skull Bones Containing Paranasal Sinuses

Bone	Number
Ethmoid	2 groups
Frontal	2
Maxillae	I each
Sphenoid	2

The **sphenoid** (sfē´-noid) **bone** forms part of the floor of the cranium, the lateral posterior portions of the eye orbits, and the lateral portions of the cranium just anterior to the temporal bones. It articulates with all other cranial bones, so it is the "keystone" of the cranium. On its superior surface at the midline is a saddle-shaped structure called the *sella turcica* (ter´-si-ka), or Turk's saddle. It has a depression that contains the pituitary gland. Two sphenoidal sinuses are located just below the sella turcica.

The **ethmoid** (eth´-moid) **bone** forms the anterior portion of the cranium, including part of the medial surface of each eye orbit and part of the roof of the nasal cavity. The lateral portions contain several air-filled sinuses. The *perpendicular plate* extends downward to form most of the nasal septum, which separates the right and left portions of the nasal cavity. It joins the sphenoid and vomer bones posteriorly and the nasal and frontal bones anteriorly.

The superior and middle **nasal conchae** (kong´-kē) extend from the lateral portions of the ethmoid toward the perpendicular plate. These delicate, scroll-like bones support the mucous membrane and increase the surface area of the nasal wall. The roof of the nasal cavity is formed by the *cribriform plates* of the ethmoid. On the superior surface where these plates join at the midline is a prominent projection called the *crista galli,* or cock's comb. The meninges that envelop the brain are attached to the crista galli.

Facial Bones

The paired bones of the face are the maxillae, palatine bones, zygomatic bones, lacrimal bones, nasal bones, and inferior nasal conchae. The single bones are the vomer and mandible.

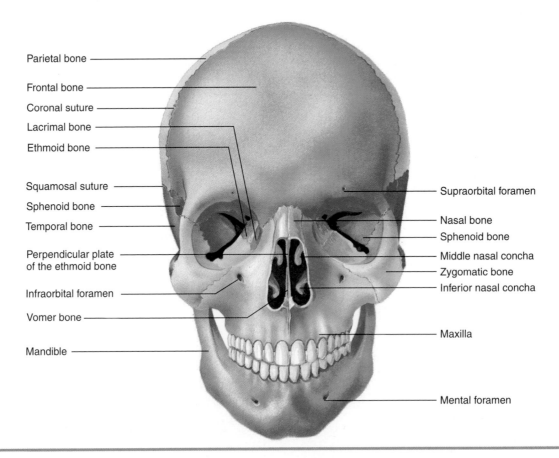

Figure 6.6 An anterior view of the skull. AP|R

Figure 6.7 The locations of the paranasal sinuses.

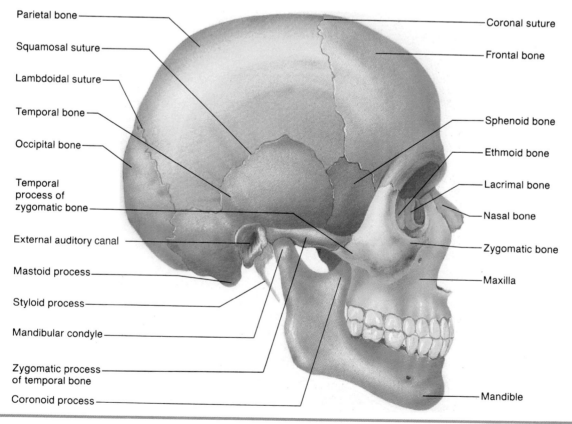

Figure 6.8 The lateral view of the skull. AP|R

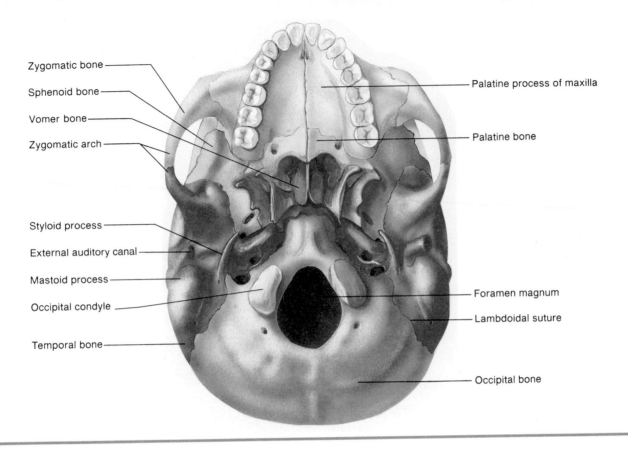

Figure 6.9 An inferior view of the skull. AP|R

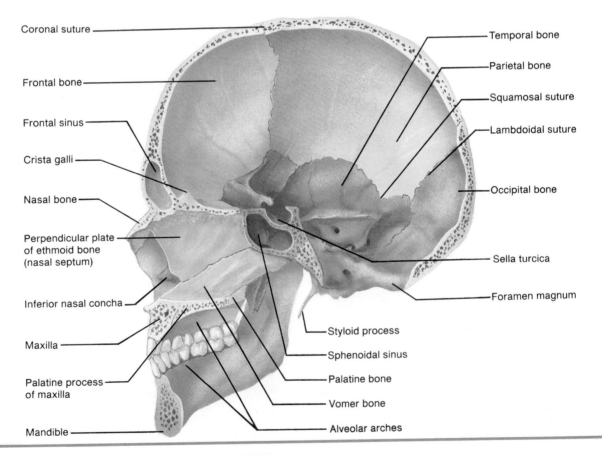

Figure 6.10 A midsagittal section of the skull. AP|R

The **maxillae** (mak-sil´-ē) form the upper jaw. Each maxilla is formed separately, but they are joined at the midline during embryonic development. The maxillae articulate with all of the other facial bones except the mandible. The palatine processes of the maxillae form the anterior portion of the hard palate (roof of the mouth and floor of the nasal cavity), part of the lateral walls of the nasal cavity, and the floors of the eye orbits.

A *cleft palate* results when the palatine processes of the maxillae and usually the palatine bones do not join before birth to form the hard palate. A *cleft lip*, a split upper lip, is often associated with a cleft palate. These conditions may be corrected surgically after birth.

Each maxilla possesses a downward projecting, curved ridge of bone that contains the teeth. This ridge is the *alveolar process*, and the sockets containing the teeth are called *alveoli*. The alveolar processes unite at the midline to form the U-shaped maxillary *alveolar*, or *dental*, *arch*. A large **maxillary sinus** is present in each maxilla just below the orbits.

The **palatine** (pal´-ah-tīn) **bones** are fused at the midline to form the posterior portion of the hard palate. Each bone has a lateral portion that projects upward (superiorly) to form part of a lateral wall of the nasal cavity.

The **zygomatic bones** are the cheek bones. They form the prominences of the cheeks and the floors and lateral walls of the eye orbits. Each zygomatic bone has a posteriorly projecting process, the *temporal process*, that extends to unite with the zygomatic process of the adjacent temporal bone. Together, they form the *zygomatic arch*.

The **lacrimal** (lak´-ri-mal) **bones** are small, thin bones that form part of the medial surfaces of the eye orbits. Each lacrimal bone is located between the ethmoid and maxilla.

The **nasal** (nā´-zal) **bones** are thin bones fused at the midline to form the bridge of the nose.

The **vomer** is a thin, flat bone located on the midline of the nasal cavity. It joins posteriorly with the perpendicular plate of the ethmoid, and these two bones form the nasal septum.

The **inferior nasal conchae** are scroll-like bones attached to the lateral walls of the nasal cavity inferior to the medial nasal conchae of the ethmoid bone. They project medially into the nasal cavity and support the mucous membrane.

The **mandible** is the lower jawbone, and it is the only movable bone of the skull. It consists of a U-shaped *body* with a superiorly (upward) projecting portion, a *ramus,* extending from each end of the body. The superior portion of the body forms the mandibular *alveolar arch,* which contains the teeth of the lower jaw. The superior part of each ramus is Y-shaped and forms two projections: an anterior *coronoid process* and a posterior *mandibular condyle.* The coronoid process is a site of attachment for muscles used in chewing. The mandibular condyle articulates with the mandibular fossa of the temporal bone to form a *temporomandibular joint.* These joints are sometimes involved in a variety of dental problems associated with an improper bite.

Hyoid Bone

The **hyoid** (hī´-oyd) is a small, U-shaped bone located in the anterior portion of the neck, inferior to the mandible. It does not articulate with any bone. Instead, it is suspended from the styloid processes of the temporal bones by ligaments. Muscles of the tongue are attached to the hyoid.

The Infant Skull

The skull of a newborn infant is incompletely developed. The face is relatively small with large eye orbits, and the bones are thin and incompletely ossified. The bones of the cranium are separated by fibrous membranes, and there are six rather large, nonossified areas called **fontanels** (fon´-tah-nels), or soft spots (table 6.5). The frontal bone is formed of two separate parts that fuse later in development. Incomplete ossification of

Table 6.5	Fontanels in an Infant Skull	
Fontanel	**Number**	**Location**
Anterior	I	On the midline at the junction of the frontal and parietal bones
Mastoid	2	Superior to the mastoid process at the junction of the occipital, parietal, and temporal bones
Posterior	I	On the midline at the junction of the occipital and parietal bones
Sphenoid	2	Superior to the temporomandibular joint at the junction of the frontal, parietal, sphenoid, and temporal bones

the skull bones and the abundance of fibrous membranes make the skull somewhat flexible and allow partial compression of the skull during birth. After birth, they allow growth of the skull without compressing the growing brain. Compare the infant skull in figure 6.11 with the adult skull in figure 6.8.

> ### Check My Understanding
> 5. What bones form the cranium?
> 6. What bones form the face?

Vertebral Column

The vertebral column extends from the skull to the pelvis and forms a somewhat flexible but sturdy longitudinal support for the trunk. It is formed of 24 slightly movable vertebrae, the sacrum, and the coccyx. The vertebrae are separated from each other by **intervertebral disks** that serve as shock absorbers and allow bending of the spinal column. The upright posture of humans produces four distinct curvatures in the vertebral column. From top to bottom they are the *cervical, thoracic, lumbar,* and *pelvic curvatures.* Locate these curvatures and the basic components of the vertebral column in figure 6.12.

Structure of a Vertebra

Vertebrae are divided into three groups: cervical, thoracic, and lumbar vertebrae. Although each type has a distinctive anatomy, they have many features in common (figure 6.13).

The anterior, drum-shaped mass is the *body,* which serves as the major load-bearing portion of a vertebra. A bony *neural arch* surrounds the large *vertebral foramen* through which the spinal cord passes. A *spinous process* projects posteriorly and *transverse processes* project laterally from each vertebra.

A pair of *superior articulating facets* (fa´-sets) of one vertebra articulates with the *inferior articulating facets* of the adjacent vertebra above it. When joined by ligaments, the vertebrae form a flexible bony cylinder that protects the spinal cord.

Small *intervertebral foramina* occur between adjacent vertebrae. They serve as lateral passageways for spinal nerves that exit the spinal cord (see figure 6.12).

Cervical Vertebrae

The first seven vertebrae are the **cervical** (ser´-vi-kul) **vertebrae** that support the neck. They are unique in having a *transverse foramen* in each transverse process. It serves as a passageway for blood vessels and nerves.

The first two cervical vertebrae are distinctly different from the rest. The first vertebra is the **atlas,** whose superior facets articulate with the condyles of the occipital bone and support the head. The second vertebra is the **axis,** which has a prominent *odontoid* (ō-don´-toyd) *process* (*dens*) that projects upward from the vertebral body, providing a pivot point for the atlas. When the head is turned, the atlas rotates on the axis (figure 6.14).

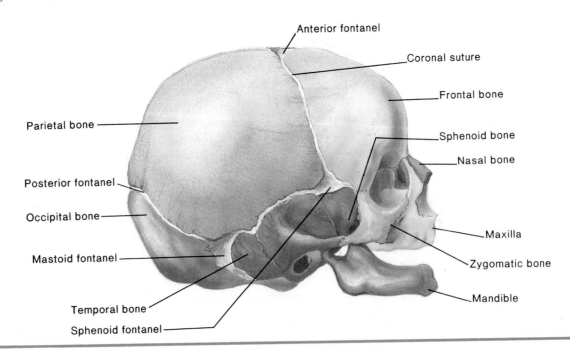

Anterior fontanel

Coronal suture

Frontal bone

Sphenoid bone

Nasal bone

Parietal bone

Posterior fontanel

Occipital bone

Mastoid fontanel

Maxilla

Zygomatic bone

Mandible

Temporal bone

Sphenoid fontanel

Figure 6.11 A lateral view of a newborn infant's skull. Note the fontanels and the membranes between the cranial bones.

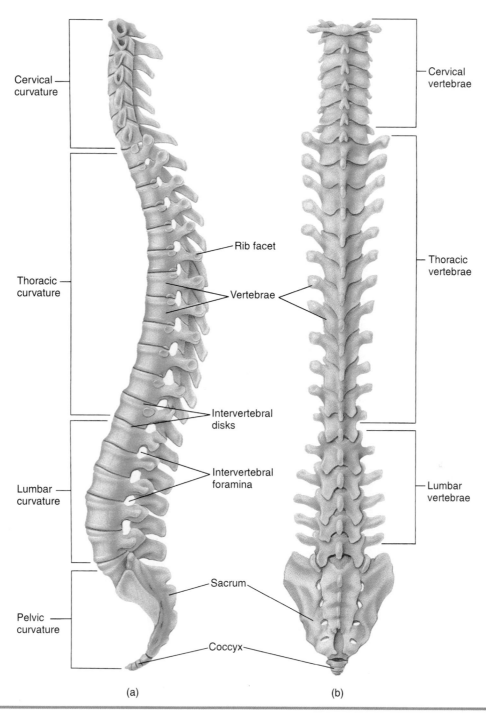

Cervical curvature

Thoracic curvature

Lumbar curvature

Pelvic curvature

Rib facet

Vertebrae

Intervertebral disks

Intervertebral foramina

Sacrum

Coccyx

Cervical vertebrae

Thoracic vertebrae

Lumbar vertebrae

(a)

(b)

Figure 6.12   The vertebral column consists of 24 movable vertebrae, separated by intervertebral disks, sacrum, and coccyx. (*a*) Lateral view. (*b*) Posterior view.   AP|R

Thoracic Vertebrae

The 12 **thoracic vertebrae** are larger than the cervical vertebrae, and their spinous processes are longer and slope downward. The ribs articulate with **facets** on the transverse processes and bodies of thoracic vertebrae.

Lumbar Vertebrae

The five **lumbar vertebrae** have heavy, thick bodies to support the greater stress and weight that is placed on this region of the vertebral column. The spinous processes are blunt, and they provide a large surface area for the attachment of heavy back muscles.

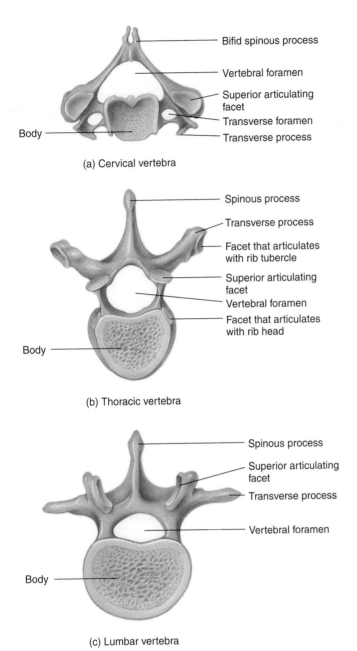

Bifid spinous process

Vertebral foramen

Superior articulating facet

Transverse foramen

Transverse process

Body

(a) Cervical vertebra

Spinous process

Transverse process

Facet that articulates with rib tubercle

Superior articulating facet

Vertebral foramen

Facet that articulates with rib head

Body

(b) Thoracic vertebra

Spinous process

Superior articulating facet

Transverse process

Vertebral foramen

Body

(c) Lumbar vertebra

Figure 6.13 Superior view of (*a*) a cervical vertebra, (*b*) a thoracic vertebra, and (*c*) a lumbar vertebra. AP|R

Sacrum

The **sacrum** (sā-k´rum) is composed of five fused vertebrae (figure 6.15). It articulates with the fifth lumbar vertebra and forms the posterior wall of the pelvic girdle. The spinous processes of the fused vertebrae are reduced to a series of **tubercles** on the posterior midline. On either side of the tubercles are the *posterior sacral foramina,* passageways for blood vessels and nerves. Foramina on the anterior surface serve a similar function. The *sacral canal* is formed

by the fused neural arches, and it continues to an inferior opening, the *sacral hiatus,* proximal to the coccyx.

Coccyx

The most inferior part of the vertebral column is the **coccyx** (kok´-six), or tailbone, which is formed of three to five fused, rudimentary vertebrae.

Thoracic Cage

The thoracic vertebrae, ribs, costal cartilages, and sternum form the **thoracic,** or **rib, cage.** It provides protection for the internal organs of the thorax and supports the upper trunk, shoulder girdle, and upper extremities (figure 6.16).

Ribs

Twelve pairs of **ribs** are attached to the thoracic vertebrae. The *head* of each rib articulates with the body of its own vertebra, and a *tubercle* near the head articulates with the transverse process. The head also articulates with the body of the next higher vertebra. The *shaft* of each rib curves around the thorax and slopes slightly downward.

The upper seven pairs of ribs are attached directly to the sternum by the **costal** (kos´-tal) **cartilages,** which extend medially from the ends of the ribs. These ribs are the *true ribs.* The remaining five pairs are the *false ribs.* The first three pairs of false ribs are attached by cartilages to the costal cartilages of the ribs just superior to them. The last two pairs of false ribs are called *floating ribs* because they lack cartilages and are not attached anteriorly. The costal cartilages give some flexibility to the thoracic cage.

Check My Understanding

7. How do cervical, thoracic, and lumbar vertebrae differ in structure and location?
8. How does the axial skeleton protect vital organs?

Sternum

The **sternum,** or breastbone, is a flat, elongated bone located at the midline in the anterior portion of the thoracic cage. It consists of three bones that are fused together. The *manubrium* (mah-nū´-brē-um) is the T-shaped upper portion that articulates with the first two pairs of ribs; the *body* is the larger middle segment; and the *xiphoid* (zī´f´-oyd) *process* is the small inferior portion.

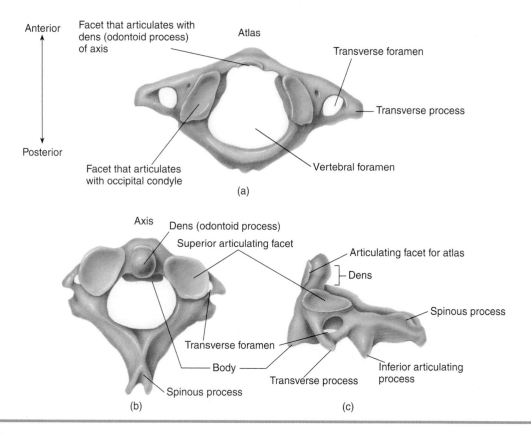

Figure 6.14 The structures of the (*a*) atlas and (*b*) axis function together to allow movement of the head. (*c*) Lateral view of the axis. APR

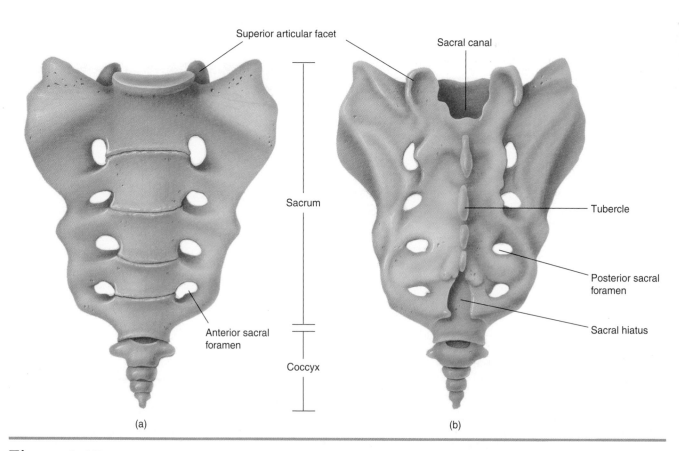

Figure 6.15 (*a*) Anterior view and (*b*) posterior view of the sacrum and coccyx. APR

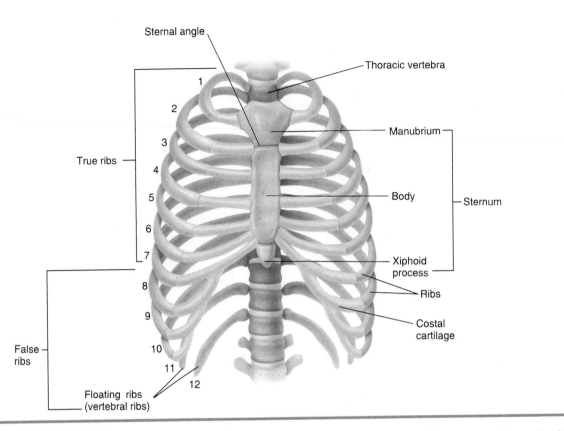

Figure 6.16 The thoracic cage is formed by thoracic vertebrae, ribs, costal cartilages, and the sternum. Note the difference between true and false ribs. AP|R

Clinical INSIGHT

A biopsy of red bone marrow may be made by a *sternal puncture* because the sternum is covered only by skin and connective tissue. Under local anesthetic, a large-bore hypodermic needle is inserted into the sternum, and red marrow is drawn into a syringe.

6.6 Appendicular Skeleton

The appendicular skeleton consists of (1) the pectoral girdle and the bones of the upper extremities and (2) the pelvic girdle and the bones of the lower extremities.

The appendicular skeleton is composed of 126 bones. The bones of the pectoral girdle and upper extremities are listed in table 6.6. Bones of the pelvic girdle and lower extremities are listed in table 6.7.

Pectoral Girdle

The **pectoral** (pek´-to-ral) **girdle,** or shoulder girdle, consists of two clavicles (collarbones) and two scapulae (shoulder blades) (figure 6.17). Each S-shaped

Table 6.6 Bones of the Pectoral Girdle and Upper Extremities	
Region and Bones	**Number of Bones**
Pectoral Girdle	
Clavicle	2
Scapula	<u>2</u>
	4
Upper Extremities	
Humerus	2
Ulna	2
Radius	2
Carpals	16
Metacarpals	10
Phalanges	<u>28</u>
	60
	Total = 64

clavicle (klav´-i-cul) articulates with the acromion process of a scapula laterally and with the sternum medially. The **scapulae** (skap´-ū-le) are flat, triangular-shaped bones located on each side of the vertebral

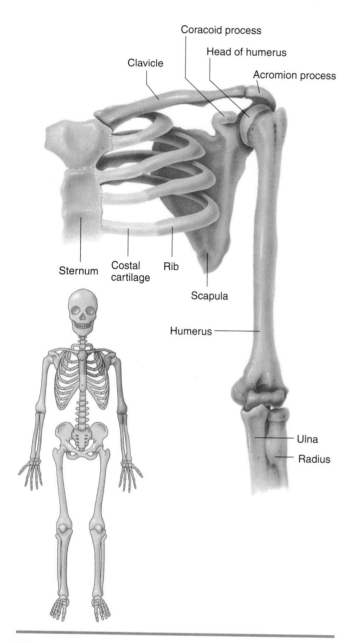

Figure 6.17 The pectoral girdle consists of a scapula and clavicle on each side of the body. Note how the head of the humerus fits into the glenoid fossa of the scapula. AP R

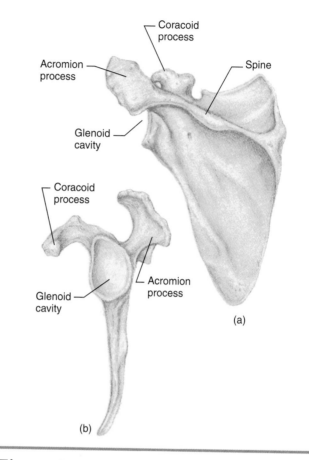

Figure 6.18 The left scapula: (*a*) posterior view; (*b*) lateral view. AP R

column, but they do not articulate with the axial skeleton (figure 6.18). Instead, they are held in place by muscles, an arrangement that enables freedom of movement for the shoulders.

The anterior surface of each scapula is flat and smooth where it moves over the ribs. The scapular *spine* runs diagonally across the posterior surface from the *acromion* (ah-krōm´-ē-on) *process* to the medial margin. On its lateral margin is the shallow *glenoid cavity,* which articulates with the head of the humerus. The *coracoid* (kor´-ah-koyd) *process* proj-

ects anteriorly from the superior margin and extends under the clavicle.

Upper Extremity

The skeleton of each **upper extremity** is composed of a humerus, an ulna, a radius, carpals, metacarpals, and phalanges. See figures 6.17 to 6.21 as you study this section.

Humerus

The **humerus** (hū´-mer-us) articulates with the scapula at the shoulder, and the ulna and radius at the elbow (figure 6.19). The rounded *head* of the humerus fits into the glenoid cavity of the scapula. Just inferior to the head are two large tubercles where muscles attach. The *greater tubercle* (tū´-ber-cul) is on the lateral surface, and the *lesser tubercle* is on the anterior surface. An *intertubercular groove* lies between them. Just below these tubercles is the *surgical neck,* which gets its name from the frequent fractures that occur in this area. Near the midpoint on the lateral surface is the *deltoid tuberosity*

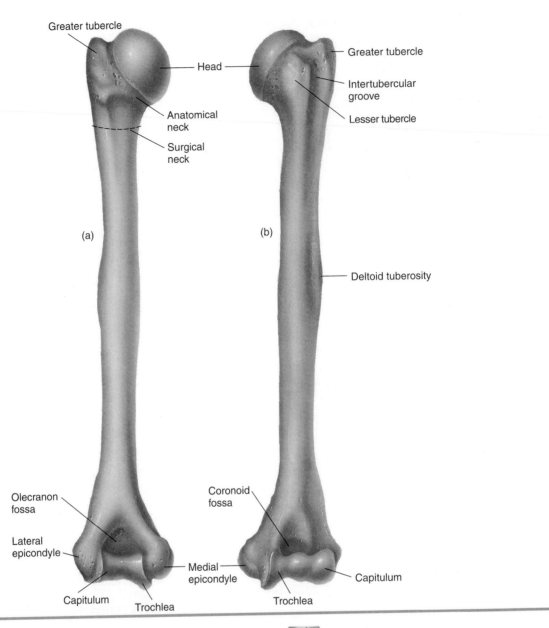

Figure 6.19 The left humerus: (*a*) posterior view; (*b*) anterior view. AP|R

(tū-be-ros´-i-tē), a rough, raised area where the del-toid muscle attaches.

The distal end of the humerus has two condyles. The *trochlea* (trok´-lē-ah) is the medial condyle, which articulates with the ulna. The *capitulum* (kah-pit´-ū-lum) is the lateral condyle, which articulates with the radius. Just above these condyles are two enlargements that project laterally and medially: the *lateral epicondyle* (ep-i-kon´-dīl) and the *medial epicondyle*. On the anterior surface between the epicondyles is a depression, the *coronoid* (kor´-o-noyd) *fossa*, that receives the coronoid process of the ulna whenever the

forearm is flexed at the elbow. The *olecranon* (o-lek´-rah-non) *fossa* is in a similar location on the posterior surface of the humerus, and it receives the olecranon process of the ulna when the arm is straightened at the elbow.

Ulna

The **ulna** (ul´-na) is the medial bone (little finger side) of the forearm (figure 6.20). The proximal end of the ulna forms the *olecranon process*, the bony point of the elbow. The large, half-circle depression just distal to the olecranon process is the *trochlear notch*, which

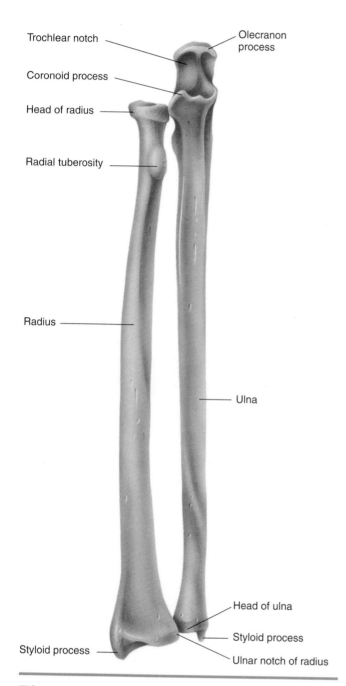

Figure 6.20 An anterior view of the right radius and ulna. AP|R

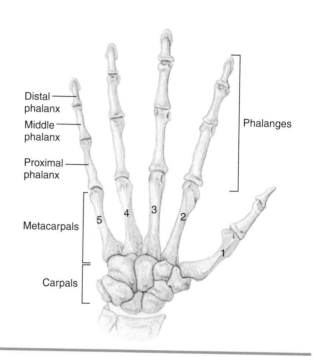

Figure 6.21 A posterior view of the bones of the left hand. AP|R

Radius

The **radius** (rā´-dē-us) is the lateral bone (thumb side) of the forearm. The disklike *head* of the radius articulates with the capitulum of the humerus in a way that enables the head to rotate freely when the hand is rotated. A short distance distally from the head is the *radial tuberosity,* a raised, roughened area where the biceps muscle attaches. At its distal end, the radius articulates with the carpal bones. A small lateral *styloid process* serves as an attachment site for ligaments of the wrist.

Carpals, Metacarpals, and Phalanges

The skeleton of the hand consists of the carpals, metacarpals, and phalanges (figure 6.21). The **carpals** (kar´-pulz), or wrist bones, consist of eight small carpal bones that are arranged in two transverse rows of four bones each. They are joined by ligaments that allow limited gliding movement.

The **metacarpals,** bones of the palm of the hand, consist of five metacarpal bones that are numbered 1 to 5 starting with the thumb. The bones of the fingers are the **phalanges** (fah-lan´-jēz). Each finger consists of three phalanges—proximal, middle, and distal—except the thumb, which has proximal and distal phalanges only.

articulates with the trochlea of the humerus. This articulation is secured by the *coronoid process* on the distal lip of the notch.

At the distal end, the knoblike *head* of the ulna articulates with the medial surface of the radius and with a fibrocartilaginous disk that separates it from the wrist bones. The *styloid process* is a small medial projection to which ligaments of the wrist are attached.

Figure 6.22 An anterior view of the bony pelvis. AP|R

Pelvic Girdle

The **pelvic** (pel´-vik) **girdle** consists of two **coxal** (kok´sal) **bones,** or hipbones, that support the attachment of the lower extremities. The coxal bones articulate with the sacrum posteriorly and with each other anteriorly to form an almost rigid, bony **pelvis,** as shown in figure 6.22. Recall that the coccyx is attached to the inferior end of the sacrum.

Coxal Bones

Each coxal bone is formed by three fused bones—ilium, ischium, and pubis—that join at the *acetabulum* (as-e-tab´-ū-lum), the cup-shaped socket on the lateral surface (figure 6.23). The **ilium** is the broad upper portion whose superior margin forms the *iliac crest,* the prominence of the hip. Interior to the posterior superior iliac spine is the *greater sciatic* (sī-at´-ik) *notch,* which allows the passage of blood vessels and nerves from the pelvis to the thigh. Each ilium joins with the sacrum to form a *sacroiliac joint.*

Table 6.7 Bones of the Pelvic Girdle and Lower Extremities	
Region and Bones	**Number of Bones**
Pelvic Girdle	
Coxal bones	<u>2</u>
	2
Lower Extremities	
Femur	2
Patella	2
Tibia	2
Fibula	2
Tarsals	14
Metatarsals	10
Phalanges	<u>28</u>
	60
	Total = 62

The **ischium** forms the inferior, posterior portion of a coxal bone and supports the body when sitting. The roughened projection at the posterior, inferior angle of the ischium is the *ischial tuberosity.* Just above this tuberosity is the *ischial spine,* which projects medially. The size of this spine in females is important during childbirth because it determines the diameter of the pelvic opening.

The **pubis** is the lower, anterior portion of a coxal bone. A portion of the pubis extends posteriorly to fuse with the anterior extension of the ischium. The large opening above this junction is the *obturator* (ob-tū-rā´-ter) *foramen,* through which blood vessels and nerves pass into the thigh. The pubic bones unite anteriorly to

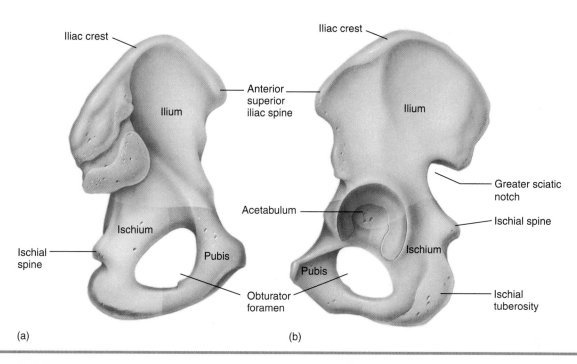

Figure 6.23 The left coxal bone. (*a*) Medial view. (*b*) Lateral view. AP|R

form the **symphysis pubis** where the bones are joined by a pad of fibrocartilage.

Table 6.8 lists the major differences between the male and the female pelvic girdles. Compare them with the male and female pelvic girdles in figure 6.24 and note the adaptations of the female pelvic girdle for childbirth.

Clinical INSIGHT

The fetus must pass through the pelvic opening during birth. Physicians carefully measure this opening before delivery to be sure that it is of adequate size. If not, the baby is delivered via a *cesarean section*. In a cesarean section, a transverse incision is made through the pelvic and uterine walls to remove the baby.

Lower Extremity

The bones of each **lower extremity** consist of a femur, a patella, a tibia, a fibula, tarsals, metatarsals, and phalanges. See figures 6.25 to 6.28 as you study this section.

Femur

The **femur** is the thighbone (figure 6.25). It is the largest and strongest bone of the body. Structures at the proximal end include the rounded *head,* a short *neck,* and two large processes that are sites of muscle attachment: a superior, lateral *greater trochanter* (trō-kan´-ter) and an inferior, medial *lesser trochanter.* The head of the femur fits into the acetabulum of the coxal bone. The neck is a common site of fractures in older people. At the enlarged distal end are the *lateral* and *medial condyles,* surfaces that articulate with the tibia.

Table 6.8	Sexual Differences of the Pelvic Girdle	
Characteristic	**Male**	**Female**
General structure	Heavier; processes prominent	Lighter; processes not so prominent
Pelvic opening	Narrower and heart-shaped	Wider and oval
Pubic arch angle	Less than 90°	More than 90°
Relative width	Narrower	Wider
Acetabulum	Faces laterally	Faces laterally but more anteriorly

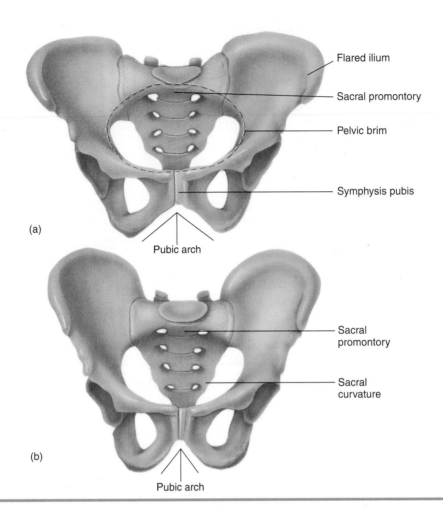

Flared ilium

Sacral promontory

Pelvic brim

Symphysis pubis

(a)

Pubic arch

Sacral promontory

Sacral curvature

(b)

Pubic arch

Figure 6.24 (*a*) Female and (*b*) male pelvic girdles. Note the obtuse angle of the pubic arch and greater pelvic width in the female pelvic girdle. AP|R

Patella

The **patella,** or kneecap, is located anterior to the knee joint. It is embedded in the tendon of the thigh muscle (quadriceps femoris), which extends over the anterior of the knee to insert on the tibia. Bones embedded in tendons are called **sesamoid bones.**

Tibia

The **tibia,** or shinbone, is the larger of the two bones of the lower leg (figure 6.26). It bears the weight of the body. Its enlarged proximal portion consists of the *lateral* and *medial condyles,* which articulate with the femur to form the knee joint. The *tibial tuberosity,* a roughened area on the anterior surface just below the condyles, is the attachment site for the patellar ligament. The distal end of the tibia articulates with the talus, a tarsus bone, and laterally with the

fibula. The *medial malleolus* (mah-lē-ō´-lus) forms the medial prominence of the ankle.

Fibula

The **fibula** is the slender, lateral bone in the lower leg. Both ends of the bone are enlarged. The proximal *head* articulates with the lateral surface of the tibia but is not involved in forming the knee joint. The distal end articulates with the tibia and tarsus. The *lateral malleolus* forms the lateral prominence of the ankle.

Tarsals, Metatarsals, and Phalanges

The skeleton of the foot consists of the tarsals (ankle), metatarsals (instep), and phalanges (toes) (figures 6.27 and 6.28). Seven bones compose the **tarsals.** The most prominent tarsal bones are the *talus,* which

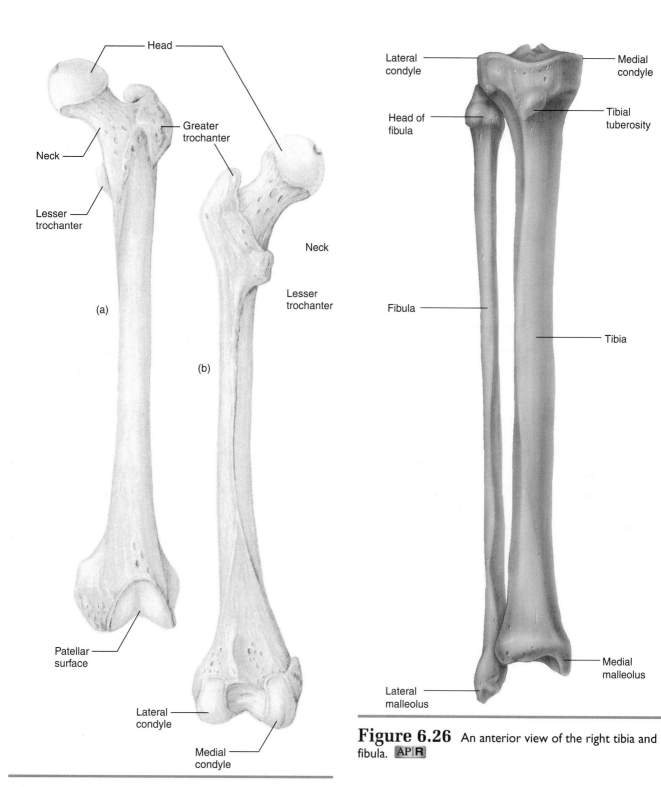

Figure 6.25 The left femur: (*a*) anterior view; (*b*) posterior view. AP|R

Figure 6.26 An anterior view of the right tibia and fibula. AP|R

articulates with the tibia and fibula, and the *calcaneus* (kal-kā′n-ē-us), or heel bone. Five **metatarsals** support the instep. They are numbered 1 to 5, starting with the great toe. The tarsals and metatarsals are bound together by ligaments to form strong, resilient arches of the foot. Each toe consists of three **phalanges**—proximal, middle, and distal—except for the great toe, which has only two.

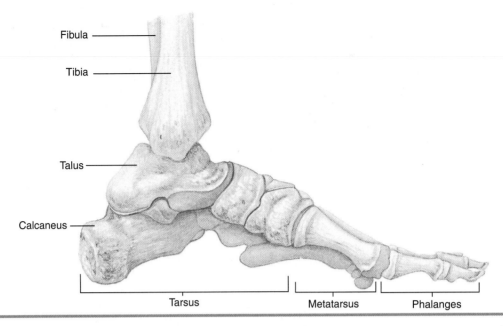

Figure 6.27 A medial view of the bones of the left foot showing articulation of the talus with the tibia. AP|R

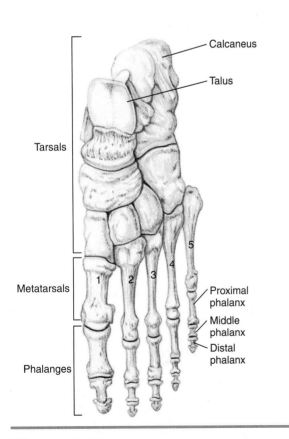

Figure 6.28 A superior view of the bones of the left foot. AP|R

Clinical   INSIGHT

Total hip replacement (THR) has become commonplace among older persons as a way to overcome the pain and immobility caused by osteoarthritis of the hip joint. This procedure utilizes two prostheses. A polyurethane cup replaces the damaged acetabular socket, and a metal shaft and ball replace the diseased fermoral head. Surfaces of the prostheses in contact with bone are porous, allowing bone to grow into them to ensure a firm attachment. Patient recovery involves stabilization of the prostheses while bone tissue grows into them as well as normal healing from the surgery.

Check My Understanding

9. What bones form the pectoral girdle and upper extremities?
10. What bones form the pelvic girdle and lower extremities?

6.7 Articulations

The junction between two bones forms an **articulation**, or **joint**. Joints allow varying degrees of movement. Joints are categorized as immovable, slightly movable, or freely movable. As you read the following descriptions, locate the different types of articulations on the corresponding illustrations of skeletal parts in figures presented earlier in the chapter.

Immovable Joints

Bones forming immovable, or **synarthrosis** (sin-ar-thrō´-sis), **joints** are tightly joined and are separated by a thin layer of fibrous connective tissue. For example, skull bones, except the mandible, are joined by immovable joints called *sutures* because they resemble stitches (see figure 6.8).

Slightly Movable Joints

Bones forming slightly movable, or **amphiarthrosis** (am-fē-ar-th-rō´-sis), **joints** are separated by a layer of cartilage or fibrous connective tissue. For example, the joints formed by adjacent vertebrae contain intervertebral disks formed of fibrocartilage. The limited flexibility of the disks allows slight movement between adjacent vertebrae. Other examples include the symphysis pubis and sacroiliac joints.

Freely Movable Joints

Most articulations are freely movable. The structure of freely movable, or **diarthrosis** (di-ar-thro´-sis), **joints** is more complex. The ends of the bones form-ing the joint are bound together by an *articular, or joint, capsule* formed of **ligaments**. A *synovial* (si-nō´-vē-al) *membrane* lines the interior of the capsule and secretes *synovial fluid* that lubricates the joint. The ends of the bones are covered with *articular cartilage*, which protects bones and reduces friction (figure 6.29). Freely movable joints are categorized into several types based on their structure and types of movements.

Gliding Joints

Gliding joints occur between small bones that slide over one another. They occur between carpal bones, between tarsal bones, and between the clavicle and scapula.

Condyloid Joints

Condyloid joints allow movements in two planes: side to side or back and forth. The joints between the carpals and bones of the forearm (radius and ulna) and the metacarpals and first phalanges are examples.

Hinge Joints

Hinge joints allow movement in one plane only, like a door hinge. The elbow, knee, and joints between phalanges are all hinge joints. Examine the sagittal section of a knee joint in figure 6.30. Note the articular capsule

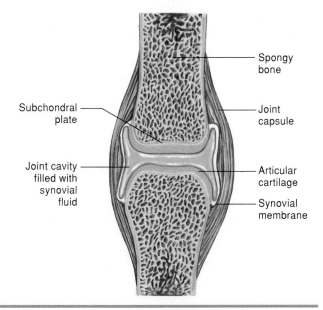

Figure 6.29 The basic structure of a freely movable joint. AP|R

Labels: Spongy bone; Joint capsule; Articular cartilage; Synovial membrane; Subchondral plate; Joint cavity filled with synovial fluid

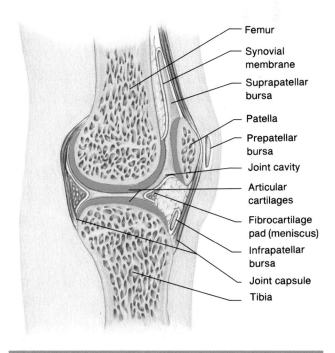

Figure 6.30 A sagittal section of a knee joint, a hinge joint. Note the articular cartilages, synovial membrane, fibrocartilage pads, bursae, and joint capsule. AP|R

Labels: Femur; Synovial membrane; Suprapatellar bursa; Patella; Prepatellar bursa; Joint cavity; Articular cartilages; Fibrocartilage pad (meniscus); Infrapatellar bursa; Joint capsule; Tibia (formed of ligaments), which binds the bones together; the bursae (sacs filled with synovial fluid); the articular cartilages, which reduce friction; and the cartilaginous pads, which cushion the ends of the bones.

Saddle Joints

Saddle joints occur where the ends of each bone are saddle-shaped: convex in one direction and concave in the other. Movement is side to side and back and forth. A joint of this type occurs between the trapezium (a carpal bone) and the metacarpal bone of the thumb.

Pivot Joints

Pivot joints allow rotational movement in a single plane. The rotation of the atlas on the axis is an example of a pivot joint.

A "torn cartilage" is a damaged cartilaginous pad (meniscus) in a knee joint, a common athletic injury. Treatment usually requires removal of the damaged cartilage by *arthroscopic surgery*. An arthroscope is a pencil-sized instrument containing lenses and a light source. It may be inserted into a joint through a small incision to enable a physician to observe the interior of the joint. While viewing the interior of the joint, the surgeon may insert small instruments to remove damaged tissue, make repairs, and flush out the joint.

Ball-and-Socket Joints

Ball-and-socket joints occur where a rounded head of one bone fits into a concavity of the other bone. These joints allow the greatest freedom of movement. Movement may be rotational or in any plane. The shoulder and hip joints are ball-and-socket joints. Examine the structure of a hip joint in figure 6.31.

Movements at Freely Movable Joints

Movement at a joint results from the contraction of skeletal muscles that span across the joint. The type of movement that occurs is determined by the type of joint and the location of the muscle or muscles involved. The more common types of movements are listed in table 6.9 and illustrated in figure 6.32.

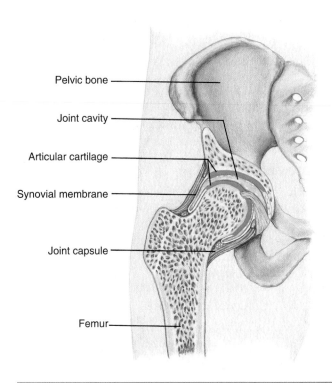

Pelvic bone

Joint cavity

Articular cartilage

Synovial membrane

Joint capsule

Femur

Figure 6.31 A coronal section of a hip joint, a ball-and-socket joint. Note the joint capsule formed of ligaments. AP|R

Check My Understanding

11. Where are immovable, slightly movable, and freely movable joints found in the skeleton?
12. What types of freely movable joints occur in the body, and where are they located?

Older persons are prone to "breaking a hip," which means that a weakened femur breaks at the neck. This usually is a consequence of osteoporosis, the excessive loss of calcium from bones. Osteoporosis is caused by a combination of factors: insufficient calcium in the diet, lack of minimal exercise, and a decline in sex hormones, especially in postmenopausal women. Older persons are not only more prone to fractures, but healing of fractures takes much longer than in younger persons.

Table 6.9   Movements at Freely Movable Joints

Movement	Description
Flexion	Decrease in the angle of bones forming joint
Extension	Increase in the angle of bones forming joint
Dorsiflexion	Flexion of the foot at the ankle
Plantar flexion	Extension of the foot at the ankle
Abduction	Movement of a bone away from the midline
Adduction	Movement of a bone toward the midline
Rotation	Movement of a bone around its longitudinal axis
Circumduction	Movement of the distal end of a bone in a circle while the proximal end forms the pivot joint
Eversion	Movement of the sole of the foot laterally
Inversion	Movement of the sole of the foot medially
Pronation	Rotation of the forearm when the palm is turned downward or posteriorly
Supination	Rotation of the forearm when the palm is turned upward or anteriorly
Protraction	Movement of the mandible anteriorly
Retraction	Movement of the mandible posteriorly
Elevation	Movement of a body part upward
Depression	Movement of a body part downward

6.8 Disorders of the Skeletal System

Common disorders of the skeletal system may be categorized as disorders of bones or disorders of joints. **Orthopedics** (or-thō-pē-diks) is the branch of medicine that specializes in treating diseases and abnormalities of the skeletal system.

Disorders of Bones

Fractures are broken bones. Fractures are the most common type of bone injury. Fractures are categorized as either complete or incomplete. There are also several specific subtypes, such as the examples noted here and in figure 6.33.

- **Complete:** The break is completely through the bone.
- **Compound:** A broken bone pierces the skin.
- **Simple:** A bone does not pierce the skin.
- **Comminuted:** The bone is broken into several pieces.
- **Segmental:** Only one piece is broken out of the bone.
- **Spiral:** The fracture line spirals around the bone.
- **Oblique:** The break angles across the bone.
- **Transverse:** The break is at right angles to the long axis of the bone.
- **Incomplete:** The bone is not broken completely through.

- **Green stick:** The break is only on one side of the bone, and the bone is bowed.
- **Fissured:** The break is a lengthwise split in the bone.

Osteomyelitis is an inflammation of bone and bone marrow caused by bacterial infection. It is treatable with antibiotics but not easily cured.

Osteoporosis (os-tē-ō-pō-rō´-sis) is a weakening of bones due to the removal of calcium salts, which increases the risk of fractures. This is a common problem in older persons due to inactivity and a decrease in hormone production. It is more common in postmenopausal women because of the lack of estrogen. Exercise and calcium supplements retard the decline in bone density. Therapy includes drugs that retard bone loss or those that promote bone formation. However, such drugs must be used with caution because they can have serious side effects.

Rickets is a disease of children that is characterized by a deficiency of calcium salts in the bones. Affected children have a bowlegged appearance due to the bending of weakened femurs, tibiae, and fibulae. Rickets results from a dietary deficiency of calcium and/or vitamin D. It is rare in industrialized nations.

Disorders of Joints

Arthritis (ar-thrī´-tis) is the general term for many different diseases of joints that are characterized by inflammation, swelling (edema), and pain.

Figure 6.32 Common movements at freely movable joints.

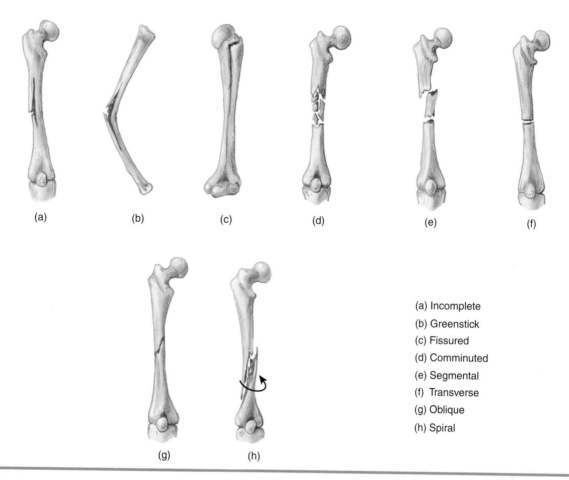

(a) Incomplete
(b) Greenstick
(c) Fissured
(d) Comminuted
(e) Segmental
(f) Transverse
(g) Oblique
(h) Spiral

Figure 6.33 Some types of bone fractures.

Rheumatoid arthritis and osteoarthritis are the most common types.

Rheumatoid (rū´-mah-toid) *arthritis* is the most painful and crippling type. The synovial membrane thickens, synovial fluid accumulates causing swelling, and articular cartilages are destroyed. The joint is invaded by fibrous connective tissue that ultimately ossifies, making the joint immovable.

Osteoarthritis, the most common type, is a degenerative disease that results from aging and wear. The articular cartilages gradually disintegrate, which causes pain and restricts movement.

Bursitis (bur-sī´-tis) is the inflammation of a bursa. It may be caused by excessive use or injury.

Dislocation is the displacement of bones forming a joint. Pain, swelling, and reduced movement are associated with a dislocation.

Herniated disk is a condition in which an intervertebral disk protrudes beyond the edge of a vertebra. A ruptured, or slipped, disk refers to the same problem. It is caused by excessive pressure on the vertebral column, which compresses a disk and causes it to bulge outward. The protruding disk may place pressure on a spinal nerve and cause considerable pain.

Spinal curvatures are usually congenital disorders. There are three major types:

1. *Kyphosis* (kī-fō-sis) is an excessive thoracic curvature of the vertebral column, which produces a humpback condition.
2. *Lordosis* is an excessive lumbar curvature of the vertebral column, which produces a swayback condition.
3. *Scoliosis* is an abnormal lateral curvature of the vertebral column. For some reason, it is more common in adolescent girls.

Sprains result from tearing or excessive stretching of the ligaments and tendons at a joint without a dislocation.

Check My Understanding

13. What are some common types of fractures?
14. How do osteoarthritis and rheumatoid arthritis differ?

CHAPTER SUMMARY

6.1 Functions of the Skeletal System

- The skeletal system provides support for the body and protection for internal organs.
- The bones of the skeleton serve as sites for the attachment of skeletal muscles.
- Blood cells are formed by red bone marrow.
- Bones serve as reservoirs for calcium salts.

6.2 Bone Structure

- The diaphysis is a long shaft of bone that lies between the epiphyses, the enlarged ends of the bone.
- Each epiphysis is joined to the diaphysis by an epiphyseal plate in immature bones, or by fusion at the epiphyseal line in mature bones.
- Articular cartilages protect and cushion the articular surfaces of the epiphyses.
- The periosteum covers the bone surface except for the articular cartilages.
- Compact bone forms the diaphysis and the surface layer of the epiphyses.
- Spongy bone forms the interior of the epiphyses.
- Red marrow fills the spaces in spongy bone.
- The diaphysis contains a medullary cavity filled with fatty yellow marrow.
- Compact bone is formed of numerous osteons fused together.
- Osteonic (central) canals contain blood vessels and nerves.
- Spongy bone lacks osteons; its cells are nourished by diffusion from blood vessels in the red marrow.

6.3 Bone Formation

- Intramembranous bones are first formed by connective tissue membranes, which are replaced by bone tissue.
- Connective tissue cells are transformed into osteoblasts, which deposit the spongy bone within the membrane.
- Osteoblasts from the periosteum form a layer of compact bone over the spongy bone.
- Endochondral bones are first formed of hyaline cartilage, which is later replaced by bone tissue.
- In long bones, a primary ossification center forms in the center of the diaphysis and extends toward the epiphyses.
- Secondary ossification centers form in the epiphyses.
- An epiphyseal plate of cartilage remains between the epiphyses and the diaphysis in immature bones.
- Growth in length occurs at the epiphyseal disk, which is gradually replaced by bone.
- Compact bone is deposited by osteoblasts from the periosteum, and they are responsible for growth in the diameter of a bone.
- Osteoclasts hollow out the medullary cavity and reshape the bone.
- Bones are dynamic, living organs that are reshaped throughout life by the actions of osteoclasts and osteoblasts.
- Calcium salts may be removed from bones for other body needs and redeposited in bones later on.
- The concentration of protein fibers decreases with age. The bones of older persons tend to be brittle and weak due to the loss of fibers and calcium salts, respectively.

6.4 Divisions of the Skeleton

- The skeleton is divided into the axial and appendicular divisions.
- The axial skeleton includes the bones that support the head, neck, and trunk.
- The appendicular skeleton includes the bones of the pectoral girdle and upper extremities and the bones of the pelvic girdle and the lower extremities.

6.5 Axial Skeleton

- The axial skeleton consists of the skull, vertebral column, and thoracic cage.
- The skull consists of cranial and facial bones; all are joined by immovable joints except the mandible.
- The cranial bones are the frontal bone (1), parietal bones (2), sphenoid bone (1), temporal bones (2), occipital bone (1), and ethmoid bone (1).
- The frontal, sphenoid, and ethmoid bones contain sinuses.
- The facial bones are the maxillae (2), palatine bones (2), zygomatic bones (2), lacrimal bones (2), nasal bones (2), inferior nasal conchae (2), vomer bone (1), and mandible (1).
- Each maxilla contains a large sinus.
- Cranial bones of an infant skull are separated by membranes and several fontanels, which allow some flexibility of the skull during birth.
- The vertebral column consists of 24 vertebrae, the sacrum, and the coccyx.
- Vertebrae are separated by intervertebral disks and are categorized as cervical (7), thoracic (12), and lumbar (5) vertebrae.
- The first two cervical vertebrae are unique. The atlas rotates on the axis when the head is turned.
- Thoracic vertebrae have facets on the body and transverse processes for articulation with the ribs.
- The bodies of lumbar vertebrae are heavy and strong.
- The sacrum is formed of five fused vertebrae and forms the posterior portion of the pelvic girdle.
- The coccyx is formed of three to five rudimentary vertebrae and forms the inferior end of the vertebral column.

- The thoracic cage consists of thoracic vertebrae, ribs, and sternum. It supports the upper trunk and protects internal thoracic organs.
- There are seven pairs of true ribs and five pairs of false ribs. The inferior two pairs of false ribs are floating ribs.
- The sternum is formed of three fused bones: manubrium, body, and xiphoid process.

6.6 Appendicular Skeleton

- The appendicular skeleton consists of the pectoral and pelvic girdles and of the bones of the extremities.
- The pectoral girdle consists of clavicles (2) and scapulae (2), and it supports the upper extremities.
- The bones of the upper extremity are the humerus, the ulna, the radius, carpals, metacarpals, and phalanges.
- The humerus articulates with the glenoid cavity of the scapula to form the shoulder joint and with the ulna and radius to form the elbow joint.
- The ulna is the medial bone of the forearm. It articulates with the humerus at the elbow and with the radius and a fibrocartilaginous disk at the wrist.
- The radius is the lateral (thumb side) bone of the forearm. It articulates with the humerus at the elbow and with the ulna and carpus at the wrist.
- The bones of the hand are the carpals (8), metacarpals (5), and phalanges (14).
- The carpal bones are joined by ligaments to form the bones of the wrist; metacarpal bones support the palm of the hand; and the phalanges are the bones of the fingers.
- The pelvic girdle consists of two coxal bones that are joined to the sacrum posteriorly and to each other anteriorly. It supports the lower extremities.
- Each coxal bone is formed by the fusion of three bones: the ilium, ischium, and pubis.
- The ilium forms the upper portion of a coxal bone and joins with the sacrum to form a sacroiliac joint.
- The ischium forms the inferior, posterior portion of a coxal bone and supports the body when sitting.
- The pubis forms the lower, anterior part of a coxal bone. The pubic bones unite anteriorly to form the symphysis pubis joint.
- Each lower extremity consists of a femur, a patella, a tibia, a fibula, tarsals, metatarsals, and phalanges.

- The head of the femur is inserted into the acetabulum of a coxal bone to form a hip joint. Distally, it articulates with the tibia at the knee joint.
- The patella is a sesamoid bone in the anterior portion of the knee joint.
- The tibia (shinbone) articulates with the femur at the knee joint and with the talus to form the ankle joint.
- The fibula lies lateral to the tibia. It articulates proximally with the tibia and distally with the talus.
- The skeleton of the foot consists of tarsals (7), metatarsals (5), and phalanges (14).
- Tarsal bones form the ankle, metatarsal bones support the instep, and phalanges are the bones of the toes.

6.7 Articulations

- There are three types of joints: immovable, slightly movable, and freely movable.
- Bones forming immovable joints are closely joined and are separated by a thin layer of fibrous connective tissue. Articulations of skull bones, except the mandible, are examples.
- Bones forming slightly movable joints are separated by fibrocartilage pads or fibrous connective tissue. Joints between vertebrae are examples.
- Bones forming freely movable joints are bound together by a ligamentous articular capsule that is lined by a synovial membrane. The articular surfaces of the bones are covered by articular cartilages. Synovial fluid lubricates the joint, and bursae may be present to reduce friction.
- There are several types of freely movable joints: gliding, condyloid, hinge, saddle, pivot, and ball-and-socket.
- Movements at freely movable joints include flexion, extension, dorsiflexion, plantar flexion, hyperextension, abduction, adduction, rotation, circumduction, inversion, eversion, protraction, retraction, elevation, and depression.

6.8 Disorders of the Skeletal System

- Disorders of bones include fractures, osteomyelitis, osteoporosis, and rickets.
- Disorders of joints include arthritis, bursitis, dislocation, herniated disk, spinal curvatures, and sprains.

BUILDING MY VOCABULARY

1. **Selected New Terms**
abduction, p. 119
adduction, p. 119
amphiarthrosis, p. 117
appendicular skeleton, p. 97
axial skeleton, p. 97
circumduction, p. 119

condyle, p. 99
diarthrosis, p. 117
epicondyle, p. 99
extension, p. 119
facet, p. 99
flexion, p. 119
foramen, p. 94

head, p. 106
pronation, p. 119
red marrow, p. 94
supination, p. 119
suture, p. 97
synarthrosis, p. 117
trochanter, p. 113
tubercle, p. 106
tuberosity, p. 109
yellow marrow, p. 94

2. **Related Clinical Terms**
Ankylosis (ang-ki-lō´-sis) Abnormal stiffness of a
   joint.
Arthralgia (ar-thral´-jē-ah) Pain in a joint.
Osteomalacia (os-tē-ō-mah-lā´-she-ah) Softening
   of bone tissue due to abnormal calcium and
   phosphorus metabolism.
Osteomyelitis (os-tē-ō-mī-e-lī´-tis) Inflammation of
   a bone and bone marrow caused by a fungus or
   bacteria.

SELF-REVIEW

Answers are located in appendix B.
1. The skeletal system provides _____ for the body and
   _____ for many internal organs.
2. The enlarged ends of a long bone are the _____,
   which are composed of _____ bone that is coated
   with a thin layer of compact bone.
3. Blood vessels and nerves enter a bone through a
   _____.
4. Cranial bones are formed by _____ ossification.
5. Growth in diameter of a long bone occurs by deposition of bone tissue by osteoblasts from the _____.
6. The skull, vertebral column, and sacrum are part of
   the _____ skeleton.
7. The bone forming the lower jaw is the _____, and it
   articulates with the _____ bone.
8. The first vertebra, the _____, articulates with the
   _____ bone of the skull.
9. True ribs are attached directly to the sternum by the
   _____.
10. The clavicles and scapulae form the _____.
11. The upper arm bone, the _____, articulates with two
    forearm bones, the _____ and the _____.
12. Each coxal bone is formed of three fused bones: the
    _____, _____, and _____.
13. The thigh bone is the _____, and it articulates distally
    with the _____.
14. Among freely movable joints, the elbow is an exam-
    ple of a _____ joint, and the shoulder is an example of
    a _____ joint.
15. _____ is a weakening of bones due to removal of cal-
    cium salts.

CRITICAL THINKING

1. Complete the learning objectives on the first page of this chapter.
2. Explain why both osteoclasts and osteoblasts are required for proper bone development.
3. Bone repairs itself faster than cartilage. Explain why.
4. What damage might result from a hyperextended knee?
5. Why is osteomyelitis more likely to occur after a compound fracture than after a greenstick fracture?

CHAPTER 7

Muscular System

Module 6
Muscular System

SELECTED KEY TERMS

Antagonist (anti = against) A muscle whose contraction opposes an action of another muscle.

Aponeurosis (apo = from; neur = cord) A broad sheet of fibrous connective tissue that attaches a muscle to another muscle or connective tissue.

Creatine phosphate A molecule that stores a small amount of energy in a muscle fiber.

Insertion The attachment of a muscle that moves when the muscle contracts.

Motor unit A motor neuron and the muscle fibers that it controls.

Muscle fiber A single muscle cell.

Muscle tone The state of slight contraction in a skeletal muscle.

Myofibril (myo = muscle; fibril = little fiber) One of many contractile fibers within a muscle cell.

Myoglobin (myo = muscle) A molecule that stores a small amount of oxygen in a muscle fiber.

Neurotransmitter (neuro = nerve; transmit = to send across) A chemical released by axon tips of neurons that activates a muscle fiber, gland, or another neuron.

Origin The attachment of a muscle that remains fixed when the muscle contracts.

Sarcomere (sarc = flesh) The smallest contractile unit of a myofibril.

Tendon A narrow band of fibrous connective tissue that attaches a muscle to a bone.

Tetanic contraction (tetan = rigid, stiff) A sustained muscle contraction.

---

uscle tissue is the only tissue in the body that is specialized for *contraction* (shortening). Contraction of muscle tissue produces the movements of the body and body parts. The body contains three types of muscle tissue: skeletal, smooth, and cardiac. Each type of muscle tissue exhibits unique structural and functional characteristics. Refresh your understanding of these tissues by referring to the discussion of muscle tissue in chapter 4. Table 7.1 summarizes the characteristics of muscle tissues.

7.1 Structure of Skeletal Muscle

Skeletal muscles are the organs of the muscular system. They are called skeletal muscles because most of them are attached to bones. A skeletal muscle is mainly composed of many skeletal **muscle fibers,** or cells, that are bound together by dense fibrous connective tissue. Muscle fibers extend the full length of a muscle, and they are arranged in small bundles called *fascicles* (fah´-si-kuls). Dense fibrous connective tissue envelopes each fiber and each fascicle, binds fascicles together, and envelops the entire muscle. Connective tissue covering a muscle is sometimes called *deep fascia* (fash´-e-ah). It extends beyond the end of the muscle tissue to form a tough, cordlike **tendon,** which attaches the muscle to a bone (figure 7.1). Fibers of the tendon and periosteum intermesh to form a secure attachment. A few muscles attach to other muscles or connective tissues rather than to bones. In these muscles, the connective tissue forms a sheetlike attachment called an **aponeurosis** (ap˝-ō-nū-rō´-sis).

Skeletal Muscle Fibers

Each muscle fiber is a multinucleated skeletal muscle cell. It is a long, thin cylinder with rounded ends that usually extends the full length of the muscle.

Table 7.1   Types of Muscle Tissue

Characteristic	Skeletal	Smooth	Cardiac
Striations	Present	Absent	Present
Nucleus	Many peripherally located nuclei	Single centrally located nucleus	Single centrally located nucleus
Fibers	Long and parallel	Short; tapered ends; parallel	Short and branching; intercalated disks join fibers end to end to form network
Neural control	Voluntary	Involuntary	Involuntary
Contractions	Fast or slow	Slow; resistant to fatigue	Rhythmic; resistant to fatigue
Location	Attached to bones	Walls of hollow visceral organs and blood vessels	Wall of the heart

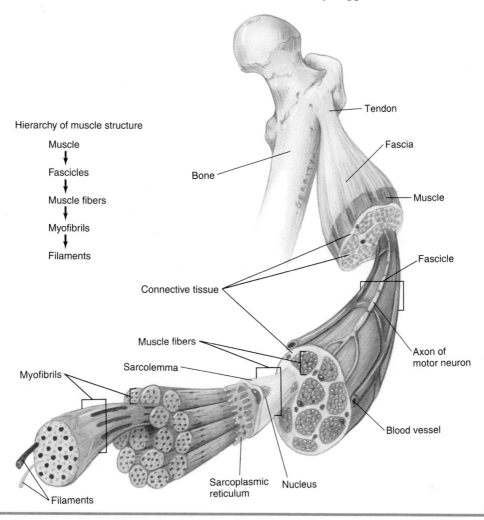

Hierarchy of muscle structure

Muscle
↓
Fascicles
↓
Muscle fibers
↓
Myofibrils
↓
Filaments

Tendon

Fascia

Bone

Muscle

Fascicle

Connective tissue

Axon of
motor neuron

Muscle fibers

Sarcolemma

Myofibrils

Blood vessel

Filaments

Sarcoplasmic
reticulum

Nucleus

Figure 7.1   A muscle is primarily composed of skeletal muscle fibers supported and bound together in fascicles by connective tissue. Myofibrils are the contractile elements of a muscle fiber.

The plasma membrane of a muscle fiber is called the **sarcolemma** (sar-kō-lem´-ah), and its cytoplasm is the **sarcoplasm**.

Each muscle fiber contains many threadlike **myofibrils,** which extend the length of the fiber, as shown in figure 7.1. Myofibrils are the contractile elements of a muscle fiber. They consist of two kinds of myofilaments that interact to produce muscle contractions: (1) *thin myofilaments* composed mostly of the protein **actin** and (2) *thick myofilaments* composed of the protein **myosin** (Table 7.2).

A thin myofilament consists of two twisted strands of actin molecules joined together like tiny strings of pearls. Two additional proteins, *troponin* and *tropomyosin,* are present on actin myofilaments and play a role in muscle contraction. Double strands of tropomyosin coil over each actin strand, and troponin occurs at regular intervals on the tropomyosin strands. A thick myofilament is composed of hundreds of myosin molecules, each shaped like a double-headed golf club. The heads are able to bind to actin myofilaments to form cross-bridges (figure 7.2). The organization of

Table 7.2 **Microscopic Anatomy of a Skeletal Muscle Fiber**	
Structure	**Description/Function**
Sarcolemma	Plasma membrane of a muscle fiber maintaining the integrity of the cell
Sarcoplasm	Cytoplasm of a skeletal muscle fiber that contains organelles
Nuclei	Contain DNA, which determines cell structure and function
Sarcoplasmic reticulum	Smooth ER in a muscle fiber that stores Ca^{++}
Transverse tubules	Extensions of the sarcolemma that penetrate into the fiber carrying nerve impulses, which trigger the release of ca^{++} from the sarcoplasmic reticulum
Myofibril	A bundle of myofilaments
Myofilaments	Thin actin myofilaments and thick myosin myofilaments that interact to produce contractions

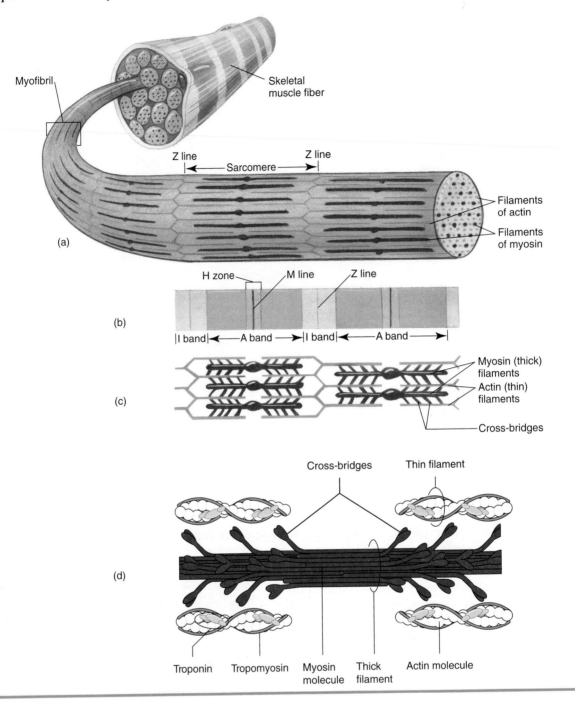

Figure 7.2 Structure of a myofibril. (*a*) A skeletal muscle fiber contains many myofibrils. Each myofibril consists of repeating contractile units called sarcomeres. (*b*) The characteristic bands of sarcomeres. (*c*) The arrangement of actin and myosin filaments within the sarcomeres. (*d*) Details of thin actin filaments and thick myosin filaments. AP|R

actin and myosin myofilaments within a muscle fiber produces *striations*—the light and dark cross bands that are characteristic of skeletal muscle fibers when viewed microscopically.

As shown in figure 7.2, the arrangement of thin actin and thick myosin myofilaments repeats itself throughout the length of a myofibril. These repeating units are called sarcomeres. A **sarcomere** is a contractile unit of skeletal muscle—that is, it

is the smallest portion of a **myofibril** capable of contraction. A sarcomere extends from a Z line to the next Z line. Z lines are composed of proteins arranged transverse to the longitudinal axis of the myofilament. Thin actin myofilaments are attached to each side of the Z lines and extend toward the middle of the sarcomeres. Note that they do not meet. Thick myosin myofilaments occur only in the A band of the sarcomere.

Figure 7.3 illustrates the arrangement of the sacroplasmic reticulum and transverse (T) tubule system to myofibrils in a skeletal muscle fiber. The **sacroplasmic reticulum** is the name given to the smooth endoplasmic reticulum in a muscle cell. It plays an important role in contraction by storing calcium (Ca^{++}) ions. The **transverse (T) tubule system** consists of invaginations of the sarcolemma that penetrate into the fiber so that they lie alongside and contact the sarcoplasmic reticulum.

Neuromuscular Interaction

A muscle fiber must be stimulated by nerve impulses in order to contract. Nerve impulses are carried from the brain or spinal cord to a muscle fiber by a long, thin process (an axon) of a motor neuron. A *motor neuron* is an action-causing neuron—its impulses produce an action in the target cells. In muscle fibers, this action is contraction. Each muscle fiber is innervated and controlled by a motor neuron.

Motor Units

A motor neuron and all of the muscle fibers to which it is attached form a **motor unit** (figure 7.4). Whereas a muscle fiber is attached to only one motor neuron, a

Clinical INSIGHT

The number of skeletal muscle fibers cannot be increased after birth. However, heavy exercise, such as weight training, increases the number of myofibrils, which increases the diameter and strength of the muscle fibers and of the whole muscle itself.

Anabolic steroids, substances similar to the male sex hormone testosterone, have been used by some athletes to promote muscle development and strength. However, physicians have warned that such use can produce a number of harmful side effects, including damage to kidneys, increased risk of heart disease and liver cancer, and increased irritability. Other side effects include decreased testosterone and sperm production in males and increased facial hair and deepening of the voice in females.

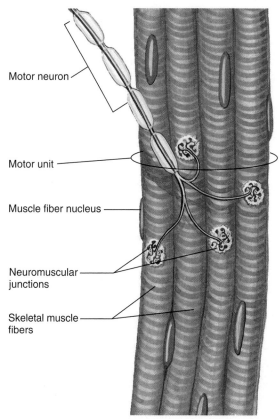

Figure 7.4 A motor unit consists of one motor neuron and all the muscle fibers that it innervates. Note the attachment of the axon terminals to the muscle fibers. AP|R

Figure 7.3 A portion of a skeletal muscle fiber showing the sarcoplasmic reticulum and the transverse (T) tubule system associated with the myofibrils.

single motor neuron may innervate from 3 to 2,000 muscle fibers. Where precise muscle control rather than strength is needed, such as in the fingers, a motor unit contains very few muscle fibers. Large numbers of motor units are involved in the manipulative movements of the fingers. In contrast, where strength rather than precise control is needed, such as in the postural muscles, a motor unit controls hundreds of muscle fibers. Whenever a motor neuron is activated, it stimulates contraction of all the muscle fibers that it controls.

Neuromuscular Junction

The part of a motor neuron that leads to a muscle fiber is called an *axon.* The connection between the terminal branches of an axon and the sarcolemma of a muscle fiber is known as a **neuromuscular junction** (figure 7.4). As shown in figure 7.5, the axon tips fit into depressions, the *motor end plates,* in the sarcolemma. The tiny space between the axon terminal and the sarcolemma is the *synaptic cleft.* Numerous secretory vesicles in the axon tip contain the **neurotransmitter** (nū-rō-trans´-mit-er) **acetylcholine** (as″-ē-til-kō´-lēn). When a motor neuron is activated and an impulse reaches the axon terminals, acetylcholine is released from secretory vesicles into the synaptic cleft. The attachment of acetylcholine to receptors on the sarcolemma triggers a series of reactions causing the muscle fiber to contract.

Figure 7.5 A neuromuscular junction is formed by the tip of a motor axon and the sarcolemma of a muscle fiber. The detailed insert shows the synaptic vesicles, the synaptic cleft, and the folded surface of the sarcolemma. **AP|R**

7.2 Physiology of Muscle Contraction

Contraction of a skeletal muscle fiber is a complex process that involves a number of rapid structural and chemical changes within the fiber. The molecular mechanism of contraction is explained by the *sliding-filament model* described in the next section.

Mechanism of Contraction **AP|R**

Contraction of a muscle fiber is initiated when the axon tip of an activated motor neuron releases acetylcholine into the synaptic cleft. Acetylcholine binds to receptors on the sarcolemma causing the formation of a muscle impulse (similar to a nerve impulse), which spreads over the sarcolemma and is carried into the muscle fiber by the transverse (T) tubule system. This triggers the release of Ca^{++} from the sarcoplasmic reticulum. When Ca^{++} binds to troponin, it causes the tropomyosin strands to change position, exposing the myosin-binding sites on actin molecules. The cross-bridges of myosin molecules bind to the binding sites on actin molecules. Then the cross-bridges exert a power stroke that pulls the thin actin filaments toward the center of the sarcomere. The cross-bridges detach from the actin molecules, become straightened ("cocked") and bind to the next myosin-binding sites, and produce another power stroke that pulls the thin actin filaments farther toward the center of the sarcomere. This cycle rapidly repeats itself to attain a maximum contraction as long as ATP and Ca^{++} are available.

Carefully study figure 7.6, which illustrates the sliding-filament model of muscle contraction. Note the configuration of thin actin filaments and thick myosin filaments in a relaxed muscle fiber, how they interact in the steps of the contraction mechanism, and how contraction is powered by ATP. Although the sliding filaments produce contraction (i.e., the shortening of the sarcomeres), the lengths of the thin actin filaments and thick myosin filaments remain unchanged (figure 7.7).

Once contraction occurs, the sarcolemma secretes the enzyme *acetylcholinesterase,* which decomposes acetylcholine in the synaptic cleft. This action of acetylcholinesterase is necessary to prevent continued stimulation of the muscle fiber and to prepare the fiber

Check My Understanding

3. What are the structure and function of a neuromuscular junction?
4. How do actin and myosin filaments interact during muscle contraction?

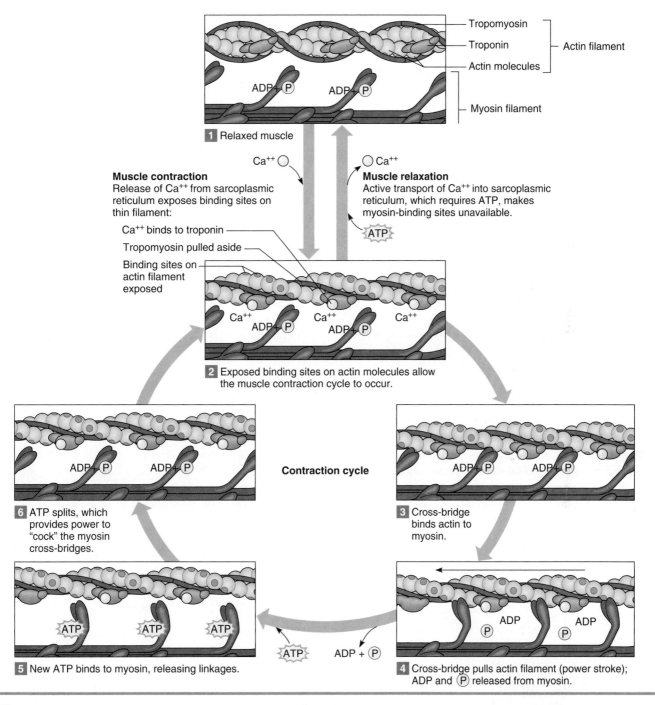

Figure 7.6   Sliding-filament model of muscle contraction. The release of Ca⁺⁺ causes the exposure of myosin-binding sites on actin molecules, enabling the contraction cycle to begin. ATP powers the contraction mechanism. **AP|R**

for the next stimulus. For each contraction, acetylcholine is released into the synaptic cleft, and then it is decomposed by acetylcholinesterase.

Energy for Contraction

The energy for muscle contraction comes from ATP molecules in the muscle cell. Recall that ATP is a product of cellular respiration. However, there is only a small amount of ATP in each muscle fiber. Once it is used up, more ATP must be formed in order for additional contractions to occur. Figure 7.8 summarizes the process of cellular respiration.

During cellular respiration, the energy released from nutrients is transferred to the high-energy phosphate bonds of ATP. Once there are sufficient amounts of ATP available in the cell, the high-energy phosphate

Figure 7.7   Contraction pulls the Z lines closer together, shortening the sarcomere. Note that the lengths of thin actin filaments and thick myosin filaments are unchanged. **AP|R**

is transferred to creatine to form **creatine phosphate,** which serves as a limited storage form of readily available energy.

When ATP supplies are decreased by muscle contractions, a high-energy phosphate group is transferred from creatine phosphate to ADP to form ATP, which can then be used to power additional contractions.

There is four to six times more creatine phosphate than ATP in a muscle cell, so it is an important source for rapid ATP formation without waiting for the slower process of cellular respiration. However, it can also be depleted rather quickly in a muscle that is contracting repeatedly.

Oxygen and Cellular Respiration

Recall from chapter 3 that cellular respiration takes place in two steps: (1) an anaerobic phase in the cytoplasm (sarcoplasm in muscle cells) and (2) an aerobic phase in mitochondria. The small amount of ATP produced by

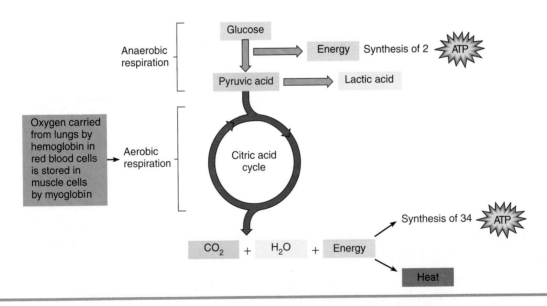

Figure 7.8   A summary of anaerobic and aerobic phases of cellular respiration. When the oxygen supply is inadequate, lactic acid accumulates in muscle cells, producing an oxygen debt.

anaerobic respiration cannot keep a person alive, except for very brief periods. Oxygen is life-sustaining because it enables the aerobic phase of cellular respiration to operate and produce adequate amounts of ATP.

Oxygen is transported from lungs to body cells in loose combination with **hemoglobin,** the red pigment in red blood cells. Muscle cells have another pigment, **myoglobin,** that can also combine loosely with oxygen. In times of muscle inactivity, some of the oxygen carried to muscle cells can be stored in combination with myoglobin and released later for aerobic cellular respiration during periods of muscle activity. This function of myoglobin reduces for a brief period the muscle cell's dependence on oxygen carried to it by the blood.

During inactivity or moderate physical activity, muscle cells receive sufficient oxygen via the blood to carry on the aerobic phase of cellular respiration. As shown in figure 7.8, this process involves the breakdown of *pyruvic acid* into carbon dioxide and water. However, during periods of strenuous exercise, the respiratory and circulatory systems cannot provide oxygen to muscle cells fast enough to maintain aerobic respiration. This causes some of the pyruvic acid to be converted to *lactic acid* as anaerobic respiration continues to break down glucose to form pyruvic acid and small amounts of ATP.

The accumulation of lactic acid causes discomfort and rapid, deep breathing in an attempt to provide adequate oxygen for aerobic respiration. About 80% of the lactic acid is carried by blood from the muscle cells to the liver, where it is later converted back into glucose and is reused. Lactic acid must be either broken down by aerobic respiration or converted back into glucose; because oxygen is required for both processes, an **oxygen debt** develops as lactic acid accumulates. The oxygen debt is the amount of oxygen required to metabolize the accumulated lactic acid and to resupply the normal amounts of ATP and creatine phosphate in the muscle cells. When the strenuous muscle activity ceases, rapid, deep breathing continues until the oxygen debt is fully paid. Endurance training enhances the efficiency of aerobic cellular respiration in muscle cells by increasing (1) the number of mitochondria, (2) the efficiency of obtaining oxygen from the blood, and (3) the concentration of myoglobin.

Fatigue

If a muscle is stimulated to contract for a long period, its contractions will gradually decrease until it no longer responds to stimulation. This condition is called **fatigue.** Fatigue seems to result primarily from an accumulation of lactic acid and carbon dioxide and the depletion of ATP, which cause chemical changes in the muscle fiber that prevent it from responding to stimulation.

Heat Production

Heat production by muscular activity is an important mechanism in maintaining a normal body temperature because muscles are active organs and form a large proportion of the body weight. Heat produced by muscles results from cellular respiration and other chemical reactions within the cells. Recall that 60% of the energy released by cellular respiration is heat energy, with only 40% of the released energy captured in ATP. The importance of muscle activity in maintaining body temperature is evident by the fact that a major response to a decrease in body temperature is shivering, which is caused by involuntary muscle contractions.

Check My Understanding

5. What are the roles of ATP and creatine phosphate in muscle contraction?
6. What is the relationship among cellular respiration, lactic acid, and oxygen debt?

Contraction Characteristics

When studying muscle contraction, physiologists consider both single-fiber contraction and whole-muscle contraction.

Contraction of a Single Fiber

It is possible to remove a single muscle fiber in order to study its contraction in the laboratory. By using electrical stimuli to initiate contraction and by gradually increasing the strength (voltage) of each stimulus, it has been shown that the fiber will not contract until the stimulus reaches a certain minimal strength. This minimal stimulus is called the **threshold stimulus.**

Whenever a muscle fiber is stimulated by a threshold stimulus or by a stimulus of greater strength, it always contracts *completely*. Thus, a muscle fiber either contracts completely or not at all—contraction is *not* proportional to the strength of the stimulus. This characteristic of individual muscle fibers is known as the **all-or-none response.**

Contraction of Whole Muscles

Much information has been gained by studying the contraction of a whole muscle of an experimental animal. In such studies, electrical stimulation is used to cause contraction, and the contraction is recorded to produce a tracing called a *myogram*.

If a single threshold stimulus is applied, some of the muscle fibers will contract to produce a single, weak contraction (a muscle twitch) and then relax, all within a fraction of a second. The myogram will look

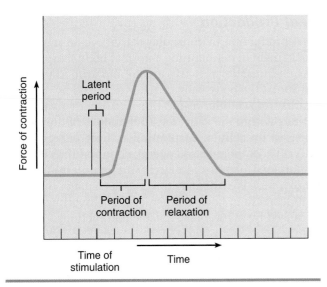

Figure 7.9 A myogram of a single muscle twitch. Note the brief latent period, rapid contraction period, and longer relaxation period.

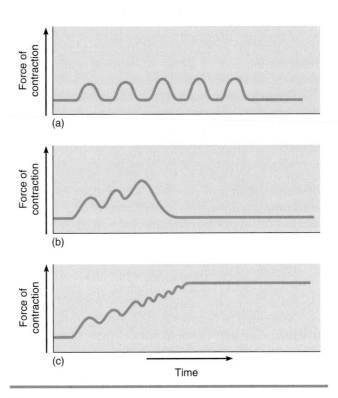

Figure 7.10 Myograms of (*a*) a series of simple twitches, (*b*) summation caused by incomplete relaxation between stimuli, and (*c*) tetanic contraction when there is no relaxation between stimuli.

like the one shown in figure 7.9. After the stimulus is applied, there is a brief interval before the muscle starts to contract. This interval is known as the *latent period.* Then, the muscle contracts (shortens) rapidly during the *period of contraction* and relaxes (returns to its former length) during the longer *period of relaxation.* If a muscle is stimulated again after it has relaxed completely, it will contract and produce a similar myogram. A series of single stimuli applied in this manner will yield a myogram like the one in figure 7.10*a*.

If the interval between stimuli is shortened so that the muscle fibers cannot completely relax, the force of individual twitches combines by *summation,* which increases the force of contraction (figure 7.10*b*). If stimuli are so frequent that relaxation is not possible, a **tetanic contraction** results (figure 7.10*c*).

Graded Responses Unlike individual muscle fibers that exhibit all-or-none responses, whole muscles exhibit *graded responses*—that is, varying degrees of contraction. Graded responses enable the degree of muscle contraction to fit the task being performed. Obviously, more muscle fibers are required to lift a 14 kg (30 lb) weight than to lift a feather. Yet both activities can be performed by the same muscles.

Graded responses are possible because a muscle is composed of many different *motor units,* each responding to different thresholds of stimulation. In the laboratory, a weak stimulus that activates only low-threshold motor units produces a minimal contraction. As the strength of the stimulus is increased, the contractions get stronger as more motor units are activated until a **maximal stimulus** (one that activates all motor units) is applied, which produces a maximal

contraction. Further increases in the strength of the stimulus cannot produce a greater contraction. The same results occur in a normally functioning body, but it is the nervous system that provides the stimulation and controls the number of motor units activated in each muscle contraction. The activation of more and more motor units is known as *recruitment.*

Sustained Contractions A sustained (tetanic) contraction lacks even partial relaxation and produces a myogram as shown in figure 7.10*c*. Sustained contractions for short time periods is the usual way in which muscles contract to produce body movements. Sustained contractions result from a rapid series of impulses carried by motor neurons to the muscle fibers.

Muscle Tone Even when a muscle is relaxed, some of its fibers are contracting. At any given time, some of the fibers in a muscle are involved in a sustained contraction that produces a constant partial, but slight, contraction of the muscle. This state of constant partial contraction is called **muscle tone** and keeps a muscle ready to respond. Muscle tone results from the alternating activation of different motor units by the nervous system so that some muscle fibers are always in sustained contraction. Muscle tone of postural muscles plays an important role in maintaining erect posture.

If a nerve to a muscle is severed, the muscle is not only paralyzed but becomes soft and flabby due to the absence of muscle tone. Such a muscle will decrease in size due to lack of use, a process known as *atrophy.*

> ### Check My Understanding
> 7. What is meant by the all-or-none response?
> 8. How are muscles able to make graded responses?

7.3 Actions of Skeletal Muscles

Skeletal muscles are usually arranged so that the ends of a muscle are attached to bones on each side of a joint. Thus, a muscle usually extends across a joint. The type of movement produced depends upon the type of joint and the locations of the muscle attachments. Common movements at joints were discussed in chapter 6.

Origin and Insertion

During contraction, a bone to which one end of the muscle is attached moves, but the bone to which the other end is attached does not. The movable attachment of a muscle is called the **insertion,** and the immovable attachment is called the **origin.** When a muscle contracts, the insertion is pulled toward the origin.

Consider the *biceps brachii* muscle in figure 7.11. It has two origins, and both are attached to the scapula.

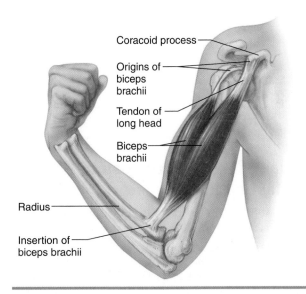

Coracoid process

Origins of biceps brachii

Tendon of long head

Biceps brachii

Radius

Insertion of biceps brachii

Figure 7.11 The biceps brachii muscle showing its two origins and single insertion. Note how the muscle extends across the elbow joint so that contraction flexes the forearm.

The insertion is on the radius, and the muscle lies along the anterior surface of the humerus. When the biceps contracts, the insertion is pulled toward the origin, which results in the flexion of the forearm at the elbow.

Most muscle contractions are *isotonic contractions,* which cause movement at a joint. Walking and breathing are examples. However, some contractions may not produce movement but only increase tension within a muscle. Pushing against an immovable object is an example. Such contractions are *isometric contractions,* and they are used by body builders to strengthen and enlarge muscles.

Exercise has a profound effect on skeletal muscles. Strength training, which involves isometric exercise and weight lifting, produces hypertrophy—an increase in muscle size and strength. Hypertrophy results from an increase in the number of myofibrils in muscle fibers, although the number of muscle fibers does not increase. Aerobic exercise, or endurance training, does not produce hypertrophy, but it increases the number of mitochondria in muscle fibers and blood vessels supplying the muscle. The enhanced supply of oxygen, nutrients, and ATP improves the efficiency of muscle action.

Muscle Interactions

Muscles function in groups rather than singly, and the groups are arranged to provide opposing movements. For example, if one group of muscles produces flexion, the opposing group produces extension. A group of muscles producing an action are called *agonists,* and the opposing group of muscles are called **antagonists.** When agonists contract, antagonists must relax, and vice versa, for movement to occur. If both groups contract simultaneously, the movable body part remains rigid.

Clinical INSIGHT

Several poisons, including *curare* (cu-rah´-re), prevent muscle contraction by blocking acetylcholine receptors at the neuromuscular junction. This causes flaccid paralysis, a condition in which the muscle is limp and cannot contract. Curare is well known as a plant extract used by South American Indians to make poisonous blowgun darts. It can cause death by asphyxiation if thoracic muscles are paralyzed. It has been used in surgery as a muscle relaxant, but it has now been replaced in most cases by other relaxants.

7.4 Naming of Muscles

Learning the complex names and functions of muscles can sometimes be confusing. However, the names of muscles are informative if their meaning is known. A few of the criteria used in naming muscles and examples of terms found in the names of muscles are listed following:

- **Function:** extensor, flexor, adductor, and pronator.
- **Shape:** trapezius (trapezoid), rhomboideus (rhomboid), deltoid (delta-shaped or triangular), biceps (two heads).
- **Relative position:** external, internal, abdominal, medial, lateral.
- **Location:** intercostal (between ribs), pectoralis (chest).
- **Site of attachment:** temporalis (temporal bone), zygomaticus (zygomatic bone).
- **Origin and insertion:** sternohyoid (sternum = origin; hyoid = insertion), sternocleidomastoid (sternum and clavicle = origins; mastoid process = insertion).
- **Size:** maximus (larger or largest), minimus (smaller or smallest), brevis (short), longus (long).
- **Orientation of fibers:** oblique (diagonal), rectus (straight), transverse (across).

7.5 Major Skeletal Muscles

This section is concerned with the name, location, attachment, and function of the major skeletal muscles. There are more than 600 muscles in the body, but only a few of the major muscles are considered here. Nearly all of them are superficial muscles. Most of this information is presented in tables and figures to aid your learning. The tables are organized according to the primary actions of the muscles. The pronunciation of each muscle is included, because being able to pronounce the names correctly will help you memorize the names of the muscles.

As you study this section, locate each muscle listed in the tables on the related figures 7.12 to 7.26. This will help you visualize the location and action of each muscle. Also, if you visualize the locations of the origin and insertion of a muscle, its action can be determined because contraction pulls the insertion toward the origin. It may help to refresh your understanding of the skeleton by referring to appropriate figures in chapter 6. Begin your study by examining figures 7.12 and 7.13 to learn the major superficial muscles that will be considered in more detail as you progress through the chapter.

Figure 7.12 Anterior view of superficial skeletal muscles.

Muscles of Facial Expression and Mastication

Muscles of the face and scalp produce the facial expressions that help communicate feelings, such as anger, sadness, happiness, fear, disgust, pain, and surprise. Most have origins on skull bones and insertions on connective tissue of the skin (Table 7.3 and figure 7.14).

The *epicranius* is an unusual muscle. It has a large aponeurosis that covers the top of the skull and two contractile portions: the *frontalis* over the frontal bone and the *occipitalis* over the occipital bone.

Temporalis
Occipitalis
Sternocleidomastoid
Trapezius
Deltoid
Teres minor
Teres major
Triceps brachii
Brachioradialis
Biceps femoris
Semitendonous
Semimembranous
Gastrocnemius
Calcaneal tendon

Brachialis
Infraspinatus
Rhomboideus
Latissiumus dorsi
External oblique
Gluteus medius
Gluteus maximus
Adductor magnus
Gracilis
Vastus lateralis
Sartorius
Soleus
Peroneus longus

Figure 7.13   Posterior view of superficial skeletal muscles.

Two major pairs of muscles raise the mandible in the process of mastication: the *masseter* and the *temporalis* (Table 7.4 and figure 7.14).

Muscles That Move the Head

Several pairs of neck muscles are responsible for flexing, extending, and turning the head. Table 7.5 lists two of the major muscles that perform this function: the *sternocleidomastoid* and the *splenius capitis*. As noted in Table 7.8, the *trapezius* can also extend the head, although this is not its major function (figures 7.14, 7.15, and 7.16).

Check My Understanding

9. What are the names and locations of the two parts of the epicranius muscle?
10. What muscles are involved in chewing your food?
11. What muscles turn your head to the side?

Muscles of the Abdominopelvic Wall

These paired muscles provide support for the anterior and lateral portions of the abdominal and pelvic regions, including support for the internal organs. The muscles are named for the direction of their muscle fibers: *rectus abdominis, external oblique, internal oblique,* and *transversus abdominis.* They are arranged in overlapping layers and are attached by larger aponeuroses that merge at the anterior midline to form the *linea alba,* or white line (Table 7.6 and figure 7.15).

Muscles of Breathing

Movement of the ribs occurs during breathing and is brought about by the contraction of two sets of muscles that are located between the ribs. The *external intercostals* lift the ribs upward and outward during inspiration, and the *internal intercostals* draw the ribs down and inward during expiration (Table 7.7 and figure 7.15). The primary breathing muscle is the *diaphragm,* a thin sheet of muscle that separates the thoracic and abdominal cavity. It is not shown in the figures.

Muscles That Move the Pectoral Girdle

These muscles originate on bones of the axial skeleton and insert on the scapula or clavicle. Because the scapula is supported mainly by muscles, it may be moved more freely than the clavicle. The *trapezius* is a superficial trapezoid-shaped muscle that covers much of the upper back. The *rhomboideus major* and the *levator scapulae* lie under the trapezius. The *serratus anterior* muscles are located on the lateral surfaces of the upper ribs near the axillary regions. The *pectoralis minor* lies under the pectoralis major. It pulls the scapula forward and downward (Table 7.8 and figures 7.15 to 7.18).

Table 7.3   Muscles of Facial Expression

Muscle	Origin	Insertion	Action
Buccinator (buk´-si-nā-tor)	Lateral surfaces of maxilla and mandible	Orbicularis oris	Compresses cheeks inward
Epicranius (ep-i-krā´-nē-us)	This muscle consists of two parts: the frontalis and the occipitalis. They are joined by the epicranial aponeurosis, which covers the top of the skull.		
Frontalis (fron-ta´-lis)	Epicranial aponeurosis	Skin and muscles above the eyes	Raises eyebrows and wrinkles forehead horizontally
Occipitalis (ok-sip-i-tal´-is)	Base of occipital bone	Epicranial aponeurosis	Pulls scalp posteriorly
Orbicularis oculi (or-bik´-ū-lar-is ok´-ū-li)	Frontal bone and maxillae	Skin around eye	Closes eye
Orbicularis oris (or-bik´-ū-lar-is- o´-ris)	Muscles around mouth	Skin around lips	Closes and puckers lips; shapes lips during speech
Platysma (plah-tiz´-mah)	Fascia of upper chest	Mandible and muscles around mouth	Draws angle of mouth downward; opens mouth
Zygomaticus (zī-gō-mat´-ik-us)	Zygomatic bone	Orbicularis oris at corners of the mouth	Pulls angle of mouth upward

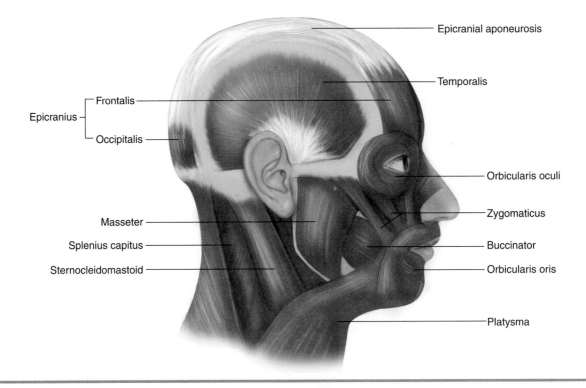

Figure 7.14 Muscles of facial expression and mastication. AP|R

Table 7.4   Muscles of Mastication

Muscle	Origin	Insertion	Action
Masseter (mas-se´-ter)	Zygomatic arch	Lateral surface of mandible	Raises mandible
Temporalis (tem-po-ra´-lis)	Temporal bone	Coronoid process of mandible	Raises mandible

Table 7.5   Muscles That Move the Head

Muscle	Origin	Insertion	Action
Sternocleidomastoid (ster-nō-klī-dō-mas´-toid)	Clavicle and sternum	Mastoid process of temporal bone	Contraction of both muscles flexes head toward chest; contraction of one muscle turns head away from contracting muscle
Splenius capitus (splē´-nē-us kap´-i-tis)	Lower cervical and upper thoracic vertebrae	Mastoid process of temporal bone	Contraction of both muscles extends head; contraction of one muscle turns head toward same side as contracting muscle

Table 7.6   Muscles of the Abdominopelvic Wall

Muscle	Origin	Insertion	Action
Rectus abdominis (rek´-tus ab-dom´-i-nis)	Pubic symphysis and pubic crest	Xiphoid process of sternum and costal cartilages of ribs 5 to 7	Tightens abdominopelvic wall; compresses internal organs; flexes the vertebral column
External oblique (eks-ter´-nal o-blēk´)	Anterior surface of lower eight ribs	Iliac crest and linea alba	Tightens abdominopelvic wall and compresses internal organs
Internal oblique (in-ter´-nal o-blēk´)	Iliac crest and inguinal ligament	Cartilage of lower four ribs, pubic crest, and linea alba	Same as above
Transversus abdominis (trans-ver´-sus ab-dom´-i-nis)	Iliac crest, cartilages of lower six ribs, processes of lumbar vertebrae	Pubic crest and linea alba	Same as above

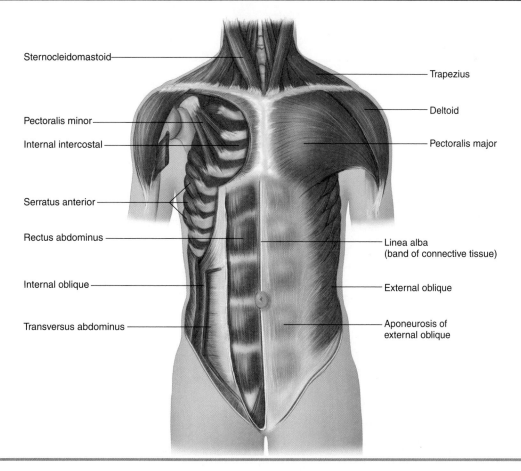

Figure 7.15 Muscles of the anterior chest and abdominal wall. The right pectoralis major is removed to show the pectoralis minor. AP|R

Table 7.7 Muscles of Breathing

Muscle	Origin	Insertion	Action
Diaphragm (dī-a-fram)	Lumbar vertebrae, costal cartilages of lower ribs, xiphoid process	Central tendon located at midpoint of muscle	Forms floor of thoracic cavity; lowers during contraction, causing inspiration
External intercostals (eks-ter´-nal in-ter-kos´-tals)	Inferior border of rib above	Superior border of rib below	Raises ribs upward and outward during inspiration
Internal intercostals (in-ter´-nal in-ter-kos´-tals)	Superior border of rib below	Inferior border of rib above	Draws ribs downward and inward during expiration

Table 7.8 Muscles That Move the Pectoral Girdle

Muscle	Origin	Insertion	Action
Trapezius (trah-pē-zē´-us)	Occipital bone; cervical and thoracic vertebrae	Clavicle; spine and acromion process of scapula	Elevates clavicle; adducts and elevates scapula; extends head
Rhomboideus major (rom-boid´-ē-us)	Upper thoracic vertebrae	Medial border of scapula	Adducts and elevates scapula
Levator scapulae (le-va´-tor skap´-ū-lē)	Cervical vertebrae	Superior medial margin of scapula	Elevates scapula
Serratus anterior (ser-ra´-tus)	Upper eight to nine ribs	Medial border of scapula	Pulls scapula downward and anteriorly
Pectoralis minor (pek-to-rah´-lis)	Anterior surface of upper ribs	Coracoid process of scapula	Pulls scapula anteriorly and downward

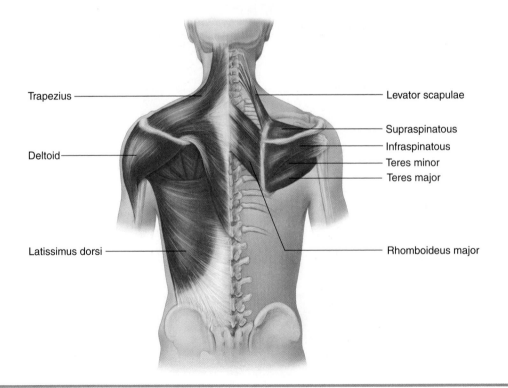

Figure 7.16 Muscles of the posterior shoulder. The right trapezius is removed to show underlying muscles. AP|R

Muscles That Move the Arm and Forearm

Movement of the humerus is enabled by the muscles that originate on the pectoral girdle, ribs, or vertebrae and insert on the humerus. The arrangement of these muscles and the ball-and-socket joint between the humerus and scapula enable great freedom of movement for the arm. The *pectoralis major* is the large superficial muscle of the chest. The *deltoid* is the thick muscle that caps the shoulder joint. The *coracobrachialis* is a relatively small muscle that lies under the pectoralis major and biceps brachii. It flexes and adducts the arm. The *supraspinatus, infraspinatus, teres major,* and *teres minor* cover the posterior surfaces of the scapulae (plural of *scapula*). The *latissimus dorsi* is a broad, sheetlike muscle that covers the lower back (Table 7.9 and figures 7.15 to 7.20).

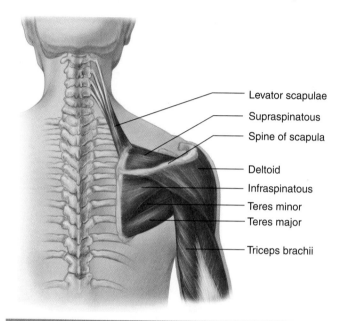

Figure 7.17 Muscles of the posterior surface of the scapula and arm. AP|R

Figure 7.18 Muscles of the anterior shoulder and arm, with the rib cage removed. AP|R

Table 7.9 Muscles That Move the Arm

Muscle	Origin	Insertion	Action
Pectoralis major (pek-tō-rah´-lis)	Clavicle; sternum, and cartilages of upper ribs	Greater tubercle of humerus	Adducts humerus; draws it forward across chest
Coracobrachialis (kōr″-a-kō-brā-kē-ah´-lis)	Coracoid process of scapula	Shaft of humerus	Adducts and flexes humerus
Deltoid (del´-toid)	Clavicle and spine, and acromion of scapula	Deltoid tuberosity of humerus	Abducts, flexes, and extends humerus
Supraspinatus (su-prah-spī´-na-tus)	Posterior surface of scapula above spine	Greater tubercle of humerus	Assists deltoid in abducting humerus
Infraspinatus (in-frah-spī´-na-tus)	Posterior surface of scapula below spine	Greater tubercle of humerus	Rotates humerus laterally
Latissimus dorsi (lah-tis´-i-mus dor´sī)	Lower thoracic, lumbar, and sacral vertebrae; lower ribs; iliac crest	Intertubercular groove of humerus	Adducts and extends humerus; rotates humerus medially
Teres major (te´r-ez)	Inferior angle of scapula	Distal to lesser tubercle of humerus	Extends, adducts, and rotates humerus medially
Teres minor	Lateral border of scapula	Greater tubercle of humerus	Rotates humerus laterally

12. What muscle separates the abdominal and thoracic cavities?
13. Name the abdominal muscles from inside out.
14. What three muscles raise the scapula?

Muscles moving the forearm originate on either the humerus or scapula and insert on either the radius or ulna. Three flexors occur on the anterior surface of the upper arm: the *biceps brachii, brachialis,* and *brachioradialis.* One extensor, the *triceps brachii,* is located on the posterior surface of the upper arm (Table 7.10 and figures 7.15, 7.19, and 7.20).

Table 7.10   Muscles That Move the Forearm

Muscle	Origin	Insertion	Action
Biceps brachii (bī´-seps brā´-kē-ī)	Coracoid process and tubercle above glenoid cavity of scapula	Radial tuberosity of radius	Flexes and rotates forearm laterally (supination)
Brachialis (brā´-kē-al-is)	Distal, anterior surface of humerus	Coronoid process of ulna	Flexes forearm
Brachioradialis (brā-kē-ō-rā-dē-a´-lis)	Lateral surface of distal end of humerus	Lateral surface of radius just above styloid process	Flexes forearm
Triceps brachii (trī´-seps brā´-kē-ī)	Lateral and medial surfaces of humerus and tubercle below glenoid cavity of scapula	Olecranon process of ulna	Extends forearm

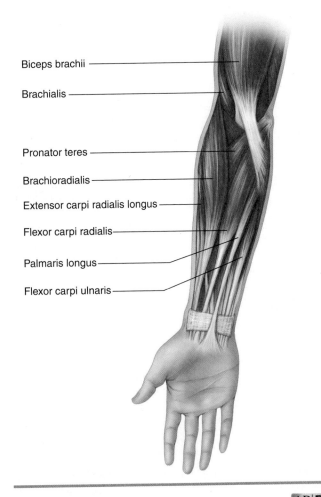

Biceps brachii
Brachialis
Pronator teres
Brachioradialis
Extensor carpi radialis longus
Flexor carpi radialis
Palmaris longus
Flexor carpi ulnaris

Figure 7.19 Muscles of the anterior forearm. AP|R

Triceps brachii
Brachioradialis
Extensor carpi radialis longus
Flexor carpi ulnaris
Extensor carpi ulnaris
Extensor digitorum

Figure 7.20 Muscles of the posterior forearm. AP|R

Muscles That Move the Wrist and Fingers

Many muscles that produce the various movements of the wrist and fingers are located in the forearm. Only a few of the larger superficial muscles are considered here. They originate from the distal end of the humerus and insert on carpals, metacarpals, or phalanges. Flexors on the anterior surface include the *flexor carpi radialis, flexor carpi ulnaris,* and *palmaris longus.* Extensors on the posterior surface include the *extensor carpi radialis longus, extensor carpi ulnaris,* and *extensor digitorum* (Table 7.11 and figure 7.20). Note that the tendons of these muscles are held in position by a circular ligament at the wrist.

Muscles That Move the Thigh and Leg

Muscles moving the thigh span the hip joint. They insert on the femur, and most originate on the pelvic girdle. The *iliacus* and *psoas major* are located anteriorly, the *gluteus maximus* is located posteriorly and forms the buttocks, the *gluteus medius* is located under the gluteus maximus posteriorly and extends laterally, and the *tensor fasciae latae* is located laterally. The *adductor longus* and *adductor magnus* are both located medially (Table 7.12 and figures 7.21, 7.22, and 7.23).

The leg is moved by muscles located in the thigh. They span the knee joint and originate on the pelvic girdle or thigh and insert on the tibia or fibula. The *quadriceps femoris* is composed of four muscles that have a common tendon that inserts on the patella. However, this tendon continues as the patellar ligament, which attaches to the tibial tuberosity—the functional insertion for these muscles. The *biceps femoris, semitendinosus,* and *semimembranosus* on the posterior surface of the thigh are often collectively called the "hamstrings." The medially located *gracilis* has two insertions that give it dual actions. The long, straplike *sartorius*

Check My Understanding

15. What muscle abducts and extends your arm?
16. What muscle extends your forearm?
17. What muscle extends your fingers?

Intramuscular injections are commonly used when quick absorption is desired. Such injections are given in three sites: (1) the lateral surface of the deltoid; (2) the gluteus medius in the upper, outer portion of the buttock; and (3) the vastus lateralis near the midpoint of the lateral surface of the thigh. These injection sites are chosen because there are no major nerves or blood vessels present that could be damaged, and the muscles have a good blood supply to aid absorption. The site chosen may vary with the age and condition of the patient.

Table 7.11 Muscles That Move the Wrist and Fingers

Muscle	Origin	Insertion	Action
Flexor carpi radialis (flek´-sor kar´-pī rā-dē-a´-lis)	Medial epicondyle of humerus	Second and third metacarpals	Flexes and abducts wrist
Flexor carpi ulnaris (flek´-sor kar´-pī ul-na´-ris)	Medial epicondyle of humerus and olecranon process of ulna	Carpal bones and fifth metacarpal	Flexes and adducts wrist
Palmaris longus (pal-ma´-ris long´-gus)	Medial epicondyle of humerus	Fascia of palm	Flexes wrist
Extensor carpi radialis longus (eks-ten´-sor kar´-pī rā-dē-a´-lis long´-gus)	Lateral epicondyle of humerus	Second metacarpal	Extends and abducts wrist
Extensor carpi ulnaris (eks-ten´-sor kar´-pī ul-na´-ris)	Lateral epicondyle of humerus	Fifth metacarpal	Extends and adducts wrist
Extensor digitorum (eks-ten´-sor dij-i-to´-rum)	Lateral epicondyle of humerus	Posterior surfaces of phalanges 2–5	Extends fingers

Table 7.12   Muscles That Move the Thigh

Muscle	Origin	Insertion	Action
Iliacus (il´-ē-ak-us)	Fossa of ilium	Lesser trochanter of femur	Flexes thigh
Psoas major (so´-as)	Lumbar vertebrae	Lesser trochanter of femur	Flexes thigh
Gluteus maximus (glū´-tē-us mak´-si-mus)	Posterior surfaces of ilium; sacrum; and coccyx	Posterior surface of femur and lateral fascia of thigh	Extends and rotates thigh laterally
Gluteus medius (glū´-tē-us mē´-dē-us)	Lateral surface of ilium	Greater trochanter of femur	Abducts and rotates thigh medially
Tensor fasciae latae (ten´-sor fash´-ē-ē lah-tē´)	Anterior iliac crest	Lateral fascia of thigh	Flexes and abducts thigh
Adductor longus (ad-duk´-tor long´-gus)	Pubic bone near symphysis pubis	Posterior surface of femur	Adducts, flexes, and rotates thigh laterally
Adductor magnus (ad-duk´-tor mag´-nus)	Inferior portion of ischium and pubis	Same as above	Same as above

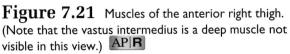

Figure 7.21 Muscles of the anterior right thigh. (Note that the vastus intermedius is a deep muscle not visible in this view.) AP|R

extends diagonally across the anterior surface of the thigh and spans both the hip and knee joints. Its contraction enables the legs to cross (Table 7.13 and figures 7.21, 7.22, and 7.23).

Figure 7.22 Muscles of the lateral right thigh.

Muscles That Move the Foot and Toes

Many muscles are involved in the movement of the foot and toes. They are located in the leg and originate on the femur, tibia, or fibula and insert on the

Table 7.13   Muscles That Move the Leg

Muscle	Origin	Insertion	Action
Quadriceps femoris (quad´-ri-seps fem´-or-is)	A composite thigh muscle formed of four parts that are usually described as separate muscles. Each muscle has a common tendon that attaches to the patella and continues as the patellar ligament to the tibial tuberosity.		
Rectus femoris (rek´-tus fem´-or-is)	Anterior inferior iliac spine and superior margin of acetabulum	Patella; tendon continues as patellar ligament, which attaches to tibial tuberosity	Extends leg and flexes thigh
Vastus lateralis (vas´-tus lat-er-a´lis)	Greater trochanter and posterior surface of femur	Same as above	Extends leg
Vastus medialis (vas´-tus me-de-a´lis)	Medial and posterior surfaces of femur	Same as above	Extends leg
Vastus intermedius (vas´-tus in-ter-mē´dē-us)	Anterior and lateral surfaces of femur	Same as above	Extends leg
Hamstrings	Three distinct muscles of the posterior thigh.		
Biceps femoris (bi´-seps fem´-or-is)	Ischial tuberosity and posterior surface of femur	Head of fibula and lateral condyle of tibia	Flexes and rotates leg laterally; extends thigh
Semitendinosus (sem-ē-ten-di-nō´-sus)	Ischial tuberosity	Medial surface of tibia	Flexes and rotates leg medially; extends thigh
Semimembranosus (sem-ē-mem-brah-nō´-sus)	Ischial tuberosity	Medial condyle of tibia	Flexes and rotates leg medially; extends thigh
Gracilis (gras´-il-is)	Pubis near symphysis	Medial surface of tibia	Flexes and rotates leg medially; adducts thigh
Sartorius (sar-to´r-ē-us)	Anterior superior iliac spine	Medial surface of tibia	Flexes thigh; rotates leg medially and thigh laterally as when crossing legs

Table 7.14   Muscles That Move the Foot and Toes

Muscle	Origin	Insertion	Action
Gastrocnemius (gas-trōk-nē´m-ē-us)	Medial and lateral condyles of femur	Calcaneus by the calcaneal tendon	Plantar flexes foot and flexes leg
Soleus (sō´l-ē-us)	Posterior surface of tibia and fibula	Calcaneus by the calcaneal tendon	Plantar flexes foot
Peroneus longus (per-ō-nē´-us long´-gus)	Lateral condyle of tibia and head and body of fibula	First metatarsal and tarsal bones	Plantar flexes and everts foot; supports arch
Tibialis anterior (tib-ē-a´l-is an-te´rē-or)	Lateral condyle and surface of tibia	First metatarsal and tarsal bones	Dorsiflexes and inverts foot
Extensor digitorum longus (eks-ten´-sor dig-i-tor´-um long´-gus)	Lateral condyle of tibia and anterior surface of fibula	Phalanges of toes 2–5	Dorsiflexes and everts foot; extends toes

tarsals, metatarsals, or phalanges. The posterior leg muscles include the *gastrocnemius* and *soleus,* which insert on a common tendon, the calcaneal tendon, which attaches to the calcaneus (heel bone). The *tibialis anterior* is anteriorly located, and the *extensor digitorum longus* lies lateral to it. Note that although the extensor digitorum extends the toes, as its name implies, it also dorsiflexes the foot. The *peroneus longus* is located on the lateral surface of the leg (Table 7.14 and figures 7.24 to 7.26).

Figure 7.23 Muscles of the posterior right thigh. **AP|R**

Repeated stress from athletic activities may cause inflammation of a tendon, a condition known as *tendonitis*. Tendons associated with the shoulder, elbow, hip, and knee joints are most commonly affected.

Check My Understanding

18. Name the muscles that flex the thigh.
19. What are the four parts of the quadriceps femoris?
20. What is the action of muscles inserting on the calcaneus?

Foot movements include moving the foot upward (dorsiflexion), moving the foot downward (plantar flexion), turning the sole inward (inversion), and turning the sole outward (eversion). Note how the tendons are held in position by the bands of ligaments at the ankle.

Figure 7.24 Muscles of the anterior right leg. **AP|R**

7.6 Disorders of the Muscular System

Some disorders of the muscle system may result from factors associated only with muscles, while others are caused by disorders of the nervous system. Certain neurological disorders are included here because of their obvious effect on muscle action.

Muscle Disorders

Cramps are involuntary, painful, sustained tetanic contractions of a muscle. The precise cause is unknown, but a cramp may result from chemical changes in the muscle, such as lactic acid accumulation or calcium deficiencies. Sometimes a severe blow to a muscle can produce a cramp.

Fibrosis (fī-brō´-sis) is an abnormal increase of fibrous connective tissue in a muscle. Usually, it

Figure 7.25 Lateral view of muscles of the right lower leg.

Figure 7.26 Muscles of the posterior right leg. **AP|R**

results from connective tissue replacing dead muscle fibers following an injury.

Fibrositis (fī-brō-sī′-tis) is the inflammation of the connective tissue, especially muscle sheaths and fascia associated with muscles. It produces soreness and stiffness that is commonly called *muscular rheumatism.*

Muscular dystrophy (dis′-trō-fē) is a general term for a number of inherited muscular disorders that are characterized by the progressive degeneration of muscles. The affected muscles gradually weaken and atrophy (shrink), producing a progressive crippling of the patient. There is no specific drug cure, but patients are encouraged to keep active and are given muscle-strengthening exercises.

Myositis (mī-ō-sī′-tis) is the inflammation of muscle tissue. It produces soreness and stiffness similar to fibrositis of the muscles.

Strains, or "pulled muscles," result when a muscle is stretched excessively. This usually occurs when an antagonist has not relaxed quickly enough as an agonist contracts. The hamstrings are a common site of muscle strains. In mild strains, only a few muscle fibers are damaged. In severe strains, both connective and muscle tissues are torn, and muscle function may be severely impaired.

Neurological Disorders Affecting Muscles

Botulism (boch′-ū-lizm) poisoning is caused by a neurotoxin produced by the bacterium *Clostridium botulinum.* The toxin prevents release of acetylcholine from the tips of motor axons. Without prompt treatment with an antitoxin, death may result from paralysis of the muscles used in breathing. Poisoning results from eating improperly canned vegetables or meats that contain *C. botulinum* and the accumulated toxins.

Myasthenia gravis (mī-as-thē′-nē-ah grav′-is) is characterized by extreme muscular weakness caused by improper functioning of the neuromuscular junctions. It is an autoimmune disease in which antibodies are produced that attach to the acetylcholine receptors on the sarcolemma and reduce or block the stimulatory effect of acetylcholine. Myasthenia gravis occurs most frequently in women between 20 and 40 years of age. Usually, it first affects ocular muscles and other muscles of the face and neck, which may lead to difficulty in chewing, swallowing, and talking. Other muscles of the body may be involved later. Treatment typically involves the use of anticholinesterase drugs and immunosuppressive drugs, such as the steroid prednisone.

Poliomyelitis (pō-lē-ō-mī-e-lī´-tis) is a viral disease of motor neurons in the spinal cord. Destruction of the motor neurons leads to paralysis of skeletal muscles. It is now rare in industrialized countries due to the availability of a polio vaccine. Virtually all children in the United States receive this vaccine, which protects them from polio.

Spasms are sudden, involuntary contractions of a muscle or a group of muscles. They may vary from simple twitches to severe convulsions and may be accompanied by pain. Spasms may be caused by irritation of the motor neurons supplying the muscle, emotional stress, or neurological disorders.

Spasms of smooth muscle in the walls of the digestive tract, respiratory passages, or certain blood vessels can be hazardous. Hiccupping is one type of spasm.

Tetanus (tet´-ah-nus) is a disease caused by the anaerobic bacterium *Clostridium tetani,* which is common in soil. Infection usually results from puncture wounds. *C. tetani* produces a neurotoxin that affects motor neurons in the spinal cord, resulting in continuous stimulation and tetanic contractions of certain muscles. Because the first muscles affected are those that move the mandible, this disease is often called "lockjaw." Without prompt treatment, mortality is high. Young children usually receive injections of tetanus toxoid to stimulate production of antibodies against the neurotoxin. Booster injections are given at regular intervals to keep the concentration of antibodies at a high level in order to prevent the disease.

CHAPTER SUMMARY

- The three types of muscle tissue in the body are skeletal, smooth, and cardiac.
- Each type of muscle tissue has unique structural and functional characteristics.

7.1 Structure of Skeletal Muscle

- Each skeletal muscle is formed of many muscle fibers (cells) that are arranged in fasciculi.
- Connective tissue envelops each fiber, each fasiculus, and the entire muscle.
- Muscles are attached to bones or connective tissue by either tendons or aponeuroses.
- The sarcolemma is the plasma membrane of a muscle fiber, and the sarcoplasm (cytoplasm) surrounds the myofibrils, the contractile elements.
- Myofibrils consist of thick (myosin) and thin (actin) myofilaments. The arrangement of the myofilaments produces the striations that are characteristic of skeletal muscle fibers.
- Each myofibril consists of many sarcomeres joined end-to-end. A sarcomere is bounded by a Z line at each end.
- The axon tip of a motor neuron is attached to each muscle fiber at the neuromuscular junction. The axon tip fits into a synaptic cleft in the sarcolemma. The neurotransmitter acetylcholine is contained in tiny vesicles in the axon tip.
- Each muscle fiber is innervated and controlled by a motor neuron.
- A motor unit consists of a motor neuron and all muscle fibers to which it is attached.

7.2 Physiology of Muscle Contraction

- An activated motor axon releases acetylcholine into the synaptic cleft. Acetylcholine attaches to receptors of the sarcolemma and causes the release of Ca^{++} molecules. This, in turn, causes the cross-bridges of myosin from the sarcoplastic reticulum to attach to binding sites on actin molecules. A series of ratchetlike movements pulls the thin filaments toward the center of the sarcomere, producing contraction.
- Acetylcholinesterase quickly breaks down acetylcholine to prevent continued stimulation and to prepare the muscle fiber for the next stimulus.
- Energy for contraction comes from high-energy phosphate bonds in ATP.
- After cellular respiration has formed a muscle cell's normal supply of ATP, excess energy is transferred to creatine to form creatine phosphate, which serves as a small reserve supply of energy.
- Small amounts of oxygen are stored in combination with myoglobin, which gives muscle cells a small reserve of oxygen for aerobic cellular respiration.
- Vigorous muscular activity quickly exhausts available oxygen, leading to the accumulation of lactic acid and producing an oxygen debt. Heavy breathing after exercise provides the oxygen required to metabolize lactic acid and pay the oxygen debt.
- Fatigue results primarily from the accumulation of lactic acid in a muscle fiber.

- Large amounts of heat are produced by the chemical and physical processes of muscle contraction.
- When stimulated by a threshold stimulus, individual muscle fibers exhibit an all-or-none contraction response.
- A simple contraction consists of a latent period, period of contraction, and period of relaxation.
- Whole muscles provide graded contraction responses, which are enabled by the number of motor units that are recruited.
- A sustained contraction of all motor units is a tetanic contraction.
- Muscle tone is a state of partial contraction that results from alternating contractions of a few motor units.

7.3 Actions of Skeletal Muscles

- The origin is the immovable attachment, and the insertion is the movable attachment.
- Muscles are arranged in groups with opposing actions: agonists and antagonists.

7.4 Naming of Muscles

- Several criteria are used in naming muscles.
- These criteria include function, shape, relative position, location, site of attachment, origin and insertion, size, and orientation of fibers.

7.5 Major Skeletal Muscles

- Muscles of facial expression originate on skull bones and insert on connective tissue of the skin. They include the epicranius, orbicularis oculi, orbicularis oris, buccinator, zygomaticus, and platysma.
- Muscles of mastication originate on fixed skull bones and insert on the mandible. They include the masseter and the temporalis.
- Muscles that move the head occur in the neck and upper back. They include the sternocleidomastoid and splenius capitis.
- Muscles of the abdominopelvic wall connect the pelvic girdle, rib cage, and vertebral column. They include the rectus abdominis, external oblique, internal oblique, and transversus abdominis.

- Muscles that move the ribs occur between the ribs. They are the external intercostals and internal intercostals.
- Muscles that move the pectoral girdle originate on the rib cage or vertebrae and insert on the pectoral girdle. They include the trapezius, rhomboideus major, levator scapulae, pectoralis minor, and serratus anterior.
- Muscles that move the arm originate on the rib cage, vertebrae, or pectoral girdle and insert on the humerus. They include the pectoralis major, coracobrachialis deltoid, supraspinatus, infraspinatus, latissimus dorsi, teres major, and teres minor.
- Muscles that move the forearm originate on the scapula or humerus and insert on the radius or ulna. They include the biceps brachii, brachialis, brachioradialis, and triceps brachii.
- Muscles that move the wrist and fingers are the muscles of the forearm. They include the flexor carpi radialis, flexor carpi ulnaris, palmaris longus, extensor carpi radialis longus, extensor carpi ulnaris, and extensor digitorum.
- Muscles that move the thigh originate on the pelvic girdle and insert on the femur. They include the iliacus, psoas major, gluteus maximus, gluteus medius, tensor fasciae latae, adductor longus, and adductor magnus.
- Muscles that move the leg originate on the pelvic girdle or femur and insert on the tibia or fibula. They include the quadriceps femoris, biceps femoris, semitendinosus, semimembranosus, gracilis, and sartorius.
- Muscles that move the foot and toes are the muscles of the lower leg. They include the gastrocnemius, soleus, peroneus longus, tibialis anterior, and extensor digitorum longus.

7.6 Disorders of the Muscular System

- Disorders of muscles include cramps, fibrosis, fibrositis, muscular dystrophy, myositis, and strains.
- Neurological disorders that directly affect muscle action include botulism, myasthenia gravis, poliomyelitis, spasms, and tetanus.

BUILDING MY VOCABULARY

1. **Selected New Terms**
   acetylcholine, p. 130
   actin myofilament, p. 127
   deep fascia, p. 126
   graded response, p. 134
   latent period, p. 134
   myosin myofilament, p. 127
   neuromuscular junction, p. 130
   recruitment, p. 134
   sarcolemma, p. 127
   sarcoplasm, p. 127

2. **Related Clinical Terms**
   Fibromyositis (fī-brō-mī-ō-sī´-tis) A general term for inflammation of a muscle and its associated connective tissue.
   Myalgia (mī-al´-jē-ah) Muscle pain from any cause.
   Myopathy (mī-op´-ah-thē) Any disease of muscles.
   Orthopedics (or-thō-pē´-diks) Branch of surgery dealing with repair of the skeletal and muscular systems.
   Spasm (Spaz´-um) An involuntary muscle contraction.

SELF-REVIEW

Answers are located in appendix B.

1. A skeletal muscle consists of many _____, which are arranged in fasciculi.
2. Muscles are attached to bones by _____.
3. A contractile unit of a myofibril is a _____.
4. A muscle contraction is triggered by _____ binding to receptors on the sarcolemma.
5. Contraction occurs when thick myosin filaments pull _____ filaments toward the center of a sarcomere.
6. Accumulation of _____ during vigorous exercise results in an oxygen debt.
7. The movable end of a muscle is its _____.
8. The lower jaw is closed by the contraction of the temporalis and the _____.
9. The abdominal muscle extending from the sternum to the pubis is the _____.
10. The broad muscle of the lower back is the _____.
11. The shoulder muscle that raises the arm is the _____.
12. The arm muscle that extends the forearm is the _____.
13. The large muscle that extends and rotates the thigh laterally is the _____.
14. The four-part thigh muscle that extends the lower leg is the _____.
15. The large calf muscle that plantar flexes the foot is the _____.

CRITICAL THINKING

1. Complete the learning objectives on the first page of the chapter.
2. Describe the interaction of thin actin and thick myosin myofilaments enabling contraction.
3. Can the origin and insertion of some muscles be interchanged? Explain.
4. Explain the roles of agonists and antagonists in body movements.
5. As a cosmetic procedure, Botox is injected in very small doses into specific facial muscles to reduce wrinkles. It is derived from a neurotoxin that competes with acetylcholine at the neuromuscular junction. Explain how Botox works.

Visit this book's website at www.mhhe.com/ gunstream5 for practice quizzes, learning exercises, case studies, and other study tools.

CHAPTER 8

Nervous System

Anatomy & Physiology REVEALED®
aprevealed.com

Module 7
Nervous System

SELECTED KEY TERMS

Autonomic nervous system
(auto = self; nom = distribute)
The involuntary portion of the
nervous system that is involved in
maintaining homeostasis.

Axon (ax = axis, central)
A neuron process that carries
impulses away from the cell body.

Central nervous system The
portion of the nervous system
composed of the brain and
spinal cord.

Dendrite (dendr = tree) A neuron
process that carries impulses
toward the cell body.

Effector A muscle or gland.

Ganglion (gangli = a swelling)
A group of neuron cell bodies.

Impulse A wave of depolarization
passing over a neuron or muscle
fiber.

Myelin sheath (myel = marrow)
The fatty insulating substance
around many axons.

Nerve A bundle of neuron processes.

Neurilemma (neur = nerve;
lemma = rind) The outer membrane covering the myelin sheath.

Neuroglial cells Supportive and
protective cells within the nervous
system.

Neuron A nerve cell.

Neurotransmitter A chemical
secreted by an axon that triggers
the formation of an impulse in the
postsynaptic neuron.

Peripheral nervous system
(peri = around) Portion of the
nervous system composed of
cranial and spinal nerves.

Plexus A network of intersecting
spinal nerves.

Receptor Portion of the peripheral
nervous system that responds to
certain stimuli by forming impulses.

Reflex An involuntary response to
a stimulus.

Somatic nervous system The
voluntary portion of the nervous
system that is involved in
conscious activities.

Synapse (syn = together) The
junction between a neuron and
another cell.

he nervous system is the primary
coordinating and controlling system of
the body. It monitors internal and external
changes, analyzes the information, makes
conscious or unconscious decisions, and then takes
appropriate action. All of these activities occur almost
instantaneously because communication within the
nervous system is by electrochemical **impulses** that
flow rapidly over neurons and from neuron to neuron.
Most of the activities of the nervous system occur below
the conscious level and serve to maintain homeostasis.

The general functions of the nervous system may
be summarized as

1. detection of internal and external changes;
2. analysis of the information received;
3. organization of the information for immediate
   and future use; and
4. initiation of the appropriate actions.

8.1 Divisions of the Nervous System

Although the nervous system functions as a coordinated whole, it is divided into anatomical and
functional divisions as an aid in understanding this
complex organ system.

Anatomical Divisions

The nervous system has two anatomical divisions.
The **central nervous system (CNS)** consists of the
brain and spinal cord. The CNS is the body's neural
control center. It receives incoming information
(impulses), analyzes and organizes it, and initiates
appropriate action. The **peripheral nervous system
(PNS)** is located outside of the CNS and consists
of cranial and spinal nerves and sensory receptors.
The PNS carries impulses formed by **receptors,**
such as pain and sound receptors, to the CNS,
and it carries impulses from the CNS to **effectors,**
glands and muscles, that carry out actions directed
by the CNS.

Functional Divisions

Similarly, the nervous system is divided into two
functional divisions. The **sensory division** carries
impulses from sensory receptors to the CNS. The
motor division carries impulses from the CNS to
effectors, muscles and glands, which perform an
action. The motor division is further divided into
two subdivisions. The **somatic nervous system
(SNS)** is involved in the *voluntary* (conscious)
control of skeletal muscles. The **autonomic nervous
system (ANS)** provides *involuntary* (subconscious)
control of cardiac muscle, smooth muscle, and
glands (figure 8.1).

8.2 Nerve Tissue

The nervous system consists of organs composed primarily of nerve tissue supported and protected by
connective tissues. There are two types of cells that
compose nerve tissue: neurons and neuroglial cells.

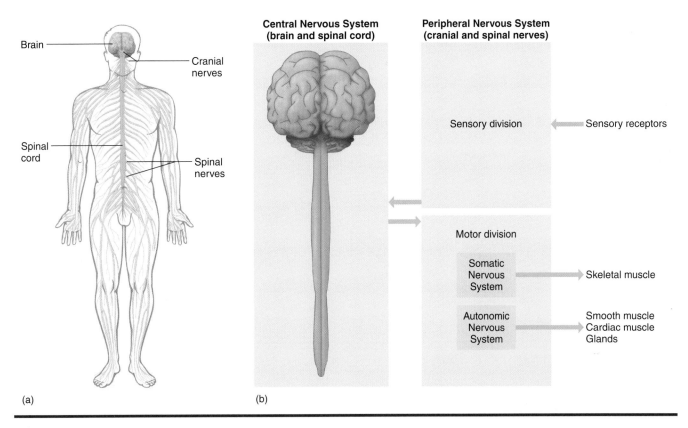

Figure 8.1 Components of the nervous system. (*a*) Anatomically, the nervous system consists of the central nervous system (brain and spinal cord) and the peripheral nervous system (cranial and spinal nerves). (*b*) Functionally, the peripheral nervous system consists of the sensory division and the motor division, which is divided into the somatic nervous system and the autonomic nervous system.

Neurons

Neurons (nū´-rahns) or nerve cells, are delicate cells that are specialized to transmit neural impulses. They are the structural and functional units of the nervous system. Neurons may vary in size and shape, but they have many common features.

As shown in figures 8.2 and 8.3, the **cell body** is the portion of a neuron that contains the large, spherical nucleus. The cell body also contains the usual cytoplasmic organelles. Two types of neuron processes extend from the cell body: dendrites and axons. A neuron may have many dendrites, but it has only one axon.

Dendrites (den´-drits) are usually short, highly-branched processes that receive impulses from other neurons and sensory receptors. Dendrites carry impulses toward the cell body and axon.

An **axon** (ak´-sahn), or *nerve fiber,* is a long, thin process of a neuron. It may have one or more side branches, and it forms a number of short, fine branches, the *axon terminals,* at its tip. The slightly enlarged tips of the axon terminals are the *synaptic knobs,* which form junctions (synapses) with other neurons, muscles, or glands. An axon carries impulses away from the cell body or dendrites.

Axons are enclosed in an insulating **myelin sheath** formed by special neuroglial cells. Such nerve fibers are said to be *myelinated.* The myelin sheath increases the speed of impulse transmission. The tiny spaces between adjacent myelin-forming cells, where the axon is exposed, are known as **nodes of Ranvier.**

Types of Neurons

Neurons may be classified according to their anatomy or their function. Structurally, there are three basic types of neurons: multipolar, bipolar, and unipolar neurons (figure 8.4).

Multipolar neurons have several dendrites and a single axon extending from the cell body. Most of the neurons whose cell bodies are located in the brain and spinal cord are multipolar neurons.

Bipolar neurons have only two processes: a dendrite and an axon extending from opposite ends of the cell body. Bipolar neurons occur in the sensory portions of the eyes, ears, and nose.

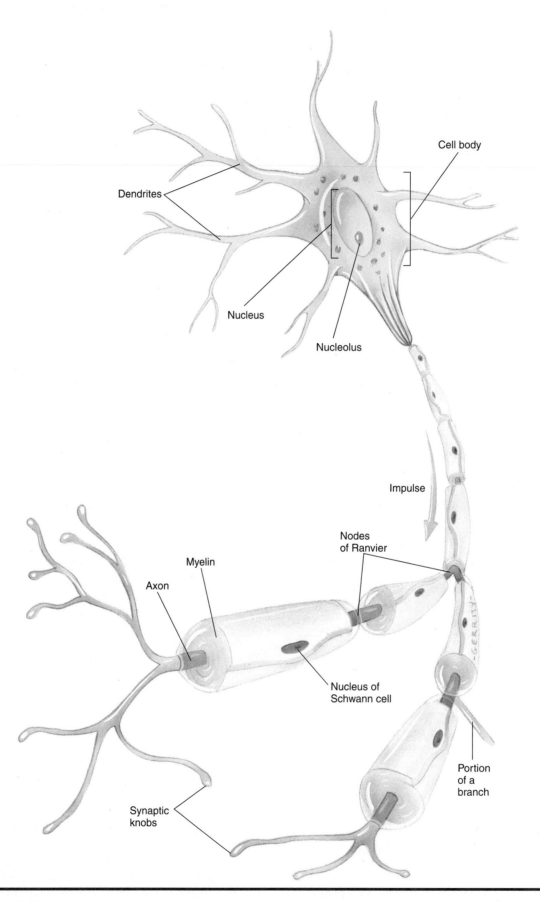

Figure 8.2 Neuron anatomy. The cell body contains the nucleus. One or more dendrites and a single axon are extensions from the cell body.

Figure 8.3 Neurons are the structural and functional units of the nervous system (50×). The dark spots in the area surrounding the neuron are nuclei of neuroglial cells. Note the location of nerve fibers (dendrites and a single axon). `AP|R`

Unipolar neurons have a single process extending from the cell body. This process quickly divides into two branches extending in opposite directions, and these branches function as a single axon. Unipolar neurons carry impulses from sensory receptors to the brain and spinal cord. Clusters of cell bodies of unipolar neurons often form **ganglia** (aggregations of neuron cell bodies) that are located outside of the central nervous system.

There are also three types of neurons based on their functions: sensory neurons, interneurons, and motor neurons.

Sensory neurons carry impulses from the peripheral parts of the body to the CNS. Their dendrites are associated with sensory receptors or are specialized to detect homeostatic changes directly. Impulses are carried over an axon within cranial or spinal nerves to the CNS. Cell bodies of sensory neurons are located outside the CNS in ganglia. Most sensory neurons are unipolar neurons.

Interneurons are located entirely within the CNS and synapse with other neurons. They are responsible for the processing and interpretation of impulses by the CNS. Interneurons receive impulses from sensory neurons and transmit them from place to place within the CNS, and they activate motor neurons to produce actions by muscles or glands. Interneurons are multipolar neurons.

Motor neurons carry impulses from the CNS to effectors, muscles, and glands to produce an action. Their cell bodies and dendrites are located within the CNS, and their axons are located in cranial and spinal nerves. Motor neurons are multipolar neurons (table 8.1).

Neuroglia

The **neuroglia** (nū-rog´-lē-ah), or **neuroglial cells,** provide support and protection for neurons. Only one type of neuroglial cell—Schwann cells—occurs in the PNS. Four types of neuroglial cells occur in the CNS, where they are even more numerous than neurons (figures 8.5 and 8.6).

Schwann cells occur only in the peripheral nervous system, where they form the myelin sheath around axons. They wrap tightly around an axon many times so the nucleus and most of the cytoplasm are squeezed into the outermost layer. The inner layers, formed of

Dendrites

Direction of impulse

Axon

(a) Multipolar

Axon

(b) Bipolar

Peripheral process

Axon

Central process

(c) Unipolar

Figure 8.4 Structural types of neurons.

Table 8.1   Functional Types of Neurons

Type	Structure	Function
Sensory neurons	Mostly unipolar	Carry impulses from peripheral receptors to the brain or spinal cord
Interneurons	Multipolar	Carry impulses between neurons in the brain and spinal cord
Motor neurons	Multipolar	Carry impulses from the brain or spinal cord to effectors (muscles and glands)

Figure 8.5   The portion of a Schwann cell that winds tightly around an axon forms a myelin sheath, and the cytoplasm and nucleus of the Schwann cell remaining outside form a neurilemmal sheath. AP|R

plasma membranes, form the myelin sheath. The outermost layer forms the **neurilemma,** which is essential for regeneration of the axon if it is injured.

Oligodendrocytes (ōl-i-gō-den´-drō-sītz) form the myelin sheath of myelinated neurons within the CNS, but they do not form a neurilemma. Destruction of neuron processes in the brain and spinal cord is permanent, because neuron processes cannot regenerate without a neurilemma.

Astrocytes (as´-trō-sītz) are the primary supporting cells for neurons in the brain. They also stimulate the growth of neurons, influence synaptic transmission, and join with the epithelium of blood vessels to form the *blood–brain barrier,* which regulates the exchange of materials between the blood and neurons.

Microglial cells are scattered throughout the CNS, where they keep the tissues clean by engulfing and digesting cellular debris and bacteria.

Ependymal (e-pen-dī´-mal) **cells** form an epithelial-like lining of cavities in the brain and spinal cord.

Check My Understanding

1. What are the general functions of the nervous system?
2. What are the structure and the function of neurons?
3. What are the roles of the five types of neuroglial cells?

Figure 8.6 Types of neuroglial cells in the central nervous system.

8.3 Neuron Physiology

Neurons have two unique functional characteristics: irritability and conductivity. **Irritability** is the ability to respond to a stimulus by forming an impulse. **Conductivity** is the ability to transmit an impulse along a neuron to other neurons, muscles, or glands. These characteristics enable the functioning of the nervous system.

Resting Potential

An inactive or resting neuron actively pumps sodium ions (Na^+) out of the cell and potassium ions (K^+) into the cell. However, the plasma membrane is more permeable to K^+ than Na^+ so some K^+ diffuse out of the neuron. Large, negatively charged proteins and ions, such as phosphate (PO_4^{---}) and sulfate (SO_4^{--}),

cannot diffuse out of the neuron. This results in a net excess of positively charged ions outside the neuron membrane and a net excess of negatively charged ions inside the neuron. This unequal distribution of electrical charges on each side of the plasma membrane makes the membrane polarized, and this condition is known as the **resting potential** (figure 8.7a). A "potential" is the difference in electrical charge between the outside and inside of the neuron's plasma membrane. The polarization of the neuron membrane does not change as long as the neuron is inactive.

Impulse Formation

When stimulated, neurons exhibit an all-or-none response. They either form an impulse, or they do not respond. The weakest stimulus that will activate a neuron is called a *threshold stimulus.* There are no strong or weak impulses. All impulses are alike.

When a neuron is activated by a stimulus, its plasma membrane instantly becomes permeable to Na⁺, so these ions quickly diffuse into the neuron as Na⁺ channels open and K⁺ channels close. The inward flow of Na⁺ for a brief instant causes the inside of the plasma membrane to become positively charged (an excess of positive ions) and the outside to become negatively charged (an excess of negative ions) at the point of stimulation. This switch in polarity is called *depolarization.* The plasma membrane is now *depolarized.* This sudden depolarization *is* the **nerve impulse,** or **action potential** (figure 8.7*b*). The wave of

depolarization then flows along the neuron. You will see how this happens momentarily.

Repolarization

Immediately after depolarization, K⁺ channels open and Na⁺ channels close, so K⁺ diffuses outward to reestablish the resting potential of the membrane, with an excess of positive charges outside and an excess of negative charges inside. In this way, the neuron membrane is repolarized. Then, Na⁺ is pumped out and K⁺ is pumped into the neuron to reestablish the resting-state distribution of ions. When this is accomplished, the neuron is ready to respond to another stimulus. Depolarization and repolarization are accomplished in about 1/1,000 of a second (figure 8.7*c*).

Impulse Conduction

When an impulse is formed at one point in a neuron, it triggers the depolarization of adjacent portions of the plasma membrane, which, in turn, depolarizes still other regions of the membrane. The result is a wave of depolarization, the conduction of a nerve impulse, that sweeps along the neuron (figure 8.8). Repolarization immediately follows an impulse.

Conduction of nerve impulses is more rapid in myelinated neuron processes than in unmyelinated processes. Recall that a myelinated neuron process is exposed only at nodes of Ranvier. Because of this, an impulse jumps from node to node and does not have to depolarize the intervening segments of the neuron process.

Synaptic Transmission

A **synapse** (sin´-aps) is a junction of an axon with either another neuron or an effector cell, such as a gland or muscle. At a synapse, the **synaptic knob** (axon tip) of the presynaptic neuron fits into a small depression on the postsynaptic neuron's dendrite or cell body, a muscle, or a gland. There is a tiny space, the **synaptic cleft,** between the neurons, so they are not in physical contact (figure 8.9).

In neuron-to-neuron synaptic transmission, when an impulse reaches the synaptic knob of the presynaptic neuron, it causes the knob to secrete a **neurotransmitter** into the synaptic cleft. Then, the neurotransmitter binds to receptors on the postsynaptic neuron's plasma membrane, which triggers a response in the postsynaptic neuron. Some neurotransmitters stimulate formation of an impulse in the postsynaptic neuron, but others inhibit impulse formation. If an impulse is formed in the postsynaptic neuron, it is carried along the neuron's axon to the next synapse where synaptic transmission takes place again.

Because only synaptic knobs can release neurotransmitters, impulses can only pass in one direction

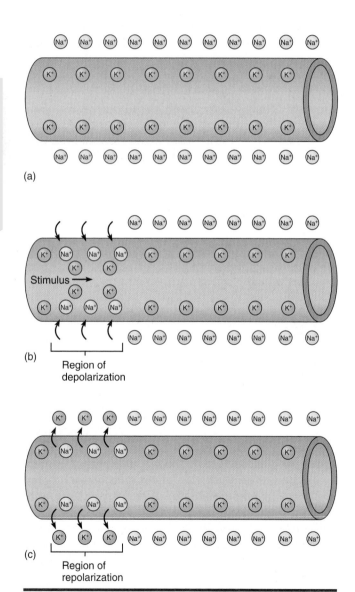

Figure 8.7 Distribution of Na⁺ and K⁺ (*a*) in a resting (polarized) neuron, (*b*) during depolarization, and (*c*) during repolarization. For simplicity, negative ions are not shown. AP|R

Figure 8.8 Distribution of excess positive charges during (*a*) impulse formation (depolarization), and (*b*) and (*c*) impulse conduction. Note that repolarization immediately follows depolarization. **AP|R**

across a synapse—from the presynaptic neuron to the postsynaptic neuron. Thus, impulses always pass in the "correct" direction, which maintains order in the nervous system.

Some neurotransmitters are reabsorbed into the synaptic knob for reuse. Others diffuse out of the synaptic cleft or are decomposed by enzymes released into the synaptic cleft. The decomposition products are then reabsorbed for reuse. Quick removal of a neurotransmitter prevents continuous stimulation or inhibition of the postsynaptic neuron (or cell) and prepares the synapse for another transmission. From start to finish, synaptic transmission takes only a fraction of a second.

Neurotransmitters

Neurotransmitters enable neurons to communicate with each other. More than 40 neurotransmitters have been identified, but they may be categorized as two basic types: excitatory and inhibitory. *Excitatory neurotransmitters* cause the formation of an impulse in postsynaptic neurons and activate other target cells. They include **acetylcholine** (as-e-til-ko´-lēn), which stimulates contraction of skeletal muscles, and **norepinephrine** (nor-ep-e-nef´-rin), which produces a sense of well-being and is an important neurotransmitter in the autonomic nervous system. *Inhibitory neurotransmitters* inhibit the formation of an impulse in postsynaptic neurons and inhibit the function of other target cells. They include dopamine (do´-pah-mēn), which creates a sense of well-being, and endorphins (in-dor´-fins), which reduce pain. Each neuron releases only one or two neurotransmitters.

Each postsynaptic neuron has synaptic knobs of hundreds of presynaptic neurons attached to its dendrites and cell body. Some presynaptic neurons secrete excitatory neurotransmitters, and others secrete inhibitory neurotransmitters. Whether or not an impulse is formed in the postsynaptic neuron depends on which type of neurotransmitter is predominant at any instant.

Check My Understanding

4. How are nerve impulses formed and conducted?
5. What is the mechanism of synaptic transmission?

8.4 Protection for the Central Nervous System

Both the brain and spinal cord are soft, delicate organs that would be easily damaged without adequate protection. Surrounding bones and fibrous membranes provide both protection and support. The brain occupies the cranial cavity formed by the cranial bones, and the spinal cord lies within the vertebral canal formed by the vertebrae. Three membranes are located between the central nervous system and the surrounding bones. These membranes are collectively called the meninges.

Meninges

The **meninges** (me-nin´-jēs) consist of three membranes arranged in layers. From innermost to outermost, they are the pia mater, arachnoid mater, and dura mater (figures 8.10 and 8.11).

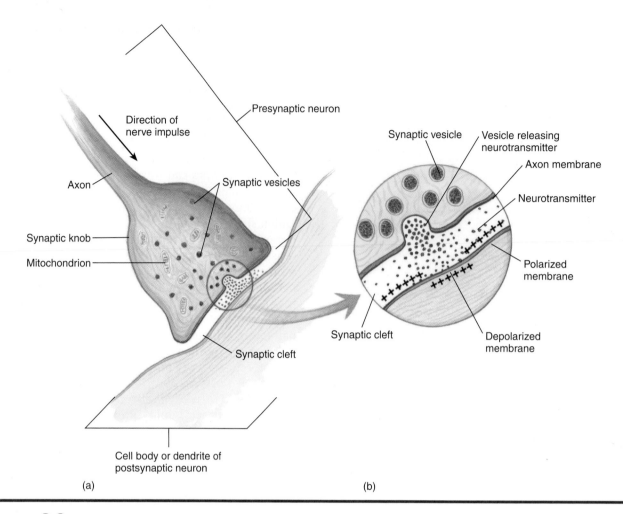

(a)

(b)

Figure 8.9 Synaptic transmission from neuron to neuron. (*a*) A synaptic knob of the presynaptic neuron fits into a depression on a dendrite or the cell body of the postsynaptic neuron. When an impulse reaches the synaptic knob, a neurotransmitter is released into the synaptic cleft. (*b*) The neurotransmitter binds with receptors on the membrane of the postsynaptic neuron, causing depolarization of the membrane. AP|R

(a)

(b)

Figure 8.10 (*a*) Membranes called meninges enclose the brain and spinal cord. (*b*) The meninges include three layers: dura mater, arachnoid mater, and pia mater. AP|R

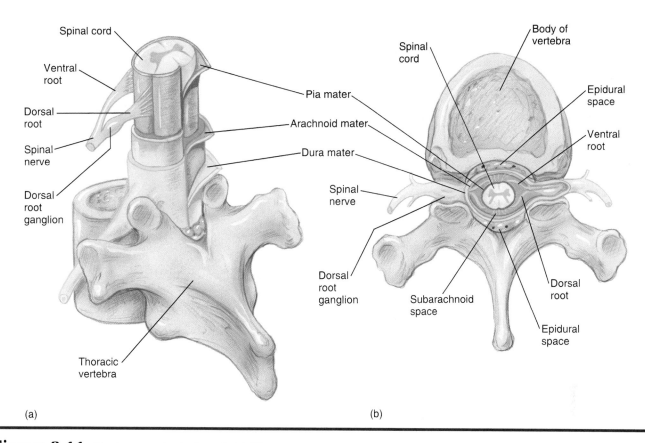

Figure 8.11 Meninges and spinal cord. (*a*) The meninges support and protect the spinal cord. (*b*) Fatty connective tissue fills the epidural space, providing a protective cushion.

Inhibitory and stimulatory drugs act by affecting synaptic transmission. *Tranquilizers* and *anesthetics* inhibit synaptic transmission by increasing the threshold of postsynaptic neurons. *Nicotine, caffeine,* and *benzedrine* promote synaptic transmission by decreasing the threshold of postsynaptic neurons.

The **pia mater** is the very thin, innermost membrane. It tightly envelops both the brain and spinal cord and penetrates into each groove and depression. It contains many blood vessels that nourish the underlying brain and spinal cord.

The **arachnoid** (ah-rak´-noyd) **mater** is the middle membrane. It is a thin, weblike membrane without blood vessels, and it does not penetrate into the small depressions as does the pia mater. Between the pia mater and arachnoid mater is the *subarachnoid space,* which contains *cerebrospinal fluid.* This clear, watery liquid serves as a shock absorber around the brain and spinal cord.

The **dura** (du´-rah) **mater** is the tough, fibrous outermost layer. In the cranial cavity, it is attached to the inner surfaces of the cranial bones and penetrates into fissures between some parts of the brain. In the vertebral canal, the dura mater forms a protective tube that extends to the sacrum. It does not attach to the bony surfaces of the vertebral canal but is separated from the bone by an *epidural space.* Fatty connective tissues fill the epidural space and serve as an additional protective cushion.

8.5 Brain AP|R

The brain is a large, exceedingly complex organ. It contains about 100 billion neurons and innumerable neuron processes and synapses. The brain consists of four major components: the cerebrum, cerebellum, diencephalon, and brain stem. Locate these structures in figure 8.12.

Cerebrum

The **cerebrum** is the largest portion of the brain. It performs the higher brain functions involved with sensations, voluntary actions, reasoning, planning, and problem solving.

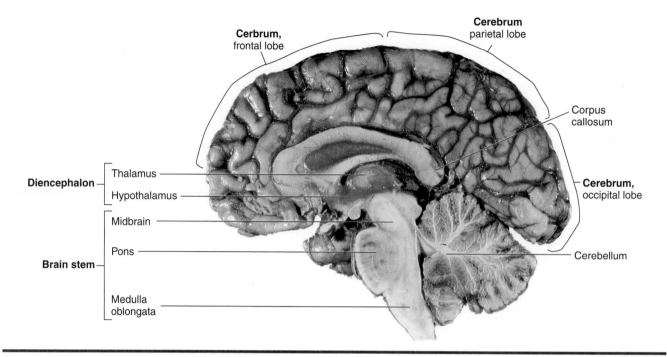

Figure 8.12 The major components of the brain as shown in a midsagittal section. Note the unlabeled gyri and sulci of the cerebrum. AP|R

Structure

The cerebrum consists of the left and right **cerebral hemispheres,** which are joined by a mass of **myelinated** neuron processes called the **corpus callosum.** The cerebral hemispheres are separated by the **longitudinal fissure,** which lies along the superior midline and extends down to the corpus callosum.

The surface of the cerebrum has numerous folds or ridges, called *gyri* (jī´-rē). The shallow grooves between the gyri are called *sulci* (sul´-sē). The surface layer of the cerebrum is composed of gray matter (neuron cell bodies and unmyelinated fibers) and is called the **cerebral cortex.** White matter, composed of myelinated fibers, lies beneath the cortex and composes most of the cerebrum. Myelinated fibers transmit impulses between the cerebral hemispheres via the corpus callosum and between the cerebral cortex and lower brain centers. Several masses of gray matter are embedded deep within the white matter of each cerebral hemisphere.

Each cerebral hemisphere is divided into four lobes. Each lobe is named for the cranial bone under which it lies. Locate the cerebral lobes in figures 8.12 and 8.13.

1. The **frontal lobe** lies anterior to the *central sulcus* and superior to the *lateral sulcus.*
2. The **parietal lobe** lies posterior to the central sulcus, superior to the temporal lobe, and anterior to the occipital lobe.
3. The **temporal lobe** lies inferior to the frontal and parietal lobes and anterior to the occipital lobe.

4. The **occipital lobe** lies posterior to the parietal and temporal lobes. The boundaries between the parietal, temporal, and occipital lobes are not distinct.

Functions

The cerebrum is involved in the interpretation of sensory impulses as sensations and in controlling voluntary motor responses, intellectual processes, the will, and many personality traits. The cerebrum has three major types of functional areas: sensory, motor, and association areas (figure 8.13).

Sensory areas receive impulses formed by sensory receptors and interpret them as sensations. These areas occur in several cerebral lobes. For example, the sensory areas for vision are in the occipital lobes and those for hearing are found in the temporal lobes. Areas identifying sensations from skin (cutaneous) stimulation lie along the *postcentral gyri* (gyri just posterior to the central sulci) of the parietal lobes. Sensory areas for taste are located at the lower end of the postcentral gyri. The sensory areas for smell are located in the inferior part of the frontal lobe.

Ascending sensory fibers cross over from one side to the other in the spinal cord or brain stem. Thus, sensory areas in the left cerebral hemisphere receive impulses from the right side of the body, and vice versa.

Motor areas are located in the frontal lobe. The primary motor areas that control skeletal muscles lie along the *precentral gyri* of the frontal lobes. The region anterior to the primary motor area is the *premotor area.*

Motor areas involved with the control of voluntary muscles

Concentration, planning, problem solving

Frontal eye field

Auditory area

Frontal lobe

Motor speech area (Broca's area)

Lateral sulcus

Interpretation of sensory experiences, memory of visual and auditory patterns

Temporal lobe

Central sulcus

Sensory areas involved with cutaneous and other senses

Understanding speech, using words

Parietal lobe

General interpretative area

Occipital lobe

Combining visual images, visual recognition of objects

Visual area

Cerebellum

Brain stem

Figure 8.13 A lateral view of the brain showing the cerebral lobes and their functional areas. AP|R

Clinical INSIGHT

The transmission of impulses by neurons in the brain produces electrical potentials that can be detected and recorded as brain waves. A recording of brain waves is called an *electroencephalogram (EEG)*. The patterns of brain waves are used in the diagnosis of certain brain disorders. The cessation of brain wave production is one criterion of brain death.

It is involved in complex learned activities, such as writing, problem solving, and planning. *Broca's area,* which controls the ability to speak, is located near the inferior end of the primary motor area. It is found in only one hemisphere—the left hemisphere in about 90% of people. Also in the premotor region is the *frontal eye field,* which controls voluntary eye movements.

Descending motor fibers cross over from one side to the other in the brain stem. Thus, the left side of the cerebrum controls skeletal muscles on the right side of the body, and vice versa.

Association areas occur in each cerebral lobe, where they interrelate sensory inputs and motor outputs. They play critical roles in the interrelationships of sensations, memory, will, and the coordination of

motor responses. The *general interpretative area* is a major association area that is located at the junction of the temporal, parietal, and occipital lobes. It is involved with the interpretation of complex sensory experiences and thought processes.

Hemisphere Specialization

The two cerebral hemispheres perform different functions in most people, although each performs basic functions of receiving sensory input and initiating voluntary motor output. In about 90% of the population, the left cerebral hemisphere controls analytical and verbal skills, such as mathematics, reading, writing, and speech. In these persons, the right hemisphere controls musical, artistic, and spatial awareness, imagination, and insight. In some persons, this pattern is reversed; in a few, there seems to be no specialization.

Diencephalon

The **diencephalon** (di-en-sef´-a-lon) is a small but important part of the brain. It lies between the brain stem and the cerebrum of the brain and consists of two major components: the thalamus and the hypothalamus.

Thalamus

The **thalamus** (thal´-ah-mus) consists of two lateral masses of neural tissue that are joined by a narrow isthmus of neural tissue called the *intermediate mass.*

Sensory impulses (except those for smell) coming from lower regions of the brain and the spinal cord are first received by the thalamus before being relayed to the cerebral cortex. The thalamus provides a general but nonspecific awareness of sensations such as pain, pressure, touch, and temperature. It seems to associate sensations with emotions, but it is the cerebral cortex that interprets the precise sensation. The thalamus also serves as a relay station for motor impulses descending from the cerebral cortex to lower brain regions.

Hypothalamus

The **hypothalamus** (hī-pō-thal´-ah-mus) is located inferior to the thalamus and anterior to the midbrain. It communicates with the thalamus, cerebrum, and other parts of the brain. The hypothalamus is a major control center for the autonomic nervous system. In this role, it controls virtually all internal organs. The hypothalamus also is the connecting link between the brain and the endocrine system, which produces chemicals (hormones) that affect every cell in the body. This link results from hypothalamic control of the hypophysis, or pituitary gland, which is suspended from its inferior surface. Although it is small, the hypothalamus exerts a tremendous impact on body functions.

The primary function of the hypothalamus is the maintenance of homeostasis, and this is accomplished through its regulation of

- body temperature;
- mineral and water balance;
- appetite and digestive processes;
- heart rate and blood pressure;
- sleep and wakefulness;
- emotions of fear and rage; and
- secretion of hormones by the pituitary gland.

Limbic System

The thalamus and hypothalamus are associated with parts of the cerebral cortex and deep nuclei (concentrations of gray matter) of the cerebrum to form a complex known as the **limbic system**. The limbic system is involved in memory and in emotions such as sadness, happiness, anger, and fear. It seems to regulate emotional behavior, especially behavior that enhances survival. Mood disorders, such as depression, are usually a result of malfunctions of the limbic system.

Check My Understanding

6. How is the CNS protected from mechanical injuries?
7. What are the functional areas of the cerebrum?
8. What are the functions of the thalamus and hypothalamus?

Brain Stem

The **brain stem** is the stalklike portion of the brain that joins higher brain centers to the spinal cord. It contains several localized masses of *gray matter,* called **nuclei,** that are surrounded by *white matter.* Ascending and descending fibers between higher brain centers and the spinal cord pass through the brain stem. The components of the brain stem include the midbrain, pons, and medulla oblongata.

Midbrain

The **midbrain** is the most superior portion of the brain stem. It is located posterior to the hypothalamus and superior to the pons. It contains reflex centers for head, eye, and body movements in response to visual and auditory stimuli. For example, reflexively turning the head to enable better vision or better hearing is activated by the midbrain.

Pons

The **pons** lies between the midbrain and the medulla oblongata and is recognizable by its bulblike anterior portion. It consists primarily of nerve fibers. Longitudinal fibers connect lower and higher brain centers, and transverse fibers connect with the cerebellum. The pons works with the medulla oblongata to control the rate and depth of breathing.

Medulla Oblongata

The **medulla oblongata** (me-dūl´-ah ob-lon-ga´-ta) is the most inferior portion of the brain, and it is the connecting link with the spinal cord. Ascending and descending fibers extending between the brain and spinal cord cross over to the opposite side of the brain within the medulla. The medulla contains three control centers that are vital for homeostasis:

1. The **respiratory control center** works with the pons to regulate the rate and depth of breathing. It is also involved in associated reflexes such as coughing and sneezing.
2. The **cardiac control center** regulates the rate of heart contractions.
3. The **vasomotor center** regulates blood pressure and blood flow by controlling the diameter of blood vessels.

Reticular Formation

The **reticular** (re-tik´-ū-lar) **formation** is a network of nerve fibers and small nuclei of gray matter scattered in the brain stem and spinal cord. Its fibers connect centers in the hypothalamus, cerebrum, and cerebellum. This network generates and transmits impulses that arouse the cerebrum to wakefulness. A decrease in activity results in sleep. Damage to the reticular formation may cause unconsciousness or a coma.

Cerebellum

The **cerebellum** (ser-e-bel´-um) is the second largest portion of the brain. It is located inferior to the occipital and temporal lobes of the cerebrum posterior to the pons and medulla oblongata. It is divided into two lateral hemispheres by a medial constriction, the *vermis* (ver´-mis). Gray matter forms a thin outer layer covering the underlying white matter, which forms most of the cerebellum.

The cerebellum is a reflex center that controls and coordinates the interaction of skeletal muscles. It controls posture, balance, and muscle coordination. Damage to the cerebellum may result in a loss of equilibrium, muscle coordination, and muscle tone.

Table 8.2 summarizes the major brain functions.

Check My Understanding

9. What are the functions of the medulla oblongata?
10. How is the cerebellum involved in skeletal muscle contractions?

Ventricles and Cerebrospinal Fluid

There are four interconnecting **ventricles,** or cavities, within the brain. Each ventricle is lined by ependymal cells and is filled with **cerebrospinal fluid.** The largest ventricles are the two *lateral ventricles* (first and second ventricles), which are located within the cerebral hemispheres. The *third ventricle* is a narrow space that lies on the midline between the lateral masses of the thalamus and hypothalamus. The *fourth ventricle* is located on the midline in the posterior portion of the brain stem just anterior to the cerebellum. It is continuous with the central canal of the spinal cord. Observe the relative positions of the ventricles in figure 8.14.

Each ventricle contains a **choroid** (kō´-royd) **plexus,** a mass of special capillaries that secrete the cerebrospinal fluid, but most of the cerebrospinal fluid is produced in the lateral ventricles. From the lateral ventricles, the cerebrospinal fluid flows into the third ventricle and on into the fourth ventricle. From the fourth ventricle, some of the fluid flows down the central canal of the spinal cord, but most of it passes into the subarachnoid space of the meninges. Within the subarachnoid space, the cerebrospinal fluid flows in two directions. Some flows upward around the brain. The remainder flows down the posterior side of the spinal cord, returns upward along its anterior surface, and continues upward around the brain in the subarachnoid space. Cerebrospinal fluid is reabsorbed into the blood-filled dural sinus that is located along the superior midline within the dura mater (figures 8.10 and 8.15). The secretion and absorption of cerebrospinal fluid normally occur at equal rates, which results in a rather constant hydrostatic pressure within the ventricles and subarachnoid space.

Table 8.2	**Summary of Brain Functions**
Part	**Function**
Cerebrum	Sensory areas interpret impulses as sensations. Motor areas control voluntary muscle actions. Association areas interrelate various sensory and motor areas and are involved in intellectual processes, will, memory, emotions, and personality traits. The limbic system is involved with emotions as they relate to survival behavior.
Cerebellum	Controls posture, balance, and the coordination of skeletal muscle contractions.
Diencephalon	
Thalamus	Receives and relays sensory impulses (except smell) to the cerebrum and motor impulses to lower brain centers. Provides a general awareness of pain, touch, pressure, and temperature and determines sensations as pleasant or unpleasant.
Hypothalamus	Serves as a major control center for the autonomic nervous system. Controls water and mineral balance, heart rate and blood pressure, appetite and digestive activity, body temperature, and sexual response. Is involved in sleep and wakefulness and in emotions of anger and fear. Regulates functions of the pituitary gland.
Brain Stem	
Midbrain	Relays sensory impulses from the spinal cord to the thalamus and motor impulses from the cerebrum to the spinal cord. Contains reflex centers that move eyeballs in response to visual stimuli and head and neck in response to auditory stimuli.
Pons	Relays impulses between the midbrain and the medulla and between the cerebellar hemispheres. Helps medulla control breathing.
Medulla	Relays impulses between the brain and spinal cord. Reflex centers control heart rate, blood vessel diameter, breathing, swallowing, vomiting, coughing, sneezing, and hiccupping. Sensory and motor fibers cross over to the opposite side. Reticular formation (also in midbrain and pons) controls wakefulness.

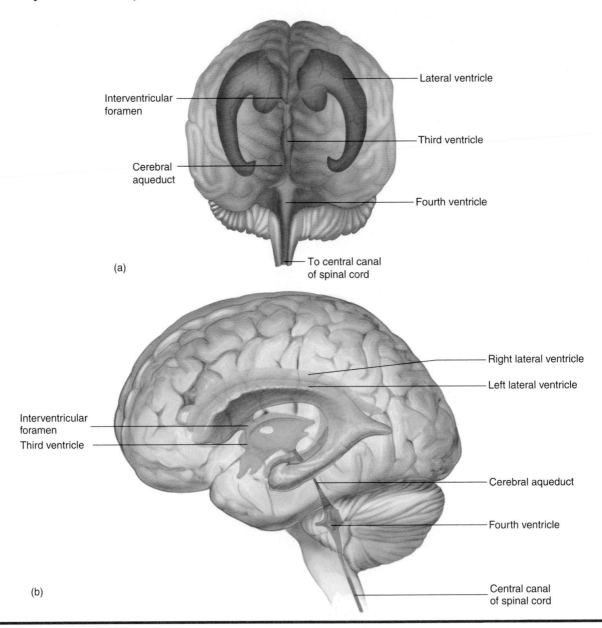

Figure 8.14 Anterior (*a*) and lateral (*b*) views of the ventricles of the brain. Note how they are interconnected. AP|R

8.6 Spinal Cord

The **spinal cord** is continuous with the brain. It descends from the medulla oblongata through the foramen magnum into the vertebral canal and extends to the second lumbar vertebra. Beyond this point, only the proximal portions of the lower spinal nerves occupy the vertebral canal.

Structure

The spinal cord is cylindrical in shape. It has two small grooves that extend throughout its length: the wider *anterior median fissure* and the narrower *posterior median sulcus*. These grooves divide the spinal cord into left and right portions. Thirty-one pairs of spinal nerves branch from the spinal cord.

The cross-sectional structure of the spinal cord is shown in figures 8.11 and 8.16. Gray matter, shaped like the outstretched wings of a butterfly, is centrally located and is surrounded by white matter. The *central canal* extends the length of the spinal cord and contains cerebrospinal fluid.

The pointed projections of the gray matter, as seen in cross section, are called horns. The *anterior horns* contain the cell bodies of motor neurons whose axons enter spinal nerves and carry impulses to muscles and glands. The *posterior horns* contain interneurons that receive impulses from sensory neurons in the spinal nerves and carry them to sites within the central nervous system. Interneurons form most of the gray matter in the central nervous system.

Figure 8.15 Circulation of cerebrospinal fluid. Choroid plexuses in ventricle walls secrete cerebrospinal fluid. The fluid flows through the ventricles, central canal of the spinal cord, and subarachnoid space. It is reabsorbed into the blood of the dural sinus. AP|R

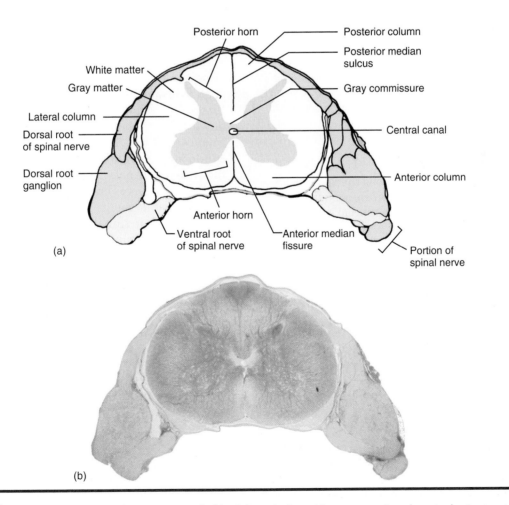

Figure 8.16 A drawing (*a*) and a photomicrograph (*b*) of the spinal cord in cross section show its basic structure. AP|R

In *hydrocephalus*, a congenital defect restricts the movement of cerebrospinal fluid from the ventricles into the subarachnoid space. In severe cases, the buildup of hydrostatic pressure within an infant's brain causes a marked enlargement of the ventricles and brain and widens the fontanels of the cranium. Without treatment, death usually results within two to three years. Treatment involves surgical insertion of a small tube to drain the excess fluid from a ventricle into the peritoneal cavity, where it is reabsorbed.

The horns of the gray matter divide the white matter into three regions: the *anterior, posterior,* and *lateral columns.* These columns are bundles of myelinated axons of interneurons that extend up and down the spinal cord. These bundles are called **nerve tracts.**

Functions

The spinal cord has two basic functions. It transmits impulses to and from the brain, and it serves as a reflex center for spinal reflexes. Impulses are transmitted to and from the brain by myelinated fibers composing the nerve tracts. *Ascending* (sensory) *tracts* carry impulses to the brain; *descending* (motor) *tracts* carry impulses from the brain.

Check My Understanding

11. What is the relationship among the ventricles, the meninges, and the cerebrospinal fluid?
12. What are the functions of the spinal cord?

8.7 Peripheral Nervous System (PNS)

The *peripheral nervous system (PNS)* consists of cranial and spinal nerves that connect the central nervous system to other portions of the body. A **nerve** consists of axons (nerve fibers) that are bound together by connective tissue. **Motor nerves** contain only axons of motor neurons; **sensory nerves** contain only axons of sensory neurons; and **mixed nerves** contain both motor nerve axons and sensory nerve axons. Most nerves are mixed. Nerves may contain fibers of both the somatic nervous system, which is involved with voluntary responses, and the autonomic nervous system, which controls involuntary (automatic) responses.

Cranial Nerves

Twelve pairs of **cranial nerves** arise from the brain and connect the brain with organs and tissues that are primarily located in the head and neck (table 8.3). Most cranial nerves arise from the brain stem. Cranial nerves are identified by both roman numerals and names. The numerals indicate the order in which the nerves arise from the inferior surface of the brain: I is most anterior; XII is most posterior (figure 8.17).

Most cranial nerves are primarily motor nerves, but a few are sensory and some are mixed.

Spinal Nerves

Thirty-one pairs of **spinal nerves** arise from the spinal cord. The first pair branches from the spinal cord between the atlas and the occipital bone. The remaining spinal nerves emerge from the spinal cord and pass between adjacent vertebrae through the *intervertebral foramina.* Spinal nerves are mixed nerves.

Spinal nerves are identified by the spinal region from which they branch and are numbered in sequence within each region. There are eight pairs of *cervical nerves* (C1–C8), twelve pairs of *thoracic nerves* (T1–T12), five pairs of *lumbar nerves* (L1–L5), five pairs of *sacral nerves* (S1–S5), and one pair of *coccygeal nerves* (figure 8.18).

As shown in figure 8.18, the spinal cord ends at the second lumbar vertebra. Proximal portions of lumbar, sacral, and coccygeal spinal nerves continue down the vertebral canal to exit between the appropriate vertebrae. The bases of these nerves form the *cauda equina,* or horse's tail, in the inferior portion of the vertebral canal.

Spinal nerves branch from the spinal cord by two short roots that merge a short distance from the spinal cord to form a spinal nerve. The **anterior root** contains axons of motor neurons whose cell bodies are located within the spinal cord. These neurons carry motor impulses from the spinal cord to effectors. The **posterior root** contains sensory neurons. The swollen region in a posterior root is a **spinal ganglion,** which contains cell bodies of sensory neurons. The long axons of these neurons carry sensory impulses to the spinal cord. Observe these structures and their relationships in figures 8.11, 8.16, and 8.19.

Spinal Plexuses

After a spinal nerve passes through an intervertebral foramen, it divides into two or three major parts: an anterior branch; a posterior branch; and, in thoracic and lumbar spinal nerves only, a visceral branch. The posterior branch continues directly to the innervated structures. The visceral branch passes to the sympathetic chain ganglia and is part of the autonomic

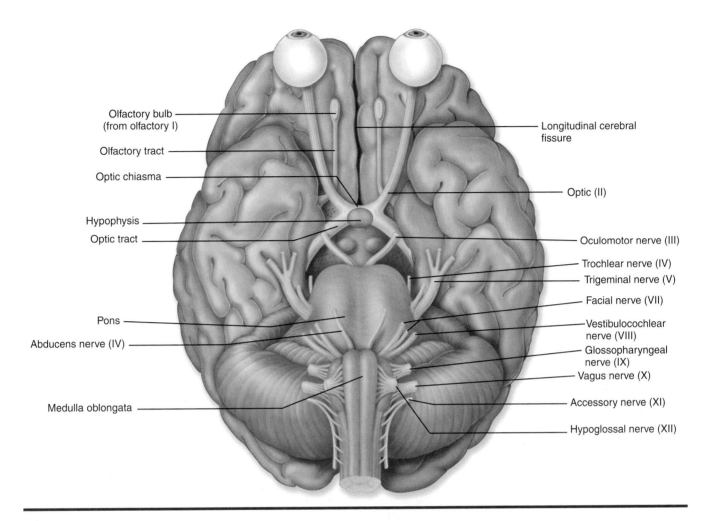

Olfactory bulb
(from olfactory I)

Olfactory tract

Optic chiasma

Hypophysis

Optic tract

Pons

Abducens nerve (IV)

Medulla oblongata

Longitudinal cerebral
fissure

Optic (II)

Oculomotor nerve (III)

Trochlear nerve (IV)

Trigeminal nerve (V)

Facial nerve (VII)

Vestibulocochlear
nerve (VIII)

Glossopharyngeal
nerve (IX)

Vagus nerve (X)

Accessory nerve (XI)

Hypoglossal nerve (XII)

Figure 8.17 A ventral view of the brain showing the roots of the 12 pairs of cranial nerves. Cranial nerves are identified by both roman numerals and names. Most cranial nerves arise from the brain stem. AP|R

system. The anterior branches of many spinal nerves merge to form a **spinal plexus** (plek´-sus), a network of nerves, before continuing to the innervated structures.

In a plexus, the nerve fibers in the anterior branches are sorted and recombined so that fibers going to a specific body part are carried in the same spinal nerve, although they may originate in several different spinal nerves. There are four pairs of plexuses: cervical, brachial, lumbar, and sacral. Because many fibers from the lumbar plexus contribute to the sacral plexus, these two plexuses are sometimes called the *lumbosacral plexuses.* The anterior branches of most thoracic spinal nerves (T2–T11) take a direct route to the skin and muscles of the trunk that they supply (figure 8.18).

Cervical Plexus   The first four cervical nerves (C1–C4) merge to form a *cervical plexus* on each side of the

neck. The nerves from these plexuses supply the muscles and skin of the neck and portions of the head and shoulders. The paired *phrenic* (fren´-ik) *nerves,* which stimulate the diaphragm to contract, producing inspiration, also arise from the cervical plexus.

Brachial Plexus   The last four cervical nerves (C5–C8) and the first thoracic nerve (T1) join to form a *brachial plexus* on each side of the vertebral column in the shoulder region. Nerves that serve skin and muscles of the arms and shoulders emerge from the brachial plexuses. The *musculocutaneous, axillary, radial, median,* and *ulnar nerves* arise here.

Lumbar Plexus   The last thoracic nerve (T12) and the first four lumbar nerves (L1–L4) unite to form a *lumbar plexus* on each side of the vertebral column just above the hip bones. Nerves from the lumbar

Table 8.3 Summary of the Cranial Nerves

Nerve	Type	Function
I Olfactory	Sensory	Transmits sensory impulses from olfactory receptors in nasal mucosa to the brain.
II Optic	Sensory	Transmits sensory impulses for vision from the retina of the eye to the brain.
III Oculomotor	Primarily motor	Transmits motor impulses to muscles that move the eyes upward, downward, and medially; control the eyelids; adjust pupil size; and control the shape of the lens. Transmits sensory impulses associated with the degree of contraction of these muscles to the brain.
IV Trochlear	Primarily motor	Transmits motor impulses to muscles that rotate the eyes. Transmits sensory impulses associated with the degree of contraction of these muscles to the brain.
V Trigeminal	Mixed	Transmits sensory impulses from scalp, forehead, face, teeth, and gums to the brain. Transmits motor impulses to chewing muscles and muscles in floor of mouth.
VI Abducens	Primarily motor	Transmits motor impulses to muscles that move the eyes laterally. Transmits sensory impulses associated with the degree of contraction of these muscles to the brain.
VII Facial	Mixed	Transmits sensory impulses from the anterior part of the tongue to the brain. Transmits motor impulses to facial muscles, salivary glands, and tear glands.
VIII Vestibulocochlear	Sensory	Transmits sensory impulses from the inner ear associated with hearing and equilibrium.
IX Glossopharyngeal	Mixed	Transmits sensory impulses from posterior portion of the tongue, tonsils, pharynx, and carotid arteries to the brain. Transmits motor impulses to salivary glands and pharyngeal muscles used in swallowing.
X Vagus	Mixed	Transmits sensory impulses from thoracic and abdominal organs, esophagus, larynx, and pharynx to the brain. Transmits motor impulses to these organs and to muscles of speech and swallowing.
XI Accessory	Primarily motor	Transmits motor impulses to muscles of the palate, pharynx, and larynx and to the trapezius and sternocleidomastoid muscles. Transmits sensory impulses associated with the degree of contraction of these muscles to the brain.
XII Hypoglossal	Primarily motor	Transmits motor impulses to the muscles of the tongue. Transmits sensory impulses associated with the degree of contraction of these muscles to the brain.

plexuses supply the skin and muscles of the lower trunk, genitalia, and part of the thighs. The *femoral* and *obturator nerves* arise here.

Sacral Plexus The last two lumbar nerves (L4–L5) and the first four sacral nerves (S1–S4) merge to form a *sacral plexus* on each side of the sacrum within the pelvic girdle. Nerves from the sacral plexuses supply the skin and muscles of the buttocks and legs. The *sciatic nerves,* which emerge from the sacral plexuses, are the largest nerves in the body.

Check My Understanding

13. What composes the peripheral nervous system?
14. What is a spinal plexus?
15. Name and locate the major spinal plexuses.

Reflexes

Reflexes are rapid, involuntary, and predictable responses to internal and external stimuli. Reflexes maintain homeostasis and enhance chances of survival. A reflex involves either the brain or spinal cord, a receptor, sensory and motor neurons, and an effector.

Most pathways of impulse transmission within the nervous system are complex and involve many neurons. In contrast, reflexes require few neurons in their pathways and therefore produce very rapid responses to stimuli. Reflex pathways are called **reflex arcs**.

Reflexes are divided into two types: autonomic and somatic. *Autonomic reflexes* act on smooth muscle, cardiac muscle, and glands. They are involved in controlling homeostatic processes such as heart rate, blood pressure, and digestion. Autonomic reflexes

Posterior view

Cervical plexus (C1–C4)

Brachial plexus (C5–T1)

Musculocutaneous nerve

Axillary nerve

Radial nerve

Median nerve

Ulnar nerve

Phrenic nerve

Intercostal nerves

C1
C2
C3
C4
C5
C6
C7
C8
T1
T2
T3
T4
T5
T6
T7
T8
T9
T10
T11
T12
L1
L2
L3
L4
L5
S1
S2
S3
S4
S5
Co

Cauda equina

Femoral nerve

Obturator nerve

Sciatic nerve

Lumbosacral plexus (T12–S5)

Figure 8.18 Thirty-one pairs of spinal nerves arise from the spinal cord. Anterior branches of spinal nerves in the thorax form the intercostal nerves. Those in other regions form nerve networks called plexuses before continuing on to their target tissues. AP|R

maintain homeostasis and normal body functions at the unconscious level, which frees the mind to deal with those actions that require conscious decisions. *Somatic reflexes* act on skeletal muscles. They enable quick movements such as moving your hand away from a painful stimulus. A person is usually unaware of autonomic reflexes but is aware of somatic reflexes.

Figure 8.19 illustrates a somatic spinal reflex, which withdraws the hand after sticking a finger with a tack. Three neurons are involved in this reflex. Pain receptors are stimulated by the sharp pin and form impulses that are carried by a sensory neuron to an interneuron in the spinal cord. Impulses pass along the interneuron to a motor neuron, which carries the impulses to a muscle that contracts to move the hand.

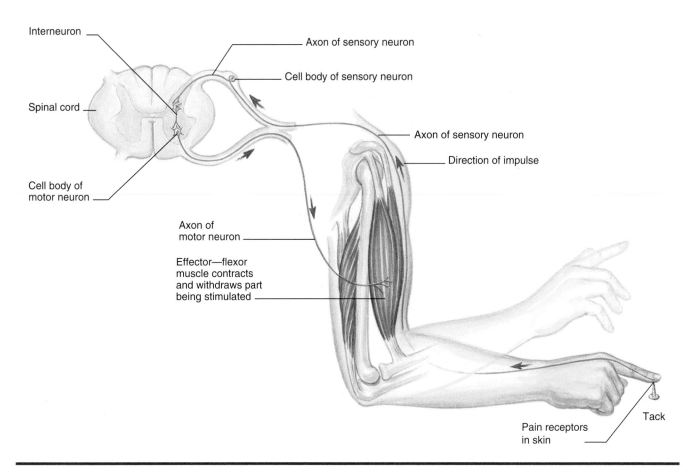

Interneuron

Axon of sensory neuron

Cell body of sensory neuron

Spinal cord

Axon of sensory neuron

Direction of impulse

Cell body of
motor neuron

Axon of
motor neuron

Effector—flexor
muscle contracts
and withdraws part
being stimulated

Tack

Pain receptors
in skin

Figure 8.19 A withdrawal reflex involves a sensory neuron, an interneuron, and a motor neuron. AP|R

Clinical **INSIGHT**

Because the spinal cord ends at the level of the second lumbar vertebra, spinal taps and epidural anesthetics are administered inferior to this point. For these procedures, a patient is placed in a fetal position in order to open the spaces between the posterior margins of the vertebrae. A hypodermic needle is inserted through the intervertebral disk either between the third and fourth lumbar vertebrae or between the fourth and fifth lumbar vertebrae. In a *spinal tap* (lumbar puncture), a hypodermic needle is inserted into the subarachnoid space to remove spinal fluid for diagnostic purposes. An *epidural anesthetic* is given by injecting an anesthetic into the epidural space with a hypodermic syringe. The anesthetic prevents sensory impulses from reaching the spinal cord via spinal nerves inferior to the injection. Epidurals are sometimes used to ease pain during childbirth.

Although the brain is not involved in this reflex, it does receive sensory impulses that make a person aware of a painful stimulus resulting in the quick withdrawal of the hand.

Check My Understanding

16. What is a reflex?
17. What are the components of a spinal reflex?

Clinical **INSIGHT**

Because the responses of reflexes are predictable, physicians usually test a patient's reflexes in order to determine the health of the nervous system. Exaggerated, diminished, or distorted reflexes may indicate a neurological disorder.

8.8 Autonomic Nervous System (ANS)

The **autonomic** (aw-to-nom´-ik) **nervous system (ANS)** consists of portions of the central and peripheral nervous systems, and it functions involuntarily without conscious control. Its role is to maintain homeostasis in response to changing internal conditions. The effectors under autonomic control are cardiac muscle, smooth muscle, and glands. The ANS functions mostly by involuntary reflexes. Sensory impulses carried to the autonomic reflex centers in the hypothalamus, brain stem, or spinal cord cause motor impulses to be carried to effectors via cranial or spinal nerves. Higher brain centers, such as the limbic system and cerebral cortex, influence the ANS during times of emotional stress.

Table 8.4 compares the somatic and autonomic nervous systems.

Organization

Autonomic nerve fibers are motor fibers. Unlike the somatic nervous system, in which a single motor neuron extends from the central nervous system to an effector, the ANS uses two motor neurons in sequence to carry motor impulses to an effector. The first neuron, or *preganglionic neuron,* extends from the CNS to an **autonomic ganglion,** a mass of neuron cell bodies. The cell body of the preganglionic neuron is located in the brain or spinal cord. The second neuron, or *postganglionic neuron,* extends from the autonomic ganglion to the visceral effector, and its cell body is located within the autonomic ganglion (figure 8.20).

The autonomic nervous system is subdivided into the **sympathetic division** and the **parasympathetic division.** The origin of their motor neurons and the organs innervated are shown in figure 8.21.

Preganglionic fibers of the sympathetic division arise from the thoracic and lumbar regions of the spinal cord—spinal nerves T1–L2. Some sympathetic fibers branch from the spinal nerves to synapse with postganglionic neurons in autonomic ganglia that are arranged in two chains, one on each side of the vertebral column. These ganglia are called *paravertebral* or *sympathetic chain ganglia.* Other sympathetic preganglionic fibers pass through a paravertebral chain ganglion without synapsing and extend to another type of ganglion, a *collateral ganglion,* before synapsing with a postganglionic neuron. Both pathways are shown in Figure 8.21.

Preganglionic fibers of the parasympathetic division arise from the brain stem and sacral region (S2–S4) of the spinal cord. They extend through cranial or sacral nerves to synapse with postganglionic neurons within ganglia that are located very near or within visceral organs (figure 8.21).

Most visceral organs receive postganglionic fibers of both the sympathetic and parasympathetic divisions; but a few, such as sweat glands and most blood vessels, receive only sympathetic fibers. Figure 8.22 summarizes the organizational differences between the sympathetic and parasympathetic divisions.

Autonomic Neurotransmitters

Preganglionic fibers of both the sympathetic and parasympathetic divisions secrete *acetylcholine* to initiate impulses in postganglionic neurons, but their postganglionic fibers secrete different neurotransmitters. Sympathetic postganglionic fibers secrete norepinephrine, a substance similar to adrenalin, and they are called *adrenergic fibers.* Parasympathetic postganglionic fibers secrete acetylcholine and thus are called *cholinergic fibers* (figure 8.22).

Table 8.4	**Comparison of Somatic and Autonomic Nervous Systems**	
	Somatic	**Autonomic**
Control	Voluntary	Involuntary
Neural Pathway	One motor neuron extends from the CNS to an effector	A preganglionic neuron extends from the CNS to an autonomic ganglion and synapses with a postganglionic neuron that extends to an effector
Neurotransmitters	Acetylcholine	Acetylcholine or norepinephrine
Effectors	Skeletal muscles	Smooth muscle, cardiac muscle, and glands
Action	Excitatory	Excitatory or inhibitory

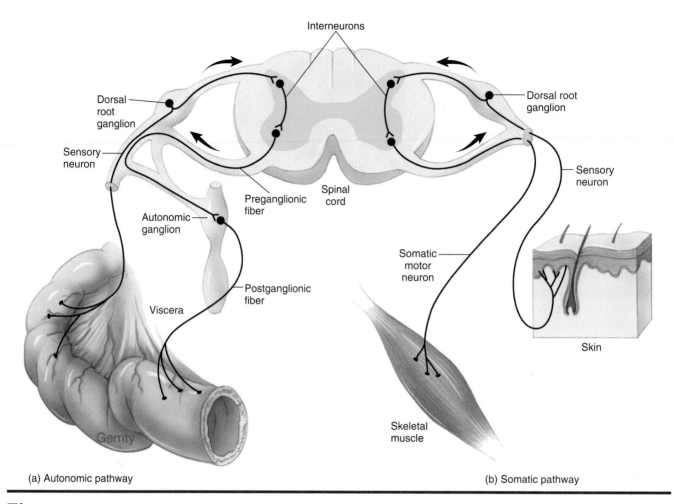

Figure 8.20 Comparison of autonomic and somatic motor pathways in spinal nerves. (*a*) An autonomic pathway involves a presynaptic neuron and a postsynaptic neuron that synapse at a ganglion outside the spinal cord. (*b*) A somatic pathway involves a single neuron.

Functions

Both sympathetic and parasympathetic divisions stimulate some visceral organs and inhibit others, but their effects on a given organ are opposite. For example, the sympathetic division increases heart rate whereas the parasympathetic division slows heart rate. The contrasting effects are due to the different neurotransmitters secreted by postganglionic sympathetic and parasympathetic fibers and the receptors of the receiving organs.

The sympathetic division prepares the body for physical action to meet emergencies. Its action has been summarized as preparing the body for *fight or flight.* The parasympathetic division is dominant under the normal, nonstressful conditions of everyday life, and its actions are usually opposite those of the sympathetic division. Table 8.5 compares some of the effects of the sympathetic and parasympathetic divisions on visceral organs.

Check My Understanding

18. How do the somatic and autonomic nervous systems differ?
19. How does the autonomic nervous system maintain homeostasis?

Clinical INSIGHT

Cocaine exerts a major effect on the autonomic nervous system. It not only stimulates the sympathetic division but also inhibits the parasympathetic division. In an overdose, this double-barreled action produces an erratic, uncontrollable heartbeat that may result in sudden death.

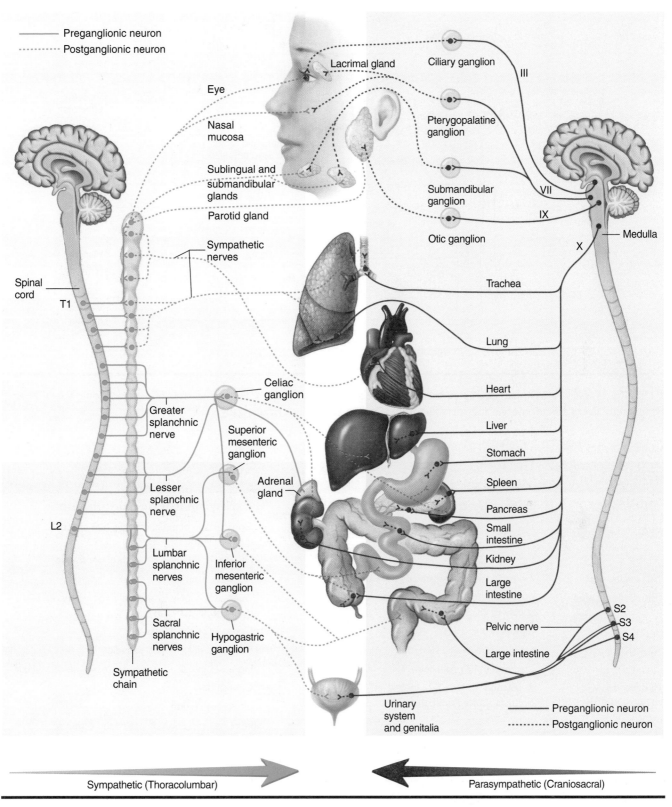

Preganglionic neuron
Postganglionic neuron

Lacrimal gland
Ciliary ganglion
III
Eye
Pterygopalatine ganglion
Nasal mucosa
Submandibular ganglion
VII
Sublingual and submandibular glands
IX
Parotid gland
Otic ganglion
Medulla
Sympathetic nerves
X
Spinal cord
Trachea
T1
Lung
Heart
Liver
Celiac ganglion
Stomach
Greater splanchnic nerve
Spleen
Superior mesenteric ganglion
Pancreas
Lesser splanchnic nerve
Adrenal gland
Small intestine
Kidney
L2
Large intestine
Lumbar splanchnic nerves
Inferior mesenteric ganglion
S2
S3
Sacral splanchnic nerves
Pelvic nerve
S4
Hypogastric ganglion
Large intestine
Sympathetic chain
Urinary system and genitalia
Preganglionic neuron
Postganglionic neuron

Sympathetic (Thoracolumbar)   Parasympathetic (Craniosacral)

Figure 8.21 Innervation of internal organs by the autonomic nervous system. AP|R

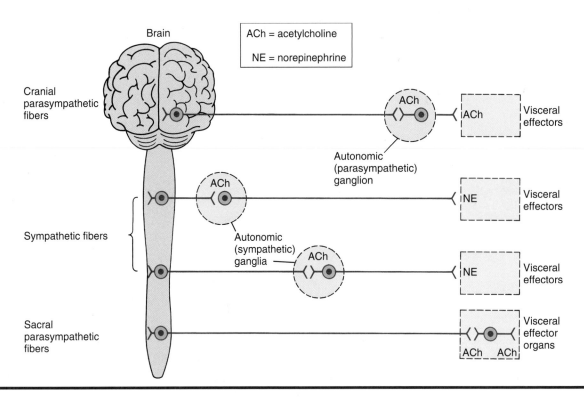

Figure 8.22 Parasympathetic fibers are cholinergic and secrete acetylcholine at the ends of postganglionic fibers. Most sympathetic fibers are adrenergic and secrete norepinephrine at the ends of postganglionic fibers.

Table 8.5	Representative Actions of the Autonomic Nervous System	
Effector	**Sympathetic Stimulation**	**Parasympathetic Stimulation**
Eye	Dilation of pupil; changes lens shape for far vision	Constriction of pupil; changes lens shape for near vision
Heart	Increases rate and strength of contraction	Decreases rate and strength of contraction
Arterioles	Constriction increases blood pressure	No known action
Blood distribution	Increases supply to skeletal muscles; decreases supply to digestive organs	Decreases supply to skeletal muscles; increases supply to digestive organs
Lungs	Dilates bronchioles	Constricts bronchioles
Digestive tract	Inhibits motility and secretion by glands	Promotes motility and secretion by glands
Liver	Decreases bile production; increases blood glucose	Increases bile production; decreases blood glucose
Gallbladder	Relaxation	Contraction
Kidneys	Decreases urine production	No known action
Pancreas	Decreases secretion of insulin and digestive enzymes	Increases secretion of insulin and digestive enzymes
Spleen	Constriction injects stored blood into circulation	No known action
Urinary bladder	Contraction of external sphincter; relaxation of bladder wall	Relaxation of external sphincter; contraction of bladder wall
Reproductive organs	Vasoconstriction; ejaculation in males; reverse uterine contractions in females; stimulates uterine contractions in childbirth	Vasodilation; erection in males; vaginal secretion in females

8.9 Disorders of the Nervous System

The disorders of the nervous system may be categorized as either inflammatory or noninflammatory disorders.

Inflammatory Disorders

Meningitis (men-in-jī´-tis) results from a bacterial, fungal, or viral infection of the meninges. Bacterial meningitis cases are the most serious, with about 20% being fatal. If the brain is also involved, the disease is called *encephalitis.* Some viruses causing encephalitis are transmitted by bites of certain mosquitoes.

Neuritis is the inflammation of a nerve or nerves. It may be caused by several factors such as infection, compression, or trauma. Associated pain may be moderate or severe.

Sciatica (sī-at´-i-kah) is neuritis involving the sciatic nerve. The pain may be severe and often radiates down the thigh and leg.

Shingles is an infection of one or more nerves. It is caused by the reactivation of the chicken pox virus, which, until that time, has been dormant in the nerve root. The virus causes painful blisters on the skin at the sensory nerve endings, followed by prolonged pain.

Noninflammatory Disorders

Alzheimer's (alts´-hī-merz) **disease (AD)** is a progressively disabling disease affecting older persons. It is associated with a loss of certain cholinergic neurons in the brain and a reduced ability of neurons to secrete acetylcholine. AD is characterized by a progressive loss of memory, disorientation, and mood swings.

Cerebral palsy (ser-ē´-bral pawl-zē) is characterized by partial paralysis and sometimes a degree of mental retardation. It may result from damage to the brain during prenatal development, often from viral infections caused by German measles, or from trauma during delivery.

Cerebrovascular accidents (CVAs) are disorders of blood vessels serving the brain. They result from blood clots, aneurysms (an´-ū-rizm), or hemorrhage. Often called strokes, CVAs cause severe damage to the brain. They are a major cause of disability and the third highest cause of death in the United States.

Comas are states of unconsciousness in which the patient cannot be aroused even with vigorous stimulation. Illness or trauma to the brain may alter the functioning of the reticular formation, resulting in a coma.

Concussion results from a severe jarring of the brain caused by a blow to the head. Unconsciousness, confusion, and amnesia may result in severe cases.

Dyslexia (dis-lek´-sē-ah) causes the afflicted person to reverse letters or syllables in words and words within sentences. It results from malfunctioning of the language center of the cerebrum.

Epilepsy (ep´-i-lep˝-sē) may have a hereditary basis, or it may be triggered by injuries, infections, or tumors. There are two types of epilepsy. *Grand mal epilepsy* is the more serious form and is characterized by convulsive seizures. *Petit mal epilepsy* is the less serious form and is characterized by momentary loss of contact with reality without unconsciousness or convulsions.

Fainting is a brief loss of consciousness due to a sudden reduction in blood supply to the brain. It may result from either physical or psychological causes.

Headaches may result from several physical or psychological causes, but they often result from a dilation of blood vessels within the meninges of the brain. Migraine headaches have visual or digestive side effects and may result from stress, allergies, or fatigue. Sinus headaches may result from inflammation that causes increased pressure within the sinuses. Some headaches result from tension in muscles of the head and neck.

Mental illnesses may be broadly categorized as either neuroses or psychoses. *Neuroses* are mild maladjustments to life situations that may produce anxiety and interfere with normal behavior. *Psychoses* are serious mental disorders that sometimes cause delusions, hallucinations, or withdrawal from reality.

Multiple sclerosis (MS) is a progressive degeneration of the myelin sheath around neuron processes in the CNS, accompanied by the formation of plaques of scar tissue called *scleroses.* This destruction results in a short-circuiting of neural pathways and an impairment of motor functions.

Neuralgia (nū-ral´-jē-ah) is pain arising from a nerve regardless of the cause of the pain.

Paralysis is the permanent loss of motor control of body parts. It most commonly results from accidental injury to the CNS.

Parkinson's disease is caused by an insufficient production of *dopamine* by neurons in certain basal nuclei within the cerebrum. It produces tremors and impairs normal skeletal muscle contractions. Parkinson's disease is more common among older persons.

CHAPTER SUMMARY

8.1 Divisions of the Nervous System

- Anatomical divisions are the central nervous system (CNS), composed of the brain and spinal cord, and the peripheral nervous system (PNS), composed of cranial and spinal nerves.
- Functional divisions are the sensory and motor divisions. The motor division is subdivided into the somatic nervous system (SNS), which is involved in voluntary actions, and the autonomic nervous system (ANS), which is involved in involuntary responses.

8.2 Nerve Tissue

- Nerve tissue consists of neurons and neuroglial cells.
- A neuron is composed of a cell body, which contains the nucleus; one or more dendrites that conduct impulses toward the cell body or axon; and one axon that conducts impulses away from the cell body or dendrites.
- Myelinated neuron processes are covered by a myelin sheath. Schwann cells form the myelin sheath and neurilemma of peripheral myelinated nerve fibers. Oligodendrocytes form the myelin sheath of myelinated nerve fibers in the CNS; these fibers lack a neurilemma.
- There are three functional types of neurons. Sensory neurons carry impulses toward the CNS. Interneurons carry impulses within the CNS. Motor neurons carry impulses from the CNS.
- Schwann cells are the only neuroglial cells in the PNS. Four types of neuroglial cells occur in the CNS: oligodendrocytes, astrocytes, microglial cells, and ependymal cells.

8.3 Neuron Physiology

- Neurons are specialized to form and conduct impulses.
- The membrane of a resting neuron is polarized with an excess of positive ions outside the cell and negative ions inside the cell.
- When a threshold stimulus is applied, the neuron membrane becomes permeable to sodium ions (Na^+), which quickly move into the neuron and cause depolarization of the membrane. This depolarization is the formation of a nerve impulse.
- The depolarized portion of the membrane causes the depolarization of adjacent portions so that a depolarization wave (impulse) flows along the neuron.
- Depolarization makes the neuron membrane permeable to potassium ions (K^+), and they quickly diffuse out of the neuron, which repolarizes the membrane.
- In synaptic transmission, the axon tip of the presynaptic neuron secretes a neurotransmitter into the synaptic cleft. The neurotransmitter reacts with receptors on the postsynaptic neuron, causing either the formation of an impulse or the inhibition of impulse formation. Then, the neurotransmitter is quickly removed by an enzymatic reaction.
- The most common peripheral neurotransmitters are acetylcholine and norepinephrine. Some neurotransmitters are excitatory, and others are inhibitory.

8.4 Protection for the Central Nervous System

- The brain is encased by the cranial bones, and the spinal cord is surrounded by vertebrae.
- Both the brain and spinal cord are covered by the meninges: the pia mater, arachnoid mater, and dura mater.
- Cerebrospinal fluid in the subarachnoid space serves as a fluid shock absorber.

8.5 Brain

- The brain consists of the cerebrum, diencephalon, brain stem, and cerebellum.
- The cerebrum consists of two cerebral hemispheres joined by the corpus callosum. Gyri and sulci increase the surface area of the cerebral cortex. Each hemisphere is subdivided into four lobes: frontal, parietal, temporal, and occipital.
- The cerebrum interprets sensations; initiates voluntary motor responses; and is involved in will, personality traits, and intellectual processes. The left cerebral hemisphere is dominant in most people.
- Sensory interpretation areas occur in the parietal, temporal, and occipital lobes. Motor areas occur in the frontal lobe. Association areas occur in all lobes of the cerebrum.
- The diencephalon consists of the thalamus and the hypothalamus.
- The thalamus is formed of two lateral masses connected by the intermediate mass. It is a relay station for sensory and motor impulses going to and from the cerebrum and provides an uncritical awareness of sensations.
- The hypothalamus is located below the thalamus and forms the floor of the third ventricle. It is a major control center for the autonomic nervous system, and it regulates several homeostatic processes such as body temperature, mineral and water balance, appetite, digestive processes, and secretion of pituitary hormones.
- The limbic system is associated with emotional behavior and memory.
- The brain stem consists of the midbrain, pons, and medulla oblongata. Ascending and descending fibers between higher brain centers and the spinal cord pass through the brain stem.

- The midbrain is a small, superior portion of the brain stem. It contains reflex centers for movements associated with visual and auditory stimuli.
- The pons is the intermediate portion of the brain stem. It works with the medulla oblongata to control breathing.
- The medulla oblongata is the lowest portion of the brain stem and is continuous with the spinal cord. It contains reflexive control centers that control breathing, heart rate, and blood pressure.
- The reticular formation consists of nuclei in the brain stem and fibers that extend to the cerebrum. It is involved with wakefulness and sleep.
- The cerebellum lies posterior to the fourth ventricle. It is composed of two hemispheres separated by the vermis, and it coordinates skeletal muscle contractions.
- The ventricles of the brain, the central canal of the spinal cord, and the subarachnoid space around the brain and spinal cord are filled with cerebrospinal fluid. Cerebrospinal fluid is secreted by a choroid plexus in each ventricle.
- Cerebrospinal fluid is absorbed into blood of the sagittal sinus in the dura mater.

8.6 Spinal Cord

- The spinal cord extends from the medulla oblongata down the vertebral canal to the second lumbar vertebra.
- Gray matter is located interiorly and is surrounded by white matter. Anterior horns of gray matter contain motor neuron cell bodies; posterior horns contain interneuron cell bodies. White matter contains ascending and descending tracts of myelinated neuron processes.
- The spinal cord serves as a reflex center and conducting pathway for impulses between the brain and spinal nerves.

8.7 Peripheral Nervous System (PNS)

- The PNS consists of cranial and spinal nerves. Most nerves are mixed nerves; a few cranial nerves are sensory only. A nerve contains bundles of nerve fibers (neuron processes) supported by connective tissue.

- The 12 pairs of cranial nerves are identified by roman numeral and name. The 31 pairs of spinal nerves are divided into 8 cervical, 12 thoracic, 5 lumbar, 5 sacral, and 1 coccygeal nerve.
- Anterior branches of many spinal nerves form plexuses where nerve fibers are sorted and recombined so that all fibers to a particular organ are carried in the same nerve. The four pairs of plexuses are cervical, brachial, lumbar, and sacral plexuses.

8.8 Autonomic Nervous System (ANS)

- The ANS involves portions of the central and peripheral nervous systems that are involved in involuntary maintenance of homeostasis.
- Two ANS neurons are used to activate an effector. The presynaptic neuron arises from the CNS and ends in an autonomic ganglion, where it synapses with a postsynaptic neuron that continues on to the effector.
- The ANS is divided into two subdivisions that generally have antagonistic effects. Nerves of the sympathetic division arise from the thorax and lumbar regions of the spinal cord and prepare the body to meet emergencies. Nerves of the parasympathetic division arise from the brain and sacral region of the spinal cord and function mainly in nonstressful situations.

8.9 Disorders of the Nervous System

- Disorders may result from infectious diseases, degeneration from unknown causes, malfunctions, and physical injury.
- Inflammatory neurological disorders include meningitis, neuritis, sciatica, and shingles.
- Noninflammatory neurological disorders include Alzheimer's disease, cerebral palsy, CVAs, comas, concussion, dyslexia, epilepsy, fainting, headaches, mental illness, multiple sclerosis, neuralgia, paralysis, and Parkinson's disease.

BUILDING MY VOCABULARY

1. **Selected New Terms**
   acetylcholine, p. 159
   action potential, p. 158
   arachnoid mater, p. 161
   cerebellum, p. 165
   cerebrum, p. 161
   dura mater, p. 161
   interneuron, p. 155
   limbic system, p. 164
   medulla oblongata, p. 164
   motor neuron, p. 155

   nerve tracts, p. 168
   norepinephrine, p. 159
   pia mater, p. 161
   resting potential, p. 157
   reticular formation, p. 164
   sensory neuron, p. 155
   spinal plexus, p. 169
   synaptic cleft, p. 158
   synaptic knob, p. 158
   ventricle, p. 165

2. **Related Clinical Terms**

Analgesic (an-al-jē´-sik) A pain-relieving drug.

Encephalopathy (en-se-fa-lop´-a-thē) Any disorder or disease of the brain.

Hemiplegia (hem-i-plē´-jē-ah) Paralysis of one side of the body.

Neurology (nū-rol´-ō-jē) Branch of medicine dealing with disorders of the nervous system.

Paraplegia (par-ah-plē´-jē-ah) Paralysis of both legs.

Psychiatry (si-kī´-ah-trē) Branch of medicine that treats mental illness.

SELF-REVIEW

Answers are located in appendix B.

1. Impulses are carried away from a neuron cell body by the _____.
2. Neurons that conduct impulses from place to place within the CNS are _____.
3. An impulse is formed by the sudden flow of _____ ions through the plasma membrane into a neuron.
4. Synaptic transmission is dependent upon the secretion of a _____ by an axon's synaptic knob.
5. Impulses pass from one cerebral hemisphere to the other over neuron processes composing the _____.
6. Voluntary muscle contractions are controlled by the _____ lobe of the cerebrum.
7. Intelligence, will, and memory are functions of the _____.
8. The _____ regulates appetite, water balance, and body temperature.
9. The _____ regulates heart and breathing rates.
10. Coordination of body movements is a function of the _____.
11. Cerebrospinal fluid fills the ventricles of the brain and the _____ space of the meninges.
12. The _____ is a conducting pathway between the brain and spinal nerves.
13. The _____ roots of spinal nerves consist of axons of motor neurons.
14. The _____ nervous system is involved in involuntary responses that maintain homeostasis.
15. The _____ division prepares the body for physical responses to emergencies.

CRITICAL THINKING

1. Complete the learning objectives on the first page of this chapter.
2. Distinguish between dendrites, axons, nerve fibers, and nerves.
3. Explain the roles of Na⁺, K⁺, negative ions, and plasma membranes in neuron function.
4. If you touch a hot stove, a reflexive withdrawal of your hand is triggered at about the same time that you feel the pain. Describe the roles of the PNS and CNS in your response and sensation.
5. What composes the ANS, and how does the ANS maintain homeostasis?

Visit this book's website at www.mhhe.com/ gunstream5 for practice quizzes, learning exercises, case studies, and other study tools.

CHAPTER 9

Senses

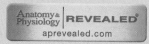

Module 7
Nervous System

SELECTED KEY TERMS

Accommodation The focusing of light rays on the retina by the lens.

Chemoreceptor A sensory receptor that is stimulated by certain chemicals.

Choroid coat (choroid = membranelike) The middle layer of the eyeball.

Cochlea (cochlea = snail) The coiled portion of the inner ear containing the receptors for hearing.

Cones Photoreceptors for color vision.

Cornea The transparent window through which light enters the eye.

Dynamic equilibrium Maintenance of balance when the head and body are in motion.

Mechanoreceptor A sensory receptor that is stimulated by certain mechanical forces such as pressure or touch.

Photoreceptor (photo = light) A sensory receptor that is stimulated by light.

Projection The process by which the brain makes a sensation seem to come from the body part being stimulated.

Referred pain The projection of pain to a site different than the source of the pain.

Retina (retin = net) The inner layer of the eye, which contains the photoreceptors.

Rods Photoreceptors for black and white vision.

Sclera (scler = hard) The outer layer of the eye.

Semicircular canals The portion of the inner ear containing the receptors for dynamic equilibrium.

Sensory adaptation The decrease in the formation of impulses by a receptor when repeatedly stimulated by the same stimulus.

Spiral organ (Organ of Corti) The sense organ in the inner ear containing the receptors for hearing.

Static equilibrium The maintenance of balance when the head and body are not in motion.

O ur senses constantly inform us of what is going on in our environment so that our body can take appropriate voluntary or involuntary action and maintain homeostasis. Several different types of **sensory receptors** are involved, and they send impulses to the central nervous system, which initiates the appropriate response.

The senses may be subdivided into two broad categories: general senses and special senses. *General senses* include pain, touch, pressure, cold, and heat. *Special senses* are taste, smell, vision, hearing, and equilibrium. Each of the senses depends upon (1) receptors, which detect environmental changes and form impulses; (2) sensory neurons (nerve fibers), which carry the impulses to the CNS; and (3) the brain, which interprets the impulses. The five types of sensory receptors, based on the specific stimuli to which they respond, are listed in table 9.1.

9.1 Sensations

Each type of sensory receptor is sensitive to a particular type of stimulus that causes the receptor to form impulses. These impulses are carried by cranial or spinal nerves to the central nervous system. **Sensations** result from an interpretation of impulses reaching sensory areas of the cerebral cortex. Because all impulses are alike, sensations are determined by the area of the cerebral cortex receiving the impulses rather than by the type of receptor forming the impulses. For example, all impulses reaching the visual center of the occipital lobe are interpreted as visual sensations.

Table 9.1	Types of Sensory Receptors
Type	**Stimulus Detected**
Thermoreceptors	Temperature changes
Mechanoreceptors	Mechanical forces
Pain receptors	Tissue damage
Chemoreceptors	Concentration of chemicals
Photoreceptors	Light energy

A strong blow to an eye or to the back of the head may produce a visual sensation (flashes of light), although the stimulus is mechanical.

The intensity of a sensation is dependent upon the frequency of impulses reaching the cerebral cortex. The greater the frequency of impulses, the greater is the intensity of the sensation. Of course, the frequency of impulses sent to the brain is, in turn, dependent upon the action of receptors. The greater the intensity of a stimulus, the greater the frequency of impulse formation by receptors.

Projection

Whenever a sensation occurs, the cerebral cortex projects the sensation back to the body region where the impulses originate so that the sensation seems to come from that region. This phenomenon is called **projection**. For example, if your thumb is injured, the pain is projected back to your thumb, and you are aware that your thumb hurts. Similarly, projection of visual and auditory sensations gives the feeling that eyes see and ears hear. The projection of sensations has obvious survival value in pinpointing the source of a sensation, because it allows corrective action to remove harmful stimuli.

Adaptation

If a receptor is repeatedly stimulated by the same stimulus, the rate of impulse formation may decline until impulses may not be formed at all. This phenomenon is called **sensory adaptation**. For example, when the odor of perfume is first encountered, it is very noticeable. But as the olfactory receptors become adapted to the stimulus, the strength of the sensation rapidly declines until the odor is hardly noticeable. Adaptation prevents overloading the nervous system with unimportant stimuli, such as clothes touching the body. Once a receptor is adapted, a stronger stimulus is needed to form impulses.

9.2 General Senses

Receptors for the general senses are widely distributed in the skin, muscles, tendons, and visceral organs.

Temperature

Two types of **thermoreceptors** are located in the skin. *Heat receptors* are located deep in the dermis, and they are most sensitive to temperatures above 25°C (77°F). Temperatures above 45°C (113°F) stimulate the formation of impulses that are interpreted as painful,

burning sensations. *Cold receptors* are located closer to the surface of the dermis. They are most sensitive to temperatures below 20°C (68°F). Temperatures below 10°C (50°F) stimulate impulses that are interpreted as very cold and painful sensations. Thermoreceptors adapt very quickly to constant stimulation.

Pressure and Touch

Pressure and touch receptors are **mechanoreceptors** (mek-ah-nō-rē-cep′tors), which are sensitive to mechanical stimuli displacing the tissue in which they are located. *Pacinian corpuscles* are pressure receptors located deep in the dermis and in ligaments and tendons of joints, where they respond to stimulation by pressure.

There are two kinds of touch receptors: Meissner's corpuscles and free nerve endings (figure 9.1). **Meissner's** (mīz′-nerz) **corpuscles** are located in the superficial layer of the dermis, often in dermal papillae. They are most abundant in hairless portions of the skin, such as fingertips, palms, and lips. Meissner's corpuscles are especially sensitive to very light stimuli, such as the motion of objects that barely touch the skin. *Free nerve endings* are abundant in epithelial and connective tissues and are widely distributed in internal organs. In the skin, they extend from the dermis upward between the cells of the epidermis. Free nerve endings are most important as pain receptors, but they also function as receptors for

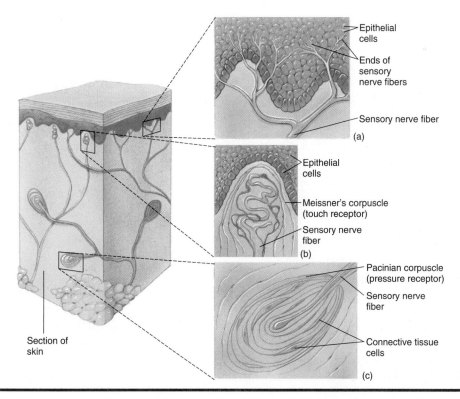

Figure 9.1 Touch and pressure receptors. (*a*) Free nerve endings and (*b*) Meissner's corpuscles are touch receptors located near the surface of the skin. (*c*) Pacinian corpuscles are pressure receptors located deep in the dermis.

touch, itch, and temperature. Some free nerve endings are wrapped around the base of hair follicles, where they are stimulated by movement of the hair shaft.

Proprioceptors

Proprioceptors are another type of mechanoreceptor. They are located in skeletal muscles and tendons. They form impulses that inform the CNS of the degree of stretching or contraction of skeletal muscles, which helps to maintain posture, equilibrium, and muscle tone. The impulses they send to the CNS also help to keep us informed about the positioning of our arms and legs.

Pain

Receptors for the sense of pain are **free nerve endings**, which are widespread in body tissues, except in the neural tissue of the brain. They are especially abundant in the skin, the organ that is in direct contact with the external environment. Pain receptors are stimulated whenever tissues are damaged, and the pain sensation initiates actions by the central nervous system to remove the source of the stimulation. Further, pain receptors do not easily adapt like many other receptors. They adapt slowly or not at all.

Referred Pain

Projection by the cerebral cortex is not always accurate when the impulses originate from pain receptors in visceral organs. When damage to visceral organs occurs, pain may seem to be located in some part of the body wall. Such pain is called **referred pain**.

Referred pain is consistent from person to person, and it is important in the diagnosis of many disorders. For example, pain caused by a heart attack seems to come from the left anterior chest wall, left shoulder, and left arm. Referred pain seems to be projected along common nerves used by neurons carrying impulses from both the body wall and visceral organs. For example, neurons carrying impulses from the heart use the same nerves as those from the left shoulder and arm (figure 9.2).

Check My Understanding

1. What parts of the nervous system are involved in the development of a sensation?
2. What sensory receptors are located within the skin?

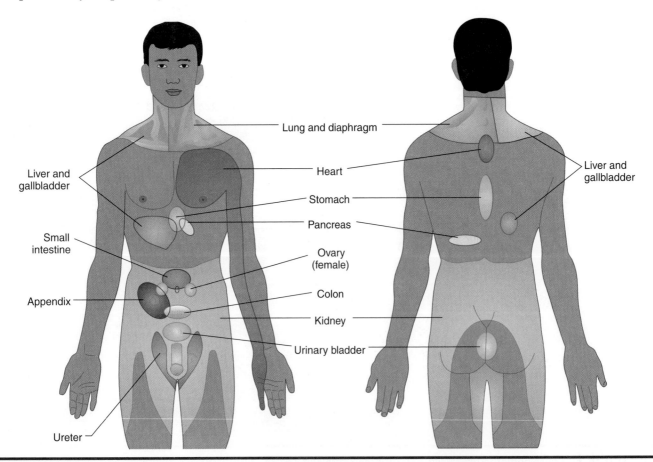

Figure 9.2 Surface regions to which visceral pain originating from various internal organs may be referred.

Clinical INSIGHT

Pain is unpleasant, but it has obvious survival value. It informs us of tissue damage and enables us to protect ourselves from further damage by either avoiding painful stimuli or seeking medical help.

9.3 Special Senses

The receptors for special senses are localized rather than widely distributed, and they, like all receptors, are specialized to respond to only certain types of stimuli. There are three different kinds of receptors for the special senses. Taste and smell receptors are **chemoreceptors**, which are sensitive to chemical substances. Receptors for hearing are **mechanoreceptors,** which are sensitive to vibrations formed by sound waves. Receptors for vision are **photoreceptors**, which are sensitive to light rays.

Taste

The chemoreceptors for taste are located in specialized microscopic organs called **taste buds**. Taste buds are located on the tongue in small, raised structures called *papillae* (figure 9.3).

A taste bud consists of several taste receptors called *taste cells* that are grouped in a bulblike arrangement within the epithelium of a papilla. *Taste hairs,* hairlike projections from the taste cells, protrude through the opening of the taste bud and are exposed to chemicals on the tongue. Sensory nerve

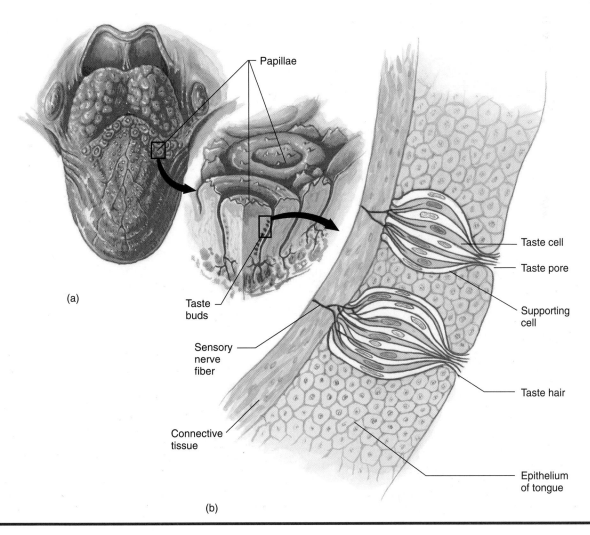

(a)

(b)

Papillae

Taste buds

Sensory nerve fiber

Connective tissue

Taste cell

Taste pore

Supporting cell

Taste hair

Epithelium of tongue

Figure 9.3 (*a*) Taste buds are located on papillae of the tongue. (*b*) A taste bud consists of taste cells whose hairlike tips protrude through the taste pore. AP|R

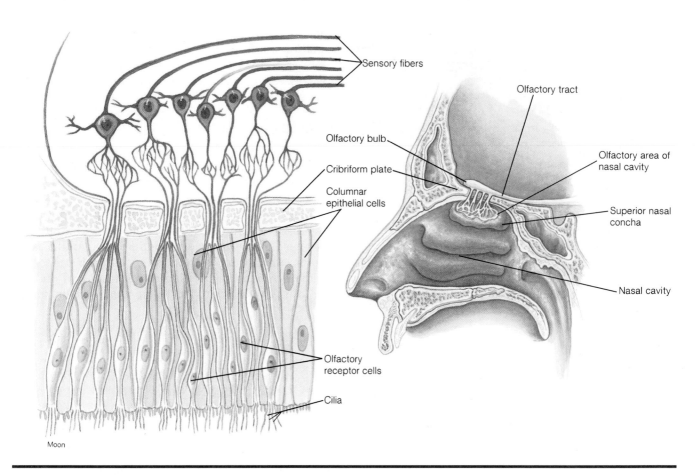

Figure 9.4 Olfactory receptors are located between columnar epithelial cells in the upper portion of the nasal cavity. `AP|R`

fibers leading to the brain are connected to the opposite ends of the taste cells. In order for a substance to activate the taste cells, it must be dissolved in a liquid—usually saliva.

There are four types of taste receptors, and each is associated with a distinct taste sensation: sweet, sour, salty, and bitter. The many flavor sensations of foods result from the stimulation of one or more of these types of receptors and, even more important, the activation of olfactory receptors discussed in the next section. Taste receptors adapt rapidly to repeated stimulation.

The pathway of impulses from taste receptors to the brain depends on where the taste receptors are located. Receptors on the anterior two-thirds of the tongue are carried by the facial (VII) nerve. Those on the posterior one-third travel over the glossopharyngeal (IX) nerve. And those located at the base of the tongue are carried by the vagus (X) nerve. These cranial nerves carry the impulses to the medulla oblongata, from which the impulses travel to the thalamus and on to the taste centers in the parietal lobe of the cerebrum. `AP|R`

Smell

The **olfactory** (ōl-fak′-tō-rē) **receptors** are located in the upper portion of the nasal cavity, including the superior conchae and nasal septum. They consist of olfactory *chemoreceptor cells,* which are supported by columnar epithelial cells of the nasal epithelium. The distal ends of the receptor cells are covered with cilia that project into the nasal cavity, where they can contact airborne molecules. Chemicals in inhaled air are in a gaseous state, but they must dissolve in the film of fluid covering the receptors in order to stimulate impulse formation (figure 9.4). When impulses are formed, they are carried by axons of receptor cells to the olfactory bulbs, where they synapse with neurons that form the olfactory tract and carry the impulses to the olfactory centers deep within the temporal lobes and at the bases of the frontal lobes of the brain.

It is common for a person to sniff the air when trying to detect faint odors. This is because the olfactory receptors are located above the usual path of inhaled air and additional force is needed to send larger amounts of air over the receptor cells. Like taste

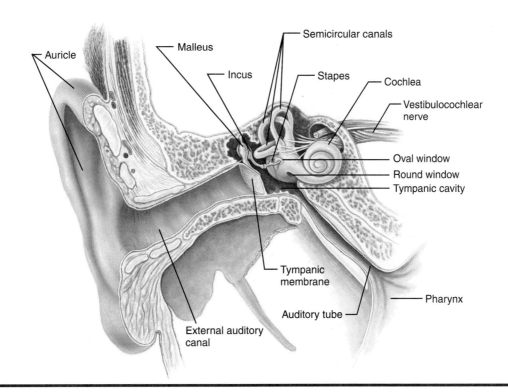

Figure 9.5 Anatomy of the ear. AP|R

receptors, olfactory receptors rapidly adapt to a particular stimulus.

Our sense of smell enables us to distinguish about 10,000 different odors. But how our olfactory receptors enable so many olfactory sensations is poorly understood, because there do not seem to be 10,000 kinds of receptors. We'll have to wait for further research.

Check My Understanding

3. Where are taste and olfactory receptors located?
4. How are the four basic taste sensations produced?

Clinical INSIGHT

The ability to distinguish various foods relies predominantly on the sense of smell. This explains why foods seem to have little taste for a person who is suffering from a head cold. The taste and smell of appetizing foods prepare the digestive tract for digestion by stimulating the flow of saliva in the mouth and gastric juice in the stomach.

Hearing

The *ear* is the organ of hearing. It is also the organ of equilibrium. The ear is subdivided into three major parts: the external ear, middle ear, and inner ear (figure 9.5).

External Ear

The external ear consists of two parts: the auricle and the external auditory canal. The *auricle* (pinna) is the funnel-like structure composed primarily of cartilage and skin that is attached to the side of the head. The **external auditory canal** is a short tube that extends from the auricle through the temporal bone to the eardrum. Sound waves striking the auricle are channeled into the auditory canal. Earwax (cerumen) and hairs in the auditory canal help to prevent foreign particles from reaching the eardrum.

Middle Ear AP|R

The tympanic membrane, tympanic cavity, auditory tube, and ear ossicles are parts of the middle ear. The **tympanic** (tim-pan′-ik) **membrane**, or eardrum, is a membrane that closes the interior end of the external auditory canal. Its exterior surface is covered with skin, and the interior surface is coated with a mucous membrane. Sound waves, or air pressure waves, entering the auditory canal cause the tympanic

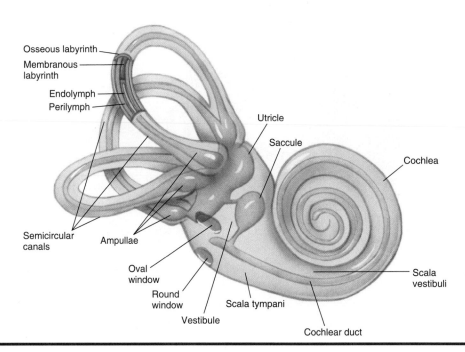

Figure 9.6 The bony and membranous labyrinths of the inner ear. Perilymph fills the space between the membranous labyrinth and the bony labyrinth. Endolymph fills the membranous labyrinth. Note that the ampullae of the semicircular canals, utricle, saccule, and cochlear duct are portions of the membranous labyrinth.

membrane to vibrate in and out at the same frequency as the sound waves. The *tympanic cavity* is an air-filled space in the temporal bone that is separated from the external auditory canal by the tympanic membrane.

The **auditory** (eustachian) **tube** connects the tympanic cavity with the pharynx. Its function is to allow air to enter or exit the tympanic cavity in order to keep the air pressure within the tympanic cavity the same as the external air pressure. Equal air pressure on each side of the eardrum is essential for the eardrum to function properly. A valve at the pharyngeal end of the tube is usually closed, but it opens when a person swallows or yawns and allows air pressure to equalize. If you have experienced a rapid change in air pressure, you probably have noticed your ears "popping," as the air pressure is equalized and the tympanic membrane snaps back into place.

The **ear ossicles** (os'-si-kulz) are three tiny bones that articulate to form a lever system from the tympanic membrane to the inner ear. Each ossicle is named for its shape. The tip of the "handle" of the club-shaped *malleus* (mal'-ē-us), or hammer, is attached to the tympanic membrane and its head articulates with the *incus* (ing'-kus), or anvil. The base of the incus articulates with the *stapes* (stā'-pēz), or stirrup, whose foot plate is inserted into the oval window of the inner ear.

The vibrations of the tympanic membrane cause corresponding movements of the ossicles, which result

Clinical **INSIGHT**

Sometimes the secretion of earwax is excessive and results in accumulations that block the auditory canal and decrease hearing. Removal of impacted earwax should be done by a physician. Irrigation with water is used to loosen the wax so that it can be safely removed.

in the stapes vibrating in the oval window. In this way, vibrations of the eardrum are transmitted to the fluid-filled inner ear.

Inner Ear

The inner ear is embedded in the temporal bone. It consists of two series of connecting tubes and chambers, one within the other: an outer *bony labyrinth* (lab'-i-rinth) and an inner *membranous labyrinth*. The two **labyrinths** are similar in shape (figure 9.6). The space between the bony and membranous labyrinths is filled with **perilymph,** whereas the membranous labyrinth contains **endolymph.** These fluids play important roles in the functions of the inner ear. The inner ear consists of three major parts: the cochlea, vestibule, and semicircular canals.

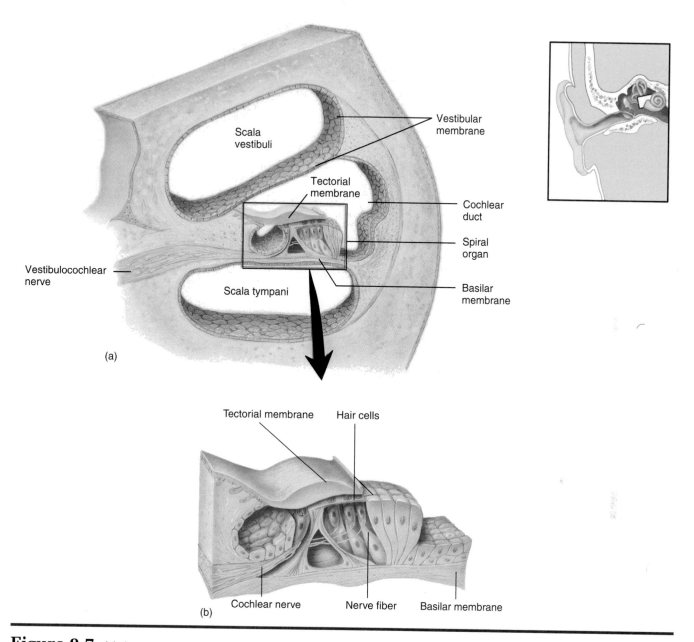

Figure 9.7 (*a*) A cross section of the cochlea shows the cochlear duct located between the scala vestibuli and the scala tympani and the spiral organ resting on the basilar membrane. (*b*) Detail of the spiral organ shows the tectorial membrane overlying the hair cells. AP|R

The **cochlea** (kok′-lē-ah) is the coiled portion of the inner ear. When viewed in cross section, as in figure 9.7, it can be seen that the cochlea is composed of three chambers that are separated from each other by membranes. The *scala vestibuli* (skā-la ves-tib′-ū-lī) and the *scala tympani* extend the length of the cochlea and are continuous with each other at the apex of the cochlea. The scala vestibuli continues into the vestibule, which houses the *oval window.* The scala tympani extends toward the vestibule to the membrane-covered *round window.*

The *cochlear duct* extends nearly to the apex of the cochlea (see figure 9.6). As shown in figure 9.7, it is separated from the scala vestibuli by the *vestibular membrane* and from the scala tympani by the **basilar membrane.** The basilar membrane contains about 20,000 cross fibers that gradually increase in length from the base to the apex of the cochlea. The fibers are attached at one end to the bony center of the cochlea. This attachment allows them to vibrate like reeds of a harmonica when activated by vibrations generated by sound.

The **spiral organ** (organ of Corti), which contains the receptors for sound stimuli, is located on the upper surface of the basilar membrane within the cochlear duct. The receptors are called **hair cells,** and they have hairlike cilia extending from their free surfaces toward the overlying *tectorial* (tek-to′-rē-al) *membrane.* Nerve fibers of the cochlear branch of the vestibulocochlear nerve (cranial nerve VIII) exit the hair cells and lead to the brain.

Physiology of Hearing

The human ear is able to detect sound waves with frequencies ranging from near 30 to 20,000 vibrations per second, but hearing is most acute between 2,000 and 3,000 vibrations per second. For hearing to occur, vibrations formed by sound waves must be transmitted to the hair cells of the spiral organ. Then, the hair cells form impulses that are transmitted to the hearing centers of the brain, where they are interpreted as sound sensations.

Figure 9.8 shows the structure of the inner ear with the cochlea uncoiled to show more clearly the relationships of its parts. Refer to this figure as you study the following outline of hearing physiology.

1. Sound waves enter the external auditory canal and strike the tympanic membrane, causing it to vibrate in and out at the same frequency and comparable intensity as the sound waves. Loud sounds cause a greater displacement of the eardrum than do soft sounds.

2. Vibration of the tympanic membrane causes movement of the ear ossicles, resulting in the in-and-out vibration of the stapes in the oval window.

3. The vibration of the stapes causes a corresponding oscillatory (back-and-forth) movement of the perilymph in the scala vestibuli and scala tympani and a corresponding movement of the membrane over the round window. This movement of the perilymph causes vibrations in the vestibular and basilar membranes.

4. The vibration of the basilar membrane causes the hairs of the hair cells to contact the tectorial membrane, which stimulates the formation of impulses by the hair cells.

5. Impulses formed by the hair cells are carried by the cochlear branch of the vestibulocochlear (VIII) nerve to the hearing centers of the temporal lobes of the cerebrum, where the sensation is interpreted. Some of the nerve fibers cross over to the opposite side of the brain so that the hearing center in each temporal lobe interprets impulses originating in each ear. AP|R

Pitch and Loudness

Because of the gradually increasing length of the fibers in the basilar membrane, different portions of the basilar membrane vibrate in accordance with the different frequencies (pitch) of sound waves. Low-pitched sounds cause the longer fibers of the membrane near

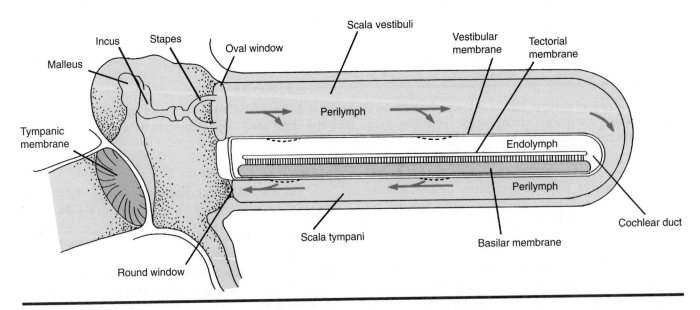

Figure 9.8 Transmission of vibrations produced by sound waves. Vibrations of the tympanic membrane are carried by the ear ossicles to the perilymph. Oscillating movements of the perilymph cause the vibration of the basilar membrane and spiral organ, which, in turn, results in the formation of impulses by the hair cells. AP|R

the apex of the cochlea to vibrate, and high-pitched sounds activate the shorter fibers of the membrane near the base of the cochlea. The pitch of a sound sensation is determined by the portion of the basilar membrane and the spiral organ that are activated by the specific sound frequency and by the parts of the hearing centers that receive the impulses. Impulses from different regions of the spiral organ go to slightly different portions of the hearing centers in the brain, which causes them to be interpreted as different pitches.

The loudness of the sound is dependent upon the intensity of the vibration of the basilar membrane and spiral organ, which, in turn, determines the frequency of impulse formation. The greater the frequency of impulses sent to the brain, the louder the sound sensation.

Check My Understanding

5. How do sound waves stimulate the formation of impulses?
6. How do the impulses produce a sound sensation?

Equilibrium

Several types of sensory receptors provide information to the brain for the maintenance of equilibrium. Receptors in joints and muscles inform the brain about the movement of body parts, and the eyes are especially important in informing the brain about the position of the body parts and equilibrium. However, the crucial receptors are located in the inner ear. There are two types of equilibrium senses that involve different receptors in the inner ear. **Static equilibrium** occurs when the head is motionless. **Dynamic equilibrium** occurs when the head is moving.

Clinical INSIGHT

The hair cells of the spiral organ are easily damaged by high-intensity sounds, such as loud music and the noise of jet airplanes. Such damage produces a form of *nerve deafness* that may be partial or total, and it is permanent. Disorders of sound transmission by the tympanic membrane or ear ossicles cause *conduction deafness*, which may be repairable by surgical means or overcome by the use of hearing aids.

Static Equilibrium

An organ of static equilibrium, the **macula** (mak′-u-lah), is located within the **utricle** (u′-tri-kul) and within the **saccule** (sak′-ul), enlarged portions of the membranous labyrinth (see figure 9.6). Each macula contains thousands of *hair cells,* the sensory receptors, whose hairlike cilia are embedded in a gelatinous material. *Otoliths* (ō′-tō-liths), crystals of calcium carbonate, are also embedded in the gelatinous mass. The otoliths increase the weight of the gelatinous mass and make it more responsive to the pull of gravity (figure 9.9).

The mechanism of static equilibrium may be summarized as follows:

1. The pull of gravity on the gelatinous mass stimulates the hair cells to form impulses that are carried by the vestibular portion of the vestibulocochlear nerve (VIII) to the brain. No matter the position of the head, impulses are formed that inform the brain of the head's position.
2. The cerebellum uses this information to maintain static equilibrium subconsciously.
3. Our awareness of static equilibrium results when the impulses are interpreted by the cerebrum.

Dynamic Equilibrium

The membranous labyrinths of the **semicircular canals** contain the receptors that detect motion of the head. Examine figure 9.6 and note that the semicircular canals are arranged at right angles to each other and that each occupies a different plane in space.

Near the attachment of each membranous canal to the utricle is an enlarged region called the **ampulla** (am-pūl′-lah). Each ampulla contains a sensory organ for dynamic equilibrium called the **crista ampullaris** (kris′-ta am-pūl-lar′-is). Each crista ampullaris contains a number of hair cells whose hairlike projections extend into a dome-shaped gelatinous mass, the *cupula.* Nerve fibers of the vestibular branch of the vestibulocochlear (VIII) nerve lead from the hair cells to the brain (figure 9.10).

The mechanism of dynamic equilibrium may be described as follows:

1. When the head is turned, the endolymph pushes against the cupula, bending the hairs of hair cells, which stimulates the formation of impulses. The impulses are carried to the brain via the vestibular branch of the vestibulocochlear (VIII) nerve (see figure 9.5).

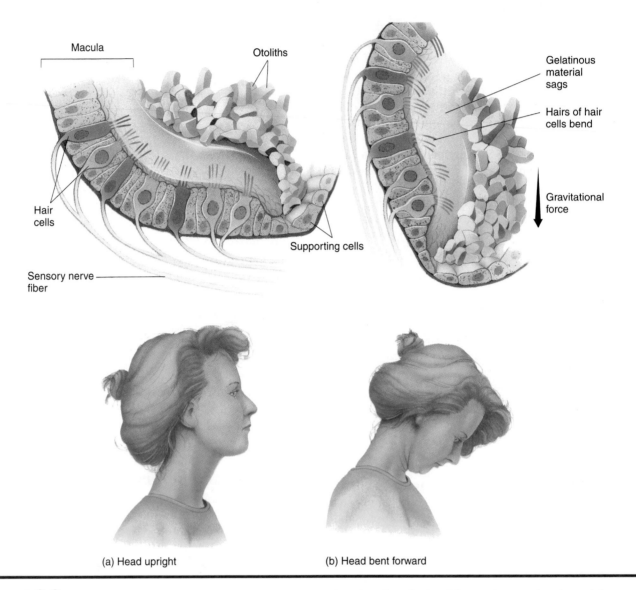

Figure 9.9 A macula is a receptor for static equilibrium. Note how bending the head forward causes bending of the hairs of the hair cells.

2. Because each semicircular canal is oriented in a different plane, the cristae and hair cells are not stimulated equally with a given head movement. Thus, the brain receives a different pattern of impulses for each type of head movement.
3. The cerebellum uses the impulses to make adjustments below the conscious level to maintain dynamic equilibrium.
4. Awareness of dynamic equilibrium, or lack of it, results from the cerebrum interpreting the pattern of impulses it receives (figure 9.11).

Table 9.2 summarizes the functions of the ear.

Check My Understanding

7. What structures are involved in static and dynamic equilibrium?
8. What are the mechanisms of static and dynamic equilibrium?

Vision

Vision is one of the most important senses supplying information to the brain. The receptors for light stimuli are located within the *eyes,* the organs of vision. The eyes are located within the *eye orbits,* where they

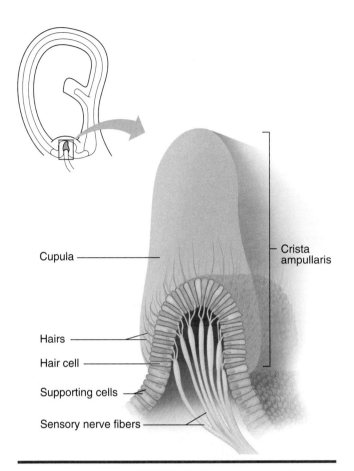

Figure 9.10 A crista ampullaris is located within the ampulla of each semicircular canal.

(a) Head in still position

(b) Head rotating

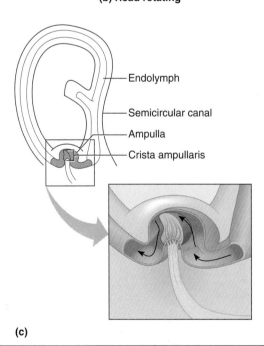

are protected by the surrounding bones. Connective tissues provide support, and fatty tissues behind the eyes provide a protective cushion.

Eyelids, Eyelashes, and Eyebrows

The exposed anterior surface of the eye is protected by the *eyelids*. The eyelids are blinked frequently to spread tears and mucus over the anterior eye surface to keep it moist. The inner surface of the eyelids is lined with a mucous membrane, the **conjunctiva** (kon-junk-tĭ′-vah), that continues across the anterior surface of the eye. Only its transparent outer epithelium covers the cornea. Mucus from the conjunctiva helps to lubricate the eye and keep it moist. The conjunctiva contains many blood vessels and pain receptors.

Eyelashes help to keep airborne particles from reaching the eye surface and provide some protection from excessive light. *Eyebrows,* located on the brow ridges, also shield the eyes from light from above. Observe the accessory structures in figure 9.12.

(c)

Figure 9.11 Dynamic equilibrium. (*a*) When the head is upright and stationary, the crista ampullaris is upright. (*b*) When the head is rotated, (*c*) the endolymph bends the cupula in the opposite direction, stimulating the hair cells to form impulses.

Table 9.2   Summary of Ear Function

Structure	Function
External Ear	
Auricle	Channels sound waves into external auditory canal
External auditory canal	Directs sound waves to tympanic membrane
Tympanic membrane	Vibrates when struck by sound waves
Middle Ear	
Tympanic cavity	Air-filled space that allows tympanic membrane to vibrate freely when struck by sound waves
Ear ossicles	Transmit vibrations produced by sound waves from the tympanic membrane to the perilymph within the cochlea
Auditory tube	Equalizes air pressure on each side of tympanic membrane
Inner Ear	
Cochlea	Fluids and membranes transmit vibrations initiated by sound waves to the spiral organ, whose hair cells generate impulses associated with hearing
Saccule	Hair cells of the macula form impulses associated with static equilibrium
Utricle	Hair cells of the macula form impulses associated with static equilibrium
Semicircular canals	Hair cells of the cristae form impulses associated with dynamic equilibrium

Figure 9.12 Accessory structures and the anterior portion of the eye as shown in a sagittal section. AP|R

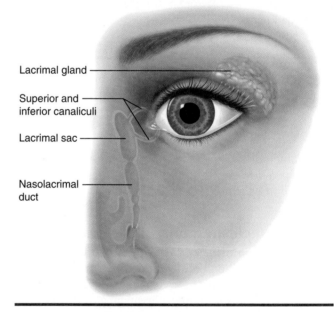

Figure 9.13 The lacrimal apparatus consists of a tear-secreting lacrimal gland and a series of ducts.

Lacrimal Apparatus

The **lacrimal** (lak'-ri-mal) **apparatus,** shown in figure 9.13, is involved in the production and removal of tears. Tears are secreted continuously by the **lacrimal gland,** which is located in the upper, lateral part of the eye orbit above the eye. Tears are carried to the surface of the eye by a series of tiny *lacrimal*

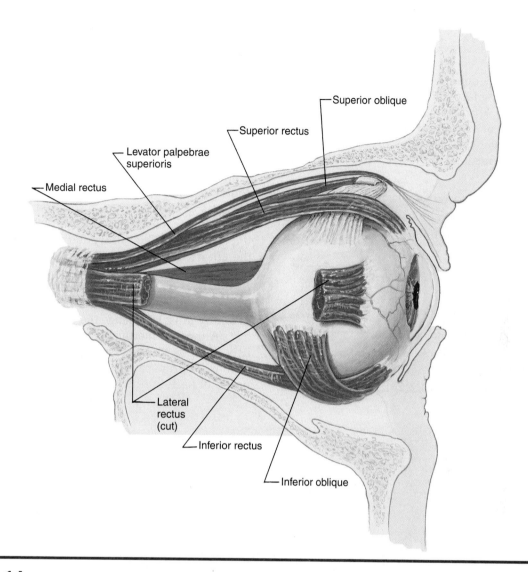

Figure 9.14 Six extrinsic muscles move the eyeball, and the levator palpebrae superioris raises the upper eyelid. AP|R

ducts. The tears flow downward and medially across the eye surface as they are spread over the eye surface by the opening and closing of the eyelids. Tears are collected at the inner corner of the eye by the *superior* and *inferior canaliculi,* flow into the *lacrimal sac,* and flow on through the *nasolacrimal duct* into the nasal cavity.

Tears perform an important function in keeping the anterior surface of the eye moist and in washing away foreign particles. An antibacterial enzyme (lysozyme) in tears helps to reduce the chance of eye infections.

Extrinsic Muscles

Movement of the eyes must be precise and in unison to enable good vision. Each eye is moved by six **extrinsic** (external) **eye muscles** that originate from the back of the eye orbit and insert on the surface of the eye. Four muscles exert a direct pull on the eye, but two muscles pass through cartilaginous loops, enabling them to exert an oblique pull on the eyeball. Although each muscle has its own action, these muscles function as a coordinated group to enable eye movements. The locations of these muscles are shown in figure 9.14, and their functions are described in table 9.3.

Check My Understanding

9. What are the functions of the accessory structures of the eye?

Structure of the Eye

The eye is a hollow, spherical organ about 2.5 cm (1 in) in diameter. It has a wall composed of three layers, and its interior spaces are filled with fluids that support the walls and maintain the shape of the eye. The major parts of the eye are shown in figure 9.15.

Outer Layer   The outer layer of the eye consists of two parts: the sclera and the cornea. The **sclera** (skle'-rah) is the opaque, white portion of the eye that forms most of the outer layer. The sclera is a tough, fibrous layer that provides protection for the delicate internal portions of the eye and for the optic nerve, which emerges from the posterior portion of the eye. The anterior portion of the sclera is covered by the conjunctiva. The **cornea** (kor'-nē-ah) is the anterior clear window of the eye. It has a greater convex curvature than the rest of the eyeball, and it bends the light rays as they pass through it. It lacks blood vessels and nerves.

Middle Layer   The middle layer includes the choroid coat, ciliary body, and iris. The **choroid** (kō'-roid) **coat** contains blood vessels that nourish the eye, plus large amounts of melanin. The absorption of light by melanin prevents back-scattering of light, which would impair vision. The **ciliary** (sil'-ē-ar-ē) **body** contains the ciliary muscles and forms a ring around the **lens** just anterior to the choroid coat. Numerous *suspensory ligaments* extend from the ciliary body to the lens, and they hold the lens in place. Contraction and relaxation of ciliary muscles change the shape of the lens.

Although entering light rays are bent by the cornea, it is the lens that focuses light rays precisely on the retina. The transparent, somewhat elastic lens is composed of protein fibers, and it lacks blood vessels and

Table 9.3	Action of Extrinsic Eye Muscles
Muscle	**Function**
Lateral rectus	Turns eye laterally
Medial rectus	Turns eye medially
Superior rectus	Turns eye upward and medially
Inferior rectus	Turns eye downward and medially
Superior oblique	Turns eye downward and laterally
Inferior oblique	Turns eye upward and laterally

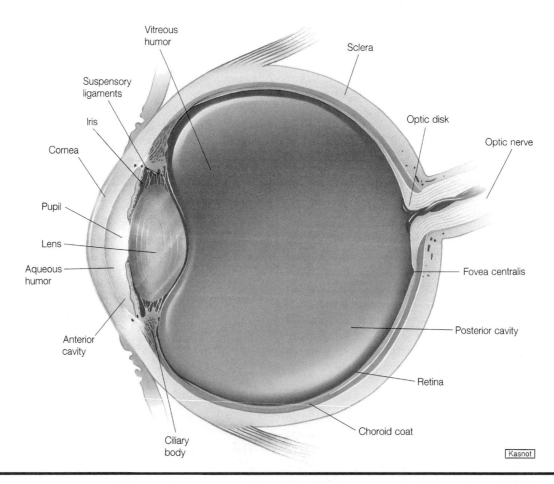

Figure 9.15   The structure of the left eye in transverse section.   AP|R

nerves. When tension is relaxed on the suspensory ligaments by the contraction of the ciliary muscles, the lens retracts to assume a thicker shape because of its elasticity. The relaxation of the ciliary muscles increases tension on the suspensory ligaments and causes the lens to take on a more flattened shape. In this way, the shape of the lens is adjusted for distance, intermediate, and near vision so that the image is focused precisely on the retina. This process is called **accommodation** (figure 9.16).

The colored portion of the eye is the **iris,** a thin disk of connective tissue and smooth muscle that extends from the ciliary body in front of the lens. The iris controls the amount of light entering the eye by controlling the size of the pupil. The **pupil** is the opening in the center of the iris through which light passes to the lens. The pupil is constricted in bright light and is dilated in dim light, and its size is constantly adjusted by the iris as lighting conditions change.

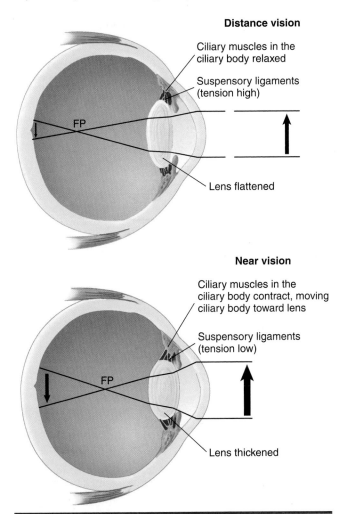

Figure 9.16 Focusing of light rays on the retina by the lens in distance vision and near vision. Note how the lens changes shape in accommodation.

Inner Layer The filmlike **retina** (ret'-i-nah) lines the interior of the eye posterior to the ciliary body. The retina contains two types of photoreceptor cells: rods and cones. The thin, elongate **rods** are photoreceptors for black-and-white vision because they are sensitive only to the presence of light. But rods enable us to see in dim light. The shorter and thicker **cones** are photoreceptors for color vision, but they require bright light and do not function in dim light.

On the retina directly behind the lens is a yellowish disk called the **macula** (mak'-u-lah). In the center of the macula is a small depression called the **fovea centralis** (fō'-vē-ah sen-trah'-lis), which contains only densely packed cones. This makes the fovea the area for the sharpest, bright-light vision. The density of cones diminishes with distance from the fovea. In contrast, the density of rods, which are absent in the fovea, increases with distance from the fovea. Therefore, dim-light vision is best at the edge of the visual field (figures 9.15 and 9.17).

The retina contains neurons in addition to rods and cones (figure 9.18). Impulses formed by rods and cones are transmitted to *ganglion neurons,* whose fibers converge at the **optic disk** to form the optic nerve. The optic disk is located medial to the fovea. Because the optic disk lacks photoreceptors, it is also known as the "blind spot." However, we usually do not notice a blind spot in our field of vision, because the visual fields of our eyes overlap.

An artery enters the eye and a vein exits the eye via the optic disk. These blood vessels are continuous with capillaries that nourish the internal tissues of the eye. These blood vessels are the only ones in the body that can be viewed directly. A special instrument called an *ophthalmoscope* (of-thal'-mō-skōp) is used to look through the lens and observe these vessels. Figure 9.17 shows the appearance of blood vessels and the retina as viewed with an ophthalmoscope.

Check My Understanding

10. How are the components of the three layers of the eye involved in vision?

Internal Cavities The space between the cornea and the lens is known as the **anterior cavity,** and it is filled with a watery fluid called **aqueous** (ā'-kwē-us) **humor.** The aqueous humor is secreted by capillaries in the ciliary body, and the pressure generated by the aqueous humor helps maintain the shape of the cornea. The aqueous humor is absorbed into blood vessels

(a)

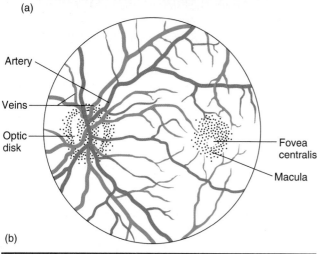

Artery

Veins

Optic
disk

Fovea
centralis

Macula

(b)

Figure 9.17 (*a*) A photo of the retina and
(*b*) a diagram of the retina showing the optic disk and fovea
centralis. Blood vessels enter and exit the eye at the optic
disk. Nerve fibers exit the eye at the optic disk to form the
optic nerve. The fovea centralis contains densely packed
cones for direct color vision. AP|R

located at the junction of the sclera and cornea.
Aqueous humor is largely responsible for the internal
pressure within the eye. Normally, it is secreted and
absorbed at the same rate so that intraocular pressure
is maintained at a constant level.

The large **posterior cavity** is located behind the
lens. It is filled with a clear, gel-like substance called
vitreous (vit′-rē-us) **humor.** The vitreous humor
presses the retina firmly against the wall of the eye
and helps to maintain the shape of the eye.

Table 9.4 summarizes the functions of eye
structures.

Sclera

Pigmented
choroid coat

Pigmented
epithelium

Rod

Cone

Receptor
cells

Retina

Bipolar
neuron

Layer of
connecting
neurons

Ganglion
cell

Nerve fibers

Vitreous humor

Impulses to
optic nerve

Light waves

Figure 9.18 The retina consists of several cell
layers. AP|R

Physiology of Vision

Light rays coming to the eye must be precisely
bent so that they are focused on the retina. This
bending of the light rays is called *refraction*

Clinical **INSIGHT**

Glaucoma results when the rate of absorption of aqueous
humor is less than its rate of secretion. This causes a
buildup of intraocular pressure that, without treatment,
can compress and close down the blood vessels nourishing the photoreceptors of the retina. If this occurs, the
photoreceptors die and permanent blindness results.

Table 9.4 Functions of Eye Structures

Structure	Function
Outer Layer	
Sclera	Provides protection and shape for eye
Cornea	Allows entrance of light and bends light rays
Middle Layer	
Choroid	Contains blood vessels that nourish interior structures and black pigment that absorbs excessive light
Ciliary body	Supports and changes shape of lens in accommodation; secretes aqueous humor
Iris	Regulates amount of light entering eye by controlling the size of the pupil
Inner Layer	
Retina	Contains photoreceptors that convert light rays into impulses; impulses transmitted to brain via optic (II) nerve
Other Structures	
Lens	Bends light rays and focuses them on the retina
Anterior cavity	Aqueous humor controls intraocular pressure, which maintains shape of the eye and presses retina against choroid
Posterior cavity	Vitreous humor helps maintain shape of the eye and holds retina against choroid

(rē-frak′-shun), and it is produced by the cornea and lens. The convex surface of the cornea produces the greatest refraction of light rays, while further bending (accommodation) by the lens provides a "fine adjustment" so that the image is focused precisely on the retina.

The optics of the eye cause the image to be inverted on the retina, as shown in figure 9.19. However, the visual centers of the cerebral cortex correct for this inversion so that objects are seen in their correct orientation. When images are incorrectly focused on the retina, poor vision results. Figure 9.20 shows common optical disorders and how they may be corrected with glasses or contact lenses.

When light rays strike the retina, the light stimuli must be converted into impulses that are sent to the brain. Both rods and cones contain light-sensitive pigments that break down into simpler substances when light is absorbed. The breakdown of these pigments results in the formation of impulses.

Rods contain a light-sensitive pigment called **rhodopsin** that breaks down into *opsin,* a protein, and *retinene,* which is derived from vitamin A. This breakdown triggers the formation of impulses that are carried via the optic nerve to the brain. Rhodopsin is resynthesized from opsin and retinene to prepare the rods for receiving subsequent stimuli. A deficiency of vitamin A may result in an insufficient amount of rhodopsin in the rods, which, in turn, may lead to *night blindness,* the inability to see in dim light.

Although the light-sensitive pigments are different in cones, they function in a similar way as rhodopsin. There seems to be three different types of cones, and each has a pigment that responds best to a different color (wavelength) of light. One type responds best to red light, another type responds best to green light, and the third type responds to blue light. The perceived color of objects results from the combination of the cones that are stimulated and the interpretation of the impulses that they form by the cerebral cortex.

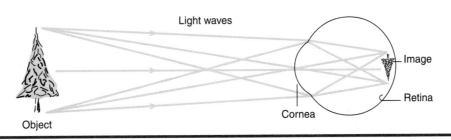

Figure 9.19 The optics of the eye cause the image to be upside down on the retina.

Figure 9.20 Comparison of (*a*) normal sight, (*b*) nearsightedness, and (*c*) farsightedness.

Clinical INSIGHT

Red-green color blindness, the most common type of color blindness, results whenever cones sensitive to red light or to green light are absent from the retina. Persons with this disorder cannot distinguish between reds and greens.

Nerve Pathway Impulses formed by the photoreceptors are transmitted via nerve fibers of the optic nerve to the brain. The optic nerves (II) merge just anterior to the pituitary gland to form an X-shaped pattern called the **optic chiasma** (kī′-as-mah) (figure 9.21). Within the optic chiasma, the fibers from the medial half of the retina in each eye cross over to the opposite optic nerve. Thus, the medial fibers of the left eye and the lateral fibers of the right eye form the right optic tract leading from the optic chiasma. Similarly, the medial fibers of the right eye and the lateral fibers of the left eye form the left optic tract leading from the optic chiasma. The fibers of the optic tracts enter the thalamus, where they synapse

with neurons that carry the impulses on to the visual centers of the occipital lobes.

The crossing of the medial fibers results in each visual center receiving images of the entire object but from slightly different views that enable stereoscopic (three-dimensional) vision. Depth perception is a result of stereoscopic vision.

The mechanism of vision may be summarized as follows:

1. Light rays are bent as they pass through the cornea.
2. The iris controls the amount of light passing through the pupil.
3. The ciliary body adjusts the shape of the lens to focus the light rays (image) on the retina.
4. Light absorbed by the rods and cones causes the formation of nerve impulses.
5. The impulses are transmitted to neurons whose fibers converge at the optic disk to form the optic nerve.
6. The medial fibers of the optic nerves cross over at the optic chiasma forming the optic tracts, which continue to the thalamus.
7. The impulses are then carried to the vision centers in the occipital lobes of the cerebrum, where they are interpreted as visual images.

Check My Understanding

11. How are light rays converted into visual sensations?

9.4 Disorders of Hearing and Vision

The disorders of hearing and vision are best considered separately, as noted next.

Disorders of the Ear

Deafness is a partial or total loss of hearing. There are two major types of hearing loss: neural deafness and conduction deafness. *Neural deafness* results from impairment of the cochlea or cochlear nerve. *Conduction deafness* results from impairment of the tympanic membrane or ear ossicles.

Labyrinthine disease is a term applied to disorders of the inner ear that produce symptoms of dizziness, nausea, ringing in the ears (tinnitis), and hearing loss. It may be caused by an excess of endolymph, infection, allergy, trauma, circulation disorders, and aging.

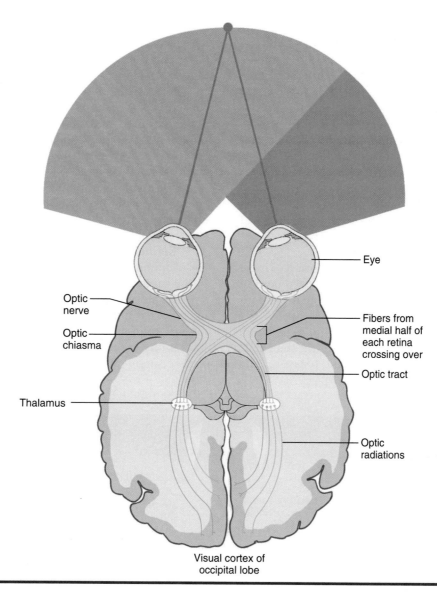

Figure 9.21 The optic nerve pathway. The medial fibers of the optic nerves cross over to the opposite side of the brain at the optic chiasma. AP|R

Motion sickness is a functional disorder that is characterized by nausea and is produced by repetitive stimulation of the equilibrium receptors in the inner ear by angular or vertical motion.

Otitis media (ō-tī′-tis mē′-dē-ah) is an acute infection of the tympanic cavity. It may cause severe pain and an outward bulging of the tympanic membrane due to accumulated fluids. Pathogens enter the middle ear from the pharynx via the auditory tube or through a perforated tympanic membrane. Young children are especially susceptible because their auditory tubes are short and horizontal, which aids the spread of bacteria from the pharynx to the tympanic cavity. AP|R

Disorders of the Eye

Astigmatism (a-stig′-mah-tizm) is the unequal focusing of light rays on the retina, which causes part of an image to appear blurred. It results from an unequal curvature of the cornea or lens.

Blindness is partial loss or lack of vision. It may be caused by a number of disorders such as cataract, glaucoma, and detachment or deterioration of the retina. It may also result from damage to the optic nerves or the visual centers in the occipital lobes of the cerebrum.

Cataract is cloudiness or opacity of the lens, which impairs or prevents vision. It is common in older people and is the leading cause of blindness.

Surgical removal of the clouded lens and implantation of a plastic lens usually restore good vision.

Color blindness is the inability to perceive certain colors or, more rarely, all colors. Red-green color blindness, the most common type, is characterized by difficulty distinguishing reds and greens due to the absence of either red or green cones. Color blindness is inherited, and it occurs more often in males than females because it is a sex-linked hereditary trait.

Conjunctivitis (con-junk-ti-vī'-tis) is inflammation of the conjunctiva. It may be caused by allergic reactions, physical or chemical causes, or infections. Inflammation that results from a bacterial or viral infection is commonly called *pinkeye.* Such bacterial infections are highly contagious.

Farsightedness (hyperopia) is blurred vision caused by light rays being incorrectly focused behind the retina. Its causes include lens abnormalities and the eye being shorter than normal.

Glaucoma (glaw-kō'-mah) is a condition in which aqueous humor is produced more rapidly than it is removed, resulting in a high intraocular pressure. The high intraocular pressure compresses blood vessels, which results in death of receptor cells. Glaucoma is the second leading cause of blindness. The tendency to develop glaucoma is inherited.

Nearsightedness (myopia) is blurred vision caused by light rays being incorrectly focused in front of the retina. Its causes include lens abnormalities and the eye being longer than normal.

Presbyopia (prez-bē-ō'pē-ah) is the diminished ability of the lens to accommodate for near vision due to a decrease in its elasticity. It is a natural result of aging. At age 20, an object can be clearly observed about 10 cm (4 in) from the eye. At age 60, an object must be about 75 cm (30 in) from the eye to be clearly observed.

Retinoblastoma (ret-i-nō-blas-tō'-mah) is a cancer of immature retinal cells. It constitutes about 2% of the cancers in children.

Strabismus (strah-biz'-mus) is a disorder of the extrinsic eye muscles in which the eyes are not directed toward the same object simultaneously. Treatment may include eye exercises, corrective lenses, or corrective surgery.

CHAPTER SUMMARY

9.1 Sensations

- Each type of sensory receptor is most sensitive to a particular type of stimulus.
- The five types of sensory receptors are thermoreceptors, mechanoreceptors, pain receptors, chemoreceptors, and photoreceptors.
- Sensations result from impulses formed by receptors that are carried to the brain and interpreted by the cerebral cortex.
- A particular sensory region of the cerebral cortex interprets all impulses that it receives as the same type of sensation.
- The brain projects the sensation back to the body region from which the impulses seem to have originated.
- Sensory receptors for touch, pressure, heat, cold, taste, and smell tend to adapt to repetitions of the same stimulus by decreasing the rate of impulse formation.

9.2 General Senses

- Thermoreceptors are located in the dermis of the skin. Heat receptors are located deeper than are cold receptors.
- Pressure receptors are located in tendons and ligaments of joints and deep in the dermis of the skin.
- Proprioceptors in skeletal muscles and tendons are involved in the maintenance of erect posture and muscle tone.

- There are two types of touch receptors. Meissner's corpuscles are located in the superficial portion of the dermis, and they are especially important in hairless skin. Free nerve endings function secondarily as touch receptors where they penetrate the epidermis or wrap around the base of hair follicles.
- Free nerve endings serve as pain receptors, and they are widely distributed throughout the body. Pain receptors are especially abundant in the skin and visceral organs.
- Referred pain is pain from visceral organs that is erroneously projected to the body wall. The pattern of referred pain is useful in diagnosing disorders of visceral organs.

9.3 Special Senses

Taste
- Taste receptors are located in taste buds, which are located on papillae of the tongue.
- There are four basic types of taste receptors: sour, sweet, salty, and bitter. Each type of taste receptor has a unique distribution on the superior surface of the tongue.
- Chemicals must be in solution in order to stimulate the taste receptors.
- Taste receptors rapidly adapt to a repeated stimulus.

Smell
- Olfactory receptors are located within the epithelium of the superior portion of the nasal cavity.

- Airborne molecules must be dissolved in the fluid film covering the olfactory epithelium in order to stimulate the olfactory receptors.
- Impulses are carried from the receptors to the olfactory bulbs and via the olfactory tracts to the brain.
- Olfactory receptors adapt quickly to a repeated stimulus.

Hearing
- The ear is subdivided into the external, middle, and inner ear.
- The external ear consists of (a) the auricle, which directs sound waves into the external auditory canal; and (b) the external auditory canal, which channels sound waves to the tympanic membrane.
- The middle ear consists of (a) the tympanic membrane, which vibrates when struck by sound waves; (b) the tympanic cavity, an air-filled space; (c) the auditory tube, which enables the equalization of air pressure on each side of the tympanic membrane; and (d) the ear ossicles, which transmit vibrations of the tympanic membrane to the oval window of the inner ear.
- The inner ear is embedded in the temporal bone. It consists of (a) the membranous labyrinth, which is filled with endolymph and lies within (b) the bony labyrinth, which is filled with perilymph. The major portions of the inner ear are the cochlea, vestibule, and semicircular canals.
- The cochlear duct, part of the membranous labyrinth, extends nearly to the apex of the cochlea. The spiral organ rests on the basilar membrane within the cochlear duct; it contains the hair cells, which are the receptors for vibrations produced by sound waves.
- Sound waves vibrate the tympanic membrane. These vibrations are transmitted to the oval window of the inner ear by the ear ossicles, which then sets up oscillatory movements of the perilymph in the cochlea. The movements of the perilymph vibrate the basilar membrane and spiral organ, resulting in the formation of impulses.
- Impulses are carried to the brain by the cochlear branch of the vestibulocochlear (VIII) nerve.

Equilibrium
- Receptors in joints, muscles, eyes, and the inner ear send impulses to the brain that are associated with equilibrium.
- The maculae within the saccule and utricle contain hair cells that are receptors for static equilibrium.

- The cristae within the ampullae of the semicircular canals contain hair cells that are the receptors for dynamic equilibrium.

Vision
- The eyes contain the receptors for vision. Accessory organs include the extrinsic eye muscles, eyelids, eyelashes, eyebrows, and lacrimal apparatus.
- The wall of the eye is composed of three layers. The outer layer consists of (a) the sclera, which supports and protects internal structures; and (b) the transparent cornea, which allows light to enter the eye. The middle layer consists of (a) the darkly pigmented choroid, which contains blood vessels nourishing internal structures and also absorbs excess light; (b) the ciliary body, which changes the shape of the lens to focus light rays on the retina; and (c) the iris, which controls the amount of light entering the posterior cavity via the pupil. The inner layer consists of the retina, which contains the photoreceptors.
- Fluids fill the cavities of the eye and give it shape. Aqueous humor fills the anterior cavity and is primarily responsible for maintaining intraocular pressure. Vitreous humor fills the posterior cavity and helps to hold the retina against the choroid.
- Light rays pass through the cornea, aqueous humor, pupil, lens, and vitreous humor to reach the retina. Light rays are primarily refracted by the cornea, but the lens focuses them on the retina.
- The photoreceptors are rods and cones. Rods are adapted for dim-light, black-and-white vision. Cones are adapted for bright-light, color vision. There are three types of cones based on the color of light that they primarily absorb: red, green, and blue.
- Impulses formed by the photoreceptors are carried to the brain by the optic (II) nerve. Fibers from the medial half of each eye cross over to the opposite side at the optic chiasma.
- The slightly different retinal images of each eye enable stereoscopic vision when the two images are superimposed by the brain.

9.4 Disorders of Hearing and Vision
- Disorders of the ears include deafness, labyrinthine disease, motion sickness, and otitis media.
- Disorders of the eyes include astigmatism, blindness, cataract, color blindness, conjunctivitis, farsightedness, glaucoma, nearsightedness, presbyopia, retinoblastoma, and strabismus.

BUILDING MY VOCABULARY

1. **Selected New Terms**
   aqueous humor, p. 197
   auditory tube, p. 188
   basilar membrane, p. 189

   conjunctiva, p. 193
   crista ampullaris, p. 191
   ear ossicles, p. 188
   endolymph, p. 188

external auditory canal, p. 187
fovea centralis, p. 197
labyrinth, p. 188
lacrimal apparatus, p. 194
macula, p. 191
Meissner's corpuscles, p. 183
olfactory, p. 186
perilymph, p. 188
rhodopsin, p. 199
saccule, p. 191
sensory receptors, p. 182
taste buds, p. 185
tympanic membrane, p. 187
utricle, p. 191
vitreous humor, p. 198

2. **Related Clinical Terms**

Audiometry (aw'-dē-om'-e-trē) Measurement of hearing acuity at various sound frequencies.

Ophthalmology (off-thal-mol'-ah-jē) Medical specialty treating disorders of the eye.

Otolaryngology (ō-tō-lar-in-gol'-ah-jē) Medical specialty treating disorders of the ear, nose, and throat.

Otosclerosis (ō-tō-skle-rō'-sis) Formation of bone tissue in joints of the ear ossicles, which prevents their movement.

Tonometry (tō-nom'-e-trē) Measurement of the pressure within the eye.

Vertigo (ver'-ti-gō) A sensation of dizziness.

SELF-REVIEW

Answers are located in appendix B.

1. There are two types of touch receptors: _____ and _____.
2. Pain originating from visceral organs but projected to parts of the body wall is called _____.
3. Receptors for taste are localized in bulblike aggregations called _____.
4. _____ receptors are located in the epithelium of the upper nasal cavity.
5. The decline in impulse formation when a receptor is repeatedly exposed to the same stimulus is called _____.
6. The cochlea of the inner ear is involved in _____, and the vestibule and semicircular canals are involved in _____.
7. The membranous labyrinth is filled with a fluid called _____.
8. The receptors for hearing are located in the _____, which rests on the _____ membrane within the cochlear duct.
9. Vibrations of the eardrum are transmitted to the inner ear by the _____.
10. The hair cell receptors for static equilibrium are located in maculae in the _____ and _____.
11. When light rays enter the eyes, they are refracted first by the _____ and focused on the retina by the _____.
12. The fovea centralis contains only _____, which are receptors for _____ vision.
13. Muscles within the _____ are responsible for changing the shape of the lens.
14. The retina is pressed against the choroid coat by the _____ in the posterior chamber.
15. The medial fibers of the optic nerve cross over at the _____.

CRITICAL THINKING

1. Complete the learning objectives listed on the first page of this chapter.
2. Explain the benefits of accommodation.
3. Free nerve endings are the most abundant sensory receptors in the body. How is this beneficial?
4. Will a hearing aid improve hearing in both neural and conduction deafness? Explain.
5. Lasix surgery, which is used to eliminate nearsightedness, changes the shape of the cornea. How does this improve vision when the problem is caused by the shape of the lens or eyeball?

Visit this book's website at www.mhhe.com/ gunstream5 for practice quizzes, learning exercises, case studies, and other study tools.

CHAPTER 10

Endocrine System

Anatomy & Physiology REVEALED®
aprevealed.com

Module 8
Endocrine System

Endocrine gland (endo = within; crin = secrete) A ductless gland whose secretions diffuse into the blood for distribution.
Hormone (hormon = to set in motion) A chemical messenger secreted by an endocrine gland.
Hypersecretion (hyper = above) Production of an excessive amount of a secretion.

Hyposecretion (hypo = below) Production of an insufficient amount of secretion.
Negative-feedback mechanism A mechanism that returns a condition to its normal state, thereby maintaining homeostasis.
Prostaglandin A chemical released by cells producing local actions by nearby cells.

Second messenger An intracellular molecule, activated by a nonsteroid hormone, that produces the specific cellular effect associated with the hormone.
Target cell A cell whose functions are affected by a specific hormone.

wo interrelated regulatory systems coordinate body functions and maintain homeostasis: the nervous system and the *endocrine* (en'-do-krin) *system.* Unlike the almost instantaneous coordination by the nervous system, the endocrine system provides slower but longer-lasting coordination. The endocrine system consists of cells, tissues, and organs, collectively called **endocrine glands**, that secrete **hormones** (chemical messengers) into the blood for transport to other tissues and organs, where they alter cellular functions. In contrast to exocrine glands, whose secretions are carried from a gland by a duct (tube), endocrine glands are ductless glands. Their secretions are simply secreted into the interstitial fluid and pass on into the blood for distribution. Figure 10.1 shows the locations of the major endocrine glands.

10.1 The Nature of Hormones

Because hormones are transported by the blood, virtually all body cells are exposed to a variety of hormones. But each hormone produces a specific effect only in its **target cells**. The target cells for a hormone may be numerous or few and may be widely distributed or localized. In addition, they may be nearby or a long distance from the endocrine gland that produces the hormone. The target cells of a particular hormone have one thing in common: specific receptors for that hormone. These receptors may be in the plasma membrane or inside the cell. Nontarget cells lack these receptors and, therefore, are unaffected by the hormone.

Hormones are secreted in very small amounts, so their concentrations in the blood are extremely low. However, because they act on cells that have specific receptors for particular hormones, large quanti-

Hypothalamus
Pituitary
Thyroid
Thymus
Adrenals
Ovaries (female)

Pineal body
Parathyroids (posterior part of thyroid)
Pancreas (islets)
Testes (male)

Figure 10.1 The major endocrine glands.

ties are not necessary to produce effects. Chemically, hormones may be classified in two broad groups: **steroids** (for steroidlike substances), which are derived from cholesterol, and *nonsteroids,* which are derived from amino acids or proteins.

Eicosanoids (i-ko'-sa-noyds) are another group of molecules secreted by cells that cause specific actions in other cells. These lipid molecules are released into the interstitial fluid by many types of cells and their effects are typically only on nearby cells. Thus, they do not fit the usual definition of hormones and are often called "local hormones." Prostaglandins and leukotrienes are examples. **Prostaglandins** produce a variety of effects ranging from promoting inflammation and blood clotting to increasing uterine contraction in childbirth and raising blood pressure.

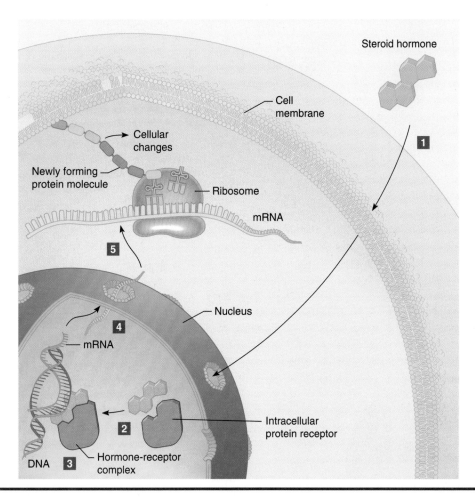

Figure 10.2 Action of a steroid hormone. (1) A steroid hormone enters the cell and (2) combines with a protein receptor usually in the nucleus. (3) The hormone-receptor complex activates the synthesis of mRNA. (4) The mRNA exits the nucleus and (5) moves to a ribosome where the encoded information in mRNA guides protein synthesis. The synthesized protein carries out the specific effect associated with the particular hormone. AP|R

Leukotrienes help regulate the immune system and promote inflammation and some allergic reactions.

Mechanisms of Hormone Action

A hormone produces its effect by binding to a target cell's receptors for that hormone. The more receptors it binds to, the greater is the effect on the target cell. All hormones affect target cells by altering their metabolic activities. For example, they may change the rate of cell processes in general, or they may promote or inhibit specific cellular processes. The end result is that homeostasis is maintained. But steroid and nonsteroid hormones produce their effects in different ways.

Steroid and Steroidlike Hormones

Steroid hormones and steroidlike hormones act on DNA in a cell's nucleus. Because they are

fat soluble (see chapter 2), they can easily move through the lipid bilayers of plasma membranes to enter the nucleus. After a steroid hormone enters a cell, it combines with a receptor protein in the nucleus to form a hormone-receptor complex. The hormone-receptor complex interacts with DNA, activating specific genes that synthesize messenger RNA (mRNA). The mRNA exits the nucleus and interacts with ribosomes, which results in the synthesis of specific proteins, usually enzymes. Then the newly formed proteins produce the specific effect that is characteristic of the particular hormone (figure 10.2).

Nonsteroid Hormones

Nonsteroid hormones are usually proteins or peptides, and they are not fat soluble. Two messengers are required for these hormones to produce their

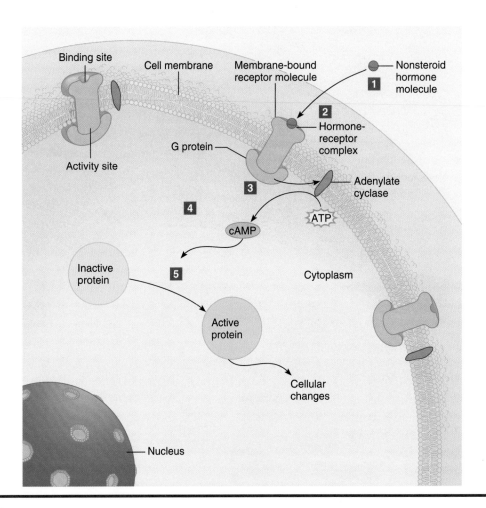

Figure 10.3 Action of a nonsteroid hormone. (1) A nonsteroid hormone in body fluids (2) binds to a receptor in the plasma membrane. (3) This activates a membrane enzyme (adenylate cyclase), which (4) catalyzes the formation of cyclic adenosine monophosphate (cAMP) from ATP. (5) cAMP activates a series of specific cellular changes associated with the particular hormone. AP|R

effect on a target cell. The *first messenger* is the nonsteroid hormone that binds to a receptor on the plasma membrane. The *second messenger* is often, but not always, *cyclic adenosine monophosphate (cAMP)*. The **second messenger** is formed within the cell, and it activates enzymes that produce the characteristic effect for the hormone (figure 10.3). When a cAMP is the second messenger, the sequence of events is as follows.

A nonsteroid hormone binds to a receptor on the target cell's plasma membrane to form a hormone-receptor complex. This complex activates a membrane protein (G protein), which, in turn, activates a membrane enzyme (adenylate cyclase), which catalyzes the formation of cyclic adenosine monophosphate (cAMP) from ATP within the cytoplasm. The cAMP activates enzymes that catalyze the activation of cellular proteins, which produce the cellular changes associated with the specific hormone.

Clinical INSIGHT

Aspirin and acetaminophen are widely used pain relievers. They function by inhibiting the synthesis of prostaglandins involved in the inflammation response, which often is the basis of pain and fever.

Control of Hormone Production

The production of hormones is normally carefully regulated so that there is no **hypersecretion** (excessive production) or **hyposecretion** (deficient production). However, hormonal disorders do occur, and they usually result from severe hypersecretion or hyposecretion. Because endocrine disorders are specifically related to individual glands, disorders in this chapter are considered when each gland is discussed rather than at the end of the chapter.

Endocrine glands are controlled in three ways. (1) The hypothalamus and anterior pituitary may stimulate other endocrine glands; (2) a gland may be stimulated by the nervous system; and (3) a gland may be stimulated directly by changes in the internal environment. These stimuli may have either stimulatory or inhibitory effects, and sometimes more than one stimulus may be involved.

Hormone secretion is usually regulated by a **negative-feedback mechanism** that works to maintain homeostasis. When a substance, whose concentration is regulated by a hormone, falls below the normal level, the endocrine gland is stimulated to increase the secretion of its hormone. The increased hormone concentration stimulates appropriate cells to raise the level of the substance back to normal. When the substance returns to normal levels, the endocrine gland is no longer stimulated to secrete the hormone, and the hormone secretion and concentration decrease. Figure 10.4 illustrates negative feedback when the concentration of one hormone controls the secretion of another hormone. Negative feedback keeps hormone levels in the blood relatively stable (figure 10.5).

Check My Understanding

1. How do steroid and nonsteroid hormones produce their effects on target cells?
2. How are hormones and prostaglandins similar but different?
3. What is negative-feedback control?

10.2 Pituitary Gland

The **pituitary** (pi-tū′-i-tar-ē) **gland**, or **hypophysis** (hī-pof′-i-sis), is attached to the hypothalamus by a short stalk. It rests in a depression of the sphenoid bone, the sella turcica, which provides protection. The pituitary consists of two major parts that have different functions: an *anterior lobe* and a *posterior lobe*. Although the pituitary gland is small, it regulates many body functions. The pituitary is controlled by neurons and chemicals that originate in the **hypothalamus,** as shown in figure 10.6. The hypothalamus serves as a link between the brain and the endocrine system and is itself an endocrine gland. Table 10.1 summarizes the hormones of the pituitary gland and their functions.

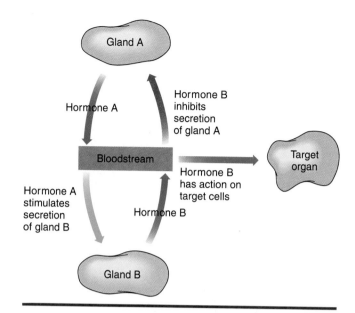

Figure 10.4 An example of a negative-feedback system. Gland A secretes a hormone that stimulates gland B to increase secretion of another hormone. The hormone from gland B alters its target cells and also inhibits activity of gland A. **AP|R**

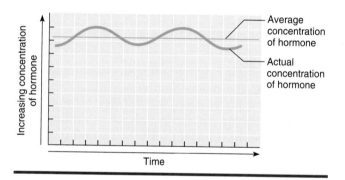

Figure 10.5 Negative feedback controls the concentration of a hormone in the blood. The concentration may fluctuate slightly above and below the hormone's average concentration.

Control of the Anterior Lobe

Special neurons (neurosecretory cells) in the hypothalamus regulate the secretion of hormones from the anterior lobe by secreting *releasing* and *release-inhibiting hormones.* The hypothalamic hormones enter the hypophyseal portal veins, which carry them directly into the anterior lobe without circulating throughout the body. In the anterior lobe, the hormones exert their effects on specific groups of cells. There is a releasing hormone for each hormone produced by the anterior lobe. There are

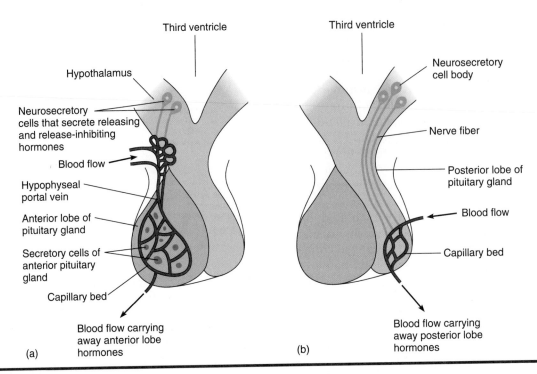

Figure 10.6 Control of pituitary secretions. (*a*) Hypothalamic hormones are secreted by modified neurons and carried by the hypophyseal portal vein to the anterior lobe of the pituitary gland, where they either stimulate or inhibit the secretion of anterior pituitary hormones. (*b*) Neural impulses stimulate modified neurons in the hypothalamus to secrete hormones that are released from their axon tips within the posterior lobe of the pituitary gland. **AP|R**

release-inhibiting hormones for growth hormone and prolactin. As the names imply, releasing hormones stimulate the production and release of hormones from the anterior pituitary. Release-inhibiting hormones have the opposite effect. The secretion of hormones by the hypothalamus is regulated by a negative-feedback control system.

Control of the Posterior Lobe

The posterior lobe is controlled by neural impulses. Special neurons that originate in the hypothalamus have axons that extend into the posterior lobe of the pituitary. Impulses passed along these neurosecretory neurons cause the release of hormones from their axons within the posterior lobe, where they are absorbed into the blood. Note that the posterior pituitary hormones are formed by neurosecretory cells originating in the hypothalamus and not by cells of the posterior pituitary. They are only released within the posterior pituitary.

Anterior Lobe Hormones

The anterior lobe of the pituitary gland is sometimes called the "master gland" because it affects so many body functions. It secretes six hormones:

growth hormone (GH), thyroid-stimulating hormone (TSH), adrenocorticotropic hormone (ACTH), follicle-stimulating hormone (FSH), luteinizing hormone (LH), and prolactin (PRL).

Growth Hormone

As the name implies, **growth hormone (GH)** stimulates the division and growth of body cells. Increased growth results because GH promotes the synthesis of proteins and other complex biological molecules. GH also increases available energy for these synthesis reactions by promoting the release of fat from adipose tissue, the use of fat in cellular respiration, and the conversion of glycogen to glucose. Although GH is more abundant during the growth years, when it determines how tall a person will be, it is secreted throughout life.

Regulation of growth hormone secretion is by two hypothalamic hormones with antagonistic functions. GH-releasing hormone (GHRH) stimulates GH secretion, and GH-inhibiting hormone (GHIH) inhibits GH secretion. Strenuous exercise, a low level of blood sugar (hypoglycemia), and an excess of amino acids in the blood trigger the secretion of GHRH. Conversely, high levels of blood sugar (hyperglycemia) stimulate the secretion of GHIH.

Table 10.1   Hormones of the Pituitary Gland

Hormone	Control	Action	Disorders
Anterior Pituitary Hormones			
Growth hormone (GH)	Growth-hormone-releasing hormone (GHRH); growth-hormone-inhibiting hormone (GHIH)	Promotes growth of body cells and cell division; promotes protein synthesis	Hyposecretion in childhood causes hypopituitary dwarfism. Hypersecretion in childhood causes gigantism; in adults, it causes acromegaly.
Thyroid-stimulating hormone (TSH)	Thyrotropin-releasing hormone (TRH)	Stimulates thyroid to produce thyroid hormone	
Adrenocorticotropic hormone (ACTH)	Corticotropin-releasing hormone (CRH)	Stimulates adrenal cortex to secrete glucocorticoids	
Follicle-stimulating hormone (FSH)	Gonadotropin-releasing hormone (GnRH)	In ovaries, stimulates development of follicles and secretion of estrogen; in testes, stimulates the production of sperm	
Luteinizing hormone (LH)	Gonadotropin-releasing hormone (GnRH)	In females, promotes ovulation, secretion of progesterone by ovaries, preparation of uterus to receive embryo, and preparation of mammary glands for milk secretion; in males, stimulates testes to secrete testosterone	
Prolactin (PRL)	Prolactin-releasing hormone (PRH); prolactin-inhibiting hormone (PIH)	Stimulates milk secretion and maintains milk production by mammary glands	
Posterior Pituitary Hormones			
Antidiuretic hormone (ADH)	Concentration of water in body fluids	Decreases excretion of water by kidneys	Hyposecretion causes diabetes insipidus.
Oxytocin (OT)	Stretching of uterus; stimulation of nipples	Stimulates contractions of uterus in childbirth and contraction of milk glands when nursing infant	

Disorders If there is an excess concentration of growth hormone during the growing years, the individual becomes very tall—sometimes nearly 2.5 m (8 ft) in height. This condition is known as **gigantism.** If the excessive concentration of growth hormone occurs in an adult after growth has been attained, it produces a condition known as **acromegaly** (ak-rō-meg′-ah-lē). Because the growth of long bones has been completed, only the bones of the face, hands, and feet continue to grow. Over time, the individual develops heavy, protruding brow ridges and a jutting lower jaw. Both gigantism and acromegaly may result from tumors of the anterior pituitary. Afflicted persons may have other health problems due to oversecretion of other anterior lobe hormones.

If the concentration of growth hormone is low during the growing years, body growth is limited. In extreme cases, this results in **hypopituitary dwarfism.** Afflicted persons have well-proportioned body parts but may be less than 1 m (3 ft) in height. They may suffer from other maladies due to a deficient supply of other anterior lobe hormones.

Thyroid-Stimulating Hormone

Thyroid-stimulating hormone (TSH) stimulates the thyroid gland to produce thyroid hormone. Blood concentrations of thyroid hormone activate the negative-feedback mechanism for TSH production. Low thyroid hormone levels activate the hypothalamus to secrete *thyrotropin-releasing hormone (TRH),* which stimulates release of TSH by the anterior pituitary. Conversely, high concentrations of thyroid hormone inhibit the secretion of TRH, which decreases production of TSH.

Adrenocorticotropic Hormone

Adrenocorticotropic (ad-re-nō-kor-ti-kō-trōp′-ik) **hormone (ACTH)** controls the secretion of hormones produced by the cortical (outer) portion of the adrenal gland. ACTH production is controlled by *corticotropin-releasing hormone (CRH)* from the hypothalamus in a negative-feedback mechanism. Excessive stress may stimulate the production of excessive amounts of ACTH by overriding the negative-feedback control.

Gonadotropins

The **follicle-stimulating hormone (FSH)** and **luteinizing** (lū-tē-in-ĭz-ing) **hormone (LH)** affect the sex glands. Their release is stimulated by *gonadotropin-releasing hormone (GnRH)* from the hypothalamus. The onset of puberty in both sexes is caused by the start of FSH secretion. In females, FSH acts on the ovaries to promote the development of ovarian follicles, which contain ova and produce estrogen, the primary female sex hormone. In males, FSH acts on testes to promote sperm production. In females, LH stimulates ovulation and the secretion of progesterone, the secondary female sex hormone. In males, it stimulates the secretion of testosterone, the male sex hormone, by the testes.

Prolactin

Prolactin (prō-lak′-tin) **(PRL)** helps to initiate and maintain milk production by the mammary glands after the birth of a child. Prolactin stimulates milk secretion after the mammary glands have been prepared for milk production by other hormones, including female sex hormones. Prolactin secretion is regulated by the antagonistic actions of *prolactin-releasing hormone (PRH)* and *prolactin-inhibiting hormone (PIH)* produced by the hypothalamus.

Posterior Lobe Hormones

The posterior lobe produces two hormones: the antidiuretic hormone and oxytocin. Both of these hormones are secreted by neurons that originate in the hypothalamus and extend into the posterior pituitary. The hormones are released into the blood within the posterior lobe and are distributed throughout the body (see figure 10.6).

Antidiuretic Hormone

The **antidiuretic** (an-ti-dī-ū-ret′-ik) **hormone (ADH)** promotes water reabsorption by the kidneys to reduce the volume of water that is excreted in urine. ADH secretion is regulated by special neurons that detect changes in the water concentration of the blood. If water concentration decreases, secretion of ADH increases to promote water reabsorption by the kidneys. If water concentration increases, secretion of ADH decreases, causing more water to be excreted in urine. By controlling the water concentration of blood, ADH helps to control blood volume and blood pressure.

Disorders   A severe hyposecretion of ADH results in the production of excessive quantities (20–30 liters per day) of dilute urine, a condition called **diabetes insipidus** (dī-ah-bē′-tēz in-sip′-i-dus). The afflicted person is always thirsty and must drink water almost constantly. This condition may be caused by injuries or tumors that affect any part of the ADH regulatory mechanism, such as the hypothalamus or posterior lobe of the pituitary.

Oxytocin

Oxytocin (ok-sē-tō′-sin) **(OT)** is released in large amounts during childbirth. It stimulates and strengthens contraction of the smooth muscles of the uterus, which culminates in the birth of the baby. It also has an effect on the mammary glands. Stimulation of a nipple by a suckling infant causes the release of oxytocin, which, in turn, contracts the milk glands of the breast, forcing milk into the milk ducts, where it can be removed by the suckling infant.

Unlike other hormones, oxytocin secretion is controlled by positive feedback. For example, the greater the nipple stimulation by a suckling infant, the more oxytocin released and the more milk available for the infant. When suckling ceases, oxytocin production ceases.

Check My Understanding

4. How does the hypothalamus control the secretions of the pituitary gland?
5. What are the functions of anterior lobe and posterior lobe hormones?

Clinical INSIGHT

Oxytocin may be used clinically to induce labor. It also may be used immediately after birth of a baby to increase the muscle tone of the uterus and to control uterine bleeding.

10.3 Thyroid Gland AP|R

The **thyroid gland** is located just below the larynx. It consists of two lobes, one on each side of the trachea, that are connected by an anterior isthmus of tissue (figure 10.7). Table 10.2 summarizes the control, action, and disorders of the thyroid gland.

Thyroxine and Triiodothyronine

Iodine atoms are essential for the formation and functioning of two similar thyroid hormones. **Thyroxine** is the primary hormone. It is also known as T_4 because each molecule contains four iodine atoms. The other hormone, **triiodothyronine** (tri″i-o″do-thi′ro-nen) or **T₃**, contains three iodine atoms in each molecule. Both T₄ and T₃ exert their effect on body cells, and they have similar functions. They increase the metabolic rate, promote protein synthesis, and enhance neuron function. T₃ and T₄ are the primary factors that determine the basal metabolic rate (BMR), the number of calories required at rest to maintain life. Moderately low levels of T₄ and T₃ cause chronic fatigue, and very low levels lead to impaired physical and mental growth and development. Secretion of these hormones is stimulated by TSH from the anterior lobe of the pituitary, and TSH, in turn, is regulated by a negative-feedback mechanism.

Disorders   Hypersecretion, hyposecretion, and iodine deficiencies are involved in the thyroid disorders: exophthalmic goiter, simple goiter, cretinism, and myxedema.

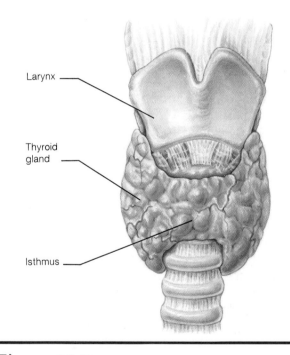

Larynx
Thyroid gland
Isthmus

Figure 10.7   The thyroid gland consists of two lobes connected anteriorly by an isthmus. **AP|R**

Exophthalmic goiter (ek-sof-thal′-mik goy′-ter), or **Graves' disease,** results from the hypersecretion of thyroxine (and T₃). It is thought to be an autoimmune disorder in which antibodies bind to TSH receptors, stimulating excessive hormone production. It is characterized by restlessness, increased metabolic rate with possible weight loss, and bulging eyes due to the swelling of tissues behind the eyes. Usually, the thyroid gland is also enlarged somewhat.

Simple goiter is the enlargement of the thyroid gland and results from a deficiency of iodine in the diet. Without adequate iodine, inadequate amounts of thyroxine and T₃ hormones are produced, and the thyroid enlarges in an attempt to produce more hormones. In some cases, the thyroid may become the size of an orange. Goiter can be prevented by including very small amounts of iodine in the diet. For this reason, salt manufacturers produce "iodized salt," which contains sufficient iodine to prevent simple goiter.

Cretinism (krē′-tin-izm) is caused by a severe deficiency of thyroxine and T₃ in infants. Without treatment, it produces severe mental and physical retardation. Cretinism is characterized by stunted growth, abnormal bone formation, mental retardation, and sluggishness.

Myxedema (mik-se-dē′-mah) is caused by severe thyroxine and T₃ deficiency in adults. It is characterized by sluggishness, weight gain, weakness, dry skin, and puffiness of the face.

Calcitonin

The thyroid gland produces a third hormone with entirely different functions. **Calcitonin** (kal-si-tō′-nin) lowers blood calcium by inhibiting the bone-resorbing action of osteoclasts and promoting calcium excretion by the kidneys. An excess of calcium ions in the blood stimulates the thyroid gland to secrete calcitonin. The concentration of calcium ions in the blood is important because it plays vital roles in metabolism, including maintenance of healthy bones, conduction of neural impulses, muscle contraction, and clotting of blood. The function of calcitonin is antagonistic to parathyroid hormone, which is discussed in the next section.

Table 10.2	Hormones of the Thyroid Gland			
Hormone	**Control**	**Action**		**Disorders**
Thyroxine (T₄) and triiodothyronine (T₃)	TSH from anterior pituitary	Increase metabolic rate; accelerate growth; stimulate neural activity		Hyposecretion in infants and children causes cretinism; in adults, it causes myxedema. Hypersecretion causes Graves' disease. Iodine deficiency causes simple goiter.
Calcitonin (CT)	Blood calcium level	Lowers blood calcium levels by promoting calcium deposition in bones; inhibits removal of calcium from bones		

10.4 Parathyroid Glands

The **parathyroid glands** are small glands that are located on the posterior surface of the thyroid gland. There are usually four parathyroid glands, two glands on each lobe of the thyroid (figure 10.8).

Parathyroid Hormone

Parathyroid glands secrete the **parathyroid hormone (PTH),** the most important regulator of blood calcium levels. PTH increases the concentration of blood calcium by promoting the removal of calcium from bones by osteoclasts and by inhibiting calcium deposition by osteoblasts. It also inhibits excretion of calcium by the kidneys and promotes calcium absorption into the blood by the intestine (figure 10.9 and table 10.3). The antagonistic actions of PTH and calcitonin maintain a normal level of calcium in the blood.

Disorders **Hypoparathyroidism,** the secretion of insufficient amounts of PTH, can produce devastating effects. Without treatment, the concentration of blood calcium may drop to levels that impair neural and muscular activity. The effect on cardiac muscle may result in cardiac arrest and sudden death. Tetanic contractions of skeletal muscles may occur, and death may result from a lack of oxygen due to the inability of breathing muscles to function normally.

Hyperparathyroidism, the secretion of excessive amounts of PTH, causes too much calcium to be removed from bones and raises blood calcium to abnormally high levels. Without treatment, calcium loss results in soft, weak bones that are prone to spontaneous fractures. The excess calcium in the blood may lead to the formation of kidney stones or may be deposited in abnormal locations.

> ### Check My Understanding
> 6. What is the function of thyroid hormones T_3 and T_4?
> 7. How is the level of blood calcium regulated?

10.5 Adrenal Glands

There are two **adrenal glands;** one is located on top of each kidney (figure 10.10). Each adrenal gland consists of two portions that are distinct endocrine glands: an inner adrenal medulla and an outer adrenal cortex. Table 10.4 summarizes the control, action, and disorders of the adrenal gland.

Hormones of the Adrenal Medulla

The **adrenal medulla** secretes **epinephrine** and **norepinephrine,** two closely related hormones that have very similar actions on target cells. Epinephrine forms about 80% of the medullary secretions.

The sympathetic division of the autonomic nervous system regulates the secretion of adrenal medullary hormones. They are secreted whenever the body is under stress, and they duplicate the action of the sympathetic division but on a bodywide scale. The medullary hormones have a stronger and longer-lasting effect in preparing the body for "fight or flight." The effects of epinephrine and norepinephrine include (1) a decrease in blood flow to the viscera and skin; (2) an increase in blood flow to the skeletal muscles, lungs, and nervous system; (3) conversion of glycogen to glucose to raise the glucose level in the blood; and (4) an increase in the rate of cellular respiration.

Hormones of the Adrenal Cortex

Several different steroid hormones are produced by the **adrenal cortex,** but the most important ones are aldosterone, cortisol, and the sex hormones.

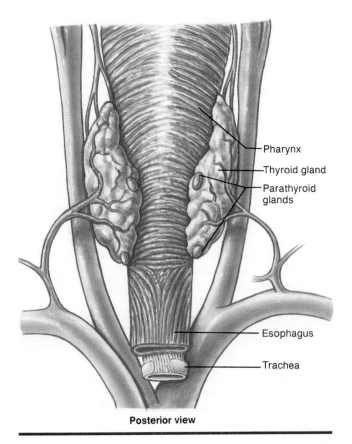

Pharynx
Thyroid gland
Parathyroid glands
Esophagus
Trachea

Posterior view

Figure 10.8 Two small parathyroid glands are located on the posterior surface of each lobe of the thyroid gland.

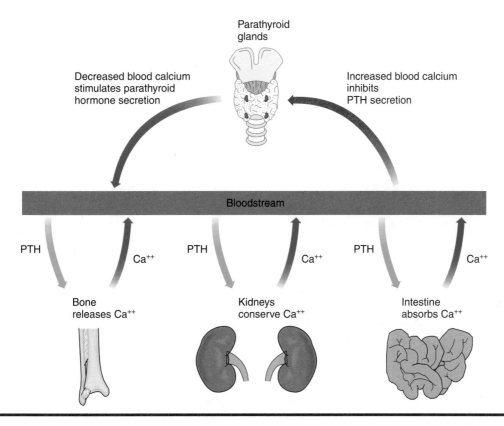

Figure 10.9 The parathyroid glands. The concentration of calcium in the blood controls parathyroid secretion. Parathyroid hormone increases the concentration of calcium in the blood. AP|R

Table 10.3	Parathyroid Hormone		
Hormone	**Control**	**Action**	**Disorders**
Parathyroid hormone (PTH)	Blood calcium level	Increases blood calcium level by promoting calcium removal from bones and calcium reabsorption by kidneys	Hyposecretion causes tetany, which may result in death. Hypersecretion causes weak, soft, deformed bones that may fracture spontaneously.

Aldosterone (al-dō-ster′-ōn) is the most important mineralocorticoid secreted by the adrenal cortex. **Mineralocorticoids** regulate the concentration of electrolytes (mineral ions) in body fluids. Aldosterone stimulates the kidneys to retain sodium ions (Na^+) and to excrete potassium ions (K^+). This action not only maintains the normal balance of sodium and potassium in body fluids but also maintains blood volume and blood pressure. The reabsorption of Na^+ into the blood causes negative ions, such as chloride (Cl^-) and bicarbonate (HCO_3^-), to be reabsorbed due to their opposing charges. And it causes water to be reabsorbed by osmosis, which maintains blood volume and blood pressure. Aldosterone secretion is stimulated by several factors, including (1) a decrease in Na^+, (2) an increase in K^+, or (3) a decrease in blood pressure.

Cortisol (kor′-ti-sol) is the most important of several glucocorticoids that are secreted by the adrenal cortex under the stimulation of ACTH. The blood levels of glucocorticoids are kept in balance because they exert a negative-feedback control on the secretion of ACTH from the anterior pituitary.

Glucocorticoids are so named because they affect glucose metabolism. There are three major actions of glucocorticoids. (1) They help to keep blood glucose concentration within normal limits by promoting the conversion of noncarbohydrate nutrients into glucose. This is important because carbohydrate sources, such as glycogen, may be exhausted after several hours without food. (2) They help the body respond to stress by making more glucose available to body cells. (3) They reduce inflammation but depress immune reactions.

The adrenal cortex also secretes small amounts of **androgens** (male sex hormones). They promote the early development of male sex organs, but in adult males

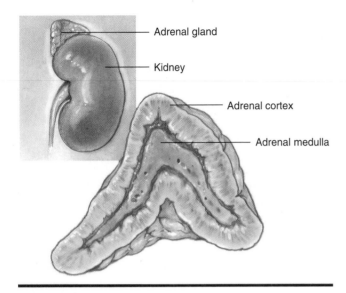

Figure 10.10 An adrenal gland consists of an outer cortex and an inner medulla. AP|R

their effects are masked by sex hormones produced by testes. In females, adrenal androgens contribute to the female sex drive. In both sexes, excessive production results in exaggerated male characteristics. AP|R

Disorders **Cushing's syndrome** results from hypersecretion by the adrenal cortex. It may be caused by an adrenal tumor or by excessive production of ACTH by the anterior pituitary gland. This syndrome is characterized by high blood pressure, an abnormally high blood glucose level, protein loss, osteoporosis, fat accumulation on the trunk, fatigue, edema, and decreased immunity. A person with this condition tends to have a full, round face and an enlarged abdomen.

Addison's disease results from a severe hyposecretion by the adrenal cortex. It is characterized by low blood pressure, low blood glucose and sodium levels, an increase in the blood potassium level, dehydration, muscle weakness, and increased skin pigmentation. Without treatment to control blood electrolytes, death may occur in a few days.

Check My Understanding

8. How do secretions of the adrenal medulla prepare the body to react in emergencies?
9. How does the adrenal cortex help to maintain blood pressure?

10.6 Pancreas

The **pancreas** (pan'-krē-as) is an elongate organ that is located posterior to the stomach (figure 10.11). It is both an exocrine gland and an endocrine gland. Its exocrine functions are performed by secretory cells that secrete digestive enzymes into tiny ducts within the gland. These ducts merge to form the pancreatic duct, which carries the secretions into the small intestine. Its endocrine functions are performed by secretory cells that are arranged in clusters or clumps called the **pancreatic islets.** Their secretions diffuse into the blood. The islets contain two major types of cells. One type produces the hormone glucagon; the other major type forms the hormone insulin. Table 10.5 summarizes the control, action, and disorders of the pancreas.

Table 10.4	Hormones of the Adrenal Glands		
Hormone	**Control**	**Action**	**Disorders**
Adrenal Medulla			
Epinephrine and norepinephrine	Sympathetic division of the autonomic nervous system	Prepare body to meet emergencies; increase heart rate, cardiac output, blood pressure, and metabolic rate; increase blood sugar by converting glycogen to glucose; dilate respiratory passages	Hypersecretion causes prolonged responses. Hyposecretion causes no major disorders.
Adrenal Cortex			
Aldosterone	Blood electrolyte levels	Increases blood levels of sodium and water; decreases blood levels of potassium	Hypersecretion inhibits neural and muscular activity, and also causes edema.
Cortisol	ACTH from anterior pituitary	Promotes normal metabolism; provides resistance to stress and inhibits inflammation; promotes formation of glucose from noncarbohydrate sources	Hyposecretion causes Addison's disease. Hypersecretion causes Cushing's syndrome.
Adrenal sex hormones		Effects are insignificant in normal adult males; contribute to the sex drive in females.	Hypersecretion as a result of tumors causes masculinization in females.

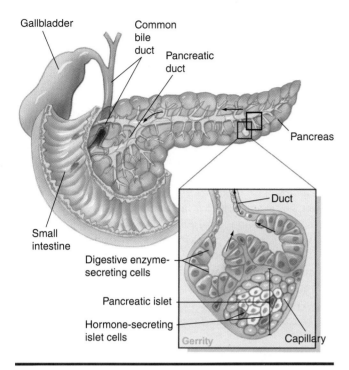

Gallbladder
Common bile duct
Pancreatic duct
Pancreas
Small intestine
Digestive enzyme-secreting cells
Pancreatic islet
Hormone-secreting islet cells
Duct
Capillary
Gerrity

Figure 10.11 The pancreas is both an endocrine and an exocrine gland. The hormone-secreting cells are grouped in clusters, called islets. Other pancreatic cells secrete digestive enzymes. AP|R

Clinical INSIGHT

Persons with inflamed joints often receive injections of *cortisone*, a glucocorticoid, to temporarily reduce inflammation and the associated pain. Such a procedure is fairly common in sports medicine.

Glucagon

Glucagon (glū′-kah-gon) increases the concentration of glucose in the blood. It does this by activating the liver to convert glycogen and certain noncarbohydrates, such as amino acids, into glucose. Glucagon helps to maintain the blood level of glucose within normal limits even when carbohydrates are depleted due to long intervals between meals. Epinephrine stimulates a similar action, but glucagon is more effective. Glucagon secretion is controlled by the blood level of glucose via a negative-feedback mechanism. A low level of blood glucose stimulates glucagon secretion, and a high level of blood glucose inhibits glucagon secretion.

Insulin

The effect of **insulin** on the level of blood glucose is opposite that of glucagon. Insulin decreases blood glucose by aiding the movement of glucose into body cells, where it can be used as a source of energy. Without insulin, glucose is not readily available to cells for cellular respiration. Insulin also stimulates the liver to convert glucose into glycogen for storage. Figure 10.12 shows how the antagonistic functions of glucagon and insulin maintain the concentration of glucose in the blood within normal limits. Like glucagon, the level of blood glucose regulates the secretion of insulin. High blood glucose levels stimulate insulin secretion; low levels inhibit insulin secretion.

Disorders   Diabetes mellitus (dī-ah-bē′-tēz mel-lī′-tus) is caused by the hyposecretion of insulin or the inability of cells to recognize it due to a loss of insulin receptors. In either case, the result is excessively high levels of glucose in the blood. With insufficient insulin, glucose cannot get into cells easily, and cells must rely more heavily on fat molecules as an energy source for cellular respiration. The products of this reaction tend to decrease the pH of the blood (acidosis), which can inactivate vital enzymes and may lead to death.

An excessive production of insulin may lead to **hypoglycemia,** a condition characterized by excessively low blood glucose levels. Symptoms include acute fatigue, weakness, increased irritability, and restlessness. In extreme conditions, it may lead to an insulin-triggered coma.

Check My Understanding

10. How does the pancreas regulate the level of blood glucose?

Table 10.5	Hormones of the Pancreas		
Hormone	**Control**	**Action**	**Disorders**
Glucagon	Blood glucose level	Increases blood glucose by stimulating the liver to convert glycogen and other nutrients into glucose	
Insulin	Blood glucose level	Decreases blood glucose by aiding movement of glucose into cells and promoting the conversion of glucose into glycogen	Hyposecretion causes diabetes mellitus. Hypersecretion may cause hypoglycemia.

Clinical INSIGHT

Everyone experiences stressful situations. Stress may be caused by physical or psychological stimuli that are perceived as threatening. Whereas mild stress can stimulate creativity and productivity, severe and prolonged stress can have serious consequences.

The hypothalamus is the initiator of the stress response. When stress occurs, the hypothalamus activates the sympathetic division of the autonomic nervous system and the secretion of epinephrine and norepinephrine by the adrenal medulla. Thus, both neural and hormonal activity prepare the body to meet the stressful situation by increasing blood glucose, heart rate, breathing rate, blood pressure, and blood flow to the muscle and nervous systems.

Simultaneously, the hypothalamus stimulates the release of ACTH from the anterior pituitary. ACTH, in turn, causes the secretion of glucocorticoids by the adrenal cortex. Glucocorticoids increase the levels of amino acids and fatty acids in the blood and promote the formation of additional glucose from noncarbohydrate sources.

All of these responses prepare the body for an immediate response to remove the stressful stimulus. Unfortunately, the complexity of modern society often prevents removing stressful stimuli promptly and tends to create prolonged stress. For example, if your boss is the cause of psychological stress, a physical or verbal assault or walking away from your job may create more problems and stress than it solves.

Prolonged stress may cause several undesirable side effects from the constant secretion of large amounts of epinephrine and glucocorticoids, such as decreased immunity and high blood pressure—problems that are common in our society.

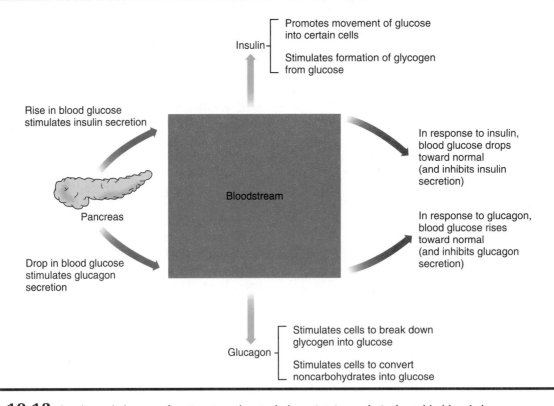

Figure 10.12 Insulin and glucagon function together to help maintain a relatively stable blood glucose concentration. Negative feedback responding to blood glucose concentration controls the levels of both hormones. AP|R

10.7 Gonads

The gonads are the sex glands: the ovaries and testes. They not only produce ova and sperm, respectively, but also secrete the sex hormones. Table 10.6 summarizes the actions of the sex hormones. The gonads and their hormones are covered in more detail in chapter 17.

Female Hormones

The **ovaries** are the female gonads. They are small, almond-shaped organs located in the pelvic cavity. The ovaries begin to function at the onset of puberty when the gonadotropic hormones (FSH and LH) are released from the anterior pituitary. Subsequently,

Table 10.6 Hormones of Ovaries and Testes

Hormone	Control	Action
Ovaries		
Estrogen	FSH	Development of female sex organs, secondary sex characteristics, and sex drive; prepares uterus to receive an embryo and helps maintain pregnancy
Progesterone	LH	Prepares uterus to receive an embryo and maintains pregnancy; prepares mammary glands for milk production
Testes		
Testosterone	LH	Development of male sex organs, secondary sex characteristics, and sex drive

Clinical INSIGHT

There are two types of diabetes mellitus. *Type I* or *insulin-dependent diabetes* is an autoimmune metabolic disorder that usually appears in persons less than 20 years of age. For this reason, it is sometimes called juvenile diabetes, although the condition persists for life. Type I diabetes results when the immune system destroys the insulin-producing cells in pancreatic islets. Because the metabolism of carbohydrates, fats, and proteins is affected, persons with type I diabetes must follow a restrictive diet. They must also check their blood glucose level several times a day and inject themselves with insulin, or receive insulin from an implanted insulin pump, to keep their blood glucose concentration within normal limits.

The vast majority of diabetics have *type 2* or *insulin-independent diabetes*, which is caused by a reduction of the insulin receptors on body cells. This form of diabetes, also called adult-onset diabetes, usually appears after 40 years of age in persons who are overweight. The symptoms are less severe than in type I diabetes and can be controlled by a careful diet and oral medications that help regulate blood levels of glucose. The current increase in obesity among children and young adults is of concern because it may lead to an increase in type 2 diabetes.

ovarian hormones, FSH, and LH interact in an approximately 28-day *ovarian cycle* in which their concentrations increase and decrease in a rhythmic pattern.

Estrogens (es'-trō-jens), the primary female sex hormones, are several related compounds that are secreted by developing ovarian follicles that also contain an ovum (egg cell). Estrogens stimulate the development and maturation of the female sex organs and the secondary sexual characteristics (e.g., female fat distribution, breasts, and broad hips). They also help to maintain the uterine lining to support a pregnancy.

Progesterone (prō-jes'-te-rōn) is secreted by an empty follicle after the ovum has been released by ovulation. It helps prepare the uterus for receiving an embryo and maintains the pregnancy. It also helps to prepare the mammary glands for milk production.

Male Hormone

The **testes** are paired, ovoid organs located outside the pelvic cavity in the scrotum, a sac of skin located posterior to the penis. The seminiferous tubules of the testes produce sperm, the male sex cell; and the interstitial cells (cells between the tubules) secrete the male hormone **testosterone** (tes-tos'-te-rōn). Testosterone stimulates the development and maturation of the male sex organs, the secondary sexual characteristics (e.g., growth of facial and body hair, low voice, narrow hips, and heavy muscles and bones), and the male sex drive.

10.8 Other Endocrine Glands and Tissues

There are a few other glands and tissues of the body that secrete hormones and are part of the endocrine system. These include the pineal gland, the thymus, and certain small glands in the lining of the stomach and small intestine. In addition, the placenta is an important temporary endocrine organ during pregnancy. It is considered in chapter 18.

Pineal Gland

The **pineal** (pin'-ē-al) **gland** is a small, cone-shaped nodule of endocrine tissue that is located in the brain between the cerebral hemispheres near the roof of the third ventricle. It secretes the hormone **melatonin** (mel-ah-tō'-nin), which seems to inhibit the secretion of gonadotropic hormones and may help control the onset of puberty. Melatonin seems to regulate wake–sleep cycles and other biorhythms associated with the cycling of day and night. The secretion of melatonin is regulated by exposure to light and darkness. When exposed to light, impulses from the retinas of the eyes are sent to the pineal gland, causing a decrease in melatonin production. During darkness, these impulses decrease, and melatonin secretion is increased. Secretion is greatest at night and lowest in the day, which keeps our sleep–wakefulness cycle in harmony with the day–night cycle.

As frequent fliers know, jet lag results when the sleep–wakefulness cycles are out of sync with the day–night cycle. Jet lag can be more quickly reversed by exposure to bright light with wavelengths similar to sunlight, because the melatonin cycle is resynchronized to the new day–night cycle.

Thymus

The **thymus** is located in the mediastinum over the heart. It is large in infants and children but it shrinks with age and is greatly reduced in adults. It plays a crucial role in the development of immunity, which is discussed in chapter 13. The thymus produces several hormones, collectively called **thymosins** (thi-mo'-sins), which are involved in the production and maturation of T lymphocytes, a type of white blood cell.

CHAPTER SUMMARY

- The endocrine system is composed of the endocrine glands and tissues. The major endocrine glands are the adrenal glands, gonads, pancreas, parathyroid glands, pineal gland, pituitary gland, thymus, and thyroid gland. In addition, the hypothalamus functions like an endocrine gland in some ways.
- The endocrine system provides a chemical control of cellular functions.

10.1 The Nature of Hormones

- Hormones are chemical messengers that are carried by the blood throughout the body, where they modify cellular functions of target cells.
- Target cells may be many or few, widely distributed or localized, and nearby or distant from the hormone source. All target cells have receptors for hormones that affect them.
- Hormones may be classified chemically as either steroid and steroidlike hormones or nonsteroid hormones.
- Steroid hormones combine with a receptor within the cell and move into the nucleus to affect production of mRNA. Nonsteroid hormones combine with a receptor in the plasma membrane, which activates a membrane enzyme that promotes synthesis of cAMP, a second messenger. Cyclic AMP, in turn, activates other enzymes that bring about cellular changes.
- Prostaglandins are not secreted by endocrine glands. They are formed by most body cells and have a distinctly local effect. They modify the amount of cAMP available in a cell, so they affect the action of a hormone whose action involves cAMP.

- Production of most hormones is controlled by a negative-feedback mechanism.
- Hormone production may be stimulated by another hormone, changes in the internal environment, or by nerve impulses.

10.2 Pituitary Gland

- The pituitary gland is attached to the hypothalamus by a short stalk. It consists of an anterior lobe and a posterior lobe.
- The hypothalamus secretes releasing hormones and release-inhibiting hormones that are carried to the anterior lobe by a portal vein. The releasing and release-inhibiting hormones regulate the secretion of anterior lobe hormones.
- Anterior lobe hormones are
  a. growth hormone (GH), which stimulates growth and division of body cells;
  b. thyroid-stimulating hormone (TSH), which activates the thyroid to secrete thyroxine;
  c. adrenocorticotropic hormone (ACTH), which stimulates the secretion of hormones by the adrenal cortex;
  d. follicle-stimulating hormone (FSH) and luteinizing hormone (LH), which affect the gonads (in females, FSH stimulates production of estrogens by the ovaries; in males, it activates sperm production by the testes; in females, LH promotes ovulation and stimulates progesterone production by the ovaries; in males, it stimulates testosterone production); and
  e. prolactin (PRL), which initiates and maintains milk production by the mammary glands.

- Hormones of the posterior lobe are formed by neurons in the hypothalamus and are released within the posterior lobe.
- There are two posterior lobe hormones:
  a. antidiuretic hormone (ADH) reduces excretion of water by the kidneys;
  b. oxytocin stimulates contraction of the uterus during childbirth.

10.3 Thyroid Gland

- The thyroid gland is located just below the larynx, with lobes on each side of the trachea.
- TSH stimulates the secretion of thyroxine (T_4) and triiodothyronine (T_3), which increase cellular metabolism, protein synthesis, and neural activity.
- Iodine is an essential component of the T_4 and T_3 molecules.
- Calcitonin lowers the level of blood calcium by promoting calcium deposition in bones. Its secretion is controlled by the level of calcium in the blood.

10.4 Parathyroid Glands

- The parathyroid glands are embedded in the posterior surface of the thyroid gland.
- Parathyroid hormone increases the level of blood calcium by promoting calcium removal from bones, calcium absorption from the intestine, and calcium retention by the kidneys.
- Parathyroid secretion is controlled by the level of blood calcium.

10.5 Adrenal Glands

- An adrenal gland is located on top of each kidney. Each gland consists of two parts: an inner medulla and an outer cortex.
- The adrenal medulla secretes epinephrine and norepinephrine, which prepare the body to deal with stressful situations. They increase the heart rate, circulation to nervous and muscle systems, and glucose level in the blood.
- The adrenal cortex secretes a number of hormones that are classified as mineralocorticoids, glucocorticoids, and sex hormones.
- Aldosterone is the most important mineralocorticoid. It helps to regulate the concentration of electrolytes in the blood, especially sodium and potassium ions.
- Cortisol is the most important glucocorticoid. It promotes the formation of glucose from noncarbohydrate sources and inhibits inflammation. Its secretion is regulated by ACTH.
- Small amounts of androgens are secreted. They have little effect in adult males but contribute to the sex drive in adult females.

10.6 Pancreas

- The pancreas is both an exocrine and an endocrine gland. Its hormones are formed by the pancreatic islets, and their secretions are controlled by the level of blood glucose.
- Glucagon increases the level of blood glucose by stimulating the liver to form glucose from glycogen and some noncarbohydrate sources.
- Insulin decreases the level of blood glucose by aiding the movement of glucose into cells.
- The antagonistic functions of glucagon and insulin keep the level of blood glucose within normal limits.

10.7 Gonads

- Gonads are the sex glands: the ovaries in females and the testes in males. They secrete sex hormones, in addition to secreting sex cells. The secretion of these hormones is controlled by FSH and LH.
- Estrogen is secreted by follicles in the ovaries, and they stimulate development of female sex organs and secondary sex characteristics. Estrogens also help to prepare the uterus for an embryo and help to maintain pregnancy.
- Progesterone is secreted by the ovaries, mostly after ovulation. It prepares the uterus for the embryo, maintains pregnancy, and prepares the mammary glands for milk production.
- The testes secrete testosterone, the male hormone that stimulates the development of the male sex organs and secondary sex characteristics.

10.8 Other Endocrine Glands and Tissues

- The pineal gland is located near the roof of the third ventricle of the brain. It secretes melatonin, which seems to inhibit the secretion of FSH and LH by the anterior pituitary. The pineal gland also seems to be involved in biorhythms.
- The thymus is located in the thorax over the heart. It secretes thymosins, which are involved in the maturation of white blood cells called T lymphocytes.
- Endocrine disorders are associated with severe hyposecretion or hypersecretion of various hormones. Hyposecretion may result from injury. Hypersecretion is sometimes caused by a tumor.
- Major endocrine disorders include acromegaly, Addison's disease, cretinism, Cushing's syndrome, diabetes insipidus, diabetes mellitus, exophthalmic goiter, gigantism, hypopituitary dwarfism, simple goiter, and myxedema.

BUILDING MY VOCABULARY

1. **Selected New Terms**
   adrenocorticotropic hormone, p. 211
   aldosterone, p. 215
   antidiuretic hormone, p. 212
   cortisol, p. 215
   estrogen, p. 219
   glucagon, p. 217
   glucocorticoid, p. 215
   growth hormone, p. 210
   insulin, p. 217
   melatonin, p. 219
   mineralocorticoids, p. 215
   oxytocin, p. 212
   parathyroid hormone, p. 214
   progesterone, p. 219

   prolactin, p. 212
   testosterone, p. 219
   thymosin, p. 220
   thyroid-stimulating hormone, p. 211
   thyroxine (T_4), p. 212
   triiodothyronine (T_3), p. 213

2. **Related Clinical Terms**
   Goiter (goi′-ter) An enlargement of the thyroid gland.
   Exophthalmos (ek-sof-thal′-mōs) An abnormal bulging of the eyes.
   Hypercalcemia (hī-per-kal-sē′-mē-ah) An excess of calcium ions in the blood.
   Hypoglycemia (hī-pō-glī-sē′-mē-ah) A deficiency of blood glucose.

SELF-REVIEW

Answers are located in appendix B.

1. Chemical coordination of body functions is the function of the _____ system, whose glands secrete _____ that serve as chemical messengers.
2. A particular hormone affects only those cells that have _____ for that hormone.
3. _____ hormones use a second messenger to produce their characteristic effects on cells.
4. The secretion of most hormones is regulated by a _____ control system.
5. The secretion of pituitary hormones is regulated by a part of the brain called the _____.
6. The pituitary secretes three hormones that regulate secretion of other endocrine glands. _____ acts on the thyroid gland; ACTH acts on the _____; _____ and _____ act on the gonads.
7. Metabolic rate is regulated by _____ secreted by the _____.
8. The concentration of calcium in the blood is regulated by two hormones with antagonistic actions: _____ promotes calcium deposition in bones; _____ promotes calcium removal from bones.
9. Secretions of the adrenal _____ prepare the body to react in emergencies.
10. The primary hormone regulating the concentration of mineral ions in the blood is _____.
11. The pancreatic hormone that increases the concentration of blood sugar is _____.
12. The primary sex hormone in females is _____; the male sex hormone is _____.

CRITICAL THINKING

1. Complete the learning objectives listed on the first page of this chapter.
2. Some hormones affect many widely distributed cells in the body but others affect relatively few, localized cells. Explain how this occurs.
3. A blood test indicates that a patient has a low level of thyroxine. What are three possible causes of this condition? Explain.
4. How do hormones regulate calcium levels in the blood?
5. How do hormones regulate glucose levels in the blood?

Visit this book's website at www.mhhe.com/ gunstream5 for practice quizzes, learning exercises, case studies, and other study tools.

CHAPTER 11

Blood

Module 9
Cardiovascular System

Agglutination (agglutin = to stick together) The clumping of red blood cells in an antigen–antibody reaction.

Antibody A protein produced by B lymphocytes in response to a specific antigen.

Antigen A substance that stimulates the production of antibodies.

Coagulation The formation of a blood clot.

Erythrocyte (erythr = red) A red blood cell.

Formed elements The cellular components of blood: erythrocytes, leukocytes, and thrombocytes.

Hemoglobin (hemo = blood) The red, oxygen-carrying pigment in red blood cells.

Hemostasis (hemo = blood; stasis = standing still) The stoppage of bleeding.

Leukocyte (leuk = white) A white blood cell.

Plasma The liquid portion of blood.

Thrombocyte (thromb = clot) A platelet; a formed element that initiates the clotting process.

Thrombus A stationary blood clot.

lood is normally confined within the heart and blood vessels as it transports materials from place to place within the body. Substances carried by blood include oxygen, carbon dioxide, nutrients, waste products, hormones, mineral ions, and water. Blood does more than just transport substances. For example, blood also helps to (1) regulate the pH of body tissues, (2) prevent excessive blood loss by hemorrhage, and (3) fight infections. In a variety of ways, blood helps to maintain a stable environment for body cells.

11.1 General Characteristics of Blood

Blood is classified as a connective tissue that is composed of **formed elements** (blood cells and *platelets*) suspended in **plasma,** the liquid portion (matrix) of the blood. It is the only fluid tissue in the body. Blood is heavier and about four times more viscous than water. It is slightly alkaline, with a pH between 7.35 and 7.45. The volume of blood varies with the size of the individual, but it averages 5 to 6 liters in males and 4 to 5 liters in females. Blood comprises about 8% of the body weight.

About 55% of the blood volume consists of plasma, and 45% is made up of blood cells and platelets. Red blood cells are so numerous that they form almost 45% of the blood volume, nearly all of the formed elements. White blood cells and platelets combined form less than 1% of the blood volume (figure 11.1).

The great number of formed elements in blood is hard to imagine. There are approximately 5 million red blood cells, 7,500 white blood cells, and 300,000 thrombocytes in each 1 cubic millimeter (mm³)— about 1 drop—of blood. And these formed elements compose only 45% of the drop!

11.2 Red Blood Cells

Erythrocytes (eh-rith′-rō-sits), or *red blood cells (RBCs),* are tiny, biconcave disks that transport oxygen to body cells and carbon dioxide from body cells. The biconcave shape exposes maximal surface area of the cell for the diffusion of these gases through the plasma membrane. Mature erythrocytes lack a nucleus, although a nucleus is present in immature RBCs (figure 11.2).

Hemoglobin

About 33% of each erythrocyte, by volume, consists of **hemoglobin** (hē′-mō-glō-bin), the red pigment that gives the red color to blood. Hemoglobin consists of *heme,* a pigment containing an iron atom in its molecule, and *globin,* a protein. Hemoglobin combines reversibly with oxygen and plays a vital role in the transport of oxygen by red blood cells. It also plays a minor role in carbon dioxide transport.

When blood flows through the lungs, oxygen diffuses from air spaces in the lungs into the blood. Oxygen enters RBCs and combines with hemoglobin to form **oxyhemoglobin,** which gives a bright red color to blood. After the release of oxygen from oxyhemoglobin to body cells, the resultant **deoxyhemoglobin** carries a small amount of carbon dioxide from body cells back to the lungs for removal. Deoxyhemoglobin gives a dark red color to blood. The mechanism of transporting oxygen and carbon dioxide is covered in chapter 14.

Concentration of RBCs

Erythrocytes are by far the most abundant blood cells. Because they are vital in the transport of oxygen, changes in the concentration of RBCs can have clinical significance. A *red blood cell count* is a routine clinical test to determine the number of red blood cells in a

(a) **Centrifuged Blood**

Withdraw blood

Centrifuge

Plasma (55% of whole blood)

White blood cells and platelets (<1% of whole blood)

Red blood cells (45% of whole blood)

Formed elements

(b) **Peripheral Blood Smear**

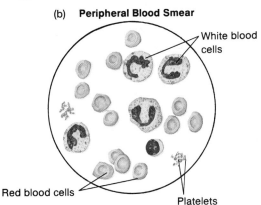

White blood cells

Red blood cells

Platelets

Figure 11.1 Blood consists of plasma and formed elements. (*a*) If blood is centrifuged, the red blood cells sink to the bottom of the tube and the liquid plasma forms the top layer. White blood cells and platelets form a thin layer between the two. (*b*) The microscopic appearance of blood cells and platelets in a smear of peripheral blood. AP|R

cubic millimeter (mm³) of blood. For adult males, normal values range from 4.5 million to 6.2 million RBCs per mm³. For adult females, normal values range from 4.2 million to 5.4 million RBCs per mm³. The higher count in males results because males have a higher metabolic rate than females, and a greater concentration of RBCs is required to provide needed oxygen for the rapidly metabolizing cells.

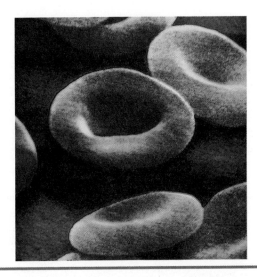

Figure 11.2 A false-color scanning electron micrograph of human erythrocytes (5000x). Note the biconcave shape and the absence of a nucleus and other organelles. AP|R

Normal values of RBCs per mm³ of blood also vary with altitude. The concentration of RBCs is greater in persons living at higher altitudes because of the reduced atmospheric pressure and oxygen concentration. This reduces the rate at which oxygen can enter the blood, causing a decline in the concentration of oxygen in the blood, which, in turn, stimulates RBC production.

Production

Prior to birth, RBCs are produced largely by the liver and spleen, but after birth production occurs only in the red bone marrow (myeloid tissue). In infants, RBCs are formed in the red marrow of all bones, but in adults RBC formation primarily occurs in the red marrow of the skull bones, ribs, sternum, vertebrae, and pelvic bones.

Erythrocyte production varies with the oxygen concentration of the blood in a negative feedback control mechanism. If blood oxygen concentration is low (hypoxia), such as after a hemorrhage, the kidneys and liver release **erythropoietin** (e-rith-ro-poi′-e-tin), a hormone that stimulates red bone marrow to produce more RBCs. When the new RBCs are added to the blood and the oxygen concentration rises to normal levels, production of erythropoietin declines, causing a decrease in RBC production (figure 11.3). A low level of erythropoietin is always present to maintain RBC production at a basal rate. Note that the concentration of oxygen in blood triggers the negative-feedback mechanism, which regulates erythropoietin secretion and, therefore, RBC production.

Iron, folic acid, and vitamin B₁₂ are required for erythrocyte production. Iron is required for hemoglobin

Figure 11.3 A negative-feedback loop corrects for a low O_2 concentration in blood. When O_2 concentration returns to normal, erythropoietin secretion declines to a basal level. **AP|R**

synthesis because each hemoglobin molecule contains four iron atoms. Folic acid and vitamin B_{12} are required for DNA synthesis during early stages of erythrocyte formation in red bone marrow. Vitamin B_{12} is sometimes called the *extrinsic factor* because it is obtained external to the body. Effective absorption of vitamin B_{12} from the digestive tract into the blood depends upon the stomach lining secreting the *intrinsic factor*. The intrinsic factor is a chemical that combines with vitamin B_{12}, enabling its absorption into the blood.

All blood cells, including erythrocytes, develop from *stem cells* called **hemocytoblasts** in red bone marrow. Hemocytoblasts divide to form myeloid stem cells and lymphoid stem cells, which, in turn, divide to produce the precursor cells that develop into specific types of blood cells and platelets. The pattern of cell division and development is shown in figure 11.4. Note that erythrocytes lose their nuclei and other organelles as they mature.

Life Span and Destruction

The life span of red blood cells is about 120 days, and billions of RBCs are destroyed and produced each day—about 2 million per second! Normally, destruction and production are kept in balance.

The plasma membranes of newly formed cells are flexible, which allows them to change shape as they pass through small blood vessels. However, with age the membranes lose their elasticity and become fragile and damaged. Worn-out RBCs are removed from circulation in the liver and spleen by phagocytic cells called **macrophages** (mak′-rō-fāj-es). Macrophages engulf and digest old and damaged erythrocytes in phagocytic vesicles. See chapter 3 to refresh your understanding of phagocytosis.

The heme portion of hemoglobin is broken down into an iron-containing compound and a yellow pigment, *bilirubin* (bil-i-rū′-bin). The iron-containing compound may be temporarily stored in the liver and spleen before being recycled to the red bone marrow and used to form more hemoglobin. Bilirubin (a bile pigment) is secreted by the liver in bile, which is carried by the bile duct into the small intestine for disposal.

Check My Understanding
1. How does hemoglobin contribute to the function of erythrocytes?
2. How is erythrocyte production regulated?

11.3 White Blood Cells

Leukocytes (lū′-kō-sīts), or *white blood cells (WBCs)*, are derived from hemocytoblasts in the red bone marrow and undergo several developmental stages in the maturation process. All WBCs retain their nuclei. Note the developmental stages and mature white blood cells

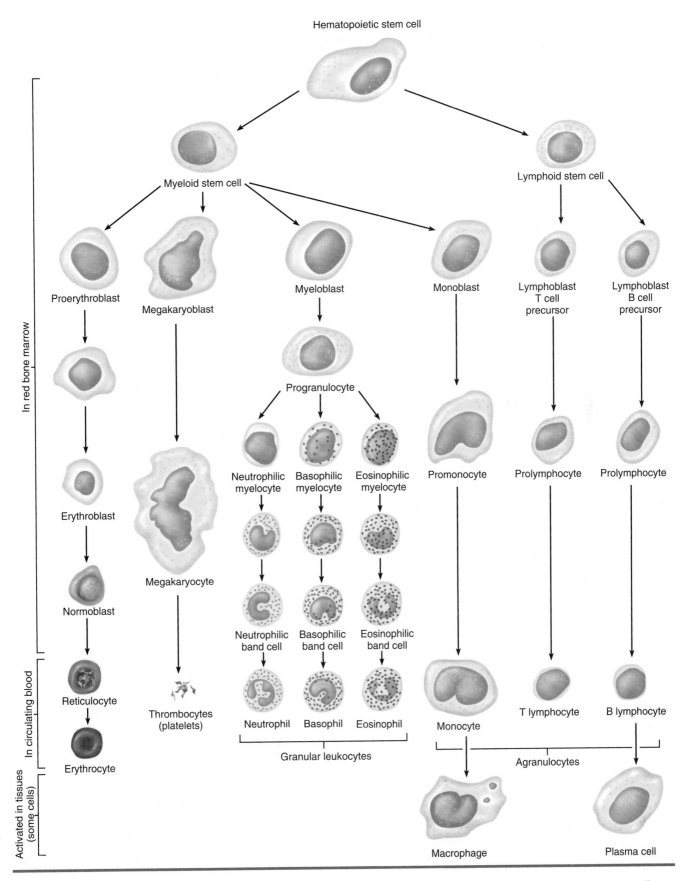

Figure 11.4 Formed elements develop from hemocytoblasts (stem cells) in red bone marrow. The color of the cells and platelets results from staining the cells with Wright's blood stain. AP|R

227

Clinical INSIGHT

Sickle-cell disease (sickle-cell anemia) is an inherited hemolytic disorder that affects about 1.3% of African-Americans. Afflicted persons have inherited two abnormal forms of the gene responsible for hemoglobin formation, which causes their hemoglobin to differ from normal hemoglobin by only a single amino acid. But this is sufficient to cause erythrocytes to be sickle-shaped (C-shaped) or elongated and pointed. Such erythrocytes tend to clump together to block tiny arteries depriving tissues of oxygen and causing intense pain and fatigue. This can lead to kidney disease, stroke, brain damage, and heart failure. The abnormal hemoglobin cannot transport oxygen efficiently, and the fragile erythrocytes rupture, further reducing the oxygen-carrying capacity of the blood. Without treatment, life expectancy is less than two years of age. With treatment, it is about age 50.

Persons who inherit only one abnormal form of the gene have a condition known as *sickle-cell trait*. They rarely have severe symptoms. About 8.3% of African-Americans have sickle-cell trait. If a man and a woman, each with sickle-cell trait, reproduce, each of their children has a 25% chance of inheriting sickle-cell disease.

Sickle-cell disease apparently originated in tropical Africa where malaria was prevalent. Persons with sickle-cell trait have a natural resistance against the malarial parasite, which invades RBCs. This resistance to malaria is what has enabled the abnormal form of the gene to persist.

A Sickle-Shaped Erythrocyte. A false-colored scanning electron micrograph of an abnormal erythrocyte characteristic of sickle-cell disease and three normal erythrocytes.

---

in figure 11.4. Leukocytes normally number 4,500 to 10,000 per mm³ of blood.

Production of a particular type of white blood cell is increased whenever the cells encounter disease-causing organisms or chemicals that they destroy. These encounters seem to cause the involved leukocytes to secrete a hormone that is carried to red bone marrow, where it stimulates increased production of that particular type of leukocyte.

Function

Leukocytes help provide a defense against disease organisms, and certain cells either promote or decrease inflammatory responses. Most of the functions of white blood cells are performed within the tissues, rather than in blood vessels. WBCs have the ability to move through capillary walls into tissues in response to chemicals released by damaged tissues. They are able to follow a "chemical trail" through the tissue spaces to reach the damaged tissues, a behavior called *chemotaxis*. WBCs congregate at the site of tissue damage to destroy dead cells and foreign substances. Leukocytes move by

ameboid movement, a motion characterized by flowing extensions of cytoplasm that pull the cell along.

Some WBCs destroy pathogens and cellular debris by phagocytosis. Others release chemicals that clump pathogens together aiding phagocytosis, and still others release chemicals that kill pathogens. How WBCs fight disease is discussed in chapter 13.

Types of Leukocytes

There are five types of white blood cells. In contrast to RBCs, WBCs are colorless. WBCs may be distinguished from RBCs by microscopic examination of fresh blood, but white blood cells must be stained in order to distinguish them from each other.

Leukocytes are broadly grouped into two categories: granulocytes and agranulocytes. **Granulocytes** (gran′-ū-lō-sīts) have small granules in their cytoplasm that are distinctively colored after staining. Neutrophils, eosinophils, and basophils are granulocytes, and they are about twice as large as red blood cells. In contrast, **agranulocytes** lack cytoplasmic granules. Lymphocytes and monocytes are agranulocytes. The five types of white

Table 11.1   Formed Elements in Blood

Formed Element	Description	Number	Function
Erythrocytes (RBCs)	Biconcave disks; no nucleus	4.2–5.4 million/mm³ in females; 4.5–6.2 million/mm³ in males	Transport O_2 and CO_2
Leukocytes (WBCs)		4,500–10,000/mm³	Help defend against invasion by microorganisms
Granulocytes	Cytoplasmic granules present		
Neutrophils	Nucleus with three to five lobes; tiny cytoplasmic granules stain lavender	60%–70% of total WBCs	Phagocytosis
Eosinophils	Nucleus bilobed; cytoplasmic granules stain red	2%–4% of total WBCs	Counteract histamine released in allergic reactions; destroy parasitic worms; phagocytosis
Basophils	Nucleus U-shaped or lobed; cytoplasmic granules stain blue	0.5%–1% of total WBCs	Intensify inflammation response in allergic reactions by releasing histamine and heparin
Agranulocytes	Cytoplasmic granules absent		
Lymphocytes	Very little cytoplasm around spherical nucleus; slightly larger than RBCs	20%–25% of total WBCs	Produce antibodies and provide immunity
Monocytes	Nucleus usually U- to kidney-shaped; two to three times larger than RBCs	3%–8% of total WBCs	Phagocytosis
Thrombocytes (platelets)	Tiny cytoplasmic fragments	150,000–400,000 per mm³	Form platelet plugs and start clotting of the blood

blood cells are distinguished by the shape of the nucleus, the presence or absence of cytoplasmic granules, and the size of the cells. See table 11.1 and figures 11.5 to 11.9. The cells in the figures have been stained with Wright's blood stain to reveal their distinguishing characteristics.

Neutrophils

Neutrophils (nū'-trō-fils) are the most abundant leukocytes and form 60% to 70% of the total WBCs. They are distinguished by a nucleus with two to five lobes and inconspicuous lavender-staining granules. Neutrophils are attracted by chemicals released from damaged tissues and are the first WBCs to respond to tissue damage. They engulf bacteria and cellular debris by phagocytosis and release the enzyme lysozyme, which destroys some bacteria. The number of neutrophils increases dramatically in acute bacterial infections. Their primary function is to destroy bacterial pathogens.

Eosinophils

Eosinophils (ē-ō-sin'-ō-fils) constitute 2% to 4% of the WBCs. They are characterized by a bilobed nucleus and red-staining cytoplasmic granules. Eosinophils neutralize histamine, a chemical released by basophils

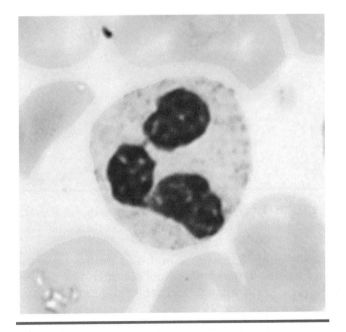

Figure 11.5 A neutrophil has a nucleus with two to five lobes and small lavender-staining cytoplasmic granules. AP|R

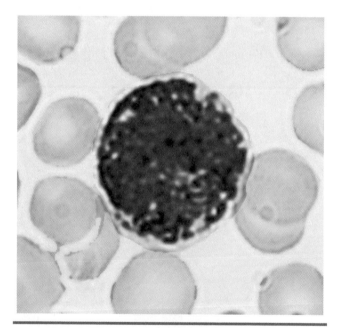

LM 1,200x

Figure 11.6 An eosinophil has red-staining cytoplasmic granules and usually a two-lobed nucleus. AP|R

Figure 11.8 A lymphocyte has a spherical nucleus and a small amount of cytoplasm that lacks cytoplasmic granules. It is the smallest of the white blood cells. AP|R

Figure 11.7 A basophil has blue-staining cytoplasmic granules and a large nucleus that is often U-shaped. AP|R

Figure 11.9 A monocyte is the largest white blood cell. It has a kidney-shaped nucleus and lacks cytoplasmic granules. AP|R

during allergic reactions, and also destroy parasitic worms. The number of eosinophils increases rapidly during allergic reactions and parasitic worm infections.

Basophils

Basophils (bā′-sō-fils) are the least numerous of the WBCs, forming only 0.5% to 1% of the WBCs. They are characterized by a nucleus that is U-shaped or

lobed and by large, blue-staining cytoplasmic granules. Basophils that have moved into the tissues are called **mast cells**. Mast cells release histamine and heparin when tissues are damaged and in allergic reactions. Histamine dilates blood vessels to increase blood flow in the affected areas, and make the blood vessels more permeable so other leukocytes can enter the affected tissues. Histamine is the primary cause of allergic symptoms. Heparin inhibits clot formation.

Lymphocytes

Lymphocytes (lim′-fō-sīts) form 20% to 25% of the circulating WBCs. They are the smallest leukocytes and are distinguished by a spherical nucleus that is enveloped by very little cytoplasm. Lymphocytes play a vital role in immunity and are especially abundant in lymphoid tissues. There are two types of lymphocytes. **T lymphocytes** directly attack and destroy pathogens (bacteria and viruses), and **B lymphocytes** produce antibodies that attack bacteria and bacterial toxins (poisons).

Clinical INSIGHT

A *complete blood count (CBC)* is one of the most common and clinically useful blood tests. It consists of several different blood tests: RBC count, WBC count, platelet count, differential white cell count (the percentage of each type of leukocyte), hematocrit, and hemoglobin percentage. Abnormal values for these tests are associated with infectious and inflammatory processes and with specific blood disorders.

Monocytes

Monocytes (mon′-ō-sīts) are the largest WBCs, and they comprise 3% to 8% of the WBCs. A U-shaped or kidney-shaped nucleus and abundant cytoplasm distinguish monocytes. Monocytes are active in phagocytosis. The number of monocytes in the blood increases during viral infections and inflammation of tissues. They carry out their functions of engulfing dead cells, cellular debris, and bacteria only after migrating into body tissues. Monocytes in body tissues are called **macrophages**. They are very active phagocytic cells that join with neutrophils to clean up damaged tissues and pathogens.

11.4 Platelets APR

Thrombocytes (throm′-bō-sīts), or **platelets**, are actually cytoplasmic fragments of *megakaryocytes,* large cells that develop from hemocytoblasts in red bone marrow (see figure 11.4). There are 150,000 to 400,000 thrombocytes per mm³ of blood. Thrombocytes clump together to plug breaks in blood vessels, and they start the clotting process.

Check My Understanding
3. What are the functions of each type of leukocyte?
4. What are the recognition characteristics of each type of leukocyte?

11.5 Plasma

Plasma is the straw-colored fluid portion of the blood and consists of over 90% water. Water is the liquid carrier of plasma solutes (dissolved substances) and formed elements and is the solvent of all living systems. Plasma contains a great variety of solutes, such as nutrients, enzymes, hormones, antibodies, waste products, electrolytes, and respiratory gases. Table 11.2 lists the major types of solutes in plasma. Plasma solutes are constantly being added and removed, so the solutes are normally in a state of dynamic balance that is maintained by a variety of homeostatic mechanisms.

Plasma Proteins

Plasma proteins are the most abundant solutes. They are not used as an energy source but remain in the plasma. The three major groups of plasma proteins are albumin, globulins, and fibrinogen. Except for gamma globulins, plasma proteins are produced by the liver and are released into the blood.

Albumins form about 60% of the plasma proteins. They are buffers that help to keep the pH of the blood within narrow limits and play an important role in maintaining the osmotic pressure of the blood. Osmotic pressure determines the water balance between the blood and body cells. If osmotic pressure of the blood declines, water moves into the body tissues and causes the tissues to swell (edema). This also decreases blood volume and, in severe cases, may decrease blood pressure as well. If osmotic pressure of the blood increases, water moves into the blood, causing an increase in blood volume and in blood pressure while reducing the amount of water available to body cells.

Globulins form about 36% of plasma proteins. The three types of globulins are alpha, beta, and gamma globulins. Alpha and beta globulins carry lipids and fat-soluble vitamins in the blood. Gamma globulins are produced in lymphoid tissues and consist of antibodies that are involved in immunity.

Fibrinogen forms only 4% of the plasma proteins, but it plays a vital role in the blood-clotting process. Fibrinogen is a soluble protein that is converted to insoluble fibrin to form blood clots.

Table 11.2   Major Solutes in Blood Plasma

Solute	Description
Albumins	60% of plasma proteins; help produce viscosity of blood; help maintain osmotic pressure and pH of blood
Globulins	Alpha and beta globulins transport lipids and fat-soluble vitamins; gamma globulins consist of antibodies
Fibrinogen	Soluble protein that is converted into insoluble fibrin during clot formation
Nonprotein nitrogen substances	Amino acids absorbed from intestine; urea and uric acid formed from protein and nucleoprotein breakdown
Nutrients	Products of digestion, such as amino acids, fatty acids, glycerol, and glucose, are carried from intestines to body cells
Enzymes and hormones	Help to regulate metabolic processes
Electrolytes	Mineral ions help to maintain osmotic pressure, pH, and ionic balance between body cells and blood
Respiratory gases	Both oxygen and carbon dioxide are dissolved in the plasma

Nonprotein Nitrogen Substances

The plasma also contains *nonprotein nitrogen (NPN) substances* that contain nitrogen in their molecules. These substances include amino acids, urea, and uric acid. Amino acids are nutrients that are formed by the digestion of protein in the intestines and are absorbed into the blood. Urea and uric acid are waste products of protein and nucleoprotein breakdown. They are carried by the blood to the kidneys for removal by excretion in the urine.

Electrolytes

Most of the plasma **electrolytes** (ē-lek′-trō-līts) are ions of inorganic compounds that are either absorbed from the intestine or released from body cells. The common electrolytes include sodium ions (Na^+), potassium ions (K^+), calcium ions (Ca^{++}), chloride ions (Cl^-), bicarbonate ions (HCO_3^-), and phosphate ions (PO_4^{---}). Electrolytes help to maintain the osmotic pressure and pH of the plasma, and most of them are essential to life processes.

Check My Understanding

5. What are the major components of blood plasma?

11.6 Hemostasis

Whenever blood vessels are broken, several homeostatic processes are implemented to prevent excessive blood loss. The stoppage of bleeding is called **hemostasis** and involves three separate but interrelated processes: blood vessel spasm, platelet plug formation, and blood clot formation.

Vascular Spasm

The first response of a damaged blood vessel is constriction, or spasm, of the vessel. A *vascular spasm* restricts blood loss from the damaged vessel and it lasts for several minutes, which allows time for formation of the platelet plug and clotting. As platelets accumulate at the site of the damage, they secrete *serotonin,* a chemical that continues the contraction of the smooth muscles in the damaged vessel.

Platelet Plug Formation

Platelets normally do not stick to each other or to the wall of the blood vessel because they are repelled by the positively charged vessel wall. However, when a vessel is damaged, the underlying connective tissue is exposed. Platelets are attracted to the site and adhere to the negatively charged connective tissue and to each other so that a cluster of platelets accumulates to plug the break. Figure 11.10 shows the stages in this process. The formation of a *platelet plug* may not seal off the damaged blood vessel but it sets the stage for the next process, blood clot formation.

Coagulation

Coagulation (kō-ag-ū-lā′-shun), or blood clotting, is the third and most effective process of hemostasis. The formation of a blood clot is a complex process involving many substances. Blood contains both *procoagulants,* substances that promote clotting, and *anticoagulants,* substances that inhibit clotting. Normally, the anticoagulants predominate, and blood does not clot. However, when a vessel is broken the increase in procoagulant activity starts the clotting process.

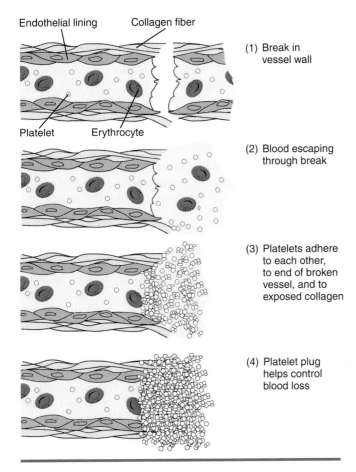

Figure 11.10 Steps in the formation of a platelet plug.

Clot formation is a complex process but it is completed within three to six minutes after a blood vessel has been damaged. The clot is restricted to the site of damage because that is where procoagulants outnumber anticoagulants. The key steps in the clotting process are summarized here and shown in figure 11.11:

1. Damaged tissues release *thromboplastin* and aggregated platelets release *platelet factors,* which react with several clotting factors in the plasma to produce **prothrombin activator**.
2. In the presence of calcium ions, prothrombin activator stimulates the conversion of **prothrombin**, an inactive enzyme, into the active enzyme **thrombin.**
3. In the presence of calcium ions, thrombin converts molecules of fibrinogen, a soluble plasma protein, into threadlike, interconnected strands of insoluble **fibrin.** Fibrin strands form a meshwork that entraps blood cells and sticks to the damaged tissue to form a **thrombus,** a blood clot.

After a clot has formed, the fibrin strands contract, which produces a more compact clot and pulls the damaged tissues closer to each other (figure 11.12).

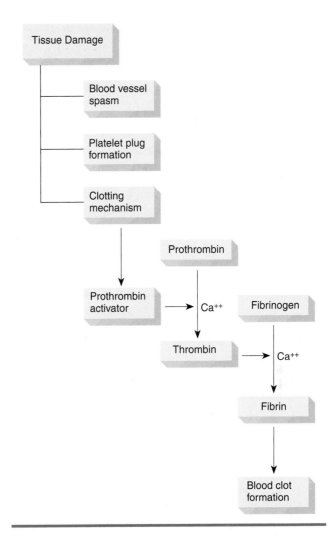

Figure 11.11 Hemostasis consists of three processes: blood vessel spasm, platelet plug formation, and blood clot formation.

Figure 11.12 A false-colored scanning electron photomicrograph of a blood clot shows blood cells trapped in a meshwork of fibrin strands.

Subsequently, fibroblasts migrate into the clot and form fibrous connective tissue that repairs the damaged area. As healing occurs, *tissue plasminogen* (plaz-min′-o-jen) *activator (t-PA)* converts *plasminogen,* an inactive enzyme in blood plasma, into *plasmin,* its active form. Plasmin breaks down fibrin and dissolves the blood clot.

Check My Understanding

6. What are the three major steps in hemostasis? How are blood clots formed?

11.7 Human Blood Types

Several different blood types occur in humans. The most familiar ones involve the ABO blood group (types A, B, AB, and O) and the Rh factor (Rh+ and Rh−).

   Blood types are determined by specific **antigens,** special proteins located on the plasma membranes of erythrocytes. Only a few of the many antigens on the surface of erythrocytes are used in blood typing. They are sometimes called *blood typing antigens* because blood is typed by identifying these antigens on the red blood cells of a blood sample. These antigens are the only ones to cause adverse reactions in blood transfusions.

   Whenever RBCs with one type of antigen are introduced into the blood of a person whose RBCs possess a different antigen, the introduced antigens (and RBCs) are recognized as foreign by the recipient's body, and they are attacked by **antibodies** present in the recipient's plasma. Antibodies are substances in plasma that react with foreign proteins in various ways to protect the body from foreign substances and pathogens. In this case, the antibodies bind to the foreign antigens, causing the foreign RBCs to clump together. The clumping of foreign RBCs is called **agglutination** (ah-glū-ti-nā′-shun).

   Whenever blood loss is substantial, transfusions of whole blood are routinely given to replace the lost blood. The blood used in the transfusion is usually of the same blood type as that of the recipient. However, a compatible but different blood type may be used in an extreme emergency. Care must be taken to ensure that the transfused blood is compatible with the blood of the recipient. A transfusion of incompatible blood can be fatal because the transfused incompatible RBCs clump together and block small blood vessels, which deprives the tissues supplied by these vessels of nutrients and oxygen.

ABO Blood Group

The ABO blood group is based on the presence or absence of two antigens on the surface of red blood cells: **antigen A** and **antigen B.** Like all antigens, they are inherited and remain unchanged from birth to death. The ABO blood group is divided into four possible types: A, B, AB, and O.

   After birth, antibodies against the ABO antigen that is *not* present are produced and accumulate in the plasma. Table 11.3 summarizes the relationships of blood type, antigens, and antibodies; figure 11.13 shows these relationships diagrammatically.

   Because antibodies anti-A and anti-B cause clumping of red blood cells with antigens A and B, respectively, the ABO blood type is easily determined. This may be done by placing two separate drops of blood to be tested on a glass slide. A drop of serum containing anti-A antibodies is added to one drop and serum containing anti-B antibodies is added to the other. The

Table 11.3   Antigens and Antibodies in ABO Blood Types*

Blood Type	Antigen on RBCs	Antibodies in Plasma
A	A	Anti-B
B	B	Anti-A
AB	A, B	None
O	None	Anti-A, anti-B

*Note that the antigen present determines the blood type.

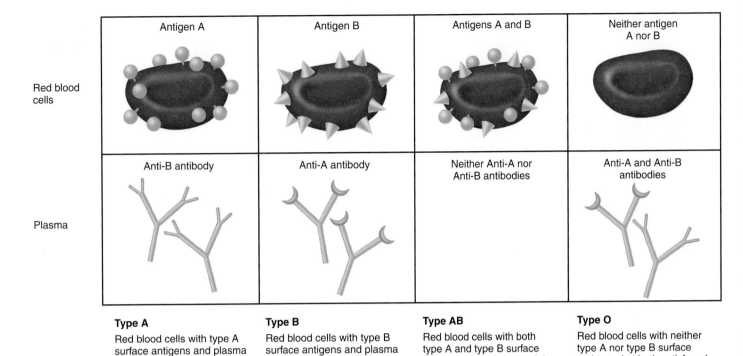

Type A
Red blood cells with type A surface antigens and plasma with anti-B antibodies

Type B
Red blood cells with type B surface antigens and plasma with anti-A antibodies

Type AB
Red blood cells with both type A and type B surface antigens, and neither anti-A nor anti-B plasma antibodies

Type O
Red blood cells with neither type A nor type B surface antigens, but both anti-A and anti-B plasma antibodies

Figure 11.13 Antigen and antibody characteristics of the ABO blood groups.

Table 11.4 Agglutination Pattern in ABO Blood Typing

Blood Type	Anti-A Serum plus Blood	Anti-B Serum plus Blood
A	Agglutination	No agglutination
B	No agglutination	Agglutination
AB	Agglutination	Agglutination
O	No agglutination	No agglutination

pattern of agglutination that occurs in the separate drops of blood indicates the blood type, as shown in table 11.4. Figure 11.14 shows how agglutination occurs when type A blood is donated to a type B recipient.

As noted earlier, blood of the patient's blood type is used for a transfusion except in extreme emergencies. When a different blood type must be used, it is crucial that the antigens of the transfused blood are compatible with the antibodies of the recipient's blood. For example, blood with antigen A or B cannot be given to a patient whose blood contains antibody anti-A or anti-B. Considering this and the pattern of antigens and antibodies in the ABO blood types, the compatibility of the blood types for transfusions may be determined.

Table 11.5 indicates the preferred ABO blood types that are used for transfusions and blood types that are "acceptable" in emergency situations when the preferred blood type is not available. Note that type AB blood may receive blood from all ABO blood types and that type O blood may be given to all ABO blood types. Therefore, type AB blood is sometimes called the *universal recipient,* and type O blood is known as the *universal donor.*

Rh Blood Type

Blood typing also routinely tests for the presence of the **Rh (D) antigen.** There are several Rh antigens, but it is the D antigen that is of prime significance. The Rh antigen is named after *Rhesus* monkeys, in which the blood group was first discovered.

If the Rh antigen is present on the red blood cells, the blood is typed as Rh-positive (Rh+). If the Rh antigen is absent, the blood is Rh-negative (Rh−). Like the A and B antigens, the presence or absence of the Rh antigen is inherited.

The Rh blood type is determined by adding serum containing anti-Rh antibodies to a drop of blood on a glass slide. If agglutination occurs, the blood is Rh+. If clumping does not occur, the blood is Rh−.

Anti-Rh antibodies are not normally present in the plasma of Rh− persons. Instead, they are formed only when Rh+ red blood cells are introduced into a person with Rh− blood. The first time this occurs, there is no clumping reaction, but the production of anti-Rh antibodies begins. The buildup of anti-Rh antibodies sensitizes the person to future introductions of Rh

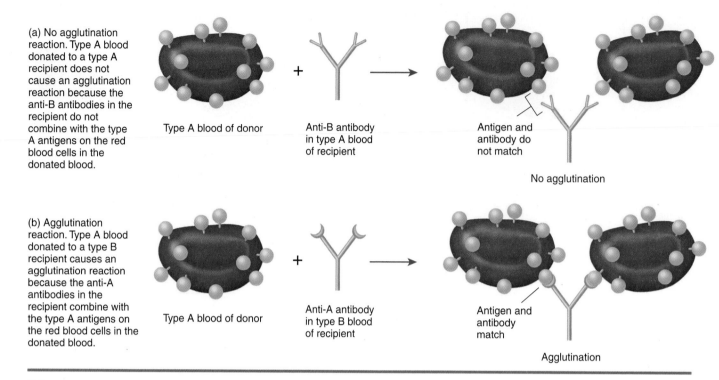

(a) No agglutination reaction. Type A blood donated to a type A recipient does not cause an agglutination reaction because the anti-B antibodies in the recipient do not combine with the type A antigens on the red blood cells in the donated blood.

Type A blood of donor

Anti-B antibody in type A blood of recipient

Antigen and antibody do not match

No agglutination

(b) Agglutination reaction. Type A blood donated to a type B recipient causes an agglutination reaction because the anti-A antibodies in the recipient combine with the type A antigens on the red blood cells in the donated blood.

Type A blood of donor

Anti-A antibody in type B blood of recipient

Antigen and antibody match

Agglutination

Figure 11.14 Compatible and incompatible transfusions.

Table 11.5   Preferred and Acceptable ABO Blood Types for Transfusions*

Blood Type of Recipient	Blood Types of Donors	
	Preferred	Acceptable
A	A	O
B	B	O
AB	AB	A, B, O
O	O	None

*Acceptable blood types are used only in emergencies when the preferred blood type is not available.

antigens. If a person with Rh− blood, who has been sensitized to the Rh antigen, receives a subsequent transfusion of Rh+ RBCs, the anti-Rh antibodies will cause agglutination of the transfused Rh+ RBCs, usually with serious or fatal results.

Erythroblastosis Fetalis

A similar kind of problem occurs in **erythroblastosis fetalis** (hemolytic disease of the newborn), a blood disorder of newborn infants that results from destruction of fetal erythrocytes by maternal antibodies.

When a woman with Rh− blood is pregnant with her first Rh+ fetus, some of the fetal Rh+ RBCs may accidentally enter the maternal blood due to broken placental blood vessels. This occurs most often during childbirth. The introduction of fetal RBCs with Rh antigens triggers the buildup of anti-Rh antibodies in the woman's blood. The buildup is slow, but the mother has become sensitized to the Rh antigen.

Erythroblastosis fetalis may develop in a subsequent pregnancy with an Rh+ fetus because the anti-Rh antibodies in maternal blood readily pass through the placenta into the fetal blood, where they agglutinate the fetal RBCs (figure 11.15). If a large number of RBCs are agglutinated and destroyed, the fetus has a decreased ability to transport oxygen.

In response to a decreased oxygen concentration, the fetal blood-forming tissues increase production of RBCs. In an attempt to rapidly produce RBCs, large numbers of nucleated, immature RBCs called *erythroblasts* are released into the blood. These immature cells are not as capable of carrying oxygen as are mature RBCs.

Also, the destruction of large numbers of RBCs produces other harmful effects. Hemoglobin freed from erythrocytes may interfere with normal kidney function and may cause kidney failure. The breakdown of large amounts of hemoglobin forms an excess of bilirubin, a yellow bile pigment that produces jaundice. Oxygen deficiency and excessive bilirubin concentrations in the fetal blood may cause brain damage in afflicted infants.

Upon birth of an infant suffering from erythroblastosis fetalis, the infant's total blood volume may be slowly replaced with Rh− blood. The transfused blood provides functional RBCs that cannot be agglutinated

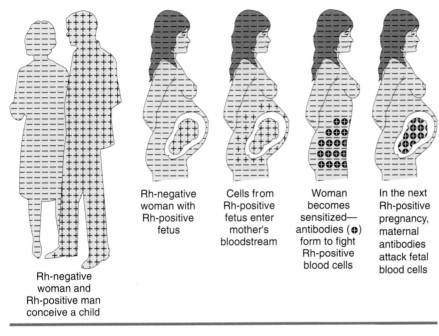

Figure 11.15 Development of erythroblastosis. A Rh− woman pregnant with a Rh+ fetus becomes sensitized to the Rh+ antigen and forms anti-Rh+ antibodies. In the next pregnancy with an Rh+ fetus, the woman's antibodies attack the fetal Rh+ red blood cells.

Rh-negative woman and Rh-positive man conceive a child

Rh-negative woman with Rh-positive fetus

Cells from Rh-positive fetus enter mother's bloodstream

Woman becomes sensitized— antibodies (⊕) form to fight Rh-positive blood cells

In the next Rh-positive pregnancy, maternal antibodies attack fetal blood cells

Check My Understanding

7. What determines an individual's ABO blood type?
8. Why is blood typing important in transfusions?
9. What is the cause of erythroblastosis fetalis?

Clinical INSIGHT

The cause of erythroblastosis fetalis is now preventable by injecting serum containing anti-Rh antibodies (trade name RhoGAM) into the blood of Rh− females within 72 hours after they have given birth to an Rh+ child, or after miscarriage or abortion. The anti-Rh antibodies agglutinate and destroy any fetal Rh+ RBCs that may have entered the mother's blood before they can stimulate the production of anti-Rh antibodies and sensitize the mother. Further, pregnant Rh− mothers may be given an injection of RhoGAM near the fifth month of subsequent pregnancies as a safety precaution.

by anti-Rh antibodies that may still be present, and it reduces the bilirubin concentration to eliminate the jaundice. Subsequently, the infant's own RBC production will again produce Rh+ RBCs, but by then all anti-Rh antibodies have been removed from the blood.

11.8 Disorders of the Blood

Blood disorders may be grouped as erythrocyte disorders, leukocyte disorders, and clotting disorders. Normal values for common blood tests are located on the inside back cover. Blood tests are valuable in diagnosing a variety of disorders. Note that many of the disorders described in the next section are associated with abnormal values of blood tests.

Erythrocyte Disorders

Anemia (ah-nē′-mē-ah) is the decreased oxygen-carrying capacity of the blood, and it is the most common blood disorder. A decreased number of RBCs or an insufficient amount of hemoglobin reduces the blood's capacity to carry oxygen. There are several different types of anemia:

- *Nutritional anemia* results from insufficient amounts of iron and vitamin B12 in the diet.
- *Hemorrhagic anemia* results from the excessive loss of RBCs through bleeding.
- *Pernicious anemia* results from a deficiency of intrinsic factor, which prevents absorption of sufficient vitamin B12 from the intestine to support adequate RBC production.
- *Hemolytic anemia* results from premature rupture of RBCs so that hemoglobin is released into the plasma.
- *Aplastic anemia* results from destruction of red bone marrow or its inability to produce a sufficient number of RBCs.
- *Sickle-cell anemia* results from abnormal hemoglobin that cannot carry sufficient oxygen. Sickled RBCs rupture easily, causing hemolytic anemia. Sickle-cell anemia is inherited and occurs primarily in descendents of African blacks who lived in malarial regions.

Erythroblastosis fetalis results from anti-Rh antibodies produced by a previously sensitized Rh− woman carrying an Rh+ fetus. The antibodies pass through the placenta into the fetal blood and agglutinate the fetal RBCs. It is characterized by anemia, jaundice, and the presence of erythroblasts in the blood.

Polycythemia (pol-ē-sī-thē-mē-ah) is a condition characterized by an excess of erythrocytes in the blood.

The excess RBCs increase blood volume and viscosity, which impairs circulation. It may result from cancer of the RBC-forming cells.

Leukocyte Disorders

Infectious mononucleosis is a contagious disease of the lymphoid tissue caused by the Epstein–Barr virus (EBV). It occurs primarily in young adults, and kissing is a common mode of transmission. Three times more females contract the disease than males. It infects B lymphocytes, which enlarge and resemble monocytes. Symptoms include fever, headache, fatigue, sore throat, and swollen lymph glands. There is no cure, but infectious mononucleosis usually persists for only about four weeks. However, in some persons it may linger for months or years, and relapses may be frequent.

Leukemia (lū-kē′-mē-ah) is a group of cancers of the red bone marrow cells that form WBCs. It is characterized by an excess production of leukocytes and the crowding out of RBC- and platelet-forming cells. Acute forms affect primarily children or young adults; chronic forms occur more often in adults. The various types of leukemia are classified according to the predominant white cell involved. Treatment usually involves chemotherapy and sometimes a transplant of bone marrow from a compatible donor.

Clotting Disorders

Hemophilia (hē-mō-fil′-ē-ah) is a group of inherited diseases that occur almost always in males because they are sex-linked disorders. Hemophilia is characterized by spontaneous bleeding and a reduced ability to form blood clots. It may be caused by a deficiency of any one of several plasma clotting factors. There is no cure for hemophilia, but it is treated by injection or transfusion of the missing clotting factors.

Thrombocytopenia (throm-bō-sī-tō-pē′-nē-ah) is a condition in which the number of platelets is so low (<50,000/mm³) that spontaneous bleeding cannot be prevented. Bleeding from many small vessels typically results in purplish blotches appearing on the skin.

Thrombosis is the condition resulting from the formation of a blood clot in an unbroken blood vessel. Such clots tend to form where the lining of a blood vessel is roughened or damaged. They can cause serious effects if they plug an artery and deprive vital tissues of blood. Blood clots form more frequently in veins than arteries, causing a condition known as *thrombophlebitis.*

Sometimes, a clot formed in a vein breaks free and is carried by the blood only to lodge in an artery, often a branch of a pulmonary artery. Such a moving clot is called an *embolus,* and when it blocks a blood vessel, the resulting condition is known as an **embolism.** An embolism can produce very serious and sometimes fatal results if it lodges in a vital organ and blocks the flow of blood.

CHAPTER SUMMARY

11.1 General Characteristics of Blood

- Blood is composed of plasma (55%) and formed elements (45%). Erythrocytes constitute nearly all of the formed elements.
- Blood is heavier and about four times more viscous than water, and it is slightly alkaline.
- About 8% of the body weight consists of blood. Blood volume ranges between 4 and 6 liters.

11.2 Red Blood Cells

- Erythrocytes, or red blood cells, are biconcave disks that lack nuclei and contain a large amount of hemoglobin. Their primary function is the transport of oxygen.
- Hemoglobin is composed of heme, an iron-containing pigment, and globin, a protein. It plays a vital role in oxygen transport and participates in carbon dioxide transport.
- Erythrocytes are very abundant in the blood. They number 4.5 million to 6.2 million per mm³ in males and 4.2 million to 5.4 million per mm³ in females.
- Erythrocytes are formed from hemocytoblasts in the red bone marrow. The rate of production is controlled by the oxygen concentration of the blood via a negative-feedback mechanism. A decreased oxygen concentration stimulates kidney cells to release erythropoietin, which stimulates increased production of RBCs by red bone marrow.
- Iron, amino acids, vitamin B_{12}, and folic acid are essential for RBC production.
- RBCs live about 120 days before they are destroyed by macrophages in the spleen and liver. In hemoglobin breakdown, the iron-containing molecules are recycled for use in forming more hemoglobin. Bilirubin, a bile pigment, is a by-product of hemoglobin breakdown.

11.3 White Blood Cells

- Leukocytes, or white blood cells, are also formed from hemocytoblasts in the red bone marrow. They retain their nuclei and number 4,500 to 10,000 per/mm³ of blood.
- White blood cells help to defend the body against invasion by disease organisms, and most of their activities occur within body tissues.

- The five types of leukocytes are categorized into two groups. Granulocytes have cytoplasmic granules and include neutrophils, eosinophils, and basophils. Agranulocytes lack cytoplasmic granules and include lymphocytes and monocytes.
- Neutrophils and monocytes are phagocytes that destroy bacteria and clean up cellular debris.
- Eosinophils help to reduce inflammation and destroy parasitic worms.
- Basophils promote inflammation.
- Lymphocytes play vital roles in immunity.

11.4 Platelets

- Thrombocytes, or platelets, are fragments of megakaryocytes in the red bone marrow. They number 150,000 to 400,000 per/mm^3 of blood.
- Platelets play a crucial role in hemostasis by forming platelet plugs and starting the clotting process.

11.5 Plasma

- Plasma, the liquid portion of the blood, consists of over 90% water along with a variety of solutes including nutrients, waste materials, proteins, electrolytes, and respiratory gases.
- There are three types of plasma proteins. Albumins are most numerous, and they help to maintain the osmotic pressure and pH of the blood. Alpha and beta globulins transport lipids and fat-soluble vitamins. Gamma globulins consist of antibodies that are involved in immunity. Fibrinogen is a soluble protein that is converted into insoluble fibrin during the clotting process.
- Nonprotein nitrogen substances in plasma include amino acids, urea, and uric acid.
- Electrolytes include ions of sodium, potassium, magnesium, calcium, carbonate, bicarbonate, phosphate, and chlorine. Electrolytes help to maintain the pH and osmotic pressure of the blood.

11.6 Hemostasis

- Hemostasis is the stoppage of bleeding. It consists of three processes: vascular spasm, platelet plug formation, and blood clotting.
- Vascular spasm is the first process in hemostasis. It reduces blood loss until the other processes can occur.
- Platelets stick to the damaged tissue and to each other to form a platelet plug.

- Platelets and damaged tissues initiate clot formation by releasing thromboplastin, which causes the formation of prothrombin activator. Prothrombin activator converts prothrombin into thrombin, which, in turn, converts fibrinogen into fibrin. Fibrin strands form the clot.
- After clot formation, fibroblasts invade the clot and gradually replace it with connective tissue as the clot is dissolved by enzymes.

11.7 Human Blood Types

- Blood types are determined by the presence or absence of blood typing antigens on the plasma membranes of RBCs.
- The four ABO blood types, A, B, AB, and O, are based on the presence or absence of antigen A and antigen B.
- Antibodies anti-A and anti-B are spontaneously formed against the antigen(s) that is (are) not present in a person's blood.
- Transfusions must be made using only compatible blood types. This means that the transfused RBCs must not have an antigen that reacts with the antibodies of the recipient's blood.
- If incompatible blood is transfused, agglutination of the transfused RBCs occurs. The clumped RBCs plug small blood vessels, depriving tissues of nutrients and oxygen. The result may be fatal.
- Blood with RBCs containing the Rh antigen is typed as Rh+. Blood without the Rh antigen is typed as Rh−.
- Anti-Rh antibodies are produced only after Rh+ RBCs are introduced into a person with Rh− blood. Once a person is sensitized in this way, a subsequent transfusion of Rh+ blood results in agglutination of the transfused RBCs.
- Erythroblastosis fetalis occurs in newborn infants when a sensitized Rh− woman is pregnant with an Rh+ fetus. Her anti-Rh antibodies pass through the placenta into the fetus and agglutinate the fetal RBCs, producing anemia and jaundice.

11.8 Disorders of the Blood

- Anemia is the most common disorder, and it may result from a variety of causes.
- Other disorders include erythroblastosis fetalis, hemophilia, infectious mononucleosis, leukemia, polycythemia, thrombocytopenia, and thrombosis.

BUILDING MY VOCABULARY

1. Selected New Terms
albumin, p. 231
basophil, p. 230
deoxyhemoglobin, p. 224
eosinophil, p. 229
erythropoietin, p. 225
fibrin, p. 233

fibrinogen, p. 231
globulin, p. 231
lymphocyte, p. 231
macrophages, p. 226
mast cell, p. 230
monocyte, p. 231
neutrophil, p. 229

oxyhemoglobin, p. 224
platelet, p. 231
prothrombin, p. 233
prothrombin activator, p. 233

2. **Related Clinical Terms**
   Hematoma (hē-mah-tō′mah) Black-and-blue marks (bruises) caused by coagulated blood in tissues.

Purpura (per′-pū-rah) Spontaneous bleeding into the tissues.
Septicemia (sep-ti-sē′mē-ah) Blood poisoning caused by bacteria or toxins in the blood.
Thalassemia (thal-ah-sē′mē-ah) A type of hemolytic anemia caused by abnormally fragile RBCs.

SELF-REVIEW

Answers are located in appendix B.

1. About _____% of blood consists of erythrocytes.
2. The red color of blood results from the presence of _____ in _____.
3. All formed elements are derived from stem cells, the _____, within red bone marrow.
4. A low blood concentration of _____ promotes the formation of the hormone _____, which stimulates RBC production.
5. Erythrocytes are destroyed in the spleen and _____.
6. Fighting disease invasion is the function of nucleated formed elements called _____.
7. The two major phagocytic WBCs are _____ and _____.
8. The release of histamine by _____ helps to promote inflammation.
9. WBCs that destroy parasitic worms and fight inflammation are the _____.
10. Immunity is the prime function of _____.
11. The fluid carrier of solutes and formed elements in blood is the _____.
12. Damaged tissues and _____ start coagulation by releasing thromboplastin.
13. Blood clot formation involves converting _____, a soluble plasma protein, into an insoluble protein called _____.
14. ABO blood types are named for the _____ on the surface of erythrocytes.
15. Type _____ blood is the universal recipient because it lacks anti-A and anti-B antibodies.

CRITICAL THINKING

1. Complete the learning objectives on the first page of this chapter.
2. Explain the role of blood oxygen concentration in the production of RBCs.
3. Why is type O blood considered the universal donor?
4. Explain how normally a blood clot forms only when tissue damage requires stopping the flow of blood.
5. In the days before RhoGAM, some Rh− women had more than one Rh+ baby and never had a problem with erythroblastosis fetalis. How do you explain this?

Visit this book's website at www.mhhe.com/ gunstream5 for practice quizzes, learning exercises, case studies, and other study tools.

CHAPTER 12

The Cardiovascular System

Anatomy & Physiology **REVEALED**
aprevealed.com

Module 9
Cardiovascular System

Arteries Blood vessels carrying blood from the heart to capillaries in body tissues.

Atrium (atrium = vestibule) A heart chamber that receives blood returned to the heart by veins.

Capillaries Tiny blood vessels in tissues where exchange of materials between the blood and tissue cells occurs.

Diastole The relaxation phase of the heart cycle.

Myocardium (myo = muscle; cardi = heart) The thick layer of cardiac muscle in the wall of the heart.

Pericardium (peri = around) The membranous sac enclosing the heart.

Pulmonary circuit (pulmo = lung) Transport of blood to and from the lungs.

Systemic circuit Transport of blood to and from all parts of the body except the lungs.

Systole The contraction phase of the heart cycle.

Vasoconstriction (vas = vessel) A decrease in the diameter of blood vessels.

Vasodilation An increase in the diameter of blood vessels.

Veins Blood vessels carrying blood from capillaries in body tissues toward the heart.

Ventricle (ventr = underside) A heart chamber that pumps blood into an artery.

he heart and blood vessels form the *cardiovascular* (kar-dē-ō-vas′-kū-lar) *system.* The heart pumps blood through a closed system of blood vessels. Arteries carry blood away from the heart to capillaries in body tissues. Veins carry blood from capillaries in body tissues back to the heart. Figure 12.1 shows the general scheme of circulation of blood in the body. Blood vessels colored blue carry deoxygenated (oxygen-poor) blood; those colored red carry oxygenated (oxygen-rich) blood. Large arteries carry blood away from the heart and branch into smaller and smaller arteries that open into capillaries, the smallest blood vessels, where materials are exchanged with body tissues. Capillaries open into small veins that merge to form larger and larger veins, and the largest veins return blood to the heart.

As shown in figure 12.1, the cardiovascular system has two closed circuits (pathways) of blood flow. In the **pulmonary circuit,** the right side of the heart pumps deoxygenated blood only to the lungs and returns oxygenated blood to the left side of the heart. In the **systemic circuit,** the left side of the heart pumps oxygenated blood to all parts of the body except the lungs and returns deoxygenated blood to the right side of the heart. AP|R

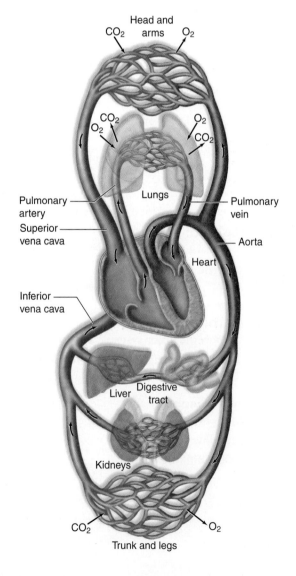

Figure 12.1 Cardiovascular system. In the pulmonary circuit, the right side of the heart pumps blood to and from the lungs. In the systemic circuit, the left side of the heart pumps blood to and from all parts of the body except the lungs. Blood vessels carrying oxygen-rich blood are colored red; those carrying oxygen-poor blood are colored blue. AP|R

12.1 Anatomy of the Heart

The heart is a four-chambered muscular pump that is located within the mediastinum in the thoracic cavity. It lies between the lungs and just superior to the diaphragm. The *apex* of the heart is the pointed end, which extends toward the left side of the thorax at the level of the fifth rib. The *base* of the heart is the superior portion, which is attached to several large blood vessels at the level of the second rib. The heart is about the size of a closed fist. Note the relationship of the heart with the surrounding organs in figure 12.2.

Protective Coverings

The heart and the bases of the attached blood vessels are enveloped by membranes that are collectively called the **pericardium** (per-i-kar′-dē-um). An outer, loosely fitting *pericardial sac* separates the heart from surrounding tissues and allows space for the heart to expand and contract as it pumps blood. The pericardial sac consists of two membranes: an outer *fibrous pericardium* and an inner *parietal pericardium.* The fibrous pericardium is a tough, unyielding membrane composed of dense connective tissue. It is attached to the diaphragm, inner surfaces of the sternum and thoracic vertebrae, and to adjacent connective tissues (figure 12.2). The delicate parietal pericardium lines the inner surface of the fibrous pericardium. At the bases of the large vessels (base of the heart), the parietal pericardium folds back to form the **epicardium** (visceral pericardium), which forms the thin membrane that tightly adheres to the surface of the heart. The potential space between the parietal pericardium and the epicardium is the **pericardial cavity** (figure 12.3).

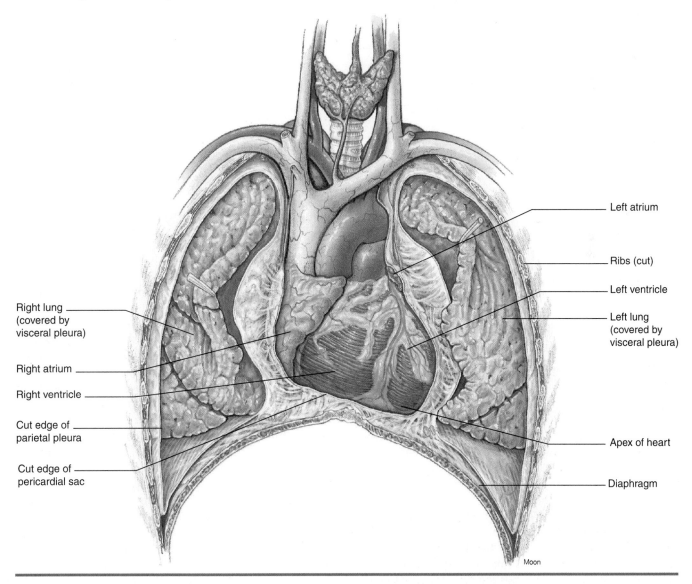

Left atrium

Ribs (cut)

Left ventricle

Left lung
(covered by
visceral pleura)

Apex of heart

Diaphragm

Right lung
(covered by
visceral pleura)

Right atrium

Right ventricle

Cut edge of
parietal pleura

Cut edge of
pericardial sac

Moon

Figure 12.2 The heart is located within the mediastinum in the thoracic cavity. AP|R

Pericardial cavity

Fibrous pericardium

Parietal pericardium

Epicardium

Myocardium

Endocardium

Epicardium

Pericardial sac

Figure 12.3   The pericardium and heart wall. The inset shows that the fibrous pericardium is lined by the parietal pericardium, which folds back to form the epicardium.

The parietal pericardium and epicardium are serous membranes, and they secrete serous fluid into the pericardial cavity. The serous fluid reduces friction between the two membranes as they rub together when the heart contracts and expands as it pumps blood.

The Heart Wall

The wall of the heart consists of a thick layer of cardiac muscle tissue, the **myocardium** (mī-ō-kar′-dē-um), sandwiched between two thin membranes. Contractions of the myocardium provide the force that pumps the blood through the blood vessels. The **epicardium,** or visceral pericardium, is the thin membrane that is firmly attached to the exterior surface of the myocardium. Blood vessels that nourish the heart itself are located within the epicardium. The internal surface of the myocardium is covered with a single layer of squamous epithelium called the **endocardium.** The endocardium not only lines the chambers of the heart, but it also is continuous with the internal lining of the blood vessels attached to the heart (figure 12.3).

Heart Chambers

The heart contains four chambers. The two upper chambers are the **atria** (ā′-trē-ah), which receive blood being returned to the heart by the veins. The two lower chambers are the **ventricles** (ven′-tri-kuls), which pump blood into the arteries carrying blood away from the heart. There is no opening between the two atria or between the two ventricles. The atria are separated from each other by a partition called the *interatrial septum.* The ventricles are separated by the *interventricular septum,* a thick partition of cardiac muscle (figure 12.4). The heart is a double pump. The left atrium and left ventricle compose the left pump. The right atrium and right ventricle compose the right pump.

The walls of the atria are much thinner than the walls of the ventricles. Differences in thickness are due to differences in the amount of cardiac muscle tissue that is present, which in turn reflects the work required of each chamber. The left ventricle has a thicker, more muscular wall than the right ventricle because it must pump blood to the entire body,

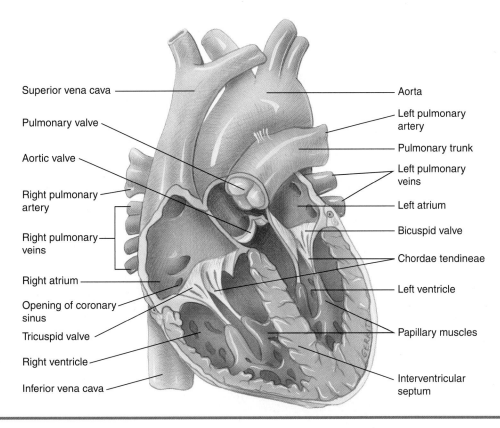

Figure 12.4 The internal structure of the heart is shown in coronal section. AP|R

except the lungs, whereas the right ventricle pumps blood only to the lungs. Locate the atria and ventricles in figure 12.4, and also in figures 12.2 and 12.5, which show external views of the heart. Table 12.1 summarizes the functions of the heart chambers.

Heart Valves

Like all pumps, the heart contains valves that allow the blood to flow in only one direction through the heart. The two types of heart valves are atrioventricular valves (A-V valves) and semilunar valves. Observe the location and structure of the heart valves in figures 12.4 and 12.6.

Atrioventricular Valves

The opening between each atrium and its corresponding ventricle is guarded by an **atrioventricular** (ā-trē-ō-ven-trik′-ū-lar) **valve** that is formed of fibrous connective tissue. Each valve allows blood to flow from the atrium into the ventricle but prevents a backflow of blood from the ventricle into the atrium. The A-V valve between the right atrium and the right ventricle is the **tricuspid** (trī-kus′-pid) **valve.** Its name

indicates that it is composed of three cusps, or flaps, of tissue. The **bicuspid valve,** or **mitral** (mī′-tral) **valve,** consists of two cusps and is located between the left atrium and the left ventricle.

The A-V valves originate from rings of thick, fibrous connective tissue that support the junction of the ventricles with the atria and the large arteries attached to the ventricles. This supporting fibrous tissue is called the *fibrous skeleton* of the heart (figure 12.6). The fibrous skeleton not only provides structural support but also serves as insulation separating the electrical activity of the atria and ventricles. This insulation enables the atria and ventricles to contract independently.

Thin strands of fibrous connective tissue, the **chordae tendineae** (kor′-de ten′-di-ne), extend from the valve cusps to the **papillary muscles,** small mounds of cardiac muscle that project from the inner walls of the ventricles (see figure 12.4). The chordae tendineae prevent the valve cusps from being forced into the atria during ventricular contraction. In fact, they are normally just the right length to allow the cusps to press against each other and tightly close the opening during ventricular contraction. Table 12.2 summarizes the functions of the heart valves.

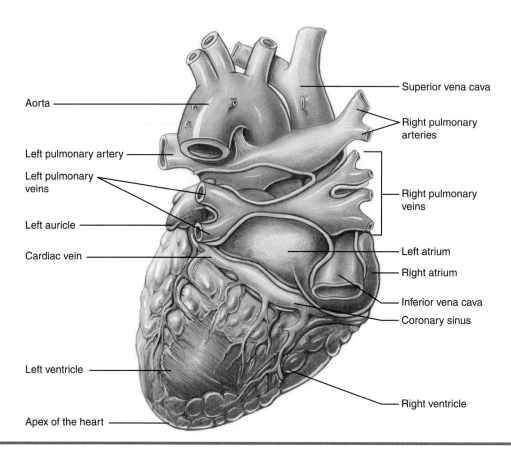

Aorta

Left pulmonary artery

Left pulmonary
veins

Left auricle

Cardiac vein

Left ventricle

Apex of the heart

Superior vena cava

Right pulmonary
arteries

Right pulmonary
veins

Left atrium

Right atrium

Inferior vena cava

Coronary sinus

Right ventricle

Figure 12.5   A posterior view of the heart and the associated blood vessels. AP|R

Table 12.1	Functions of the Heart Chambers
Chamber	**Function**
Right atrium	Receives deoxygenated blood from the superior and inferior venae cavae and passes this blood through the tricuspid A-V valve to the right ventricle
Right ventricle	Receives deoxygenated blood from the right atrium and pumps this blood through the pulmonary semilunar valve into the pulmonary trunk
Left atrium	Receives oxygenated blood from the pulmonary veins and passes this blood through the bicuspid A-V valve to the left ventricle
Left ventricle	Receives oxygenated blood from the left atrium and pumps this blood through the aortic semilunar valve into the aorta

Semilunar Valves

The **semilunar valves** are located in the bases of the large arteries that carry blood from the ventricles. The **pulmonary semilunar valve** is located at the base of the pulmonary trunk, which extends from the right ventricle. The **aortic semilunar valve** is located at the base of the aorta, which extends from the left ventricle.

Each semilunar valve is composed of three pocketlike cusps of fibrous connective tissue. They allow blood to be pumped from the ventricles into the arteries during ventricular contraction, but they prevent a backflow of blood from the arteries into the ventricles during ventricular relaxation.

Check My Understanding

1. What are the names and functions of the heart chambers?
2. What are the names and functions of the heart valves?

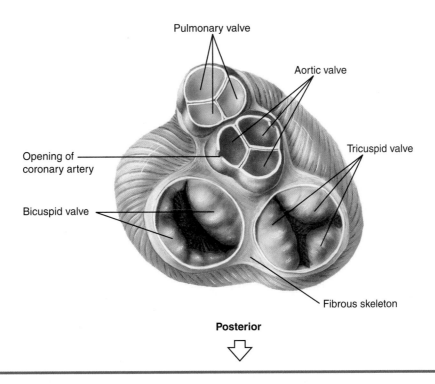

Pulmonary valve

Aortic valve

Opening of coronary artery

Tricuspid valve

Bicuspid valve

Fibrous skeleton

Posterior

Figure 12.6   The valves of the heart as seen from above. Note the fibrous skeleton of the heart.

Clinical   **INSIGHT**

If cusps of an A-V valve bulge into the atrium, some blood may regurgitate (backflow) into the atrium during ventricular contractions. This is what happens in a disorder known as *mitral valve prolapse (MVP)*. In some cases, it causes no serious dysfunction. In others, fatigue and shortness of breath may occur. Persons with MVP are susceptible to *endocarditis*, inflammation of the endocardium, caused by some species of *Streptococcus* bacteria. Endocarditis can result in scarring of the valve cusps, which further decreases valve function. Persons with MVP are often advised to take antibiotics prior to dental work to prevent bacteria from entering the blood and being carried to the heart.

Table 12.2   Heart Valves

Valve	Location	Function
Atrioventricular Valves		
Bicuspid (mitral) valve	Opening between the left atrium and left ventricle	Prevents the backflow of blood from the left ventricle into the left atrium
Tricuspid valve	Opening between the right atrium and right ventricle	Prevents backflow of blood from the right ventricle into the right atrium
Semilunar Valves		
Aortic valve	Entrance to the aorta	Prevents backflow of blood from the aorta into the left ventricle
Pulmonary valve	Entrance to the pulmonary trunk	Prevents backflow of blood from the pulmonary trunk into the right ventricle

12.2 Cardiac Cycle

The cardiac cycle includes both contraction and relaxation phases. Contraction is known as **systole** (sis′-to-lē); relaxation is called **diastole** (dĭ′-as-to-lē). These phases are illustrated in figure 12.7. Note that the ventricles are relaxed when the atria contract, and the atria are relaxed when the ventricles contract.

When both the atria and ventricles are relaxed between beats, blood flows into the atria from the large veins leading to the heart and on into the ventricles. Then, the atria contract (atrial systole), forcing more blood into the ventricles so that they are filled. Immediately thereafter, the ventricles contract. Ventricular systole suddenly produces high blood pressure within the ventricles, and this blood pressure closes both atrioventricular valves and opens both semilunar valves as blood is pumped into the arteries

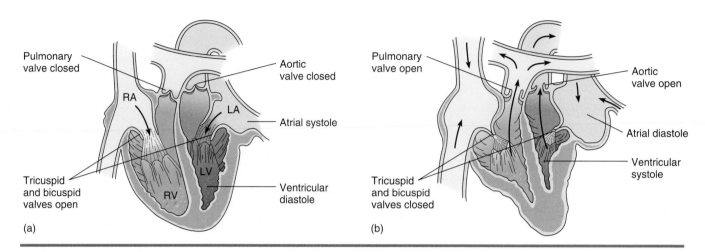

Figure 12.7 The cardiac cycle. (*a*) Blood flows from the atria into the ventricles during ventricular diastole. (*b*) Blood is pumped from the ventricles during ventricular systole. AP|R

leading from the heart. Ventricular diastole immediately follows, enabling the atrioventricular valves to open. Simultaneously, the semilunar valves close because of the greater blood pressure within the arteries. The cardiac cycle is then repeated. Study these relationships in figure 12.7.

Heart Sounds

The sounds of the heartbeat are usually described as *lub-dup* (pause) *lub-dup,* and so forth. These sounds are produced by the closing of the heart valves. The first sound results from the closing of the atrioventricular valves during ventricular systole. The second sound results from the closing of the semilunar valves during ventricular diastole. If any of the heart valves are defective and do not close properly, an additional sound, known as a heart murmur, may be heard.

Flow of Blood Through the Heart

Figure 12.8 diagrammatically shows the flow of blood through the heart and the great vessels attached to the heart. Chambers and vessels colored blue carry deoxygenated blood; those colored red carry oxygenated blood. Blood is oxygenated as it flows through the lungs, and it becomes deoxygenated as it releases oxygen to body tissues. Trace the flow of blood through the heart and major vessels in figure 12.8 as you read the following description.

The right atrium receives deoxygenated blood from all parts of the body except the lungs via two large veins: the superior and inferior venae cavae. The **superior vena cava** (vē′-nah kā′-vah) returns blood from the head, neck, shoulders, and arms. The **inferior vena cava** returns blood from body regions below the heart. Simultaneously, the left atrium receives oxygenated

blood returning to the heart from the lungs via the **pulmonary veins.** Blood flows from the left and right atria into the corresponding ventricles. About 70% of the blood flow into the ventricles is due to gravity, and about 30% results from atrial contraction.

After blood has flowed from the atria into their respective ventricles, the ventricles contract. The right ventricle pumps deoxygenated blood into the **pulmonary trunk.** The pulmonary trunk branches to form the **left** and **right pulmonary arteries,** which carry blood to the lungs. The left ventricle pumps oxygenated blood into the **aorta** (ā-or′-tah). The aorta branches to form smaller arteries that carry blood to all parts of the body except the lungs. Locate these major blood vessels associated with the heart in figure 12.5.

Because the heart is a double pump, there are two basic pathways, or circuits, of blood flow as shown in figure 12.8. The **pulmonary circuit** carries deoxygenated blood from the right ventricle to the lungs and returns oxygenated blood from the lungs to the left atrium. The **systemic circuit** carries oxygenated blood to all parts of the body except the lungs and returns deoxygenated blood to the right atrium.

Blood Supply to the Heart

The heart requires a constant supply of blood to nourish its own tissues. Blood is supplied by left and right **coronary** (kor′-ō-na-rē) **arteries,** which branch from the aorta just distal to the aortic semilunar valve. Blockage of a coronary artery may result in a heart attack. After passing through capillaries in cardiac tissues, blood is returned via **cardiac** (kar′-dē-ak) **veins,** which lie next to the coronary arteries. These veins empty into the **coronary sinus,** which drains into the right atrium. Locate these blood vessels in figure 12.5 and note the fat deposits that lie alongside

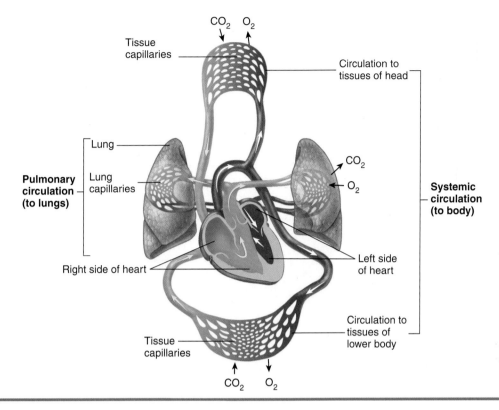

Figure 12.8 Blood flow through the heart and the pulmonary and systemic circuits. Heart chambers and vessels colored blue carry deoxygenated blood. Those colored red carry oxygenated blood.

the vessels. Also, study the relationships of the atria, ventricles, and large blood vessels associated with the heart.

Check My Understanding

3. What are the events of a cardiac cycle?
4. What produces the heart sounds?
5. Trace a drop of blood as it flows through the heart and the pulmonary and systemic circuits.

12.3 Heart Conduction System

The heart contains specialized muscle tissue that functions somewhat like neural tissue. It spontaneously forms impulses and transmits them to the myocardium to initiate contraction. This specialized tissue forms the *conduction system* of the heart, which consists of the sinoatrial node (S-A node), atrioventricular node (A-V node), A-V bundle, and Purkinje fibers. Observe the location of the conduction system and its parts in figure 12.9.

Clinical INSIGHT

If a coronary artery is partially obstructed by the fatty deposits of atherosclerosis, portions of the myocardium may be deprived of adequate blood. This produces chest pain known as *angina pectoris*. In severe cases, treatment may involve one of two approaches: coronary angioplasty or coronary bypass surgery.

In *coronary angioplasty*, a catheter that contains a balloon at its tip is inserted into an artery of an arm or leg and is threaded into the affected coronary artery. The balloon is positioned at the obstruction and is inflated for a few seconds to compress the fatty deposit and enlarge the lumen of the affected coronary artery. A meshlike metal tube called a stent is then inserted and positioned at the site of the obstruction to hold open the artery. The stent may be coated with a chemical that inhibits the growth of cells to minimize the chances that the artery will become obstructed again.

In *coronary bypass surgery*, a portion of a vein from elsewhere in the body is removed and is surgically grafted, providing a bypass around the obstruction to supply blood to the distal portion of the affected coronary artery.

Figure 12.9 The heart conduction system. Arrows indicate the flow of impulses from the S-A node. AP|R

Figure 12.10 A normal electrocardiogram showing five cardiac cycles.

Clinical **INSIGHT**

Some irregularities in heart rhythms result from improper transmission of impulses by the heart conduction system. In patients in whom the S-A node or A-V node malfunctions, a normal heartbeat may be obtained by implanting an artificial *pacemaker* in the chest wall. Wires (leads) are threaded through a vein to connect the pacemaker to the heart. This battery-operated device synchronizes heart contractions and controls the heart rate by sending weak electrical pulses to the heart to initiate contraction.

The **sinoatrial** (sī-nō-ā′-trē-al) **node (S-A node),** the pacemaker of the heart, is located in the right atrium at the junction of the superior vena cava. It rhythmically forms electrical impulses to initiate each heartbeat. The impulses are transmitted to the myocardium of the atria, where they produce a simultaneous contraction of the atria. The flow of impulses causes contraction of the atria from the top to the bottom, forcing blood into the ventricles. At the same time, the impulses are carried to the **atrioventricular node (A-V node),** which is located in the right atrium near the junction with the ventricular septum.

There is a brief time delay as the impulses pass through the A-V node, which allows time for the ventricles to fill with blood. From the A-V node, the impulses pass along the **A-V bundle** (bundle of His), a group of large fibers that divide into left and right branches extending down the ventricular septum and up the lateral walls of the ventricles. The smaller **Purkinje fibers** arise from the branches of the A-V bundle and carry the impulses to the myocardium of the ventricles, where they stimulate ventricular contraction. The distribution of the A-V bundle and the Purkinje fibers causes the ventricles to contract from the apex upward so that blood is forced into the pulmonary trunk and aorta.

Electrocardiogram

The origination and transmission of impulses through the conduction system of the heart generate electrical currents that may be detected by electrodes placed on the body surface. An instrument called an *electrocardiograph* is used to transform the electrical currents picked up by the electrodes into a recording called an **electrocardiogram** (**ECG** or **EKG**).

Figure 12.10 shows a normal EKG of five cardiac cycles, and figure 12.11 shows an enlargement of a normal EKG of one cardiac cycle. Note that an EKG consists of several deflections, or waves. These waves correlate with the flow of impulses during particular portions of the cardiac cycle.

An electrocardiogram has three distinct waves: the P wave, QRS wave, and T wave. The *P wave* is a small upward wave. It is produced by the depolarization of the atria. The *QRS wave* is produced by the depolarization of the ventricles. The greater size of the QRS wave is due to the greater muscle mass of the ventricles. The last wave is the *T wave,* which is produced by the repolarization of the ventricular myocardium. The repolarization of the atria is not detected because it is masked by the stronger QRS wave.

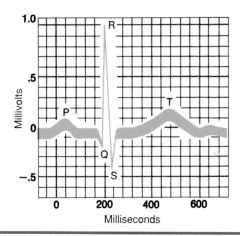

Figure 12.11 A normal electrocardiogram. The P wave results from depolarization of the atria. The QRS wave results from the depolarization of the ventricles. The T wave results from the repolarization of the ventricles.

Check My Understanding

6. What composes the cardiac conduction system?
7. What events produce the waves of an electrocardiogram?

Clinical **INSIGHT**

An electrocardiogram provides important information in the diagnosis of heart disease and abnormalities. In reading an EKG, physicians pay close attention to the height of each wave and to the time required for each wave.

12.4 Regulation of Heart Function

Cardiac output is the amount of blood pumped from the heart in one minute, and it is an important measure of heart function. It is determined by two factors: **stroke volume** and **heart rate.** Stroke volume (SV) is the amount of blood pumped per ventricle at each contraction. Multiplying this volume by the heart rate (HR), heart beats per minute, yields the cardiac output (CO).

$$CO = SV \times HR$$

At normal resting values of a stroke volume of 70 ml/beat and a heart rate of 72 beats/min, the cardiac output is 5,040 ml/min. This means that the total volume of blood, 4 to 6 liters, passes through the heart

each minute. Cardiac output increases with exercise because both stroke volume and heart rate increase.

Heart function is regulated by factors both internal and external to the heart. For example, *venous return,* the amount of blood returning to the heart during diastole, is an internal factor that affects stroke volume. If venous return increases, more blood enters and is pumped from the ventricles, increasing the stroke volume and cardiac output. Heart rate is **primarily** controlled by the autonomic nervous system, although hormones and certain ions also affect it.

Autonomic Regulation

Heart rate regulation is primarily under the control of the **cardiac control center** located within the medulla oblongata of the brain. It receives sensory information about the level of blood pressure from pressure receptors (baroreceptors) located in the aortic arch and in the carotid sinuses of the carotid arteries. It is also affected by emotions, which generate impulses from the cerebrum and hypothalamus.

The cardiac control center consists of both sympathetic and parasympathetic components. Impulses transmitted to the heart via sympathetic fibers cause an increase in heart rate; impulses transmitted by parasympathetic fibers cause a decrease in heart rate. The cardiac control center constantly adjusts the frequency of sympathetic and parasympathetic impulses to produce a heart rate that meets the changing needs of body cells (figure 12.12).

Neurons of the sympathetic division extend from the cardiac control center down the spinal cord to the thoracic region. There the sympathetic fibers exit the spinal cord via thoracic nerves to innervate the S-A node, A-V node, and portions of the myocardium. The transmission of impulses causes the sympathetic fibers to secrete *norepinephrine* at synapses in the heart. Norepinephrine increases the heart rate and strengthens the force of myocardial contraction. Physical and emotional stresses, such as exercise, excitement, anxiety, and fear, stimulate sympathetic fibers to increase the heart rate.

Parasympathetic nerve fibers arise from the cardiac control center and exit in the vagus nerve (X) to innervate the S-A and A-V nodes. The transmission of impulses causes the parasympathetic fibers to secrete *acetylcholine* at the heart synapses, which slows the heart rate. The greater the frequency of parasympathetic impulses sent to the heart, the slower the heart rate. Excessive blood pressure and emotional factors, such as grief and depression, stimulate the parasympathetic nerve fibers to slow the heart rate.

A predominance of parasympathetic impulses reaches the heart when the body is at rest, and they

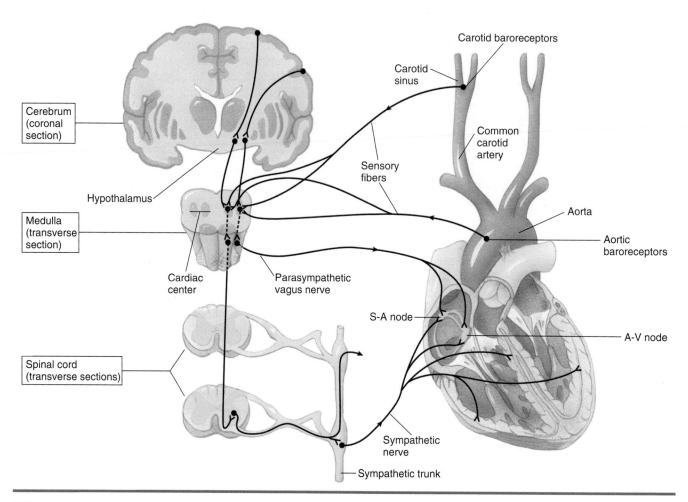

Figure 12.12 The rate and strength of heart contractions are regulated by the antagonistic actions of sympathetic and parasympathetic divisions of the autonomic nervous system. AP|R

slow the heart rate to produce the resting heart rate. As cellular needs for blood increase, a decrease in the frequency of parasympathetic impulses and an increase in sympathetic impulses cause the heart rate to increase.

Other Factors Affecting Heart Rate

Age, sex, physical condition, temperature, epinephrine, thyroxine, and the blood levels of calcium and potassium ions also affect the heart rate.

The resting heart rate gradually declines with age, and it is slightly faster in females than in males. Average resting heart rates in females are 72 to 80 beats per minute, as opposed to 64 to 72 beats per minute in males. People who are in good physical condition have a slower resting heart rate than those in poor condition. Athletes may have a resting heart rate of only 40 to 60 beats per minute. An increase in body temperature, which occurs during exercise or when feverish, increases the heart rate.

Epinephrine, which is secreted by the adrenal glands during stress or excitement, affects the heart like norepinephrine—it increases and strengthens the heart rate. An excess of thyroxine produces a lesser, but longer-lasting, increase in heart rate.

Reduced levels of Ca^{++} slow the heart rate, and increased Ca^{++} levels increase the heart rate and prolong contraction. In extreme cases, an excessively prolonged contraction may result in death. Excessive levels of K^+ decrease both heart rate and force of contraction. Abnormally low levels of K^+ may cause potentially life-threatening abnormal heart rhythms.

Check My Understanding

8. How is the heart rate regulated?
9. What other factors affect the heart rate?

12.5 Types of Blood Vessels

There are three basic types of blood vessels: arteries, capillaries, and veins. They form a closed system of tubes that carry blood from the heart to the body cells and back to the heart. Table 12.3 compares these three types.

Structure of Arteries and Veins

The walls of arteries and veins are composed of three distinct layers. The *tunica externa,* the outer layer, is formed of fibrous connective tissue that includes both collagenous and elastic fibers. These fibers provide support and elasticity for the vessel. The *tunica media,* the middle layer, usually is the thickest layer. It consists of smooth muscle fibers that encircle the blood vessel. The smooth muscle fibers not only provide support but also produce changes in the diameter of the blood vessel by contraction or relaxation. The *tunica interna,* the inner layer, forms the inner lining of blood vessels. It consists of a single layer of squamous epithelial cells, called the *endothelium.* It is supported by thin layers of connective tissue that lie between it and the smooth muscle fibers.

The walls of arteries and veins have the same basic structure. However, arterial walls contain more smooth muscle and elastic connective tissues as an adaptation to the higher blood pressure found in them. Another difference is that large veins, but not arteries, contain valves formed of endothelium. Venous valves prevent a backflow of blood. Compare the structure of arteries and veins in figure 12.13.

Arteries

Arteries carry blood away from the heart. They branch repeatedly into smaller and smaller arteries and ultimately form microscopic arteries called **arterioles** (ar-te′-rē-ōls). As arterioles branch and form smaller arterioles, the thickness of the muscle layer decreases. The walls of the smallest arterioles consist of only endothelium and a few encircling smooth muscle fibers. Arteries, especially the arterioles, play an important role in the control of blood flow and blood pressure.

Capillaries

Arterioles connect with **capillaries,** the most numerous and the smallest blood vessels. A capillary's diameter is so small that red blood cells must pass through

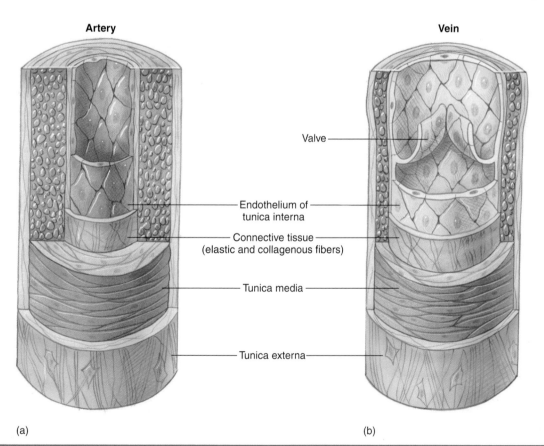

Artery

Vein

Valve

Endothelium of
tunica interna

Connective tissue
(elastic and collagenous fibers)

Tunica media

Tunica externa

(a)

(b)

Figure 12.13 (*a*) The wall of an artery. (*b*) The wall of a vein. APR

Table 12.3   Comparison of Arteries, Capillaries, and Veins

Type of Vessel	Function	Structure
Arteries	Carry blood from the heart to the capillaries	Relatively thick muscular layer to withstand higher blood pressure
Capillaries	Enable exchange of materials between blood and tissue cells	Microscopic vessels composed of a single layer of endothelial cells
Veins	Return blood from the capillaries to the heart	Relatively thin muscular layer; internal valves located at intervals to prevent backflow of blood

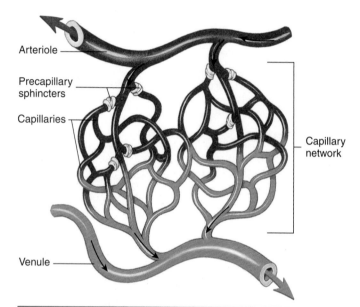

Figure 12.14 A capillary network. Precapillary sphincters regulate the blood flow from an arteriole into a capillary. Oxygenated blood (red) enters a capillary network. Deoxygenated blood (blue) exits the capillaries and enters a venule.

it in single file. The wall of capillaries consists only of endothelium, which allows the exchange of materials between blood in capillaries and body cells.

The distribution of capillaries in body tissues varies with the metabolic activity of each tissue. Capillaries are especially abundant in active tissues, such as muscle and nerve tissues, where nearly every cell is near a capillary. Capillaries are less abundant in connective tissues, and they are absent in some tissues, such as cartilage, epidermis, and the lens and cornea of the eye.

Blood flow in capillaries is controlled by *precapillary sphincters,* smooth muscle fibers encircling the bases of capillaries at the arteriole–capillary junctions (figure 12.14). Contraction of a precapillary sphincter inhibits blood flow to its capillary network.

Relaxation of the sphincter allows blood to flow into its capillary network to provide oxygen and nutrients for the tissue cells. The flow of blood in capillary networks occurs intermittently. When some capillary networks are filled with blood, others are not. Capillary networks receive blood according to the needs of the cells that they serve. For example, during physical exercise blood is diverted from capillary networks in the digestive tract to fill the capillary networks in skeletal muscles. This pattern of blood distribution is largely reversed after a meal.

Exchange of Materials

The continual exchange of materials between the blood and tissue cells is essential for life. Cells require oxygen and nutrients to perform their metabolic functions, and they produce carbon dioxide and other metabolic wastes that must be removed by the blood.

The cells of tissues are enveloped in a thin film of extracellular fluid called **interstitial fluid,** or *tissue fluid,* that fills the tissue spaces and lies between the tissue cells and the capillaries. Therefore, all materials that pass between the blood and tissue cells must pass through the interstitial fluid. Dissolved substances such as oxygen and nutrients diffuse from blood in the capillary into the interstitial fluid and from the interstitial fluid into body cells. Carbon dioxide and metabolic wastes diffuse in the opposite direction.

Recall that the capillary walls are formed of a single layer of endothelial cells so materials can readily diffuse through them. And the junctions between these cells are not tight so fluid is able to move between the cells. Two opposing forces determine the movement of fluid between capillary blood and interstitial fluid: blood pressure and osmotic pressure. Blood pressure against the capillary walls results from the force of ventricular contractions. It tends to push fluid out of the capillaries into the interstitial fluid. Osmotic pressure of the blood results from proteins in blood plasma. Osmotic

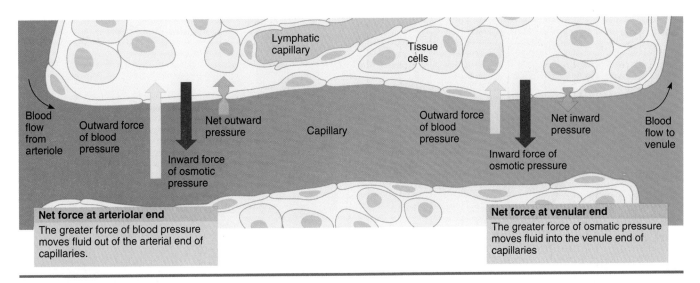

Figure 12.15 Fluid exchange. Fluid moves out of or into capillaries according to the net difference between blood pressure and osmotic pressure. Solutes diffuse out of or into capillaries according to each solute's concentration gradient. AP|R

pressure tends to "pull" fluid from interstitial fluid into the capillaries by osmosis.

Recall that capillaries connect the smallest arteries with the smallest veins. At the arterial end of a capillary, blood pressure exceeds osmotic pressure, so fluid moves out of the capillary into the interstitial fluid. In contrast, at the venous end of the capillary, osmotic pressure exceeds blood pressure, so fluid moves from the interstitial fluid into the capillary by osmosis (figure 12.15). About nine-tenths of the fluid that moves from the arteriole end of a capillary into the interstitial fluid returns into the venous end of the capillary. The remainder is picked up by the lymphatic system and ultimately is returned to the blood (see chapter 13).

Veins

After blood flows through the capillaries, it enters the **venules,** the smallest **veins.** Several capillaries merge to form a venule. The smallest venules consist only of endothelium and connective tissue, but larger venules also contain smooth muscle tissue. Venules unite to form small veins. Small veins combine to form progressively larger veins as blood is returned to the heart. Larger veins, especially those in the legs and arms, contain valves that prevent a backflow of blood and aid the return of blood to the heart.

Because nearly 60% of the blood volume is in veins at any instant, veins may be considered as storage areas for blood that can be carried to other parts of the body in times of need. Venous sinusoids in the liver and spleen are especially important reservoirs. If blood is lost by hemorrhage, both blood volume and

pressure decline. In response, the sympathetic nervous system sends impulses to constrict the muscular walls of the veins, which reduces the venous volume and compensates for the blood loss. A similar response occurs during strenuous muscular activity in order to increase the blood flow to skeletal muscles.

Check My Understanding

10. Compare the structure and function of arteries, capillaries, and veins.
11. How does the exchange of materials occur between blood in capillaries and tissue cells?

12.6 Blood Flow

Blood circulates because of differences in blood pressure. Blood flows from areas of higher pressure to areas of lower pressure. Blood pressure is greatest in the ventricles and lowest in the atria. Figure 12.16 shows the decline of blood pressure in the systemic circuit with increased distance from the left ventricle.

Contraction of the ventricles creates the blood pressure that propels the blood through the arteries. However, the pressure declines as the arteries branch into an increasing number of smaller and smaller arteries and finally connect with the capillaries. The decline in blood pressure occurs because the overall cross-sectional area of the combined arteries is greatly increased as the arteries continue to branch. By the time blood has left the capillaries and entered the

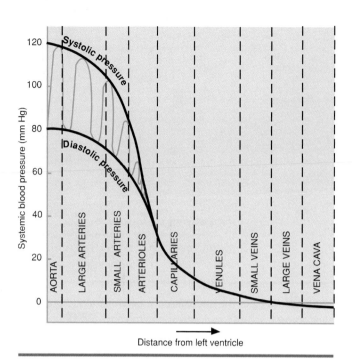

Figure 12.16 Blood pressure decreases as distance from the left ventricle increases.

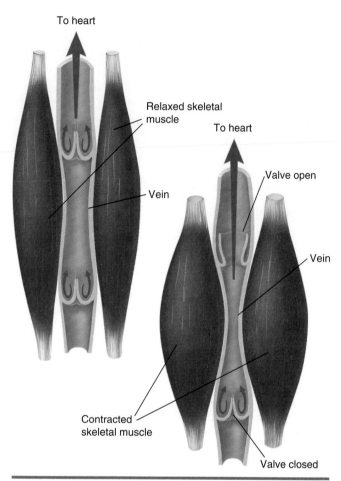

Figure 12.17 Contraction of skeletal muscles compresses veins and aids the movement of blood toward the heart.

veins, there is very little blood pressure remaining to return the blood to the heart. The return of venous blood is assisted by three additional forces: *skeletal muscle contractions, respiratory movements,* and *gravity.*

Contractions of skeletal muscles compress the veins, forcing blood from one valved segment to another and on toward the heart because the valves prevent a backflow of blood. This method of moving venous blood toward the heart is especially important in the return of blood from the arms and legs, and it is illustrated in figure 12.17.

Respiratory movements aid the movement of blood upward toward the heart in the abdominal and thoracic cavities. The downward contraction of the diaphragm during inspiration decreases the pressure within the thoracic cavity and increases the pressure within the abdominal cavity. The higher pressure on abdominal veins forces blood upward into thoracic veins, where the pressure is reduced because valves in leg veins prevent a backflow of blood.

Gravity aids the return of blood in veins superior to the heart.

Velocity of Blood Flow

The velocity of blood flow varies inversely with the overall cross-sectional area of the *combined* blood vessels. Therefore, the velocity progressively decreases as blood flows through an increasing number of smaller

and smaller arteries and into the capillaries. Then, the velocity progressively increases as the blood flows into a decreasing number of larger and larger veins on its way back to the heart.

Blood velocity is fastest in the aorta and slowest in the capillaries, an ideal situation providing for the rapid circulation of the blood and yet sufficient time for the exchange of materials between blood in the capillaries and tissue cells.

12.7 Blood Pressure

The term *blood pressure* usually refers to arterial blood pressure in the systemic circuit—in the aorta and its branches. Arterial blood pressure is greatest during ventricular contraction (systole) as blood is pumped into the aorta and its branches. This pressure is called the **systolic blood pressure,** and it optimally averages 110 mm Hg (mercury) when measured in the brachial artery. The lowest arterial pressure occurs during ventricular relaxation (diastole). This pressure is called the **diastolic blood pressure,** and it optimally averages 70 mm Hg (see figure 12.17).

The difference between the systolic and diastolic blood pressures is known as the *pulse pressure.* The alternating increase and decrease in arterial blood pressure during ventricular systole and diastole causes a comparable expansion and contraction of the elastic arterial walls. This pulsating expansion of the arterial walls follows each ventricular contraction, and it may be detected as the *pulse* by placing the fingers on a surface artery. Figure 12.18 identifies the name and location of surface arteries where the pulse may be detected.

Clinical INSIGHT

A blood pressure of 110/70 mm Hg is optimal. Each 20 mm Hg of systolic pressure over 115, and each 10 mm Hg of diastolic pressure over 75 doubles the risk of heart attack, stroke, and kidney disease.

Factors Affecting Blood Pressure

Four major factors affect blood pressure: cardiac output, blood volume, peripheral resistance, and blood viscosity. An increase in any of these factors causes an increase in blood pressure.

Cardiac output is the volume of blood pumped by the heart in one minute. It is determined by the heart rate and the volume of blood pumped at each contraction. An increase or decrease in cardiac output causes a comparable change in blood pressure. Changes in cardiac output occur primarily by changes in heart rate.

Blood volume may be decreased by severe hemorrhage, vomiting, diarrhea, or reduced water intake. As soon as the lost fluid is replaced, blood pressure returns to normal. Conversely, if the body retains too much fluid, blood volume and blood pressure increase.

Peripheral resistance is the friction of blood against the walls of blood vessels. Arterioles play an important role in controlling blood pressure by changing their diameters, which alters peripheral resistance. As arterioles constrict, peripheral resistance and blood pressure increase. As arterioles dilate, peripheral resistance and blood pressure decrease.

Viscosity is the resistance of a liquid to flow. For example, water has a low viscosity, while honey has a high viscosity. The viscosity of blood is determined by the concentration of blood cells and plasma proteins,

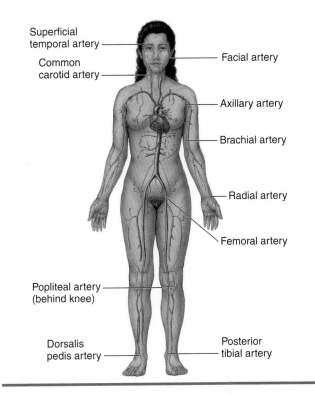

Figure 12.18 Locations and arteries where the pulse may be detected.

so an increase in either of these factors increases blood viscosity, which, in turn, increases blood pressure.

Control of Peripheral Resistance

The sympathetic nervous system primarily controls peripheral resistance by regulating the diameter of blood vessels, especially arterioles. The control center is the **vasomotor center** in the medulla. An increase in the frequency of sympathetic impulses to the smooth muscle of blood vessels produces **vasoconstriction,** which raises the blood pressure and increases blood velocity. This response accelerates the rate of oxygen transport to cells and the removal of carbon dioxide from blood by the lungs. A decrease in impulse frequency results in **vasodilation,** which lowers blood pressure and slows blood velocity.

Like the cardiac control center, the activity of the vasomotor center is modified by epinephrine, impulses from higher brain areas, and sensory impulses from pressure receptors and chemoreceptors in the aorta and carotid arteries. For example, a decrease in pressure, pH, or oxygen concentration of the blood stimulates vasoconstriction. Conversely, an increase in these values promotes vasodilation.

In addition, arterioles and precapillary sphincters are affected by localized changes in blood concentrations of oxygen, carbon dioxide, and pH. These local effects override the control by the vasomotor center, a process called *autoregulation,* and increase the rate of exchange of materials between tissue cells and the capillaries. For example, if a particular muscle group is active for an extended period, a localized decrease in oxygen concentration and an increase in carbon dioxide concentration results. These chemical changes stimulate the dilation of local arterioles and precapillary sphincters, which increases the flow of blood into capillary networks of the affected muscles to provide more oxygen and to remove more carbon dioxide.

Check My Understanding

12. How does blood pressure affect the flow of blood through blood vessels?
13. Compare systolic and diastolic blood pressure.
14. How do cardiac output, blood volume, and peripheral resistance affect blood pressure?

12.8 Circulation Pathways

As noted earlier, the heart is a double pump that serves two distinct circulation pathways: the pulmonary and systemic circuits. These circuits were shown earlier in figures 12.1 and 12.8.

Pulmonary Circuit

The **pulmonary circuit** carries deoxygenated blood to the lungs, where oxygen and carbon dioxide are exchanged between the blood and the air in the lungs. The right ventricle pumps deoxygenated blood into the **pulmonary trunk,** a short, thick artery that divides to form the left and right **pulmonary arteries.** Each pulmonary artery enters a lung and divides repeatedly to form arterioles, which continue into the capillary networks that surround the air sacs (alveoli) of the lungs. Oxygen diffuses from the air in the lungs into the capillary blood, and carbon dioxide diffuses from the blood into the air in the lungs. Blood then flows from the capillaries into venules, which merge to form small veins, which, in turn, join to form progressively larger veins. Two **pulmonary veins** emerge from each lung to carry oxygenated blood back to the left atrium of the heart.

Systemic Circuit

The **systemic circuit** carries oxygenated blood to the tissue cells of the body and returns deoxygenated blood to the heart. The left ventricle pumps the freshly oxygenated blood, received from the pulmonary circuit, into the **aorta** for circulation to all parts

of the body except the lungs. The aorta branches to form many major arteries, which continually branch to form arterioles leading to capillaries, where the exchange of materials between the blood and tissue cells takes place. Oxygen diffuses from the capillary blood into the tissue cells, while carbon dioxide diffuses from the tissue cells into the blood. From the capillaries, blood enters venules, which merge to form small veins, which join to form progressively larger veins. Ultimately, veins from the arms, shoulders, head, and neck join to form the **superior vena cava,** which returns blood from these regions back to the right atrium. Similarly, veins from the legs and lower trunk enter the **inferior vena cava,** which also returns blood into the right atrium.

12.9 Systemic Arteries

All of the systemic arteries are branch arteries of the aorta, which carries oxygenated blood from the left ventricle of the heart.

Major Branches of the Aorta

The aorta ascends from the heart, arches to the left and behind the heart, and descends through the thorax and abdomen just anterior to the vertebral column. Figure 12.19 shows the major branches of the aorta and their relationships to the internal organs. Tables 12.4 and 12.5 list the major branches of the aorta and the organs and body regions that they supply.

The first arteries to branch from the aorta are the left and right **coronary arteries,** which supply blood to the heart. They branch from the aorta just distal to the aortic semilunar valve in the base of the *ascending aorta.*

Three major arteries branch from the *aortic arch.* In order of branching, they are the **brachiocephalic** (brāk-ē-ō-se-fal′-ik) **artery,** the **left common carotid** (kah-rot′-id) **artery,** and the **left subclavian** (sub-klā′-vē-an) **artery.**

Pairs of small **intercostal** (in-ter-kos′-tal) **arteries** branch from the *thoracic aorta* to supply the intercostal muscles between the ribs and other organs of the thoracic wall. A number of other small arteries supply the organs of the thorax.

Once the aorta descends through the diaphragm, it is called the *abdominal aorta,* and it gives off several branch arteries to the abdominal wall and visceral organs. The **celiac** (sē′-lē-ak) **artery** is a short artery that divides to form three branch arteries: (1) the **left gastric artery** supplies the stomach, (2) the **splenic artery** supplies the spleen and pancreas, and (3) the **hepatic artery** supplies the liver.

Figure 12.19 The major arteries that branch from the aorta. (a. = artery) AP|R

The **superior mesenteric** (mes-en-ter'-ik) **artery** supplies most of the small intestine and the first portion of the large intestine. The left and right **renal arteries** supply the kidneys. The left and right **gonadal** (gō-nad'-al) **arteries** supply the ovaries in females and the testes in males.

Several pairs of **lumbar arteries** supply the walls of the abdomen and back. The **inferior mesenteric artery** supplies the distal half of the large intestine.

At the level of the iliac crests, the aorta divides to form two large arteries, the left and right **common iliac** (il'-ē-ak) **arteries,** which carry blood to the lower portions of the trunk and to the legs.

Arteries Supplying the Head and Neck

The head and neck receive blood from several arteries that branch from the carotid and subclavian arteries. Note in figures 12.19 and 12.20 that the brachiocephalic artery branches to form the **right common carotid artery** and the **right subclavian artery.** The left common carotid and left subclavian arteries branch directly from the aorta.

Each common carotid artery divides in the neck to form an **external carotid artery** and the **internal carotid artery.** The slight enlargement at the junction

Table 12.4 Major Arteries Branching from the Ascending Aorta, Aortic Arch, and Thoracic Aorta

Artery	Origin	Region Supplied
Coronary	Ascending aorta	Heart
Brachiocephalic	Aortic arch	Head and right arm
Right common carotid	Brachiocephalic	Right side of head and neck
Right subclavian	Brachiocephalic	Right shoulder and arm
Left common carotid	Aortic arch	Left side of head and neck
External carotid	Common carotid	Scalp, face, and neck
Internal carotid	Common carotid	Brain
Left subclavian	Aortic arch	Left shoulder and arm
Vertebral	Subclavian	Neck and brain
Axillary	Subclavian	Armpit
Brachial	Axillary	Upper arm
Radial	Brachial	Forearm and hand
Ulnar	Brachial	Forearm and hand
Intercostal	Thoracic aorta	Thoracic wall

Table 12.5 Major Arteries Branching from the Abdominal Aorta

Artery	Origin	Region Supplied
Celiac	Abdominal aorta	Liver, stomach, spleen
Hepatic	Celiac	Liver
Gastric	Celiac	Stomach
Splenic	Celiac	Spleen
Renal	Abdominal aorta	Kidney
Superior mesenteric	Abdominal aorta	Small intestine; part of colon
Gonadal	Abdominal aorta	Ovaries or testes
Lumbar	Abdominal aorta	Lumbar region of back
Inferior mesenteric	Abdominal aorta	Colon and rectum
Common iliac	Abdominal aorta	Pelvic region and leg
Internal iliac	Common iliac	Reproductive and urinary organs; rectum
External iliac	Common iliac	Pelvic region and leg
Femoral	External iliac	Thigh
Popliteal	Femoral	Knee
Anterior tibial	Femoral	Lower leg (anterior) and foot
Posterior tibial	Femoral	Lower leg (posterior) and foot

of these arteries is a *carotid sinus,* the site of pressure receptors and chemoreceptors that send sensory impulses to the cardiac and vasomotor centers in the medulla. The external carotids give rise to a number of smaller arteries that carry blood to the neck, face, and scalp. The internal carotids enter the cranium through foramina in the temporal bones and provide the major supply of blood to the brain.

The neck and brain are also supplied by the **vertebral arteries.** They branch from the subclavian

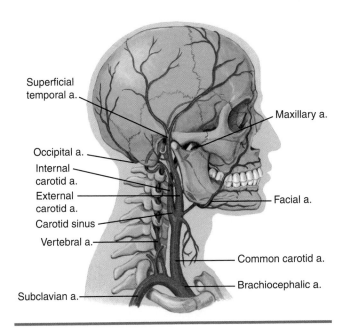

Figure 12.20 Major arteries supplying the head and neck. (a. = artery) AP|R

arteries and pass upward through the foramina of the transverse processes of cervical vertebrae to enter the cranium.

Arteries Supplying the Shoulders and Arms AP|R

The subclavian artery provides branches to the shoulder and passes under the clavicle to become the **axillary artery,** which supplies branches to the thorax wall and axillary region. The axillary artery continues into the arm to become the **brachial artery,** which provides branches to serve the arm. At the elbow, the brachial artery divides to form a **radial artery** and an **ulnar artery,** which supply the forearm and wrist and merge to form a network of arteries supplying the hand (figure 12.21 and table 12.4).

Arteries Supplying the Pelvis and Legs AP|R

As noted earlier, the left and right common iliac arteries branch from the inferior end of the aorta. Each common iliac branches within the pelvis to form internal and external iliac arteries. The **internal iliac artery** is the smaller branch that supplies the pelvic wall, pelvic organs, external genitalia, and medial thigh muscles. The **external iliac artery** is the larger

branch, and it supplies the anterior pelvic wall and continues into the leg, where it becomes the femoral artery (figure 12.21).

The **femoral artery** gives off branches that supply the anterior and medial muscles of the thigh. The largest branch is the **deep femoral artery,** which serves the posterior and lateral thigh muscles. As the femoral artery descends, it passes posterior to the knee and becomes the **popliteal** (pop-li-tē′-al) **artery,** which supplies certain muscles of the thigh and leg, as well as the knee. The popliteal artery branches just below the knee to form the anterior and posterior tibial arteries.

The **anterior tibial artery** descends between the tibia and fibula to supply the anterior and lateral portions of the leg, and it continues to become the **dorsal pedis artery,** which supplies the ankle and foot. The **posterior tibial artery** lies posterior to the tibia and supplies the posterior portion of the leg, and it continues to supply the ankle and the plantar surface of the foot. Its largest branch is the **peroneal** (per-ō-nē′-al) **artery,** which serves the lateral leg muscles (table 12.5).

Check My Understanding

15. What is the arterial pathway of blood from the left ventricle to the right side of the brain?
16. What is the arterial pathway of blood from the left ventricle to the small intestine?
17. What is the arterial pathway of blood from the left ventricle to the dorsal surface of the foot?

Clinical INSIGHT

Determination of the pulse and blood pressure involves certain arteries. The pulse may be taken at any surface artery, but the radial artery at the wrist and the common carotid artery in the neck are the most commonly used sites. Blood pressure is usually taken in the brachial artery of the upper arm.

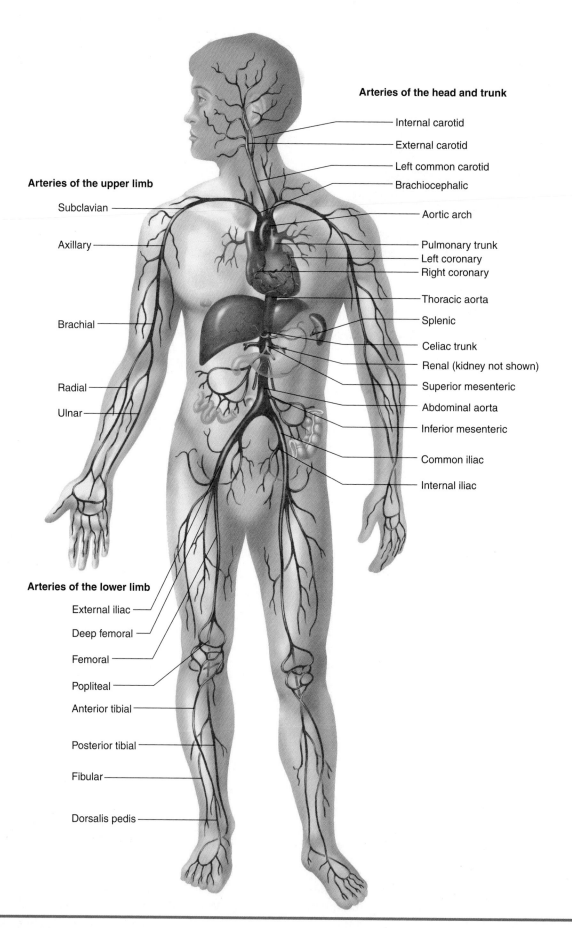

Arteries of the head and trunk

Internal carotid
External carotid
Left common carotid
Brachiocephalic
Aortic arch
Pulmonary trunk
Left coronary
Right coronary
Thoracic aorta
Splenic
Celiac trunk
Renal (kidney not shown)
Superior mesenteric
Abdominal aorta
Inferior mesenteric
Common iliac
Internal iliac

Arteries of the upper limb

Subclavian
Axillary
Brachial
Radial
Ulnar

Arteries of the lower limb

External iliac
Deep femoral
Femoral
Popliteal
Anterior tibial
Posterior tibial
Fibular
Dorsalis pedis

Figure 12.21 Major systemic arteries.

12.10 Systemic Veins

The systemic veins receive deoxygenated blood from capillaries and return the blood to the heart. Ultimately, all systemic veins merge to form two major veins, the superior and inferior venae cavae, that empty into the right atrium of the heart.

Veins Draining the Head and Neck

As shown in figure 12.22, superficial areas of the head and neck are drained by the left and right **external jugular** (jug´-ū-lar) **veins,** which lead into the left and right **subclavian veins,** respectively. The left and right **vertebral veins** carry blood from the brain and deep neck regions into the subclavian veins as well.

Most of the blood from the brain, face, and neck is carried by the left and right **internal jugular veins.** Each internal jugular vein merges with a subclavian vein to form a **brachiocephalic vein.** The left and right brachiocephalic veins join to form the **superior vena cava,** which returns blood to the right atrium of the heart (table 12.6).

Veins Draining the Shoulders and Arms AP|R

Deep regions of the forearm are drained by the **radial** and **ulnar veins.** These two veins join at the elbow to form the **brachial vein,** which drains the deep areas of the arm (figure 12.23).

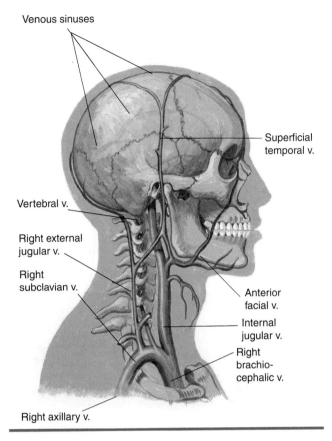

Figure 12.22 Major veins draining the head and neck. (v. = vein) AP|R

Vein	Region Drained and Location	Receiving Vein
Table 12.6 Major Veins Draining to the Superior Vena Cava		
Head and Neck		
External jugular	Face, scalp, and neck	Subclavian
Vertebral	Head and neck (deep)	Subclavian
Internal jugular	Brain and neck (deep)	Brachiocephalic
Arm and Shoulder		
Radial	Hand and forearm	Brachial
Ulnar	Hand and forearm	Brachial
Basilic	Upper arm	Axillary
Cephalic	Forearm and upper arm (deep)	Axillary
Brachial	Upper arm	Axillary
Axillary	Armpit	Subclavian
Subclavian	Shoulder	Brachiocephalic
Upper Trunk		
Brachiocephalic	Upper trunk	Superior vena cava
Azygos	Upper trunk (deep)	Superior vena cava

Veins of the head and trunk

Superior sagittal sinus

Facial

Internal jugular

External jugular

Veins of the upper limb

Subclavian

Cephalic

Axillary

Basilic

Brachial

Median cubital

Ulnar

Radial

Veins of the lower limb

External iliac

Left brachiocephalic

Superior vena cava

Right pulmonary

Great cardiac

Small cardiac

Inferior vena cava

Hepatic

Splenic

Hepatic portal

Superior mesenteric

Inferior mesenteric

Left common iliac

Internal iliac

Femoral

Great saphenous

Popliteal

Posterior tibial

Anterior tibial

Small saphenous

Fibular

Figure 12.23 Major systemic veins.

264

Superficial regions of the hand, forearm, and arm are drained by the laterally located **cephalic** (se-fal′-ik) **vein** and the medially located **basilic** (bah-sil′-ik) **vein.** Note the **median cubital** (kyū′-bi-tal) **vein,** which connects the basilic and cephalic veins.

The basilic and brachial veins merge in the axilla to form the **axillary vein,** which, in turn, joins with the cephalic vein to form the **subclavian vein.** As noted earlier, the subclavian vein joins with the internal jugular vein to form the brachiocephalic vein (table 12.6).

Veins Draining the Pelvis and Legs AP|R

The **anterior** and **posterior tibial veins** drain the foot and deep regions of the leg. They join below the knee to form the **popliteal vein.** The **small saphenous** (sah-fē′-nus) **vein** drains the superficial posterior part of the leg and merges with the popliteal vein. The **peroneal vein** drains the lateral portion of the leg and joins with the popliteal vein at the knee to form the **femoral vein,** which drains the deep regions of the thigh and hip.

The median cubital and great saphenous veins have important clinical uses. The median cubital vein is the vein of choice when drawing a sample of blood for clinical tests. It is easily located just under the skin on the anterior surface of the elbow joint. In coronary bypass surgery, the great saphenous vein is sometimes removed from a leg, and a segment of this vein is grafted to the afflicted coronary artery on each side of the blockage. This allows blood to flow through the segment of vein, bypassing the blockage to reach the distal part of the coronary artery.

The **great saphenous vein** originates from the venous arches in the foot, and it drains the medial and superficial portions of the foot, leg, and thigh. It merges with the femoral vein to form the **external iliac vein.** The external iliac vein and the **internal iliac vein** receive branches that drain the upper thigh and pelvic areas, and they merge to form the **common iliac vein.** The left and right common iliac veins merge to form the **inferior vena cava,** which returns blood to the right atrium of the heart (see figure 12.23).

Veins Draining the Abdominal and Thoracic Walls AP|R

The **azygos** (az′-i-gōs) **vein** drains most of the thoracic and abdominal walls, and it empties into the superior vena cava near the right atrium. The azygos vein receives blood from a number of smaller veins,

including the **intercostal veins** and the **ascending lumbar vein,** which drains the wall of the abdomen.

Veins Draining the Abdominal Viscera AP|R

The **inferior mesenteric vein** and the **superior mesenteric vein** drain the large and small intestines and merge to form the **hepatic portal vein.** The **gastric veins,** which drain the stomach, the **splenic vein,** which drains the spleen, and the **pancreatic vein,** which drains the pancreas, all empty into the hepatic portal vein. All of these veins compose the **hepatic portal system.**

The hepatic portal vein carries blood from the stomach, intestines, spleen, and pancreas to the liver instead of the inferior vena cava. After entering the liver, the blood flows through the venous sinusoids, where materials are either removed or added before the blood enters the **hepatic veins,** which empty into the inferior vena cava (figure 12.24). The hepatic portal system allows the liver to monitor and adjust the concentrations of substances in blood coming from the digestive tract before it enters the general circulation.

The left and right **renal veins** carry blood from the kidneys, and the left and right **gonadal veins** return blood from the ovaries in females and the testes in males. Both renal veins and the right gonadal vein drain into the inferior vena cava. The left gonadal vein empties into the left renal vein (table 12.7).

Check My Understanding

18. What is the venous pathway of blood from the left side of the head to the right atrium?
19. What is the venous pathway of blood from the small intestine to the right atrium?
20. What is the venous pathway of blood from the posterior portion of the ankle to the right atrium?

12.11 Disorders of the Heart and Blood Vessels

These disorders are grouped according to whether they affect primarily the heart or blood vessels. In some cases, the underlying cause of a heart ailment is a blood vessel disorder.

Heart Disorders

Arrhythmia (ah-rith′-mē-ah), or dysrhythmia, refers to an abnormal heartbeat. It may be caused by a number of factors, including damage to the heart conduction system, drugs, electrolyte imbalance, or a diminished

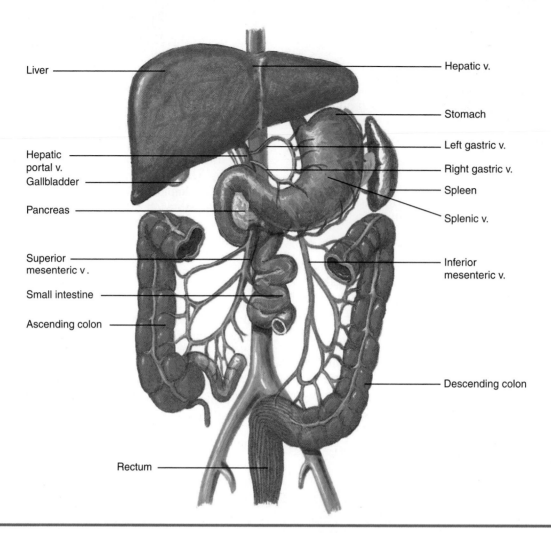

Figure 12.24 Veins that drain the abdominal viscera. (v. = vein) AP|R

Table 12.7	Major Veins Draining to the Inferior Vena Cava	
Vein	**Region Drained and Location**	**Receiving Vein**
Leg		
Anterior and posterior tibial	Foot and lower leg	Popliteal
Popliteal	Knee	Femoral
Small saphenous	Posterior leg	Popliteal
Great saphenous	Foot, leg, and thigh	Femoral
Femoral	Thigh	External iliac
Trunk		
Hepatic portal	Intestines and stomach	Liver sinusoids
Hepatic	Liver	Inferior vena cava
Renal	Kidneys	Inferior vena cava
Right gonadal	Right ovary or testis	Inferior vena cava
Left gonadal	Left ovary or testis	Left renal
External iliac	Pelvic wall	Common iliac
Internal iliac	Viscera in pelvis and lower abdomen	Common iliac
Common iliac	Pelvic and lower abdominal regions	Inferior vena cava

(a) Lumen   Artery wall

(b) Fatty deposit   Lumen   Artery wall

Figure 12.25 Cross sections of (*a*) a normal artery and (*b*) an atherosclerotic artery whose lumen is diminished by fatty deposits. Atherosclerosis promotes the formation of a blood clot within the artery.

supply of blood via the coronary arteries. In addition to irregular heartbeats, arrhythmia includes

- Bradycardia—a slow heart rate of less than 60 beats per minute.
- Tachycardia—a fast heart rate of over 100 beats per minute.
- Heart flutter—a very rapid heart rate of 200 to 300 beats per minute.
- Fibrillation—a very rapid heart rate in which the contractions are uncoordinated so that blood is not pumped from the ventricles. Ventricular fibrillation is usually fatal without prompt treatment.

Congestive heart failure (CHF) is the acute or chronic inability of the heart to pump out the blood returned to it by the veins. Symptoms include fatigue; edema (accumulation of fluid) of the lungs, feet, and legs; and excess accumulation of blood in internal organs. CHF may result from atherosclerosis of the coronary arteries, which deprives the myocardium of adequate blood.

Heart murmurs are unusual heart sounds. They are usually associated with defective heart valves, which allow a backflow of blood. Unless there are complications, heart murmurs have little clinical significance.

Myocardial infarction (mī-ō-kar′-dē-al in-fark′-shun) is the death of a portion of the myocardium due to an obstruction in a coronary artery. The obstruction is usually a blood clot that has formed as a result of atherosclerosis. This event is commonly called a "heart attack," and it may be fatal if a large portion of the myocardium is deprived of blood.

Pericarditis is the inflammation of the pericardium and is usually caused by a viral or bacterial infection. It may be quite painful as the inflamed membranes rub together during each heart cycle.

Blood Vessel Disorders

An **aneurysm** (an′-yū-rizm) is a weakened portion of a blood vessel that bulges out, forming a balloonlike sac filled with blood. Rupture of an aneurysm in a major artery may produce a fatal hemorrhage.

Arteriosclerosis (ar-te″-rēō-skle-rō′-sis) is hardening of the arteries. It results from calcium deposits that accumulate in the tunica media of arterial walls and is usually associated with atherosclerosis.

Atherosclerosis is the formation of fatty deposits (cholesterol and triglycerides) in the tunica interna of arterial walls. The atherosclerotic plaques reduce the lumen of the arteries and increase the probability of blood clots being formed. Such deposits in the coronary, carotid, or cerebral arteries may lead to serious circulatory problems (figure 12.25).

Hypertension refers to chronic high blood pressure. It is the most common disease affecting the heart and blood vessels. Blood pressure that exceeds 140/90 is indicative of hypertension. A systolic blood pressure of 120 to 139 and a diastolic blood pressure of 80 to 89 is considered to be *prehypertension*. Hypertension may be caused by a variety of factors, but persistent stress and smoking are commonly involved.

Phlebitis (flē-bī′-tis) is inflammation of a vein, and it most often occurs in a leg. If it is complicated by the formation of a blood clot, it is called *thrombophlebitis*.

Varicose veins are veins that have become dilated and swollen because their valves are not functioning properly. Heredity seems to play a role in their occurrence. Pregnancy, standing for prolonged periods, and lack of physical activity reduce venous return and promote varicose veins in the legs. Chronic constipation promotes their occurrence in the anal canal, where they are called **hemorrhoids** (hem′o-royds).

12.1 Anatomy of the Heart

- The heart is enveloped by the pericardial membranes, which provide protection and support.
- The heart wall consists primarily of the myocardium, a thick layer of cardiac muscle. It is lined on the inside by the thin endocardium and on the outside by the thin epicardium.
- The heart contains four chambers. The upper chambers are the left and right atria, which receive blood returning to the heart. The lower chambers are the left and right ventricles, which pump blood from the heart. There are no openings between the atria or between the ventricles.
- Atrioventricular valves allow blood to flow between each atrium and its corresponding ventricle but prevent a backflow of blood. The bicuspid A-V valve lies between the left atrium and left ventricle. The tricuspid A-V valve lies between the right atrium and right ventricle.
- Semilunar valves allow blood to be pumped from the ventricles into their associated arteries. The aortic semilunar valve is located in the base of the aorta. The pulmonary semilunar valve is located in the base of the pulmonary trunk.

12.2 Cardiac Cycle

- The cardiac cycle includes both contraction (systole) and relaxation (diastole) phases.
- During atrial diastole, blood returns to the atria and flows on into the ventricles. Atrial systole forces more blood into the ventricles to fill them.
- During ventricular diastole, blood flows into the ventricles. Ventricular systole pumps blood from the ventricles into their associated arteries.
- The normal lub-dup heart sound is caused by the closure of the heart valves. The first sound results from the closure of the atrioventricular valves. The second sound results from the closure of the semilunar valves.
- The right atrium receives deoxygenated blood from the superior and inferior venae cavae, and the left atrium receives oxygenated blood from the pulmonary veins.
- The right ventricle pumps deoxygenated blood into the pulmonary trunk, which divides into the left and right pulmonary arteries, which lead to the lungs. At the same time, the left ventricle pumps oxygenated blood into the aorta, which leads to all parts of the body except the lungs.
- The heart tissues receive blood from the coronary arteries, which branch from the ascending aorta. Blood is returned from the heart tissues by the cardiac veins, which open into the coronary sinus, which leads to the right atrium.

12.3 Heart Conduction System

- The S-A node is the pacemaker, which rhythmically initiates impulses that cause the heart contractions.
- Impulses pass through the atria, causing atrial systole and simultaneously reach the A-V node.
- Impulses pass from the A-V node along the A-V bundle to the Purkinje fibers, which transmit the impulses to the myocardium, causing ventricular contraction.
- An electrocardiogram is a recording of the formation and transmission of impulses through the heart conduction system.
- An electrocardiogram consists of a P wave, a QRS wave, and a T wave, and it is used in the diagnosis of heart ailments.

12.4 Regulation of Heart Function

- Cardiac output is a measure of heart function. It is determined by stroke volume and heart rate:

$$CO = SV \times HR$$

- Cardiac output is regulated by factors internal and external to the heart.
- Heart rate is controlled by the autonomic nervous system. The cardiac control center is in the medulla oblongata. It receives sensory impulses from pressure receptors in the aorta and carotid arteries.
- Sympathetic fibers release norepinephrine at heart synapses, which causes an increase in the heart rate. Parasympathetic fibers release acetylcholine at heart synapses, which causes a decrease in heart rate.
- The dynamic balance in the frequency of sympathetic and parasympathetic impulses reaching the heart adjusts the heart rate to meet body needs.
- Heart rate is also affected by age, sex, physical condition, temperature, epinephrine, thyroid hormone, and the concentration of Ca^{++} and K^+.

12.5 Types of Blood Vessels

- The three basic types of blood vessels are arteries, capillaries, and veins. Large arteries and veins are formed of an outer fibrous layer of connective tissue, a middle layer of smooth muscle, and an inner layer of simple squamous epithelium.
- Arteries have thick, muscular walls and carry blood from the heart. Large arteries divide repeatedly to form the smallest arteries, arterioles, which connect with capillaries.
- Capillaries are the smallest and most numerous blood vessels. Their thin walls of endothelial cells allow an exchange of materials between the blood and the interstitial fluid. Dissolved molecules are

exchanged by diffusion. Fluid exits the arteriole end of a capillary because blood pressure is greater than osmotic pressure, and it reenters the venule end of the capillary because osmotic pressure is greater than blood pressure. Capillaries merge to form venules.

- Veins have thinner walls than arteries and carry blood from capillaries toward the heart. The smallest veins are venules, which lead from capillaries and merge to form small veins. Veins contain valves that prevent a backflow of blood.

12.6 Blood Flow

- Blood circulates from areas of higher pressure to areas of lower pressure. Blood pressure is highest in the ventricles and lowest in the atria.
- Systemic blood pressure declines as blood is carried to the capillaries. Skeletal muscle contractions and respiratory movements are important forces that aid the return of venous blood.
- Blood velocity varies inversely with the cross sectional area of the combined blood vessels. Blood velocity is highest in the aorta and lowest in the capillaries.

12.7 Blood Pressure

- Optimal systolic blood pressure is 115 mm Hg. Optimal diastolic blood pressure is 75 mm Hg.
- The difference between systolic and diastolic pressures is the pulse pressure. The pulse may be detected by palpating surface arteries.
- Blood pressure is determined by four factors: cardiac output, blood volume, peripheral resistance, and blood viscosity.
- The vasomotor center in the medulla oblongata provides the autonomic control of blood vessel diameter. In this way, the autonomic nervous system controls peripheral resistance and blood pressure.
- Local autoregulation of arterioles overrides autonomic control and regulates blood flow in capillaries according to the needs of the local tissues.

12.8 Circulation Pathways

- The pulmonary circuit carries blood from the heart to the lungs and back again.
- The systemic circuit carries blood from the heart to all parts of the body, except the lungs, and back again.

12.9 Systemic Arteries

- The major branch arteries of the aorta are the coronary, brachiocephalic, left common carotid, left subclavian, intercostals, celiac, superior mesenteric, renal, gonadal, lumbar, inferior mesenteric, and common iliac arteries.
- The major arteries supplying the head and neck are paired arteries. Each common carotid artery branches to form the external and internal carotid arteries. The external carotid supplies the neck, face, and scalp. The internal carotid is the major artery supplying the brain. The vertebral arteries supply the neck and brain.
- Each shoulder and arm is supplied by a subclavian artery, which becomes the axillary artery, which becomes the brachial artery of the arm. The brachial artery branches to form the radial and ulnar arteries of the forearm.
- Each common iliac artery branches to form internal and external iliac arteries. The external iliac enters the leg to become the femoral artery, which becomes the popliteal artery near the knee. The popliteal branches below the knee to form the anterior and posterior tibial arteries.

12.10 Systemic Veins

- Veins draining the head and neck are paired veins. On each side, the external jugular and vertebral veins empty into the subclavian vein. The internal jugular vein and subclavian merge to form the brachiocephalic vein. The left and right brachiocephalic veins join to form the superior vena cava.
- The ascending lumbar vein and the intercostal veins enter the azygos vein, which opens into the superior vena cava.
- Radial and ulnar veins of the forearm join to form the brachial vein of the arm. The basilic vein joins the brachial vein to form the axillary vein, which, in turn, receives the cephalic vein to form the subclavian vein.
- Anterior and posterior tibial veins merge below the knee to form the popliteal vein. The popliteal vein receives the small saphenous and peroneal veins to form the femoral vein. The great saphenous vein extends from the foot to join with the femoral vein near the hip, which forms the external iliac vein. The external iliac vein joins with the internal iliac vein to form the common iliac vein. The left and right common iliac veins merge to form the inferior vena cava.
- The inferior and superior mesenteric veins merge to form the hepatic portal vein, which then receives the gastric, splenic, and pancreatic veins. These veins form the hepatic portal system. The hepatic portal vein empties into the liver sinusoids. The hepatic vein carries blood from the liver to the inferior vena cava.
- The paired gonadal and renal veins empty into the inferior vena cava.

12.11 Disorders of the Heart and Blood Vessels

- Disorders of the heart include arrhythmia, congestive heart failure, heart murmurs, myocardial infarction, and pericarditis.
- Disorders of blood vessels include aneurysm, arteriosclerosis, atherosclerosis, hypertension, phlebitis, and varicose veins.

BUILDING MY VOCABULARY

1. Selected New Terms

atrioventricular bundle (A-V bundle), p. 249
atrioventricular node (A-V node), p. 249
bicuspid valve, p. 245
cardiac control center, p. 251
cardiac output, p. 257
chordae tendineae, p. 245
electrocardiogram, p. 250
interstitial fluid, p. 254
pericardial cavity, p. 243
peripheral resistance, p. 257
sinoatrial node (S-A node), p. 250
tricuspid valve, p. 245

2. Related Clinical Terms

Angiospasm (an'-jē-ō-spa-zum) Muscular spasm of a blood vessel.

Arteriography (ar-ter-ē-og'-rah-fē) An X-ray of arteries after injection of a radiopaque dye.

Cardiology (kar-dē-ol'-ō-jē) Medical specialty treating disorders of the heart.

Phlebitis (flē-bī'-tis) Inflammation of a vein, most often in a leg.

Thrombophlebitis (throm-bō-flē-bī'-tis) A blood clot in a vein resulting from inflammation; usually forms in a leg.

SELF-REVIEW

Answers are located in appendix B.

1. The membranous sac around the heart is the _____.
2. The _____ is the heart chamber receiving oxygenated blood from the lungs.
3. The _____ valve prevents a backflow of blood from the right ventricle into the _____.
4. During _____ diastole blood fills the atria; during ventricular _____ blood is pumped into arteries leading from the heart.
5. The heartbeat originates in the _____ node: the _____ node relays impulses along the A-V bundle and Purkinje fibers to the ventricular myocardium.
6. Impulses from _____ fibers increase the heart rate; impulses from the _____ fibers decrease the heart rate.
7. Blood is carried from the heart in _____ and returned to the heart in _____.
8. Vessels with the thickest walls are _____; those with the thinnest walls are _____.
9. The exchange of materials between capillary blood and tissue fluid occurs by _____ and _____.
10. The heart chambers and vessels in the pulmonary circuit are _____ ventricle, pulmonary _____, pulmonary _____, capillaries in the lungs, pulmonary _____, _____ atrium.
11. The arterial pathway of blood from the heart to the right side of the brain is ascending aorta, aortic arch, _____, common carotid, and _____.
12. The arterial pathway of blood from the heart to the liver is ascending aorta, aortic arch, _____ aorta, abdominal aorta, _____, and _____.
13. The venous pathway returning blood from the small intestine to the heart is _____, liver, _____, and _____ vena cava.
14. The venous pathway returning blood from the back of the knee is _____, femoral, _____, _____, and _____ vena cava.
15. The venous pathway from the little finger to the heart is basilic, _____, _____, _____, and _____ vena cava.

CRITICAL THINKING

1. Complete the learning objectives on the first page of this chapter.
2. How do the heart valves keep blood flowing in one direction?
3. What factors are involved in creating blood pressure?
4. What enables the heart to change its rate and strength of contraction as needed?
5. What is the advantage of the hepatic portal system?

Visit this book's website at www.mhhe.com/ gunstream5 for practice quizzes, learning exercises, case studies, and other study tools.

CHAPTER 13

Lymphatic System and Defenses Against Disease

Module 10
Lymphatic System

Allergen A foreign substance that stimulates an allergic reaction.
Antibody (anti = against) A substance produced by B cells in response to a specific antigen.
Antigen A foreign substance capable of stimulating the production of antibodies.
Complement A group of plasma proteins that works with antibodies to destroy cells of pathogens.

Immunity (immun = free) Resistance to specific disease-producing antigens.
Inflammation (inflam = to set on fire) A localized response to damaged or infected tissues that is characterized by swelling, redness, pain, and heat.
Lymph (lymph = clear water) The fluid transported in lymphatic vessels.

Lymph node A lymph-filtering node of lymphatic tissue located on a lymphatic vessel.
Lymphatic vessel A vessel that transports lymph.
Pathogen A disease-causing organism.
Spleen The largest lymphatic organ.

uring the exchange of materials between capillary blood and interstitial fluid, slightly more fluid enters the interstitial fluid than is returned to the blood. The *lymphatic system,* which consists of lymphatic vessels and organs, returns the excess interstitial fluid to the blood for reuse. By recycling interstitial fluid, the lymphatic system helps to maintain homeostasis by conserving water and dissolved substances. In this way, the lymphatic system helps maintain water balance in the body. The relationship of the lymphatic system to the cardiovascular system is shown diagrammatically in figure 13.1.

The lymphatic system also is involved in the absorption of fats from the digestive tract. In the small intestine, lymphatic vessels called **lacteals** (lak'-te-alz) absorb fat molecules and other substances from the digestive tract. Fats are carried by lymphatic vessels to the venous circulation.

The lymphatic system also works with white blood cells to protect the body against **pathogens** (path'-ō-jens)— disease-causing organisms. Pathogens include viruses, bacteria, fungi, protozoa, and other parasites that may invade the body. The body's defense mechanisms are categorized into two broad groups: nonspecific resistance and specific resistance, or immunity.

13.1 Lymph

Interstitial fluid is derived from blood plasma as materials move from the blood in capillaries to the tissue cells. It tends to accumulate in tissue spaces because the forces that move fluid from capillaries into

tissue spaces are greater than the forces that return fluid into the capillaries. The excess interstitual fluid is picked up by lymphatic capillaries and returned to the blood by lymphatic vessels. After interstitual fluid enters a lymphatic capillary, it is called **lymph**. The removal of excess interstitial fluid by the lymphatic system prevents

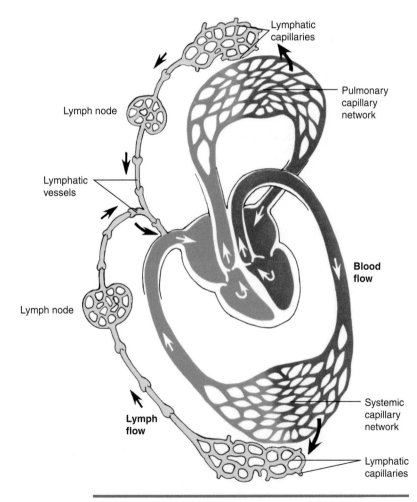

Figure 13.1 Lymphatic vessels transport fluid from interstitial spaces to the bloodstream. AP|R

edema, the swelling of tissues due to fluid accumulation, and helps maintain the normal blood volume.

13.2 Lymphatic Capillaries and Vessels

Lymphatic vessels provide a pathway for the one-way movement of lymph from body tissues to the subclavian veins. The smallest lymphatic vessels are the microscopic *lymphatic capillaries,* closed-ended tubes that are found in spaces within body tissues (figure 13.2). Lymphatic capillaries are immersed in interstitial fluid. Like blood capillaries, lymphatic capillaries consist of a single layer of endothelial cells (squamous epithelium). The edges of adjacent cells overlap each other slightly, which forms tiny flaplike valves between the cells. Fluid can move easily into the lymphatic capillary, but the valves inhibit movement of fluid out of the capillary.

Lymphatic capillaries merge to form **lymphatic vessels**, which are about as numerous as the veins in the body. Lymphatic vessels have a structure similar to veins, including valves that prevent a backflow of lymph. The smaller lymphatic vessels merge to form larger vessels called *lymphatic trunks* that drain large body regions. Locate these trunks in figure 13.3.

Lymphatic trunks drain into one of two lymphatic *collecting ducts.* Lymphatic trunks from the right side of the head and neck, right arm and shoulder, and right side of the thorax empty into the *right lymphatic duct.* The right lymphatic duct is very short, and it empties into the right subclavian vein. Lymphatic trunks from the rest of the body drain into the *thoracic duct,* a large lymphatic duct that extends from the upper abdomen and through the thorax to empty into the left subclavian vein. In this way, all of the lymph is returned to venous blood for reuse via either the right lymphatic duct or the thoracic duct.

13.3 Transport of Lymph

The movement of lymph is dependent upon outside forces because there is no pumping mechanism within the lymphatic system. These forces are the contractions of skeletal muscles, respiratory movements, and gravity—the same forces that aid the return of venous blood to the heart.

The contraction of skeletal muscles compresses lymphatic vessels. Because the backflow of lymph is prevented by the valves in the vessels, compression of a lymphatic vessel forces lymph from one valved segment to another. This mode of lymph movement is especially important in the arms and legs.

Movement of lymph in vessels within the thorax and abdomen is enabled by respiratory movements that

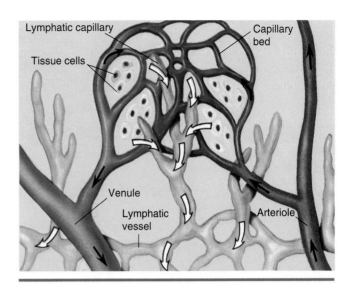

Figure 13.2 Lymphatic capillaries (green) are microscopic, closed-ended tubes that begin in the interstitial spaces of most tissues.

Clinical **INSIGHT**

Edema is the swelling of localized tissues due to the accumulation of excess interstitial fluid. It results from either too much fluid exiting the blood in capillaries or insufficient removal of fluid by lymphatic vessels. There are a variety of causes for edema. For example, a sedentary lifestyle, which leads to the breakdown of valves in leg veins, can result in edema of the lower legs. Also, removal of lymphatic vessels and lymph nodes during cancer surgery often leads to edema of the affected area.

change the pressure within these body cavities. During inspiration, the pressure within the thoracic cavity is decreased and the pressure within the abdominal cavity is increased. This difference in pressure causes lymph to flow from abdominal vessels upward into the thoracic vessels along the pressure gradient. Of course, the valves play an important role as well by preventing a backflow of lymph.

Gravity helps to move lymph along in vessels located superior to the subclavian veins.

Table 13.1 outlines the components of the lymphatic system.

Check My Understanding

1. What is lymph and how is it returned to the blood?
2. Why is the return of lymph to the blood important?

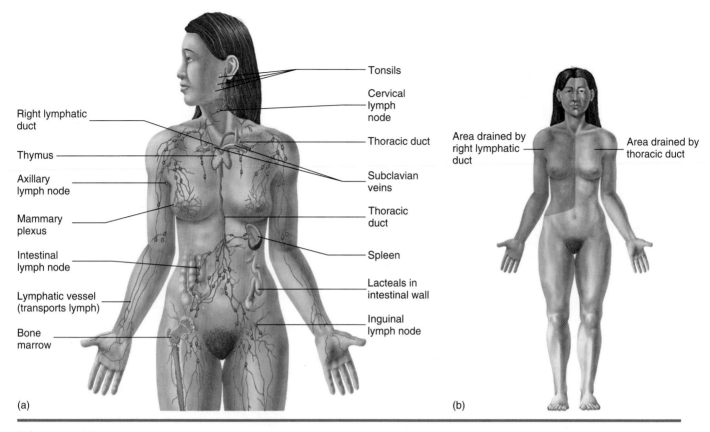

(a)

(b)

Figure 13.3 The lymphatic system. (*a*) Major organs and vessels of the lymphatic system. The right lymphatic duct empties into the right subclavian vein. The thoracic duct drains into the left subclavian vein. (*b*) Body regions drained by the right lymphatic duct and the thoracic duct. AP|R

Table 13.1 Components of the Lymphatic System

Component	Characteristics	Function
Lymphatic Capillaries	Microscopic closed-ended tubes in tissue spaces	Collect interstitial fluid from tissue spaces; once in a lymphatic capillary, interstitial fluid is called *lymph*
Lymphatic Vessels	Formed by merging of lymphatic capillaries; structure similar to veins; contain valves; merge to form lymphatic trunks that drain into either the *right lymphatic duct* or the *thoracic duct*	Transport lymph and empty it into the subclavian veins
Lymphatic Organs		Sites of lymphocyte production and immune responses
Lymph nodes	Small, bean-shaped organs arranged in groups along lymphatic vessels	Filter and cleanse lymph; destroy pathogens carried by lymph
Tonsils	Masses of lymphatic tissue at entrance to throat	Intercept and destroy pathogens entering throat from nasal and oral cavities
Spleen	Large lymphatic organ containing venous sinuses	Filters and cleanses blood; destroys pathogens carried by blood; contains reservoir of blood; primary site for removal of old RBCs; stores platelets
Thymus	Bilobed gland located above heart; size decreases with age	Site of T cell maturation; secretes hormone *thymosin,* which stimulates maturation of T cells

13.4 Lymphatic Organs

There are several lymphatic organs in the body, including the lymph nodes, tonsils, spleen, and thymus gland. All lymphatic organs are sites of lymphocyte production. Many of the lymphocytes remain in the lymphatic organs, but some are released into the blood and are carried to other sites, especially when a pathogen invades the body.

Lymph Nodes

Lymph nodes, or lymph glands, usually occur in groups along the larger lymphatic vessels. They are widely distributed in the body, but they do occur more frequently in inguinal, axillary, and cervical regions of the body. Interestingly, there are no lymph nodes in the central nervous system.

Structure of Lymph Nodes

Lymph nodes are roughly bean-shaped and 1.0 to 2.5 cm in length. Figure 13.4 is a photograph of a lymph node *in situ* that shows lymphatic vessels leading to and from the node. Figure 13.5 shows the structure of a section of a lymph node. Note that the lymph node consists of a number of small subunits called **nodules.** The nodules are production sites for new lymphocytes.

Lymph enters a lymph node through several *afferent* (af′-er-ent) *lymphatic vessels* and flows through the *lymph sinuses,* which surround the nodules. Lymph is collected from the sinuses and enters *efferent* (ef′-er-ent) *lymphatic vessels,* which carry lymph away from the lymph node. The indentation of the node where efferent lymphatic vessels emerge is called the *hilum.*

Function of Lymph Nodes

A major function of lymph nodes is the filtration and cleansing of the lymph as it passes through a node. They are the only lymphatic organs that filter the lymph. Damaged cells, cancerous cells, cellular debris, bacteria, and viruses become trapped in the fibrous network of the lymph node and are destroyed by the action of lymphocytes and macrophages. Lymphocytes act against cancerous cells and pathogens, such as bacteria and viruses. Macrophages engulf cellular debris, immobilized or dead bacteria, and viruses.

Tonsils AP|R

Tonsils (ton′-sils) are clusters of lymphatic tissue located just under the mucous membrane at the back of the nasal and oral cavities. Like all lymphatic tissue, they produce lymphocytes and contain both lymphocytes and macrophages to fight disease. Their function is to intercept and destroy pathogens that enter through the nose and mouth before they can reach the blood.

Figure 13.4 A lymph node and its associated vessels.

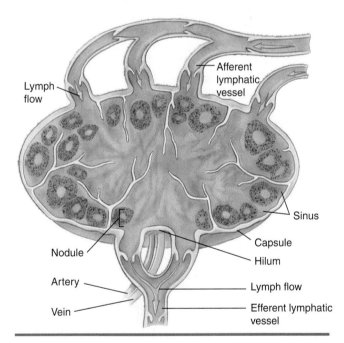

Figure 13.5 Section of a lymph node. AP|R

There are three kinds of tonsils that are strategically located to carry out this function:

1. The *palatine* (pal′-ah-tine) *tonsils* are located on each side at the junction of the oral cavity and the pharynx (throat).
2. The *pharyngeal* (fah-rin′-jē-al) *tonsil* is located on the back wall of the nasal cavity, a region known as the nasopharynx. This tonsil is commonly called the *adenoid.*
3. The *lingual* (ling′-gwal) *tonsils* are located on the back of the tongue.

Tonsils are larger in young children and play an important role in their defense against disease. Sometimes the palatine tonsils and pharyngeal tonsil become so overloaded and swollen with bacteria that they must be surgically removed by a tonsillectomy. But this is usually avoided, if possible.

Thymus AP|R

The **thymus** is a soft, bilobed gland located in the mediastinum above the heart (figure 13.6). It is large in infants and children, but after puberty it begins to atrophy and becomes quite small in adults. The thymus plays a key role in the development of the immune system before birth and during early childhood. Until the immune system matures at about two years of age, an infant is more susceptible to disease than older children. Only after the immune system is well developed can vaccination provide protection for children against certain diseases.

The major function of the thymus is the differentiation (maturation) of a class of lymphocytes called **T lymphocytes,** or *T cells.* The *thymosin* hormones promote the differentiation and division of T cells, which makes them *immunocompetent,* that is, capable of recognizing and attacking foreign antigens. After maturation, T cells are distributed by blood to lymphatic tissues throughout the body.

Spleen

The **spleen** is the largest lymphatic organ. It is located behind the stomach near the diaphragm in the upper left quadrant of the abdominal cavity (figure 13.7). The lower ribs provide protection against physical injury. The spleen is a soft, purplish organ 5 to 7 cm (2–3 in) wide and 13 to 16 cm (5–6 in) long. It contains

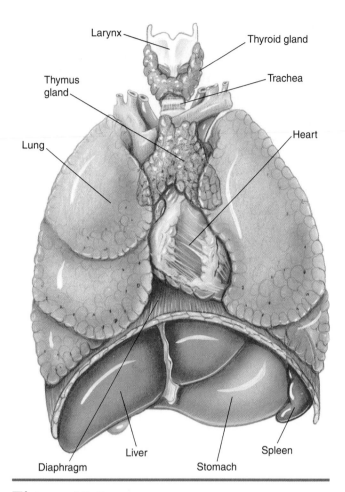

Figure 13.6   The thymus is located in the mediastinum above the heart. It is the site of T lymphocyte maturation.   AP|R

numerous centers for lymphocyte production and a large venous sinus filled with blood.

The spleen resembles a large lymph node. Like lymph nodes, it is enveloped by a thin capsule of connective tissue and is subdivided by connective tissue into many compartments. The compartments contain two basic types of tissues that are named for their appearance in fresh, unstained tissue. *White pulp* consists of large numbers of lymphocytes that cluster around tiny branches of the splenic artery. This tissue is mostly concerned with the immune functions of the spleen. *Red pulp* occupies the rest of a compartment, surrounding the white pulp and the venous sinuses, which are filled with blood. The red pulp is named for the numerous erythrocytes that it contains in addition to many macrophages and lymphocytes. It is a storage area for erythrocytes and a site where worn-out erythrocytes and pathogens are removed from the blood (figure 13.7). Before birth, the spleen is a major blood-forming organ, but this function is later taken over by red bone marrow. After birth, the spleen's role is related to both lymphatic and cardiovascular functions:

The spread of cancerous cells occurs when cells break away from the primary tumor and are carried to other sites via the lymphatic system or the blood. This process, called *metastasis* (me-tas′-ta-sis), generates secondary cancerous growths called *metastases* wherever the cancerous cells lodge. Because metastatic cells are frequently carried in the lymph, secondary cancerous growths often occur in lymph nodes on lymphatic vessels draining the region of the primary cancer. Knowledge of the location of lymphatic vessels and lymph nodes, and the direction of lymph flow, is important in the detection and treatment of metastases.

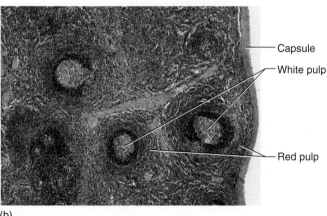

Figure 13.7 The spleen. (*a*) The spleen is subdivided into compartments by connective tissue. (*b*) A photomicrograph of spleen tissue showing white pulp and red pulp. AP|R

- It cleanses and filters the blood much like lymph nodes cleanse lymph. Lymphocytes and macrophages destroy pathogens, and macrophages clean up the debris.
- It stores a reserve supply of red blood cells, which can be released into the blood in times of need, such as after a hemorrhage.
- It is a major site for red blood cell destruction and removal. Macrophages play a major role in this process.

- It is a major site of lymphocyte production.
- The spleen stores about one-third of the body's supply of platelets.

In spite of these important functions, the spleen is not essential for life. But following a splenectomy, a person may be more susceptible to potent pathogens and the effects of hemorrhage.

> ### Check My Understanding
> 3. What are the functions of the lymph nodes, tonsils, spleen, and thymus?

13.5 Nonspecific Resistance Against Disease

Nonspecific resistance provides protection against all pathogens and foreign substances, but it is not directed against a specific pathogen. Nonspecific defense mechanisms include mechanical barriers, chemical actions, phagocytosis, inflammation, and fever.

Mechanical Barriers

The most obvious *mechanical barriers* against infectious agents are the skin and the mucous membranes that line the digestive, respiratory, urinary, and reproductive passages. The closely packed epidermal cells of the skin make penetration by pathogens very difficult, and the acid pH of the skin discourages bacterial growth. Mucous membranes are less effective barriers than the skin. However, they secrete mucus that entraps microorganisms and airborne particles and usually prevents their contact with the underlying membranes. The continuous flow of tears over the eyes, the production and swallowing of saliva, and the passage of urine through the urethra are examples of fluid mechanical barriers that help to flush away microbes before they can attack body tissues.

Chemical Actions

Various body chemicals, including certain enzymes, provide a nonspecific defense against pathogens. A few examples will illustrate the effect of these chemicals.

Tears, saliva, nasal secretions, and perspiration contain the enzyme *lysozyme*, which destroys bacteria and helps to protect underlying tissues.

Mucus is continuously produced by epithelium lining the respiratory and digestive passageways. Microorganisms entering the nose and mouth tend to be trapped in the mucus, which is carried to the throat and is swallowed at frequent intervals. Upon reaching the stomach, most microorganisms are destroyed by the gastric juice, either by its low pH or by the enzyme *pepsin*. Pepsin acts by digesting the proteins composing the microbes.

When infected with a virus, lymphocytes and macrophages produce *interferon*, a substance that stimulates uninfected cells to synthesize special proteins that inhibit the replication of viruses within cells. In this way, the rapid growth of viruses may be inhibited. Interferon is now produced commercially by biotechnology and may be used, via injections, to fight serious viral diseases.

Phagocytosis

Phagocytosis (fag-ō-sǐ-tō′-sis) is the engulfing and destruction (by digestion) of microorganisms, damaged cells, and cellular debris by granulocytic leukocytes and macrophages. When an infection occurs, neutrophils and monocytes are quickly attracted to the infected tissues. Monocytes entering the tissues become transformed into **macrophages** (mak′-rō-fāj-es), large cells that are especially active in phagocytosis.

Some macrophages wander among the tissues, searching out and phagocytizing microorganisms and cellular debris. Others become fixed (stationary) in particular locations in the body, where they phagocytize microbes that are passing by. Fixed macrophages are especially abundant along the inner walls of blood and lymphatic vessels and in the spleen, lymph nodes, liver, brain, and bone marrow. The wandering and fixed macrophages compose the **tissue macrophage system** (formerly called the reticuloendothelial system), which plays a major role in the destruction of potential pathogens.

Inflammation

Inflammation is a localized response to infection or injury that promotes the destruction of pathogens and the healing process. It is characterized by redness, pain, heat, and swelling of the affected tissues.

When infection occurs, cells release several types of chemicals, such as histamine, that cause a dilation of the arterioles and increase the permeability of capillaries in the affected area. The increased blood flow to the local area produces redness and heat. Blood from deeper tissues carries heat to inflamed surface tissues. The increased movement of fluids from the capillaries produces swelling (edema) of the tissues. Pain results from irritation of nerve endings by pathogens, swelling, or chemicals released by infected cells.

White blood cells are attracted to the affected area to fight the infection. In bacterial infections, neutrophils and macrophages actively phagocytize the pathogens and damaged cells. The accumulated mass of living and dead leukocytes, tissue cells, and bacteria may form a thick, whitish fluid called **pus.**

Fluids from capillaries that enter the affected area contain both fibrinogen and fibroblasts. Fibrinogen may be converted into fibrin to form a clot that is subsequently penetrated and enveloped by fibers formed by the fibroblasts. This action tends to seal off the infected area and prevent the spread of pathogens to neighboring tissues.

The continued action of leukocytes usually brings the infection under control. Then, the dead pathogens and cells are cleaned up by phagocytes, and new cells are produced by cell division to repair any damage to the tissues.

Fever

Fever is an abnormally high body temperature that accompanies widespread infections. It serves a useful purpose as long as the body temperature does not get too high. The increased body temperature inhibits growth of certain pathogens and increases the rate of body processes, including those that fight infection.

Table 13.2 summarizes the major components of nonspecific resistance.

Clinical **INSIGHT**

The most common pathogens affecting humans are bacteria and viruses. Bacteria are very small, single-celled organisms that lack a true nucleus and other complex cellular organelles. Their DNA is concentrated, but it is not enclosed in a nuclear envelope as in higher organisms. Bacteria are simple organisms but they have the necessary metabolic machinery required for life and reproduction. Bacterial pathogens may cause disease by releasing toxins (poisons), releasing enzymes that damage cells, or entering and destroying cells. Antibiotics are effective in treating bacterial infections.

In contrast, viruses are ultrasmall particles of nucleic acid and protein—thousands of times smaller than bacteria. They are not organisms, and they are not alive. A virus is simply composed of either a DNA or RNA molecule enveloped by a protein coat. It causes disease by dismantling the metabolic machinery of the host cell and by destroying host cells. A virus attaches to a cell's surface receptor and penetrates into the cell. Once inside, it takes over the cell's DNA and metabolic machinery, causing the cell to replicate hundreds or thousands of viruses, which burst forth as the cell is destroyed. The released viruses then move on to attack other cells. Antibiotics are not effective in treating viral infections.

Table 13.2   Summary of Major Components of Nonspecific Resistance

Component	Function
Mechanical Barriers	
Intact skin	Closely packed cells and multiple cell layers prevent entrance of pathogens
Intact mucous membranes	Closely arranged cells retard entrance of pathogens; not as effective as intact skin
Mucus	Traps pathogens in digestive and respiratory tracts
Saliva	Washes pathogens from oral surfaces
Tears	Washes pathogens from surface of eye
Urine	Flushes pathogens from urethra
Chemical Actions	
Acid pH of skin	Retards growth of many bacteria
Gastric juice	Kills pathogens that are swallowed
Interferon	Helps to prevent viral infections
Lysozyme	Antimicrobial enzyme in nasal secretions, perspiration, saliva, and tears kills some pathogens
Other Mechanisms	
Fever	Speeds up body processes and inhibits growth of pathogens
Inflammation	Promotes nonspecific resistance; confines infection
Phagocytosis	Macrophages and granulocytic leukocytes engulf and destroy pathogens

Check My Understanding

4. Identify and explain the method of action of mechanical barriers, chemical actions, and cellular mechanisms providing nonspecific resistance against disease.

13.6 Immunity

In contrast to nonspecific resistance, **immunity** (i-mū′-ni-tē), or specific resistance, is directed at specific pathogens and foreign cells. An immune response involves the production of specific cells and substances to attack a specific invader. And immunity has a "memory." If the same pathogen should reenter the body at a later date, the immune response is quicker and stronger than during the first encounter. Lymphocytes and macrophages play important roles in immunity.

An immune response involves one or both of two distinct processes: **cell-mediated immunity** and **antibody-mediated immunity** (figure 13.8).

Specialization of Lymphocytes

During fetal development and in newborn infants, lymphocytes are formed in red bone marrow, but they must mature and become specialized before they can participate in immunity. About half of the unspecialized

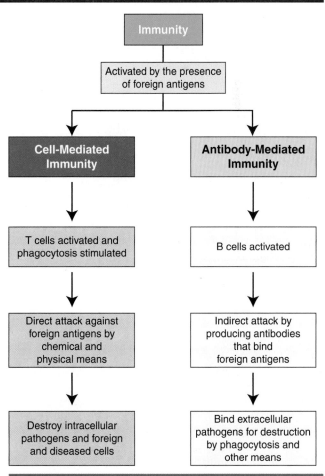

Figure 13.8 Overview of immunity.

(undifferentiated) lymphocytes pass to the thymus, where they become specialized (differentiated) to become **T lymphocytes,** or *T cells.* The other half of the lymphocytes become specialized in a presently unknown site, perhaps in the bone marrow, to become **B lymphocytes,** or *B cells.* T and B lymphocytes are carried by blood to lymphatic organs, such as the lymph nodes, spleen, and tonsils, where they divide to form large populations of T and B cells, and some are released into the blood. About 75% of circulating lymphocytes are T cells, and about 25% are B cells (figure 13.9).

Recognizing Pathogens

All cells, including human cells, have surface recognition molecules called **antigens**. (Recall that antigens are used in typing blood.) In fact, the cells of each person have a unique set of antigens. Antigens are large molecules, such as proteins and glycoproteins.

During the specialization process, lymphocytes "learn" to distinguish "self" antigens from "nonself," or foreign, antigens. Thereafter, lymphocytes can recognize an invading pathogen or cells with abnormal antigens, such as cancer cells and cells infected by a virus, and launch an attack. Unfortunately, lymphocytes also recognize a transplanted organ as foreign, as in graft rejection, and in some cases fail to recognize certain body tissues as "self" and attack the body's own tissues, as in autoimmune diseases.

The maturation process produces thousands (and perhaps millions) of different kinds of T and B cells, each with specific receptors capable of binding with (recognizing) a specific antigen. Therefore, when an antigen of a pathogen or foreign cell enters the body, only the T or B cells that have a receptor that can bind with the specific antigen are involved in the immune response. Table 13.3 summarizes the roles of B and T cells in immunity.

Cell-Mediated Immunity

In cell-mediated immunity, T lymphocytes directly attack and destroy foreign cells or diseased body cells, such as cancer cells, and develop a memory of their antigens in case they should reappear in the future. Cell-mediated immunity also destroys *intracellular* pathogens.

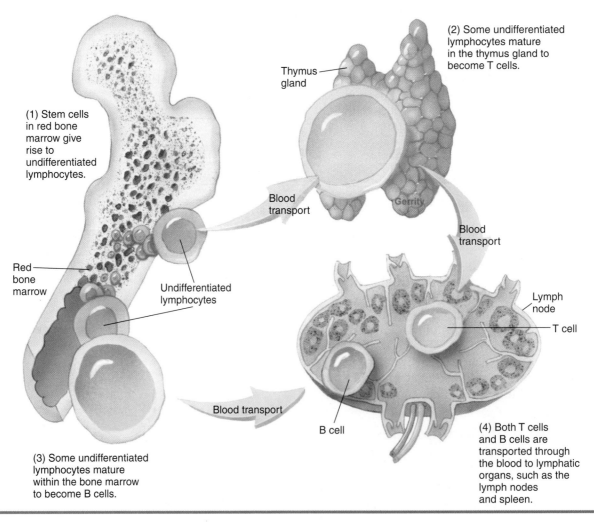

(1) Stem cells in red bone marrow give rise to undifferentiated lymphocytes.

(2) Some undifferentiated lymphocytes mature in the thymus gland to become T cells.

Thymus gland

Blood transport

Blood transport

Red bone marrow

Undifferentiated lymphocytes

Lymph node

T cell

Blood transport

B cell

(3) Some undifferentiated lymphocytes mature within the bone marrow to become B cells.

(4) Both T cells and B cells are transported through the blood to lymphatic organs, such as the lymph nodes and spleen.

Figure 13.9 Differentiation of T lymphocytes and B lymphocytes.

Table 13.3 Roles of B Cells and T Cells in an Immune Response

Cell	Function
B cells	When activated, produce a clone of plasma cells and memory B cells that have the same antigen receptors as the activated parent B cell
Plasma cells	Produce specific antibodies against the antigen that activated the parent B cell
Memory B cells	Dormant cells that are activated if an antigen that fits their antigen receptors reenters the body; launch a secondary immune response
Helper T cells	When activated, start an immune response by releasing cytokines, which activate B cells, promote clone formation by B and T cells, and stimulate phagocytosis; form a clone of active helper T cells and memory T cells
Cytotoxic T cells	When activated, form a clone of cytotoxic T cells and memory T cells programmed to bind to the same antigen that activated the parent cytotoxic T cell; kill cells possessing the targeted antigen with toxic chemicals
Memory T cells	Dormant cells that are activated if an antigen that fits their antigen receptors reenters the body; launch a secondary immune response

A cell-mediated immune response begins when an **antigen-presenting cell (APC)**, often a macrophage, engulfs a foreign (nonself) antigen and displays the antigen, in combination with its own self proteins, on its plasma membrane. When a T cell, which has been programmed during maturation to recognize this particular antigen, binds to the antigen and the APC self proteins, it becomes activated. The activated T cell undergoes repeated mitotic divisions to form a **clone** of identical T cells capable of binding with the same antigen that activated the parent T cell (figure 13.10).

If the activated T cell is a **helper T cell (T_H)**, it produces a clone consisting mostly of active T_H cells along with some *memory T cells (T_M)* capable of binding with the same antigen as the activated parent T cell. When active T_H cells bind with the antigen, they secrete *cytokines* (chemicals) that (1) attract neutrophils and macrophages to the site and stimulate their phagocytic activity, and (2) stimulate mitotic division and immune responses of activated B and T cells.

If the activated T cell is a **cytotoxic T cell (T_C)**, it produces a clone consisting mostly of active T_C cells along with some memory T cells (T_M). When an active T_C cell binds to any cell displaying the targeted antigen, it injects a lethal dose of chemicals to kill the cell. It then detaches and searches out and destroys other cells with the same antigen.

As more and more active T cells are produced and the pathogen is eliminated, the immune response slows and stops. The long-lived T_M cells remain to launch a stronger attack if the targeted antigen should reappear.

Antibody-Mediated Immunity

Antibody-mediated immunity involves both B cells and helper T cells. It provides a defense against *extracellular* pathogens. Rather than directly attacking foreign antigens, it involves the production of antibodies that bind to foreign antigens tagging them for destruction by other means.

An antibody-mediated immune response begins when foreign (nonself) antigens bind to receptors of a B cell. The B cell engulfs the antigens and displays the antigen on its plasma membrane along with its own self antigens. When a helper T cell, which has been programmed to recognize this antigen, binds to this nonself antigen and self protein complex, the helper T cell secretes cytokines that activate the B cell. The activated B cell produces a clone of identical B cells programmed against the same antigen. Most of the B cells in the clone become **plasma cells** but some become *memory B cells* (figure 13.11).

Plasma cells rapidly produce and release antibodies capable of binding with the targeted antigen. Antibodies circulate throughout the body in blood and other body fluids binding to the nonself antigens so they are more easily destroyed by phagocytosis and other means. After the pathogen has been destroyed, antibodies remain to provide protection. If the targeted antigen reenters the body, memory B cells launch an even quicker and stronger attack.

Antibodies do not destroy pathogens directly. Instead, they bind to the antigens, forming *antigen–antibody complexes* that tag pathogens for destruction by other means. For example, an antigen–antibody complex involving bacteria, or other cellular pathogens, creates a site for binding **complement**, a group of plasma proteins. The binding of complement is known as *complement fixation.* The fixed complement punches holes in the pathogen's plasma membrane,

Check My Understanding

5. What is immunity?
6. How is an immune reaction started?

1. Antigen recognition
T cell binds to nonself antigen and self proteins of APC and becomes activated.

2. Clone formation
Activated T cell undergoes repeated mitotic division producing a clone of identical T cells.

3. Action of clone cells
T_C cells bind to cells displaying the targeted antigen and inject chemicals to destroy them.

T_H cells bind to antigen and self proteins on APC, become activated, and release cytokines, which promote activity of B and T_C cells, inflammation, and phagocytosis by neutrophils and macrophages.

T_M cells launch a secondary response if the targeted antigen reappears.

Figure 13.10 T cell activation and cell-mediated immunity. (APC = antigen presenting cell; T_H = helper T cell; T_C = cytotoxic T cell; T_M = T memory cell) AP|R

Clinical INSIGHT

Scientists have developed ways to harvest antibodies from a single clone, a monoclone, of B cells. Each monoclone produces specific *monoclonal antibodies* against a specific antigen. Monoclonal antibodies may be used in a variety of ways. They are used to quickly diagnose a number of diseases and cancers; to treat certain cancers, such as leukemia and lymphomas; and to determine an early pregnancy.

causing the cell to burst and the pathogen to be destroyed. Subsequently, the resulting debris is cleaned up by phagocytes (neutrophils and macrophages).

Antibodies neutralize bacterial toxins by binding to the antigens, which prevents the toxins from attaching to receptors of body cells. Body cells escape damage because the toxins cannot enter the cells. Subsequently, the antigen–antibody complexes are engulfed and destroyed by macrophages and neutrophils.

Antibodies are proteins known as globulins, so another name for antibodies is **immunoglobulins,** which have a shorthand designation, *Ig.* There are several classes of antibodies, and each class plays a special role in antibody-mediated immunity, as noted in table 13.4.

13.7 Immune Responses AP|R

When an antigen is encountered for the first time, it stimulates T cells and B cells to produce clones that attack and destroy the invading antigen. This is the *primary immune response*, and it also produces memory cells that are able to recognize the same antigen if it should reenter the body. If another invasion of the same antigen occurs at a later date, the memory T cells and memory B cells recognize it and launch a *secondary immune response*, which is more rapid and intense than the primary immune response. A secondary immune response occurs each time the same antigen is detected by the memory cells. Figure 13.12 shows that the concentration of antibodies in the secondary immune response is much higher than in the primary response.

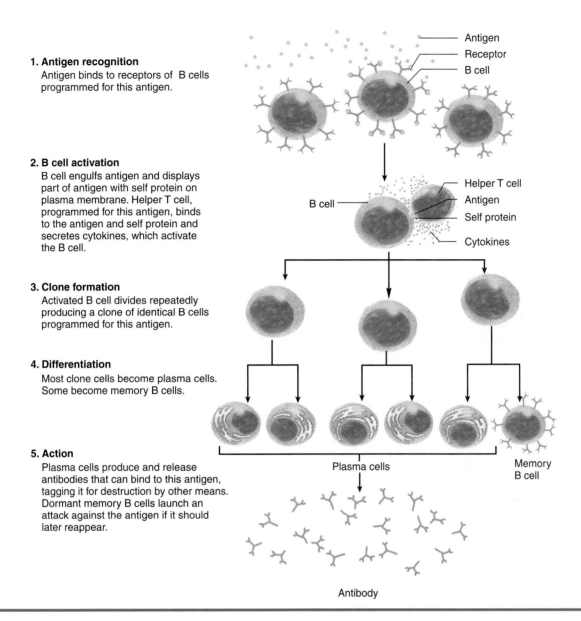

1. Antigen recognition
Antigen binds to receptors of B cells programmed for this antigen.

2. B cell activation
B cell engulfs antigen and displays part of antigen with self protein on plasma membrane. Helper T cell, programmed for this antigen, binds to the antigen and self protein and secretes cytokines, which activate the B cell.

3. Clone formation
Activated B cell divides repeatedly producing a clone of identical B cells programmed for this antigen.

4. Differentiation
Most clone cells become plasma cells. Some become memory B cells.

5. Action
Plasma cells produce and release antibodies that can bind to this antigen, tagging it for destruction by other means. Dormant memory B cells launch an attack against the antigen if it should later reappear.

Antigen
Receptor
B cell

Helper T cell
Antigen
Self protein
Cytokines

B cell

Plasma cells

Memory B cell

Antibody

Figure 13.11 B cell activation and antibody-mediated immunity. AP|R

Table 13.4 Classes of Antibodies

Class	Location	Functions
IgA	Saliva, tears, mucus, breast milk	Protects mucous membranes from pathogens; provides passive immunity for breast-fed infants
IgD	B lymphocytes	Serves as a receptor on B cells
IgE	Binds to mast cells and basophils	Triggers allergic reactions by causing release of histamine when it binds with allergen
IgG	Blood plasma	Provides long-term immunity following vaccination or recovery from infection; crosses placenta to provide passive immunity for newborn infant
IgM	B lymphocytes	Released from B cells and agglutinates antigens

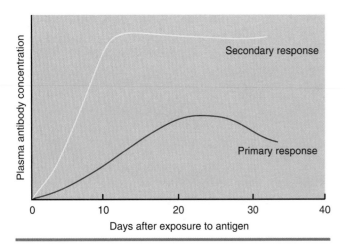

Figure 13.12 Antibodies are produced more rapidly and at a higher concentration during a secondary immune response.

Types of Immunity

There is more than one way for a person to be immune to a particular disease, and these mechanisms may be grouped into two broad categories: active immunity and passive immunity. A person is directly involved in the development of **active immunity** but not in **passive immunity**. Also, active immunity is longer lasting than passive immunity, but the duration of active immunity varies in different diseases.

Naturally acquired active immunity results after a person contracts a disease and recovers, leaving antibodies and memory B and T cells to fight the pathogen if it reenters the body.

Artificially acquired active immunity results after a person receives a vaccine (vak-sēn′) of dead or weakened (attenuated) pathogens or inactivated toxins (toxoid), which trigger a primary immune response, leaving antibodies and memory B and T cells to fight the pathogen if it reenters the body. Booster shots may be used to trigger a secondary immune response to build up the concentration of antibodies even higher.

Naturally acquired passive immunity occurs in infants who have received maternal antibodies via the placenta and in mother's milk after birth. You can see that breast-feeding provides more benefits to the infant than nutrients.

Artificially acquired passive immunity results from receiving injections of antibodies (immunoglobulins) produced in another person or animal. Tetanus antitoxin, commercially produced in horses, is an example (table 13.5).

Check My Understanding

7. Why are helper T cells so important to immunity?
8. How does a vaccination provide immunity against disease?

13.8 Rejection of Organ Transplants

Organ transplants are viable treatment options for persons with terminal disease of certain organs such as the heart, kidneys, and liver. Except for the surgery, the major problem encountered is that the patient's immune system recognizes the transplanted organ as foreign (nonself) and launches an attack against it. The problem is reduced by carefully determining compatibility of the tissues of both donor and recipient. This is usually done by comparing the antigens on the surfaces of leukocytes, called the *human leukocyte antigens (HLAs) group A,* of donor and recipient. A match of 75% is considered minimal for making a transplant.

To overcome the normal immune reaction and organ rejection, immunosuppressive therapy is administered following transplant surgery. The immune system must be suppressed sufficiently to prevent rejection of the organ but not enough to eliminate immunity against pathogens. Achieving this delicate balance has

Table 13.5	Types of Immunity	
Type	**Mechanism**	**Result**
Naturally acquired active immunity	Infection by live pathogens	Person is ill with the disease; immune response destroys pathogens and leaves memory T and B cells to prevent later infection
Artificially acquired active immunity	Receives vaccine of weakened or dead pathogens or their antigenic parts	Immune response occurs without the person becoming ill; memory T and B cells remain to prevent later infection
Artificially acquired passive immunity	Receives injection of antibodies or antitoxin against a specific antigen	Enables short-term immunity without stimulating an immune response
Naturally acquired passive immunity	Antibodies passed from mother with active immunity to fetus in utero or to newborn via breast milk	Enables short-term immunity for newborn without stimulating an immune response

been aided by the use of *cyclosporine,* a selective immunosuppressive drug derived from fungi. Cyclosporine inhibits T cell functions but has minimal effects on B cells. Because T cells are primarily responsible for organ rejection, rejection is minimized, and B cells are able to provide antibody-mediated immunity against pathogens. In spite of advances in immunosuppressive therapy, bacterial and viral infections are the primary causes of death among organ transplant recipients.

13.9 Disorders of the Lymphatic and Immune Systems

These disorders may be grouped according to infectious or noninfectious origins.

Infectious Disorders

Acquired immunodeficiency syndrome (AIDS) is a viral disease that is approaching epidemic proportions. It is caused by the *human immunodeficiency virus (HIV),* which attacks and kills helper T cells and invades macrophages, which serve as a reservoir for the virus. In time, the immune defenses of the victim are greatly reduced, and the patient becomes susceptible to opportunistic diseases that ultimately lead to death. These secondary diseases include pneumonia caused by *Pneumocystis carinii* and a cancer known as Kaposi's sarcoma, disorders that are rarely encountered except in AIDS patients. At present, there is no cure for AIDS, although a major research effort has provided drugs to slow its progress.

Although HIV has been found in most body fluids, it appears that sufficient HIV concentrations for transmission to other persons are not present in tears or saliva. Transmission does not occur through routine, nonintimate contact; instead, it primarily occurs through blood exchanges and sexual intercourse. Transmission occurs through exchanges of blood, most commonly by the use of contaminated hypodermic needles and by exposure of open wounds or mucous membranes to infected blood. Vaginal fluids and semen of infected persons are effective transmitting agents in sexual intercourse. Also, infected mothers may transmit HIV to infants during childbirth.

Elephantiasis (el-e-fan-tī′-ah-sis) is a tropical disease. It is a chronic condition characterized by greatly swollen (edematous) legs or other body parts, which become "elephantlike" in appearance. This occurs because the lymphatic vessels are blocked by masses of microscopic roundworms, which causes fluid to accumulate excessively in the tissues drained by the plugged lymphatic vessels. The microscopic worms are transmitted by the bites of certain species of mosquitoes.

Immunization is dependent on recognition by memory cells of antigens to which they have previously been sensitized. The injection of vaccines produces the primary immune reaction. A secondary immune response occurs if the pathogen actually invades the body or if additional injections of the vaccine are given. Booster shots of vaccines trick the memory cells into producing a secondary immune response as if a real reinvasion of the antigen has occurred. This secondary immune response raises the concentration of T cells, B cells, and antibodies, which increases the person's immunity against that antigen.

This secondary immune response is the basis for repeated childhood immunizations. Most children in the United States receive *DPT vaccine,* which stimulates immune reactions against diphtheria, pertussis (whooping cough), and tetanus, at selected ages: 2 to 3 months, 4 to 5 months, 6 to 7 months, 15 to 19 months, and 4 to 6 years. Similarly, *oral poliomyelitis vaccine* is administered at 4 to 5 months, 6 to 7 months, 15 to 19 months, and 4 to 6 years.

Tonsillitis is the inflammation of the tonsils. It usually results from bacterial infections that cause the tonsils to become sore and swollen. If this condition becomes chronic and interferes with breathing or swallowing, or becomes a persistent focal point for spreading infections, the tonsils may be surgically removed. Tonsillectomies are much less common now that effective antibiotics are available and the role of tonsils in immunity is better understood.

Noninfectious Disorders

Allergy (al′-er-jē), or *hypersensitivity*, refers to an abnormally intense immune response to an antigen that is harmless to most people. Such antigens are called **allergens** to distinguish them from antigens associated with disease. Once a person is sensitized to an allergen, an allergic reaction results whenever subsequent exposure to that allergen occurs. Allergic reactions may be either immediate or delayed.

Immediate reactions result when allergens bind with IgE antibodies on the surface of basophils and mast cells. This interaction causes these cells to secrete substances—such as histamine—that stimulate an inflammatory response. Immediate allergic reactions may be either localized or systemic (whole body). Localized reactions, such as hay fever, hives, allergy-based asthma, and digestive disorders, are unpleasant but rarely life threatening. In contrast, systemic allergic reactions, also known as *anaphylaxis* (an-ah-fi-lak′-sis), are often life threatening. They quickly impair breathing and may cause circulatory failure due to a sudden drop in blood volume as blood vessels dilate and fluid moves into the tissues. Allergic reactions to penicillin and bee stings are examples of systemic allergic responses. **AP|R**

Delayed allergic reactions appear one to three days after exposure to the antigen. Delayed allergic reactions result from cytokines released by T cells. The dermatitis that occurs following contact with poison ivy and some cosmetic chemicals is a common delayed allergic reaction. A positive skin test for tuberculosis also results from a delayed allergic reaction to the tubercle antigen.

Autoimmune diseases result when T and B cells, for unknown reasons, recognize certain body tissues as foreign antigens and produce an immune response against them. This problem may result because certain body molecules have changed slightly and are no longer recognizable as self. Some of the most common autoimmune diseases are

- *rheumatoid arthritis (RA)*, which destroys joints;
- *type 1 diabetes*, which destroys insulin-producing cells in the pancreas;
- *multiple sclerosis (MS)*, which destroys the white matter in the brain and spinal cord;
- *Graves' disease*, which stimulates the thyroid gland to produce excessive amounts of thyroid hormone; and
- *myasthenia gravis*, which impairs impulse transmission at neuromuscular junctions.

Lymphoma (lim-fō'-mah) is a general term referring to any tumor of lymphatic tissue. There are several types of lymphomas. One type of malignant lymphoma is *Hodgkin's lymphoma*, which is cancer of lymphoid tissue involving the production of B lymphocytes. It is characterized by enlarged but painless lymph nodes, fatigue, and sometimes fever and night sweats. Early treatment with chemotherapy or radiation yields a high cure rate.

Severe combined immunodeficiency (SCID) is a group of disorders resulting from several different genetic defects. They are characterized by a marked deficit or absence of both T cells and B cells. Thus, the immune system of affected individuals is basically nonfunctional. Infants have little or no protection against disease-causing pathogens and usually die within a year without treatment. Transplants of normal stem cells from bone marrow or umbilical-cord blood have proved to be successful in some cases, and gene therapy trials look promising for treating this devastating disease.

> *Check My Understanding*
>
> 9. What is so serious about the AIDS virus destroying helper T cells?
> 10. What is the cause of autoimmune diseases?

CHAPTER SUMMARY

13.1 Lymph

- As interstitial fluid accumulates in tissue spaces, it is picked up by lymphatic capillaries. Once the fluid is within a lymphatic vessel, it is called lymph.

13.2 Lymphatic Capillaries and Vessels

- Lymph is carried by lymphatic vessels and is ultimately returned to the blood. Lymphatic vessels contain valves that keep the lymph moving in one direction.
- Lymphatic vessels merge to form lymphatic trunks, which drain major regions of the body. Lymphatic trunks ultimately join one of two collecting ducts.
- The right lymphatic duct receives lymphatic trunks that drain the upper right portion of the body; it empties into the right subclavian vein.
- The thoracic duct receives lymphatic trunks from the rest of the body; it empties into the left subclavian vein.

13.3 Transport of Lymph

- The propulsive forces that move lymph through the vessels are skeletal muscle contractions and respiratory movements.

13.4 Lymphatic Organs

- Lymphatic organs include lymph nodes, tonsils, the spleen, and the thymus. Lymphatic organs are sites of lymphocyte production and immune reactions.
- Lymph nodes occur in groups along lymphatic vessels, where they cleanse lymph as it passes through them.
- Tonsils are groups of lymphatic tissues located near the entrance to the pharynx. They intercept pathogens entering the pharynx from the mouth and nose.
- The spleen filters and cleanses the blood and contains a reservoir of blood that is squeezed into circulation if more blood is needed. It destroys old and damaged red blood cells.
- The thymus is located above the heart within the mediastinum. It is the site of T lymphocyte differentiation.

13.5 Nonspecific Resistance Against Disease

- Nonspecific resistance provides general protection against all pathogens, but it is not directed at any particular pathogen.

- Mechanical barriers include the skin, mucous membranes, mucus, tears, saliva, and urine.
- Protective chemicals include gastric juice, interferon, enzymes such as lysozyme and pepsin, and fluids with an acid pH.
- Phagocytosis is a major mechanism of nonspecific resistance. Neutrophils, monocytes, and wandering and fixed macrophages actively engulf and destroy microorganisms. The wandering and fixed macrophages form the tissue macrophage system, which plays a major role in protection against disease.
- Inflammation helps control infection by attracting leukocytes and macrophages and by increasing the blood supply to the affected area.
- Fever increases the rate of defense processes and inhibits the growth of certain microorganisms.

13.6 Immunity

- Immunity provides protective mechanisms against specific antigens. Lymphocytes and macrophages play key roles in immunity.
- Maturing lymphocytes learn to distinguish molecules composing the body (self) from foreign (nonself) molecules. Large nonself molecules that can stimulate an immune response are called antigens.
- Undifferentiated lymphocytes are formed in fetal bone marrow and are released into the blood. About half of the lymphocytes are carried to the thymus, where they mature to become T lymphocytes. The remainder mature in unknown tissues to become B lymphocytes. Differentiated T cells and B cells are disbursed to lymphatic organs throughout the body and also circulate in the blood.
- T cells provide cell-mediated immunity. T_H cells and T_C cells are activated when they bind to an antigen and self protein presented by an APC. Activated T_H cells form a clone of active T_H cells and memory T cells; activated T_C cells form a clone of active T_C cells and memory T cells.
- T_H cells release cytokines that stimulate cell division and immune action of T and B cells and phagocytosis. T_C cells destroy foreign and diseased cells with chemicals. After the antigen is destroyed, memory T cells remain to attack the antigen if it reenters the body.
- B cells provide antibody-mediated immunity. When an antigen binds to receptors on a B cell, it is engulfed and displayed on the cell surface along with self antigens. A T_H cell binds to the antigen–self protein complex and secretes cytokines, which activate the B cell. The B cell forms a clone of identical B cells. Most of the cloned B cells become plasma cells, and a few become memory B cells. Plasma cells produce antibodies that bind to the antigen, enabling easier destruction of the antigen by phagocytosis and other means. Memory cells remain to attack the antigen if it reenters the body.
- Antibodies are specific proteins produced by plasma cells against specific antigens. There are five classes of antibodies: IgA, IgD, IgE, IgG, and IgM. Each performs a special role.

13.7 Immune Responses

- The first contact with a specific antigen produces the primary immune response. Subsequent contacts with the same antigen produce secondary immune responses that are more rapid and intense.
- There are two basic types of immunity: active and passive. Active immunity results when the body produces its own memory cells and antibodies. Passive immunity results from introduced antibodies that have been produced by another organism. The use of monoclonal antibodies provides passive immunity.

13.8 Rejection of Organ Transplants

- The normal response of the immune system is to attack and destroy organ transplants because they are foreign. Rejection is minimized by a good match between donor and recipient and by the administration of immunosuppressive drugs.
- The use of cyclosporine inhibits functions of T cells but leaves functions of B cells essentially intact.

13.9 Disorders of the Lymphatic and Immune Systems

- Infectious disorders include AIDS, elephantiasis, and tonsillitis.
- Noninfectious disorders of the immune system include allergy, autoimmune diseases, and lymphoma.

BUILDING MY VOCABULARY

1. **Selected New Terms**
   active immunity, p. 284
   antigen-presenting cell, p. 280
   B lymphocyte, p. 280
   clone, p. 282
   cytokine, p. 282
   cytotoxic T cell, p. 282
   fever, p. 279
   helper T cell, p. 282

   immunoglobulin, p. 286
   memory B cell, p. 283
   memory T cell, p. 282
   passive immunity, p. 284
   plasma cell, p. 283
   T lymphocyte, p. 276
   thymus, p. 276
   tonsil, p. 276

2. **Related Clinical Terms**

Immunocompetence (im-mū-nō-kom′-pe-tens) The ability of the immune system to respond to a foreign antigen.

Immunodeficiency (im-mū-nō-dē-fish′-en-sē) The inability of the immune system to respond to a foreign antigen.

Lymphadenectasis (lim-fad-in-nek′-tah-sis) Enlargement of a lymph node.

Splenectomy (splē-nek′-tō-mē) The surgical removal of the spleen.

SELF-REVIEW

Answers are located in appendix B.

1. The lymphatic system removes excess _____ from tissue spaces.
2. Lymphatic vessels carry _____ from body tissues to the _____ veins.
3. Filtering and cleansing lymph is the function of _____, which also are sites of _____ production.
4. Filtering and cleansing blood is a function of the _____, which also removes worn-out _____ cells.
5. Mucous membranes, tears, and gastric juice provide _____ resistance against disease.
6. The major phagocytes involved in nonspecific resistance are _____ and _____.
7. Fighting infection is aided by _____, which increases the blood flow and attracts phagocytes to the affected area.
8. Lymphocytes that are processed by the _____ become T lymphocytes.
9. To start an immune response, part of an antigen must be displayed by an _____ cell where a specific _____ cell can bind to it.
10. Subtype cells formed in a clone of T cells are _____ T cells, _____ T cells, _____ T cells, and _____ T cells.
11. B cells produce _____-mediated immunity, and T cells produce _____-mediated immunity.
12. Cytokines released by _____ cells promote rapid cell division in activated _____ cells and _____ cells.
13. An activated B cell forms a clone consisting of _____ cells, which produce _____, and memory B cells.
14. Immunity acquired by contact with a pathogen and producing antibodies against it is known as _____ immunity.
15. _____ artificially introduces an antigen into the body and produces a primary immune response, so if the real pathogen subsequently enters the body, a faster, more intense _____ immune response destroys it.

CRITICAL THINKING

1. Complete the learning objectives listed on the first page of this chapter.
2. How do lymphatic capillaries differ from blood capillaries?
3. How do lymph nodes help reduce the spread of disease organisms?
4. How do vaccinations help prevent disease?
5. How would a nonfunctional thymus affect immunity?

Visit this book's website at www.mhhe.com/ gunstream5 for practice quizzes, learning exercises, case studies, and other study tools.

CHAPTER 14

Respiratory System

Module 11
Respiratory System

Alveolus (alveol = small cavity) A microscopic air sac within a lung.

Bronchial tree (bronch = windpipe) The branching tubes that carry air to the alveoli of the lungs.

Expiration (ex = from; spirat = breathe) Movement of air out of the lungs.

External respiration The exchange of oxygen and carbon dioxide between the air in alveoli and the blood in alveolar capillaries.

Glottis The opening between the vocal cords within the larynx.

Inspiration Movement of air into the lungs.

Internal respiration The exchange of oxygen and carbon dioxide between the tissue cells and the blood in tissue capillaries.

Larynx (laryn = gullet) The cartilaginous box containing the vocal cords.

Pharynx (pharyn = throat) The throat; the passageway for air from the nasal cavity and mouth to the larynx.

Surfactant A chemical in alveoli that reduces the cohesion of water molecules.

Trachea (trache = windpipe) The tube carrying air from the larynx to the bronchi.

---

*T*he cells of the body require a continuous supply of oxygen for cellular respiration, which produces carbon dioxide as a waste product. Both the respiratory and cardiovascular systems work together to provide oxygen to the cells and to remove carbon dioxide from them. The overall process of the exchange of respiratory gases (oxygen and carbon dioxide) between the atmosphere and the body cells is called *respiration,* and it involves four distinct events:

1. The movement of air into and out of the lungs is accomplished by breathing (pulmonary ventilation).
2. The exchange of respiratory gases between the air and the blood in the lungs occurs by diffusion. Oxygen moves from the air in the lungs into the blood, and carbon dioxide moves from the blood into the air in the lungs. This exchange is known as **external respiration.**
3. The transport of respiratory gases between the lungs and the body cells is accomplished by the cardiovascular system.
4. The exchange of gases between the blood and the body cells occurs by diffusion. Oxygen moves from the blood into the body cells, and carbon dioxide moves from the body cells into the blood. This exchange is known as **internal respiration.**

14.1 Organs of the Respiratory System

The *respiratory system* is subdivided into upper and lower respiratory tracts. The *upper respiratory tract* is that portion not located within the thorax: nose, pharynx, larynx, and part of the trachea. The *lower respiratory tract* is located within the thorax: part of the

trachea, the bronchial tree, and the lungs. Figure 14.1 illustrates the major components of the respiratory system. Figure 14.2 shows the major parts of the upper respiratory tract.

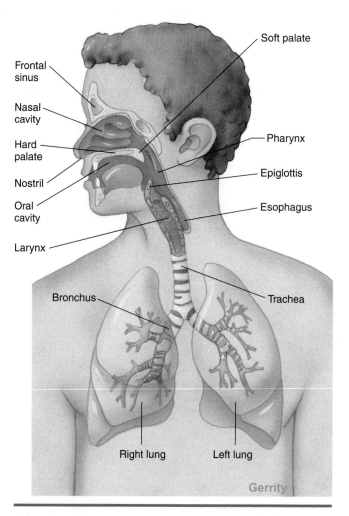

Figure 14.1 The respiratory system. AP|R

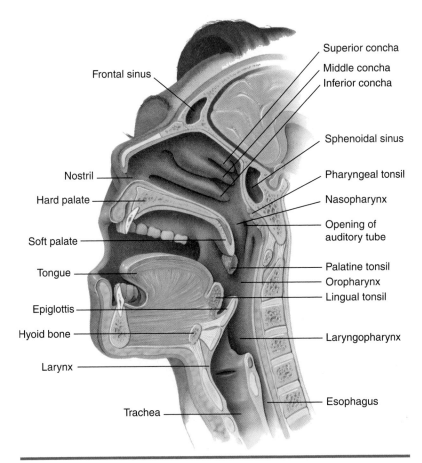

Figure 14.2 Major structures of the upper respiratory tract. **AP|R**

flows through the nasal cavity, it is warmed by the blood-rich mucous membranes and is moistened by the mucus. In addition, airborne particles, including microorganisms, are trapped in the mucous layer. Cilia of the epithelium slowly move the layer of mucus with its entrapped particles toward the pharynx (figure 14.3), where it is swallowed. Upon reaching the stomach, most microorganisms in the mucus are destroyed by the gastric juice.

Several bones surrounding the nasal cavity contain **paranasal sinuses,** air-filled cavities. Sinuses are located in the ethmoid, frontal, maxillary, and sphenoid bones adjacent to the nasal cavity. The sinuses lighten the skull and serve as sound-resonating chambers during speech. The sinuses open into the nasal cavity, and they are lined with ciliated mucous membranes that are continuous with the mucous membranes of the nasal cavity.

Pharynx

The **pharynx** (fayr´-inks), commonly called the throat, is a short passageway that lies posterior to the nasal and oral cavities and extends to the larynx and esophagus. It has a muscular wall and it is lined with mucous

Nose

The protruding portion of the *nose* is supported by bone and cartilage. The nasal bones form a rigid support for the bridge of the nose, and cartilage supports the remaining portions and is responsible for the flexibility of the nose. The *nostrils,* the two external openings in the nose, allow air to enter and leave the nasal cavity. Stiff hairs around the nostrils tend to keep out large airborne particles and insects.

The **nasal cavity** is the interior chamber of the nose, and it is surrounded by skull bones. It is separated from the oral cavity by the **palate** (roof of the mouth), which consists of two basic portions. The anterior *hard palate* is supported by bone; the posterior *soft palate* is not. The nasal cavity is divided into left and right portions by the **nasal septum,** a vertical partition of bone and cartilage that is located on the midline. Three *nasal conchae* (kong´-kē) project from each lateral wall and serve to increase the surface area of the nasal cavity.

The nasal cavity is lined with pseudostratified ciliated columnar epithelium, whose goblet cells produce mucus that coats the epithelial surface. As air

The paranasal sinuses are lined with mucous membranes that are continuous with those of the nasal cavity. The secreted mucus drains into the nasal cavity. **Sinusitis** results from allergic reactions or infections, and it may cause the membranes to swell so that drainage is reduced or prevented. When this occurs, the increased fluid pressure may cause sinus headaches.

Figure 14.3 Mucus and entrapped particles are moved by cilia from the nasal cavity to the pharynx. **AP|R**

membranes. As shown in figure 14.2, the pharynx consists of three parts: the *nasopharynx* lies posterior to the nose; the *oropharynx* lies posterior to the mouth; and the *laryngopharynx* lies posterior to the larynx.

The auditory (eustachian) tubes, which extend to the middle ear, open into the nasopharynx. Air moves in or out of the auditory tubes to equalize the air pressure on each side of the tympanic membrane.

The tonsils, clumps of lymphatic tissue, occur at the openings to the pharynx. The *palatine tonsils* are located on each side of the pharynx at the junction with the oral cavity. The *pharyngeal tonsil* (adenoids) is located at the upper end of the pharynx, and the *lingual tonsils* are found on the back of the tongue. Tonsils are sites of immune reactions and may become sore and swollen when infected. Enlargement of the palatine tonsils tends to make swallowing painful and difficult. A swollen pharyngeal tonsil tends to block the flow of air from the nasal cavity into the pharynx, which promotes mouth breathing. When breathing through the mouth, air is not adequately warmed, filtered, and moistened.

Larynx

The **larynx** (layr´-inks) is a cartilaginous, boxlike structure that provides a passageway for air between the pharynx and the trachea. The three largest cartilages are the *thyroid cartilage,* which projects anteriorly to form the Adam's apple; the *cricoid cartilage,* which forms the attachment to the trachea; and the *epiglottis,* a cartilaginous flap that helps to keep food from entering the larynx. The larynx is supported by ligaments that extend from the hyoid bone (figure 14.4).

The **vocal cords,** folds of the mucous membrane, are located within the larynx (figure 14.5). They are

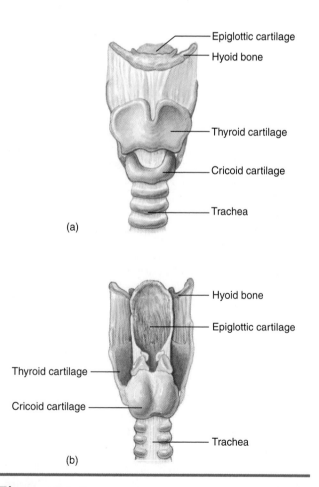

Figure 14.4 The larynx. (*a*) Anterior view. (*b*) Posterior view. AP|R

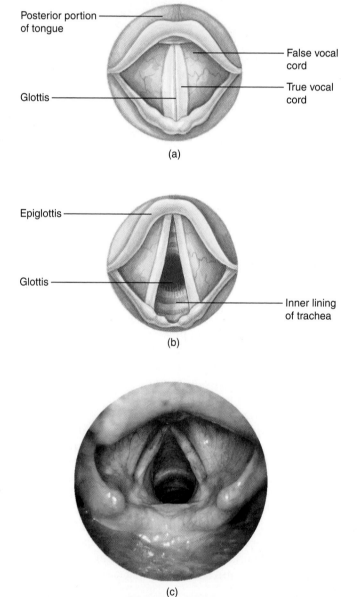

Figure 14.5 Vocal cords as viewed from above with the glottis (*a*) closed and (*b*) open. (*c*) Photograph of the glottis and vocal folds.

relaxed during normal breathing, but when contracted, they vibrate to produce vocal sounds when exhaled air passes over them. The opening between the vocal cords, the **glottis,** leads to the trachea.

The oropharynx and laryngopharynx are also passageways for food, and a mechanism exists to prevent food from entering the larynx and to direct food into the esophagus (ē-sof´-ah-gus), the flexible tube that carries food to the stomach. When swallowing, muscles lift the larynx upward, which causes the epiglottis to flop over and cover the opening into the larynx. This action directs food into the esophagus, whose opening is located just posterior to the larynx. Sometimes this mechanism does not work perfectly and a small amount of food or drink enters the larynx, stimulating a coughing reflex that usually expels the substance.

Check My Understanding

1. What are the functions of the nose?
2. What are the three divisions of the pharynx, and where are they located?
3. What are the functions of the glottis and epiglottis?

Trachea

The **trachea** (trā´-kē-ah), or windpipe, is a tube that extends from the larynx into the thoracic cavity, where it branches to form the primary bronchi. The walls of the trachea are supported by C-shaped *cartilaginous rings* that hold the passageway open in spite of the air pressure changes that occur during breathing. The open portion of the cartilaginous rings is oriented posteriorly against the esophagus. This orientation allows the esophagus to expand slightly as food passes down to the stomach.

The inner wall of the trachea is lined with pseudostratified ciliated columnar epithelium, the same type of epithelium lining the upper respiratory passages. Mucus produced by the goblet cells coats the surface of the epithelium and traps airborne particles, including microorganisms. The beating cilia move the mucus and entrapped particles upward to the pharynx where they are swallowed. Microorganisms are usually killed by gastric juice in the stomach.

Infections of the mucous membranes lining the nasal cavity and pharynx may spread to the middle ear via the auditory (eustachian) tubes to cause *otitis media,* a middle ear infection that is common in young children.

Bronchial Tree

The trachea branches at about midchest into the left and right *primary bronchi* (brong´-kī). Each primary bronchus enters its respective lung, where it branches to form smaller *secondary bronchi,* one for each lobe of the lung. Within each lobe, the bronchi continue to branch into smaller and smaller tubules. Because the trachea, bronchi, and smaller tubules resemble a tree and its branches, they are collectively called the **bronchial tree** (figure 14.6).

The walls of the bronchi contain cartilaginous rings similar to those of the trachea, but as the branches get progressively smaller, the amount of cartilage gradually decreases and finally is absent in the very small tubes called the **bronchioles** (brong´-kē-ōls). As the amount of cartilage decreases, the amount of smooth muscle increases. Air passageways larger than bronchioles are lined with ciliated mucous membranes that continue to trap and remove airborne particles. Bronchioles and smaller tubules are composed of simple cuboidal epithelium, so foreign particles that reach them are not effectively removed. Bronchioles branch to form smaller and smaller bronchioles that lead to microscopic **alveolar ducts,** which terminate in tiny air sacs called **alveoli** (al-vē´-ō-lī; singular, *alveolus*). Alveoli resemble tiny grapes clustered about an alveolar duct (figure 14.7).

The primary function of the bronchial tree is to carry air into and out of the alveoli during breathing. The exchange of respiratory gases occurs between the air in the alveoli and the blood in the capillary networks that surround the alveoli. Alveoli are extremely numerous—about 300 million in each lung. They have a combined surface area of about 75 square meters and can hold about 6,000 ml of air.

Alveoli contain very small spaces, which are coated with a watery fluid. The attraction (cohesion) between water molecules would cause the alveoli to collapse if it were not for surfactant. **Surfactant**

Tobacco smoke paralyzes cilia of epithelium lining the air passages. As a result, mucus and entrapped particles are not effectively removed. Prolonged irritation by tobacco smoke causes the ciliated epithelium to be replaced with stratified squamous epithelium, which cannot clear the airways of mucus. The resulting mucus accumulations lead to smoker's cough and provide a fertile site for the growth of microorganisms.

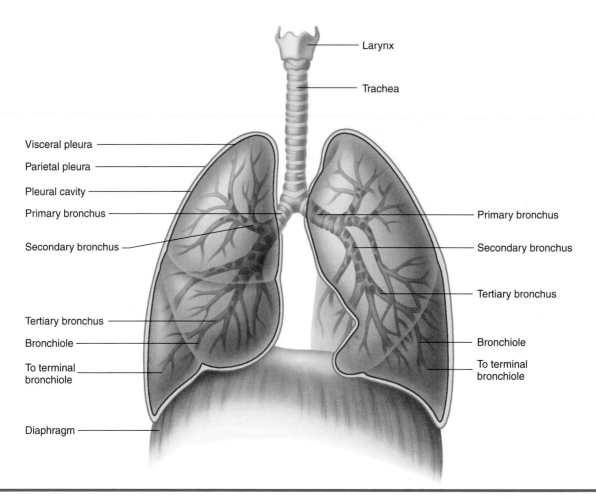

Larynx

Trachea

Visceral pleura

Parietal pleura

Pleural cavity

Primary bronchus

Secondary bronchus

Primary bronchus

Secondary bronchus

Tertiary bronchus

Tertiary bronchus

Bronchiole

Bronchiole

To terminal bronchiole

To terminal bronchiole

Diaphragm

Figure 14.6 Lungs and the bronchial tree. As the air passages branch, they increase in number and decrease in size. **AP|R**

(ser-fak'-tant) is a mixture of lipoproteins secreted by special cells in alveoli. It reduces the attraction between water molecules and keeps alveoli open so they may fill with air during inspiration. Without surfactant, alveoli would collapse and become nonfunctional.

Lungs

The paired **lungs** are large organs that occupy much of the thoracic cavity. They are roughly cone-shaped and are separated from each other by the mediastinum and the heart. Each lung is divided into lobes. The left lung has two lobes and it is somewhat smaller than the right lung, which is composed of three lobes (see figure 14.6). Each lobe is supplied by a secondary bronchus, blood and lymphatic vessels, and nerves. The lungs consist primarily of air passages, alveoli, blood and lymphatic vessels, and connective tissues giving the lungs a soft, spongy texture.

Two serous membranes enclose and protect each lung. The **visceral pleura** is firmly attached to the surface of each lung, and the **parietal pleura** lines the inner wall of the thorax and forms part of the mediastinum. The potential space between the visceral and parietal pleurae is known as the **pleural cavity.** A thin film of serous fluid occupies the pleural cavity and reduces friction between the pleural membranes as the lungs inflate and deflate during breathing. Although lungs are elastic and tend to contract, the attraction of water molecules in the serous fluid within the pleural cavity keeps the visceral and parietal pleurae pressed together (figure 14.8).

Table 14.1 summarizes the functions of the respiratory organs.

Check My Understanding
4. What is the function of cartilaginous rings in the walls of the trachea and bronchi?
5. What is the function of the bronchial tree?
6. Why is surfactant important?

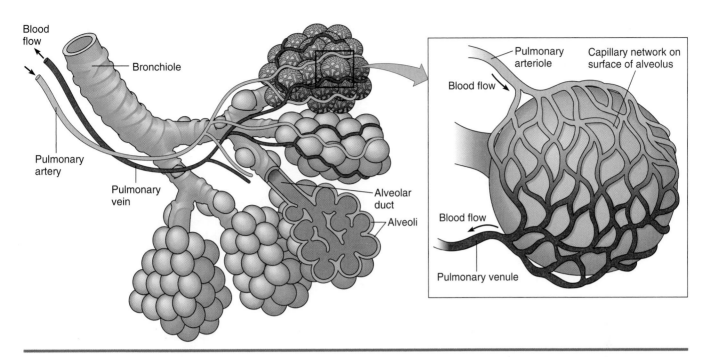

Figure 14.7 Bronchioles branch to form smaller and smaller bronchioles, which lead to microscopic alveolar ducts that terminate in a cluster of alveoli. Each alveolus is enveloped by a capillary network. `AP|R`

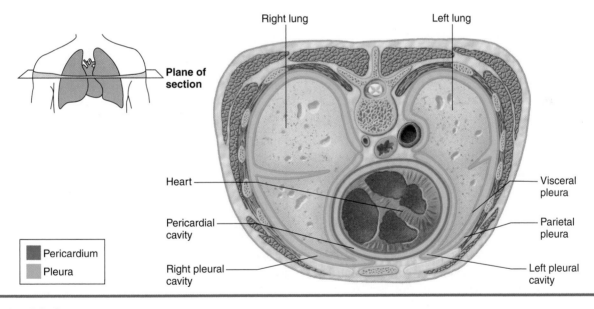

Figure 14.8 A transverse section of the thoracic cavity shows the pleural membranes and the relationship of the lungs to other thoracic organs. For clarity, the potential spaces of the pleural cavities are shown as actual spaces. `AP|R`

14.2 Breathing

Breathing (pulmonary ventilation) is the process that exchanges air between the atmosphere and the alveoli of the lungs. Air moves into and out of the lungs along an air pressure gradient—from regions of higher pressure to regions of lower pressure. There are three pressures that are important in breathing:

1. *Atmospheric pressure* is the pressure of the air that surrounds the earth. Atmospheric pressure at sea level is 760 mm Hg (mercury), but at higher elevations it decreases because there is less air at higher elevations. Atmospheric pressure forces air into the lungs.

2. *Intra-alveolar (intrapulmonary) pressure* is the air pressure within the lungs. As we breathe

Table 14.1   Summary of Functions of the Respiratory Organs

Component	Function
Nose	Nostrils allow air to enter the nasal cavity; the nasal cavity filters, warms, and moistens air as it passes toward the pharynx
Pharynx	Carries air from the nasal cavity to the larynx; filters, warms, and moistens the air; also serves as passageway for food from the mouth to the esophagus
Larynx	Carries air from the pharynx to the trachea; contains vocal cords that produce sounds in vocalization; prevents objects from entering the trachea
Trachea	Receives air from the larynx and carries it to the primary bronchi; filters, warms, and moistens the air
Bronchial tree	Air from the trachea enters the primary bronchi, which enter the lungs and branch repeatedly to form the bronchial tree; passageways larger than bronchioles filter, warm, and moisten the air
Lungs	Gas exchange occurs between air in the alveoli and blood in surrounding capillaries

in and out, this pressure fluctuates between being lower than atmospheric pressure and then higher than atmospheric pressure.

3. *Intrapleural pressure* is the pressure within the pleural cavity. It is normally about 756 mm Hg, which is slightly less than atmospheric pressure. This lower intrapleural pressure is often described as a "negative pressure," and it keeps the lungs pressed against the inner walls of the thorax, even as the thorax expands and contracts during breathing. If the intrapleural pressure were to equal atmospheric pressure, the lungs would collapse and be nonfunctional.

Inspiration

The process of breathing air into the lungs is called **inspiration,** or inhalation. When the lungs are at rest, the air pressure in the lungs is the same as the atmospheric air pressure. In order for air to flow into the lungs, the air pressure within the lungs must be reduced to less than the atmospheric air pressure. This is accomplished by the contraction of the primary breathing muscles: the diaphragm and the external intercostals.

The dome-shaped **diaphragm** is a thin sheet of skeletal muscle separating the thoracic and abdominal cavities. When it contracts, the diaphragm pulls downward and becomes flattened, which increases the volume of the thoracic cavity. At the same time, contraction of the *external intercostal muscles* lifts the ribs upward and outward and pushes the sternum forward, which further increases the volume of the thoracic cavity (figure 14.9).

Because intrapleural pressure keeps the lungs pressed against the thoracic wall, the lungs are pulled along when the thorax expands. Therefore, the expansion of the thoracic cavity increases the volume of the lungs, which decreases the intra-alveolar pressure. Then, the higher atmospheric pressure forces air through the air passageways into the lungs until intra-alveolar and atmospheric pressures are equal (figure 14.10).

The presence of air in the pleural cavity is called a *pneumothorax* (nū-mō-thō´-raks). This may occur due to a thoracic injury or surgery that allows air to enter the pleural cavity. It also occurs in emphysema patients when air escapes from ruptured alveoli into the pleural cavity. The result of a pneumothorax is that the affected lung collapses and is nonfunctional. Because each lung is in a separate pleural cavity, the collapse of one lung does not adversely affect the other lung. Treatment involves removing the intrapleural air to restore the normal pressure so that the lungs may inflate.

Expiration

Expiration, or exhalation, occurs when the diaphragm and external intercostal muscles relax, allowing the thoracic cage and lungs to return to their original size. This results in a decrease in the volume of the thoracic cavity and lungs. The decrease in lung volume increases intra-alveolar pressure to a level higher than atmospheric pressure. The higher intra-alveolar pressure forces air out of the lungs until intra-alveolar and atmospheric pressures are equal.

Expiration during quiet breathing is a rather passive process because the abundant elastic tissue in the lungs and thoracic wall causes them to return to their original size as soon as the muscles of inspiration relax. However, a forceful expiration is possible by contraction of the *internal intercostal muscles,* which pull the ribs down and inward, and by the muscles of the abdominal wall, which force the abdominal viscera and diaphragm upward. These contractions further decrease the volume of the lungs, which increases the air pressure in the lungs, causing more air to flow out of the lungs.

Check My Understanding

7. How do intrapleural pressure and serous fluid in the pleural cavity affect breathing?
8. Describe the mechanisms of inspiration and expiration.

Figure 14.9 Inspiration results when the thoracic cavity is increased by contraction of the diaphragm and the external intercostal muscles. At the end of inspiration, these muscles relax, which decreases the thoracic cavity, resulting in expiration. AP|R

External intercostal muscles pull ribs up and out

Diaphragm contracts

14.3 Respiratory Volumes

Normal adults average 12 to 15 quiet breathing cycles per minute. A *breathing cycle* is one inspiration followed by one expiration. The volume of air inhaled and exhaled in a quiet or forceful breathing cycle

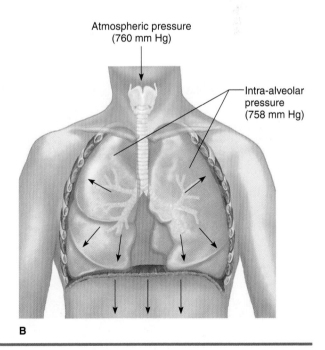

Intra-alveolar pressure (760 mm Hg)

Diaphragm

A

Atmospheric pressure (760 mm Hg)

Intra-alveolar pressure (758 mm Hg)

B

Figure 14.10 The mechanics of inspiration. (*a*) When at rest, both intra-alveolar pressure and atmospheric pressure are 760 mm Hg. (*b*) During inspiration, the expansion of the thoracic cavity and lungs reduces the intra-alveolar pressure to 758 mm Hg. Because of the difference in pressure, atmospheric pressure forces air into the lungs. AP|R varies with size, sex, age, and physical condition. The average respiratory volumes have been determined by size, age, and sex in order to enable evaluation of pulmonary functions. Respiratory volumes that are 80% or less than the normal average usually indicate some form of pulmonary disease.

An instrument called a *spirometer* is used to determine respiratory volumes. It produces a *spirogram,* a graphic record of the volume of air exchanged.

The volume of air exchanged in a quiet breathing cycle is about 500 ml, and it is known as the *tidal volume (TV).* Forceful inspirations and expirations can exchange a much greater volume of air. The maximum volume of air that can be forcefully inhaled after a tidal inspiration is about 3,000 ml, and it is known as the *inspiratory reserve volume (IRV).*

The maximum volume of air that can be forcefully exhaled after a tidal expiration is about 1,100 ml, and it is known as the *expiratory reserve volume (ERV).* About 1,200 ml of air remains in the lungs after a maximum forced expiration. This residual air is known as the *residual volume (RV).* Once an infant takes its first breath, there is always residual air in the lungs. The residual air keeps the alveoli open, preventing collapse of the lungs.

The maximum amount of air that can be forcefully exchanged is known as the *vital capacity (VC),* and it is equal to the sum of the tidal volume, inspiratory reserve volume, and the expiratory reserve volume—about 4,600 ml. The *total lung capacity (TLC)* is equal to the sum of the vital capacity and the residual volume—about 5,800 ml.

The respiratory volumes are summarized in table 14.2 and are graphically shown in figure 14.11.

Table 14.2 Summary of Respiratory Volumes

Name	Definition	Average Volume
Tidal volume (TV)	Volume of air inhaled or exhaled during quiet breathing	500 ml
Inspiratory reserve volume (IRV)	Volume of air that can be forcefully inhaled after a tidal volume inhalation	3,000 ml
Expiratory reserve volume (ERV)	Volume of air that can be forcefully exhaled after a tidal volume expiration	1,100 ml
Vital capacity (VC)	Maximum volume of air that can be forcefully exhaled after a maximum forceful inhalation VC = TV + IRV + ERV	4,600 ml
Residual volume (RV)	Volume of air that always remains in the lungs	1,200 ml
Total lung capacity (TLC)	Maximum volume of air that the lungs can contain TLC = VC + RV	5,800 ml

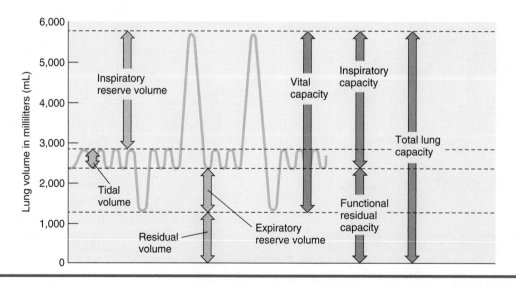

Figure 14.11 Respiratory volumes and capacities. The wavy blue line is a spirogram tracing that indicates the volume of air exchanged as the respiratory movements are performed.

14.4 Control of Breathing

The normal rhythmic cycle of breathing is involuntary—we don't have to think about it. It continues when we are sleeping or even unconscious. However, we can voluntarily override the normal pattern and take deep breaths and breathe faster or slower if we wish. The centers for involuntary control of breathing lie in the brain stem where two groups of neurons in the medulla oblongata and one group of neurons in the pons regulate breathing. Of course, the voluntary override of breathing is controlled by the motor area of the cerebral cortex (figure 14.12).

Respiratory Centers

Two bilateral groups of neurons compose the respiratory center in the medulla: the ventral respiratory group and the dorsal respiratory group. The *ventral respiratory group (VRG)* is responsible for the normal rhythmic cycle of breathing. It sends neural impulses to the diaphragm and external intercostal muscles causing them to contract, which results in inspiration. Inspiration continues as long as the VRG sends out the neural impulses; but when impulses cease, the muscles of inspiration relax and expiration occurs. This pattern of alternating neural activity and inactivity of the VRG produces the cyclic nature of inspiration and expiration. In quiet breathing, inspiration lasts about two seconds, and expiration lasts about three seconds.

However, breathing can be deeper or shallower and faster or slower as the needs of the body change. The VRG receives input from other sources that result in such changes in the breathing cycle. The *dorsal respiratory group (DRG)* serves as a center for receiving and integrating input from sensory sources. It sends impulses to the VRG to make necessary changes in the breathing pattern in accordance with the sensory input. Sensory input is considered in the next section.

A third respiratory center, the *pontine respiratory group (PRG)* is located in the pons. It receives input from

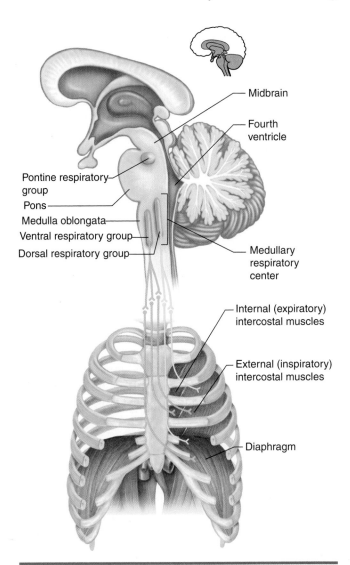

Midbrain
Fourth ventricle
Pontine respiratory group
Pons
Medulla oblongata
Ventral respiratory group
Dorsal respiratory group
Medullary respiratory center
Internal (expiratory) intercostal muscles
External (inspiratory) intercostal muscles
Diaphragm

Figure 14.12 Respiratory control centers are located in the medulla oblongata and the pons.

Clinical INSIGHT

The determination of the lung volumes is useful in identifying the two basic categories of pulmonary disease: obstructive and restrictive disorders. Each category has a characteristic pattern of abnormal test results. It is possible for a patient to exhibit both patterns simultaneously.

The *obstructive pattern* occurs where there is airway obstruction from any cause, such as in asthma, bronchitis, and emphysema. In this pattern, residual volume (RV) is increased and the RV/TLC ratio is increased.

The *restrictive pattern* occurs when there is a loss of lung tissue or when expansion of the lungs is limited. This pattern may result from lung tumors, weakness of respiratory muscles, pulmonary edema, or fibrosis of the lungs. In this pattern, the TLC is decreased, the RV/TLC ratio is normal or increased, and the VC is decreased.

higher brain centers and sends impulses to the DRG and VRG that modify the breathing pattern. The PRG contains two types of neurons: those that stimulate and those that inhibit the DRG and VRG. Thus, the PRG can either speed up or slow down the transition from inspiration to expiration, which alters the rate and depth of breathing. The PRG also plays a key role in adapting breathing to speaking, singing, exercise, sleep, and emotional respiratory responses such as crying or laughing.

14.5 Factors Influencing Breathing

The respiratory areas of the medulla and pons are influenced by a number of factors that cause modifications in the rate and depth of breathing. Factors involved in involuntary control are detected by sensory neurons, which forward impulses to the respiratory control areas. One cluster of sensory neurons associated with involuntary control is located in the medulla adjacent to the respiration control areas, but other sensors are located outside of the central nervous system. Higher brain centers involved in voluntary control send impulses to the pons respiratory group, which, in turn, transmits impulses to the medullary control areas.

Chemicals

The most important chemical factors affecting respiration are the concentrations of CO_2, hydrogen ions (H^+), and O_2 in the blood. Sensory receptors that are sensitive to these factors are called **chemoreceptors,** and they are located in the medulla oblongata, the carotid bodies, and the aortic bodies. The *carotid bodies* are located in both common carotid arteries, where they divide into the internal and external carotid arteries. The *aortic bodies* are located in the aortic arch. You can see that they are strategically located, especially to monitor blood going to the brain.

You may wonder why the concentration of H^+ is involved in respiratory control. This occurs because the mechanism for transporting CO_2 in the blood releases H^+ as a by-product. Therefore, an increase in CO_2 concentration produces an increase in the H^+ concentration.

The chemoreceptors are sensitive to changes in CO_2 and H^+ concentrations in the blood and cerebrospinal fluid. If the concentrations of CO_2 and H^+ increase, the VRG and DRG are stimulated to increase the rate and depth of breathing, which increases the rate of CO_2 and H^+ removal and returns their concentrations to normal resting levels. The result is that the rate and depth of breathing also return to normal quiet levels.

If the CO_2 and H^+ concentrations are abnormally low, breathing is slow and shallow until their concentrations increase to normal levels.

The medullary chemoreceptors are not sensitive to a decline in O_2 concentration in the blood. Chemoreceptors that detect oxygen levels, as well as concentrations of CO_2 and H^+, are located in the carotid bodies and the aortic bodies. These chemoreceptors send their sensory information via sensory nerves to the DRG and VRG in the medulla. Usually, a drop in O_2 concentration is not a strong stimulus for increasing the rate and depth of breathing, and its main effect seems to be to increase the sensitivity of chemoreceptors in the medulla to changes in the CO_2 concentration. The oxygen level of the blood has little effect on normal breathing unless it is very low.

Inflation Reflex

Stretch receptors in the visceral pleurae are sensitive to the degree of stretching by the lungs. During inspiration, impulses from the stretch receptors are sent to the DRG via the vagus nerve, where they inhibit the formation of impulses causing inspiration. This promotes expiration and prevents excessively deep inspirations that may damage the lungs.

Higher Brain Centers

Impulses from higher brain centers may alter the rhythmic cycle of breathing. These impulses may be voluntarily generated in the cerebrum, as when a person chooses to alter the normal pattern of quiet breathing. However, these voluntary controls are limited. For example, if a little child tries to "punish" his mother by holding his breath, as soon as the level of CO_2 in his blood increases to a critical point, the impulses from higher brain centers are ignored and involuntary breathing resumes.

Involuntary impulses may be formed by higher brain centers during emotional experiences, such as anxiety, fear, and excitement, which activate the autonomic nervous system. At such times, the breathing rate is increased. Similarly, a sudden emotional experience, a sharp pain, or a sudden cold stimulus tends to momentarily stop breathing, a condition called *apnea* (ap´-nē-ah).

Body Temperature

An increase in body temperature, such as occurs during strenuous exercise or a fever, increases the breathing rate. Conversely, a decrease in body temperature lowers the breathing rate.

Check My Understanding

11. How is breathing controlled by the nervous system?
12. What factors influence the control of breathing?

14.6 Gas Exchange

Respiratory gases are exchanged between the air in the alveoli and the blood in the capillaries that surround them. Oxygen and carbon dioxide must diffuse through the **respiratory membrane,** which is composed of the cells forming an alveolar wall and the cells forming a capillary wall (figure 14.13).

Alveolar air has a higher concentration of oxygen and a lower concentration of carbon dioxide than does the capillary blood. Because molecules tend to move from an area of higher concentration to areas of lower concentration, oxygen diffuses from the alveolar air into the blood, and carbon dioxide diffuses from the blood into the alveolar air.

Blood entering a capillary network of an alveolus is oxygen poor and carbon dioxide rich. Following the gas exchange, blood leaving the capillary is oxygen rich and carbon dioxide poor (figure 14.14).

After blood has been oxygenated, it returns to the heart and is pumped throughout the body to supply the tissue cells. Blood in capillaries supplying body tissues contains a higher concentration of oxygen and a lower concentration of carbon dioxide than the tissue cells. Therefore, oxygen diffuses from the blood into the tissue cells, and carbon dioxide diffuses from the tissue cells into the blood. In this way, cells are supplied with oxygen for their metabolic activities, and carbon dioxide, which is produced by cellular metabolism, is removed.

Blood entering a capillary network at the tissue level is oxygen rich and carbon dioxide poor. Following gas exchange, blood leaving the capillary is oxygen poor and carbon dioxide rich. AP|R

14.7 Transport of Respiratory Gases

The red blood cells play a major role in the transport of both oxygen and carbon dioxide.

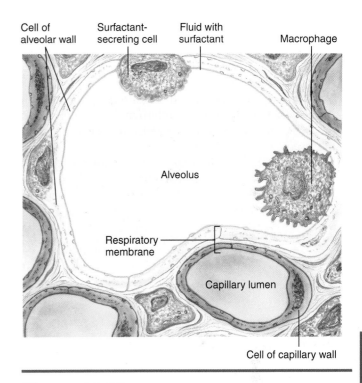

Figure 14.13 The respiratory membrane consists of alveolar and capillary walls. AP|R

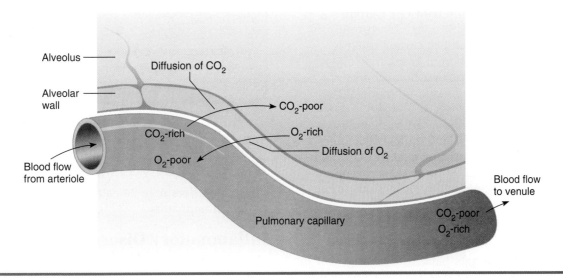

Figure 14.14 Exchange of oxygen and carbon dioxide between air in an alveolus and blood in a pulmonary capillary occurs by diffusion. AP|R

Oxygen Transport

In the lungs, oxygen diffuses from the air in alveoli into the blood of surrounding capillaries. Most of the oxygen enters red blood cells and combines with the heme (iron-containing) portions of hemoglobin (Hb) to form **oxyhemoglobin (HbO$_2$).** About 97% of the oxygen is transported as oxyhemoglobin. Only 3% is dissolved in the plasma.

In body tissues, oxyhemoglobin releases oxygen, and it diffuses from capillary blood into the tissue cells. Actually, only about 25% of the oxygen is released, so oxyhemoglobin is present even in deoxygenated blood.

The reason that hemoglobin is such an effective carrier of oxygen is because the chemical bond between oxygen and hemoglobin is relatively unstable. When the surrounding oxygen concentration is high, as in the lungs, hemoglobin combines readily with oxygen; but when the surrounding oxygen concentration is low, as in body tissues, hemoglobin releases oxygen. The pickup and release of oxygen are summarized as follows:

$$Hb \quad + \quad O_2 \quad \underset{\text{In tissues}}{\overset{\text{In lungs}}{\rightleftharpoons}} \quad HbO_2$$

Hemoglobin   Oxygen   Oxyhemoglobin

Carbon Dioxide Transport

The transport of carbon dioxide is more complex. When carbon dioxide diffuses from body cells into the capillary blood, it takes three pathways:

1. About 7% is dissolved in the plasma.
2. About 23% enters red blood cells and combines with hemoglobin to form **carbaminohemoglobin (HbCO$_2$).** Carbon dioxide combines with the globin (protein) portion of hemoglobin, so carbon dioxide and oxygen have different combining sites on hemoglobin. Therefore, hemoglobin can transport oxygen and carbon dioxide at the same time.
3. The remaining 70% of the carbon dioxide also enters red blood cells, but it quickly combines with water to form **carbonic acid (H$_2$CO$_3$).** This reaction is catalyzed by the enzyme **carbonic anhydrase.** Carbonic acid rapidly breaks down (dissociates) into hydrogen ions (H$^+$) and **bicarbonate ions (HCO$_3^-$).** Carbon dioxide is now part of the bicarbonate molecule (figure 14.15).

When the blood gets back to the lungs, all of these reactions run in reverse, releasing carbon dioxide, which diffuses into the alveoli. The pickup and release of carbon dioxide are summarized as follows:

$$CO_2 \quad + \quad Hb \quad \underset{\text{In lungs}}{\overset{\text{In tissues}}{\rightleftharpoons}} \quad HbCO_2$$

Carbon dioxide   Hemoglobin   Carbaminohemoglobin

$$CO_2 \quad + \quad H_2O \quad \underset{\text{In lungs}}{\overset{\text{In tissues}}{\rightleftharpoons}} \quad H_2CO_3$$

Carbon dioxide   Water   Carbonic acid

$$H_2CO_3 \quad \underset{\text{In lungs}}{\overset{\text{In tissues}}{\rightleftharpoons}} \quad H^+ \quad + \quad HCO_3$$

Carbonic acid   Hydrogen ion   Biocarbonate ion

Check My Understanding

13. How does gas exchange occur in the lungs and in body tissues?
14. How are oxygen and carbon dioxide transported by the blood?

Clinical INSIGHT

Carbon monoxide (CO) is an odorless, colorless gas that is produced by burning carbon fuels. It competes with oxygen for the same binding sites on hemoglobin molecules, and it combines with hemoglobin about 200 times more readily than oxygen. Further, CO binds so tightly with hemoglobin that it is hard to remove. Therefore, even small concentrations of CO can displace oxygen from hemoglobin molecules and deprive tissues of needed oxygen. CO poisoning is the leading cause of death from fires. It is especially treacherous because it kills quietly without attracting attention. Treatment includes the administration of 100% oxygen to flush out the CO.

14.8 Disorders of the Respiratory System

These disorders may be categorized as inflammatory or noninflammatory.

Inflammatory Disorders

Chronic obstructive pulmonary disease (COPD) is a group of disorders in which there is a long-term obstruction that reduces airflow to and from the lungs. The two most important COPDs are chronic bronchitis and emphysema. Asthma is another COPD but differs

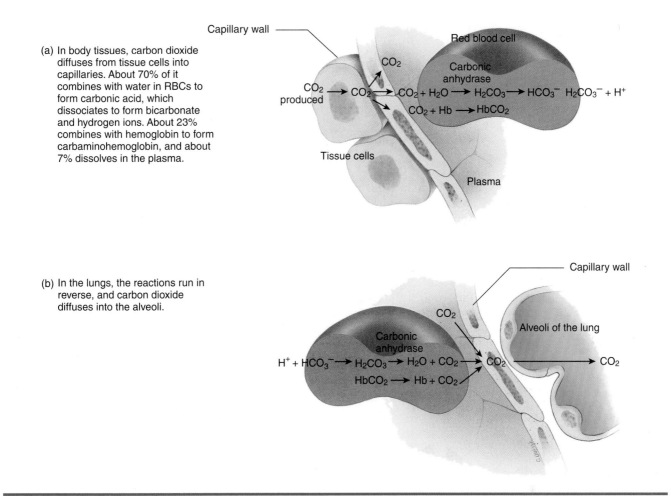

(a) In body tissues, carbon dioxide diffuses from tissue cells into capillaries. About 70% of it combines with water in RBCs to form carbonic acid, which dissociates to form bicarbonate and hydrogen ions. About 23% combines with hemoglobin to form carbaminohemoglobin, and about 7% dissolves in the plasma.

(b) In the lungs, the reactions run in reverse, and carbon dioxide diffuses into the alveoli.

Figure 14.15 Transport of carbon dioxide.

in that reduction in airflow is usually intermittent rather than constant.

Asthma (az´-mah) is characterized by wheezing and **dyspnea** (labored breathing) that result from constriction of the bronchioles by the contraction of smooth muscles in their walls. It is often caused by an allergic reaction to airborne substances but also may result from hypersensitivity to bacteria or viruses infecting the bronchial tree.

Bronchitis is inflammation of the bronchi, and it is characterized by excessive mucus production that partially obstructs air flow. Acute bronchitis is usually caused by viral or bacterial infections. Chronic bronchitis occurs in chronic asthmatics, and it is common in smokers due to persistent exposure to irritants in tobacco smoke.

Emphysema (em-fi-sē´-mah) results from long-term exposure to airborne irritants, especially tobacco smoke. It is characterized by a rupture of the alveoli, forming larger spaces in the lungs, and excess mucus production, which plugs terminal bronchioles, trapping air in the alveoli. This reduces the respiratory surface area and impairs gas exchange.

A reduced expiratory reserve volume and an increased residual volume are symptomatic. Exhaling requires voluntary effort by the patient. The disease is uncommon except among long-term smokers. It usually can be prevented and progressive deterioration can be stopped by removing the airborne irritant—usually tobacco smoke. Otherwise, there is no cure.

The **common cold** may be caused by a number of viruses, and it often involves rhinitis, laryngitis, and sinusitis. Excessive mucus production, sneezing, and congestion are common symptoms.

Influenza, or flu, is caused by one of several viruses. Symptoms are fever, chills, headache, and muscular aches followed by coldlike symptoms.

Laryngitis is the inflammation of the mucous membrane lining the larynx. It usually causes a thickening of the vocal cords, which lowers the voice. Viral or bacterial infections or allergens may cause laryngitis.

Pleurisy (pler´-i-sē) is inflammation of the pleural membranes. It often results in a decrease in secretion of serous fluid, which causes sharp pains with each breath. Pleurisy can also cause the opposite effect—an increase in serous fluid secretion. This type exerts pressure on the lungs and impairs expansion of the lungs.

Pneumonia (nū-mōn´-yah) is an acute inflammation of the alveoli that may be caused by viral or bacterial infections. The alveoli become filled with fluid, pathogens, and white blood cells, which reduce space for air exchange. Blood oxygen levels may be greatly reduced. Pneumonia is one of the common causes of death among older people. AP|R

Rhinitis (rī-nī´-tis) is inflammation of the membranes lining the nasal cavity. It is characterized by an increased mucus secretion. Causes may be viral or bacterial infections or airborne allergens.

Sinusitis is the inflammation of the sinuses, and it is characterized by an increased mucus secretion and a buildup of pressure within the sinuses. Causes may be viral or bacterial infections or airborne allergens.

Tuberculosis (tū-ber″-kū-lō´-sis) is an inflammation caused by the bacterium *Mycobacterium tuberculosis,* which is transmitted by inhalation. When it infects the lungs, the destroyed lung tissue is replaced by fibrous connective tissue that retards gas exchange and reduces lung elasticity. Fortunately, modern drugs are effective in treating this disease.

Noninflammatory Disorders

Lung cancer usually develops from long-term exposure to irritants, and the most common irritant producing this malignancy is tobacco smoke. The link between lung cancer and cigarette smoking has been firmly established. Lung cancer metastasizes rapidly and is not usually detected until it has spread to other parts of the body. Treatment includes surgical removal of the diseased lung, if detected prior to metastasis, and anticancer drug therapy. More than 90% of lung cancers occur in smokers, so the most effective prevention is the elimination of cigarette smoking.

Pulmonary edema is the accumulation of fluid in the lungs. It results from excessive fluid passing from lung capillaries into the alveoli, which may be due to congestive heart failure. Symptoms include labored breathing and a feeling of suffocation. Treatment includes administration of oxygen, diuretics, drugs that dilate the bronchioles, suctioning air passageways, and mechanical ventilation.

Pulmonary embolism refers to a blood clot or gas bubble that blocks a pulmonary artery and prevents blood from reaching a portion of a lung. Gas exchange cannot occur in the affected parts of the lung. A massive embolism affecting a large portion of a lung may cause a cardiac arrest.

Respiratory distress syndrome (RDS), or hyaline membrane disease, is a disease of newborn infants, especially premature infants. It results from an insufficient production of surfactant in the alveoli, leading to alveolar collapse.

At birth, the respiratory system of an infant goes through a transition from a nonfunctional, fluid-filled system to a functional, air-filled system. Normally, an infant's first breath is the most difficult because it must open the collapsed alveoli. Succeeding breaths are easier because surfactant keeps the alveoli open after expiration. Without adequate surfactant, alveoli tend to collapse at each expiration and the infant must expend a great amount of energy to force them open at each inspiration. RDS causes about 20,000 infant deaths every year.

CHAPTER SUMMARY

14.1 Organs of the Respiratory System

- The major organs of the respiratory system are the nose, pharynx, larynx, trachea, bronchial tree, and lungs.
- The external portion of the nose is supported by bone and cartilage, whereas the nasal cavity is surrounded by skull bones. The nasal conchae increase the surface area of the ciliated mucous membrane that lines the nasal cavity.
- Air enters and leaves the nasal cavity via the nostrils. Inhaled air is filtered, warmed, and moistened by the mucous membrane of the nasal cavity.
- The pharynx is a short passageway for both air moving from the nasal cavity to the larynx and food passing from the mouth to the esophagus. The pharyngeal, lingual, and palatine tonsils are clumps of lymphoid tissue associated with the pharynx.
- The larynx is a cartilaginous boxlike structure that conducts air from the pharynx to the trachea, and it houses the vocal cords. During swallowing, the epiglottis prevents food from entering the larynx and directs it into the esophagus.
- The trachea extends from the larynx into the thoracic cavity, where it branches to form the primary bronchi, which enter the lungs.
- The bronchial tree consists of the trachea, primary bronchi, secondary bronchi, tertiary bronchi, bronchioles, and alveolar ducts that lead to the alveoli. The bronchial tree carries air into and out of the alveoli.
- Portions of the bronchial tree (except the bronchioles) are supported by cartilaginous rings and are lined with ciliated mucous membranes. These portions filter, warm, and moisten the air.

- Lungs fill most of the thoracic cavity. They consist of air passageways of the bronchial tree, alveoli, blood and lymphatic vessels, nerves, and connective tissues. Gas exchange occurs between air in the alveoli and the blood in the alveolar capillaries.
- Surfactant in the alveoli prevents the collapse of the alveoli.
- The visceral pleurae cover the outer surfaces of the lungs, and the parietal pleurae line the thoracic cavity. The pleural cavity is the potential space between the pleural membranes.

14.2 Breathing

- Breathing involves inspiration and expiration. Air moves into and out of the lungs along a pressure gradient.
- Inspiration results from contraction of the diaphragm and external intercostal muscles, which increases the volume and decreases the pressure within the thoracic cavity and lungs. The higher atmospheric pressure causes air to flow into the lungs until the atmospheric and intra-alveolar pressures are equalized.
- Expiration results from relaxation of these muscles, which decreases the volume and increases the pressure within the thoracic cavity and lungs. The higher intra-alveolar pressure causes air to flow out of the lungs until the intra-alveolar and atmospheric pressures are equalized. A forced expiration involves the contraction of internal intercostal and abdominal muscles.

14.3 Respiratory Volumes

- Respiratory air volumes vary with size, sex, age, and physical condition. Variations from the norm usually indicate a pulmonary disorder.
- The average values for respiratory volumes are tidal volume—500 ml; inspiratory reserve volume—3,000 ml; expiratory reserve volume—1,100 ml; vital capacity—4,600 ml; residual volume—1,200 ml; and total lung capacity—5,800 ml.

14.4 Control of Breathing

- Breathing is controlled by the respiratory centers, located in the pons and medulla oblongata.
- The two groups of neurons in the medulla controlling breathing are the ventral respiratory group (VRG) and the dorsal respiratory group (DRG).
- The VRG controls the normal rhythmic breathing cycle. The DRG integrates sensory input and stimulates the VRG to modify breathing to be faster or slower and deeper or shallower.
- The pontine respiratory group (PRG) in the pons relays impulses, especially from higher brain centers, to the DRG and VRG to modify the breathing cycle.

14.5 Factors Influencing Breathing

- Chemoreceptors in the medulla are sensitive to changes in concentrations of carbon dioxide and hydrogen ions in the blood. An increase in their concentrations is the primary stimulus for inspiration. The breathing rate and depth vary directly with changes in carbon dioxide and hydrogen ion concentrations.
- Chemoreceptors in the carotid and aortic bodies are sensitive to the concentration of oxygen, carbon dioxide, and hydrogen ions in the blood. They send impulses to the DRG and VRG in the medulla. Oxygen concentration must be very low to produce a direct effect on breathing.
- The stretching of the visceral pleurae during inspiration triggers the inflation reflex, which inhibits excessive inspiration and promotes expiration.
- Higher brain centers can influence the respiratory centers either voluntarily or involuntarily. Sudden pain or cold produces momentary apnea. Chronic pain and anxiety increase the breathing rate.
- The breathing rate varies directly with changes in body temperature.

14.6 Gas Exchange

- Gas exchange between air in the alveoli and the blood in alveolar capillaries occurs by diffusion, and it is called external respiration.
- Oxygen diffuses from air in the alveoli into the blood; carbon dioxide diffuses from the blood into air in the alveoli.
- Gas exchange between tissue cells and blood in capillaries occurs by diffusion, and it is called internal respiration.
- Oxygen diffuses from the blood into the tissue cells; carbon dioxide diffuses from the tissue cells into the blood.

14.7 Transport of Respiratory Gases

- In the lungs, oxygen combines with hemoglobin to form oxyhemoglobin. In tissues, oxyhemoglobin releases oxygen to tissue cells. About 97% of the oxygen is carried as oxyhemoglobin; only about 3% is carried dissolved in blood plasma.
- Carbon dioxide is mostly carried in bicarbonate ions. When carbon dioxide diffuses from tissues into the blood, most of it enters the red blood cells. Carbonic anhydrase in red blood cells catalyzes the combination of carbon dioxide and water to form carbonic acid, which ionizes to form hydrogen and bicarbonate ions. In the lungs, the reaction reverses to release carbon dioxide into the alveoli.
- Some carbon dioxide is carried as carbaminohemoglobin, and a little carbon dioxide is carried dissolved in the plasma.

14.8 Disorders of the Respiratory System

- Inflammatory disorders include asthma, bronchitis, emphysema, common cold, influenza, laryngitis, pleurisy, pneumonia, rhinitis, sinusitis, and tuberculosis. Asthma, chronic bronchitis, and emphysema are COPDs.
- Noninflammatory disorders include lung cancer, pulmonary edema, pulmonary embolism, and respiratory distress syndrome.

BUILDING MY VOCABULARY

1. **Selected New Terms**
   atmospheric pressure, p.295
   bicarbonate ion, p. 302
   carbaminohemoglobin ($HbCO_2$), p. 302
   carbonic anhydrase, p. 302
   intra-alveolar (intrapulmonary) pressure, p. 295
   intrapleural pressure, p. 296
   laryngopharynx, p. 292
   lower respiratory tract, p. 290
   nasopharynx, p. 292
   oropharynx, p. 292

   oxyhemoglobin (HbO_2), p. 302
   respiratory membrane, p. 301
   upper respiratory tract, p. 290

2. **Related Clinical Terms**
   Apnea (ap´-nē-ah) Cessation of breathing.
   Dyspnea (disp-nē´-ah) Labored breathing.
   Hyperventilation Rapid, deep breathing.
   Pneumothorax (nū-mō-thor´-aks) Air in the pleural cavity causing collapse of a lung.

SELF-REVIEW

Answers are located in appendix B.

1. Inhaled air is moistened, _____, and warmed by the _____ lining the nasal cavity and most of the bronchial tree.
2. Vocal cords are located within the _____, and the space between relaxed vocal cords is the _____.
3. The walls of the trachea and bronchi are supported by _____, which are absent in _____ and alveolar ducts.
4. The lungs consist largely of blood vessels, air passageways, and tiny air sacs called _____ where gas exchange occurs.
5. The potential space between the visceral and parietal pleurae is the _____.
6. Alveoli do not collapse because _____ reduces the cohesion of water molecules within alveoli.
7. During inspiration, air moves into the lungs because _____ pressure is greater than _____ pressure.
8. The _____ volume, about _____ ml, is the amount of air inhaled and exhaled in quiet breathing.
9. The rhythmic cycle of breathing is controlled by the VRG in the _____, and it is influenced by the _____ in the medulla and the _____ in the pons.
10. The rate and depth of breathing increase when the blood levels of _____ and _____ increase.
11. In the lungs, _____ moves from alveoli into capillary blood and _____ moves from capillary blood into alveoli.
12. In the blood, oxygen is primarily carried as _____ and carbon dioxide is primarily carried as _____.

CRITICAL THINKING

1. Complete the learning objectives listed on the first page of this chapter.
2. How does the mucous blanket in air passages help protect against airborne microorganisms?
3. If an athlete had a transfusion of RBCs a few hours before an athletic event, would it provide a physiological advantage? Explain.
4. Explain how strenuous exercise increases the rate of breathing.
5. Explain the importance of carbonic anhydrase in the transport of carbon dioxide.

Visit this book's website at www.mhhe.com/ gunstream5 for practice quizzes, learning exercises, case studies, and other study tools.

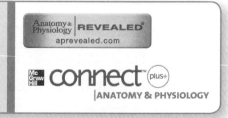

CHAPTER 15

Digestive System

Anatomy & Physiology REVEALED®
aprevealed.com

Module 12
Digestive System

SELECTED KEY TERMS

Absorption The process by which nutrients pass from the digestive tract into the blood.

Accessory organs Organs that have a digestive function but are not part of the alimentary canal.

Alimentary canal (aliment = food) The tube through which food passes from the mouth to the anus.

Chyme (chym = juice) Liquified food entering the small intestine from the stomach.

Digestion (digest = to dissolve) Mechanical and chemical processes that convert nonabsorbable foods into absorbable nutrients.

Duodenum The first part of the small intestine, which receives bile and pancreatic juice.

Nutrient (nutri = to nourish) A substance required for the functioning of body cells.

Peristalsis (peri = around; stalsis = constriction) Wavelike

contractions that move food through the alimentary canal.

Sphincter (sphin = squeeze) A circular muscle that closes an opening.

Substrate A chemical that is acted upon and changed by an enzyme.

Villi (vill = hairy) Tiny projections of the mucous membrane in the small intestine.

Vitamin (vita = life) An organic compound required by the body in minute amounts.

$\mathcal{B}$ody cells require a continuous supply of **nutrients** in order to carry out their vital functions. Nutrients include carbohydrates, proteins, lipids, vitamins, and minerals, and they come from the food we eat. However, most food molecules are too large to pass directly into the blood, so they must be digested to break them down into absorbable molecules. **Digestion** of food and **absorption** of nutrients are the major functions of the digestive system.

The *digestive system* consists of the *alimentary canal,* a long tube through which food passes, and *accessory organs.* The major parts of the alimentary canal are the mouth, pharynx, esophagus, stomach, small intestine, large intestine, and anus. The major accessory organs are the teeth, salivary glands, liver, gallbladder, and pancreas (figures 15.1 and 15.2).

15.1 Digestion: An Overview

Digestion involves both mechanical and chemical processes. *Mechanical digestion* is the physical breakdown of food into smaller pieces, which provides a greater surface area for contact with digestive secretions. *Chemical digestion* is the splitting of complex, nonabsorbable food molecules into small, absorbable nutrient molecules by the addition of water—a process known as *hydrolysis* (hī-drol´-i-sis). Because hydrolysis is normally very slow, it is the action of digestive enzymes that speeds up digestion and enables the formation of small, absorbable nutrients within the alimentary canal. Chemical digestion may be summarized as follows. **AP|R**

Nonabsorbable food molecules + Water $\xrightarrow{\text{Digestive enzymes}}$ Absorbable nutrient molecules

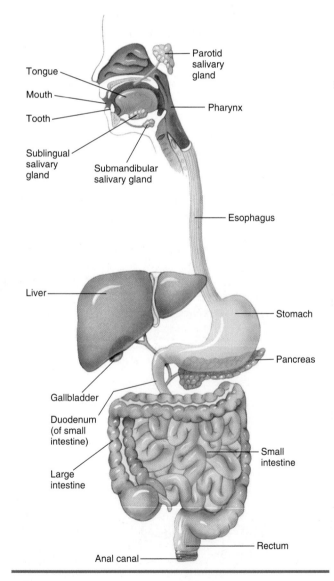

Figure 15.1 Major organs of the digestive system. **AP|R**

Figure 15.2 The wall of the alimentary canal consists of four tissue layers as shown here in a section of the small intestine. From outside in, they are the serous layer, muscular layer, submucosa, and mucosa.

A number of different types of enzymes are involved in digestion. Each type of digestive enzyme acts on a specific **substrate,** for example, a particular type of food molecule, and speeds up its breakdown into smaller molecules. A series of digestive reactions involving several digestive enzymes from different parts of the digestive system are usually required to break down complex food molecules into absorbable nutrients.

15.2 Alimentary Canal: General Characteristics

The **alimentary canal** is a muscular tube about 9 m (29 ft) in length that extends from the mouth to the anus. Various portions of the alimentary canal are specialized to perform different digestive functions. The hollow space within the alimentary canal through which food passes is called the *lumen.*

Structure of the Wall

The wall of the alimentary canal consists of four layers. From the outside of the alimentary canal to the inside, they are the serosa, muscular layer, submucosa, and mucosa. These layers may be modified in the various regions but remain as distinct layers. Compare figure 15.2 to the discussion that follows.

The **serosa** is the outermost layer. It is formed of the *visceral peritoneum* and is continuous with the *parietal peritoneum,* which lines the inner abdominal wall. Cells of the peritoneum secrete serous fluid, which keeps the membrane surfaces moist and reduces friction as parts of the alimentary canal rub against each other and the abdominal wall.

The **muscular layer** lies just under the serosa. It consists of two layers of smooth muscle that differ in the orientation of their muscle fibers. Fibers of the outer muscular layer are arranged longitudinally. Their contractions shorten the tube. Fibers of the inner muscular layer are arranged circularly around the tube. Their contractions constrict the tube. Contractions of these muscular layers mix food with digestive secretions and move food through the alimentary canal.

The **submucosa** lies between the muscular layer and the mucosa. It contains nerves, lymphatic vessels, and blood vessels embedded in loose connective tissue.

The innermost layer is the **mucosa.** It consists of a surface layer of columnar epithelial tissue supported by underlying connective tissue that contains a few smooth muscle cells. The epithelial cells produce digestive secretions and mucus. The epithelium is often folded to increase the surface area that is in contact with food. The mucosa has different functions in different parts of the digestive tract. In some regions, it secretes only mucus, which protects underlying cells. In others, it secretes mucus and digestive fluids containing enzymes and it absorbs nutrients.

Movements

Contraction of the smooth muscle layers produces two different types of movement in the alimentary canal: mixing movements and propelling movements. Mixing movements are called *segmentation* and involve ringlike contractions at multiple places along the alimentary canal followed by relaxation as the contractions form at other locations. The alternating segmental contractions help to mix the food contents with the digestive secretions. These are especially frequent in the small intestine.

The movements that propel food through the alimentary canal are called **peristalsis** (per-i-stal´-sis). In peristalsis, contraction of circular muscle fibers produces a ringlike constriction that moves along the alimentary canal in a wavelike manner, pushing food in front of it. In this way, peristaltic contractions move food from one portion of the alimentary canal to another.

15.3 Mouth

The *mouth,* or *oral cavity,* is involved in the intake of food, mechanically breaking it into small pieces, mixing it with saliva, and swallowing it. The mouth is surrounded by the cheeks, palate, and tongue. Examine figures 15.3 and 15.4.

Cheeks

The *cheeks* form the lateral walls of the mouth. Skin covers their outer surfaces, and nonkeratinized squamous epithelium lines their inner surfaces.

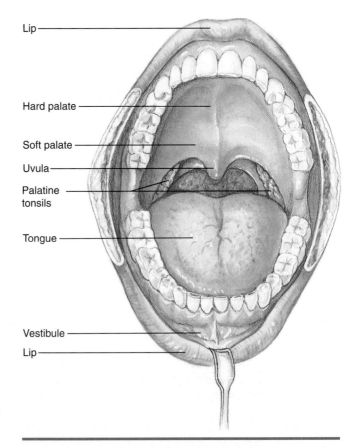

Lip

Hard palate

Soft palate

Uvula

Palatine tonsils

Tongue

Vestibule

Lip

Figure 15.3 Major structures associated with the mouth.

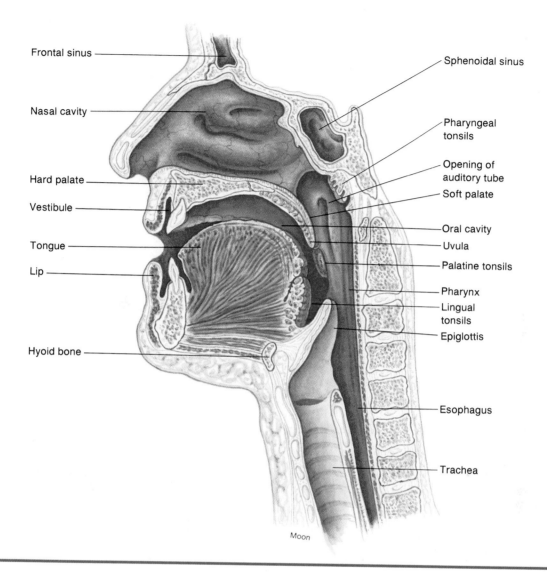

Labels (clockwise from top left):
Frontal sinus — Nasal cavity — Hard palate — Vestibule — Tongue — Lip — Hyoid bone — Sphenoidal sinus — Pharyngeal tonsils — Opening of auditory tube — Soft palate — Oral cavity — Uvula — Palatine tonsils — Pharynx — Lingual tonsils — Epiglottis — Esophagus — Trachea

Moon

Figure 15.4 The structural relationships of the nasal cavity, mouth, pharynx, esophagus, and larynx are shown in sagittal section. AP|R

Contractions of muscles located in the cheeks produce facial expressions. The anterior portions of the cheeks form the *lips,* which surround the opening into the mouth. Lips are sensitive, highly mobile structures. Their pinkish color results from numerous blood vessels near their surfaces.

Palate

The *palate* forms the roof of the mouth and separates the oral cavity from the nasal cavity. The anterior portion is known as the *hard palate* because it is supported by bone. The posterior *soft palate* lacks bony support. The soft palate ends posteriorly in a cone-shaped *uvula* that hangs downward at the back of the oral cavity. The uvula is very sensitive to touch stimuli. This sensitivity causes the soft palate to move upward during swallowing, which closes off the nasal cavity and directs food downward into the pharynx.

Tongue

The *tongue* forms the floor of the oral cavity. It is composed primarily of skeletal muscle that is covered by a mucous membrane. An anterior fold of the mucous membrane on the undersurface of the tongue attaches the tongue to the floor of the mouth. This membranous attachment is known as the *lingual frenulum* (ling´-gwal fren´-ū-lum), and it limits the posterior movement of the tongue.

The upper surface of the tongue contains numerous tiny projections called **papillae** (pah-pil´-ē) that give a rough texture to the tongue and aid in its manipulation of food. Taste buds are located on the papillae.

The tongue moves the food about during chewing and aids in mixing it with saliva. In swallowing, the tongue pushes food posteriorly into the pharynx.

Teeth

Teeth are important accessory digestive structures that mechanically break food into smaller pieces during **mastication** (mas-ti-kā'-shun), or chewing. Humans develop two sets of teeth: deciduous and permanent teeth.

The **deciduous teeth,** the first set, start to erupt through the gums at about six months of age. Central incisors (in-sī-zers) come in first, and second molars erupt last. There are 20 deciduous teeth, 10 in each jaw, and all of them are in place by three years of age. Deciduous teeth are gradually shed starting at about six years of age, and they are lost in the same order as their emergence. The loss of a deciduous tooth occurs because the growth of a permanent tooth underneath it causes resorption of the root. Later, the emerging permanent tooth pushes out the deciduous tooth.

The **permanent teeth** begin appearing at about six years of age when the first molars (six-year molars) erupt. All of the permanent teeth, except the third molars, are in place by age 16. The third molars (wisdom teeth) erupt between 17 and 21 years of age, or they may never emerge. In many persons, there is insufficient room for the third molars, so they become impacted and often must be surgically removed. The 32 permanent teeth, 16 in each jaw, consist of four different types: incisors, cuspids, bicuspids, and molars (figure 15.5).

There are four chisel-shaped *incisors* at the anterior of each jaw. Incisors are adapted for biting off pieces of food. Lateral to the incisors are the *cuspids* (kus'-pids), or canines, two in each jaw, that are used to grasp and tear tough food morsels. Posterior to the cuspids are four *bicuspids* (premolars) and six *molars* in each jaw. Their somewhat flattened surfaces are used to crush and grind the food. Examine figure 15.5 and table 15.1.

Figure 15.6 shows the basic structure of a tooth. Each tooth consists of two major parts: a root and a crown. The *crown* is the portion that protrudes above

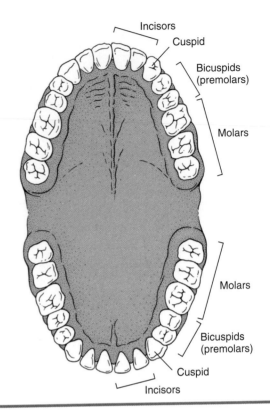

Figure 15.5 There are 32 permanent teeth, 16 in each jaw. Note the location and shape of the incisors and molars. AP|R

Table 15.1	Deciduous and Permanent Teeth	
	Number	
Type	**Deciduous**	**Permanent**
Incisors		
Central	4	4
Lateral	4	4
Cuspid	4	4
Bicuspid		
First	0	4
Second	0	4
Molar		
First	4	4
Second	4	4
Third	0	4
Totals	20	32

the *gingiva* (jin-ji-vah), or gum, covering the alveolar bone. The *root* is embedded in a socket in the alveolar bone of the jaw. The junction of the crown and root is known as the *neck* of the tooth.

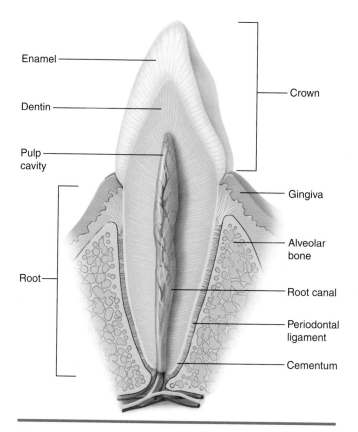

Enamel

Dentin

Pulp cavity

Root

Crown

Gingiva

Alveolar bone

Root canal

Periodontal ligament

Cementum

Figure 15.6 The structure of a tooth is shown in this section of a cuspid. AP|R

The root of a tooth is attached firmly to the alveolar bone of the jaw. A hard substance called *cementum* attaches the root to the tough *periodontal membrane,* whose fibers penetrate into the bone.

Most of a tooth is composed of **dentin,** a hard, bonelike substance. The crown of the tooth has a layer of **enamel** overlying the dentin. Enamel is the hardest substance in the body, and it is appropriately located to resist the abrasion caused by chewing hard foods. Each tooth is supplied with blood vessels and a nerve, which enter the tip of a root and pass through a tubular *root canal* into the *pulp cavity,* a central space in the interior of a tooth. In a molar, the pulp cavity is relatively large and roughly box-shaped. But in a cuspid, the pulp cavity is an elongated enlargement of the root canal. *Pulp* is soft connective tissue that supports the blood vessels and nerves.

Salivary Glands

The **salivary glands** secrete **saliva** into the mouth, where it is mixed with food during chewing. The presence of food (or nonfood objects) in the mouth activates neural reflexes that stimulate the flow of saliva. The mere thought of appetizing food can stimulate the flow of saliva. The functions of saliva include binding food particles together, dissolving certain foods, cleansing and lubricating the mouth, and starting carbohydrate digestion. The sense of taste is dependent upon saliva because only dissolved food molecules can stimulate the taste buds. There are three pairs of major salivary glands: the parotid, submandibular, and sublingual salivary glands (figure 15.7).

The largest salivary glands are the *parotid* (pah-rot´-id) *glands.* A gland is located in front of each ear over the masseter muscle. Parotid glands secrete saliva that is rich in amylase. Parotid secretions are emptied through a duct into the vestibule of the mouth near the upper second molars.

The *submandibular* (sub-man-dib´-ū-lar) *glands* are found in the floor of the mouth. They produce a watery saliva that contains relatively little mucus. Secretions of the submandibular glands are emptied through ducts into the anterior part of the mouth at the base of the lingual frenulum.

The *sublingual* (sub-ling´-gwal) *glands* lie on the floor of the mouth under the tongue. They are the smallest of the major salivary glands. Their secretions consist mostly of mucus, and they are emptied by several ducts into the floor of the mouth under the tongue.

Saliva consists mostly of water (99.5%), which helps to dissolve food substances, plus a small amount of other substances. Mucus helps to hold food particles together during chewing and swallowing. Saliva contains two enzymes. *Salivary amylase* is a digestive enzyme that speeds up the breakdown of starch and glycogen, and *lysozyme* is an enzyme that kills certain bacteria.

Clinical **INSIGHT**

Enamel and dentin are not replaced after they have been eroded by tooth decay. The repair of a decayed tooth requires removal of the decayed material, sterilization of the area, and the insertion of a filling. A filling seals the area and provides an abrasion-resistant surface.

Clinical **INSIGHT**

Mumps is a common childhood disease. Infection by the mumps virus causes inflammation of the parotid glands. The glands become swollen and sore, making opening the mouth, chewing, and swallowing quite painful.

Tongue

Parotid duct

Parotid gland

Masseter muscle

Submandibular gland

Sublingual gland

Submandibular duct

Mandible

Figure 15.7 The major salivary glands. AP|R

Digestion in the Mouth

Both mechanical and chemical digestion take place in the mouth. Mechanical digestion in the mouth consists of breaking food into smaller pieces and mixing it with saliva during chewing. This improves chemical digestion because the smaller pieces have an increased surface area upon which digestive secretions may act. Chemical digestion starts in the mouth with the breakdown of certain complex carbohydrates. *Salivary amylase* acts on *starch* and *glycogen* (polysaccharides) and speeds up their breakdown into *maltose,* a disaccharide sugar. The action of salivary amylase continues for a few minutes after food enters the stomach, but it soon stops because it is inactivated by the strong acidity of gastric juice.

Check My Understanding

4. What is the structure of a tooth?
5. What digestive processes occur in the mouth?

15.4 Pharynx and Esophagus

The **pharynx** (fayr´-inks) is the passageway that connects the nasal and oral cavities with the larynx and esophagus. It is part of both the respiratory and digestive systems. Its digestive function is the transport of food from the mouth to the esophagus during swallowing (see figure 15.4).

The swallowing reflex is activated when food is pushed into the pharynx by the tongue. The soft palate contracts upward, preventing food from entering the nasal cavity, and directs food downward into the pharynx. At the same time, muscle contractions raise the larynx, and this causes the epiglottis to flop over and cover the opening into the larynx. This action prevents food from entering the larynx and directs it into the esophagus.

The **esophagus** (ē-sof´-ah-gus) is a muscular tube that extends from the pharynx down through the thoracic cavity and the diaphragm to join with the stomach. When food is swallowed and enters the esophagus, peristaltic contractions propel the food toward the stomach. The esophageal mucosa produces mucus that lubricates the esophagus and aids the passage of food.

At the junction of the esophagus and stomach, there is a thickened ring of circular muscle fibers known as the *lower esophageal,* or *cardiac, sphincter* (sfink´-ter) muscle. Normally, this sphincter is constricted to prevent regurgitation of stomach contents into the esophagus. But when the peristaltic wave that is propelling food toward the stomach reaches the sphincter, it relaxes, allowing food to enter the stomach. **AP|R**

Check My Understanding

6. Describe the swallowing reflex.
7. How does the esophagus carry food to the stomach?

15.5 Stomach

As shown in figure 15.8, the J-shaped **stomach** is a pouchlike portion of the alimentary canal. It lies just below the diaphragm in the upper left quadrant of the abdomen. The basic functions of the stomach are temporary storage of food, mixing food with gastric juice, and starting the digestion of proteins.

Structure

The stomach may be subdivided into four regions: the cardiac, fundic, pyloric regions, and body. The *cardiac region* (closest to the heart) is a relatively small area that receives food from the esophagus. The *fundic region* expands above the level of the cardiac region and serves as a temporary storage area. The *pyloric region* is the narrow portion located near the junction with the duodenum. The *body* is the largest region of the stomach, and it is located between the fundic and pyloric regions.

The *pyloric sphincter* is a thickened ring of circular muscle fibers that is located at the junction of the stomach and duodenum. This muscle usually is contracted, closing the stomach outlet, but it relaxes to let food pass into the small intestine.

The mucous membrane lining the stomach is quite thick and, in an empty stomach, is organized into numerous folds called *rugae* (rū-jē). These folds allow the mucosa to stretch as the stomach fills with food. The mucosa is dotted with numerous pores called *gastric pits.* Gastric pits are openings of the **gastric glands** that extend deep into the mucosa.

Gastric Juice

The secretion of the gastric glands is known as **gastric juice.** Cells near the opening of the gastric glands secrete mucus that coats and protects the mucosa from

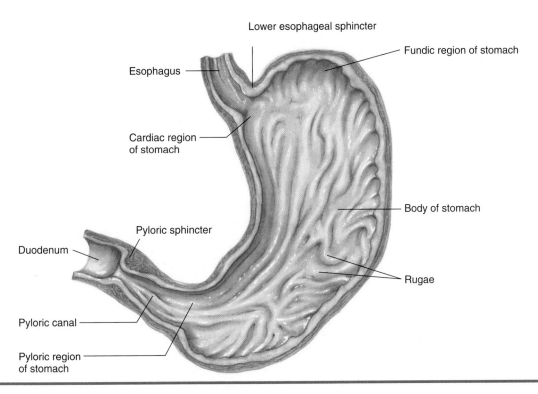

Figure 15.8   The pouchlike stomach receives food from the esophagus and releases chyme into the duodenum. **AP|R**

the action of digestive secretions. *Chief cells,* located at the bottom of the glands, secrete digestive enzymes. *Parietal cells,* located in the midportion of the glands, secrete hydrochloric acid (figure 15.9).

Clinical **INSIGHT**

Sometimes the lower esophageal sphincter inadvertently allows a small amount of gastric juice to regurgitate into the base of the esophagus. When this occurs, the acidic gastric juice irritates the esophageal lining and produces a burning sensation called *heartburn*.

As food is mixed with gastric juice and as digestion occurs, it is converted into a semiliquid substance called **chyme** (kīm). Small amounts of chyme are released intermittently into the duodenum by the opening of the pyloric sphincter.

Control of Gastric Secretion

The rate of gastric secretion is controlled by both neural and hormonal means. Gastric juice is produced continuously, but its secretion is greatly increased whenever food is on the way to, or already in, the stomach. The sight, smell, or thought of appetizing food, food in the mouth, or food in the stomach stimulates the transmission of parasympathetic impulses that increase the secretion of gastric juice. These impulses also stimulate certain stomach cells to secrete a hormone called **gastrin.** Gastrin is absorbed into the blood and is carried to stomach mucosal cells, increasing their secretions (figure 15.10).

As stomach contents are gradually emptied into the small intestine, there is a decrease in the frequency of parasympathetic impulses to the stomach, which reduces the secretion of gastric juice. When chyme passes from the stomach into the small intestine, it stimulates the intestinal mucosa to release two hormones: **cholecystokinin** (kō-lē-sis-tō-kīn´-in) **(CCK)** and **secretin** (se´-krē´-tin), which reduce the secretion of gastric juice.

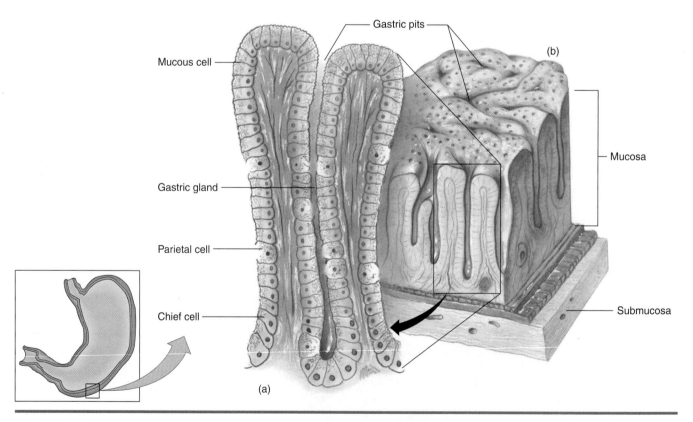

Figure 15.9 (*a*) An enlargement of the gastric glands shows the locations of mucous cells, parietal cells, and chief cells. (*b*) The thick stomach mucosa is dotted with gastric pits, the openings of the gastric glands. **AP|R**

1 Parasympathetic preganglionic nerve fiber (in vagus nerve)

2 Parasympathetic postganglionic impulses stimulate the release of gastric juice from gastric glands

3 Impulses stimulate the release of gastrin

4 Gastrin stimulates glands to release more gastric juice

Release into bloodstream

Stimulation

Bloodstream

Figure 15.10 Neural and hormonal control of gastric secretions. AP|R

Digestion and Absorption

Food entering the stomach is thoroughly mixed with gastric juice by ripplelike, mixing contractions of the stomach wall. Gastric juice is very acidic (pH 2) due to an abundance of hydrochloric acid. **Pepsin** is the most important digestive enzyme in gastric juice, and it is secreted in an inactive form that prevents digestion of the cells secreting it. Once it is released into the stomach, pepsin is activated by the strong acidity of gastric juice. Pepsin acts on proteins and breaks these complex molecules into smaller molecules called *peptides.* However, peptides are still much too large to be absorbed, and they will be further digested in the small intestine.

Rennin is an enzyme in the gastric juice of infants. It curdles milk proteins, which keeps them in the stomach longer and makes them more easily digestible by pepsin. Gastric juice also contains a substance known as **intrinsic factor** that is essential for the absorption of vitamin B_{12} by the small intestine. Except for a few substances such as water, minerals, some drugs, and alcohol, little absorption occurs in the stomach.

Check My Understanding

8. What digestive processes occur in the stomach?
9. How are gastric secretions controlled?

Clinical INSIGHT

Gastric ulcers produce stomach pain one to three hours after eating. Without treatment, they can perforate the stomach wall, producing internal bleeding or peritonitis. Gastric ulcers result from persistent erosion of the alkaline mucus that coats the stomach lining. Most recurring gastric ulcers are caused by an acid-resistant bacterium, *Helicobacter pylori,* which erodes the protective mucous layer, allowing gastric juice to attack the underlying cells. Other contributing factors that promote hydrochloric acid (HCl) secretion or reduce mucus production include stress, smoking, alcohol, coffee, aspirin, and nonsteroidal antiinflammatory drugs. Treatment involves antibiotics to kill the bacteria and drugs to reduce gastric secretion.

When semiliquid chyme passes from the stomach into the **duodenum**, the first part of the small intestine, secretions from the pancreas and liver are emptied into the duodenum. The secretions from these **accessory organs** play important roles in digestion within the small intestine.

15.6 Pancreas

The **pancreas** is a small, pennant-shaped gland located posterior to the pyloric portion of the stomach. It is connected by a duct to the inner curve of the duodenum, the first part of the small intestine. The pancreas has both endocrine and exocrine functions. The digestive function of the pancreas is the secretion of **pancreatic juice,** and the cells that produce it compose most of the pancreas. Pancreatic juice is collected by tiny ducts that merge to form large ducts, which enter the **pancreatic duct**. The pancreatic duct extends the length of the pancreas and usually divides into a *main pancreatic duct* and a smaller *accessory pancreatic duct*. The main pancreatic duct joins with the common bile duct where they both open into the duodenum. This opening is controlled by the *hepatopancreatic sphincter*, which dilates to allow pancreatic juice and bile to enter the duodenum. The accessory pancreatic duct allows pancreatic juice to enter the duodenum independently of bile (figure 15.11).

Control of Pancreatic Secretion

Pancreatic secretion, like gastric secretion, is controlled by both neural and hormonal mechanisms. Neural control is via parasympathetic fibers. When parasympathetic

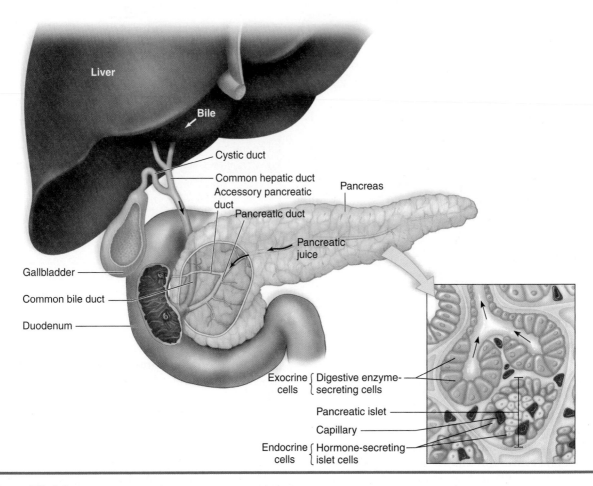

Figure 15.11 The pancreas is closely associated with the liver and duodenum. The inset shows secretory cells involved in the exocrine and endocrine functions of the pancreas. AP|R

impulses activate the stomach mucosa, they also stimulate the pancreas to secrete pancreatic juice.

Hormonal control of pancreatic secretion results from two hormones that stimulate different types of pancreatic cells. Acid chyme entering the duodenum stimulates the intestinal mucosa to release the hormone **secretin**, which is carried by blood to the pancreas, where it stimulates secretion of pancreatic juice that is rich in carbonates (figure 15.12). Carbonates neutralize the acidity of the chyme entering the small intestine. Fat-laden chyme stimulates production of **cholecystokinin (CCK)** by the intestinal mucosa. CCK stimulates secretion of pancreatic juice that is rich in digestive enzymes.

Table 15.2 summarizes the major hormones that regulate digestive secretions.

Digestion by Pancreatic Enzymes

Pancreatic juice contains enzymes that act on each of the major classes of energy foods: carbohydrates, fats, and proteins. Their digestive actions occur within the small intestine.

Pancreatic amylase, like salivary amylase, acts on *starch* and *glycogen,* splitting these polysaccharides into *maltose,* a disaccharide.

Pancreatic lipase acts on *fats* (triglycerides) and splits them into *monoglycerides* and *fatty acids* that are absorbable. A monoglyceride is a glycerol molecule with one fatty acid attached.

Trypsin is the major pancreatic enzyme in pancreatic juice. Trypsin splits *proteins* into shorter amino acid chains called *peptides.* Like pepsin in the stomach, it is secreted in an inactive form and is activated only when mixed with intestinal secretions within the small intestine. This mode of secretion prevents the pancreatic cells from being digested by their own enzymatic secretions.

Check My Understanding
10. What composes pancreatic juice?
11. How is pancreatic secretion controlled?

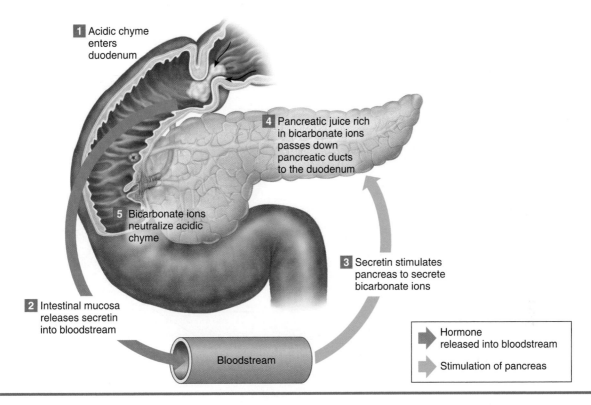

Figure 15.12 Acidic chyme entering the duodenum triggers the release of secretin, a hormone that stimulates the secretion of pancreatic juice.

Table 15.2	**Major Hormones Regulating Digestive Secretions**	
Hormone	**Action**	**Source**
Gastrin	Stimulates gastric glands to increase their rate of secretion	Gastric mucosa; food in the stomach stimulates release of gastrin
Cholecystokinin	Reduces secretion of gastric glands; stimulates secretion of pancreatic juice that is rich in digestive enzymes; stimulates contraction of gallbladder, causing release of bile	Intestinal mucosa; fatty chyme stimulates the release of cholecystokinin
Secretin	Stimulates secretion of pancreatic juice that is rich in carbonates; inhibits gastric secretion	Intestinal mucosa; acid chyme stimulates the release of secretin

15.7 Liver

The **liver** is the largest gland in the body. It weighs about 1.4 kg (3 lb) and is dark reddish brown in color. The liver is located mostly in the upper right quadrant of the abdomen just below the diaphragm, where it is protected by the lower ribs.

The liver has many important and vital functions, but most are not associated with digestion. Its only digestive function is the secretion of bile. Later in this chapter, you will see how the liver plays a key role in carbohydrate, lipid, and protein metabolism. In addition to these functions, the liver detoxifies poisons and harmful chemicals, such as alcohol and other drugs; removes worn-out blood cells; and stores fat, glycogen, iron, and several vitamins.

The liver is encased in a fibrous connective tissue capsule that, in turn, is covered by the peritoneum, which provides support. A ligament of connective tissue joins the liver to the diaphragm and the anterior abdominal wall and separates the two main lobes: a larger right lobe and a smaller left lobe. Blood vessels enter and leave the liver, and the hepatic duct, carrying bile, exits from a small area on the posterior surface of the liver (figure 15.13).

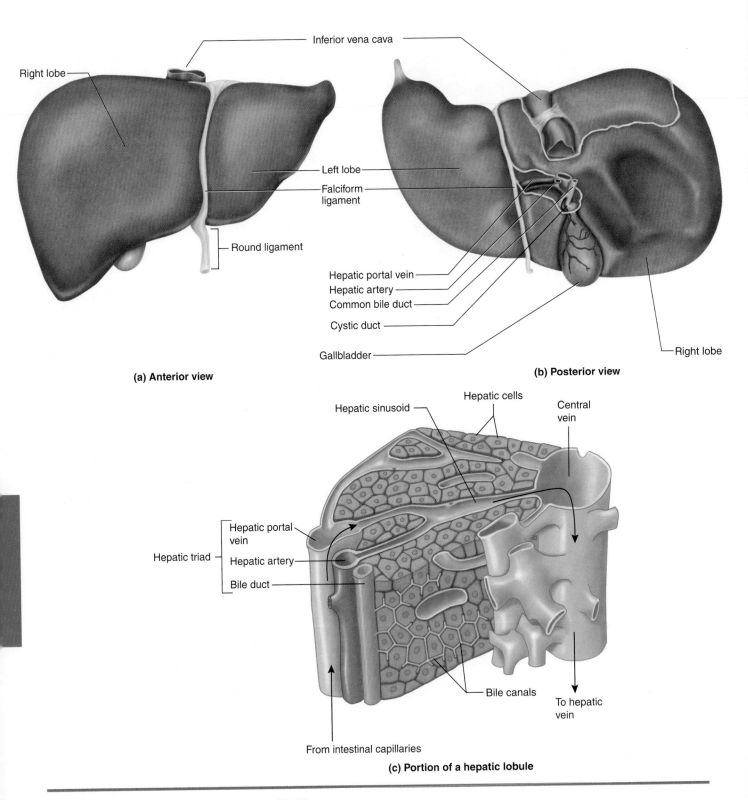

Figure 15.13 Anatomy of the liver. AP|R

The liver receives blood from two sources. The *hepatic artery* brings oxygenated blood to the liver cells. The *hepatic portal vein* brings deoxygenated, nutrient-rich blood from the digestive tract. As blood flows through the liver, liver cells remove, modify, or add substances to the blood before it leaves the liver via the *hepatic vein*.

Microscopically, the liver consists of multitudes of **hepatic lobules,** which serve as the structural and functional units. Each lobule is a short, roughly hexagonal cylinder with a central vein running through its core from which thin sheets of liver cells (hepatocytes) radiate. At corners where several lobules meet, there are *hepatic triads* composed of three vessels: a branch of the hepatic artery carrying oxygenated blood to the liver; a branch of the hepatic portal vein bringing nutrients from the intestines; and a small bile duct. Between the sheets of liver cells are *hepatic sinusoids,* blood-filled spaces that carry blood from the hepatic artery and hepatic portal vein to the central vein of the lobule. As blood flows through the hepatic sinusoids, an exchange of materials occurs between the blood and the liver cells, and macrophages in the epithelium lining the sinusoids remove cellular debris and bacteria. The central veins of the lobules ultimately merge to form the hepatic vein.

As noted, the production of bile is the only digestive function of the liver. Bile is collected in tiny ducts that merge to form the bile ducts of the hepatic triads, which, in turn, join to form the *hepatic duct,* which carries bile from the liver. The hepatic duct and the *cystic duct,* a short duct that extends from the gallbladder, merge to form the **common bile duct,** which carries bile to the duodenum. The cystic duct carries bile to and from the **gallbladder,** a small, pear-shaped sac that stores bile temporarily between meals (figures 15.11 and 15.13).

Bile

Liver cells continuously produce **bile,** a yellowish green liquid. Bile consists of water, bile salts, bile pigments, cholesterol, and minerals. Bile pigments, mostly *bilirubin,* are waste products of hemoglobin breakdown.

Bile salts are the only bile components that play a digestive role. When in contact with fatty substances, they break up the lipid globules into very small droplets, a process called *emulsification* (ē-mul-si-fi-kā´-shun). Emulsification greatly increases the surface area of the lipid substances exposed to water and lipid-digesting enzymes. In this way, bile salts aid the digestion of lipids. Bile salts also aid the absorption of fatty acids, cholesterol, and fat-soluble vitamins by the small intestine.

Release of Bile

Bile normally enters the duodenum only when food is present. When the intestine is empty, the hepatopancreatic sphincter at the base of the common bile duct is closed, and this forces bile to enter the gallbladder, where it is stored temporarily.

When fat-laden chyme enters the duodenum, it stimulates the release of cholecystokinin from the intestinal mucosa. CCK is carried by the blood to the gallbladder, where it stimulates contraction of muscles in the gallbladder wall ejecting bile from the gallbladder into the common bile duct. Further, CCK relaxes the hepatopancreatic sphincter muscle so bile is injected into the small intestine. Note that this hormonal control releases bile only when it is needed in the small intestine (figure 15.14).

Check My Understanding

12. Where is the liver located?
13. What is the digestive function of the liver?
14. How is bile release controlled?

15.8 Small Intestine

The small intestine is about 2.5 cm (1 in) in diameter and 6.4 m (21 ft) in length. It begins at the pyloric sphincter of the stomach, fills much of the abdomen, and empties into the large intestine. Most of the digestion of foods and absorption of nutrients occur in the small intestine.

Structure

There are three sequential segments composing the small intestine. The **duodenum** (dū-o-dē´-num) is a very short section, about 25 cm long, that receives chyme from the stomach. The middle section is the *jejunum* (je-jū´-num), and it is about 2.5 m long. The last and longest segment is the *ileum* (il´-ē-um), which is about 3.6 m long. The ileum joins with the large intestine at the *ileocecal* (il-ē-ō-sē´-kal) *sphincter.*

The small intestine is suspended from the posterior abdominal wall by the **mesentery** (mes´-en-ter-ē), double folds of the peritoneum that provide support but allow movement. Blood vessels, lymphatic vessels, and nerves serving the small intestine are also supported by the mesentery (figure 15.15).

The mucosa of the small intestine is modified to provide a very large surface area. The distinctive velvety appearance of the intestinal mucosa results from the presence of **intestinal villi,** tiny projections from the mucosa that are extremely abundant (see figure 15.2). Each villus, like all of the mucosa, is covered by columnar epithelium and contains a centrally located **lacteal,** a lymphatic capillary. A blood capillary network surrounds the lacteal. At the bases of the villi are tiny pits that open into **intestinal glands,** which secrete intestinal juice and mucus (figure 15.16).

The mucosal surface area in contact with chyme and digestive fluids is further increased by the presence

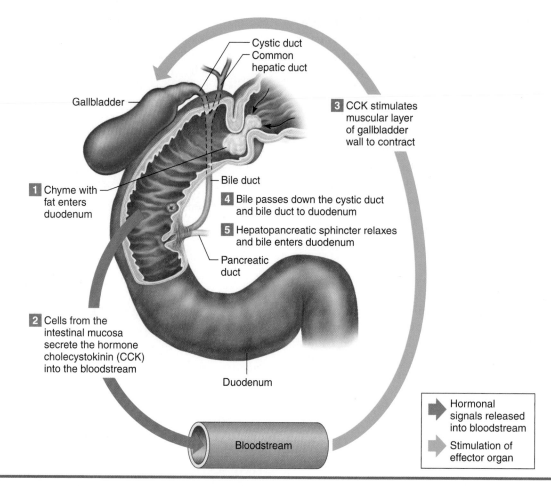

Figure 15.14 Fatty chyme entering the duodenum triggers the secretion of cholecystokinin, the hormone that stimulates release of bile from the gallbladder.

of numerous **microvilli.** The microscopic microvilli are formed by folds of the plasma membranes that form the exposed surfaces of the epithelial cells.

Intestinal Juice

The fluid secreted by the intestinal glands is known as **intestinal juice.** It is slightly alkaline and contains abundant water and mucus. Intestinal juice provides an appropriate environment for the action of bile salts and pancreatic digestive enzymes within the small intestine. Recall that trypsin in pancreatic juice is activated only after being mixed with intestinal secretions.

Regulation of Intestinal Secretion

The presence of chyme in the small intestine provides mechanical stimulation of the mucosa that activates the secretion of intestinal juice and enzymes. Also, the chyme causes an expansion of the intestinal wall, which triggers a neural reflex, sending parasympathetic

impulses to the mucosa. The impulses stimulate an increase in the rate of intestinal secretions.

Digestion and Absorption

Vigorous contractions of the small intestine mix chyme with bile, pancreatic juice, and intestinal juice. The emulsification of fats by bile and the continued digestion of carbohydrates, fats, and proteins by pancreatic and intestinal enzymes occur within the small intestine. The digestive process is completed by intestinal enzymes within the small intestine.

There are three intestinal enzymes that split disaccharides into monosaccharides. (1) **Maltase** converts *maltose* into *glucose;* (2) **sucrase** converts *sucrose* into *glucose* and *fructose;* and (3) **lactase** converts *lactose* into *glucose* and *galactose.*

Enzymes acting on fats and proteins are also present. **Intestinal lipase** splits *fats* (triglycerides) into *monoglycerides* and *fatty acids.* **Peptidase** splits *peptides* into *amino acids.* Table 15.3 summarizes the

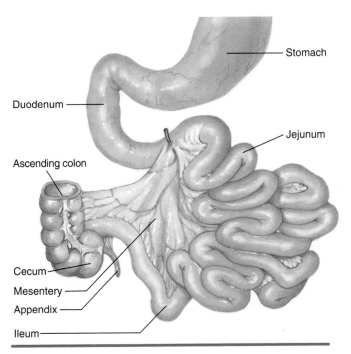

Figure 15.15 The small intestine consists of the duodenum, jejunum, and ileum. Chyme from the stomach enters the duodenum. After digestion and absorption, food residues pass from the ileum into the large intestine. AP|R

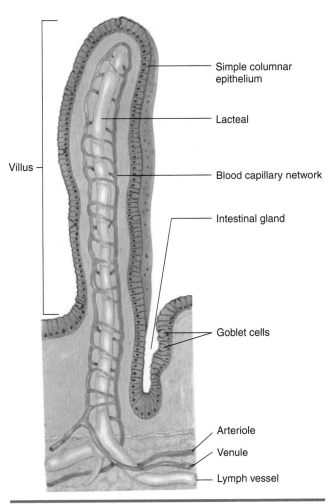

Figure 15.16 The structure of a villus.

enzymes involved in the digestion of carbohydrates, fats, and proteins.

Carbohydrate digestion begins in the mouth and concludes in the small intestine. The end products of carbohydrate digestion are monosaccharides, the simple sugars *glucose, fructose,* and *galactose.* These sugars are absorbed into the capillaries of the villi primarily by active transport, although diffusion accounts for some of the absorption.

Fat (triglyceride) digestion occurs in the small intestine. The end products are *monoglycerides* and *fatty acids,* and they diffuse into the epithelial cells of the villi. Once inside the epithelial cells, they recombine to form fat molecules. Then, the fat molecules combine in small clusters, along with cholesterol and phospholipids, and become coated with protein, forming particles known as **chylomicrons** (kĭ-lō-mĭ´-krons). The protein coat makes chylomicrons water-soluble. Chylomicrons move from the epithelial cells and enter the lacteals of the villi, as shown in figure 15.17. They are carried by lymphatic vessels to the left subclavian vein, where lymph from the intestine enters the blood. Very small fatty acids seem to enter the capillary networks of villi directly without being recombined to form fat molecules.

Protein digestion begins in the stomach and concludes in the small intestine. The end products are *amino acids,* and they are actively absorbed in the capillaries of villi.

In addition to the end products of digestion, other needed substances are absorbed in the small intestine. For example, water, minerals, and vitamins are absorbed into the capillaries of villi. Materials absorbed into the blood are carried from the intestines to the liver via the hepatic portal vein. After processing by the liver, appropriate concentrations of nutrients are released into the general circulation to serve the needs of tissue cells.

Check My Understanding

15. What are the three parts of the small intestine?
16. What digestive processes occur in the small intestine?
17. How are end products of digestion absorbed?

Table 15.3	Summary of the Major Digestive Enzymes and Their Actions	
Enzyme	**Substrate**	**Product**
Saliva		
Amylase	Starch and glycogen	Maltose
Gastric Juice		
Pepsin	Proteins	Peptides
Pancreatic Juice		
Amylase	Starch and glycogen	Maltose
Lipase	Triglycerides	Monoglycerides* and fatty acids*
Trypsin	Proteins	Peptides
Intestinal Juice		
Maltase	Maltose	Glucose*
Sucrase	Sucrose	Glucose* and fructose*
Lactase	Lactose	Glucose* and galactose*
Lipase	Triglycerides	Monoglycerides* and fatty acids*
Peptidase	Peptides	Amino acids*

*End products of digestion.

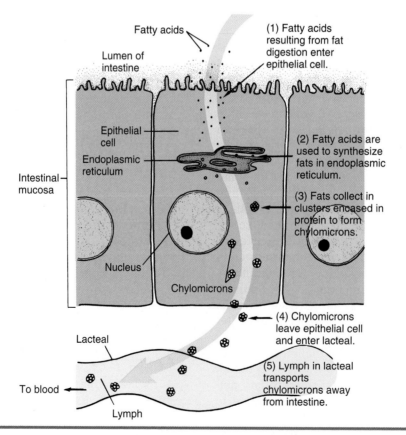

Figure 15.17   Absorption of fatty acids.

15.9 Large Intestine

The small intestine joins with the large intestine at the ileocecal sphincter. This valve is closed most of the time but opens to allow food residues to enter the large intestine.

Structure

The *large intestine* gets its name because its diameter (6.5 cm; 2.5 in) is larger than that of the small intestine, although its length (1.5 m; 5 ft) is much shorter. The large intestine consists of three segments: cecum, colon, and rectum.

The first portion of the large intestine is the pouchlike *cecum,* which bulges below the ileocecal sphincter. The slender wormlike **appendix** extends from the cecum and has no digestive function.

The **colon** forms most of the large intestine, and it is subdivided into four segments. The *ascending colon* extends upward from the cecum along the right side of the abdomen. As it nears the liver, it turns left to become the *transverse colon.* Near the spleen, the transverse colon turns downward to become the *descending colon* along the left side of the abdomen. Near the pelvis, the descending colon becomes the *sigmoid colon,* which is characterized by an S-shaped curvature leading to the rectum (figure 15.18).

The **rectum** is the short, terminal portion of the large intestine. The last portion of the rectum is known as the *anal canal* and its exterior opening is the **anus.** The mucosa of the anal canal is folded to form the *anal columns,* which contain networks of arteries and veins. The anus is kept closed except during defecation by the involuntarily controlled *internal anal*

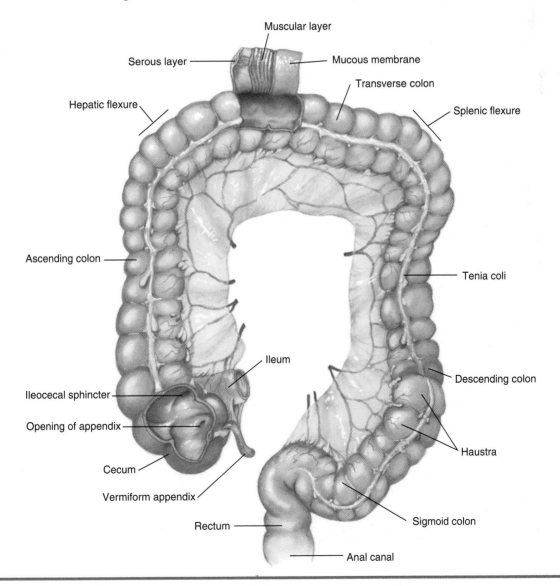

Figure 15.18 Anterior view of the large intestine. **AP|R**

sphincter and the voluntarily controlled *external anal sphincter* (figure 15.19).

The large intestine has a puckered appearance when viewed externally. This results because the longitudinal muscles are not uniformly layered but are reduced to three longitudinal bands, the *taeniae coli,* that run the length of the colon. Contractions of these muscle fibers gather the colon into a series of pouches, the *haustra.* Like the small intestine, the large intestine is supported by the mesentery.

The mucosa of the large intestine is also different from that of the small intestine. Villi are absent, and the columnar epithelium contains numerous mucus-producing goblet cells.

Functions

Food residue entering the large intestine contains water, minerals, bacteria, and other substances that were not digested or absorbed while in the small intestine. There are no digestive enzymes formed by the large intestine. Instead, intestinal bacteria decompose the nondigested food residues. This action yields certain B vitamins and vitamin K and also produces gas (flatus). The mucosa of the large intestine secretes large quantities of mucus that lubricate the intestinal lining and reduce abrasion as materials are moved along.

A major function of the large intestine is the absorption of water, some minerals, and vitamins as the contents slowly move through the colon. Much of this absorption occurs before the contents reach the descending colon, where they are congealed to form the **feces** (fē-sēz). Feces contain large amounts of bacteria, mucus, and water as well as nondigested food residues.

Lactose intolerance is caused by a deficiency or absence of intestinal lactase. The presence of undigested lactose in the intestines produces an osmotic gradient that prevents the normal reabsorption of water into the blood and, even worse, actually causes water to be drawn into the intestines from interstitial fluid. The result is diarrhea, flatulence, bloating, and intestinal cramps. Afflicted persons can avoid this problem if they take a tablet or liquid containing lactase before meals containing milk or milk products.

Movements

The mixing and propelling movements of the large intestine are more sluggish than those of the small intestine. Vigorous peristalsis occurs only two to four times a day, usually following a meal. Such peristaltic contractions are called *mass movements* because they move the contents of the descending and sigmoid colons toward the rectum. The defecation reflex is activated when the rectum fills with feces and its wall is stretched. This reflex stimulates contractions that increase pressure within the rectum and open the internal anal sphincter. If the voluntarily controlled external anal sphincter is relaxed, the feces are expelled through the anus. If its contraction is voluntarily maintained, defecation is postponed.

Check My Understanding

18. What are the parts of the large intestine?
19. What is the function of the large intestine?

15.10 Nutrients: Sources and Uses

Nutrients are chemicals in foods that provide energy for powering life processes; chemicals aiding or enabling life processes; or materials to construct molecules for the normal development, growth, and maintenance of the body. There are six groups of nutrients: carbohydrates, lipids, proteins, vitamins, minerals, and water. All six groups provide raw materials for constructing new molecules, but only carbohydrates, lipids, and proteins provide energy to sustain life processes.

Essential nutrients are those nutrients that the body cannot synthesize and must obtain in food in order to construct other molecules necessary for life. The essential nutrients include certain amino acids, certain fatty acids, most vitamins, minerals, and water. Because the

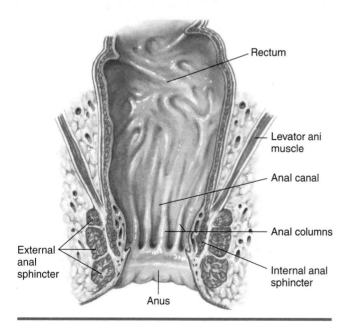

Figure 15.19 The rectum and the anal canal are located at the distal end of the alimentary canal.

essential nutrients are not all present in any one food, a balanced diet is required. The conversion of raw materials into molecules for life processes is a major role of the liver. Table 15.4 summarizes liver functions.

Energy Foods and Cellular Respiration

Carbohydrates, fats, and proteins are called "energy foods" because they are used in cellular respiration to release the energy in their chemical bonds for ATP production. Recall from the discussion in chapter 7 that cellular respiration includes both anaerobic and aerobic components. The anaerobic process, *glycolysis,* occurs within the cytoplasm of a cell, and the aerobic processes occur within mitochondria, where the enzymes catalyzing the reactions are located. There are two sequential, linked aerobic processes: the **citric acid cycle** and the *electron transport chain.* When oxygen is available, a nutrient, such as glucose, is completely degraded to carbon dioxide, water, and released energy. Some of the energy, about 40%, is captured in ATP molecules, and the remainder is lost as heat. ATP does not store energy, but it carries it to where it is needed to power life processes. The released heat energy is important in maintaining a normal body temperature.

Follow the cellular respiration of glucose in figure 15.20. A molecule of glucose (containing 6 carbon atoms) is split by glycolysis to form 2 molecules of pyruvic acid (each containing 3 carbon atoms), and 2 ATP molecules are formed. Each pyruvic acid molecule is converted to acetyl-CoA (each molecule containing 2 carbon atoms), and CO_2 is released. Each acetyl-CoA molecule enters the citric acid cycle. With each turn of the cycle, one acetyl-CoA molecule is broken down to release CO_2, H^+, and high-energy electrons.

The higher-energy electrons pass along the molecular carriers of the electron transport chain from a higher-energy level to a lower-energy level—much like water flowing down a staircase. At each transfer (step) within the chain, energy is released to form ATP and the electrons move to the next lower energy level (next lower step in the staircase). Ultimately, all of the available energy is extracted, and the electrons, H^+, and O_2 combine to form water (H_2O). Electron transfer yields a total of 34 ATP molecules, which when added to 2 ATP molecules from glycolysis, gives a total of 36 ATP molecules for each glucose molecule respired. One molecule of glucose yields 36 to 38 ATP molecules, depending upon the cell in which cellular respiration occurs.

The end products of digestion for lipids (fats) and proteins also may be used in cellular respiration, either directly or after conversion into compatible molecules. Figure 15.20 shows the major points of entry into cellular respiration for these molecules. The number of ATP molecules produced varies with the type of molecule respired.

Carbohydrates

Nearly all **carbohydrates** in the diet come from plant foods. Glycogen is the only carbohydrate in animal foods, and there is very little of it in meat. Monosaccharide sugars are in honey and fruits; disaccharides are found in table sugar and dairy products; and starch, a polysaccharide, occurs in cereals, vegetables, and legumes (e.g., beans, peas, peanuts). The recommended daily allowance (RDA) for carbohydrates is 125 to 175 g, or 55% to 60% of the total daily caloric intake.

Clinical **INSIGHT**

Evidence suggests that high-fiber, low-fat diets reduce the risk of certain colon disorders, such as diverticulitis and cancer.

Table 15.4	**Summary of Liver Functions**
Function	**Action**
Carbohydrate metabolism	Regulates glucose levels of the blood; converts excess glucose into glycogen or fat for storage; converts glycogen, glycerol, and amino acids into glucose as needed
Lipid metabolism	Forms lipoproteins for transport of fatty acids, triglycerides, and cholesterol; synthesizes cholesterol and uses it to form bile salts
Protein metabolism	Removes amine groups from amino acids, making the remainder of amino acid molecules available for cellular respiration or conversion into glucose or fat; converts ammonia into urea; forms plasma proteins, including fibrinogen and immunoglobulins
Storage	Stores fat, glycogen, iron, and vitamins A, D, E, K, and B_{12}
Detoxification	Modifies many drugs and toxic chemicals to form less toxic compounds
Phagocytosis	Removes worn-out blood cells and any bacteria that are present
Secretion	Produces bile, which is emptied into the small intestine; releases heparin, an anticoagulant, into the blood

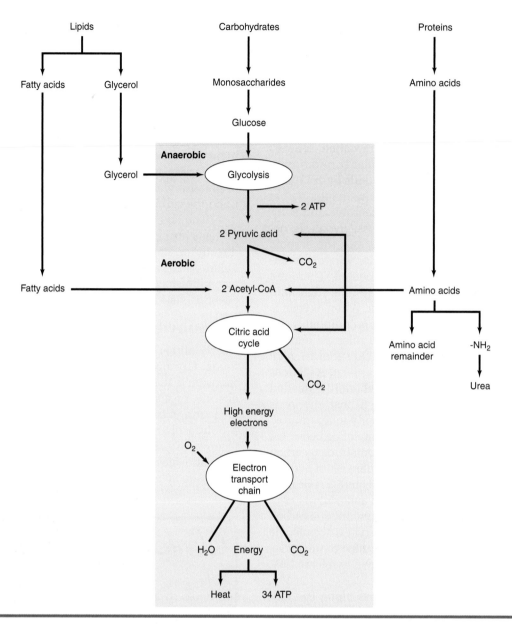

Figure 15.20 Energy foods and cellular respiration. Lipids, carbohydrates, and proteins may be respired to release energy for ATP production. Note the three major parts of cellular respiration.

Cellulose is a polysaccharide that is abundant in plant foods, but it cannot be digested by humans. However, it is an important dietary component, because it provides fiber (roughage) that increases the bulk of the intestinal contents, which aids the function of the large intestine.

Carbohydrates are used mostly as an energy source, and glucose is the primary carbohydrate molecule used in cellular respiration. Recall that the hormone insulin plays a crucial role in moving glucose into cells. Most cells can live by obtaining energy from fatty acids or amino acids via cellular respiration, but some cells, notably nerve cells, are dependent upon a steady supply of glucose. For this reason, if the concentration of blood glucose drops too low, the nervous system and brain functions decline.

The liver, along with the hormones insulin and glucagon, is involved in the regulation of glucose concentration in the blood. Excess glucose is converted into glycogen and is stored in the liver and skeletal muscles. If excess glucose still remains, it is converted into triglycerides (fats) and is stored in adipose tissues. When blood glucose levels decline, the liver converts glycogen into glucose. If still more glucose is needed, fats are converted into glycerol and fatty acids. Then glycerol may be converted into glucose.

Lipids

Lipids include triglycerides (fats), phospholipids, and fat-soluble vitamins, but triglycerides are the most common lipids in the diet. Triglycerides may be either saturated or unsaturated. Saturated fats have fatty acids without any double bonds between carbon atoms, and they are solid at room temperature (e.g., butter and margarine). Unsaturated fats have fatty acids with at least one double bond between their carbon atoms, and they are liquid at room temperatures. Fats and oils contain a mixture of saturated, monounsaturated (one double bond), and polyunsaturated (more than one double bond) fatty acids. Coconut and palm oils, dairy products, and beef fat contain mostly saturated fatty acids. Peanut, olive, and canola oils consist mostly of monounsaturated fatty acids. Safflower, sunflower, and corn oils contain mostly polyunsaturated fatty acids. Cholesterol, a steroid, is present in dairy products, red meats, and egg yolks.

The recommended daily allowance for lipids is 80 to 100 g, or no more than 30% of the total caloric intake. The American Heart Association recommends that dietary fats consist of less than 10% saturated fats and that cholesterol should not exceed 300 mg per day (about one egg yolk).

Lipids are essential components of the diet, although excessive amounts are not desirable. Phospholipids form the major portion of cellular membranes, and fatty acids help form the myelin sheaths of neurons. Triglycerides are important energy sources for many cells, including liver and skeletal muscle cells. Excess triglycerides are stored in adipose tissue, where they form the largest energy reserve in the body.

Cholesterol is not used as an energy source, but it forms parts of plasma membranes and is used in the synthesis of bile salts and steroid hormones. The liver helps to regulate the concentration of triglycerides and cholesterol in the blood.

Lipids are hydrophobic and do not dissolve in the aqueous blood plasma. This poses a problem for their transport to and from body cells. To overcome this problem, lipids are combined with protein to form complexes called *lipoproteins.* A lipoprotein has a core of triglycerides and cholesterol with a coating of protein, making the complex soluble in blood plasma. Lipoproteins are classified by their density. The greater the proportion of protein, the greater the density of a lipoprotein.

Low-density lipoproteins (LDLs), the "bad" cholesterol, are formed in the liver and transport cholesterol and triglycerides to body cells, including cells of arteries where dangerous plaques can form.

High-density lipoproteins (HDLs), the "good" cholesterol, are formed in the liver as an almost empty shell of protein. They pick up cholesterol from cells of other organs, including arterial cells, as they circulate through the body and return the cholesterol to the liver for disposal in bile. Thus LDLs transport cholesterol from the liver to body cells, and HDLs transport cholesterol from body cells to the liver.

High-fat diets and high blood levels of triglycerides and cholesterol are associated with an increased risk of atherosclerosis and coronary heart disease. To minimize the risk of coronary heart disease, the American Heart Association recommends that the concentrations of cholesterol in the blood be as follows: total cholesterol <200 mg/dl; LDL cholesterol <130 mg/dl; HDL cholesterol >40 mg/dl in males and >50 mg/dl in females. The LDL/HDL ratio ideally should be about 3.5:1.

Proteins

Prime sources of proteins include red meat, poultry, fish, milk products, eggs, nuts, cereals, and legumes. Of the 20 kinds of amino acids composing proteins, eight cannot be synthesized from other amino acids by the liver. These eight amino acids are the **essential amino acids.** All essential amino acids must be present in the body in order for the body to synthesize proteins necessary for normal growth and maintenance. Animal proteins contain all of the essential amino acids, but plant proteins lack one or more of them. However, if cereals and legumes (e.g., beans, peas) are eaten together, this combination provides all of the essential amino acids. The recommended daily allowance for proteins is at least 0.8 g per kilogram (2.2 lb) of body weight.

Amino acids are used by the body primarily to synthesize proteins: plasma proteins, certain hormones, enzymes, and proteins that form structural components of cells. However, they may be used as an energy source in cellular respiration if there is a deficient supply of glucose or fats. If there is an excess of amino acids, they may be converted to glucose or fat.

For amino acids to be used as an energy source or converted to glucose or fat, the liver first removes the amine groups ($-NH_2$) so that the remainders of the amino acid molecules are available for these alternative pathways.

The amine groups react to form ammonia, a toxic substance. However, the liver converts ammonia into *urea,* a less toxic substance that is released into the blood and is excreted by the kidneys in urine (figure 15.20).

Vitamins

Vitamins are organic compounds that are required in minute amounts for the normal functioning of the body. They are not an energy source, but they are essential for the utilization of energy foods. Most vitamins act with enzymes to bring about particular metabolic reactions.

Vitamins are classified according to their solubility: water-soluble or fat-soluble. Water-soluble vitamins include vitamin C and the B vitamins. They are sensitive to heat and easily destroyed by cooking. Fat-soluble vitamins are vitamins A, D, E, and K. They are more resistant to heat and are not easily destroyed by cooking.

The sources and functions of vitamins are shown in tables 15.5 and 15.6.

Table 15.5   Water-Soluble Vitamins

Vitamin	Sources	Importance
C (ascorbic acid)	Citrus fruits, cabbage, tomatoes, leafy green vegetables	Required for synthesis of steroid hormones, absorption of iron, and formation of connective tissues
B_1 (thiamine)	Meats, eggs, cereals, beans, peas, leafy green vegetables	Required for cellular respiration and the synthesis of ribose sugars
B_2 (riboflavin)	Meats, cereals, leafy green vegetables; formed by colon bacteria	Required for cellular respiration
Niacin	Meats, liver, beans, peas, peanuts	Required for cellular respiration and synthesis of proteins, nucleic acids, and fats
B_6	Meats, poultry, fish, cereals, beans, peas, peanuts; formed by colon bacteria	Required for protein synthesis and formation of antibodies
Pantothenic acid	Meats, fish, cereals, beans, peas, fruits, vegetables, milk; formed by colon bacteria	Required for cellular respiration, conversion of amino acids and lipids into glucose, synthesis of cholesterol and steroid hormones
B_{12}	Meats, poultry, fish, milk, eggs, cheese	Required for synthesis of nucleic acids, formation of red blood cells, and cellular respiration of amino acids
Folic acid	Liver, cereals, leafy green vegetables; formed by colon bacteria	Required for synthesis of DNA, RNA, and normal blood cells
Biotin	Liver, eggs, beans, peas, peanuts; formed by colon bacteria	Required for cellular respiration and synthesis of fatty acids

Table 15.6   Fat-Soluble Vitamins

Vitamin	Sources	Importance
A	Eggs, milk, butter, liver; green, yellow, and orange vegetables and fruits	Required for healthy skin and mucous membranes; for development of visual pigments in rods and cones; for healthy bones and teeth
D	Formed by skin when exposed to ultraviolet light; fish liver oils, milk, eggs	Required for healthy bones and teeth; promotes absorption of calcium and phosphorus
E	Cereals, vegetable oils, fruits, and vegetables	Prevents oxidation of fatty acids and vitamin A; helps keep plasma membranes intact
K	Synthesized by colon bacteria; leafy green vegetables, cabbage, pork, liver, soybean oil	Required for formation of prothrombin, an enzyme involved in the formation of blood clots

Table 15.7 Major Minerals in the Body

Mineral	Sources	Importance
Calcium (Ca)	Milk, milk products, leafy green vegetables	Forms bones and teeth; required for blood clotting, conduction of nerve impulses, and muscle contraction
Phosphorus (P)	Meats, cereals, nuts, milk, milk products, legumes	Forms bones and teeth; component of proteins, nucleic acids, ATP, and phosphate buffers
Potassium (K)	Meats, nuts, potatoes, bananas, cereals	Required for conduction of nerve impulses and muscle contractions
Sulfur (S)	Meats, milk, eggs, legumes	Component of vitamins biotin and thiamine, the hormone insulin, and some amino acids
Sodium (Na)	Table salt, cured meats, cheese	Helps maintain osmotic pressure of body fluids; required for nerve impulse transmission
Chlorine (Cl)	Table salt, cured meats, cheese	Helps maintain osmotic pressure of body fluids; required for formation of HCl in gastric juice
Magnesium (Mg)	Milk, milk products, cereals, legumes, nuts, leafy green vegetables	Required for normal nerve and muscle functions; involved in ATP–ADP conversions

Minerals

Minerals are inorganic substances that plants absorb from the soil. They are present in both plant foods and animal foods because animals obtain them by eating plants. Humans need adequate amounts of the seven major minerals noted in table 15.7 but require only trace amounts of other minerals that occur in the body. About 4% of the body weight consists of minerals. Calcium and phosphorus, the most abundant minerals, account for about 75% of the total minerals in the body.

In the body, minerals may be incorporated into organic molecules, deposited as mineral salts (as in bone), or occur as ions in body fluids. Table 15.7 identifies the sources and functions of the major minerals.

Check My Understanding

20. How are monosaccharides, fatty acids, and amino acids used in the body?
21. What are the major functions of the liver?

15.11 Disorders of the Digestive System

These disorders may be grouped as inflammatory or noninflammatory.

Inflammatory Disorders

Appendicitis is an acute inflammation of the appendix. First symptoms include referred pain in the umbilical region and nausea. Later, pain is localized in the right lower quadrant of the abdomen. Surgical removal of the appendix is the standard treatment.

Inflammatory bowel disease (IBD) is a group of chronic disorders that cause painfully swollen, inflamed intestines; abdominal cramps; and bloody diarrhea. IBDs result from an overactive immune system that continuously promotes the inflammation, and there is a genetic predisposition to the disease. IBDs cause permanent changes in the intestinal tissues. Patients with IBDs are at a greater risk of intestinal cancer. Treatment includes corticosteroids and immunosuppressant drugs. Surgical removal of the affected portions of the intestines is necessary when drug therapy fails to provide remission. The major IBDs are ulcerative colitis and Crohn's disease. *Crohn's disease* may affect any portion of the alimentary canal but most often affect the distal portion of the ileum. *Ulcerative colitis* affects only the large intestine and/or rectum.

Irritable bowel syndrome (IBS) is an intestinal disorder causing abdominal bloating, cramping pain, and diarrhea. Unlike IBDs, IBS does not permanently damage intestinal tissues, and symptoms can usually be controlled by dietary and lifestyle changes.

Diverticulitis (dī-ver-tik-ū-lī´-tis) is a disorder of the large intestine. Small, saclike outpockets of the colon often develop from a diet lacking sufficient fiber (bulk). Diverticulitis is the inflammation of these diverticula, and it may cause considerable pain, bloating, or diarrhea.

Hemorrhoids is a condition in which one or more veins in the anal canal become enlarged and inflamed. Chronic constipation contributes to the development of hemorrhoids.

Hepatitis is inflammation of the liver, and it may be caused by several factors, including viruses, drugs, or alcohol. It is characterized by jaundice, fever, and liver enlargement. There are three basic types of hepatitis.

Hepatitis A (infectious hepatitis) is caused by the hepatitis A virus, which is spread by person-to-person contact and fecal contamination of food and water.

It is highly contagious, but an effective vaccine and treatment are available. Symptoms are usually mild. Recovery takes four to six weeks.

Hepatitis B (serum hepatitis) is a serious infection. It is spread through contaminated blood, saliva, vaginal secretions, and semen. Most people recover completely, but some retain live viruses for years and unknowingly serve as carriers of the disease. Chronic hepatitis may produce cirrhosis or lead to liver cancer. Hepatitis B vaccine is the best protection against hepatitis B infection. It consists of a series of three spaced injections and may be given to persons of all ages, including infants. Chronic hepatitis B patients are treated with antiviral medications.

Hepatitis C is spread primarily by contaminated blood but also by contaminated food and water. Symptoms are usually so mild a person may not even know he or she has it until liver damage shows up, maybe decades later. It can lead to liver failure, cirrhosis, and cancer. In some cases, the symptoms are mild and short-lived so medications are usually not needed. But most cases progress to the chronic form of the disease and require antiviral medications.

Periodontal disease refers to a variety of conditions characterized by inflammation; bleeding gums; and degeneration of the gingivae, cementum, periodontal ligaments, and alveolar bone, which causes loosening of the teeth. Poor dental hygiene contributes to this condition.

Peritonitis is the acute inflammation of the peritoneum that lines the abdominal cavity and covers abdominal organs. It may result from bacteria entering the peritoneal cavity due to contamination in accidents or surgery or by a ruptured intestine or appendix.

Noninflammatory Disorders

Cirrhosis of the liver is characterized by scarring, which results from connective tissue replacing destroyed liver cells. It may be caused by hepatitis, alcoholism, nutritional deficiencies, or liver parasites.

Constipation is a condition in which defecation is difficult and the feces are hard and dry. This results from feces remaining in the colon for a longer than normal period, which allows more water to be absorbed.

Dental caries—tooth decay—result from the excess acid produced by certain microorganisms that live in the mouth and use food residues for their nutrients. Residues of carbohydrates, especially sugars, nurture microorganisms that cause decay.

Diarrhea is the production of watery feces due to the abnormally rapid movement of food residues through the colon. Increased peristalsis may result from a number of causes, including inflammation and chronic stress.

Eating disorders result from an obsessive concern about weight control, especially among young adult females. There are two major types of eating disorders: anorexia and bulimia.

Anorexia nervosa is self-imposed starvation that results in malnutrition and associated physiological changes. Patients with this disorder see themselves as overweight, although others see them as very thin. Death can occur due to the complications of prolonged starvation.

Bulimia is characterized by frequent overeating and purging by self-induced vomiting. Fears of being overweight, depression, and stress are associated factors. The exact cause is unknown. Bulimia may lead to such complications as an imbalance of electrolytes, erosion of tooth enamel by stomach acids, and constipation.

Gallstones result from crystallization of cholesterol in bile. They commonly occur in the gallbladder, but they may be carried into bile ducts, where they block the flow of bile. Severe pain—and often jaundice—accompanies such blockage. Treatment may include drugs that dissolve the gallstones, shock-wave therapy to break up the stones, or surgical removal of the gallstones and gallbladder.

Clinical INSIGHT

Obesity has become a national health concern. Studies have shown that obesity is a significant health risk, perhaps second in importance only to smoking. Obesity results from consuming food containing more kilocalories than is necessary to meet the body's energy needs. Underlying causes of obesity include heredity, eating habits, inadequate exercise, and poor diet. People who are genetically predisposed toward obesity have a very difficult time controlling their weight. Excess kilocalories are stored as fats in adipose tissue. An excess of 3,500 kcal equals one pound of fat. The only way to get rid of stored fat is to consume fewer kilocalories than needed so the stored fat will be mobilized and respired. Exercise increases the body's need for energy, which helps burn fat more rapidly.

An effective way to determine if a person is overweight or obese is to calculate the **body mass index (BMI)**. It is calculated by dividing a person's weight in kilograms by the square of his or her height in meters: $BMI = Wt/Ht^2$. To determine the weight in kilograms, divide the weight in pounds by 2.2. To determine the height in meters, divide the height in inches by 39.37. A BMI higher than 25 to 27 is considered overweight, and a value of 30 or more is considered obese.

15.1 Digestion: An Overview

- Digestion involves both mechanical and chemical processes. Mechanical digestion is the physical process of breaking food into smaller particles. Chemical digestion is an enzymatic process that converts non-absorbable foods into absorbable nutrients.
- A number of different digestive enzymes are required for the chemical digestion of foods.

15.2 Alimentary Canal: General Characteristics

- The alimentary canal is the long tube through which food passes from the mouth to the anus. Digestion of food and absorption of nutrients occur in some portions of the alimentary canal.
- The wall of the alimentary canal is composed of four layers. From outside in, they are the serosa, muscular layer, submucosa, and mucosa.
- Food is moved through the alimentary canal by peristaltic contractions. Ripplelike contractions mix food with digestive secretions.

15.3 Mouth

- The mouth is surrounded by the cheeks, palate, and tongue. Teeth are embedded in the dental arches of the maxilla and mandible.
- Humans have two sets of teeth: deciduous and permanent. There are 32 permanent teeth divided into four types: incisors, cuspids, bicuspids, and molars.
- A tooth is composed of two major parts: a crown covered with enamel and a root embedded in alveolar bone. Dentin forms most of the tooth. The centrally located pulp cavity contains blood vessels and nerves. The root is anchored to bone by cementum and by a periodontal membrane.
- Three pairs of salivary glands (parotid, submandibular, and sublingual) secrete saliva into the mouth. Salivary secretion is under reflexive neural control. Saliva cleanses and lubricates the mouth and binds food together.
- Saliva contains salivary amylase, which breaks down starch and glycogen into maltose.

15.4 Pharynx and Esophagus

- The pharynx connects the oral and nasal cavities with the esophagus and larynx. Its digestive function is to transport food from the mouth to the esophagus.
- The swallowing reflex causes the epiglottis to cover the laryngeal opening, directing food into the esophagus.
- Pharyngeal, palatine, and lingual tonsils are located near the entrance to the pharynx.
- The esophagus carries food by peristalsis from the pharynx to the stomach.
- The lower esophageal sphincter opens to let food enter the stomach.

15.5 Stomach

- The stomach is a pouchlike enlargement of the alimentary canal. It is located in the upper left quadrant of the abdomen and consists of four regions: cardiac, fundic, and pyloric regions and the body.
- The pyloric sphincter opens to allow chyme to enter the duodenum.
- The stomach mucosa contains gastric glands that secrete gastric juice, whose components include hydrochloric acid and pepsin. Gastric juice converts food into chyme.
- The secretion of gastric juice is regulated by neural reflexes and the hormones gastrin and cholecystokinin.
- Pepsin acts on proteins and breaks them into peptides.
- Rennin is a gastric enzyme secreted by infants. It curdles milk, which aids digestion of milk proteins.
- Gastric juice contains intrinsic factor, which is necessary for absorption of vitamin B_{12}.
- Little absorption occurs in the stomach.

15.6 Pancreas

- The pancreas is located adjacent to the duodenum and pyloric region of the stomach. The pancreas secretes pancreatic juice, which is carried to the duodenum by the pancreatic duct. The hormones secretin and cholecystokinin stimulate the secretion of pancreatic juice.
- Pancreatic digestive enzymes act on each of the three types of energy food. Amylase converts starch and glycogen into maltose. Lipase converts fats into monoglycerides and fatty acids. Trypsin converts proteins into peptides.

15.7 Liver

- The liver is located in the upper right quadrant of the abdomen. The liver removes, modifies, or adds substances to the blood as it flows through the sinusoids.
- Hepatic lobules are the structural and functional units of the liver.
- Bile is continuously secreted by the liver. Between meals, bile is stored in the gallbladder. It is released when the hormone cholecystokinin, formed by the intestinal mucosa, stimulates contraction of the gallbladder. Bile is carried to the duodenum by the common bile duct.
- Bile emulsifies lipids, which aids their digestion by lipases.

15.8 Small Intestine

- The small intestine occupies much of the abdominal cavity, and it consists of three parts: duodenum, jejunum, and ileum. Most of the digestion and absorption of food occur in the small intestine.
- The mucosa contains numerous intestinal glands that secrete intestinal juice and villi that absorb nutrients.

Secretion of intestinal juice is activated by a neural reflex. Intestinal digestive enzymes act on all three types of energy foods.

- The enzymes maltase, sucrase, and lactase act on corresponding disaccharides to form the monosaccharides: glucose, fructose, and galactose. Lipase converts fats into monoglycerides and fatty acids. Peptidase converts peptides into amino acids.
- End products of digestion are absorbed into the villi. Monosaccharides, amino acids, water-soluble vitamins, and minerals enter the capillaries of the villi. Monoglycerides and fatty acids enter mucosal cells and are recombined to form fat molecules. Clusters of fat molecules are coated with protein to form chylomicrons, which, along with fat-soluble vitamins, enter the lacteals of the villi.
- Nondigested and nonabsorbed materials exit the small intestine and enter the large intestine through the ileocecal sphincter.

15.9 Large Intestine

- The large intestine consists of the cecum, colon, and rectum. The appendix is a nonfunctional appendage of the cecum.
- The large intestine is gathered into a series of pouches by the taeniae coli. Its mucosa lacks villi and secretes only mucus.
- The absorption of water and the formation and expulsion of feces are major functions of the large intestine. Bacteria decompose the nondigested materials.
- Mass peristaltic movements propel the feces into the rectum, initiating the defecation reflex, which opens the internal anal sphincter. Voluntary relaxation of the external sphincter allows expulsion of the feces.

15.10 Nutrients: Sources and Uses

- Nutrients include carbohydrates, lipids, proteins, vitamins, minerals, and water. The liver is involved in the metabolism of many nutrients.
- Essential nutrients are nutrients that must be consumed because they cannot be synthesized by the body.
- Cellular respiration consists of glycolysis, the citric acid cycle, and an electron transport chain. Respiration of a molecule of glucose yields 36 ATP molecules.
- End products of carbohydrate, lipid, and protein digestion may be used in cellular respiration either directly or after modification.
- Dietary carbohydrates come primarily from plant foods. Cellulose is a nondigestible polysaccharide that provides fiber in the diet.

- The liver regulates the concentration of glucose in the blood. Excess glucose is converted to glycogen or fats for storage, and these reactions may be reversed to release more glucose into the blood.
- Dietary lipids are mostly triglycerides that occur either as saturated fats, usually in animal foods, or as unsaturated fats, usually in plant foods. Cholesterol occurs in egg yolks, milk, and meats.
- Lipids form important parts of plasma membranes and myelin sheaths of neurons. Fats are an energy source for many cells. Excess fats are stored in adipose tissue. The liver helps to regulate the concentration of triglycerides and cholesterol in the blood.
- Dietary proteins occur in meats, milk, eggs, cereals, nuts, and legumes. The eight essential amino acids cannot be synthesized by the body. Only animal proteins contain all of the essential amino acids.
- Amino acids are used primarily to synthesize protein in the body. These proteins form plasma proteins, enzymes, certain hormones, and structural parts of cells. Amino acids may be deaminated by the liver and used to form glucose or fat or may be used as an energy source by cells.
- Vitamins are organic molecules required in minute amounts for normal functioning of the body. Water-soluble vitamins include the B vitamins and vitamin C. Fat-soluble vitamins include vitamins A, D, E, and K.
- Vitamins act with enzymes to bring about essential chemical reactions, such as cellular respiration, in cells.
- Minerals are inorganic substances that are necessary for the normal functioning of the body. Minerals are obtained by plants from the soil, and they are passed on to animals, including humans, eating the plants.
- Many minerals are a part of organic molecules in the body. Other minerals are deposited as salts in bones and teeth, and some occur as ions in body fluids.
- There are seven major minerals that are required in moderate amounts in the diet: calcium, phosphorus, potassium, sulfur, sodium, chloride, and magnesium. Other minerals of the body are required in trace amounts.

15.11 Disorders of the Digestive System

- Inflammatory disorders include appendicitis, inflammatory bowel disease (IBD), irritable bowel syndrome (IBS), diverticulitis, hemorrhoids, hepatitis, periodontal disease, and peritonitis.
- Other disorders include eating disorders (anorexia nervosa and bulimia), cirrhosis, constipation, dental caries, diarrhea, and gallstones.

BUILDING MY VOCABULARY

1. **Selected New Terms**
   bile, p. 321
   cholecystokinin, p. 316, 318
   chylomicrons, p. 323
   dentin, p. 313

   enamel, p. 313
   essential amino acids, p. 329
   gastrin, p. 316
   lactase, p. 322
   lipase, p. 322

maltase, p. 322
mastication, p. 312
pepsin, p. 317
peptidase, p. 322
rennin, p. 317
saliva, p. 313
secretin, p. 318
sucrase, p. 322
trypsin, p. 318

2. Related Clinical Terms

Dysphagia (dis-fā´-jē-ah) Difficulty in swallowing.
Colonoscopy (kō-lon-os´-kō-pē) Viewing the interior of the colon with a flexible, tubelike instrument called an endoscope.

Gastrectomy (gas-trek´-tō-mē) Removal of all or part of the stomach.

Gastroenterology (gas-trō-en-ter-ol´-ō-jē) Medical specialty treating disorders of the digestive tract.

Ileus (il´-ē-us) Paralysis of the digestive tract.

SELF-REVIEW

Answers are located in appendix B.

1. It is _____ that speed up the hydrolysis of food molecules to yield absorbable _____.
2. Digestive secretions are produced by the _____, the inner lining of the alimentary canal.
3. Food is moved through the digestive tract by wavelike contractions called _____.
4. A tooth is composed mostly of _____, but the crown of a tooth is covered by _____.
5. Chemical digestion begins in the mouth, where the enzyme _____ acts on starch to yield _____.
6. When food enters the esophagus, it is carried by _____ and enters the stomach when the _____ opens.
7. Gastric juice contains HCl and the enzyme _____, which breaks down _____ to peptides.
8. Gastric secretion is stimulated by impulses carried by _____ fibers and by the hormone _____.
9. The hormones _____ and _____ activate the production of pancreatic juice, and the hormone _____ stimulates the release of bile from the gallbladder.
10. The three enzymes in pancreatic juice are _____, which acts on starch; _____, which acts on fats; and _____, which acts on proteins.
11. Digestion is completed in the _____, where disaccharides are converted to _____ and peptides are converted to _____.
12. End products of digestion are absorbed into _____ of the small intestine; amino acids and monosaccharides enter the _____, and fatty acids and monoglycerides enter the _____.
13. Absorption of water and dissolved minerals and vitamins is the primary function of the _____.
14. The _____ processes and modifies absorbed nutrients before they enter the general circulation.
15. Organic substances that are essential to health in minute amounts are called _____.

CRITICAL THINKING

1. Complete the learning objectives on the first page of this chapter.
2. How does swallowing channel food into the esophagus and not the larynx?
3. Sometimes medications or aging can cause "dry mouth" (xerostomia), a condition of insufficient saliva production. What effects would this cause in a patient?
4. What is the advantage of blood from the intestines passing to the liver before entering the general circulation?
5. How do the stomach and small intestine avoid digesting themselves as they digest food?

Visit this book's website at www.mhhe.com/ gunstream5 for practice quizzes, learning exercises, case studies, and other study tools.

CHAPTER 16

Urinary System

Anatomy & Physiology REVEALED®
aprevealed.com

Module 13
Urinary System

Glomerular filtration The forcing of water and small solutes from the blood in a glomerulus into a glomerular capsule.

Glomerulus (glomus = ball) The cluster of capillaries enveloped by the glomerular capsule.

Juxtaglomerular apparatus (juxta = next to) Specialized cells next to the glomerulus that help to regulate blood pressure.

Micturition (micture = to urinate) Urination.

Nephron (nephros = kidney) The structural and functional unit of the kidneys.

Peritubular capillaries (peri = around) Capillaries surrounding a renal tubule.

Renal corpuscle (ren = kidney) The portion of a nephron composed of a glomerulus and its enveloping glomerular capsule.

Renal tubule The portion of a nephron composed of a proximal convoluted tubule, a nephron loop, and a distal convoluted tubule.

Tubular reabsorption The movement of substances from the filtrate in a renal tubule into blood in the peritubular capillaries.

Tubular secretion The movement of substances from blood in peritubular capillaries into the filtrate in a renal tubule.

T he normal metabolic activities of body cells produce a number of waste materials which tend to change the balance of water and dissolved substances in body fluids. The basic function of the *urinary system* is to maintain the volume and composition of body fluids within normal limits.

The urinary system consists of the kidneys, ureters, urinary bladder, and urethra. The paired *kidneys* maintain the composition and volume of body fluids by removing wastes and excess substances in the formation of urine. *Ureters* are slender tubes that carry urine from the kidneys to the *urinary bladder* for temporary storage. Urine is carried from the urinary bladder and is expelled from the body through the *urethra* (figure 16.1).

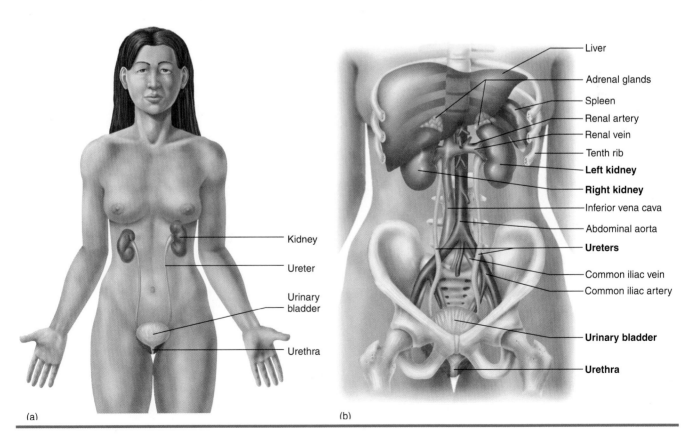

(a)   (b)

Figure 16.1 The urinary system. (*a*) It consists of two kidneys, two ureters, a urinary bladder, and a urethra. (*b*) Orientation of urinary organs in the body. AP|R

16.1 Kidneys

The *kidneys* are reddish brown, bean-shaped organs located on each side of the vertebral column and against the upper, posterior wall of the abdominal cavity. They lie posterior to the parietal peritoneum, which covers their anterior surfaces. The kidneys are located between the levels of the twelfth thoracic vertebra and the third lumbar vertebra, and they are protected by the lower ribs. Each kidney is protected by three layers of connective tissue. A thin *renal capsule* tightly envelops each kidney supporting the soft internal tissues. A thick layer of adipose tissue serves as a cushioning shock absorber, and a fibrous *renal fascia* joins each kidney to the abdominal wall.

Structure

Each kidney is convex laterally and concave medially with a medial indentation called the *hilum.* Blood vessels, lymphatic vessels, nerves, and the ureter enter or exit at the hilum. An adult kidney is about 12 cm long, 7 cm wide, and 2.5 cm thick.

The internal macroscopic structure of a kidney is best observed in coronal section, as shown in figure 16.2*a.* Three regions of the kidney are evident:

the cortex, medulla, and pelvis. The **renal cortex** is the relatively thin, outermost layer. Interior to the cortex is the **renal medulla,** which contains the cone-shaped *renal pyramids.* Renal pyramids contain microscopic **collecting ducts** that extend from the base of each pyramid to its apex. The apex, or *renal papilla,* of each pyramid extends toward the renal pelvis. Narrow portions of the cortex, the *renal columns,* extend into the medulla between the renal pyramids.

The work of the kidneys is performed by microscopic tubules called **nephrons** (nef´-rons). Nephrons originate in the cortex, dip into the medulla, return to the cortex, and ultimately join a collecting duct, as shown in figure 16.2*b.* Nephrons form urine that flows into the collecting ducts of renal pyramids.

The renal papilla of each renal pyramid fits into a funnel-shaped **minor calyx** (kā´-lix), which receives urine from the collecting ducts. Two or three minor calyces (kā´-li-sēz) converge to form a **major calyx,** and two or three major calyces merge to form the funnel-like **renal pelvis.** The renal pelvis is contiguous with the ureter. Thus, the pathway of urine from nephrons to ureter is: nephrons → collecting ducts → minor calyces → major calyces →

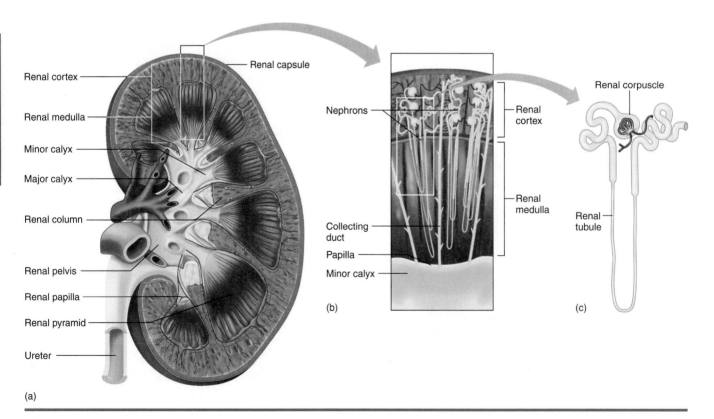

(a)

(b)

(c)

Figure 16.2   Internal structure of the kidney. (*a*) Coronal section of a kidney. (*b*) A renal pyramid showing the orientation of nephrons and collecting ducts. (*c*) A single nephron. **AP|R**

renal pelvis → ureter. Urine is carried by the ureter to the urinary bladder by peristalsis.

Nephron

Each kidney contains about 1 million nephrons, the functional units of the kidneys. A nephron consists of two major parts: a renal corpuscle and a renal tubule. Figure 16.3 shows the structure of a nephron and its associated blood vessels.

Renal corpuscles are located in the renal cortex of the kidneys. Each renal corpuscle is composed of a **glomerulus** (glō-mer´-ū-lus), a tuft of arterial capillaries, which is enclosed in a double-walled **glomerular (Bowman's) capsule.** The glomerular capsule is an expanded extension of a renal tubule.

A **renal tubule** leads away from the glomerular capsule and consists of three sequential segments. The first part of the renal tubule is the *proximal convoluted tubule.* It leads from the glomerular capsule to the *nephron loop,* the U-shaped second part of the tubule. The thin descending arm of the nephron loop dips into the kidney medulla, and the ascending arm of the nephron loop returns to the region of the proximal convoluted tubule. The ascending arm of the nephron loop is continuous with the *distal convoluted tubule,* the third segment of the renal tubule, which unites with a collecting duct. Several nephrons unite with a single collecting duct. Collecting ducts begin in the cortex and extend the length of a renal pyramid to its papilla, where the collecting ducts open into a minor calyx.

Cortical and Juxtamedullary Nephrons

There are two types of nephrons in the kidney: about 80% are cortical nephrons, and about 20% are juxtamedullary nephrons. The glomerular capsules of *cortical nephrons* are located near the outer surface of the kidney cortex. The nephron loops of these nephrons are located almost entirely in the cortex of the kidney. In contrast, the glomerular capsules of *juxtamedullary nephrons* are located in the

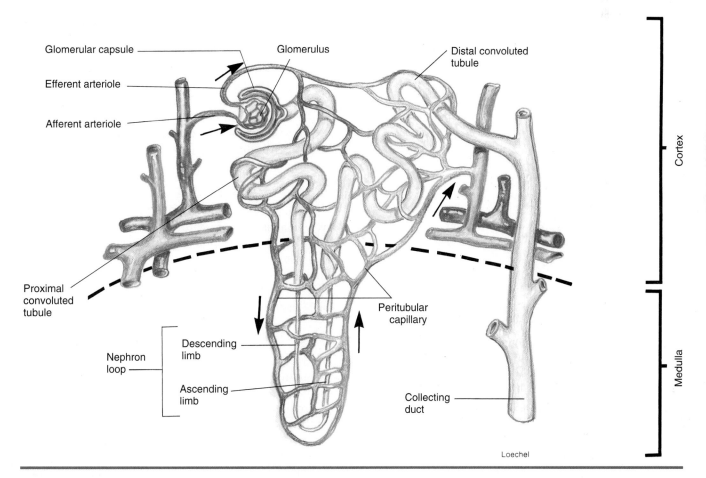

Figure 16.3 A nephron and its associated blood vessels. The nephron has been stretched out to show its parts more clearly. Arrows show the direction of blood flow. **AP|R**

cortex near the medulla. The nephron loops of these nephrons dip deep into the medulla. Juxtamedullary nephrons play an important role in regulating water content of the blood.

Blood Supply

The kidneys receive a large volume of blood—1,200 ml per minute, which is about one-fourth of the total cardiac output. Each kidney receives blood via a *renal artery,* which branches from the abdominal aorta. Within each kidney, the renal artery branches to form a number of *interlobar arteries* that run along the renal columns between the renal pyramids to the cortex. These arteries branch to form smaller and smaller arteries and finally form arterioles.

In the cortex, **afferent arterioles** branch from the smallest arteries, and each afferent arteriole carries blood to a glomerulus. Blood leaves a glomerulus in an **efferent arteriole.** Note that a glomerulus is an arterial capillary tuft sandwiched between two arterioles. The efferent arteriole leads to **peritubular capillaries,** which are entwined around the renal tubule. Blood from the peritubular capillary enters a venule, progressively larger veins that merge to form *interlobar veins,* which finally join to form the renal vein. A *renal vein* carries blood from each kidney to the inferior vena cava (figures 16.3 and 16.4).

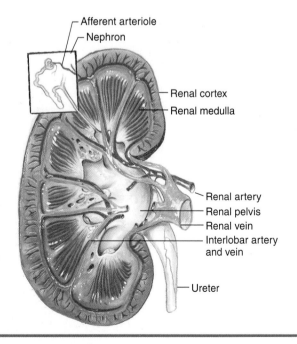

Afferent arteriole
Nephron

Renal cortex
Renal medulla

Renal artery
Renal pelvis
Renal vein
Interlobar artery and vein

Ureter

Figure 16.4 Main branches of the renal artery and renal vein. **AP|R**

Juxtaglomerular Apparatus

The **juxtaglomerular** (juks-tah-glo-mer'-u-lar) **apparatus** of each nephron is located where the ascending arm of the nephron loop contacts the afferent and efferent arterioles near the glomerulus (figure 16.5). It consists of two groups of specialized cells: juxtaglomerular cells and the macula densa. *Juxtaglomerular cells* are large smooth muscle cells in the walls of the afferent and efferent arterioles near their attachment to the glomerulus. The *macula densa* consists of rather narrow, tightly packed cells composing the nephron tubule where it contacts the afferent and efferent arterioles. The juxtaglomerular apparatus helps to regulate blood pressure, as you will see shortly.

Overview of Kidney Functions

1. **Production of urine.** The major function of the kidneys is to keep the volume and composition of blood plasma within normal limits. This is accomplished by the removal of waste products and excess substances from the blood through the formation of urine.
2. **Secretion of renin.** Whenever systemic blood pressure decreases, the kidneys secrete **renin.** Renin is an enzyme that triggers the **renin–angiotensin mechanism,** which increases blood pressure.
3. **Secretion of erythropoietin.** When the blood oxygen level falls below normal (hypoxia), the kidneys release more **erythropoietin,** which stimulates red blood cell formation by red bone marrow. The added red blood cells help increase the blood oxygen level.

Check My Understanding

1. What organs compose the urinary system, and what are their functions?
2. What is the general function of the urinary system?
3. Describe the structure of a kidney.
4. Name the parts of a nephron.

16.2 Urine Formation

The formation of urine is a homeostatic mechanism that maintains the composition and volume of blood plasma within normal limits. In the production of urine, nephrons perform three basic functions: (1) They regulate the concentration of solutes, such as nutrients and ions, in blood plasma, and this also regulates blood pH. (2) They regulate the concentration of water in blood plasma, which in turn helps regulate blood pressure. (3) They remove metabolic wastes and excess substances from the blood plasma.

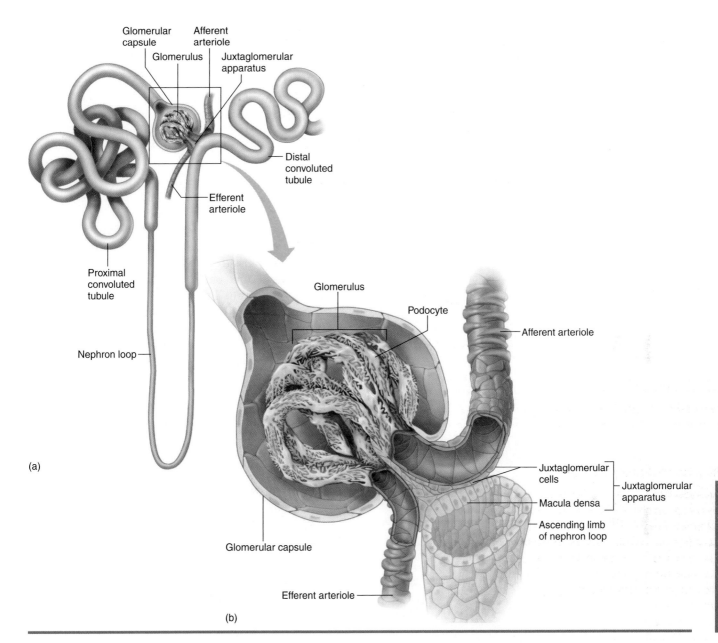

Figure 16.5 Juxtaglomerular apparatus. (*a*) The juxtaglomerular apparatus is located where the ascending arm of the nephron loop contacts the afferent and efferent arterioles near a glomerulus. (*b*) Enlargement showing the juxtaglomerular cells and macula densa, which compose the juxtaglomerular apparatus.

Three processes are crucial to the formation of urine: (1) **Glomerular filtration** moves water and solutes, except plasma proteins, from blood plasma into the nephron to form the filtrate. Blood cells and platelets normally are not part of the filtrate. (2) **Tubular reabsorption** removes useful substances from the filtrate and returns them into the blood, and **tubular secretion** moves additional wastes and excess substances from the blood into the filtrate. (3) **Water reabsorption** removes water from the filtrate and returns it into the blood (figure 16.6).

Glomerular Filtration

Urine formation starts with glomerular filtration, a process that forces some of the water and dissolved substances in blood plasma from the glomeruli into the glomerular (Bowman's) capsules. Two major factors are responsible for filtration: (1) the greater permeability of glomerular capillary walls and (2) the higher blood pressure within the glomeruli.

Glomerular capillaries are much more permeable to substances in the blood than are other capillaries

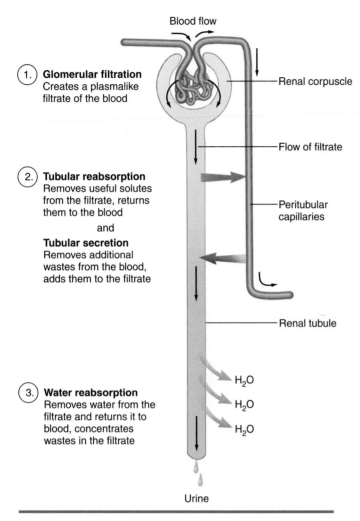

1. **Glomerular filtration**
   Creates a plasmalike filtrate of the blood

2. **Tubular reabsorption**
   Removes useful solutes from the filtrate, returns them to the blood
   and
   Tubular secretion
   Removes additional wastes from the blood, adds them to the filtrate

3. **Water reabsorption**
   Removes water from the filtrate and returns it to blood, concentrates wastes in the filtrate

Renal corpuscle

Flow of filtrate

Peritubular capillaries

Renal tubule

H_2O

H_2O

H_2O

Blood flow

Urine

Figure 16.6   The major steps of urine formation.

because their walls contain numerous pores, as shown in figure 16.7. These pores allow water and most dissolved substances to easily pass through the capillary walls into the glomerular capsules. Unlike other capillaries, glomerular capillaries are enveloped by specialized cells called *podocytes*, which have numerous fingerlike cellular extensions that wrap around the capillaries. Podocytes help prevent plasma proteins, platelets, and blood cells from entering glomerular capsules.

The higher glomerular blood pressure results because the diameter of the efferent arteriole is smaller than that of the afferent arteriole. Because blood can enter a glomerulus at a faster rate than it can leave it, a buildup of blood pressure within the glomerulus occurs. The glomerular blood pressure provides the force for filtration.

The fluid that enters the glomerular capsule is known as the **filtrate.** It consists of the same substances as those composing the blood plasma, except for plasma proteins that are too large to pass through the pores of the glomerular capillaries. Because filtration is a nonselective process, the concentrations of these substances are the same in both blood plasma and filtrate (table 16.1).

Filtration Rate

Glomerular filtration rate (GFR) is about 125 ml per minute, or 7.5 liters per hour. This means that the entire volume of blood is filtered every 40 minutes! In 24 hours, about 180 liters (nearly 45 gallons) of filtrate is produced. However, most of the filtrate is reabsorbed, as you will see shortly.

Maintenance of a relatively stable GFR is necessary for normal kidney function. The GFR varies

Figure 16.7   Filtration is the first step in urine formation. Water and dissolved substances in plasma are filtered through pores in the glomerular capillaries into the glomerular capsule.

Table 16.1	Concentrations of Selected Chemicals in Plasma, Filtrate, and Urine*		
Chemicals	**Plasma (g/l)**	**Filtrate (g/l)**	**Urine (g/l)**
Protein	44.4	0.0	0.0
Chloride (Cl⁻)	3.5	3.5	6.3
Sodium (Na⁺)	3.0	3.0	3.8
Bicarbonate (HCO₃⁻)	1.7	1.7	0.4
Glucose	1.0	1.0	0.0
Urea	0.3	0.3	31.3
Potassium (K⁺)	0.2	0.2	5.0
Uric acid	0.05	0.05	1.0
Creatinine	0.01	0.01	1.9

*Based on 180 liters of filtrate and 1.25 liters of urine produced in a 24-hour period.

directly with glomerular blood pressure, which, in turn, is primarily determined by systemic blood pressure. The GFR is regulated by three homeostatic processes: renal autoregulation, sympathetic control, and the renin–angiotensin mechanism. These processes operate primarily by controlling the diameter of afferent arterioles to keep the GFR within normal limits.

Autoregulation is the mechanism that keeps the GFR within normal limits, without outside neural or hormonal control, in spite of moderate variations in systemic blood pressure. One way this occurs is by the response of smooth muscle in the afferent arteriole wall to blood pressure changes. If the afferent arteriole is stretched by increased blood pressure, it contracts, keeping glomerular blood pressure and the GFR about the same. A decline in blood pressure causes the arteriole to dilate, which keeps the GFR stable.

Another autoregulatory mechanism involves the juxtaglomerular apparatus. If the GFR increases, the juxtaglomerular cells constrict the afferent arteriole, keeping the GFR normal. If the GFR declines, the afferent arteriole relaxes to maintain a normal GFR.

Sympathetic control is a function of the sympathetic nervous system. If a drop in blood pressure is detected, afferent arterioles are constricted, which decreases glomerular pressure and GFR. This decreases urine formation, which conserves water to maintain normal blood pressure and volume. If an increase in blood pressure is detected, the afferent arteriole is dilated, which increases glomerular pressure and the GFR. This results in an increase in urine production and water excretion to maintain normal blood pressure and volume.

The *renin–angiotensin mechanism* is triggered when the juxtaglomerular apparatus detects a reduced filtration rate and releases the enzyme *renin*. Renin is secreted in response to (1) sympathetic stimulation; (2) a drop in blood pressure in the afferent arteriole; and (3) detection of a reduction of sodium, potassium, and chloride ions in the ascending arm of the nephron loop

by the macula densa (see figure 16.5). Renin converts a plasma protein (angiotensinogen), which is formed by the liver, into angiotensin I. Angiotension I is rapidly converted into angiotensin II by the *angiotensin-converting enzyme (ACE)* released from endothelial cells of capillaries in the lungs and other organs. Angiotensin II constricts the efferent arterioles to maintain blood pressure in glomeruli, which maintains an adequate GFR in spite of a decline in blood pressure. It also acts to restore blood volume and blood pressure by (1) constricting systemic arterioles; (2) stimulating aldosterone secretion by the adrenal cortex, which promotes the reabsorption of sodium ions and water; (3) stimulating secretion of antidiuretic hormone by the posterior pituitary, which also promotes water reabsorption; and (4) stimulating thirst, which promotes water intake (figure 16.8).

Clinical **INSIGHT**

Autoregulatory mechanisms cannot maintain glomerular pressure when the mean (average) systemic blood pressure drops to 70 mm Hg or less. At this point, filtration ceases and urine is not formed.

The GFR is increased by the *atrial natriuretic hormone (ANH)*, which is secreted by atria of the heart when they are stretched by an excessive blood volume. ANH also promotes water excretion, which, with the increased GFR, decreases blood pressure and volume.

Tubular Reabsorption and Tubular Secretion

Tubular reabsorption and tubular secretion involve both active and passive transport mechanisms. *Active transport* is powered by ATP and uses carrier molecules

Figure 16.8 The renin–angiotensin mechanism. The multiple actions of angiotensin II help to maintain the GFR and systemic blood pressure.

to reabsorb substances against a concentration gradient. *Passive transport* includes diffusion, osmosis, and electrochemical attraction. The effectiveness of passive transport of any substance depends upon (1) the permeability of the tubule to the substance, and (2) the concentration gradient of the substance.

Events in the Proximal Convoluted Tubule

About 65% of the filtrate is reabsorbed in the proximal convoluted tubule. All nutrients, such as glucose and amino acids, are actively reabsorbed here. Positively charged ions, such as those of sodium (Na^+), potassium (K^+), and calcium (Ca^{++}), are also actively reabsorbed. The active reabsorption of positively charged ions causes negatively charged ions, such as chloride ions (Cl^-) and bicarbonate ions (HCO_3^-), to be passively reabsorbed by electrochemical attraction. The reabsorption of these substances increases the osmotic pressure of the blood plasma in the peritubular capillary and decreases the osmotic pressure of the filtrate. This causes water to be reabsorbed from the filtrate by osmosis (figure 16.9).

Tubular secretion is the process that extracts substances from blood in the peritubular capillary

Figure 16.9 Reabsorption in the proximal convoluted tubule. About 65% of the filtrate volume is reabsorbed from the proximal convoluted tubule into blood in peritubular capillaries.

and secretes them into the filtrate in the renal tubule. Metabolic wastes, such as urea and uric acid, drugs, and hydrogen and bicarbonate ions, are removed from the blood in this way. It not only removes unwanted wastes but also helps regulate the pH of body fluids.

Events in the Nephron Loop

Water is passively reabsorbed by osmosis from the thin-walled descending limb of the nephron loop into the peritubular capillaries, and solutes diffuse in the opposite direction to a lesser extent. Both the thin-walled and the thick-walled portions of the ascending limb are impermeable to water, but solutes are reabsorbed passively by diffusion from the filtrate in the thin-walled segment into the peritubular capillaries (figure 16.10).

The thick-walled segment actively pumps sodium ions out of the filtrate, and potassium and chloride ions follow passively into the interstitial fluid (figure 16.11). Some potassium ions reenter the tubule, but Na^+ and Cl^- remain in the interstitial fluid. The accumulation of ions in the interstitial fluid of the medulla establishes a strong osmotic gradient for the reabsorption of water from the collecting duct. Establishing this osmotic gradient is a major function of the nephron loop.

Tubular secretion does not occur in the nephron loop. At the end of the nephron loop, the filtrate is quite dilute due to the removal of many solutes. It still contains about 20% of the water and 10% of the salts that were present in the glomerular filtrate.

Events in the Distal Convoluted Tubule

Reabsorption in the distal convoluted tubule is under hormonal control. The active reabsorption of sodium ions from the filtrate into peritubular capillaries is promoted by the hormone aldosterone. Passive reabsorption of negative ions, such as chloride and bicarbonate ions, then occurs by electrochemical attraction. The reabsorption of ions decreases the osmotic pressure of the filtrate, which causes water to be reabsorbed into the blood by osmosis. However, the amount of water reabsorbed from the filtrate in the distal convoluted tubule is controlled by the antidiuretic hormone (ADH) (figure 16.12).

Tubular secretion actively moves potassium ions from blood in the peritubular capillary into the distal tubule under the influence of aldosterone. Hydrogen ions are also actively secreted, as necessary, to maintain the normal pH of the blood.

Reabsorption from the Collecting Duct

The filtrate entering the collecting duct is isotonic with (has the same osmotic pressure as) the blood, so it still contains a lot of water. Because the collecting duct extends from the cortex to a renal papilla, the concentration of ions in the surrounding interstitial fluid increases along the length of the collecting duct. Recall that sodium, potassium, and chloride ions have been pumped into the interstitial fluid by the ascending nephron loop. This creates a strong osmotic gradient that causes the passive reabsorption of water from the filtrate in the collecting duct by osmosis. The reabsorption of water causes the filtrate to become concentrated and hypertonic to blood plasma by the time it exits the collecting duct. The reabsorption of water from the collecting duct is regulated by antidiuretic hormone (ADH), which increases the collecting duct's permeability to water (figure 16.12). The remaining filtrate is now called urine. Only 1% of the original filtrate volume remains as urine.

Table 16.2 summarizes the functions of each segment of a nephron in the formation of urine. AP|R

Check My Understanding

5. What are the mechanisms of filtration, tubular reabsorption, and tubular secretion?
6. For each section of a nephron, plus a collecting duct, what substances are reabsorbed from the filtrate and secreted into the filtrate?

16.3 Maintenance of Blood Plasma Composition

The composition and volume of blood plasma are affected by diet, cellular metabolism, and urine production. The intake of food and liquids provides the body with water and a variety of nutrients, including minerals, that are absorbed into the blood. Cellular metabolism depletes nutrients and produces waste products, including nitrogenous wastes. Urine production retains essential nutrients and minerals in the blood but removes some water along with excess substances and nitrogenous wastes. In healthy people, the kidneys are able to keep the composition and volume of the blood plasma relatively constant in spite of variations in diet and cellular activity.

Water and Electrolyte Balance

Two important components of blood plasma and other body fluids are water and electrolytes, and their concentrations in body fluids must be maintained within normal limits. Recall that water is the solvent of body fluids in which the chemical

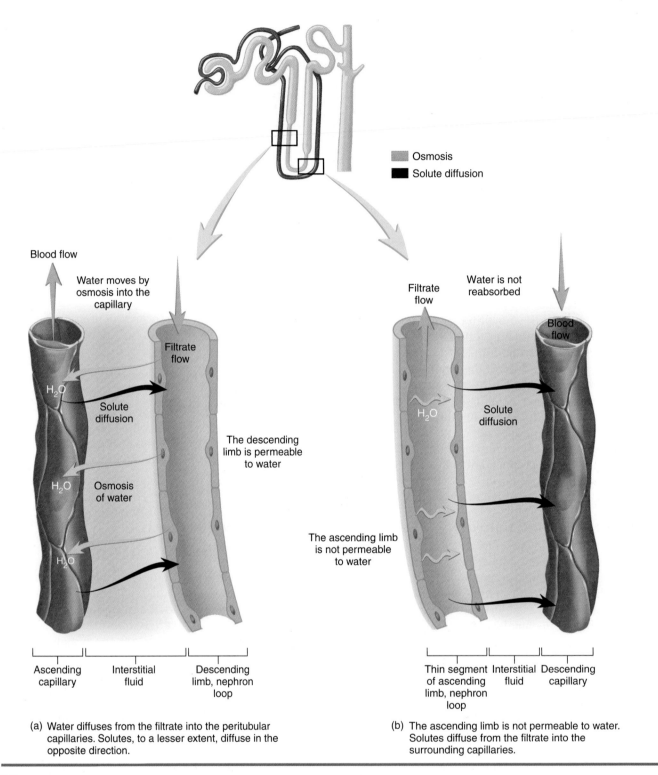

(a) Water diffuses from the filtrate into the peritubular capillaries. Solutes, to a lesser extent, diffuse in the opposite direction.

(b) The ascending limb is not permeable to water. Solutes diffuse from the filtrate into the surrounding capillaries.

Figure 16.10   Reabsorption in the nephron loop: the descending limb and thin segment of the ascending limb.

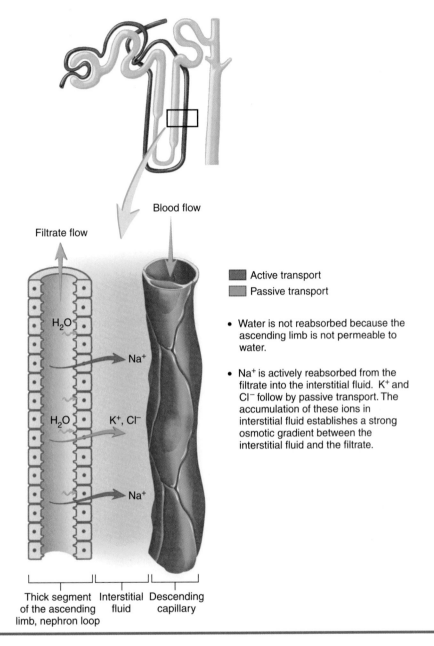

Blood flow

Filtrate flow

■ Active transport
□ Passive transport

- Water is not reabsorbed because the ascending limb is not permeable to water.

- Na⁺ is actively reabsorbed from the filtrate into the interstitial fluid. K⁺ and Cl⁻ follow by passive transport. The accumulation of these ions in interstitial fluid establishes a strong osmotic gradient between the interstitial fluid and the filtrate.

H_2O

Na^+

H_2O K^+, Cl^-

Na^+

Thick segment of the ascending limb, nephron loop

Interstitial fluid

Descending capillary

Figure 16.11 Reabsorption in the nephron loop: the thick segment of the ascending limb.

reactions of life occur. **Electrolytes** are substances that form ions when dissolved in water, and they are so named because they can conduct an electric current when dissolved in water. For example, sodium chloride is an electrolyte that forms sodium and chloride ions (Na^+ and Cl^-, respectively) when dissolved in water.

The concentrations of water and electrolytes in body fluids are interrelated because the concentration of one affects the concentration of the other. For example, the concentration of electrolytes

establishes the concentration gradient that enables water to be reabsorbed by osmosis.

Clinical **INSIGHT**

Substances that increase the production of urine are known as *diuretics*. Physicians often prescribe a diuretic to reduce the volume of body fluids in patients with edema or hypertension.

Figure 16.12 Reabsorption in the distal convoluted tubule and collecting duct.

Water Balance

The intake of water is largely regulated by the *thirst center* located in the hypothalamus of the brain. The thirst center is activated when it detects a decrease in water concentration in the blood. It is also activated by angiotensin II when blood pressure declines significantly. An awareness of thirst stimulates water intake to replace water lost from body fluids. Water intake must balance water loss, and this averages about 2,500 ml per day.

The body loses water in several ways, but about 60% of the total water loss occurs in urine. In addition, water is lost in the humidified air exhaled from the lungs, in feces, and in perspiration (figure 16.13).

However, it is the kidneys that regulate the concentration of water in the blood plasma by controlling the volume of water lost in urine.

The volume of water lost in urine varies with both the volume of water lost by other means and the volume of water intake. These factors affect the action of the kidneys simultaneously, but we consider them separately to better understand how they influence kidney function.

In general, the more water that is lost through other means, the less water that is lost in urine. For example, if excessive water loss occurs through perspiration or diarrhea, more water is reabsorbed from the renal

Table 16.2 Summary of Nephron Functions

Structure	Function
Renal Corpuscle	
Glomerulus	Filtration
	Glomerular blood pressure forces some of the water and dissolved substances (except proteins) from the blood plasma through the pores in the glomerular capillary walls
Glomerular capsule	Receives filtrate from glomerulus
Renal Tubule	
Proximal convoluted tubule	Reabsorption
	Active reabsorption of all nutrients, including glucose and amino acids
	Active reabsorption of positively charged ions like sodium, potassium, calcium, and magnesium in addition to organic acids like lactic, ascorbic, and uric acids
	Passive reabsorption by electrochemical attraction of negatively charged ions such as bicarbonate
	Passive reabsorption of water by osmosis
	Secretion
	Active secretion of hydrogen ions and substances such as histamine and creatinine
Nephron loop	
Descending limb	Reabsorption
	Passive reabsorption of water by osmosis
Ascending limb	Reabsorption
	Active reabsorption of sodium ions into the interstitial fluid of the medulla
	Passive reabsorption of chloride and potassium ions
Distal convoluted tubule	Reabsorption
	Active reabsorption of sodium ions under influence of aldosterone
	Passive reabsorption by electrochemical attraction of negatively charged ions such as chloride and bicarbonate
	Passive reabsorption of water by osmosis under the influence of ADH
	Secretion
	Active secretion of hydrogen ions
	Secretion of potassium ions by passive electrochemical attraction under the influence of aldosterone

tubule. The result is a smaller volume of more concentrated urine. Conversely, if water loss through other means is minimal, water reabsorption is reduced, and a larger volume of more dilute urine is produced.

Similarly, the greater the intake of water, the less water is reabsorbed and a larger volume of more dilute urine is produced. Conversely, the less the intake of water, the more water is reabsorbed and a smaller volume of more concentrated urine is produced.

You can see that regulating water balance is a dynamic process and that water balance is largely controlled by the amount of water reabsorbed from renal tubules and collecting ducts into peritubular capillaries. Whether more or less water is reabsorbed is dependent upon antidiuretic hormone (ADH) secreted by the posterior lobe of the pituitary gland. ADH promotes

Clinical INSIGHT

If water loss significantly exceeds water intake for several days, extracellular fluids may become more concentrated, causing water to move out of the cells by osmosis. This condition, known as *cellular dehydration,* may lead to serious complications unless the water loss is quickly restored. In serious cases, dehydration may result in fever, mental confusion, or coma.

water reabsorption by increasing the permeability of the distal tubules and collecting ducts to water.

When the water concentration of blood is excessive, atrial natriuretic hormone (ANH) is secreted, and

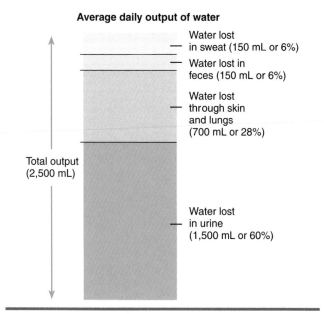

Average daily output of water

Water lost
in sweat (150 mL or 6%)

Water lost in
feces (150 mL or 6%)

Water lost
through skin
and lungs
(700 mL or 28%)

Total output
(2,500 mL)

Water lost
in urine
(1,500 mL or 60%)

Figure 16.13 Pathways of water loss. Urine formation is the most important process that regulates water loss.

Clinical **INSIGHT**

If ADH secretion is deficient, a condition known as *diabetes insipidus* results. It is characterized by an excessive production of dilute urine due to the inability to reabsorb sufficient water from the filtrate. Up to 15 liters of urine may be produced in a single day, which triggers extreme thirst and the almost continuous intake of water. Without treatment, the excessive water loss may lead to severe dehydration and electrolyte imbalances. Patients with this disorder are treated with synthetic ADH to promote water reabsorption.

ADH secretion declines. The combined effect is that less water is reabsorbed and a greater volume of urine (and water) is excreted. The result is a decrease in water concentration in the blood. Conversely, when the water concentration of blood decreases, ANH is not secreted, ADH secretion is increased, more water is reabsorbed, and a smaller volume of urine is produced. ADH minimizes water loss in urine, but it cannot prevent it. Thus, water must be replenished daily by fluid intake.

Electrolyte Balance

Important electrolytes in body fluids include ions of sodium, potassium, calcium, chloride, phosphate, sulfate, and bicarbonate. Electrolytes are obtained from the intake of food and fluids. A craving for salt results when electrolytes are in low concentration in body fluids.

Electrolyte balance is regulated largely by active reabsorption of positively charged ions, which, in turn, secondarily controls the passive reabsorption of negatively charged ions by electrochemical attraction. Sodium ions are the most important ions to be regulated because they compose about 90% of the positively charged ions in extracellular fluids. Certain hormones play important roles in maintaining electrolyte balance.

Aldosterone is a hormone that regulates the balance of sodium and potassium ions in the blood by stimulating the reabsorption of sodium ions and the secretion of potassium ions by the distal tubule. Thus, aldosterone causes an exchange of sodium and potassium ions between the filtrate and the blood until the blood concentrations of these two ions returns to normal. The adrenal cortex is stimulated to secrete aldosterone by (1) an increase of potassium ions (K^+) in the blood, (2) a decrease of sodium ions (Na^+) in the blood, and (3) angiotensin II. As long as blood concentrations of sodium and potassium ions are normal, aldosterone is not secreted. In contrast to aldosterone, atrial natriuretic hormone (ANH) promotes the excretion of sodium ions and water when excess blood volume is detected by the atria of the heart.

The blood concentration of calcium ions (Ca^{++}) is regulated mainly by the antagonistic actions of parathyroid hormone and calcitonin. When the blood calcium concentration declines, the parathyroid glands are stimulated to secrete *parathyroid hormone (PTH)*. PTH promotes an increase in blood calcium by stimulating three different processes: (1) the reabsorption of calcium ions from renal tubules, (2) the resorption of calcium from bones into the blood, and (3) the absorption of calcium in foods by the small intestine. When the blood calcium level returns to normal, parathyroid hormone secretion is curtailed. Table 16.3 summarizes the effect of hormones that act on the kidneys.

In contrast, *calcitonin* is secreted by the thyroid gland when the level of blood calcium is too high. Calcitonin promotes the deposition of calcium in bones, which reduces the level of blood calcium.

Nitrogenous Wastes

A major function of the kidneys is the removal of excess nitrogenous wastes. The kidneys do not remove all of these wastes but keep their concentrations in the blood within tolerable limits. The primary nitrogenous wastes produced by cellular metabolism are urea, uric acid, and creatinine (see table 16.1).

Urea is a waste product of amino acid metabolism. For amino acids to be used as an energy source in cellular respiration or converted into glucose or fat, the liver removes the amine (—NH_2) groups from them. The amine groups react to form ammonia, which is

Table 16.3   Hormones Acting on the Kidneys

Hormone	Source	Action
Aldosterone	Adrenal cortex	Stimulates reabsorption of Na^+ from the filtrate into the blood; stimulates the secretion of K^+ from blood into the filtrate
Antidiuretic hormone	Posterior pituitary	Stimulates the reabsorption of water from the filtrate into the blood by making the distal tubule and collecting ducts more permeable to water; decreases the volume of urine produced
Atrial natriuretic hormone	Heart	Inhibits reabsorption of Na^+ and water from distal convoluted tubules and collecting ducts
Parathyroid hormone	Parathyroid glands	Stimulates the reabsorption of Ca^{++} from the filtrate into the blood; stimulates the secretion of PO_4^-

converted to the less toxic urea by the liver. About 40% of the urea in the filtrate is passively reabsorbed by diffusion, and the remainder is excreted in urine.

Uric acid is a waste product of nucleic acid metabolism. Much of the uric acid in the filtrate is reabsorbed by the renal tubules, but enough is actively secreted into the filtrate to keep the blood concentration of uric acid within normal limits.

Creatinine is a waste product of muscle metabolism and, specifically, the breakdown of creatine phosphate. It is actively secreted by the distal tubule.

pH Balance

The pH of the blood must be maintained within rather narrow limits—pH 7.35 to pH 7.45—for body cells to function properly. Cellular metabolism produces products that tend to upset the pH balance. These

An abnormally high concentration of uric acid in the blood and the deposition of uric acid crystals in joints are characteristic of a hereditary disorder called *gout*. Joints of the hands and feet are often the sites of uric acid deposition, which produces inflammation and severe pain.

products, such as lactic acid, phosphoric acid, and carbonic acid, tend to make the blood more acidic, as shown in figure 16.14.

Acids are substances that release hydrogen ions (H^+) when they are in water, which lowers the pH and increases the acidity of the liquid. Strong acids release

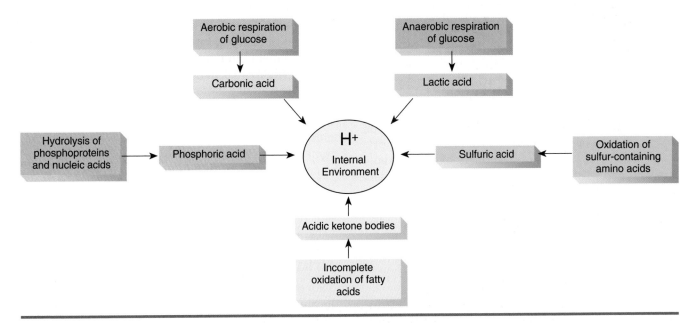

Figure 16.14 Examples of metabolic processes that increase the hydrogen ion concentration of body fluids.

Clinical INSIGHT

The kidneys have a tremendous functional reserve. Renal insufficiency becomes evident only after about 75% of the renal functions have been lost. As the development of renal failure progresses, patients must rely on *hemodialysis* as a means of removing wastes and excessive substances from the blood. In hemodialysis, the patient's blood is pumped through selectively permeable tubes that are immersed in a dialyzing solution within a "kidney machine." Nitrogenous wastes and excessive electrolytes diffuse from the blood into the dialyzing solution, while certain needed substances, such as buffers, diffuse from the dialyzing solution into the blood. In this way, the concentration of wastes and electrolytes in the patient's blood are temporarily restored within normal limits. Hemodialysis may be required two to three times per week for patients with chronic kidney failure.

An alternative method is called *continuous ambulatory peritoneal dialysis (CAPD)*. In this technique, 1 to 3 liters of dialyzing fluid are introduced into the peritoneal cavity through an opening made in the abdominal wall. Waste products and excessive substances diffuse from blood vessels in the peritoneal membrane into the dialyzing solution, which is drained after two to three hours. This technique is less costly, may be done at home, and allows the patient to move about during the procedure. However, it must be done more frequently than dialysis using a kidney machine, and there is a greater chance of serious infection.

more hydrogen ions than weak acids. **Bases** are substances that, when placed in water, release ions that can combine with hydrogen ions, such as hydroxide or bicarbonate ions (OH^- or HCO_3^-). Body fluids contain both acids and bases.

The blood and other body fluids contain chemicals known as **buffers** that prevent significant changes in pH. Buffers are able to combine with or release hydrogen ions as needed to stabilize the pH. If the hydrogen ion concentration is excessive, buffers combine with some hydrogen ions to reduce their concentration. Conversely, if too few hydrogen ions are present, buffers release some hydrogen ions to increase their concentration to within normal limits. In this way, buffers help to keep the pH of the blood relatively constant.

$$\text{Buffer} + H^+ \rightleftharpoons \text{Buffer}-H^+$$

The removal of excess hydrogen ions by the kidneys prevents the buffers from being overwhelmed. Tubular secretion actively transports excess hydrogen ions from blood in peritubular capillaries into the filtrate in the renal tubules. By excreting excess hydrogen ions in urine, kidneys help to maintain the normal pH of body fluids.

The respiratory system also plays a significant role in regulating H^+ concentration of body fluids. Recall that the production of CO_2 results in the formation of carbonic acid, which dissociates to release H^+. When CO_2 production increases, blood pH increases, and this stimulates the respiratory center in the brain stem to increase the depth and rate of breathing to remove the excess CO_2. Conversely, when the H^+ concentration of the blood is too low, the depth and rate of breathing are decreased until the H^+ concentration increases to normal.

Check My Understanding

7. Describe the action of hormones regulating water and electrolyte concentrations in blood.
8. What are the nitrogenous wastes in urine, and how are they formed?

16.4 Excretion of Urine

Once the filtrate passes from collecting ducts into the renal pelvis, it is called urine. Urine passes from the renal pelvis into the ureter and is carried by peristalsis to the urinary bladder. Urine is voided from the bladder through the urethra.

Ureters

Each **ureter** is a slender tube about 25 cm (10 in) long that extends from a kidney to the urinary bladder. It begins at the kidney with the funnel-shaped renal pelvis and enters the lower lateral margin of the urinary bladder (figures 16.1 and 16.15).

The wall of a ureter is formed of three layers. The outer fibrous layer is composed of supportive connective tissue. The middle layer consists of smooth muscle fibers that produce peristaltic waves for urine transport. The inner layer is a mucous membrane that is continuous with that of the kidney pelvis and the urinary bladder. A flaplike fold of mucous membrane in the urinary bladder covers the opening of the ureter, and it functions as a valve that prevents urine from backing up into the ureter.

Urinary Bladder

The **urinary bladder** is a hollow, muscular organ located posterior to the symphysis pubis within the pelvic cavity. It lies inferior to the parietal peritoneum. The urinary bladder provides temporary storage

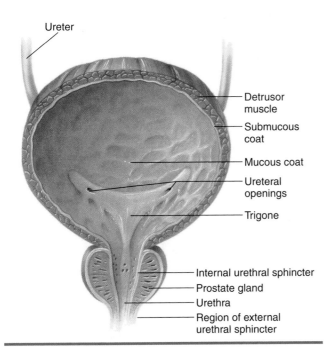

Figure 16.15 A male urinary bladder in coronal section. AP|R

of urine, and its shape varies with the volume of urine that it contains. When distended with urine, it is almost spherical as its upper surface expands upward. When empty, its upper portion is lowered, giving a deflated appearance.

The internal floor of the bladder contains the *trigone* (tri´-gōn), a smooth, triangular area that contains an opening at each of its angles. The openings of the ureters are located at the two posteriorly located base angles, and the opening of the urethra is located at the anteriorly located apex angle (figure 16.15).

Four layers compose the wall of the bladder. The innermost layer is the *mucosa,* which is composed of transitional epithelium that is adapted to the repeated stretching of the bladder wall. The epithelium stretches, and its thickness decreases as the bladder fills with urine.

The mucosa is supported by the underlying *submucosa* formed of connective tissue containing an abundance of elastic fibers. Blood vessels and nerves supplying the urinary bladder are present in the submucosa.

Smooth muscle fibers compose the third, and thickest, layer. These fibers form the *detrusor* (dē-trū´-sor) *muscle.* The detrusor muscle is relaxed as the bladder fills with urine, and it contracts as urine is expelled. Fibers of the detrusor muscle form an *internal urethral sphincter* at the junction of the bladder and urethra.

The outermost layer consists of the parietal peritoneum, but it covers only the upper portion of the

urinary bladder. The remainder of the bladder surface is coated with fibrous connective tissue.

Urethra

The **urethra** is a thin-walled tube that carries urine from the bladder to the outside. The urethral wall contains smooth muscle fibers and is supported by connective tissue. The inner lining is a mucous membrane that is continuous with the mucous membrane of the urinary bladder. An *external urethral sphincter,* which is composed of skeletal muscle fibers in the floor of the pelvis, is located where the urethra penetrates the pelvic floor.

The female urethra is quite short, about 3 to 4 cm (1.5 in) in length. Its external opening lies anterior to the vagina. The male urethra is much longer, about 16 to 20 cm (6–8 in) in length, because the urethra runs the length of the penis. The external opening is at the tip of the penis.

An infant is not able to be toilet trained until neural development allows control of the external urethral sphincter muscle. Voluntary control is possible shortly after two years of age.

Micturition AP|R

Micturition (mik-tū-rish´un), or urination, is the act of expelling urine from the bladder. Although the bladder may hold up to 1,000 ml of urine, micturition usually occurs long before that volume is attained. When 200 to 400 ml of urine have accumulated in the urinary bladder, stretch receptors in the bladder wall are stimulated and they trigger the *micturition reflex.* This reflex sends parasympathetic impulses to the detrusor muscle, causing rhythmic contractions. As this reflex continues, it causes the involuntarily controlled internal urethral sphincter to open. If the voluntarily controlled external urethral sphincter is relaxed, micturition occurs; if it is not relaxed, micturition is postponed.

Micturition may be postponed by keeping the external sphincter voluntarily closed, and in a few moments the urge to urinate subsides. After more urine enters the urinary bladder, the micturition reflex is activated again, and the urge to urinate returns. Micturition cannot be postponed for long periods of time. After a while, the reflex overwhelms voluntary control and micturition occurs, ready or not.

16.5 Characteristics of Urine

The volume of urine produced in a 24-hour period usually is 1.5 to 2.0 liters. In healthy persons, fresh urine is usually clear with a pale yellow to light amber color and a characteristic odor. The color is due to the presence of *urochrome,* a substance produced by the breakdown of bile pigments in the intestine. The more concentrated the urine, the darker is its color.

Urine is usually slightly acidic (about pH 6), although the normal pH range extends from 4.7 to 8.0. Variations in pH usually result from the diet. High-protein diets increase the acidity. Conversely, vegetarian diets tend to make the urine more alkaline.

Urine is heavier than water because of the many solutes it contains. The term *specific gravity* is used to compare how much heavier urine is than water. Pure water has a specific gravity of 1.000, and the specific gravity of normal urine ranges from 1.001 (dilute urine) to 1.035 (concentrated urine). Specific gravity is a measure of the concentration of a urine sample.

The usual solutes of urine have been discussed earlier in the section on urine formation. Substances not normally found in urine are glucose, proteins, red or white blood cells, hemoglobin, and bile pigments. The presence of any of these substances suggests possible pathological conditions. Normal values of urine components and some indications of abnormal values are listed on the inside back cover.

Check My Understanding

9. How is micturition controlled?
10. What substances, if present in urine, indicate a urinary disorder?

16.6 Disorders of the Urinary System

These disorders are grouped as inflammatory or noninflammatory.

Inflammatory Disorders

Cystitis (sis-tī´-tis) is the inflammation of the urinary bladder. It is often caused by bacterial infection. Females are more prone to cystitis because their shorter urethra makes it easier for bacteria to reach the urinary bladder.

Glomerulonephritis (glō-mer-ū-lō-ne-frī´-tis) is the inflammation of a kidney involving the glomeruli. It may be caused by bacteria or bacterial toxins. The inflamed glomeruli become more permeable, allowing blood cells and proteins to leak into the filtrate and remain in the urine.

Pyelonephritis (pī-e-lō-ne-frī´-tis) is the inflammation of the renal pelvis and nephrons. If only the renal pelvis is involved, the condition is called *pyelitis.* These conditions result from bacteria carried by blood from other places in the body or by migration of bacteria from lower portions of the urinary tract.

Urethritis is the inflammation of the urethra. It may be caused by several types of bacteria, but the bacterium *Escherichia coli* is the most common. Urethritis is more common in females.

Noninflammatory Disorders

Diuresis is the excessive production of urine. It results from inadequate tubular reabsorption of water and is characteristic of diabetes insipidus.

Renal calculi (kal´-kū-li), or kidney stones, result from crystallization of uric acid or of calcium or magnesium salts in the renal pelvis. They can cause extreme pain, especially when moving through a ureter by peristalsis. A new treatment using ultrasound waves to break up the stones is proving successful as an alternative to surgery.

Renal failure is characterized by a reduction in urine production and a failure to maintain the normal volume and composition of body fluids. It may occur suddenly (acute) or gradually (chronic). Renal failure leads to *uremia,* a toxic condition caused by excessive nitrogenous wastes in the blood, and ultimately to *anuria,* a cessation of urine production. Hemodialysis and/or a kidney transplant may be necessary.

Clinical INSIGHT

A routine urinalysis is a common clinical test that provides information about kidney function and also about general health of the body. Kidney function is also assessed by two blood tests. The *blood urea nitrogen (BUN)* test evaluates how effectively the kidney removes urea from the blood and other substances as well. The normal BUN value is 5 to 25 mg per 100 ml of blood. In acute kidney failure and in later stages of chronic kidney failure, BUN may range from 50 to 200 mg per 100 ml of blood. *Blood (serum) creatinine* is another test that assesses kidney effectiveness. Creatinine levels in the blood are normally stable (0.6–1.5 mg/100 ml), so an increase indicates a decrease in kidney function.

CHAPTER SUMMARY

16.1 Kidneys

- The paired kidneys are located against the upper posterior abdominal wall, posterior to the parietal peritoneum.
- Internal structure of a kidney consists of three recognizable parts: an outer cortex, a medulla composed of renal pyramids, and a medially located renal pelvis, which is continuous with a ureter.
- Nephrons are the functional units of the kidneys. Each nephron consists of a renal corpuscle and a renal tubule. A renal corpuscle is composed of a glomerulus and a glomerular (Bowman's) capsule. A renal tubule is composed of a proximal convoluted tubule, the loop of Henle, and a distal convoluted tubule.
- Each nephron joins with a collecting duct that empties into a calyx of the renal pelvis.
- The blood supply for each kidney is provided by a renal artery and renal vein.
- An afferent arteriole brings blood to a glomerulus. Blood exits the glomerulus via an efferent arteriole and flows through the peritubular capillary, which entwines around the renal tubule.
- The juxtaglomerular apparatus consists of modified cells of the afferent arteriole and the distal convoluted tubule at their point of contact.
- The functions of the kidneys are the production of urine and the secretion of renin and erythropoietin.

16.2 Urine Formation

- The process of urine formation regulates the composition and volume of blood plasma by removing excess nitrogenous wastes and surplus substances from the blood plasma.
- Urine is formed by three sequential processes: filtration, tubular reabsorption and secretion, and water reabsorption.
- In filtration, water and dissolved substances (except plasma proteins) in blood plasma are filtered from the glomerulus into the glomerular capsule. Filtration results from the greater permeability of glomerular capillaries and the greater blood pressure within the glomerulus.
- About 180 liters of filtrate are formed in a 24-hour period.
- Filtration rate is proportional to the glomerular blood pressure. Glomerular blood pressure is maintained by mechanisms that control the diameters of the afferent and efferent arterioles.
- Glomerular blood pressure generally varies directly with systemic blood pressure. Glomerular filtration rate is regulated by autoregulation, sympathetic control, and the renin–angiotensin mechanism.

- In tubular reabsorption, needed substances are reabsorbed back into the blood of the peritubular capillary by either active or passive transport.
- Positively charged ions, amino acids, and glucose are actively reabsorbed. Negatively charged ions are passively reabsorbed by electrochemical attraction to the positively charged ions. Water is passively reabsorbed by osmosis, and substances not actively absorbed, such as urea, may be partially reabsorbed by diffusion.
- Most tubular reabsorption occurs in the proximal tubule, but other portions of the tubule are also involved.
- In tubular secretion, certain substances are actively or passively secreted into the filtrate from the blood. Uric acid and hydrogen ions are actively secreted. Potassium ions are secreted passively.
- The filtrate is concentrated by water reabsorption from the collecting duct so it is hypertonic to blood plasma.

16.3 Maintenance of Blood Plasma Composition

- The prime function of the kidneys is to maintain the volume and composition of the blood plasma in spite of variations in diet and metabolic processes.
- Water intake must equal water loss. Most water is lost in urine, but other avenues include exhaled air, perspiration, and feces.
- The volume of water lost in urine is decreased when water loss via other means is increased, and vice versa.
- Antidiuretic hormone (ADH), which is released from the posterior pituitary gland, increases the permeability of distal tubules and collecting ducts to water and thereby promotes water reabsorption by osmosis.
- Electrolyte intake must replace electrolyte loss. Electrolytes are conserved largely by the active reabsorption of positively charged ions that passively pull along negatively charged ions by electrochemical attraction.
- Aldosterone regulates the plasma concentration of sodium and potassium ions by stimulating the active reabsorption of sodium ions and the secretion of potassium ions.
- Atrial natriuretic hormone (ANH) promotes the excretion of sodium ions and water to decrease the concentration of water in the blood.
- The concentration of calcium ions in the blood is regulated by the antagonistic actions of two hormones. Parathyroid hormone increases Ca^{++} in blood by stimulating the reabsorption of calcium from bones into the blood, the reabsorption of calcium ions by the kidneys, and the absorption of

calcium by the small intestine. In contrast, calcitonin decreases Ca++ in blood by promoting the deposition of calcium in bones.

- A major function of the kidneys is the removal of excess nitrogenous wastes—urea, uric acid, and creatinine—in order to keep their concentrations in the blood within normal limits.
- The maintenance of the pH of the blood between 7.35 and 7.45 includes three major mechanisms: buffers in the blood either combine with or release hydrogen ions as needed; carbon dioxide is removed by the lungs; and renal tubules secrete excess hydrogen ions into the filtrate.

16.4 Excretion of Urine

- Urine is the fluid that flows from collecting tubules into the renal pelvis and on into the ureter. A ureter is a slender tube that carries urine by peristalsis into the urinary bladder.
- Urine is temporarily held in the urinary bladder. The urinary bladder is located posterior to the symphysis pubis in the pelvic cavity.
- The wall of the urinary bladder consists of the mucosa, submucosa, muscle layer, and fibrous connective tissue. The parietal peritoneum covers only its upper surface. The muscular layer consists of smooth muscle fibers forming the detrusor muscle.
- A thickening of the detrusor muscle at the bladder–urethra junction forms the internal urethral sphincter. The external urethral sphincter is formed of skeletal muscle fibers in the floor of the pelvis.

- Micturition is the process of voiding urine from the urinary bladder. Urine is expelled from the urinary bladder through the urethra.
- When the bladder contains 200 to 400 ml of urine, the micturition reflex is triggered, causing the detrusor muscle to contract rhythmically. Continued contractions open the involuntarily controlled internal urethral sphincter. If the voluntarily controlled external urethral sphincter is relaxed, micturition occurs. If not, micturition is postponed.

16.5 Characteristics of Urine

- The daily production of urine is 1.5 to 2.0 liters. Normal urine is a clear, pale yellow to amber fluid with a characteristic odor. The color is due to the presence of urochrome.
- Urine is usually slightly acidic but the pH may range from 4.7 to 8.0.
- Urine is heavier than water due to the dissolved substances that it contains.
- Abnormal substances that may be in urine are glucose, proteins, blood cells, hemoglobin, and bile pigments.

16.6 Disorders of the Urinary System

- Inflammatory disorders include cystitis, glomerulonephritis, pyelonephritis, and urethritis.
- Noninflammatory disorders include diuresis, renal calculi, and renal failure.

BUILDING MY VOCABULARY

1. **Selected New Terms**
   afferent arteriole, p. 340
   angiotensin, p. 340
   calyx, p. 338
   creatinine, p. 351
   efferent arteriole, p. 340
   renal cortex, p. 338
   renal medulla, p. 338
   renal pelvis, p. 338
   renin, p. 340
   urea, p. 350
   ureter, p. 352
   urethra, p. 353
   uric acid, p. 351

2. **Related Clinical Terms**
   Cystocoele (sis´-tō-sel) Herniation of the urinary bladder into the vagina; often a result of tearing pelvic muscles during childbirth.
   Enuresis (en-ū-rē´-sis) Involuntary urination.
   Incontinence (in-kon´-ti-nens) Inability to control urination or defecation.
   Pyelogram (pī-el´-ō-gram) An X-ray of the kidney and ureter, usually after intravenous injection of a contrast material.
   Uremia (u-rē´-mē-ah) An excessive level of urea in the blood.
   Urology (ū-rol´-ō-jē) The medical specialty dealing with disorders of the urinary system.

SELF-REVIEW

Answers are located in appendix B.

1. The functional units of the kidneys are called _____.
2. Renal corpuscles, proximal convoluted tubules, and distal convoluted tubules are located in the _____ of a kidney.
3. Renal pyramids are located in the _____ of a kidney, and they are composed mostly of _____.
4. The force powering filtration is _____ blood pressure, which, in turn, is primarily determined by the _____ blood pressure.
5. In filtration, water and dissolved substances that are forced from blood in the glomerulus into the _____ compose the _____.
6. In tubular reabsorption, certain substances pass from the _____ in the renal tubules into blood in the _____.
7. Glucose, amino acids, and positively charged ions are _____ reabsorbed, and water is _____ reabsorbed by _____.

8. A severe drop in blood pressure causes the juxtaglomerular apparatus to secrete _____, which triggers a mechanism to raise blood pressure by chemical means.
9. The _____ hormone promotes the reabsorption of water by making the distal tubule and _____ more permeable to water.
10. The hormone _____ promotes the reabsorption of sodium ions and secretion of _____ ions.
11. Fluid in the renal pelvis is called _____.
12. The _____ carry urine to the urinary bladder by _____.
13. Urine is voided from the urinary bladder via the _____.
14. The _____ urethral sphincter is involuntarily controlled, and the _____ sphincter is voluntarily controlled.
15. Water lost in urine composes about _____% of the total water loss from the body.

CRITICAL THINKING

1. Complete the learning objectives on the first page of this chapter.
2. What mechanisms help ensure an adequate glomerular blood pressure?
3. How would perspiring heavily on a hot day affect a person's urine production?
4. How do the kidneys help regulate erythrocyte production?
5. How is the acid–base balance of the blood maintained?

Visit this book's website at www.mhhe.com/ gunstream5 for practice quizzes, learning exercises, case studies, and other study tools.

CHAPTER 17

Reproductive Systems

Chapter Preview & Learning Objectives

Male Reproductive System
1. Identify the organs of the male reproductive system and describe the functions of each one.
2. Describe spermatogenesis.

Male Sexual Response
3. Describe the male sexual response.

Hormonal Control of Reproduction in Males
4. Describe the actions of testosterone.
5. Describe the hormonal control of testosterone secretion.

Female Reproductive System
6. Identify the organs of the female reproductive system and describe the functions of each one.
7. Describe oogenesis.

Female Sexual Response
8. Describe the female sexual response.

Hormonal Control of Reproduction in Females
9. Describe the ovarian and menstrual cycles and their regulation by hormones.

Mammary Glands
10. Describe the structure of mammary glands and breasts.

Birth Control
11. Identify the various methods of birth control, describe how they work, and outline the effectiveness of each one.

Disorders of the Reproductive Systems
12. Describe the common disorders of the reproductive systems.

Chapter Summary
Building My Vocabulary
Self-Review
Critical Thinking

Anatomy & Physiology REVEALED
aprevealed.com

Module 14
Reproductive System

Gamete A sex cell, either a sperm or an ovum.

Gonads (gone = seed) The sex glands—the ovaries and testes—that produce sex cells.

Meiosis (mei = less) A form of cell division in which the daughter cells contain one-half the number of chromosomes as the parent cell.

Menopause (men = month; paus = stop) The cessation of monthly female reproductive cycles.

Menstrual cycle The monthly female reproductive cycle.

Oogenesis (oo = ovum, egg; genesis = origin) The process of ova formation in the ovaries.

Ovulation The release of a female sex cell from an ovary.

Puberty (puber = grown up) The age at which reproductive organs mature.

Semen (semin = seed) Fluid composed of sperm and secretions of male accessory reproductive glands.

Spermatogenesis The process of sperm formation in the testes.

---

eproduction is the process by which life is sustained from one generation to the next. The human male and female reproductive systems are specially adapted for their roles in reproduction. The **gonads** (gō´-nads)—the ovaries and testes—form the **gametes** (sex cells). Other reproductive organs nurture or transport male and female sex cells to sites where they may unite. The fertilized egg develops within the female reproductive system and culminates in the birth of a baby. Sexual maturation and the development of sex cells in both sexes and pregnancy in females are regulated by hormones secreted by the pituitary gland and the gonads.

17.1 Male Reproductive System

The primary functions of the male reproductive system are the production of male hormones, the formation of sperm cells (spermatozoa), and the placement of sperm cells in the female reproductive tract, where one sperm can unite with a female sex cell. The organs of the male reproductive system include (1) paired testes, which produce sperm and male hormones; (2) ducts that store and transport sperm; (3) accessory glands, whose secretions form part of the semen; and (4) external accessory structures including the scrotum and penis (figure 17.1).

Testes

The paired **testes** (tes´-tēz), or **testicles** (tes´-ti´kulz), are the male gonads, or sex glands. Each testis is protected and supported by a capsule of fibrous connective tissue. Septa (partitions) of connective tissue radiate into the testis from its posterior surface, dividing the testis into internal subdivisions called *lobules*. Each lobule contains several highly coiled **seminiferous** (se-mi-nif´-er-us) **tubules.** Seminiferous tubules are lined with **germinal** (jer´-mi-nal) **epithelium,** which is formed of spermatogenic cells and supporting cells. *Spermatogenic cells* divide to produce sperm, and *supporting cells* support and nourish the spermatogenic cells and help regulate sperm formation. The cells that fill the spaces between the seminiferous tubules are known as **interstitial** (in-ter-stish´-al) **cells,** and they produce the male sex hormone (figure 17.2).

Spermatogenesis

Spermatogenesis (sper-mah-tō-jen´-e-sis) is the process that produces sperm cells by the division of the spermatogenic cells in the germinal epithelium. Sperm production begins at **puberty** (pū´-ber-tē), the development of reproductive potential, and continues throughout the life of a male. Sexual maturity and sperm production are controlled by follicle-stimulating hormone (FSH) and luteinizing hormone (LH) from the anterior pituitary gland and by testosterone from interstial cells of the testes. LH is often called interstitial cell–stimulating hormone (ICSH) in males. Hormonal relationships are discussed later in this chapter.

Seminiferous tubules have a thick epithelium and a small lumen. The epithelium consists of *spermatogenic cells*, cells that form sperm, embedded in *supporting cells* (sustentacular cells) that support and nourish the cells undergoing spermatogenesis. The large, outermost cells of a seminiferous tubule are known as **spermatogonia** (sper-mah-to-gō´-nē-ah), and they compose the germinal epithelium. Each spermatogonium contains 46 chromosomes (23 pairs), the normal number of chromosomes for human body cells. Each spermatogonium divides by mitosis to produce two spermatogonia, each with 46 chromosomes. One spermatogonium (type A) remains next to the margin of the tubule. It will serve as the "stem" spermatogonium and will divide

Figure 17.1 Male reproductive system in a midsagittal section. AP|R

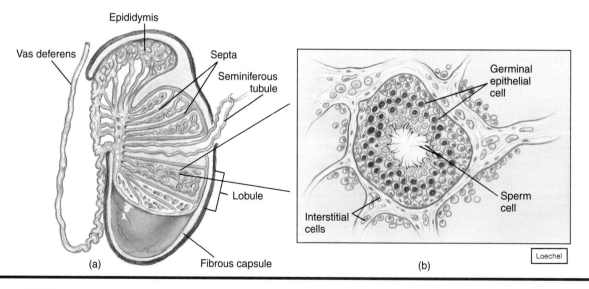

Figure 17.2 (*a*) Testis in sagittal section; (*b*) seminiferous tubule in cross section. AP|R

repeatedly by mitosis. The spermatogonium (type B) that is pushed inward toward the lumen of the tubule undergoes changes to become a **primary spermatocyte** (figure 17.3).

Primary spermatocytes divide by **meiosis** (mī-ō´-sis), a special type of cell division. Meiosis requires two successive divisions and reduces the number of chromosomes in the daughter cells by one-half.

(a)

Sperm cells

Spermatogonia

Seminiferous tubule

Interstitial cells

Figure 17.3 Spermatogenesis. (*a*) A photomicrograph of seminiferous tubules in cross section (200×); (*b*) a diagram showing the sequence of stages in spermatogenesis. Note that cells in developmental stages are embedded in a supporting cell until sperm are released into the lumen of a seminiferous tubule. AP|R

(b)

Changes in chromosome structure

Spermatozoa (Sperm cells, 23 chromosomes, 1 chromatid per chromosome)

Supporting cells

Nucleus of supporting cell

Spermatid (23 chromosomes, 1 chromatid per chromosome)

Meiosis II

Secondary spermatocyte (23 chromosomes, 2 chromatids per chromosome)

Meiosis I

Primary spermatocyte (46 chromosomes, 2 chromatids per chromosome)

Spermatogonium mitosis

Daughter cell in late interphase (type B spermatogonium, 46 chromosomes, 2 chromatids per chromosome)

Daughter cell in late interphase (new type A spermatogonium, 46 chromosomes, 2 chromatids per chromosome)

Basement membrane

Lumen of seminiferous tubule

Wall of seminiferous tubule

Developmental sequence

Meiotic divisions in spermatogenesis are summarized in figures 17.3 and 17.4. Each primary spermatocyte, containing 46 chromosomes, divides in the first meiotic division to form two **secondary spermatocytes,** each containing 23 chromosomes. Prior to meiosis I, the chromosomes replicate. Each replicated chromosome is composed of two *chromatids* joined together at a region called a *centromere.* During metaphase of meiosis I, the replicated chromosomes are arranged as homologous pairs. During cytokinesis, the members of each chromosome pair are separated into different daughter cells. Thus, each secondary spermatocyte is haploid, containing 23 replicated chromosomes (figure 17.4).

In the second meiotic division, the chromatids separate into different daughter cells so each secondary spermatocyte divides to form two **spermatids,** each containing 23 chromosomes. Each spermatid attaches to a supporting cell, gradually loses much of its cytoplasm, and develops a flagellum to form a sperm cell containing 23 chromosomes.

Examine figure 17.3 and note how cells in stages of spermatogenesis are arranged in sequence from outside inward, with sperm cells located in the lumen of the tubule. Once the sperm cells are completely formed, they are carried into the epididymis, where they are temporarily stored while they mature.

A mature **sperm** consists of a head, body, and flagellum. The flattened *head* is composed of a compact nucleus containing 23 chromosomes. The anterior portion of the head is covered by a caplike structure, the *acrosome.* The acrosome contains an enzyme that helps the sperm penetrate a female sex cell. The *body* contains mitochondria, where ATP is formed to power the movements of the *flagellum,* which enables movement (figure 17.5).

Accessory Ducts

Sperm cells pass through a series of accessory ducts as they are carried from the testes to outside the body. These accessory ducts include the epididymis, vas deferens, ejaculatory duct, and urethra.

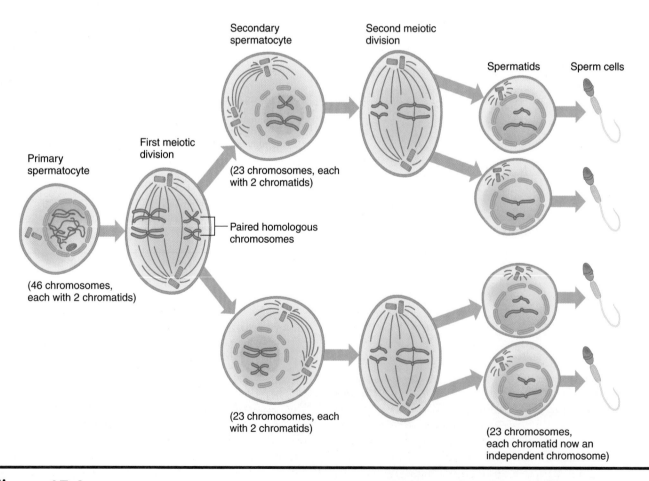

Figure 17.4 Spermatogenesis requires two successive meiotic divisions plus the development of spermatids into sperm cells. AP|R

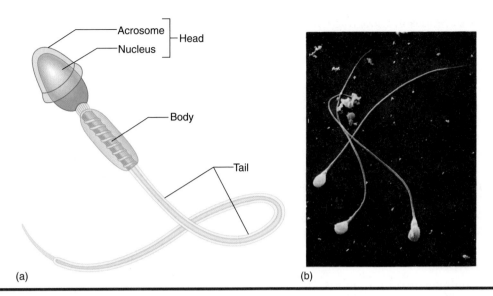

Figure 17.5 (*a*) Parts of a mature sperm cell. (*b*) Scanning electron photomicrograph of human sperm cells (1,400×).

Epididymis

The seminiferous tubules of a testis lead to a number of small ducts that open into the epididymis. The **epididymis** (ep-i-did´-i-mis) (plural, *epididymides*) appears as a comma-shaped organ that lies along the superior and posterior margins of a testis (see figure 17.1). Upon close examination, the epididymis is shown to be a long (6 m), tightly coiled, slender tube that is continuous with the vas deferens (see figure 17.2).

Sperm cells mature as they are slowly moved (10–14 days) through the epididymis by weak peristaltic contractions.

Vas Deferens

As shown in figure 17.1, a **vas deferens** (vas def´-er-enz) (plural, *vasa deferentia*) extends from the epididymis upward in the scrotum, passes through the inguinal canal, and enters the pelvic cavity. It runs along the lateral surface of the urinary bladder and merges with the duct from a seminal vesicle under the urinary bladder. The duct formed by this merger is an ejaculatory duct. The vasa deferentia have rather thick, muscular walls that move the sperm by peristalsis.

Ejaculatory Duct

Each short **ejaculatory duct** is formed by the merger of a vas deferens and a duct from a seminal vesicle. The ejaculatory ducts enter the prostate gland and merge with the urethra within the prostate. During ejaculation, muscular contractions of the ejaculatory ducts mix seminal vesicle secretions with sperm and propel them into the urethra.

Urethra

The **urethra** is a thin-walled tube that extends from the urinary bladder to the end of the penis. The urethra serves a dual role in the male. It transports urine from the urinary bladder during micturition, as noted in chapter 16, and it also carries semen, which includes sperm, during ejaculation. Control mechanisms prevent both fluids passing at the same time.

Check My Understanding
1. Describe how sperm cells are formed.
2. Trace the path of sperm from a testis to outside the body.

Accessory Glands

Three different types of glands produce secretions involved in the reproductive process. These glands are the seminal vesicles, prostate gland, and bulbourethral glands (see figure 17.1).

Seminal Vesicles

The **seminal vesicles** are paired glands located on the posterior surface of the urinary bladder. The duct of each seminal vesicle merges with the vas deferens on the same side to form an ejaculatory duct near the posterior surface on the prostate gland. The alkaline secretions of the seminal vesicles help to keep semen slightly alkaline and contain fructose sugar and prostaglandins. Secretions by the seminal vesicles compose about 60% of semen.

Prostate Gland

The **prostate gland** is a doughnut-shaped gland that encircles the urethra where it exits the urinary bladder. The ejaculatory ducts pass through the posterior portion of the prostate to join with the urethra within the prostate. Prostatic fluid is forced through 20 to 30 tiny ducts into the urethra during ejaculation. The secretion is an alkaline, milky fluid containing a mix of substances, including prostate-specific antigen (PSA). It forms about 30% of semen and contains substances that activate the swimming movements of sperm.

Bulbourethral Glands

The **bulbourethral** (bul-bō-ū-rē´-thral) **glands** are two small, spherical glands that are located below the prostate gland near the base of the penis (see figure 17.1). These glands secrete an alkaline, mucuslike fluid into the urethra in response to sexual stimulation. This secretion neutralizes the acidity of the urethra and lubricates the end of the penis in preparation for sexual intercourse.

Semen

The seminal fluid, or **semen** (sē´-men), is the fluid passed from the urethra during ejaculation. It consists of the fluids secreted by the bulbourethral glands, seminal vesicles, and prostate gland along with sperm cells from the testes. It is slightly alkaline (pH 7.5) and contains substances that protect and nourish the sperm. Fructose from seminal vesicles provides the nutrient energy for sperm, and prostatic fluid activates their swimming movements. After semen is deposited in the vagina during sexual intercourse, prostaglandins in seminal vesicle secretions stimulate reverse peristalsis of the uterus and uterine tubes, which accelerates the movement of sperm through the female reproductive tract. The volume of semen in a single ejaculation may vary from 2 to 5 ml, with 50 to 150 million sperm per milliliter. Although only one sperm participates in fertilization, many sperm are necessary for fertilization to occur.

Clinical INSIGHT

Male infertility may be caused by a number of factors, such as hormone imbalances, duct blockage, a low sperm count, abnormal sperm, or a low fructose concentration in the semen. The minimum sperm count for male fertility is considered to be at least 20 million sperm per milliliter of semen.

Scrotum

The **scrotum** (skrō´-tum) is the external sac of skin and subcutaneous tissue that contains the testes. It hangs from the trunk midline posterior to the penis. A medial partition keeps each testis in a separate chamber within the scrotum. Testes develop within the pelvic cavity but descend into the saclike scrotum through the inguinal canals near the end of the seventh month of fetal development. This migration occurs under the stimulation of testosterone, the male sex hormone, and it is essential for the production of viable sperm.

The subcutaneous layer of the scrotum contains smooth muscle fibers that reflexively contract or relax to shorten or lengthen the scrotum in response to temperature. In addition, the *cremaster muscles,* which are composed of skeletal muscle fibers attached to the testes, respond similarly. Through the actions of these muscles, the testes are raised closer to the body in cold temperatures and lowered in warm temperatures. In this way, the temperature of the testes is kept about 3°F lower than the normal body temperature. This lower temperature is necessary for the production of viable sperm.

Clinical INSIGHT

Failure of the testes to descend into the scrotum produces sterility and increases the chance of testicular cancer. Undescended testes may be stimulated to descend by testosterone administration, or surgical means may be used to move the testes into the scrotum. Both treatments are done in early childhood.

Penis

The **penis** is the male copulatory organ that deposits semen in the female vagina during sexual intercourse. It contains specialized erectile tissues that enable it to become enlarged and rigid during sexual excitement.

Three columns of erectile tissue compose the body of the penis. The *corpora cavernosa* are two columns of erectile tissue located dorsally, and the *corpus spongiosum* is located ventrally. The urethra extends throughout the length of the corpus spongiosum (see figure 17.1). The corpora spongiosum expands at the tip to form the *glans penis,* which contains numerous sensory nerve endings and the urethral opening. A loose sheath of skin, the *prepuce,* extends forward to cover the glans.

Table 17.1 summarizes the functions of male reproductive organs.

Table 17.1   Summary of Functions of Male Reproductive Organs AP|R

Organ	Function
Testis	Seminiferous tubules produce sperm and secrete inhibin; interstitial cells secrete testosterone
Epididymis	Site of sperm maturation and temporary storage; carries sperm to vas deferens
Vas deferens	Carries sperm to ejaculatory duct
Ejaculatory duct	Carries sperm and secretion from seminal vesicle to the urethra
Urethra	Carries semen to outside the body
Bulbourethral gland	Secretes watery fluid that neutralizes acidity of the urethra
Seminal vesicle	Secretes alkaline fluid containing nutrients for sperm and prostaglandins; helps keep semen slightly alkaline
Prostate gland	Secretes alkaline fluid that helps keep semen slightly alkaline and activates motility of sperm
Scrotum	Contains and protects testes; regulates temperature of testes
Penis	Inserted into vagina during sexual intercourse; deposits semen in vagina; contains sensory nerve endings associated with feelings of sexual pleasure

Check My Understanding

3. What composes semen?
4. What is the function of the scrotum?

Clinical INSIGHT

For many American male babies, *circumcision*, the surgical removal of the prepuce, is performed in the delivery room or within three days after birth. In Jewish culture, it may be performed on the eighth day as a religious rite. It is believed that circumcision improves male hygiene and decreases the risk of penile infections, and it may reduce the risk of cervical cancer in female sexual partners.

17.2 Male Sexual Response

In the absence of sexual stimulation, the vascular sinusoids in the erectile tissue of the penis contain a small amount of blood, and the penis is flaccid (flak´-sid), or soft. Sexual stimulation initiates parasympathetic nerve impulses that dilate arterioles and constrict venules supplying the erectile tissue. These vascular changes cause the erectile tissue to become engorged with blood, which produces **erection,** a condition in which the penis swells, lengthens, and becomes erect.

Continued sexual stimulation of the glans, as in sexual intercourse, culminates in **orgasm,** which is characterized by **ejaculation** (ē-jak-ū-lā´-shun) of semen and a feeling of intense pleasure. Just prior to

ejaculation, sympathetic nerve impulses stimulate peristaltic contractions of the epididymides, vasa deferentia, and ejaculatory ducts along with contractions of the seminal vesicles and prostate gland. These contractions force semen (sperm and glandular secretions) into the urethra. Then, ejaculation occurs as certain skeletal muscles at the base of the penis contract rhythmically, forcing semen through the urethra to the outside. A feeling of general relaxation follows.

Immediately after ejaculation, the vascular changes that produced erection are reversed. Sympathetic impulses constrict the arterioles and dilate the venules supplying the erectile tissue, allowing the accumulated blood to leave the penis. The penis becomes flaccid again, as blood is carried away. After orgasm, erection is not possible for a time period that varies from less than an hour to several hours.

17.3 Hormonal Control of Reproduction in Males

The onset of male sexual development begins around the ages of 11 or 12 and is completed by ages 15 to 17. Processes initiating the onset of puberty are not well understood, but the sequence of events is known. Hormones of the hypothalamus, anterior pituitary gland, and testes are involved.

Puberty begins when unknown stimuli trigger the hypothalamus to secrete **gonadotropin-releasing hormone (GnRH),** which is carried to the anterior pituitary gland by the blood. GnRH activates the release of **luteinizing hormone (LH)** and **follicle-stimulating hormone (FSH)** from the anterior pituitary gland. In males, LH is sometimes called *interstitial cell–stimulating hormone (ICSH).* LH (ICSH) promotes growth of the interstitial cells of the testes and stimulates their secretion of **testosterone** (tes-tos´-te-rōn), the primary male hormone. FSH and testosterone in combination act on the seminiferous tubules, stimulating spermatogenesis.

Action of Testosterone

Male hormones are collectively called **androgens** (an´-dro-jens), and testosterone is the most important one. Testosterone secretion starts in fetal development, continues for a brief time after birth, and then nearly ceases until puberty.

At puberty, testosterone stimulates the maturation of the male reproductive organs, the continuation of spermatogenesis, and the development of the male secondary sexual characteristics. Male *secondary sexual characteristics* include (1) growth of body hair, especially on the face, axillary, and pubic regions; (2) increased muscular development; (3) development of heavy bones, broad shoulders, and narrow pelvis; and (4) deepening of the voice due to enlargement of the larynx and thickening of the vocal cords. Less obvious effects are increases in the rate of cellular metabolism and red blood cell production. Both metabolic rate and the concentration of red blood cells in the blood are greater in males than in females.

Regulation of Testosterone Secretion

Like many other hormones, testosterone production is controlled by a *negative-feedback system,* as shown in figure 17.6. Note that the secretion of GnRH starts the hormonal negative-feedback control mechanism. After puberty, this mechanism maintains the testosterone level in the blood within normal limits.

As testosterone concentration increases in the blood, it inhibits the production of GnRH by the hypothalamus, which, in turn, reduces the release of LH from the anterior pituitary gland. The decrease in LH production causes a decrease in testosterone secretion by the interstitial cells of the testes, which reduces testosterone concentration in the blood.

Conversely, as testosterone concentration in the blood declines, the hypothalamus is stimulated to secrete GnRH, which, in turn, promotes the release of LH by the anterior pituitary. The increase in LH production causes an increase in testosterone secretion by the testes, which increases the testosterone concentration in the blood.

Testosterone maintains the male reproductive organs and spermatogenesis. However, sperm production is fine-tuned by the hormone **inhibin,** which is secreted by supporting cells within the seminiferous tubules. When the sperm count is high, secretion of

Figure 17.6 Hormonal control of spermatogenesis and testosterone secretion.

inhibin is increased, which decreases sperm production by decreasing FSH secretion by the anterior pituitary. When the sperm count is low, inhibin secretion decreases, and sperm production is increased by an increase in FSH secretion. Thus, inhibin works to keep sperm concentration in semen within normal limits without altering the secretion of LH and testosterone.

Check My Understanding

5. How is sperm production regulated?
6. What are the functions of testosterone?
7. How is testosterone secretion regulated?

Clinical   INSIGHT

Testosterone production starts to decline at about 40 years of age, resulting in a gradual decline in sexual activity. However, male sexual activity continues into old age.

17.4 Female Reproductive System

The female reproductive system produces female hormones and female sex cells and transports the sex cells to a site where they may unite with a sperm cell. In addition, the female reproductive system provides a suitable environment for the development of the embryo and fetus and is actively involved in the birthing process. The organs of the female reproductive system include the paired ovaries, which produce female hormones and sex cells; paired uterine tubes, which transport the female sex cells; a uterus, where internal development of the embryo and fetus occurs; a vagina, which serves as the female copulatory organ and birth canal; and accessory glands and external organs (figure 17.7).

Ovaries

The **ovaries** are located in the upper, lateral portions of the pelvic cavity, one on each side of the uterus. They are about the same size and shape as large almonds, and they are supported by several ligaments. The outer surface of an ovary is covered by **germinal epithelium.** Interior to the germinal epithelium is a

Uterine tube — Fimbriae
Ovary
Uterus
Urinary bladder — Cervix
Symphysis pubis — Rectum
Urethra
Clitoris — Vagina
Labium minus
Labium majus — Anus
Vaginal orifice

Waldrop

Figure 17.7 Female reproductive system in a midsagittal section. AP|R more dense region, which contains immature ovarian follicles. The interior of an ovary consists of loose connective tissue supporting nerves and blood vessels.

Oogenesis

Oogenesis (ō-ō-jen´-e-sis) is the process of producing ova (eggs), the female sex cells. Oogenesis is similar to spermatogenesis with a few notable exceptions. The process of oogenesis is summarized in figure 17.8, and the sequential stages within an ovary are shown in figure 17.9. Oogenesis is closely tied to the ovarian cycle, which is discussed later in this chapter.

By the fifth month of prenatal development of a human female, the ovaries contain several million **oogonia** (ō-ō-gō-nē-ah), the diploid stem cells of the

ovaries. Gradually, most of the oogonia are transformed into **primary oocytes** (ō-ō-sītz) and are surrounded by a thin layer of cells forming the *primordial follicles*. At puberty, some of the primordial follicles mature to become *primary follicles* whose follicular cells envelop a primary oocyte. Primary oocytes contain the normal diploid number of chromosomes (46) found in human body cells, so they are capable of meiotic cell division. A female's lifetime supply of oocytes, about two million, is present at birth; the oocytes remain inactive until puberty. Starting at puberty, a few primary oocytes are activated each month. However, only one will continue development and complete meiosis I each month.

As shown in Figure 17.8, chromosomes are replicated prior to meiosis 1 and line up as homologous

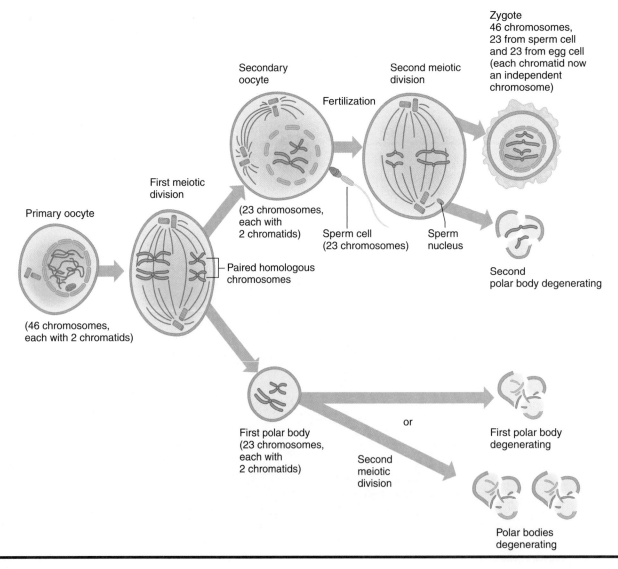

Figure 17.8 Oogenesis. In meiosis I, the primary oocyte divides to form a secondary oocyte and a polar body. If the secondary oocyte is penetrated by a sperm, it divides in meiosis II to form an ovum and a polar body. Union of ovum and sperm nuclei forms a zygote. Polar bodies disintegrate.

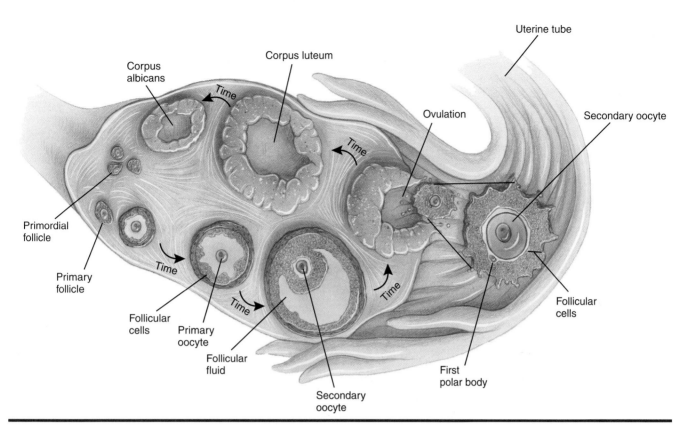

Figure 17.9 Stages of follicle development, release of a secondary oocyte at ovulation, and the formation of a corpus luteum.

pairs at metaphase. Each chromosome consists of two chromatids joined by the centromere. In meiosis I, the primary oocyte divides to form two dissimilar cells, each with only 23 chromosomes. Only one member of each chromosome pair is distributed to each daughter cell. The smaller cell, the first **polar body,** contains almost no cytoplasm, and it performs no further function. It is formed as a convenient way to get rid of 23 chromosomes. The larger cell is the **secondary oocyte,** and it contains nearly all of the cytoplasm that was present in the primary oocyte. The follicle containing the secondary oocyte is now called a *secondary follicle*, and it has enlarged. A thicker layer of follicular cells envelop the secondary oocyte, and follicular fluid fills much of the follicle. Prior to ovulation, the follicular cells surrounding the oocyte gradually separate from the wall of the follicle so that the oocyte, enveloped by follicular cells, floats freely in the follicular fluid. It is the secondary oocyte that is released from an ovary each month during a female's reproductive life. **Ovulation** is the process of an ovary releasing a secondary oocyte.

Meiosis II is completed only if the secondary oocyte is penetrated by a sperm. Meiosis II forms another polar body and an **ovum,** an egg cell, which receives nearly all of the cytoplasm. The chromatids of each chromosome separate, and they are distributed into different daughter cells. Therefore, both ovum and second polar body contain 23 chromosomes. The fusion of ovum and sperm nuclei forms a **zygote,** the first cell of an embryo. The polar bodies simply disintegrate (figures 17.8 through 17.10).

Uterine Tubes

The paired **uterine tubes** are sometimes called fallopian tubes, or oviducts. Each uterine tube extends laterally from the superior lateral surface of the uterus to an ovary. The end of each tube forms a funnel-shaped expansion, the *infundibulum* (in-fun-dib´-ū-lum), that partially envelops an ovary but is not connected to it. Each infundibulum is subdivided into a number of fingerlike processes called *fimbriae* (fim´-brē-ē) that may touch the ovary (figure 17.11).

The inner lining of a uterine tube consists of simple ciliated columnar epithelium and secretory cells. The beating of the cilia creates a current that helps draw the ovulated secondary oocyte into the infundibulum. Then, the beating cilia move the oocyte slowly toward the uterus.

Figure 17.10 Photomicrograph of a maturing follicle showing an oocyte covered by follicular cells (250×). AP|R

Infections of the female reproductive tract can easily migrate up the uterine tubes into the pelvic cavity, where the infections become far more serious.

Uterus

The **uterus** (ū´-ter-us) is located in the pelvic cavity posterior to the urinary bladder. As shown in figure 17.7, it is located superior to the vagina and is bent anteriorly over the urinary bladder. The uterus is a hollow organ with thick, muscular walls. Its primary function is to provide an appropriate internal environment for a developing embryo and fetus.

The uterus has two major regions. The *cervix,* the lower tubular portion, is inserted into the upper end of the vagina. The *body,* the upper portion, is enlarged and rounded, and it joins with the uterine tubes laterally.

The walls of the uterus are composed of three layers. The *endometrium* (en-dō-mē´-trē-um) is the mucosal layer that lines the interior of the uterus. The *myometrium* is the thick layer of smooth muscle that forms most of the wall thickness. The *perimetrium* is

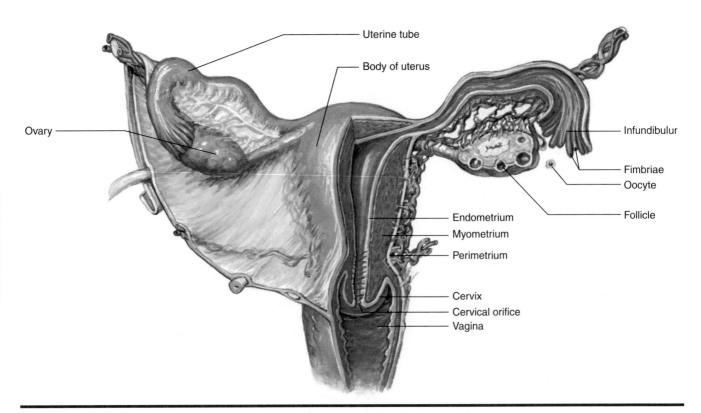

Uterine tube

Body of uterus

Ovary

Infundibulur

Fimbriae

Oocyte

Follicle

Endometrium

Myometrium

Perimetrium

Cervix

Cervical orifice

Vagina

Figure 17.11 Female reproductive organs. AP|R

the thin, serous layer that covers the exterior of the uterus (see figure 17.11).

Vagina

The **vagina** (vah-ji´-nah) is the collapsible tube that extends from the uterus to the exterior. It serves as the female copulatory organ and the birth canal. The vagina is located posterior to the urethra and anterior to the rectum.

The vaginal wall consists of three layers: an inner mucosa of stratified squamous epithelium and supportive connective tissue, a thin muscle layer consisting of smooth muscle, and an outer fibrous layer composed of dense connective tissue.

External Accessory Organs

The openings of the urethra and vagina are surrounded by external accessory reproductive organs that compose the external genitals, or **vulva** (see figure 17.7). Figure 17.12 illustrates the female external genitals and **perineum** (per-i-nē´-um), the pelvic floor. The portion of the perineum between the vaginal opening and the anus is often called the *obstetrical perineum.*

The paired **labia majora** (lā´-bē-ah ma-jō´-rah) (singular, *labium majus*) are rounded longitudinal folds of adipose tissue and a thin layer of smooth muscle covered by skin. The labia majora enclose the other external accessory structures, and their medial margins are separated by a narrow cleft. They join

anteriorly at the *mons pubis,* a rounded cushion of adipose tissue over the anterior surface of the pubic symphysis. The labia majora are formed of the same embryonic tissues that form the scrotum in males.

The **labia minora** (singular, *labium minus*) are paired, thinner, longitudinal folds that lie medial to the labia majora. They join anteriorly to form a hood-like covering of the clitoris. Posteriorly, they join with the labia majora.

The narrow space between the labia minora is known as the **vestibule.** The urethra opens into its anterior region, and the vagina opens into its posterior region. A pair of *vestibular (Bartholin's) glands* lie on each side of the vaginal opening and release their secretions into the vestibule.

The **clitoris** (kli´-tōr-is) is a nodule of erectile tissue located at the anterior union of the labia minora. It consists of erectile tissue and corresponds to the penis in males. The *glans,* its anterior portion, contains abundant sensory nerve endings whose stimulation leads to the female sexual response.

Table 17.2 summarizes the functions of the female reproductive organs.

Check My Understanding

8. Describe oogenesis and ovulation.
9. What are the parts of the vulva?

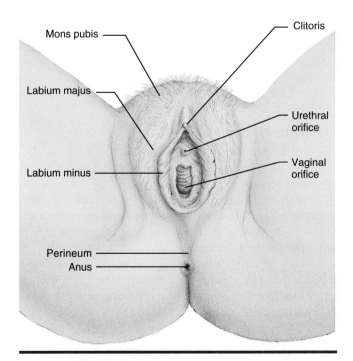

Figure 17.12 Female external genitals. [AP|R]

Mons pubis

Labium majus

Labium minus

Perineum

Anus

Clitoris

Urethral orifice

Vaginal orifice

17.5 Female Sexual Response

In the absence of sexual stimulation, the erectile tissue of the clitoris contains a small amount of blood. Sexual stimulation causes parasympathetic nerve impulses to dilate the arterioles and constrict the venules supplying the erectile tissue. These vascular changes cause the erectile tissue to become engorged with blood and produce erection of the clitoris.

Simultaneously, nerve impulses cause enlargement of the vaginal mucosa and breasts and erection of the nipples due to increased blood flow to these areas. Secretion of the vestibular glands is increased, lubricating the vestibule and aiding entry of the penis.

As in the male, the female sexual response culminates in orgasm. Muscles of the pelvic floor and walls of the uterus and uterine tubes contract rhythmically due to neural reflexes and prostaglandins in semen. These contractions aid the movement of sperm through the uterus and toward the upper ends of the uterine tubes. Orgasm produces a sensation of intense

Table 17.2   Summary of Functions of Female Reproductive Organs AP|R

Organ	Function
Ovary	Produces egg cells; secretes estrogen, progesterone, and inhibin
Uterine tube	Receives secondary oocyte, site of fertilization; carries early embryo to uterus
Uterus	Holds embryo and fetus during pregnancy
Vagina	Receives penis in sexual intercourse; serves as birth canal
Labia majora	Protect other external reproductive organs
Labia minora	Enclose vestibule; protect vaginal and urethral openings
Clitoris	Contains sensory nerve endings associated with feelings of sexual pleasure
Vestibular glands	Secrete fluid that lubricates vaginal opening and vestibule

pleasure followed by general relaxation and a feeling of warmth throughout the body.

17.6 Hormonal Control of Reproduction in Females

Reproduction in females is controlled by hormones produced by the hypothalamus, anterior pituitary gland, and ovaries.

Female Sex Hormones

The ovaries produce the two major groups of female sex hormones—estrogen and progesterone—plus inhibin, which aids estrogen in its negative-feedback control function. Ovarian follicles under the stimulation of FSH produce **estrogen** (es´-trō-jen), which stimulates the maturation of the female sex organs and the development and maintenance of the female *secondary sexual characteristics.* The female secondary sexual characteristics include development of the mammary glands and breasts, a broad pelvis, increased deposition of adipose tissue in the subcutaneous layer (especially in the breasts, buttocks, and thighs), and increased blood supply to the skin. The development of axillary and pubic hair probably is stimulated by the small amount of androgen produced by the adrenal glands.

After ovulation, the remainder of the ovarian follicle becomes a **corpus luteum** (kor´-pus lū´-tē-um) (see figure 17.9). Under stimulation by LH, the corpus luteum secretes the other female sex hormone, **progesterone** (prō-jes´-te-rōn), as well as estrogen. The major role of progesterone is the development and maintenance of the uterine lining in pregnancy, but it also inhibits uterine contractions and dilation of the cervix. Both estrogen and progesterone play major roles in the regulation of the female reproductive cycles.

Female Reproductive Cycles

The two female reproductive cycles are hormonally controlled and occur simultaneously starting at puberty: ovarian cycles and menstrual cycles. **Ovarian cycles** involve the monthly formation and release of a secondary oocyte and the ovarium events that take place in anticipation of pregnancy. **Menstrual cycles** involve repetitive changes in the uterine lining that lead to monthly menstrual bleeding. The lengths of these cycles range from 24 to 35 days in different women, but 28 days is about average. Figure 17.13 illustrates the stages of menstrual and ovarian cycles along with the concentrations of the hormones that control them in a 28-day cycle. Table 17.3 summarizes the events of the ovarian and menstrual cycles.

Except for periods of pregnancy and nursing, women experience monthly reproductive cycles from puberty (menarche) until menopause. **Menopause,** the cessation of reproductive cycles, usually occurs between 45 and 55 years of age.

Ovarian Cycle

Puberty in females begins at about 11 years of age, with the first menses occurring at about 13 years of age. The female reproductive cycles begin when the hypothalamus secretes gonadotropin-releasing hormone (GnRH), which activates the anterior pituitary gland to release follicle-stimulating hormone (FSH) and luteinizing hormone (LH).

Recall that the primary ooctyes are formed within the ovary prior to birth. At the time of puberty, each primary oocyte is enveloped by a layer of cuboidal follicular cells forming a *primary follicle.* FSH promotes the development of a few primary follicles each month. In each monthly cycle, one of these follicles becomes the dominant follicle

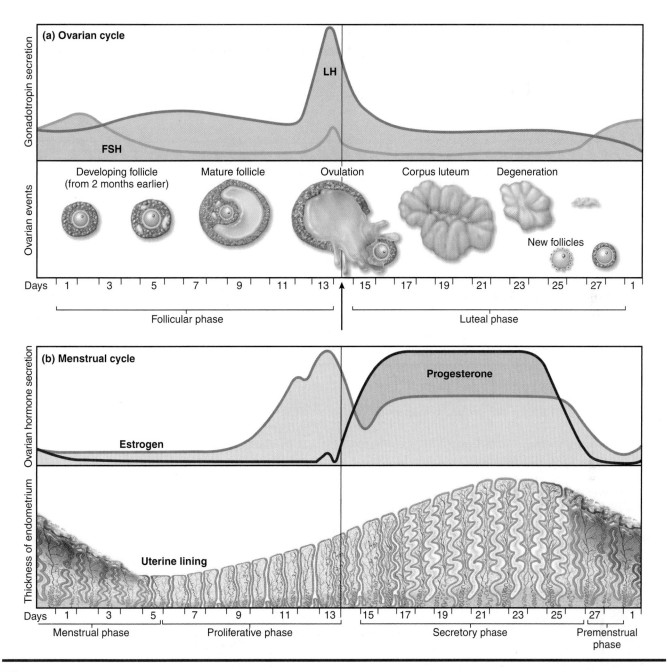

Figure 17.13 Female reproductive cycle. AP|R

that will continue development. The growth of other follicles is curtailed.

The follicular cells multiply by mitosis, forming several layers around the primary oocyte. FSH stimulates the follicular cells to secrete estrogens, but LH also is involved. A fluid-filled space soon appears between inner and outer layers of the follicular cells. The appearance of this space marks the formation of the *secondary follicle* (figure 17.9). The developing follicle continues to secrete low concentrations of estrogen and progesterone and now produces *inhibin,* as well. The low level of estrogen, aided by inhibin, exerts a

negative-feedback inhibition on FSH secretion, which prevents development of additional follicles. The secretion of estrogen increases as the follicle continues to develop.

In a 28-day cycle, increased sensitivity of the follicular cells to FSH results in a rapid rise in estrogen production starting on day 7 and reaching a peak on day 12 (see figure 17.13). At this high concentration, estrogen exerts a *positive-feedback control* that stimulates the hypothalamus to secrete GnRH and the release of LH from the anterior pituitary. This results in a sharp increase in LH and a lesser increase

Table 17.3 Major Events in the Female Reproductive Cycle
1. GnRH secreted by the hypothalamus stimulates the anterior pituitary to release FSH and LH.
2. FSH stimulates enlargement of a few primary ovarian follicles and the subsequent maturation of the dominant follicle. FSH (with LH involvement) promotes estrogen secretion by follicular cells.
3. Estrogen stimulates the thickening of the uterine lining and, aided by inhibin, exerts a negative-feedback inhibition on FSH secretion, which prevents development of additional follicles.
4. A rapid rise in estrogen concentration peaks on day 12 as the dominant follicle enlarges.
5. The anterior pituitary produces a sharp increase in LH and a smaller increase in FSH that peak on day 13.
6. The primary oocyte undergoes the first meiotic division, forming the secondary oocyte, and the surge of LH causes ovulation on day 14.
7. LH transforms the ruptured follicle into a corpus luteum and stimulates the corpus luteum to secrete increasing amounts of progesterone and lesser amounts of estrogen during days 15 to 25.
a. Estrogen promotes the continued thickening of the uterine lining.
b. Progesterone promotes the formation of blood vessels and glands in the uterine lining, preparing it to receive an embryo.
c. Progesterone and estrogen, aided by inhibin, exert a negative feedback on GnRH secretion by the hypothalamus, inhibiting the release of FSH and LH from the anterior pituitary.
8. If fertilization does not occur, the corpus luteum degenerates, and the secretion of estrogen and progesterone declines rapidly from days 25 to 28.
9. The reproductive cycle starts again as the low levels of estrogen and progesterone
a. result in the breakdown of the uterine lining with menstruation starting on day 1 of the next menstrual cycle;
b. no longer inhibit the hypothalamus, allowing the secretion of GnRH, which stimulates release of FSH and LH from the anterior pituitary, starting a new ovarian cycle.

in FSH concentrations in the blood, which peak on day 13.

The abrupt increase in LH and FSH causes the rapid maturation of the secondary follicle to form a *mature follicle* that contains much fluid and bulges from the ovary surface. LH stimulates the completion of meiosis I by the primary oocyte to form a secondary oocyte and the first polar body as one of the last events in the maturation process. Thereafter, the high level of LH stimulates **ovulation,** the rupture of the mature follicle, which releases the secondary oocyte surrounded by follicular cells. Ovulation occurs 14 days before the onset of the next mensis, regardless of the length of the cycle.

After ovulation, the empty follicle is transformed into a corpus luteum under the stimulation of LH. Prior to ovulation, the follicular cells secrete estrogen and a small amount of progesterone, but after ovulation the corpus luteum secretes large amounts of progesterone as well as estrogen. The high concentration of progesterone exerts a *negative-feedback control* that inhibits the secretion of GnRH by the hypothalamus and FSH and LH by the anterior pituitary.

If the secondary oocyte is not penetrated by a sperm leading to fertilization of the ovum, the corpus luteum degenerates, causing a rapid decline in estrogen and progesterone levels from days 25 to 28. Once the low level of progesterone no longer inhibits the hypothalamus, allowing secretion of GnRH, the next reproductive cycle begins.

Menstrual Cycle

The menstrual, or uterine, cycle refers to the series of changes in the endometrium that occur each month unless pregnancy occurs. These changes are responses to fluctuating levels of estrogen and progesterone. The menstrual cycle has three phases: menstruation, proliferative phase, and secretory phase (see figure 17.13).

The low progesterone and estrogen levels at the end of the previous reproductive cycle cause the breakdown of the uterine lining, leading to menstruation. *Menstruation* starts a new menstrual cycle. It begins on the first day of the next menstrual cycle and lasts from three to five days.

The *proliferative phase* is characterized by a buildup of the endometrium under stimulation by estrogen, whose concentration in the blood increases as the dominant primary follicle develops. This phase begins at the end of menstruation and ends at ovulation.

Following ovulation, both progesterone and estrogen are produced by the corpus luteum, and they continue the development of the uterine lining in the *secretory phase.* Estrogen promotes the continued thickening of the endometrium. Progesterone stimulates the formation of blood vessels and glands in the uterine lining, preparing it to receive an early embryo. If fertilization of an ovum does not occur, the low levels of progesterone and estrogen drop rapidly, triggering the breakdown of the endometrium, which leads to menstruation on the first day of the next menstrual cycle. The secretory phase begins at ovulation and ends with the onset of menstruation.

Menopause, the cessation of regular menstrual cycles, usually occurs between 45 and 55 years of age. The onset is usually gradual with menstrual cycles becoming irregular. During this time, a woman can still conceive, so menopause is not considered to be complete until the cycles have not occurred for one year.

Aging of the ovaries is the cause of menopause. There are fewer primary follicles to respond to gonadotropins from the pituitary, and ovulation does not occur. Therefore, the secretion of estrogen and progesterone by the ovaries is greatly curtailed.

The decline in female hormones often is accompanied by physical symptoms such as headaches, insomnia, and depression. Hot flashes, caused by sudden and temporary dilation of dermal blood vessels, is perhaps the most common symptom. Hormone replacement therapy (HRT), the administration of estrogen and progesterone, was previously used to treat the unpleasant symptoms of menopause. But its use has been greatly curtailed, because studies have shown that it increases the risk of breast cancer, strokes, and heart disease.

Check My Understanding

10. How are FSH, LH, estrogen, and progesterone involved in ovarian and menstrual cycles?

17.7 Mammary Glands

Both males and females possess **mammary glands.** The mammary glands of males and immature females are similar. At puberty, estrogen and progesterone stimulate the development of female mammary glands. Estrogen starts breast and mammary gland development, and progesterone stimulates the maturation of the mammary glands so that they are capable of secreting milk. Another anterior pituitary hormone, *prolactin*, is required for milk production.

Mature mammary glands are female accessory reproductive structures that are specialized for milk production (figure 17.14). They are located in the subcutaneous tissue of female breasts. The breasts are formed external to the pectoralis muscles. Breasts contain large amounts of fatty tissue that surround and cushion the mammary glands. Dense connective tissue within the

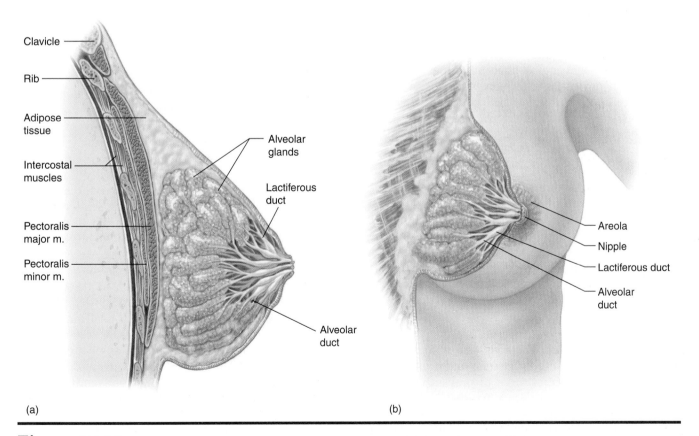

(a)

(b)

Figure 17.14 Anatomy of the female breast and mammary glands. (*a*) Sagittal section. (*b*) Anterior view. (m. = muscle) APR breasts is attached to the dermis and to the fascia of the pectoral muscles to provide support for the breasts and mammary glands. Externally, a circle of pigmented skin, the *areola* (ah-rē´-ō-lah), is located near the anterior portion of each breast. A *nipple* containing erectile tissue is located in the center of each areola.

Each mammary gland consists of 15 to 25 lobes containing *alveolar glands.* Alveolar glands produce milk under stimulation by prolactin after the birth of a baby. Milk is carried from the alveolar glands by *alveolar ducts*, which open into *lactiferous ducts* that lead to the nipple and outside. Regulation of lactation is discussed in chapter 18.

Because breast cancer has the highest fatality rate among cancers in women, early detection is crucial. After 35 years of age, annual mammograms are advised and women are encouraged to develop the habit of monthly self-examinations.

17.8 Birth Control

Birth control methods may be categorized into several groups based on their mode of action: hormonal, chemical and behavioral contraceptive methods, anti-implantation devices, sterilization, and induced abortion. Figure 17.15 shows a few birth control devices, and Table 17.4 summarizes the effectiveness of the various birth control methods.

Contraception

Contraception is the prevention of conception, which is the union of sperm and egg. Contraceptive methods are designed to prevent sperm from reaching and penetrating a secondary oocyte, which leads to fertilization of an ovum. There are several types of contraceptives, including the use of hormones, barriers to sperm, spermicides (chemicals that kill sperm), and behavioral methods.

Hormonal Methods

Hormonal birth control methods use a higher concentration of synthetic progesterone and a lower concentration of synthetic estrogen to prevent ovulation. These hormones provide a negative-feedback control that inhibits the secretion of GnRH by the hypothalamus, which reduces the secretion of FSH and LH by the anterior pituitary. This prevents maturation of ovarian follicles so ovulation does not occur. Use of hormonal birth control methods is timed to a woman's menstrual cycle.

Hormonal birth control methods are very effective, but some women may experience unpleasant side effects, such as headache, irregular menstruation, nausea, and bloating. Women who smoke or have a history of blood clots, stroke, heart disease, liver disease, or uncontrolled diabetes have an elevated health risk when using hormonal birth control methods.

There are several ways to use hormonal birth control.

The **oral contraceptive,** "the pill," was the first available method of delivery, and it is still widely used. Several types are available, but the combination pill, which contains both synthetic progesterone and estrogen, is most commonly used. One pill is taken each day for three weeks of the menstrual cycle.

Some combination birth control pills may be used in higher dosages as *morning after pills (MAPs),* for postcoital emergency contraception. When used within 72 hours of unprotected intercourse, the hormone combination disrupts normal hormonal controls and tends to prevent either fertilization or implantation.

A **birth control patch** is a small adhesive skin patch containing the synthetic hormones. It is applied to the skin, and the hormones are absorbed through the skin. A new patch is used each week for three weeks.

A **vaginal ring** is a soft plastic ring that is wedged into the upper part of the vagina, where it remains and releases synthetic hormones over a three-week period. It is removed at the start of the fourth week.

Norplant is a set of tiny silicone rods containing synthetic progesterone that are surgically implanted under the skin of the upper arm or over the shoulder blade. The released progesterone acts similarly to an oral contraceptive by inhibiting ovulation, and the implant is effective for up to five years. The implant may be removed to terminate contraception.

Depo-Provera is a synthetic progesterone that is administered by muscular injection at three-month intervals. It protects against pregnancy by preventing ovulation and altering the uterine lining to inhibit implantation of an embryo. Its use often causes weight gain as a side effect, and it can be a considerable health risk, so it must be used under a physician's care. Women with a personal or strong family history of high blood pressure, asthma, kidney disease, migraine headaches, or breast cancer are at increased risk if using Depo-Provera.

Figure 17.15 Examples of birth control devices and chemicals: (*a*) intrauterine device (IUD), (*b*) diaphragm and spermicide, (*c*) spermicide gel, (*d*) oral contraceptive, and (*e*) male and female condoms.

Barriers

There are three types of **barriers** that are designed to prevent sperm from entering the uterus: condom, diaphragm, and cervical cap.

Condoms act by preventing sperm from being deposited in the vagina. A *male condom* is a thin sheath of latex rubber that is slipped over the penis prior to sexual intercourse. A *female condom* is a thin polyurethane bag with a flexible ring at each end. The woman inserts the bag into the vagina prior to sexual intercourse. Condoms reduce but do not eliminate the chance of infection by sexually transmitted diseases (STDs).

A **diaphragm** is a dome-shaped sheet of rubber supported by a firm but somewhat flexible ring. It is placed in the upper vagina over the cervix prior to intercourse. It prevents sperm from entering the uterus. Spermicidal substances are used along with a diaphragm.

A **cervical cap** is a thimble-shaped piece of latex rubber that fits snugly over the cervix. Spermicidal substances are used with a cervical cap. Females with abnormal Pap smears or cervical infections should not use a cervical cap.

Spermicides

A variety of **spermicides** are available, including creams, jellies, and suppositories. These chemicals kill sperm by destroying their plasma membranes.

Behavioral Methods

The **rhythm method** requires abstinence from sexual intercourse from three days before the day of ovulation to three days after ovulation, for a total of seven

Table 17.4 Effectiveness of Birth Control Methods

Effectiveness values are approximate because they vary with how the birth control methods are used.

Method	Effectiveness*
Vasectomy	Nearly 100%
Tubal ligation	Nearly 100%
Depo-Provera	99%
Norplant	99%
Oral contraception	97%
Skin patch	97%
Vaginal ring	97%
Intrauterine device (IUD)	95%
Male condom	85%
Female condom	85%
Diaphragm with spermicide	80%
Cervical cap with spermicide	80%
Withdrawal	75%
Rhythm method	70%

*Effectiveness is the percentage of women who do not become pregnant in one year while using this method of birth control.

days. It is based on the fact that the secondary oocyte may be penetrated by a sperm for only about 24 hours after ovulation. One difficulty with this method is determining the time of ovulation, because few women have perfectly regular cycles. The failure rate is higher in women who have irregular cycles.

Withdrawal, or **coitus interruptus,** is the removal of the penis from the vagina just prior to ejaculation. Failures of this method result from preejaculatory emission of semen or failure to withdraw before ejaculation.

Anti-Implantation Devices

An *intrauterine device (IUD)* is a small plastic and copper object that is inserted into the uterus by a physician. The IUD causes inflammation of the uterine lining, preventing implantation of an embryo. An IUD may remain in place for long periods of time, but it should be checked at regular intervals by a physician because an IUD may be spontaneously expelled from the uterus. Undesirable side effects include excessive menstrual bleeding, painful cramps, and an increased risk of pelvic inflammatory disease and infertility.

Sterilization

Sterilization surgeries may be performed on both males and females. In males, a **vasectomy** is performed by cutting and tying the vasa deferentia within the scrotum so that sperm do not form part of the semen. The sperm disintegrate and are reabsorbed. In females, a **tubal ligation** is performed through a small abdominal incision. The uterine tubes are cut and tied to prevent the transport of a secondary oocyte toward the uterus. The ovulated oocytes disintegrate and are reabsorbed. Vasectomies and tubal ligations do not affect the production of sex hormones or the sexual response.

Induced Abortion

An **abortion** is the premature expulsion of an embryo or fetus from the uterus. Spontaneous abortions are called *miscarriages.* They usually result from hormonal disorders or serious abnormalities of the developing embryo. An *induced abortion* may be used to terminate an unwanted pregnancy. Induced abortion involves dilation of the cervix and removal of the embryo or fetus by suction or surgical means. Possible side effects of induced abortions include prolonged bleeding, perforation of the uterus, and emotional trauma.

The so-called abortion pill, *mifepristone* (RU 486), is a progesterone antagonist. It causes the endometrium to break down, thereby detaching the embryo or fetus, which is passed from the uterus after administration of prostaglandins to promote uterine contractions. Its use is limited to the first five weeks of pregnancy and requires the supervision and care of a physician.

Check My Understanding

11. How do hormonal birth control methods work?
12. How does an IUD prevent pregnancy?

17.9 Disorders of the Reproductive Systems

These disorders are grouped as male disorders, female disorders, and sexually transmitted diseases.

Male Disorders

Prostatitis is the inflammation of the prostate gland. It is caused by acute or chronic infections that often are associated with tenderness and enlargement of the prostate.

An **enlarged prostate** without inflammation occurs in about 33% of males over 60 years of age. In some cases, it may restrict the flow of urine and prevent the control of micturition. Enlarged prostates are usually detected by rectal examinations. Surgical correction usually is by *transurethral resection,* a procedure in which an instrument is inserted into the urethra to remove portions of the prostate gland compressing the urethra.

Cancer of the prostate is the second leading cause of death from cancer in males. Males over 40 years of age should have annual prostate examinations.

Erectile dysfunction (ED) is the inability to attain and maintain an erection long enough for sexual intercourse. It may result from organic or psychological factors. Treatment is available in most cases.

Infertility is the inability of a male to produce and deposit sufficient numbers of viable sperm in the vagina to bring about fertilization of an ovum. A low sperm count is a common cause.

Female Disorders

Amenorrhea is the absence of menstruation. *Primary amenorrhea* is the failure of a woman to begin menstruation, and it is caused by endocrine disorders or abnormal reproductive development. *Secondary amenorrhea* is the absence of one or more menstrual periods without pregnancy. This may result from excessive physical exertion or excessive weight loss.

Dysmenorrhea refers to painful menstruation that prevents a woman from doing her normal activities for one or more days during the menses. Uterine contractions are thought to be responsible for the pain.

Premenstrual syndrome is characterized by severe physical or emotional distress after ovulation and prior to menstruation. The cause is unknown, although it is probably related to ovarian hormone production.

Toxic shock syndrome is characterized by high fever, fatigue, headache, sore throat, vaginal irritation, vomiting, and diarrhea. It results from a toxin produced by a strain of bacteria *(Staphylococcus aureus)* whose growth is apparently enhanced by the use of highly absorbent tampons.

Endometriosis is the growth of endometrial tissue outside the uterus. The tissue migrates up the uterine tubes and enters the pelvic cavity. It may cause premenstrual or menstrual pain due to its breakdown during menstruation. Infertility may result from tubal obstruction.

Infertility in females is the inability to conceive. It may be caused by tubal obstruction, ovarian disease, or a lack of maintenance of the uterine lining.

Pelvic inflammatory disease (PID) is a collective term referring to any infection of the female reproductive organs and/or other pelvic tissues. The most common pathogens are those of sexually transmitted diseases that migrate into the pelvic cavity via the uterine tubes.

Cancer of the female reproductive system most often occurs as breast cancer or cervical cancer. *Breast cancer* rarely occurs before 30 years of age and is more prevalent after menopause. Any lump in a breast should be brought to a physician's attention immediately because breast cancer has a high fatality rate unless it is treated early. *Cervical cancer* is a rather slow-growing cancer and seems to be associated with penile papillomavirus infections of sexual partners. An association with multiple sex partners and uncircumcised sex partners may also be causes. Cervical cancer usually can be detected early by a Pap smear. Annual examinations for possible breast and cervical cancers are recommended for women over 30 years of age.

Sexually Transmitted Diseases (STDs)

Acquired immunodeficiency syndrome (AIDS) results from infection with the *human immunodeficiency virus (HIV),* which attacks a group of lymphocytes known as helper T (T_H) cells. The AIDS virus is transmitted via sexual intercourse and by blood transfer, including infected needles shared by drug users. Also, it may be passed from an infected mother to her developing fetus. It is not transmitted by casual contact. AIDS is discussed in more detail in the disorders section of chapter 13.

Gonorrhea is caused by the bacterium *Neisseria gonorrhoeae.* In males, it infects the urethra, causing painful urethritis. In females, it infects the vagina and may spread to the urethra, uterus, uterine tubes, and pelvic cavity. Females may not experience symptoms until advanced stages. Gonorrhea is a major cause of female sterility due to damage to the uterine tubes, and it can cause blindness in newborn babies. Antibiotics usually provide effective treatment. Most newborn infants born in hospitals receive eyedrops of antibiotics at birth to protect against possible gonorrhea infection.

Syphilis is caused by the bacterium *Treponema pallidum.* Without treatment, syphilis progresses through several recognizable stages. The *first stage* is characterized by an open sore, a *chancre* (shang´-ker), at the site of entrance by the bacterium. It may not be readily noticed, especially in females. The chancre heals within one to five weeks. Several weeks later, the *second stage* appears as muscle and joint pain, fever, and skin rash; it persists from four to eight weeks. Then, the disease enters a latent period of variable length. When the bacterium begins to destroy organs, such as the brain and liver, the *third stage* is recognized. Treatment with antibiotics is effective prior to the third stage.

Chlamydia (klah-mid´-ē-ah) is caused by the bacterium *Chlamydia trachomatis,* and it infects nearly 5 million people each year. In males, it causes painful urethritis. In females, it may spread throughout the reproductive tract, causing damage to uterine tubes that can lead to sterility. Chlamydia may also be transmitted from an infected mother to her baby during childbirth when the bacterium enters the baby's eyes. Antibiotics are an effective treatment.

Genital herpes is caused by the herpes simplex virus type 2. This disorder is characterized by painful blisters on the reproductive organs and may be accompanied by fever or flulike symptoms. It may be transmitted from an infected mother to her baby during delivery. In the newborn baby, it may cause only mild discomfort, serious neural damage, or death. Treatment with the drug acyclovir inhibits viral replication but does not eliminate the virus. The virus remains in the body and intermittently produces the genital blisters.

Genital warts are caused by another virus, the human papillomavirus (HPV). About 1 million new cases occur each year. Patients with genital warts may have an increased risk of certain cancers of the reproductive organs. Although there is no treatment that eliminates the virus, the warts can be removed by electrocautery (burning), cryosurgery (freezing), or laser surgery.

CHAPTER SUMMARY

17.1 Male Reproductive System

- The male reproductive system consists of the testes, accessory ducts, accessory glands, and accessory external organs.
- Testes are the male gonads. Each testis is divided into lobules containing seminiferous tubules that produce sperm cells. Interstitial cells between the tubules produce testosterone.
- Spermatogenesis is the process of producing sperm cells from spermatogonia. Meiotic division of a primary spermatocyte produces four spermatids that mature into sperm cells, each with 23 chromosomes.
- Sperm cells pass from the seminiferous tubules into the highly coiled epididymis, where they mature. From the epididymis, sperm pass in sequence through the vas deferens, ejaculatory duct, and the urethra to the outside.
- Accessory glands secrete alkaline fluids. Two bulbourethral glands secrete fluids that neutralize the acidity of the urethra. Seminal vesicles release their secretions into the ejaculatory ducts. The prostate gland secretes its sperm-activating fluid directly into the urethra.
- Semen consists of sperm cells and fluids from the accessory glands. About 3 to 6 ml of semen is produced in each ejaculation, with 50 to 150 million sperm in each milliliter.
- Testes are contained in the saclike scrotum outside the body. Muscle fibers control the distance the testes are from the body to keep the temperature of the testes at about 95.6°F.
- The penis contains three columns of erectile tissue that become engorged with blood during sexual excitement. The erect penis is inserted into the vagina in sexual intercourse.

17.2 Male Sexual Response

- Sexual stimulation causes erection of the penis. In sexual intercourse, continued stimulation results in orgasm, which is characterized by ejaculation and intense pleasure.
- After orgasm, blood leaves the erectile tissues and the penis returns to its flaccid state.

17.3 Hormonal Control of Reproduction in Males

- At puberty, the hypothalamus secretes GnRH, which stimulates the anterior pituitary to release FSH and LH (ICSH). LH stimulates the production of testosterone. FSH and testosterone stimulate the production of sperm.
- Testosterone stimulates the maturation of the male sex organs, the continuation of sperm production, and the male sex drive. It also develops and maintains the male secondary sexual characteristics.
- Testosterone secretion is regulated by a negative-feedback control system.
- Sperm production is kept within normal limits by inhibin exerting a negative-feedback control on FSH secretion.

17.4 Female Reproductive System

- The female reproductive system consists of the ovaries, uterine tubes, uterus, vagina, accessory glands, and external accessory organs.
- Ovaries are the female gonads, which produce female sex cells and female hormones. They are located in the pelvic cavity on each side of the uterus.
- Oogenesis is the process of producing female sex cells from oogonia. Millions of oogonia are formed during fetal development, but most degenerate. Those that remain become primary oocytes containing 46 chromosomes and are enveloped by follicular cells, forming primordial follicles.
- Starting at puberty, a few primary follicles are stimulated to grow each month. The dominant primary follicle enlarges, and its primary oocyte undergoes the first meiotic division, forming a secondary oocyte and the first polar body.
- The secondary follicle grows until it ruptures, releasing the secondary oocyte in ovulation.
- The infundibulum of a uterine tube receives the secondary oocyte, and the uterine tube carries it toward the uterus. If the secondary oocyte is penetrated by a sperm, the second meiotic division occurs, forming the ovum and a second polar body. Then, the sperm and ovum nuclei unite at fertilization.

- The uterus is located in the pelvic cavity posterior to the urinary bladder. Its major function is to provide a suitable environment for the developing offspring. The layers composing the uterine wall are the endometrium, myometrium, and perimetrium.
- The vagina receives the penis in sexual intercourse and serves as the birth canal in childbirth.
- External female reproductive organs are collectively called the vulva, which includes the outer labia majora, the inner labia minora enclosing the vestibule, and the clitoris, a small nodule of erectile tissue located at the anterior juncture of the labia minora.

17.5 Female Sexual Response

- Sexual stimulation causes erection of the clitoris and nipples and secretion by the vestibular glands.
- Sexual response culminates in orgasm, which produces rhythmic contractions of muscles in the walls of the uterus and uterine tubes and a feeling of intense pleasure.

17.6 Hormonal Control of Reproduction in Females

- The ovaries secrete estrogen and progesterone, the female sex hormones. Estrogen stimulates the maturation of the female reproductive organs and the development and maintenance of female secondary sexual characteristics. Progesterone maintains the uterine lining during pregnancy.
- Female reproductive cycles involve simultaneous ovarian and menstrual cycles, which are controlled by interactions of FSH, LH, estrogen, and progesterone.
- The start of an ovarian cycle is initiated by the secretion of GnRH by the hypothalamus, which stimulates the release of FSH and LH from the anterior pituitary gland. FSH promotes the development of ovarian follicles. The dominant follicle enlarges and secretes estrogen and some progesterone. Estrogen, aided by inhibin, suppresses FSH secretion to prevent development of additional follicles. Ovulation results from follicle stimulation by a sharp increase in LH and FSH.
- After ovulation, the follicle remnants become a corpus luteum under stimulation by LH. A large amount of progesterone and a lesser amount of estrogen, plus inhibin, are secreted by the corpus luteum, which suppress GnRH secretion. If fertilization does not occur, secretion of progesterone and estrogen declines rapidly, which allows the hypothalamus to secrete GnRH, starting another ovarian cycle.

- A menstrual cycle begins with the first day of menstruation, which results from the decline in progesterone and estrogen levels. Increasing levels of estrogen cause thickening of the endometrium during the proliferative phase. After ovulation, estrogen stimulates continued development of the uterine lining, and progesterone promotes the formation of blood vessels and glands in the uterine lining in the secretive phase. If fertilization does not occur, the drop in progesterone and estrogen levels triggers breakdown of the uterine lining, followed by menstruation.
- Menopause is the cessation of menstrual cycles. It usually occurs between ages 45 and 55.
- Menopause results when primary follicles no longer respond to pituitary gonadotropins.
- There is a marked decline in estrogen and progesterone secretion.

17.7 Mammary Glands

- Mammary glands are adapted to secrete milk after childbirth. They are located within the female breasts.
- Estrogen stimulates development of the mammary glands and breasts.

17.8 Birth Control

- Contraceptive methods include hormonal methods, barriers, spermicides, and behavioral methods.
- Anti-implantation methods use intrauterine devices that change the uterine lining, preventing implantation.
- Sterilization methods involve a vasectomy in males or a tubal ligation in females.
- Induced abortion involves dilation of the cervix and evacuation of the uterine contents.

17.9 Disorders of the Reproductive Systems

- Male disorders include an enlarged prostate, prostate cancer, impotence, and infertility.
- Female disorders include amenorrhea, dysmenorrhea, premenstrual syndrome, toxic shock syndrome, endometriosis, infertility, pelvic inflammatory disease, and cancer.
- Sexually transmitted diseases include AIDS, gonorrhea, syphilis, chlamydia, genital herpes, and genital warts.

BUILDING MY VOCABULARY

1. **Selected New Terms**
   bulbourethral gland, p. 364
   clitoris, p. 371
   contraception, p. 375

   ejaculatory duct, p. 363
   endometrium, p. 370
   epididymis, p. 363
   labia, p. 371

2. **Related Clinical Terms**

Endometriosis (en-dō-mē-tri-ō´-sis) Spread of endometrial tissue into the pelvic cavity.

Gynecology (gĭ-ne-kol´-o-jē) The medical specialty dealing with the female reproductive system.

Hysterectomy (his-to-rek´-to-mē) The surgical removal of the uterus.

Orchitis (or-kĭ´-tis) Inflammation of the testes.

Prostatectomy (pros-tah-tek´-to-mē) Surgical removal of the prostate gland.

SELF-REVIEW

Answers are located in appendix B.

1. Male gonads, the _____, are formed in the pelvic cavity and migrate into the saclike _____ before birth.
2. Sperm cells are formed within _____ in the testes by a process called _____.
3. Sperm cells mature within the _____ and pass through the vas deferens, _____, and _____ to the outside.
4. During sexual stimulation, the erectile tissue of the penis becomes engorged with _____.
5. The hormone _____ stimulates the secretion of _____ by interstitial cells.
6. Female sex cells are formed in the _____ by a process called _____.
7. At ovulation, a _____ is released from an ovary and enters a _____, which carries it toward the uterus.
8. Oogenesis is completed if a _____ is penetrated by a sperm, forming an ovum and a second _____.
9. The _____ serves as the female copulatory organ and birth canal.
10. The onset of puberty begins with the release of _____ from the hypothalamus, which stimulates secretion of FSH and _____ by the anterior lobe of the pituitary gland.
11. FSH promotes the secretion of _____ by the ovarian follicles.
12. After ovulation, the empty follicle becomes a _____, which secretes progesterone, which promotes buildup of the _____ of the uterus.
13. If fertilization does not occur, a rapid _____ in FSH and LH causes a breakdown of the endometrium, triggering the onset of _____.
14. Hormonal birth control methods act by preventing _____, whereas an IUD prevents _____ of an embryo.
15. Secondary sexual characteristics are produced by _____ in females and _____ in males.

CRITICAL THINKING

1. Complete the learning objectives on the first page of this chapter.
2. Considering the reproductive roles of males and females, contrast spermatogenesis and oogenesis.
3. Can an HIV-infected man who has had a vasectomy transmit HIV to his sexual partner? Explain.
4. Will a tubal ligation trigger the onset of menopause? Explain.
5. If an adult male is castrated (testes removed), how will this affect the blood concentrations of testosterone, FSH, LH, and GnRH?

Visit this book's website at www.mhhe.com/ gunstream5 for practice quizzes, learning exercises, case studies, and other study tools.

CHAPTER 18

Pregnancy, Prenatal Development, and Genetics

aprevealed.com

Module 14
Reproductive System

SELECTED KEY TERMS

Allele An alternate form of a gene.

Embryo The developmental stage extending from the second week through the eighth week of pregnancy.

Fertilization The union of sperm and ovum nuclei.

Fetus The prenatal developmental stage extending from the ninth week of pregnancy to birth.

Gene A unit of heredity; part of a DNA molecule in a chromosome.

Genotype The genetic composition of an individual.

Germ layer One of three embryonic tissues from which all subsequent tissues develop.

Heterozygous (hetero = different) A condition in which alleles of a gene pair are different.

Homozygous (homo = the same) A condition in which alleles of a gene pair are identical.

Implantation The attachment of an early embryo to the uterine lining.

Labor The series of events composing the birth process.

Parturition The process of giving birth.

Phenotype (phen = visible) The observable characteristics of inherited traits.

Placenta (plac = flat) Temporary organ formed of fetal and maternal tissues that attaches fetus to the uterine wall.

Umbilical cord (umbil = navel) The organ connecting the fetus with the placenta.

Zygote (zygo = yolk) A fertilized egg.

ach new baby begins as a single cell formed by the fusion of a sperm cell and an ovum. At the instant of its formation, this first cell contains all of the inherited information necessary for growth and development, plus all of the inherited characteristics that provide an individual's unique identity. After about 38 weeks of *prenatal* (before birth) growth and development (40 weeks from the last menses), a baby is born.

18.1 Fertilization and Early Development

Recall from chapter 17 that each **primary oocyte** undergoes the first meiotic division while still in the ovarian follicle. This division forms a **secondary oocyte** and the first **polar body,** and each cell contains 23 chromosomes. At ovulation, a secondary oocyte and the first polar body, still enclosed within a sphere of follicular cells, are released into a uterine tube. They are slowly moved toward the uterus by the beating cilia of epithelial cells lining the uterine tube.

Fertilization

After semen is deposited in the vagina, sperm begin their long journey into the uterus and on into the uterine tubes. Sperm inherently swim against the slight current of fluid that moves down the uterine tubes and uterus, and this behavior guides them into the uterus and up the tubes. Of the millions of sperm in the semen, probably only a few thousand sperm actually enter the uterine tubes. Prostaglandins in semen stimulate wavelike muscular contractions of the uterus and uterine tubes that greatly aid the migration of sperm. Sperm reach the upper portions of uterine tubes within one hour after sexual intercourse. Usually, only one uterine tube contains a secondary oocyte because only one secondary oocyte is usually released at ovulation. Sperm entering an empty uterine tube have no chance for fertilization.

When sperm reach a secondary oocyte, they are chemically attracted to it and cluster around it, trying to penetrate through the follicular cells (figure 18.1). The acrosomes of the sperm release an enzyme that dissolves the "glue" holding follicular cells together so they can reach the oocyte. It takes many sperm cells to disperse the follicular cells, so that one sperm can eventually wriggle between the follicular cells to contact the oocyte. The acrosome then releases a different enzyme that enables the sperm to penetrate the oocyte membrane and enter the oocyte. Once this happens, changes in the oocyte membrane prevent other sperm from entering (figure 18.2).

Figure 18.1 Scanning electron photomicrograph of sperm cells clustered on the surface of a secondary oocyte (1,200X). Only one sperm may enter the oocyte.

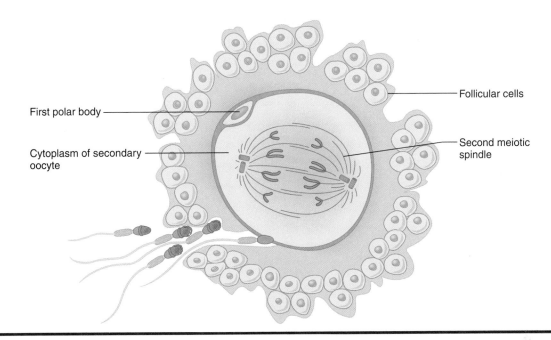

First polar body

Cytoplasm of secondary oocyte

Follicular cells

Second meiotic spindle

Figure 18.2 Enzymes from many sperm cells are required to separate the follicular cells, enabling one sperm to penetrate the plasma membrane of the secondary oocyte.

When a sperm enters the secondary oocyte, it triggers the second meiotic division, which forms the **ovum** and a second polar body. Then, the sperm and ovum nuclei unite in **fertilization** to form a **zygote,** the first cell of the baby-to-be. The zygote contains 46 chromosomes, 23 from the sperm and 23 from the ovum.

A secondary oocyte remains viable for about 24 hours after ovulation. Most sperm remain viable in the female reproductive tract for about 72 hours, although some may be viable for five days. Therefore, conception is most likely to occur when sexual intercourse occurs three days before ovulation to one day after ovulation.

Preembryonic Development

Immediately after fertilization, the zygote begins to divide by mitotic cell division. The early cell divisions are collectively known as *cleavage.* These divisions occur so rapidly that maximum cellular growth between divisions is not possible, so increasingly smaller cells are formed. During this time, the *preembryo* is carried down the uterine tube by the beating cilia of epithelial cells lining it. By the time the preembryo reaches the uterus, it consists of a solid ball of cells called a *morula* (mor´-u-lah) that is not much larger than the zygote.

Continued but slightly slower mitotic divisions form a larger hollow ball of cells called a **blastocyst** (blas´-to-sist) that soon develops within it the *inner cell mass,* a specialized group of cells from which the **embryo** later develops. The outer wall of the blastocyst is now called the *trophoblast,* which later will form the embryonic portion of the placenta.

Clinical **INSIGHT**

Identical, or monozygotic, twins come from a single zygote whose cells separate after the first cell division. Identical twins have a common placenta and chorion and have identical genetic characteristics. Fraternal, or dizygotic, twins are derived from two zygotes—separate ova that were fertilized by different sperm during the same female reproductive cycle. Fraternal twins do not have identical genetic traits.

Clinical **INSIGHT**

Pregnancy is measured in weeks from the last menses. A full-term pregnancy lasts about 40 weeks, 10 lunar months, or 280 days from the last menses. Pregnancy is also often divided into three *trimesters,* each with a duration of three calendar months.

About the seventh day after ovulation, the blastocyst attaches to the uterine lining. Digestive enzymes, released from the trophoblast, enable the blastocyst to penetrate into the endometrium, where it is soon covered by surface layers of the uterine lining. This entire process is called **implantation,** and it is completed by the fourteenth day (figure 18.3).

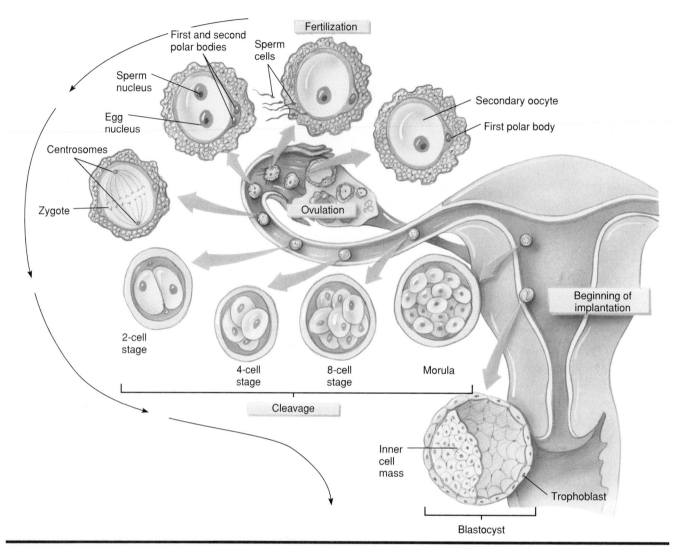

Figure 18.3 The stages of fertilization, cleavage, and implantation. Implantation begins about seven days after fertilization. AP|R

18.2 Hormonal Control of Pregnancy

Without the formation of an early embryo, the corpus luteum disintegrates about two weeks after ovulation. The resulting decline in estrogen and progesterone levels causes the uterine lining to break down and to be shed in the menses. Pregnancy causes hormone changes that maintain the uterine lining.

The trophoblast cells of the blastocyst secrete **human chorionic gonadotropin (HCG)** (kō-rē-on´-ik gōn-ah-dō-trō´-pin), an LH-like hormone that overrides hypothalamus–pituitary controls and maintains the corpus luteum. Under stimulation of HCG, the corpus luteum continues to secrete progesterone and estrogen to maintain the uterine lining. Pregnancy tests are designed to detect the presence of HCG in a woman's blood or urine, and it is usually detectable by the end of the third week after fertilization.

The concentration of HCG in the blood rises sharply between the third and fourth week and then declines to level off at about the fourth month of pregnancy, causing the degeneration of the corpus luteum. Between

Clinical INSIGHT

If the corpus luteum stops secreting progesterone and estrogen too quickly or if the placenta is too slow in starting to secrete these hormones, a decline in their concentrations results. Such a decline may detach the placenta from the uterine wall, causing a miscarriage.

the second and third month, the placenta takes over the role of producing estrogen and progesterone, and the corpus luteum degenerates. The ovaries remain inactive during the remainder of the pregnancy because the high level of progesterone suppresses secretion of gonadotropin-releasing hormone (GnRH) by the hypothalamus, preventing the release of follicle-stimulating hormone (FSH) and luteinizing hormone (LH) from the anterior pituitary.

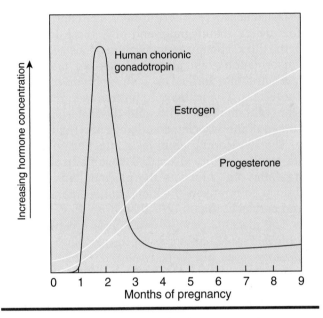

Figure 18.4 Relative concentrations of human chorionic gonadotropin (HCG), estrogen, and progesterone during pregnancy.

The concentrations of estrogen and progesterone continue to increase throughout pregnancy (figure 18.4). Note that the level of estrogen increases faster than that of progesterone. As pregnancy continues, placental estrogen and progesterone stimulate development of the mammary glands in preparation for milk secretion.

Check My Understanding

3. What hormonal changes are triggered by the presence of an implanted embryo?

18.3 Embryonic Development

The embryonic stage of development begins at the end of the second week and is completed at the end of the second month (eighth week). During this time, the embryo undergoes rapid development, forming the rudiments of all body organs, extraembryonic membranes, and the placenta. By the end of the eighth week, it has a distinct human appearance.

Germ Layers

After implantation, the inner cell mass grows to become the *embryonic disk,* which is supported by a short stalk extending from the wall of the blastocyst. The embryonic disk consists of three embryonic tissues: ectoderm, mesoderm, and endoderm. These embryonic tissues are called **germ layers** because all body tissues and organs are formed from them. Figure 18.5 illustrates the formation of the germ layers.

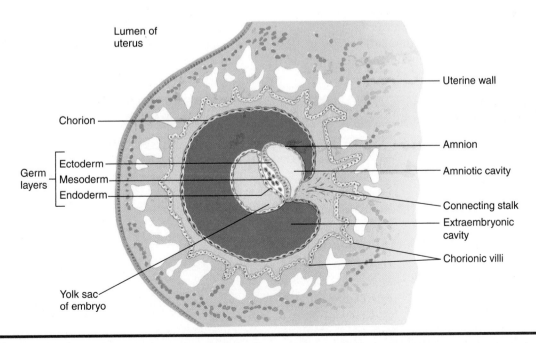

Figure 18.5 Development of the germ layers and three extraembryonic membranes—chorion, amnion, and yolk sac—in an early embryo. Note the chorionic villi.

Briefly, **ectoderm** forms all of the nervous system and the epidermis of the skin. **Mesoderm** forms muscles, bones, blood, and other forms of connective tissues. **Endoderm** forms the epithelial lining of the digestive, respiratory, and urinary tracts. Table 18.1 provides a more detailed listing of the major structures formed by each primary germ layer.

Extraembryonic Membranes

While the embryonic disk is forming, slender extensions from the trophoblast grow into the surrounding endometrium, firmly anchoring the blastocyst. The trophoblast of the blastocyst is now called the **chorion** (kō´-rē-on), the outermost extraembryonic membrane, and the slender extensions are known as **chorionic** (kō-rē-on´-ik) **villi.**

At about the same time, two other extraembryonic membranes separate from the embryonic disk. The **amnion** (am´-nē-on) is formed dorsal (posterior) to the embryo, and the **yolk sac** is formed ventral (anterior) to the embryo (figure 18.5). Amniotic fluid fills the space between the embryonic disk and the amnion. As the embryo develops, the amnion margins move toward the ventral surface of the embryo. In a short time, the embryo is enveloped by the amnion (figure 18.6).

The space between the embryo and the amnion becomes filled with *amniotic fluid.* It serves as a shock absorber for the developing embryo, and it also prevents adhesions from developing between various parts of the embryo. Later in development, the fetus swallows and inhales amniotic fluid and discharges dilute urine into it.

While the amnion is forming, the yolk sac branches, giving rise to the **allantois** (al-lan´-to-is), the last of the extraembryonic membranes. Both the allantois and the yolk sac subsequently become part of

the **umbilical** (um-bil´-i-kal) **cord,** which attaches the embryo to the placenta (figure 18.6). The yolk sac forms the early blood cells for the embryo. The allantois also forms blood cells and brings embryonic blood vessels to the placenta.

Placenta

As the embryo continues to grow and the chorion enlarges, the layer of the endometrium covering the blastocyst becomes increasingly thinner. The chorionic villi in this region disintegrate, and only those in contact with the thick, spongy endometrium persist. This leads to the formation of the **placenta** (plah-sen´-tah), a disk-shaped structure formed of both embryonic and maternal tissues. The embryonic portion is formed of the chorion and chorionic villi, and the maternal portion is formed of the associated endometrium (figure 18.6).

The developing embryo is attached to the placenta by the umbilical cord. Two umbilical arteries bring embryonic blood to the placenta, and a single umbilical vein returns the blood to the embryo. There are no nerves in the umbilical cord.

The placenta provides an interface between embryonic and maternal bloods for the exchange of water, respiratory gases, nutrients, wastes, hormones, and antibodies. The embryonic blood must receive all required substances from the mother's blood, and it must pass metabolic wastes into the mother's blood. The placenta is usually fully functional by the end of the eighth week.

The embryonic and maternal bloods do not mix in the placenta. The maternal blood vessels open into blood-filled spaces called *lacunae* into which the embryonic blood vessels extend and branch repeatedly. This arrangement provides a large surface area for the exchange of substances between embryonic and maternal bloods. Observe this relationship in figure 18.7.

Table 18.1 Structures Formed by the Primary Germ Layers		
Ectoderm	**Mesoderm**	**Endoderm**
All nervous tissue	All connective tissues including bone and cartilage	Epithelial lining of digestive system (except oral cavity and anal canal)
Sensory epithelium of sense organs	Skeletal, cardiac, and smooth muscles	Liver and pancreas
Hypophysis, pineal gland, and adrenal medulla	Blood, bone marrow, and lymphatic tissue	Epithelial lining of respiratory system
Epidermis of the skin including nails, hair follicles, sebaceous glands, and sweat glands	Blood and lymphatic vessels	Epithelial lining of urethra and bladder
	Dermis of the skin	Thymus, thyroid and parathyroid glands
Cornea and lens of eye	Kidneys, ureters, gonads, and reproductive ducts	
Epithelial lining of oral and nasal cavities, paranasal sinuses, and anal canal	Adrenal cortex	
Salivary glands	Epithelial lining of joints and the ventral body cavity	

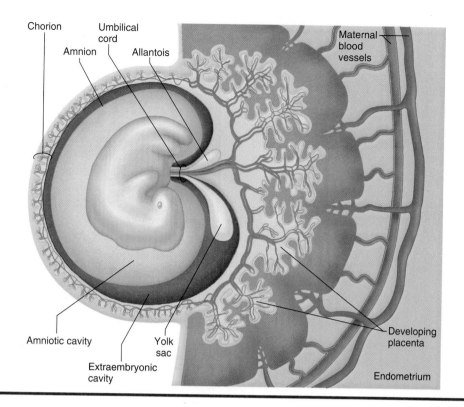

Figure 18.6 Amniotic fluid surrounds the embryo as the amnion continues to grow. The yolk sac and allantois become part of the developing umbilical cord. The chorion surrounding the embryo becomes thinner, the chorionic villi grow into the endometrium, and embryonic blood vessels extend into the chorionic villi as the placenta develops.

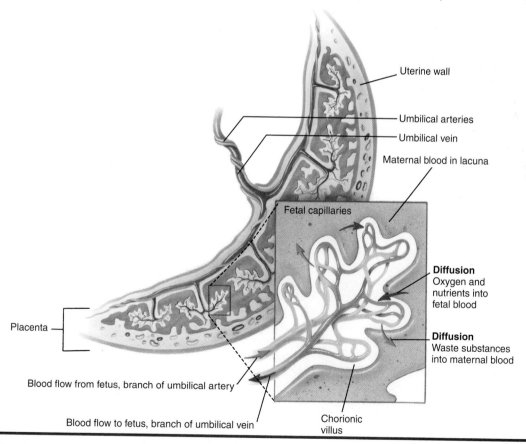

Figure 18.7 The placenta is formed of both embryonic and maternal tissues. The chorion and chorionic villi form the embryonic portion, and the endometrium of the uterine wall forms the maternal portion. Materials are exchanged between embryonic and maternal bloods by diffusion.

External Appearance

By the fourth week, the head and limb buds of the embryo are recognizable. By the seventh week, the rudiments of body organs are present, and the eyes and ears are visible. Figure 18.8 illustrates the visible changes in the embryo from the fourth to the seventh week.

Check My Understanding

4. What are the germ layers, and what happens to them?
5. What are the extraembryonic membranes, and what are their roles?
6. What composes the placenta, and what is its function?

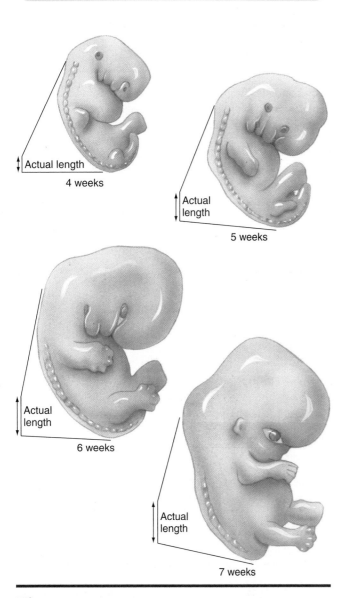

Figure 18.8 External appearance of the embryo from the fourth to the seventh week of development.

Actual length
4 weeks

Actual length
5 weeks

Actual length
6 weeks

Actual length
7 weeks

Clinical INSIGHT

Many substances that are harmful to the embryo, such as alcohol, cocaine, heroin, nicotine, caffeine, and many therapeutic drugs, can pass across the placenta into the embryonic blood. Physicians recommend that no drugs be taken during pregnancy except those that are crucial for the mother's health.

In addition, pathogens of certain maternal infections can also pass across the placenta and infect the fetus. These infections include AIDS, German measles, syphilis, and toxoplasmosis (transmitted from cat feces). All of these diseases may cause serious fetal disorders.

18.4 Fetal Development

When the embryo has reached the end of the eighth week of development, it has a distinctly human appearance. At this time it is called a **fetus** (figure 18.9). Table 18.2 highlights the changes in physical appearance that take place during fetal development.

At the start of the fetal stage, the head is as large as the body, and all organs are present in rudimentary form. The ossification of bones begins in the third month, and organs continue to develop. The fetus weighs about 45 grams.

In the fourth month, the eyes and ears reach their final positions, and a heartbeat may be detected with a stethoscope. During the fifth month, fine hair (lanugo) covers the body, hair appears on the scalp, and sebum from sebaceous glands forms the *vernix caseosa*, which protects the skin from the surrounding amniotic fluid. Amniotic fluid contains digestive and urinary wastes. Movements of the fetus may now be detected by the mother. The fetus weighs about 460 grams.

Continued growth of organ systems in the sixth and seventh months enables head, body, and limbs to attain infant proportions, but the fetus is lean with wrinkled, rather translucent skin. The fetus weighs about 1,300 grams.

Clinical INSIGHT

Some pregnant women develop hemorrhoids or varicose veins in the latter stages of pregnancy. These conditions result from inadequate venous return in veins serving the legs and anal canal due to pressure of the fetus on blood vessels in the pelvic area.

Deposition of subcutaneous fat plus continued growth and development of organ systems and descent of the testes in males occur in the eighth and ninth months. By the time the fetus is full term, the lanugo has been shed, the skin is pinkish with ample

Figure 18.9 A photograph of an eight-week embryo showing the umbilical cord and the enveloping amniochorionic membrane.

subcutaneous fat, hair covers the scalp, and all organ systems are ready for birth. The fetus weighs about 3,400 grams.

18.5 Birth

During the latter stages of pregnancy, the concentration of estrogen becomes increasingly greater than that of progesterone, as noted earlier. Whereas progesterone inhibits uterine contractions, estrogen promotes them. Therefore, there is an increasing tendency toward the onset of uterine contractions as the pregnancy approaches full term. Late in the pregnancy, the hormone **relaxin** is secreted by the placenta. It helps to relax the ligaments of the symphysis pubis and sacroiliac joints and softens the cervix as the time of birth approaches.

Birth usually occurs within two weeks of the calculated due date, which is 280 days from the last menses. The birth process is called **parturition** (par-tū-rish´-un), and the events associated with parturition are collectively called **labor.** The onset of labor involves both hormonal and neural aspects. As the fetus reaches full term, the high estrogen level overrides progesterone's inhibition of uterine contractions, allowing uterine contractions to occur. Pressure of the fetus on the cervix stretches the cervix, stimulating neural activity that results in uterine contractions. In fact, physicians

Table 18.2	**Changes During Fetal Development**
Month	**Changes**
2	Recognizable human shape; head as large as the body; eyes far apart; arms and legs present with digits present; body systems present in rudimentary form
3	Head nearly as large as the body; body is growing in length; eyes nearly fully developed but eyelids still fused; brain enlarging; arms and legs well formed; nails forming on digits; ossification beginning; organ systems continuing to develop
4	Head still dominant but body getting longer; facial features well developed; eyes and ears reach characteristic positions; bones distinct; heartbeat detectable by stethoscope
5	Head still dominant; fine hair (lanugo) covers body; hair appears on head; sebaceous gland secretions (vernix caseosa) cover body; eyelashes and eyebrows develop; limb movements detectable by mother; fetus assumes fetal position due to limited space
6	Head less dominant as body grows; substantial weight gain; limbs attain final proportions
7	Body is lean; head and body are proportionate; skin is wrinkled and pinkish; eyelids separate; body systems continue development
8	Skin smoother due to subcutaneous fat deposition; skull bones ossifying but cranial bones are soft; testes descend into scrotum; sex determination possible by ultrasound; distal limb bones ossifying
9	More subcutaneous fat deposited; skin smoother and whitish pink; skull bones continue to ossify
10	More subcutaneous fat deposited; nails extend to end of toes and fingers; skull bones largely ossified but cranial bones are not firmly joined; lanugo has been shed; vernix caseosa still present; skin pinkish even in fetuses of dark-skinned parents because melanin is not produced until skin is exposed to light

Figure 18.10 A full-term fetus positioned with the head against the cervix.

sometimes initiate labor by breaking the amnion so that increased pressure is placed on the cervix. Usually, the fetus is positioned headfirst, as shown in figure 18.10.

The *first stage of labor* is the dilation of the cervix. The stretching of the cervix triggers the formation of nerve impulses that are sent to the hypothalamus. When these reach a critical frequency, the hypothalamus activates the posterior pituitary gland to secrete *oxytocin,* increasing its concentration in the blood. Oxytocin stimulates the characteristic rhythmic contractions that begin at the upper end of the uterus and move toward the cervix, pushing the fetus toward the *vagina,* or birth canal.

The continued stretching of the cervix by uterine contractions forcing the baby's head against the cervix sends more impulses to the hypothalamus, resulting in a greater release of oxytocin from the posterior pituitary, which produces stronger and more frequent uterine contractions. This *positive-feedback mechanism* produces increasingly stronger contractions until birth occurs.

Dilation of the cervix is the longest stage of labor. It may last from 6 to 12 hours, depending on the size of the baby and whether the mother has had other children. During this time, the amnion ruptures, and the cervix dilates to the size of the baby's head (figure 18.11).

The *second stage of labor* is the delivery (expulsion) of the infant. It usually lasts less than an hour, with contractions occurring every two to three minutes and lasting about one minute. Once the head is expelled, the rest of the body exits rather quickly.

The *third stage of labor* is the delivery of the placenta. Within 15 minutes after birth of the baby, the

placenta detaches. Continued contractions expel the placenta (the afterbirth). The placenta is checked carefully to see that all of it has been removed from the uterus because any residue may cause a serious uterine infection. Detachment of the placenta produces some bleeding because endometrial blood vessels at the placental site are ruptured. However, uterine contractions compress the broken blood vessels so that serious bleeding is usually avoided. Subsequently, the uterus decreases in size rather quickly.

Check My Understanding

7. How does an increased estrogen level contribute to the onset of labor?
8. What is the neural–hormonal mechanism that increases uterine contractions?

About 5% of births are *breech births* in which the fetus is presented buttocks first. This complicates the delivery and may require delivery by *cesarean section.* In a cesarean section, a low, transverse incision is made through the walls of the abdomen and uterus, through which the baby is extracted.

(a) Fetal position before labor

(b) Dilation of the cervix

(c) Expulsion of the fetus

(d) Expulsion of the placenta

Figure 18.11 Stages of labor.

First Breath

Immediately after birth, the infant's nose and mouth are aspirated to remove mucus or fluid that would impair breathing. The umbilical cord is clamped and cut, separating the infant from the placenta, which has served as its prenatal respiratory organ. As carbon dioxide increases in the infant's blood, the respiratory center in the medulla is activated, and it stimulates the infant's first inspiration.

The first breath is difficult because the lungs are collapsed. In a full-term fetus, surfactant in alveolar

Premature infants born with less than 24 weeks of development seldom survive. The respiratory system of such infants is not sufficiently developed, even with the use of synthetic surfactant, to enable rapid gas exchange with blood in the lungs.

fluids reduces surface tension, making the first breath and subsequent breathing easier.

18.6 Circulatory Adaptations

Fetal circulation is quite different than adult circulation because the digestive tract, lungs, and kidneys are not functioning. Oxygen and nutrients are obtained from the maternal blood in the placenta, and carbon dioxide and other metabolic wastes are removed via the maternal blood. The pattern of fetal circulation is an adaptation to these conditions. Birth immediately separates the baby from its supply of nutrients and oxygen and stimulates circulatory changes to accommodate independent living as an air-breathing human.

Fetal Circulation

Figure 18.12 illustrates the pattern of fetal circulation. Oxygenated and nutrient-rich blood is carried from the placenta to the fetus by the *umbilical vein,* which enters the fetus at the umbilicus (navel).

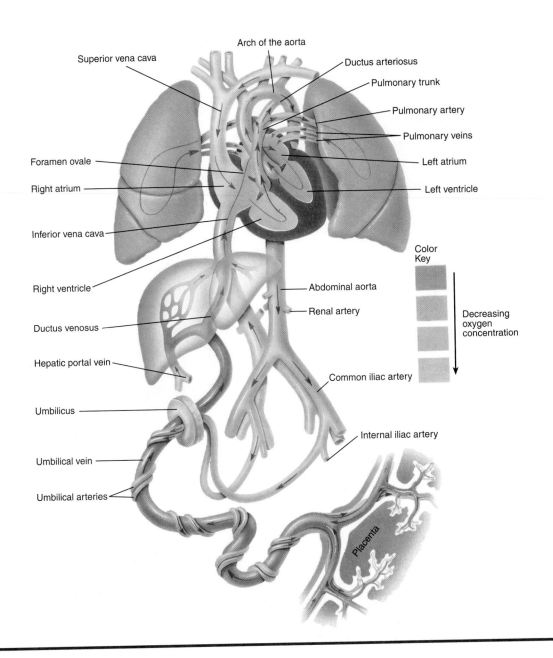

Figure 18.12 The pattern of circulation in a fetus.

Within the fetus, the umbilical vein passes toward the liver, where it divides into two branches. About half of the blood enters the liver, and the other half bypasses the liver through the **ductus venosus** (duk´-tus ven-ō´-sus) to enter the inferior vena cava. The oxygenated blood from the umbilical vein is mixed with deoxygenated blood in the inferior vena cava. The addition of blood from the ductus venosus increases the blood pressure within the inferior vena cava and the right atrium, which keeps the foramen ovale open.

Most of the blood entering the right atrium of the fetal heart passes directly through the **foramen ovale** (ō-vah´-lē), an opening into the left atrium. The blood in the left atrium flows into the left ventricle,

is pumped into the aorta, and is carried throughout the body. The blood entering the right ventricle is pumped through the pulmonary trunk, but most of it bypasses the lungs by flowing through the **ductus arteriosus** (duk´-tus ar-te-rē-ō´-sus) into the aortic arch. This bypass provides additional blood for transport to the body. However, sufficient blood flows through the pulmonary circuit to maintain the nonfunctional lungs.

Blood is returned to the placenta by two *umbilical arteries* that branch from the internal iliac arteries. Trace the flow of blood through the fetal cardiovascular system shown in figure 18.12. Table 18.3 summarizes these fetal circulatory adaptations.

Structure	Function
Umbilical vein	Carries oxygen-rich and nutrient-rich blood from the placenta to the fetus
Ductus venosus	Carries about half of the blood in the umbilical vein into the inferior vena cava, bypassing the liver and mixing oxygenated and deoxygenated blood
Foramen ovale	Allows a large portion of the blood entering the right atrium to pass through the atrial septum directly into the left atrium, bypassing the pulmonary circuit and providing as much oxygen and as many nutrients as possible for body cells via the systemic circuit
Ductus arteriosus	Carries most blood from the pulmonary trunk directly into the aorta, bypassing the nonfunctional lungs and providing more blood with available oxygen and nutrients for the systemic circuit
Umbilical arteries	Carry blood from the internal iliac arteries back to the placenta

Table 18.3   Fetal Circulatory Adaptations

Clinical INSIGHT

Fetal hemoglobin can carry up to 30% more oxygen than can adult hemoglobin. Because fetal arterial blood is almost always a mixture of oxygenated and deoxygenated bloods, this adaptation ensures adequate oxygen for the fetal cells.

Postnatal Circulatory Changes

After the baby is breathing, changes are made to convert the pattern of fetal circulation into that of an air-breathing infant. This involves closure of the foramen ovale and the constriction of all of the vessels used to get blood quickly from the umbilical vein into the aorta.

The distal portions of umbilical arteries constrict, inhibiting the flow of blood to the placenta. Subsequently, the proximal portions of the umbilical arteries persist as *superior vesical arteries* and the distal portions become *umbilical ligaments*. Blood continues to flow through the umbilical vein from the placenta to the newborn for about one minute, and then it constricts. It will become the *ligamentum teres*. At the same time, the ductus venosus constricts. It will subsequently become the *ligamentum venosum* in the wall of the liver.

As the umbilical vein constricts and the pulmonary circulation becomes functional, blood pressure in the right atrium decreases, whereas blood pressure in the left atrium increases due to increased blood flow to and from the lungs. The higher blood pressure in the left atrium closes a tissue flap in the left atrium over the foramen ovale, separating the pulmonary and systemic circuits. A slight depression called the *fossa ovalis* remains at the site of closure. About the same time, the ductus arteriosus constricts and ultimately becomes the *ligamentum arteriosum*. These circulatory changes

Check My Understanding
9. What are the circulatory adaptations in a fetus?
10. What circulatory changes occur in a newborn infant?

Clinical INSIGHT

Umbilical cord blood is rich in blood-forming stem cells, which are required for blood cell production. After delivery and after the umbilical cord is cut, cord blood may be collected, saved, and kept frozen and available in case it is needed by the child later in life. If the child in later life develops leukemia and needs a transfusion of blood-forming stem cells, the cord blood is available for transfusion. Because it is essentially a self-transfusion, rejection is not a problem.

are functionally complete within 30 minutes after birth, but it takes about one year for tissue growth to make them permanent (figure 18.13).

18.7 Lactation

High levels of estrogen and progesterone during pregnancy stimulate the development of the mammary glands and enlargement of the breasts in preparation for milk production, or **lactation** (lak-tā´-shun). Although the mammary glands are capable of secreting milk, the high levels of estrogen and progesterone inhibit the hypothalamus so that milk production does not occur during pregnancy.

After birth, the levels of estrogen and progesterone drop dramatically, removing the inhibitory effect

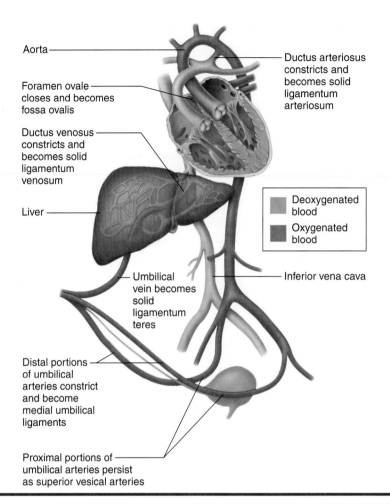

Aorta

Foramen ovale closes and becomes fossa ovalis

Ductus venosus constricts and becomes solid ligamentum venosum

Liver

Umbilical vein becomes solid ligamentum teres

Distal portions of umbilical arteries constrict and become medial umbilical ligaments

Proximal portions of umbilical arteries persist as superior vesical arteries

Ductus arteriosus constricts and becomes solid ligamentum arteriosum

Deoxygenated blood

Oxygenated blood

Inferior vena cava

Figure 18.13   Circulatory changes in a newborn infant.

and enabling the hypothalamus to secrete *prolactin-releasing hormone (PRH)*. PRH activates the anterior pituitary to secrete **prolactin,** which stimulates milk production.

Prolactin stimulates the mammary glands to secrete milk, but its effects are not evident for two to three days. In the meantime, the mammary glands produce *colostrum* (kō-los´-trum), which differs from true milk by containing higher concentrations of protein and essentially no fat. The high protein content provides an added boost of essential nutrients for protein synthesis, which is needed for the continued development and growth of the baby.

The continued secretion of prolactin and milk production are maintained by mechanical stimulation of the nipples by the suckling infant. Suckling forms neural impulses that stimulate the hypothalamus to secrete PRH, which, in turn, causes continued prolactin secretion by the anterior pituitary. Thus, lactation is maintained by a *positive-feedback system.*

Milk does not simply flow from the breasts. Instead, it is ejected after about 30 seconds of suckling

Clinical **INSIGHT**

Breast-feeding seems to provide advantages for the baby, including (1) better nutrition because nutrients are easier to absorb, (2) rapid bonding due to prolonged contact with the mother, (3) antibodies that prevent digestive inflammation, and (4) enhanced cognitive development.

Check My Understanding

11. How do hormones control lactation?

by the infant. Stimulation of the nipple by suckling sends impulses to the hypothalamus, which triggers the release of oxytocin by the posterior pituitary. *Oxytocin* stimulates contraction of smooth muscles in the lactiferous ducts, resulting in milk ejection, or "letdown."

Milk production may continue for as long as the infant is suckled, but the volume of milk produced gradually declines. If suckling is stopped, milk accumulates, the secretion of prolactin is inhibited, and milk production ceases in about a week.

18.8 Disorders of Pregnancy and Prenatal Development

These disorders are grouped as pregnancy disorders of the mother and prenatal disorders of the fetus.

Pregnancy Disorders

Eclampsia (ē-klamp´-sē-ah), or *toxemia of pregnancy,* is a disorder that occurs in two forms. *Preeclampsia* of late pregnancy is characterized by increased blood pressure, edema, and proteinuria (protein in the urine). The cause is unknown. If unsuccessfully treated, it may develop into *eclampsia,* a far more serious disorder that may lead to convulsions and coma. Both infant and maternal mortality are high in eclampsia. Rapid termination of the pregnancy may be indicated.

An **ectopic pregnancy** is the implantation of an embryo anywhere other than in the uterus. A common site is in a uterine tube. Treatment involves surgical removal of the embryo.

A **miscarriage** is a spontaneous abortion. Most miscarriages occur early in pregnancy as a result of gross abnormalities of the embryo or placenta. Another cause is the untimely transfer of estrogen and progesterone production from the corpus luteum to the placenta during the second and third month of pregnancy.

Morning sickness is characterized by nausea and vomiting upon getting up in the morning. It lasts from one to six weeks, and the cause is unknown. About 60% of pregnant women experience this discomfort.

Prenatal Disorders

Birth defects may be inherited or may be caused by a variety of *teratogens* (ter-ah´-to-jens), substances or influences that produce physical abnormalities. Teratogens include alcohol, illegal drugs, some therapeutic drugs, X-rays, and certain diseases such as German measles (Rubella). Generally, the earlier the embryo is exposed, the greater is the defect produced. Alcohol is the most common teratogen. It produces *fetal alcohol syndrome,* which is characterized by a small head; mental retardation; facial deformities; and abnormalities of the heart, genitals, and limbs.

Physiological jaundice sometimes occurs in a newborn infant due to the destruction of fetal red blood cells faster than the liver can process the bilirubin. This results in excess bilirubin in the blood. Phototherapy (exposure to ultraviolet light) is a common treatment to speed up bilirubin breakdown. Jaundice may be a more serious problem in premature babies.

Infant respiratory distress syndrome (IRDS), or infant crib death, is the major cause of death in newborn infants. It occurs more often in premature babies. One cause of IRDS is insufficient surfactant production by the alveoli. Breathing is labored, and gas exchange is inadequate.

18.9 Genetics

Gentics is the study of heredity, the passing of inherited traits from one generation to the next. The determiners of hereditary traits are located on **chromosomes.** A chromosome consists of DNA and protein, and it is the DNA that controls inheritance and directs cellular functions.

Each human body cell contains 46 chromosomes, 23 pairs. Chromosome pairs 1 through 22 are called *autosomes* because they control most inherited traits except gender. Gender is determined by chromosome pair 23, the *sex chromosomes.* There are two types of sex chromosomes, a large X chromosome and a small Y chromosome. The Y chromosome determines maleness, so males possess one X chromosome and one Y chromosome (XY). Females possess two X chromosomes (XX).

A person's chromosomes, including the sex chromosomes, may be examined by making a *karyotype.* The chromosomes in a dividing cell are photographed during metaphase, and the photograph is enlarged. Then the chromosomes are cut out, matched in pairs and arranged by size and location of the centromere. Figure 18.14 is a karyotype of a normal male. Note the X and Y chromosomes and that the chromosomes are arranged in pairs.

Sex Determination

Recall that gametes are formed by meiotic cell division, a process that places one member of each chromosome pair in each gamete. Each human gamete contains 23 chromosomes—22 autosomes and 1 sex chromosome. We will consider only the sex chromosomes here.

Figure 18.14   Karyotype of a normal human male. The only difference in a female karyotype would be the presence of a pair of X chromosomes in place of the XY pair of the male.

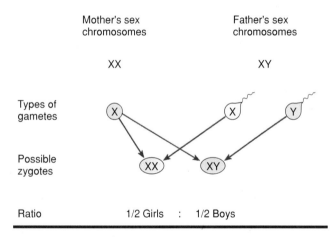

Figure 18.15   The inheritance of sex.

Because a female has two X chromosomes in her cells, all of her gametes contain an X chromosome. A male has both an X chromosome and a Y chromosome in his cells. Therefore, half of his gametes are X-bearing, and half are Y-bearing. If an egg is fertilized by an X-bearing sperm, the child will be a girl. If an egg is fertilized by a Y-bearing sperm, the child will be a boy. Obviously, the probability of any zygote being a girl (or a boy) is one-half or 50%. Figure 18.15 illustrates the determination of sex.

Genes

Recall from chapter 2, page 38, that DNA consists of a double strand of nucleotides that are joined by complementary pairing of their nitrogenous bases: adenine (A),

thymine (T), cytosine (C) and guanine (G). The sequence of these bases forms the genetic code, which regulates cellular functions and determines the inheritance of genetic traits.

A specific part of a chromosome's DNA molecule that codes for the synthesis of a specific protein is called a **gene.** A gene is the unit of inheritance. Chemically, a gene is a specific sequence of nucleotides, so genes occur in a linear sequence in a chromosome. The DNA of a chromosome may contain hundreds of genes.

The *human genome,* all of the DNA in human chromosomes, consists of a sequence of about 3 billion base pairs and about 25,000 genes. Scientists have now determined the sequence of bases in more than 90% of the human genome, and they have mapped the sequence of known genes on chromosomes. This information has greatly accelerated the rate of genetic discoveries, especially the identification of genes that cause human genetic disorders. This new knowledge will speed up the development of drugs to treat genetic disorders and, perhaps in the more distant future, enable correction of genetic defects through genetic engineering.

Because chromosomes occur in pairs, genes also occur in pairs. An inherited trait is determined by at least one pair of genes. There may be two or more alternate forms of a gene controlling the expression of a particular trait. These alternate forms are called **alleles** (ah-lēls´), and each allele affects the expression of a trait differently. So, in the simplest case, a trait is determined by one pair of alleles present in a person's cells. If the two alleles for a trait are identical, the person is **homozygous** for that trait; if they are different, the person is **heterozygous** for that trait.

Gene Expression

Each person's chromosomes contain a unique catalog of genes, the **genotype** for that person. The expression of those genes yields the observable characteristics known as the **phenotype.** What we see is the phenotype, but it is the genotype that is involved in the transmission of traits.

Dominant and Recessive Inheritance

Some alleles are dominant, and some are recessive. A *dominant allele* is always expressed, whereas a *recessive allele* is expressed only when both recessive alleles are present.

Consider the example of skin pigmentation. Normal skin pigmentation is controlled by a dominant allele *(A)*. The absence of pigment (albinism) is controlled by a recessive allele *(a)*. The possible genotypes and phenotypes are shown below. Note that it requires only one dominant allele to express the dominant trait but that both recessive alleles must be present for the recessive trait to be expressed.

Genotype	Phenotype
AA	Normal
Aa	Normal
aa	Albino

Table 18.4 indicates a few human traits that are determined by dominant and recessive alleles.

Codominance

In some traits, both alleles are equally expressed, so they both affect the phenotype. This type of inheritance is known as *codominance.* An example is sickle-cell anemia, a condition characterized by defective hemoglobin that cannot carry adequate oxygen. Erythrocytes with the defective hemoglobin assume a characteristic sickled or crescent shape. Sickle-cell anemia occurs

Table 18.4 Examples of Traits Determined by Dominant and Recessive Alleles

Traits Determined by Dominant Alleles	Traits Determined by Recessive Alleles
Freckles	Absence of freckles
Dimples in cheeks	Absence of dimples
Dark hair	Light hair or red hair
Full lips	Thin lips
Free earlobes	Attached ear lobes
Normal	Thalassemia
Feet with arches	Flat feet
Huntington's disease	Normal
Astigmatism	No astigmatism
Farsightedness	Not farsighted
Panic attacks	Normal
Extra fingers or toes	Normal number of digits
Normal	Cystic fibrosis
Normal	Hemophilia*
A or B blood types	O blood type
Rh+ blood type	Rh− blood type
Color vision	Red–green color blindness*
Normal	Gout*

*X-linked trait.

among people whose ancestors lived in central Africa. About 8% of African-Americans possess the allele for sickle-cell anemia.

A person who inherits both alleles for sickle-cell anemia (H^sH^s) produces abnormal hemoglobin, leading to the formation of sickled cells that cannot carry sufficient oxygen, and the sickled cells tend to plug capillaries. Symptoms include pain in joints and the abdomen and chronic kidney disease.

In the heterozygous state (HH^s), some hemoglobin molecules are normal, but others are abnormal. Fortunately, few red blood cells become sickled when oxygen is at normal levels, and clinical symptoms are absent at such times. However, more red blood cells become sickled during times of oxygen deficit, a characteristic that allows detection of carriers of the sickle-cell allele. The heterozygote state affords some protective advantage against the pathogen causing malaria.

Multiple Alleles

Some traits are determined by genes that have more than two alleles. An example is the ABO blood groups. There are three alleles involved: I^A causes the production of the A antigen; I^B causes the production of the B antigen; and i^o produces neither antigen. Both I^A and I^B are dominant over the recessive i^o. If both I^A and I^B are present, both are expressed. The possible genotypes and phenotypes are

Genotypes	Phenotypes
I^AI^A; I^Ai^o	Type A blood
I^BI^B; I^Bi^o	Type B blood
I^AI^B	Type AB blood
i^oi^o	Type O blood

Polygenes

To this point, we have considered either-or traits, but some traits do not fit this mode of inheritance. For example, people are not either tall or short. Instead, the human population exhibits a gradation of heights that fits a standard bell curve. Such traits are controlled by *polygenes,* a number of different genes that may be located on different chromosomes. Examples of such traits are height, intelligence, and skin pigment concentration. It is difficult to predict the inheritance of polygenic traits.

Let's consider height. Four pairs of genes seem to be involved. The two alleles are T and t. Each T allele exerts a small increase in height, and each t allele exerts no increase in height. If all eight alleles are T alleles, the person will be very tall; if all eight alleles are t alleles, the person will be very short. Various combinations of the two alleles produce a variety of intermediate heights.

Predicting Inheritance

Parents often wonder about the chances of their child developing certain inherited traits. This can be predicted for some traits for which the inheritance pattern has been determined and if the genotypes of the parents are known. Such predictions indicate the *probability,* rather than absolute certainty, that a trait will be inherited.

Let's consider freckles. Freckles are determined by a dominant allele *(F)*, and normal pigment distribution is determined by a recessive allele *(f)*. The possible genotypes and phenotypes are

Genotypes	Phenotypes
FF	Freckled
Ff	Freckled
ff	Normal

Figure 18.16 shows how to determine the probability of the freckled or nonfreckled trait in the next generation if the genotypes of the parents are known. In this example, the parents are known to be heterozygous for freckles. What is the probability that their children will be freckled?

Because each parent is heterozygous, meiotic division during gamete formation causes half of the gametes of each parent to contain an allele for freckles *(F)*, and

Figure 18.16 The probability of freckles being inherited by children of parents who are heterozygous for freckles.

half to carry an allele for normal pigmentation *(f)*. The union of sperm and egg occurs at random (by chance), so we must allow for all possible combinations of gametes. This is accomplished by using a *Punnett square* (a chart named after Reginald Punnett, a geneticist).

The alleles in eggs are placed along the horizontal axis, and the alleles in sperm are placed along the vertical axis. Then, the allele of each egg is written in the squares below each egg, and the allele of each sperm is written in the squares to the right of each sperm. Each square now contains a possible genotype of an individual in the next generation. The Punnett square now shows all possible genotypes that may occur in the next generation.

From this information, the predicted genotype ratio may be determined. Then, knowing that the trait for freckles is dominant and that the presence of a single dominant allele *(F)* produces freckles, the predicted phenotype ratio may be determined. Note in figure 18.16 that it is possible for two heterozygous freckled parents to have a child with normal pigmentation. However, if one parent is homozygous for freckles and the other is heterozygous for freckles, all children would be freckled.

The inheritance of any dominant/recessive trait may be determined in a similar manner.

X-Linked Traits

A few traits are determined by genes on the X chromosome. These are **X-linked,** or *sex-linked,* **traits**. They affect males much more frequently than females. Recessive X-linked traits are expressed in males because males possess only one X chromosome, so alleles on the X chromosome are always expressed. Females have two X chromosomes, so they usually possess a dominant normal allele, which prevents expression of a recessive allele.

Red-green color blindness is a common X-linked recessive trait. A color-blind male inherits the allele for color blindness from his mother, who provides his X chromosome. The mother may have either normal vision or be red-green color-blind (table 18.5).

Table 18.5 Possible Genotypes and Phenotypes for Red-Green Color Blindness, an X-Linked Trait

	Genotype	Phenotype
Females	$X^C X^C$	Normal
	$X^C X^c$	Normal carrier
	$X^c X^c$	Color-blind
Males	$X^C Y$	Normal
	$X^c Y$	Color-blind

C = Allele for normal vision; *c* = Allele for color blindness.

Check My Understanding

12. What are the relationships among chromosomes, DNA, genes, and alleles?
13. What distinguishes the dominant/recessive pattern of inheritance?
14. Why are recessive X-linked traits expressed more often in males than in females?

18.10 Inherited Diseases

Inherited, or genetic, diseases are caused by either chromosome abnormalities or specific alleles. The development of advanced techniques and new knowledge makes an understanding of genetic disease increasingly important.

Chromosome Abnormalities

Some genetic diseases are related to the presence of an additional chromosome or to the absence of a chromosome. These disorders result from errors that occur during meiotic cell division, causing some gametes to receive both members of a chromosome pair while other gametes receive neither member. If such gametes are involved in zygote formation, a genetic disorder occurs. The genetic damage usually is so severe that it causes a spontaneous abortion. In some cases, the effect is not lethal but disabling.

An example of a disabling genetic disorder is Down syndrome, one of the more common genetic disorders. It is caused by the presence of an extra chromosome 21, as shown in figure 18.17. Down syndrome is characterized by mental retardation, short stature, short digits, slanted eyes, and a protruding tongue. A girl with Down syndrome is shown in figure 18.18. Babies with Down syndrome are born more often to mothers over 40 years of age.

Single-Gene Disorders

These disorders usually affect the baby's metabolism after birth, when it must depend on its own life processes, or they may appear later in life. Consider a few examples of single-gene disorders.

Cystic fibrosis, a recessive disorder, is the most common genetic disorder among Caucasians. It is caused by a missing chloride channel on mucus-secreting cells. This causes production of thick mucus that blocks respiratory airways, and it leads to an early death from respiratory infections.

Phenylketonuria (PKU), a recessive disorder, is due to a missing enzyme needed to metabolize phenylalanine (an amino acid). Without treatment, mental and physical retardation results. A special diet

Figure 18.17 A karyotype of a male with Down syndrome caused by trisomy 21.

Figure 18.18 A girl with Down syndrome.

that limits phenylalanine can prevent these effects if it is started at birth and continued to adulthood.

Tay–Sachs disease, a recessive disorder, primarily affects Jewish people of central European ancestry. An enzyme needed to metabolize a fatty substance associated with neurons is missing. The results are mental retardation, muscle weakness, seizures, and finally death, usually by two years of age.

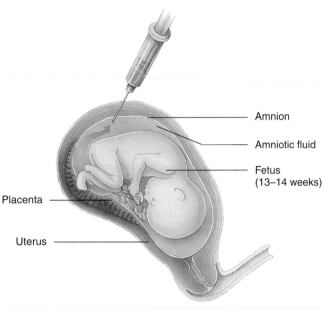

Figure 18.19 In amniocentesis, a sample of amniotic fluid is withdrawn and the suspended fetal cells are examined for genetic abnormalities.

Huntington's disease, a dominant disorder, results from one or more missing enzymes needed in cellular respiration. This causes a buildup of lactic acid in neurons in the brain. Uncontrollable muscle contractions, memory loss, and personality changes begin between 30 and 50 years of age. Death occurs within 15 years after the appearance of symptoms.

Hemophilia A and *hemophilia B,* X-linked recessive disorders, result from missing clotting factors. Prolonged bleeding can be life threatening, and joints may be painfully disabled. Patients are dependent upon frequent transfusions of normal plasma or intravenous injections of the missing clotting factor.

Genetic Counseling

Prospective parents who have genetic disorders in one or both of their families may benefit from genetic counseling. By collecting genetic information, a genetic counselor can inform prospective parents of the probability of a genetic disorder appearing in their children. Genetic information may be collected from family histories and blood tests of the prospective parents and family members. If the woman is pregnant, ultrasound may be used to detect gross fetal abnormalities, and fetal cells may be obtained for examination. Fetal cells are obtained in two ways: amniocentesis and chorionic villi sampling.

In *amniocentesis,* a hollow needle is inserted through the abdominal and uterine walls of the mother and into the amnion to draw out a sample of amniotic fluid (figure 18.19). Fetal cells in the sample are grown by tissue culture and are analyzed to see if there are chromosomal abnormalities. Also, the amniotic fluid is analyzed for the presence of specific proteins that indicate serious neural defects. Amniocentesis is not done earlier than the 14th week of pregnancy, when ample amniotic fluid is available for sampling without injury to the fetus.

In *chorionic villi sampling,* a narrow tube is inserted through the cervix and fetal tissue from chorionic villi is suctioned out. Chromosomes in the fetal cells are examined for abnormalities. Chorionic villi sampling may be performed at 10 weeks, and chromosome examination can be done immediately.

Both amniocentesis and chorionic villi sampling have inherent risks for mother and fetus. Fetal risks seem to be greater in chorionic villi sampling.

A new way of obtaining fetal cells for analysis called *fetal cell sorting* is in early stages of development. This procedure is based on the discovery that a small amount of fetal cells enter the mother's blood in about 70% of all pregnancies. A fluorescent cell sorter can identify and separate out the rare fetal cells for analysis. Although it is still experimental, this method shows promise, and it circumvents the health risks inherent in amniocentesis and chorionic villi sampling.

CHAPTER SUMMARY

18.1 Fertilization and Early Development

- Sperm usually encounter the secondary oocyte in the upper third of a uterine tube. Only one sperm can enter an oocyte.
- When a secondary oocyte is penetrated by a sperm, it undergoes the second meiotic division, forming an ovum and a second polar body. Fertilization occurs with the fusion of the sperm and ovum nuclei, forming a zygote.
- The zygote undergoes cleavage divisions, forming a morula. Continued mitotic divisions form a blastocyst containing an inner cell mass.
- About the seventh day, the blastocyst becomes implanted in the endometrium.

18.2 Hormonal Control of Pregnancy

- The trophoblast and chorion secrete HCG, taking over the role of maintaining the corpus luteum whose progesterone maintains the uterine lining.
- In the second or third month, the placenta takes over the production of progesterone and estrogen, and the corpus luteum disintegrates. Ovaries remain inactive for the remainder of the pregnancy.

18.3 Embryonic Development

- The embryonic disk separates into the three germ layers: ectoderm, mesoderm, and endoderm.
- The trophoblast becomes the chorion, the first and outermost extraembryonic membrane. The chorionic villi will become part of the placenta.
- The amnion develops dorsal to the embryo, envelops the embryo, and becomes filled with amniotic fluid that serves as a shock absorber.
- The yolk sac develops ventral to the embryo. It subsequently branches to form the allantois. Both of these extraembryonic membranes form blood cells prior to their production by the liver and bone marrow. The allantois brings fetal blood vessels to the placenta.
- The placenta is formed of both embryonic and maternal tissues, and it is functional by the eighth week. It allows the exchange of materials between embryonic and maternal bloods.
- By the seventh week, the embryo exhibits a head, body, limbs with digits, eyes, and ears.

18.4 Fetal Development

- The embryo is called a fetus after the eighth week, and it clearly resembles a human. Organ systems are in rudimentary form, and the cardiovascular system is functioning.
- Fetal development includes development of the organ systems to functional levels, an increase in size and weight, ossification of bones, and development of hair.

18.5 Birth

- Placental relaxin softens the cervix and relaxes the symphysis pubis and sacroiliac joints in the late stage of pregnancy.
- The high level of estrogen in the late stage of pregnancy counteracts the inhibitory action of progesterone against uterine contractions.
- The onset of labor involves nerve impulses and oxytocin. Pressure of the fetus on the cervix forms nerve impulses that are sent to the hypothalamus, which stimulates oxytocin secretion by the posterior pituitary. Oxytocin stimulates uterine contractions, dilating the cervix and forming more nerve impulses. These interactions set up a positive-feedback control that strengthens contractions until birth.
- Labor involves three stages: (a) dilation of the cervix, (b) delivery of the infant, and (c) delivery of the placenta.
- After birth, an accumulation of carbon dioxide stimulates the respiratory center to trigger the first breath. Surfactant in alveolar fluids makes breathing easier.

18.6 Circulatory Adaptations

- The pattern of fetal circulation is adapted to a life in which the lungs and digestive system are nonfunctional and nutrients and oxygen are derived from the mother's blood via the placenta. Embryonic blood is carried to the placenta by umbilical arteries and is returned by an umbilical vein.
- Circulatory adaptations pass oxygen-rich and nutrient-rich blood as quickly as possible from the umbilical vein to the aorta to meet the needs of body cells. These adaptations include the ductus venosus, foramen ovale, and ductus arteriosus.
- When the baby starts breathing, fetal circulatory adaptations are eliminated to enable an efficient separation of the pulmonary and systemic circuits.

18.7 Lactation

- The high levels of estrogen and progesterone during pregnancy prepare the mammary glands for lactation but prevent hormone stimulation of lactation until birth.
- After birth, the low levels of progesterone and estrogen allow the hypothalamus to secrete PRH, which stimulates the anterior pituitary to secrete prolactin. Prolactin stimulates the mammary glands to produce milk.
- Colostrum is secreted first, followed by true milk after two to three days.
- Suckling stimulates the formation of impulses that are sent to the hypothalamus, which (a) secretes PRH, ensuring the continued release of prolactin and milk production; and (b) stimulates the posterior pituitary to secrete oxytocin, which produces ejection of the milk.

18.8 Disorders of Pregnancy and Prenatal Development

- Pregnancy disorders include eclampsia, ectopic pregnancy, miscarriage, and morning sickness.

- Prenatal disorders include birth defects, physiological jaundice, and respiratory distress syndrome.

18.9 Genetics

- The determiners (genes) of hereditary traits are located on chromosomes. There are 46 chromosomes in human body cells: 22 pairs of autosomes and one pair of sex chromosomes.
- Sex chromosomes for females are XX; for males, XY.
- A gene is the unit of heredity. It is a portion of a DNA molecule that codes for a specific protein. Alternate forms of a gene are called alleles. A person with identical alleles for a trait is homozygous for that trait. If the alleles are different, the person is heterozygous.
- The genotype is all of the genes determining a trait. The phenotype is the observable characteristics expressed for a trait.
- Many genes have only two alleles whose expression is either by dominant/recessive inheritance or by incomplete dominance. Some traits are determined by multiple alleles, and others are determined by polygenes.
- The probability of transmitting traits to the next generation may be predicted using a Punnett square.
- X-linked traits are determined by genes located on the X chromosome.

18.10 Inherited Diseases

- Genetic diseases may result from either chromosomal abnormalities or defective alleles.
- Prospective parents who have genetic diseases in their family histories may benefit from genetic counseling.

BUILDING MY VOCABULARY

1. **Selected New Terms**
   allantois, p. 394
   amnion, p. 394
   chorion, p. 394
   codominance, p. 405
   ductus arteriosus, p. 400
   ductus venosus, p. 400
   ectoderm, p. 394
   endoderm, p. 394
   foramen ovale, p. 400
   human chorionic gonadotropin (HCG), p. 392
   lactation, p. 401
   mesoderm, p. 394
   oxytocin, p. 398
   prolactin, p. 402

   relaxin, p. 397
   X-linked traits, p. 407
   yolk sac, p. 394

2. **Related Clinical Terms**
   Monozygotic (mon-o-zi-got´-ik) One zygote.
   Obstetrics (ob-ste t´-riks) Medical specialty dealing with pregnancy and childbirth.
   Placenta abruptio (ah-brup´-she-o) Premature separation of the placenta from the uterus.
   Placenta previa (pre´-ve-ah) Placenta located over or adjacent to the opening into the uterus.
   Postpartum (post-par´-tum) Occurring after birth.
   Teratogen (te-rah´-to-jen) A substance or condition causing birth defects.

SELF-REVIEW

Answers are located in appendix B.

1. Usually a sperm meets a secondary oocyte in the _____.
2. Fusion of sperm and ovum nuclei is called _____.
3. A _____ is implanted in the endometrium on about the _____ day of development.
4. Secretion of _____ by the trophoblast and chorion maintain the secretion of estrogen and _____, which maintains the endometrium.
5. The embryonic disk forms the three _____ that subsequently form all other tissues of the embryo and fetus.
6. The _____ contains fluid in which the embryo develops, and the chorionic villi become the embryonic part of the _____.
7. After the _____ week, the embryo is called a _____, and it clearly resembles a human.
8. The first and longest stage of _____ is the dilation of the cervix, which results from uterine contractions stimulated by the hormone _____.

9. In a fetus, the _____ enables oxygenated blood to pass from the right atrium into the left atrium, and the _____ passes blood from the pulmonary trunk into the aorta.
10. Lactation begins after _____ from the hypothalamus stimulates secretion of _____ by the anterior pituitary gland.
11. The units of inheritance are _____, which are small segments of _____ that make up chromosomes.
12. Humans possess _____ chromosomes in their cells, and a person possessing two X chromosomes is a _____.
13. X-linked recessive traits occur more often in _____.
14. In dominant/recessive inheritance, a recessive allele is expressed only when the person is _____ for the recessive trait.
15. It is possible to predict the _____ of a trait appearing in children if the genotypes of parents are known.

CRITICAL THINKING

1. Complete the learning objectives on the first page of this chapter.
2. Describe the various roles of the placenta during pregnancy.
3. Explain why a miscarriage is likely if the placenta is too slow to take over its hormone-producing role.
4. If you are pregnant and a genetic test indicates the potential of a debilitating abnormality in the fetus, would you consider induced abortion? What would you want to know before making your decision? Explain.
5. DNA analysis can determine if a person's genome contains any of the known defective genes. At present, there are no cures or effective treatments for most of the disorders caused by these genes. Would you like to know if you possess defective genes? Explain.

1. Anatomy and Physiology

Write the terms that match the phrases in the spaces at the right.

1) The study of cells. _____

2) The study of body organization and structure. _____

3) The study of body functions. _____

2. Levels of Organization

a.   List the levels of organization from the most complex to the simplest.

   1) _____   4) _____

   2) _____   5) _____

   3) _____   6) _____

b.   Write the terms that match the phrases in the spaces at the right.

   1) A coordinated group of organs.   _____

   2) Structural and functional units of the body.   _____

   3) An aggregation of similar cells.   _____

c.   Match the names of the organ systems with the phrases.

Cardiovascular	Lymphatic	Reproductive, male
Digestive	Muscle	Respiratory
Endocrine	Nervous	Skeletal
Integumentary	Reproductive, female	Urinary

   1) Stomach, liver, intestines.   _____

   2) Brain, spinal cord, nerves.   _____

   3) Provides chemical coordination.   _____

   4) Skin, hair, nails.   _____

   5) Returns lymph to blood; provides immunity.   _____

   6) Bones, ligaments, cartilages.   _____

   7) Contraction enables movement.   _____

   8) Transports materials to and from cells. _____

   9) Kidneys, ureters, urinary bladder.   _____

   10) Testes, penis, prostate gland.   _____

   11) Ovaries, oviducts, uterus, vagina.   _____

   12) Blood, heart, arteries, veins.   _____

   13) Supports the body.   _____

   14) Secretes hormones that regulate functions. _____

   15) Regulates volume of body fluids.   _____

   16) Protects underlying tissues.   _____

   17) Rapid coordination of body functions.   _____

   18) Digests food and absorbs nutrients.   _____

19) Gas exchange between air and blood.   _____

20) Larynx, trachea, bronchi, and lungs.   _____

3. Directional Terms

Provide the term that correctly completes each statement.

1) The head is _____ to the neck.   _____

2) The hand is _____ to the wrist.   _____

3) The skin is _____ to the muscles.   _____

4) The mouth is _____ to the nose.   _____

5) The elbow is _____ to the wrist.   _____

6) The ear is on the _____ surface of the head.   _____

7) The umbilicus is on the _____ body surface.   _____

8) The hip is on the _____ body surface.   _____

9) The buttocks are on the _____ body surface.   _____

4. Body Regions

Label the body regions by placing the number of the label line in the space by the correct label.

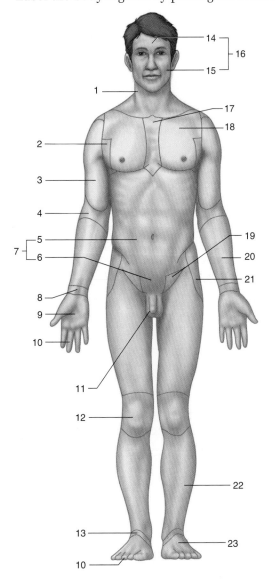

_____ Abdominal

_____ Abdominopelvic

_____ Antebrachial

_____ Antecubital

_____ Axillary

_____ Brachial

_____ Carpal

_____ Cephalic

_____ Cervical

_____ Coxal

_____ Cranial

_____ Crural

_____ Digital

_____ Facial

_____ Genital

_____ Inguinal

_____ Palmar

_____ Patellar

_____ Pectoral

_____ Pedal

_____ Pelvic

_____ Sternal

_____ Tarsal

_____ Brachial

_____ Dorsum

_____ Femoral

_____ Gluteal

_____ Lumbar

_____ Olecranal

_____ Plantar

_____ Perineal

_____ Popliteal

_____ Sacral

_____ Sural

_____ Vertebral

5. Body Planes and Sections

Name the planes that match the statements.

1) Divides the body into equal left and right halves.

2) Divides the body into superior and inferior portions.

3) Divides the body into left and right portions.

4) Divides the body into anterior and posterior portions.

6. Body Cavities

a. Label the body cavities and related structures by placing the number of the label line in the space by the correct label.

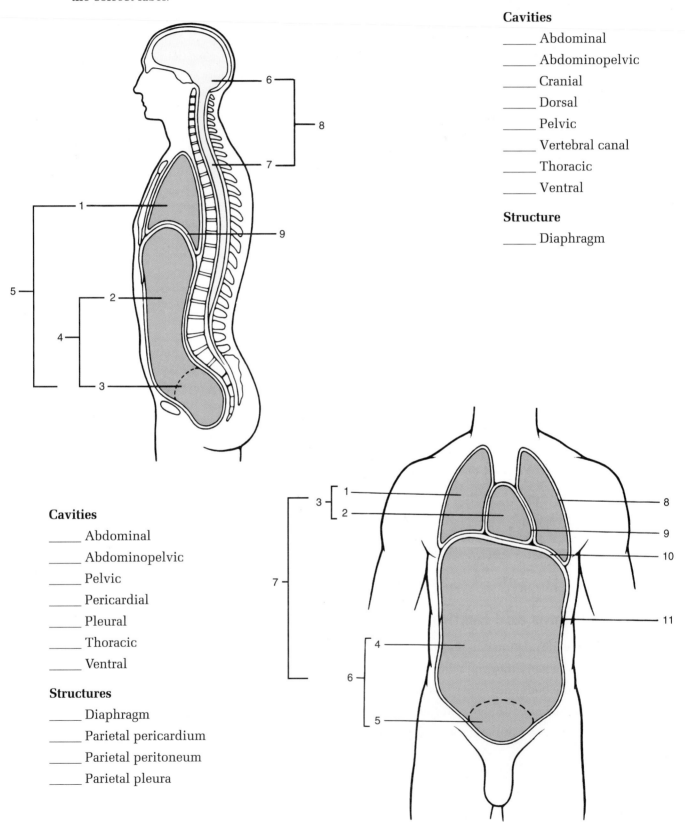

Cavities

_____ Abdominal

_____ Abdominopelvic

_____ Cranial

_____ Dorsal

_____ Pelvic

_____ Vertebral canal

_____ Thoracic

_____ Ventral

Structure

_____ Diaphragm

Cavities

_____ Abdominal

_____ Abdominopelvic

_____ Pelvic

_____ Pericardial

_____ Pleural

_____ Thoracic

_____ Ventral

Structures

_____ Diaphragm

_____ Parietal pericardium

_____ Parietal peritoneum

_____ Parietal pleura

b. Place the number of the cavity in which the organ occurs in the space by the organ.

1) Abdominal 3) Pelvic 5) Thoracic, lateral parts

2) Cranial 4) Vertebral canal 6) Thoracic, mediastinum

_____ Brain _____ Kidneys _____ Spinal cord

_____ Gallbladder _____ Liver _____ Thymus

_____ Heart _____ Lungs _____ Urinary bladder

_____ Intestine, small _____ Pancreas _____ Rectum

c. Write the names of the membranes that match the statements in the spaces at the right.

1) Covers the surface of the heart. _____

2) Covers the surface of the stomach. _____

3) Lines the abdominal cavity. _____

4) Covers the brain. _____

5) Lines the thoracic cavity. _____

6) Lines the spinal cavity. _____

7) Covers the surface of the lungs. _____

8) Forms double-membrane sac around heart. _____

9) Double-layered membranes supporting
abdominal organs. _____

7. Abdominopelvic Subdivisions

Select the abdominopelvic quadrant and abdominopelvic region in which the following structures are located.

Quadrants **Regions**

1. Right upper 5. Epigastric 10. Right hypochondriac

2. Left upper 6. Hypogastric 11. Right iliac

3. Right lower 7. Left hypochondriac 12. Right lumbar

4. Left lower 8. Left iliac 13. Umbilical

9. Left lumbar

_____ Gallbladder _____ Stomach

_____ Spleen _____ Ascending colon

_____ Rectum _____ Urinary bladder

_____ Right kidney _____ Left kidney

_____ Appendix _____ Pancreas

8. Maintenance of Life

Write the terms that match the statements in the spaces at the right.

1) Maintenance of a dynamic balance of substances
in body fluids. _____

2) The sum of all life processes. _____

3) Breakdown of complex substances. _____

4) Synthesis of complex substances. _____

5) Mechanism regulating homeostasis. _____

6) Sum of the chemical reactions that occur in the body. _____

7) List the five basic needs essential for human life. _____

_____

_____

_____

_____

8) Components of a negative-feedback mechanism. _____

_____

_____

9. Clinical Insights

a.   A patient complains of pain in the epigastric region. What organs may be involved?

_____

_____

b.   A patient complains of pain in the right lower quadrant. What organs may be involved?

_____

_____

c.   How is homeostasis related to health and disease?

_____

_____

1. Atoms and Elements

   a.   Write the terms that match the phrases in the spaces at the right.

      1) Smallest unit of an element.   _____

      2) Positively charged subatomic particle.   _____

      3) Negatively charged subatomic particle.   _____

      4) Subatomic particle with no charge.   _____

      5) Substance that cannot be broken down into any
         simpler substance.   _____

      6) Atoms of the same element, with different
         numbers of neutrons.   _____

      7) Most abundant element in the body.   _____

   b.   Label the atom shown by placing the letter of the component in the space by the label, then provide the responses to the phrases below.

      _____ 1) Nonvalence electrons

      _____ 2) Nucleus

      _____ 3) Valence electron(s)

      4) Atomic number of this atom.

      5) Atomic weight of this atom.   _____

      6) Number of electrons needed to complete its
         outer shell.   _____

      7) Type of chemical bond that is likely to join
         this atom to another atom.   _____

      8) Symbol of this atom.   _____

   c.   Diagram an atom of these elements.

Oxygen

Nitrogen

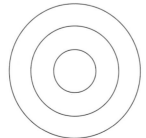

2. Molecules and Compounds

a. Write the terms that match the phrases in the spaces at the right.

1) Composed of two elements combined in
   a fixed ratio.   _____

2) Smallest unit of a compound.   _____

3) Number of chlorine atoms in $CaCl_2$.   _____

4) Chemical bond resulting from the donation
   of electron(s) from one atom to another.   _____

5) Chemical bond resulting from the sharing of
   valence electrons by two atoms.   _____

6) An atom with a net electrical charge.   _____

7) The attractive force between a slightly positive
   H atom and a slightly negative O or N atom.   _____

8) Chemical bonds forming organic molecules.   _____

9) Electrons in the outer shell.   _____

b. Indicate the kinds and numbers of atoms in a glucose molecule ($C_6H_{12}O_6$).

Kinds of Atoms   **Numbers of Atoms**

_____   _____

_____   _____

_____   _____

c. Identify the pH values as acid (A) or base (B). Circle the pH with the highest concentration of H^+.

_____ pH 2.8   _____ pH 6.8   _____ pH 7.4   _____ pH 9.5   _____ pH 3.7

3. Compounds Composing the Human Body

a. Identify the following compounds as either organic (O) or inorganic (I).

_____ NaCl   _____ Lipids   _____ $CaPO_4$

_____ Nucleic acids   _____ Salts   _____ $C_6H_{12}O_6$

_____ Proteins   _____ Most acids   _____ CH_4

_____ Most bases   _____ Carbohydrates   _____ CO_2

_____ Amino acids   _____ Steroids   _____ Monosaccharides

_____ Fatty acids   _____ Glycerol   _____ Nucleotides

b. Write the terms that match the phrases in the spaces at the right.

1) Most abundant compound in the body.   _____

2) Substances dissolved in a liquid.   _____

3) A compound that releases H^+.   _____

4) Splitting of ionic compounds into ions.   _____

5) A measure of the H^+ concentration in a solution.   _____

6) Chemicals that keep the pH of a solution
   relatively constant.   _____

7) Class of compounds formed of many simple
   sugars joined together.   _____

8) Type of reaction that joins two glucose
   molecules to form maltose.   _____

9) Storage form of carbohydrates in the body.   _____

10) Composed of three fatty acids and one glycerol.   _____

11) Composed of two fatty acids and a phosphate
    group joined to one glycerol.   _____

12) Type of fat whose fatty acids contain no
    carbon–carbon double bonds.   _____

13) Compound used to store excess energy reserves.   _____

14) Class of lipids that includes sex hormones.   _____

15) Class of compounds formed of 50 to thousands
    of amino acids.   _____

16) Chemical bonds that determine the
    three-dimensional shape of proteins.   _____

17) Bonds joining amino acids together in proteins.   _____

18) A single-stranded nucleic acid that is involved
    in protein synthesis.   _____

19) Building units of nucleic acids.   _____

20) Steroid that tends to plug arteries when
    in excess.   _____

21) Sugar in DNA molecules.   _____

22) Primary carbohydrate fuel for cells.   _____

23) Building units of proteins.   _____

24) Water compartment containing 65% of water
    in the body.   _____

25) Molecule releasing energy to power chemical
    reactions within cells.   _____

26) Double-stranded nucleic acid.   _____

27) Molecules catalyzing chemical reactions in cells.   _____

28) Type of reaction breaking a large molecule
    into smaller molecules.   _____

29) Molecule controlling protein synthesis in cells.   _____

30) Element whose atoms form the backbone of
    organic molecules.   _____

c. Match the four classes of organic compounds with the listed substances.

1) Carbohydrates	2) Lipids	3) Proteins	4) Nucleic acids
_____ Amino acids	_____ Nucleotides	_____ Enzymes	
_____ Steroids	_____ Monosaccharides	_____ RNA	
_____ Glycogen	_____ Triglycerides	_____ DNA	
_____ Cholesterol	_____ Starch	_____ Fatty acids	

d. Label the parts of the small portion of an RNA molecule shown and draw a line around one nucleotide.

_____ Nitrogen bases   _____ Ribose sugars   _____ Phosphate groups

e. Show the interaction of ADP, ATP, P, and energy in the formation and breakdown of ATP by placing the numbers of the responses in the correct spaces provided.

1) ADP   3) Energy from cellular respiration + $\ominus$P

2) ATP   4) Energy released for cellular work + $\ominus$P

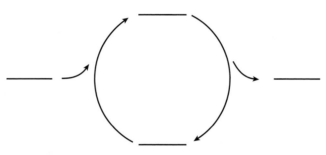

f. Explain the importance of the shape of an enzyme. _____
_____

g. How does a change in pH change the shape of and inactivate an enzyme? _____
_____

4. Clinical Insights

a. Why does a diet high in saturated fats increase the risk of coronary heart disease? _____
_____
_____
_____

b. A patient in a coma is brought to the emergency room. A blood test shows that he has severe hypoglycemia (abnormally low blood glucose) and acidosis. Treatment is begun immediately to increase both blood sugar and pH.

1) Why is a normal level of blood glucose important? _____
_____

2) Why is severe acidosis a problem? _____
_____

1. Cell Structure

a. Label the diagram of the cell by placing the numbers of the structures by the labels listed.

_____ Centrioles   _____ Microvilli   _____ Plasma (cell) membrane

_____ Cilia   _____ Mitochondrion   _____ RER

_____ Cytoplasm   _____ Nuclear envelope   _____ Ribosome in cytoplasm

_____ Golgi complex   _____ Nucleolus   _____ Ribosome on RER

_____ Lysosome   _____ Nucleus   _____ Secretory vesicles

_____ Microtubule   _____ Phagocytic vesicle   _____ SER

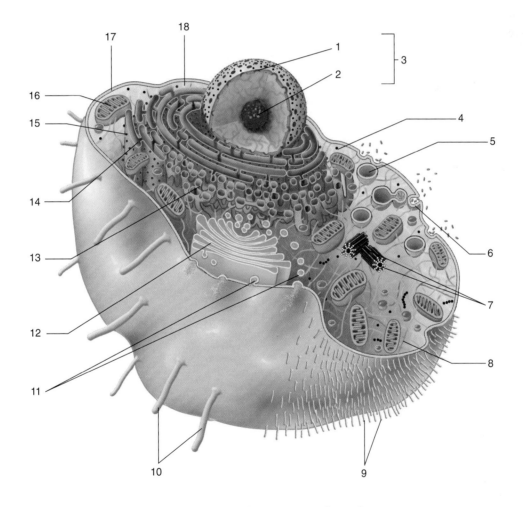

b. Write the terms that match the phrases in the spaces at the right.

1) Endoplasmic reticulum with ribosomes.   _____

2) Forms cytoskeleton (two answers).   _____

     _____

3) Packages materials for export from cell.   _____

4) Sites of protein synthesis. _____

5) Composed of DNA and protein. _____

6) Intranuclear site of rRNA synthesis. _____

7) Sites of cellular respiration. _____

8) Controls movement of materials between
    nucleus and cytoplasm. _____

9) Endoplasmic reticulum without ribosomes. _____

10) Vesicles of digestive enzymes. _____

11) Provides motility for sperm. _____

12) Short cylinders formed of microtubules. _____

13) Semiliquid around organelles. _____

14) Short, hairlike projections that move substances
    across cell surfaces. _____

15) Controls movement of materials into and out of
    the cell. _____

16) Sites of aerobic cellular respiration. _____

17) Contains chromosomes. _____

18) Forms channels for material transport in the
    cytoplasm. _____

19) Molecule determining inheritance. _____

20) Organelle controlling cell functions. _____

2. Transport Through Plasma Membranes

a. Match the terms and phrases. More than one answer may apply.

Diffusion   Osmosis   Phagocytosis   Pinocytosis

1) Diffusion of water. _____

2) Engulfment of small particles. _____

3) Engulfment of liquid droplets. _____

4) Movement of molecules from an area of higher
   concentration to areas of lower concentration. _____

5) Results from random molecular movement. _____

b. Identify the transport processes as either active (A) or passive (P).

_____ By carrier proteins   _____ Osmosis

_____ Diffusion   _____ Pinocytosis

_____ Phagocytosis   _____ Exocytosis

c. Consider the solutions below that are separated by a selectively permeable membrane. Use arrows to show the direction of molecular movement. In 1, show the direction of *water* movement. In 2, show the direction of *solute* movement.

1)	A	B	2)	A	B
	10% protein solution	5% protein solution		10% salt solution	5% salt solution

3) In 1, which solution is hypotonic? _____

4) In 2, which solution is hypertonic? _____

5) Describe what happens when a human cell is placed in a hypotonic solution. _____

_____

3. Cellular Respiration

a.   Write the summary equation for the cellular respiration of glucose. Words may be used instead of chemical formulas.

b.   Completion
   1) List the products of cellular respiration.   _____

   _____   _____
   2) The source of energy captured in ATP. _____
c.   Explain why cellular respiration is a continuous process._____

_____

_____

4. Protein Synthesis

Completion
1) The genetic code consists of the sequence of
    bases in _____ molecules.   _____

2) The genetic code is transcribed to the sequence
    of bases in _____ molecules.   _____

3) Molecule that carries instructions for protein
    synthesis to ribosomes.   _____

4) Molecule that carries amino acids to ribosome
    for addition to amino acid chain.   _____

5) Small molecules that join to form a protein
    during translation.   _____

5. Cell Division

a.   Indicate the type of cell division described by the statements.
   1) Provides new cells for growth and repair.   _____
   2) Forms sperm and ova.   _____
   3) Daughter cells have same chromosome number
       and composition as parent cell.   _____
   4) Daughter cells have half the number of
       chromosomes as the parent cell.   _____

b.   Select the phase of the cell cycle described by the statements.

Interphase   Prophase   Metaphase   Anaphase   Telophase

1) Division of the cytoplasm.   _____
2) Replication of chromosomes.   _____
3) Chromosomes appear as threadlike bodies.   _____
4) Chromatids move toward ends of spindle.   _____

5) New nuclei start to form.   _____

6) Occupies most of cell cycle.   _____

7) Chromosomes line up at equator of spindle.   _____

8) Cell performs its normal functions.   _____

c. Human body cells have 46 chromosomes. How many chromosomes are in daughter cells formed by mitotic cell division? _____

d. Write the names of the mitotic phases in the spaces provided and place the numbers of the cell parts in the spaces by the correct label.

_____ Centrioles   _____ Chromosome   _____ Spindle fiber

_____ Centromere   _____ Chromatid

6) _____   7) _____

8) _____   9) _____

6. Clinical Insights

a. When you drink a glass of water, how does the water enter the blood? _____
    Why does this occur? _____

b. Explain why a chemical therapy drug that disrupts formation of spindle fibers kills cancerous cells.

    _____

    _____

1. Basic Tissues

Select the tissues described by the statements.

Epithelial   Connective   Muscle   Nerve

1) Adapted for contraction.   _____

2) Contains scattered cells in a matrix.   _____

3) Sheets of closely packed cells.   _____

4) Composed of neurons and supporting cells.   _____

5) Lacks blood vessels.   _____

6) Supports and protects organs.   _____

7) Lines body cavities and covers organs.   _____

8) Forms and conducts impulses.   _____

9) Functions in absorption and secretion.   _____

2. Epithelial Tissues

a. Write the names of the tissues in the spaces provided and place the number of each structure in the space by the correct label.

6) _____   7) _____   8) _____

_____ Basement membrane

_____ Cell nucleus

_____ Cilia

_____ Connective tissue

_____ Goblet cell

9) _____   10) _____

b.   Write the number of the appropriate tissue described in the space provided.

1) Simple squamous   5) Stratified keratinized squamous

2) Simple cuboidal   6) Stratified nonkeratinized squamous

3) Simple columnar   7) Transitional

4) Pseudostratified ciliated columnar

_____ Forms secretory cells of glands.   _____ Forms outer layer of skin.

_____ Lines interior of blood vessels.   _____ Lines interior of urinary bladder.

_____ Lines interior of stomach and intestines.   _____ Lines mouth and vagina.

_____ Lines upper respiratory passages.   _____ Contain goblet cells.

_____ Lines ventral body cavity.   _____ Forms air sacs of lungs.

3. Connective Tissue Proper

a.   Write the names of the tissues in the spaces provided and place the number of each structure in the
space by the correct label.

_____ Collagenous fiber

_____ Elastic fiber

_____ Fat droplet

_____ Fibroblast

_____ Ground substance

_____ Nucleus

7) _____

8) _____

b.   Select the connective tissues described by the statements.

1) Loose   2) Adipose   3) Fibrous   4) Elastic

_____ Storage area for fat.   _____ Poor blood supply.

_____ Binds skin to muscles.   _____ Insulates body.

_____ Forms ligaments and tendons.   _____ Tightly packed collagenous fibers.

_____ In walls of arteries.   _____ Enables expansion and contraction of lungs.

_____ Supporting framework for internal organs.   _____ Protective cushion for internal organs.

_____ Very strong but pliable.   _____ Inner layer of skin.

4. Special Connective Tissues

a. Write the names of the tissues in the spaces provided and place the number of each structure in the space by the correct label.

_____ Canaliculi   _____ Lamellae

_____ Chondrocyte in a lacuna   _____ Nonfibrous matrix

_____ Elastic fibers   _____ Osteocyte in a lacuna

_____ Osteonic canal

8) _____

9) _____

10) _____

b. Select the connective tissues described by the statements.

1) Elastic cartilage   2) Fibrocartilage   3) Hyaline cartilage

4) Bone   5) Blood

_____ Intervertebral disks.   _____ Smooth, glassy matrix.

_____ Pinna of outer ear.   _____ Fibers impart increased flexibility.

_____ Forms embryonic bones.   _____ Hard, rigid matrix.

_____ Liquid matrix.   _____ Dense collagenous fibers resist strong pressures.

5. Muscle Tissues

a. Write the names of the muscle tissues in the spaces provided and place the number of each structure in the space by the correct label.

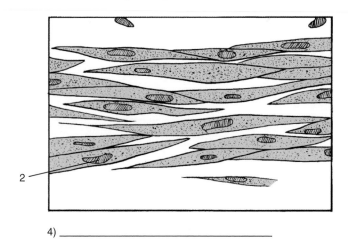

_____ Intercalated disk

_____ Nucleus

_____ Striations

4) _____

5) _____

6) _____

b. Select the muscle tissues described by the statements.

1) Cardiac   2) Skeletal   3) Smooth

_____ Voluntary   _____ Slow contractions

_____ Involuntary   _____ Rapid contractions

_____ In walls of intestine   _____ Rhythmic contractions

6. Nerve Tissue

a. Indicate whether each statement is true (T) or false (F).

_____ Nerve cells are called neurons.

_____ The nucleus of a nerve cell is located in the cell body.

_____ Nerve cells form and transmit neural impulses.

_____ Supporting cells in nerve tissue are fibroblasts.

b.   Write the name of the cell in the space below the figure and place the number of each structure in the space by the correct label.

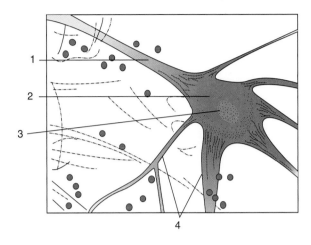

_____ Axon

_____ Cell body

_____ Dendrites

_____ Nucleus

_____

7. Body Membranes

Select the membranes identified by the statements.

1) Cutaneous membrane   4) Perichondrium   6) Serous membranes

2) Meninges   5) Periosteum   7) Synovial membranes

3) Mucous membranes

_____ Line the abdominal cavity and cover most
         abdominal organs.

_____ Protective covering of the brain and
         spinal cord.

_____ Covers the entire body.

_____ Epithelial membranes. (3 answers)

_____ Covers the surfaces of cartilage.

_____ Line tubes and cavities that open to the
         exterior.

_____ Line cavities of freely movable joints.

_____ Covers surfaces of bones.

_____ Secrete a watery fluid to reduce frictions.
         (2 answers)

8. Clinical Insights

a.   Most cancers are carcinomas. How do you explain this? _____

_____

b.   Judy tore a knee cartilage on a skiing vacation. Can she expect a rapid recovery? _____ Explain. _____

_____

1. Functions of the Skin

List five functions of the integumentary system.

1) _____

2) _____

3) _____

4) _____

5) _____

2. Structure of the Skin and Hypodermis

Select the structure described by each statement.

Dermis   Epidermis   Stratum basale   Stratum corneum   Hypodermis

1) Contains abundant adipose tissue. _____

2) Innermost layer of the epidermis. _____

3) Composed of stratified squamous epithelium. _____

4) Contains collagen and elastic fibers. _____

5) Attaches skin to underlying tissues. _____

6) Lacks blood vessels. _____

7) Outermost layer of the epidermis. _____

8) Contains sensory receptors of the skin. _____

9) Forms new epidermal cells. _____

10) Formed of dead keratinized cells. _____

11) Provides insulation for the body. _____

12) Provides strength and elasticity of skin. _____

13) Inner layer of the skin. _____

14) Outer cells are continuously sloughed off. _____

15) Formed of fibrous connective tissue. _____

3. Skin Color

a. Provide the term described by each statement.

1) Three pigments that determine skin color. Indicate the color of each pigment.

_____

_____

_____

2) Protects against ultraviolet radiation. _____

3) Cells producing melanin. _____

4) Stimulates melanin production. _____

5) Ultimate determiner of skin color. _____

b.   Explain why a summer tan is only temporary. _____

_____

_____

4. Diagram of the Skin

Label the diagram.

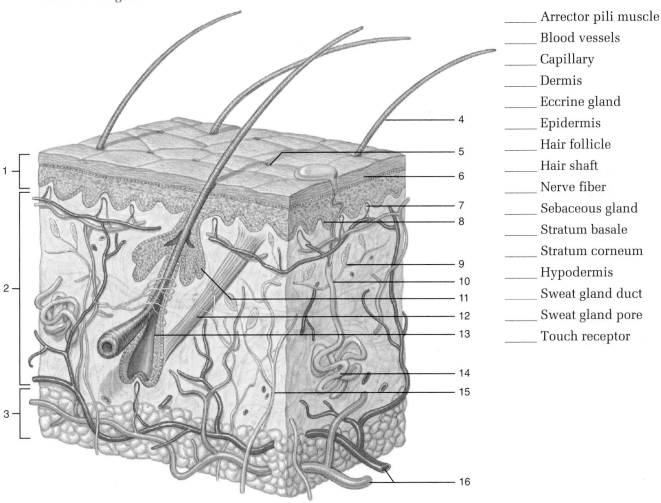

_____ Arrector pili muscle
_____ Blood vessels
_____ Capillary
_____ Dermis
_____ Eccrine gland
_____ Epidermis
_____ Hair follicle
_____ Hair shaft
_____ Nerve fiber
_____ Sebaceous gland
_____ Stratum basale
_____ Stratum corneum
_____ Hypodermis
_____ Sweat gland duct
_____ Sweat gland pore
_____ Touch receptor

5. Accessory Structures

Provide the term that matches each statement.

1) Tubular sheath surrounding hair root.

2) Gland producing sebum.

3) Muscle raising hair more erect.

4) Gland producing perspiration.

5) Gland producing cerumen.

6) Sweat gland opening into hair follicle.

7) Sweat gland producing watery perspiration.

8) Protein in cells forming hair and nails.

9) Basic function of hair and nails.

10) Secretion containing salts and urea.

_____

11) Oily secretion that helps keep skin soft.

_____

12) Waxy secretion found in external ear canal.

_____

13) Normal color of nail beds.

_____

6. Temperature Regulation

Provide the missing words in the paragraph below.
Humans have a normal body temperature of
__1__ °C, or __2__ °F. The heat that maintains the
body temperature is generated as a by-product of
cellular __3__, especially in active organs like the
liver and skeletal __4__. Overall regulation of body
temperature is controlled by the __5__, and the
__6__ serves as an important regulatory organ.

1) _____
2) _____
3) _____
4) _____
5) _____
6) _____

When the body temperature falls below normal,
the flow of __7__ to the skin is decreased, which
reduces secretion of __8__ by sweat glands and
minimizes heat __9__ by radiation. Shivering
increases cellular respiration in muscles, which
generates more __10__.

7) _____
8) _____
9) _____
10) _____

When the body temperature rises above normal,
blood flow to the skin is __11__, which increases
heat loss by __12__ and activates __13__ glands
to produce perspiration. The __14__ of perspiration
from the surface of the skin increases __15__
loss and cools the body surface.

11) _____
12) _____
13) _____
14) _____
15) _____

A person with a body temperature less than
__16__ °F suffers from hypothermia. A body
temperature over __17__ °F indicates hyperthermia.

16) _____
17) _____

7. Aging of the Skin

Indicate whether each statement is true (T) or false (F).

_____ A baby's skin is thinner than an adult's.

_____ A decrease in melanin production often occurs in the elderly.

_____ Wrinkled skin results from an excess of active elastic fibers.

_____ Ultraviolet radiation accelerates the aging of the skin.

_____ Excess subcutaneous fat increases sensitivity to temperature changes.

8. Disorders of the Skin

Write the name of the disorder described by each statement.

1) Results from a chronic deficiency of circulation to a portion of skin. _____

2) Cancer of the melanocytes. _____

3) Numerous red, itchy bumps resulting from an allergic reaction. _____

4) Skin-colored tumors caused by a virus. _____

5) Slow-growing, pigmented tumors. _____

6) A burn that destroys all of the dermis. _____

7) Loss of hair as in male pattern baldness. _____

8) Thickened areas of skin on hands and feet. _____

9) Inflammation causing red, itching, scaling skin; may involve sebaceous glands. _____

10) Contagious infection in which pustules rupture and form a yellow crust. _____

11) Reddish, raised scaly patches on scalp, knees, or elbows. _____

12) Condition caused by excessive shedding of epidermal cells of the scalp. _____

13) Blisters on lips caused by *Herpes simplex.* _____

14) Itching, flaking skin between toes due to a fungus infection. _____

15) Bacterial infection of a hair follicle, sebaceous gland, and surrounding tissues. _____

16) The general term for any inflammation of the skin. _____

9. Clinical Insights

a. Name two major clinical problems expected in a patient with third-degree burns. _____

_____

b. Hypodermal injections of medications are frequently used. Why is the hypodermis especially good for rapid absorption of medications? _____

_____

1. Functions of the Skeletal System

List five functions of the skeletal system.

1) _____   3) _____   5) _____

2) _____   4) _____

2. Bone Structure

a.   Label the diagram by placing the number of each structure by the correct label.

_____ Articular cartilage

_____ Bone, compact

_____ Bone, spongy

_____ Diaphysis

_____ Epiphyseal lines

_____ Epiphysis, distal

_____ Epiphysis, proximal

_____ Marrow, red, in spaces

_____ Marrow, yellow

_____ Medullary cavity

_____ Periosteum

b.   Match the terms with the statements.

1) Periosteum   3) Marrow, red

2) Epiphyseal plate   4) Marrow, yellow

_____ Fills spaces in spongy bone.

_____ Hyaline cartilage.

_____ Covers surface of bone.

_____ Fills medullary cavity.

3. Microscopic Structure

Match the terms with the statements.

1) Lacunae   4) Osteonic canals

2) Lamellae   5) Periosteum

3) Osteon   6) None of these

_____ Channel for blood vessels and nerves.

_____ Spaces containing osteocytes.

_____ Concentric layers of compact bone.

_____ Source of osteoblasts.

_____ Structural unit of compact bone.

_____ Spaces containing red marrow.

4. Bone Formation

Write the answers to the statements in the spaces provided.

1) Cells that deposit bone matrix. _____

2) Cells that remove bone matrix. _____

3) Cells that occupy the lacunae. _____

4) Site of growth in length of long bones. _____

5) Type of ossification in most skull bones. _____

6) Type of ossification in bones preformed in cartilage. _____

7) Cells that hollow out the medullary cavity. _____

5. Bones of the Skeleton

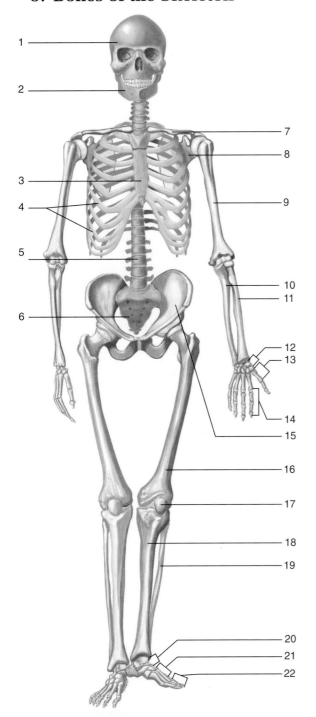

Write the names of the labeled bones in the spaces provided.

1) _____

2) _____

3) _____

4) _____

5) _____

6) _____

7) _____

8) _____

9) _____

10) _____

11) _____

12) _____

13) _____

14) _____

15) _____

16) _____

17) _____

18) _____

19) _____

20) _____

21) _____

22) _____

6. Axial Skeleton

a. Label the diagram of the skull, anterior view, by placing the number of each structure in the space by the correct label.

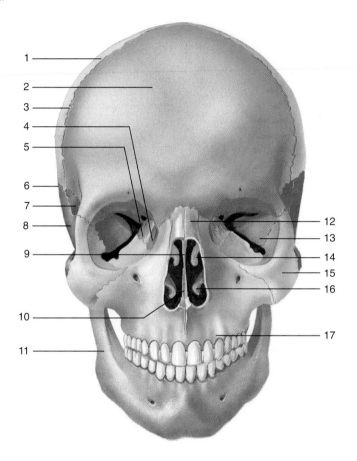

_____ Coronal suture

_____ Ethmoid (eye orbit)

_____ Ethmoid, perpendicular plate

_____ Frontal

_____ Lacrimal

_____ Mandible

_____ Maxilla

_____ Nasal

_____ Nasal concha, inferior

_____ Nasal concha, middle

_____ Parietal

_____ Squamosal suture

_____ Sphenoid (2 places)

_____ Temporal

_____ Vomer

_____ Zygomatic

b. List the skull bones that contain sinuses. _____

_____

c.   Label the diagram of the skull, lateral view, by placing the number of each structure in the space by the correct label.

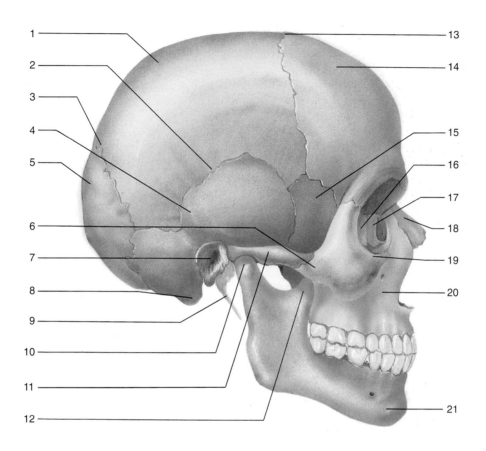

_____ Coronal suture

_____ Coronoid process

_____ Ethmoid

_____ External auditory canal

_____ Frontal

_____ Lacrimal

_____ Lambdoidal suture

_____ Mandible

_____ Mandibular condyle

_____ Mastoid process

_____ Maxilla

_____ Nasal

_____ Occipital

_____ Parietal

_____ Sphenoid

_____ Squamosal suture

_____ Styloid process

_____ Temporal

_____ Temporal, zygomatic process

_____ Zygomatic

_____ Zygomatic, temporal process

d. Write the terms that match the statements in the spaces provided.

   1) Contains the foramen magnum.

   2) Forms anterior portion of hard palate.

   3) Contains external auditory canal.

   4) The seven vertebrae of the neck.

   5) Weight-bearing portion of a vertebra.

   6) Foramen through which spinal cord passes.

   7) Vertebrae-bearing ribs.

   8) Number of pairs of true ribs.

   9) Attaches true ribs to sternum.

  10) First cervical vertebra.

  11) Cartilaginous pads between vertebrae.

  12) Forms posterior wall of pelvic girdle.

  13) Vertebrae with heaviest bodies.

  14) The breastbone.

e. Name the group of bones that provides protection for the

   1) Brain _____ 2) Heart and lungs _____

f. Label the vertebra by placing the number of the structure in the space by the correct label.

_____ Body

_____ Facet for rib

_____ Spinous process

_____ Superior articular process

_____ Transverse process

_____ Vertebral foramen

7. Appendicular Skeleton

a. Write the missing words in the spaces at the right.

The pectoral girdle is formed of two __1__
and two __2__. Its function is to support the
upper __3__. Each __4__ articulates with
the scapula at one end and the __5__ at the
other. The scapulae are attached to the axial
skeleton by __6__ instead of ligaments.

1) _____

2) _____

3) _____

4) _____

5) _____

6) _____

b.   Label these diagrams by placing the number of each structure in the space by the correct label.

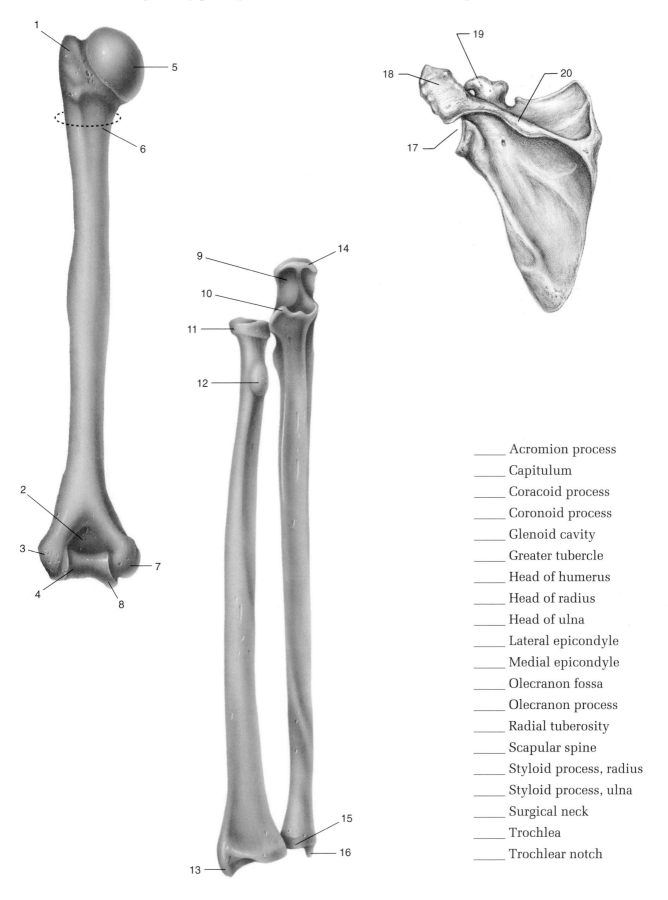

_____ Acromion process
_____ Capitulum
_____ Coracoid process
_____ Coronoid process
_____ Glenoid cavity
_____ Greater tubercle
_____ Head of humerus
_____ Head of radius
_____ Head of ulna
_____ Lateral epicondyle
_____ Medial epicondyle
_____ Olecranon fossa
_____ Olecranon process
_____ Radial tuberosity
_____ Scapular spine
_____ Styloid process, radius
_____ Styloid process, ulna
_____ Surgical neck
_____ Trochlea
_____ Trochlear notch

c. Label the diagrams by placing the number of each structure in the space by the correct label.

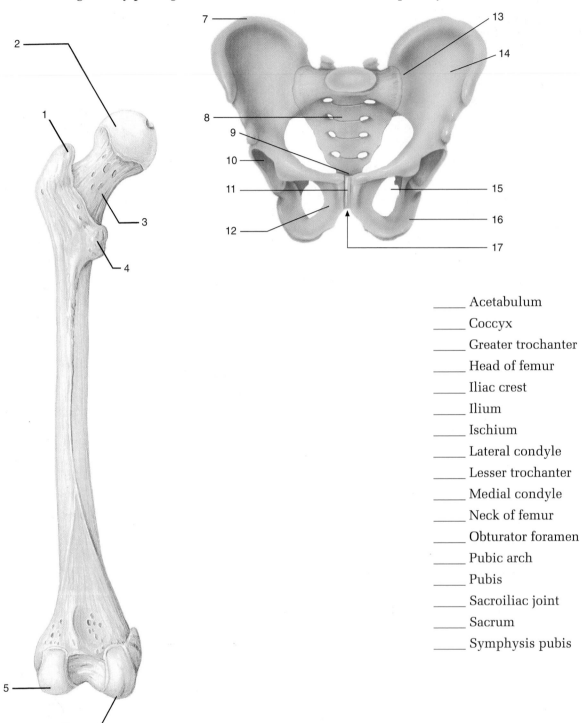

_____ Acetabulum

_____ Coccyx

_____ Greater trochanter

_____ Head of femur

_____ Iliac crest

_____ Ilium

_____ Ischium

_____ Lateral condyle

_____ Lesser trochanter

_____ Medial condyle

_____ Neck of femur

_____ Obturator foramen

_____ Pubic arch

_____ Pubis

_____ Sacroiliac joint

_____ Sacrum

_____ Symphysis pubis

d. Indicate whether each statement is associated with the fibula (F) or tibia (T).

_____ Lateral malleolus   _____ Medial malleolus

_____ Lateral condyle   _____ Medial condyle

_____ Articulates with femur   _____ Articulates with talus

8. Articulations

a. Match the type of joint with the articulation formed by the bones.

1) Immovable   3) Ball-and-socket   5) Gliding   7) Pivot

2) Slightly movable   4) Condyloid   6) Hinge   8) Saddle

_____ Femur–tibia   _____ Carpal–carpal

_____ Frontal–parietal   _____ Trapezium–metacarpal 1

_____ Humerus–scapula   _____ Coxa–femur

_____ Vertebra–vertebra   _____ Maxilla–zygomatic

_____ Atlas–axis   _____ Metacarpal–phalanx

b. Match the terms with the correct definitions.

1) Articular cartilage   3) Cartilage pads   5) Sesamoid bone

2) Bursa   4) Joint capsule   6) Synovial fluid

_____ Lubricates joints.   _____ Protects articular surfaces of bones.

_____ Sacs of synovial fluid.   _____ Bone embedded in a tendon.

_____ Support knee joint and cushion bones.   _____ Formed of ligaments.

c. Match the movements with the descriptions.

1) Abduction   5) Extension   9) Eversion   13) Pronation

2) Adduction   6) Flexion   10) Inversion   14) Supination

3) Depression   7) Dorsiflexion   11) Circumduction   15) Protraction

4) Elevation   8) Plantar flexion   12) Rotation   16) Retraction

_____ Opposite of dorsiflexion.   _____ Turning head from side to side.

_____ Pushing mandible anteriorly.   _____ Decrease in angle of joint.

_____ Movement of arm toward midline.   _____ Raising shoulders.

_____ Straightening arm at elbow.   _____ Drawing circle on chalkboard.

_____ Turning palm of hand upward.   _____ Turning sole of foot inward.

9. Disorders of the Skeletal System

Write the name of each disorder described in the space provided.

1) Displacement of bones forming a joint.

2) A lateral curvature of vertebral column.

3) Protrusion of intervertebral disk.

4) Bone broken into several pieces.

5) Broken bone pierces through skin.

6) Arthritis with invasion of fibrous tissue that calcifies, making joint immovable.

7) Tearing of ligaments of joint capsule.

8) Severe loss of calcium salts from bones.

10. Clinical Insights

a. A member of the soccer team is diagnosed with a torn knee cartilage. Would you expect rapid or slow recovery? Explain your answer. _____

_____

b. Specifically, what is a broken hip? _____

Why is it more common among older persons? _____

_____

1. Types of Muscle Tissues

Match the types of muscle tissues with the words and phrases.

1) Skeletal   2) Smooth   3) Cardiac

_____ Striated

_____ Single nucleus

_____ Involuntary

_____ Intercalated disks

_____ Branching network

_____ Walls of blood vessels

_____ Heart muscle

_____ Walls of digestive tract

_____ Skeletal muscles

_____ Easily fatigued

2. Structure of Skeletal Muscle

Write the terms that match the statements in the spaces at the right.

1) A bundle of fibers enveloped by connective tissue.   _____

2) Binds all fasciculi together.   _____

3) Connective tissue covering entire muscle.   _____

4) Cordlike attachment of a muscle.   _____

5) Sheetlike attachment of a muscle.   _____

6) Plasma membrane of muscle cell.   _____

7) Cytoplasm of a muscle cell.   _____

8) Threadlike contractile elements.   _____

9) Most abundant molecules in thin myofilaments.   _____

10) Molecules composing thick myofilaments.   _____

11) Portion of a myofibril between Z lines.   _____

12) Light and dark bands on myofibrils.   _____

13) Attachment of motor axon to sarcolemma.   _____

14) Depression in sarcolemma receiving axon tip.   _____

15) Motor neuron and its attached muscle fibers.   _____

3. Physiology of Muscle Contraction

a. Write the words that complete the sentences in the spaces at the right.

The axon tip of an activated motor neuron releases __1__ into the __2__ where it binds to receptors on the __3__. The impulse is carried into the muscle fiber by __4__, causing the release of Ca^{++} from the __5__. Ca^{++} binds with troponin in thin myofilaments causing __6__ to shift, exposing the myosin-binding sites on __7__ molecules. Cross-bridges of __8__ attach to the binding sites, and a power stroke pulls thin myofilaments and the attached __9__ toward the center of the sarcomere. This process is rapidly repeated until __10__ is complete.

1) _____

2) _____

3) _____

4) _____

5) _____

6) _____

7) _____

8) _____

9) _____

10) _____

b. Write the terms that match the statements in the spaces provided.

1) Decomposes acetylcholine. _____

2) Combines with oxygen to store small amounts
   of oxygen in muscle cells. _____

3) Phase of cellular respiration that requires oxygen. _____

4) Products of pyruvic acid breakdown when
   adequate oxygen is present. _____

5) Substance formed from pyruvic acid when adequate
   oxygen is not available. _____

6) Provides direct energy for muscle contraction. _____

7) Process releasing energy from nutrients in cells. _____

8) Chemical whose accumulation produces an
   oxygen debt. _____

9) Released from creatine phosphate to quickly
   re-form ATP. _____

c. Write the terms that match the statements in the spaces at the right.

1) Smallest stimulus causing a contraction. _____

2) Activation of a muscle fiber causes a/an
   (all-or-none, graded) contraction. _____

3) Primary cause of fatigue. _____

4) Type of contractions observed in whole
   muscles (all-or-none, graded). _____

5) Smallest stimulus that activates all motor
   units of a muscle. _____

6) Activation of an increasing number of motor
   units in a series of contractions. _____

7) Controls the number of motor units that are
   activated. _____

8) State of constant, partial contraction. _____

9) State of constant, complete contraction. _____

4. Actions of Skeletal Muscles

a. Write the terms that match the statements in the spaces provided.

1) Fixed end of a muscle. _____

2) Movable end of a muscle. _____

3) Muscles opposing agonists. _____

b. Write the names of the muscles that match the actions.

1) Closes and puckers lips. _____

2) Pulls angle of mouth upward. _____

3) Helps masseter raise the mandible. _____

4) Compresses cheeks. _____

5) Pair of neck muscles that flex head. _____

6) Pair of neck muscles that extend head.   _____

7) Innermost muscle of abdominal wall.   _____

8) Raises ribs during inspiration.   _____

9) Elevates clavicle and scapula.   _____

10) Draws scapula downward and anteriorly.   _____

11) Adducts and draws humerus across chest.   _____

12) Sheetlike muscle of lower back that adducts
    and extends humerus.   _____

13) Abducts, flexes, and extends humerus.   _____

14) Rotates humerus laterally.   _____

15) Assists deltoid in abducting humerus.   _____

16) Assists latissimus dorsi.   _____

17) Assists biceps brachii (two muscles).   _____

    _____

18) Extends forearm.   _____

19) Flexes and rotates forearm laterally.   _____

20) Flexes and abducts wrist.   _____

21) Flexes and adducts wrist.   _____

22) Extends fingers.   _____

23) Extends and adducts wrist.   _____

24) Extends and abducts wrist.   _____

25) Adducts, flexes, and rotates thigh laterally
    (two muscles).   _____

    _____

26) Abducts and rotates thigh medially.   _____

27) Extends and rotates thigh laterally.   _____

28) Flexes and abducts thigh.   _____

29) Flexes thigh only (two muscles).   _____

    _____

30) Flexes leg and thigh.   _____

31) Flexes leg and adducts thigh.   _____

32) Group of four muscles that extend leg.   _____

33) Three muscles that flex the leg and extend
    the thigh.   _____

    _____

    _____

34) Dorsiflexes and inverts foot.   _____

35) Flexes leg and plantar flexes foot.   _____

36) Extends toes and dorsiflexes and everts foot.   _____

37) Plantar flexes and everts foot.   _____

5. Major Skeletal Muscles

Label the muscles and associated structures in the following diagrams by writing the names of the labeled parts in the spaces provided.

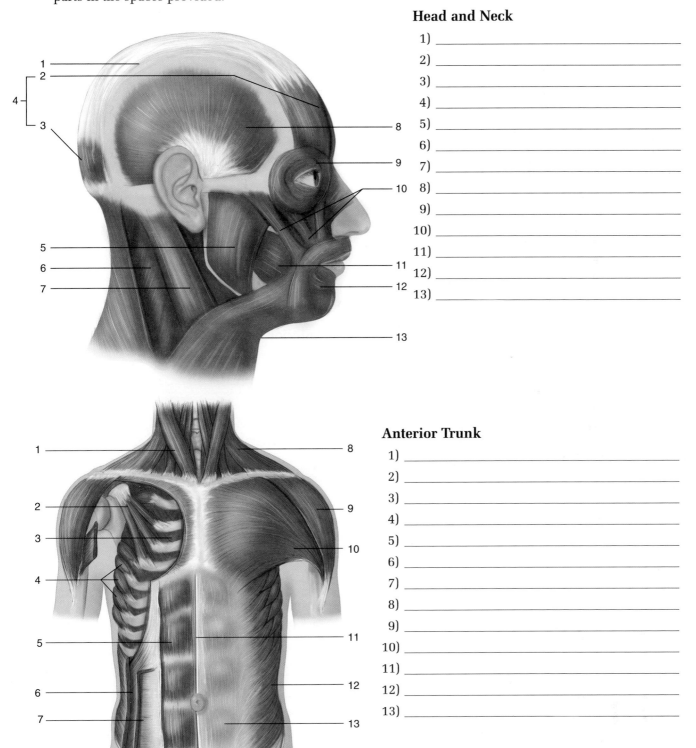

Head and Neck

1) _____
2) _____
3) _____
4) _____
5) _____
6) _____
7) _____
8) _____
9) _____
10) _____
11) _____
12) _____
13) _____

Anterior Trunk

1) _____
2) _____
3) _____
4) _____
5) _____
6) _____
7) _____
8) _____
9) _____
10) _____
11) _____
12) _____
13) _____

Posterior Trunk

1) _____

2) _____

3) _____

4) _____

5) _____

6) _____

7) _____

8) _____

9) _____

Anterior Forearm

1) _____

2) _____

3) _____

4) _____

5) _____

6) _____

7) _____

Posterior Forearm

1) _____

2) _____

3) _____

4) _____

5) _____

6) _____

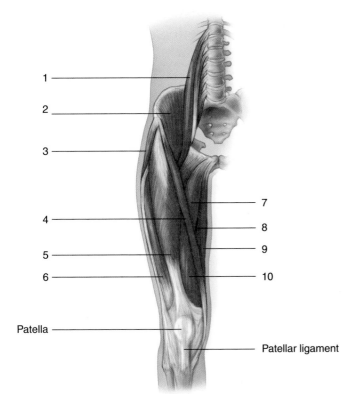

Patella

Patellar ligament

Anterior Thigh

1) _____

2) _____

3) _____

4) _____

5) _____

6) _____

7) _____

8) _____

9) _____

10) _____

Posterior Thigh

1) _____

2) _____

3) _____

4) _____

5) _____

6) _____

7) _____

8) _____

Anterior Leg

1) _____
2) _____
3) _____
4) _____
5) _____
6) _____
7) _____

Lateral Leg

1) _____
2) _____
3) _____
4) _____
5) _____
6) _____
7) _____
8) _____

6. Disorders of the Muscular System

Write the names of the disorders in the spaces provided.

1) Inflammation of connective tissues of muscles. _____

2) Involuntary, tetanic contraction of a muscle. _____

3) Antibodies attach to acetylcholine receptors, preventing normal stimulation of muscles. _____

4) Inflammation of muscle tissue. _____

5) A pulled muscle. _____

6) Abnormal increase of fibrous connective tissue in a muscle. _____

7) Viral disease that destroys motor neurons and paralyzes skeletal muscles. _____

8) Group of diseases characterized by the progressive degeneration of muscles. _____

9) A bacterial disease that prevents the release of acetylcholine from axon tips. _____

10) A bacterial disease commonly called "lockjaw." _____

11) Sudden, involuntary weak contractions of a muscle or group of muscles. _____

7. Clinical Insights

a. The accumulation of lactic acid can make muscles sore. Would heat or cold applications be best to alleviate the soreness? _____ Explain. _____

_____

b. While playing tennis, Jim had a sudden pain on the back of his left thigh. Was this a sprain or a strain? _____ What muscles were probably involved? _____

_____

_____

c. Tom has been working out to build up his muscles. At the microscopic level, how does a muscle increase in size and strength? _____

_____

_____

1. Divisions of the Nervous System

    a.   List the anatomical subdivisions.

        _____

        _____

    b.   List the functional subdivisions.

        _____

        1) _____

        2) _____

2. Nerve Tissue

    a.   Write the terms that match the statements in the spaces at the right.

        1) Portion of a neuron containing the nucleus. _____

        2) Neuron processes receiving impulses from
other neurons. _____

        3) Structural type of neuron having several
dendrites. _____

        4) Functional type of neuron carrying impulses
toward the CNS. _____

        5) Neuron process carrying impulses to muscles
and glands. _____

        6) Functional type of neuron carrying impulses
to effectors. _____

        7) Fatty insulation around some neuron processes. _____

        8) Functional type of neuron carrying impulses
within the CNS. _____

        9) Structural type of neuron having a single
dendrite. _____

        10) Membrane required for regeneration of neuron
processes. _____

        11) Small spaces between Schwann cells on an axon. _____

    b.   Write the names of the neuroglial cells that match the statements.

        1) Line the ventricles of the brain. _____

        2) Form myelin of neurons in the CNS. _____

        3) Engulf bacteria and debris. _____

        4) Form myelin of neurons in the PNS. _____

        5) Bind neurons with blood vessels. _____

c. Label the figure by placing the number of the structure by the correct label. Draw arrows to show direction of impulse transport from dendrite tip to axon tip.

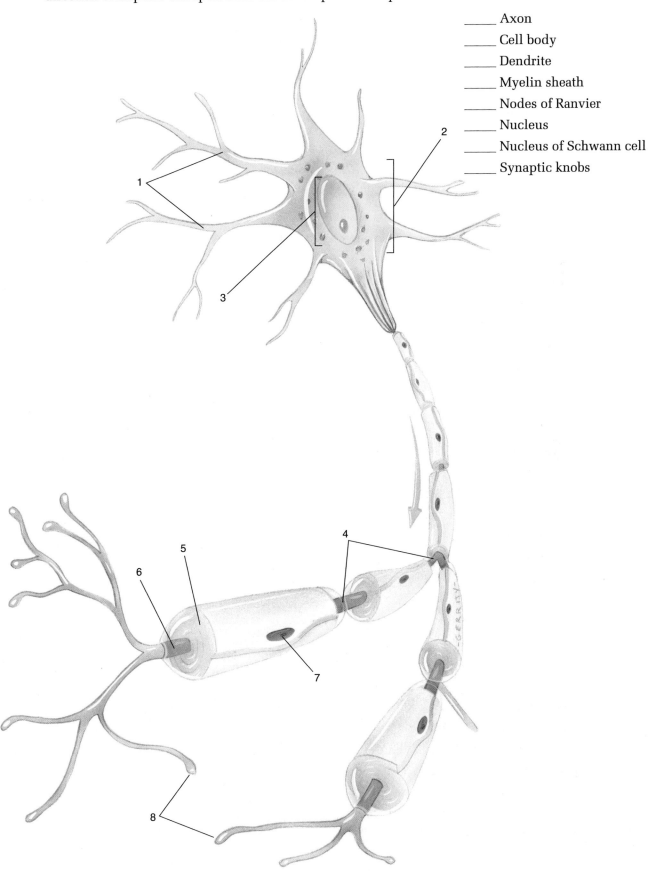

_____ Axon

_____ Cell body

_____ Dendrite

_____ Myelin sheath

_____ Nodes of Ranvier

_____ Nucleus

_____ Nucleus of Schwann cell

_____ Synaptic knobs

3. Neuron Physiology

a.   Write the terms that complete the sentences in the spaces at the right.

In a resting neuron, __1__ ions are actively

pumped out, which causes the membrane to be

__2__ with an excess of positive ions __3__

the membrane and an excess of negative ions

__4__ the neuron. A threshold stimulus makes

the membrane permeable to __5__ ions that

rapidly diffuse into the neuron, which depolarizes

the membrane forming a nerve __6__. An

impulse is conducted as a __7__ wave passes

along a neuron. A depolarized membrane is

repolarized when __8__ ions diffuse out of the

neuron and replace the __9__ ions that entered

the neuron. Impulse conduction is more rapid

in __10__ nerve fibers.

In synaptic transmission, an impulse

reaching a synaptic knob causes the release of a

__11__ into the __12__. The __13__ binds

with __14__ on the postsynaptic neuron, causing

an __15__ to be formed. An enzyme

quickly breaks down the __16__ and restores

the synapse to its resting state.

1) _____

2) _____

3) _____

4) _____

5) _____

6) _____

7) _____

8) _____

9) _____

10) _____

11) _____

12) _____

13) _____

14) _____

15) _____

16) _____

b.   Indicate the excitatory (+) and inhibitory (−) transmitters.

_____ Acetylcholine   _____ Dopamine

_____ Endorphins   _____ Norepinephrine

c.   If a drug prevents an excitatory neurotransmitter from binding to receptors of the postsynaptic neuron, will synaptic transmission occur? _____ How might such a drug be useful in a clinical situation?

_____

_____

_____

_____

4. Protection for the Central Nervous System

Write the terms that match the phrases in the spaces at the right.

1) Outermost membrane of meninges.   _____

2) Intermediate membrane of meninges.   _____

3) Innermost membrane of meninges.   _____

4) Portion of skull protecting brain.   _____

5) Meningeal space with cerebrospinal fluid.   _____

6) Space filled with fatty connective tissue in
    vertebral canal.   _____

7) Provides bony protection for spinal cord.   _____

5. Brain

a. Label the figure by placing the number of the structure by the correct label.

_____ Brain stem

_____ Cerebellum

_____ Cerebrum, frontal lobe

_____ Cerebrum, occipital lobe

_____ Cerebrum, parietal lobe

_____ Corpus callosum

_____ Diencephalon

_____ Hypothalamus

_____ Medulla oblongata

_____ Midbrain

_____ Pons

_____ Thalamus

b. Write the names of the structures that match the phrases.

1) Connects the cerebral hemispheres.   _____

2) Surface layer of cerebral gray matter.   _____

3) Ridges on cerebral surface.   _____

4) Shallow grooves on cerebral surface.   _____

5) Groove separating cerebral hemispheres.   _____

6) Cerebral lobe anterior to central sulcus.   _____

7) Cerebral lobe posterior to central sulcus.   _____

8) Most posterior cerebral lobe.   _____

9) Cerebral lobe inferior to lateral sulcus.   _____

10) Portion of the brain that is continuous with
    the spinal cord.   _____

11) Two lateral masses of gray matter connected
    by the intermediate mass.   _____

12) Forms the floor of third ventricle.   _____

13) Formed of pons, midbrain, and medulla.   _____

14) Lowest portion of the brain.   _____

15) Superior portion of brain stem.   _____

16) Consists of two lateral hemispheres separated
    by the vermis.   _____

17) Cavities in the cerebral hemispheres.   _____

18) Cavity continuous with the central canal of
    the spinal cord.   _____

19) Cavity between lateral masses of the thalamus
    and above the hypothalamus.   _____

20) Second largest portion of the brain.   _____

c. Match the parts of the brain with the functions described.

   1) Cerebrum   4) Medulla oblongata   7) Pons
   2) Cerebellum   5) Limbic system   8) Reticular formation
   3) Hypothalamus   6) Midbrain   9) Thalamus

   _____ Controls body temperature and water balance.
   _____ Coordinates body movements, posture, and equilibrium.
   _____ Controls moods and emotional behavior.
   _____ Controls voluntary actions, will, and intellect.
   _____ Provides general, nonspecific awareness of sensations.
   _____ Provides specific interpretation of sensations.
   _____ Controls wakefulness and arouses cerebrum.
   _____ Controls heart rate and blood pressure.
   _____ Assists medulla oblongata in control of breathing.
   _____ Major center controlling homeostasis.

d. Match parts of the cerebrum with the functions described.

   1) Association areas   6) Precentral gyrus
   2) Broca's area   7) Premotor area
   3) Corpus callosum   8) Postcentral gyrus
   4) Left hemisphere   9) Temporal lobe
   5) Occipital lobe   10) Right hemisphere

   _____ Identifies sensations from the skin.
   _____ Center for visual sensations.
   _____ Center for sound sensations.
   _____ Controls ability to speak.
   _____ Primary control area for contractions of skeletal muscles.
   _____ Hemisphere controlling verbal and computational skills in most people.
   _____ Hemisphere controlling artistic and spatial skills in most people.
   _____ Conducts impulses between cerebral hemispheres.
   _____ Controls complex and sequential learned motor activities.
   _____ Controls will, memory, and intellectual processes.

e.   Write the terms that complete the sentences in the spaces at the right.

Cerebrospinal fluid (CSF) is produced by a

___1___ in each ventricle. Most of the CSF is

formed within the ___2___ ventricles and

flows through two small openings into the

median ___3___ ventricle. From here, it passes

into the fourth ventricle in the posterior portion

of the brain stem. From the ___4___ ventricle,

some CSF flows into the ___5___ of the

spinal cord, but most of it enters the ___6___

space and flows around the spinal cord and

brain. CSF is absorbed into the blood of the

___7___ located in the ___8___ above the longitudinal

fissure of the cerebrum.

1) _____

2) _____

3) _____

4) _____

5) _____

6) _____

7) _____

8) _____

6. Spinal Cord

a.   Write the terms that match the phrases in the spaces at the right.

1) Contain cell bodies of motor neurons.   _____

2) Composed of myelinated nerve fibers.   _____

3) Contain cell bodies of interneurons.   _____

4) Carry impulses toward brain.   _____

5) Carry impulses from brain.   _____

6) Vertebra where spinal cord ends.   _____

7) Part of brain continuous with spinal cord.   _____

8) Nerves arising from spinal cord.   _____

b.   Label the figure by placing the number of the structure in the space by the correct label.

_____ Anterior median fissure

_____ Central canal

_____ Gray matter, commissure

_____ Gray matter, anterior horn

_____ Gray matter, posterior horn

_____ Posterior median fissure

_____ Spinal nerve, anterior (ventral) root

_____ Spinal nerve, posterior (dorsal) root

_____ Spinal nerve, posterior root gangelion

_____ White matter, anterior column

_____ White matter, lateral column

_____ White matter, posterior column

c. Write the terms that match the phrases in the spaces at the right.

1) Tissue binding nerve fibers together in a nerve. _____

2) Nerves arising from the spinal cord. _____

3) Nerves arising from the brain. _____

4) Nerves composed of both axons and dendrites. _____

5) Sensory neuron processes in spinal nerves. _____

6) Neurons carrying impulses from the CNS. _____

7) Neurons carrying impulses to the CNS. _____

8) Nerves composed of both sensory and motor
   neuron processes. _____

7. **Peripheral Nervous System (PNS)**

a. Write the numerals and names of the cranial nerves described by the phrases.

1) Transmits motor impulses to facial muscles. _____

2) Transmits sensory impulses from retina. _____

3) Transmits motor impulses to muscles that
   move the eyes (three nerves). _____
   _____
   _____

4) Transmits sensory impulses from thoracic
   and abdominal viscera. _____

5) Transmits motor impulses to tongue muscles. _____

6) Transmits sensory impulses from the ear. _____

7) Transmits sensory impulses from "smell" receptors. _____

8) Transmits motor impulses to chewing muscles. _____

9) Transmits sensory impulses from the face. _____

10) Transmits motor impulses to muscles of the
    larynx and to the trapezius muscle. _____

11) Transmits motor impulses to salivary glands. _____

12) Transmits motor impulses to thoracic and
    abdominal viscera. _____

13) Transmits sensory impulses from the teeth. _____

14) Transmits motor impulses to the eye that
    adjust pupil size and lens shape. _____

b. Write the terms that match the phrases in the spaces at the right.

1) Number of pairs of spinal nerves. _____

2) Root containing axons of motor nerves. _____

3) Root containing sensory neurons. _____

4) Spinal nerves that do *not* form plexuses. _____

5) Plexuses from which nerves to the legs emerge. _____

6) Rapid, involuntary, predictable responses. _____

7) Where spinal nerve fibers are sorted and recombined. _____

c. Write the terms that complete the sentences in the spaces at the right.

In a somatic spinal reflex, a painful stimulus
causes a receptor to form impulses that are   1) _____
carried by a __1__ neuron to the spinal cord.   2) _____
This neuron enters the spinal cord via the __2__ 3) _____
root and synapses with an __3__ in the __4__   4) _____
horn. This second neuron extends to the __5__   5) _____
horn, where it synapses with a __6__ neuron that 6) _____
exits the spinal cord via the __7__ root and   7) _____
carries impulses to an __8__.   8) _____

8. Autonomic Nervous System (ANS)

a. Write the terms that match the phrases in the spaces at the right.

1) Division arising from brain stem and
   sacral region of spinal cord.   _____

2) Division arising from thorax and lumbar
   regions of spinal cord.   _____

3) Autonomic ganglia forming a chain on each
   side of the vertebral column.   _____

4) Neurotransmitter secreted by postganglionic
   sympathetic neurons.   _____

5) Neurotransmitter secreted by postganglionic
   parasympathetic neurons.   _____

6) Division preparing body for emergencies.   _____

7) Division promoting digestion.   _____

8) Division increasing blood pressure.   _____

b. Write the terms that complete the sentences in the spaces at the right.

In a spinal autonomic visceral reflex, a __1__   1) _____
neuron exits the spinal cord via an __2__ root and   2) _____
extends to an autonomic __3__, where it synapses   3) _____
with a __4__ neuron that continues to an effector.   4) _____

9. Disorders of the Nervous System

Write the disorders described by the phrases.

1) Infection of the meninges.   _____

2) Caused by a deficiency of dopamine.   _____

3) Severe memory loss caused by a loss of certain
   cholinergic neurons in the brain.   _____

4) Blood clot, aneurysm, or hemorrhage in brain.   _____

5) Destruction of myelin sheath in CNS.   _____

6) Prenatal brain damage, often caused by viral infections
   like German measles.   _____

7) Convulsive seizures.   _____

8) A severe jarring of the brain.   _____

9) Neuritis by reactivation of chicken pox virus.   _____

10) Results from inactive reticular formation.   _____

10. Clinical Insights

a. A stroke patient is paralyzed on the right side of the body and cannot speak. What part of the brain is
    affected by the stroke? _____

    _____

    _____

b. A patient complains of severe pain in the left lower back that extends down the thigh. A nurse
    describes the pain as neuralgia. What is neuralgia? _____

    _____

    What nerve is the likely source of the pain? _____

c. The poliomyelitis virus destroys neuron cell bodies in the anterior horn of the spinal cord. If the
    affected spinal nerve innervates the left leg, what will be the effect on the patient? _____

    _____

    Will the patient fully recover? _____ Explain. _____

    _____

1. Sensations

a. Match the structures with the statements that follow.

1) Cerebral cortex 2) Nerve fiber 3) Receptor

_____ Carries impulses.

_____ Forms sensory impulses.

_____ Interprets impulses as sensations.

_____ Decreases impulse formation when repeatedly stimulated.

_____ Projects sensation back to region where impulses seem to originate.

_____ Sensitive to a particular type of stimulus.

_____ Exhibits adaptation.

b. Define adaptation. _____

_____

2. General Senses

a. Match the responses with the statements that follow.

1) Cold receptors

2) Free nerve endings

3) Heat receptors

4) Meissner's corpuscles

5) Pressure receptors

6) Proprioceptors

_____ Pain receptors.

_____ Touch receptors.

_____ Most sensitive to temperatures over 25°C.

_____ Most sensitive to temperatures under 10°C.

_____ May be located in epidermis.

_____ Located in visceral organs.

_____ Located in superficial portion of dermis.

_____ Located in muscles and tendons.

_____ Temperature receptors closest to epidermis.

_____ Touch receptor abundant in hairless skin.

_____ Involved in maintenance of erect posture.

b. What is referred pain? _____

_____

_____

3. Taste and Smell

Write the terms described by the statements in the spaces at the right.

1) Organs containing taste receptors. _____

2) Receptors located in nasal epithelium. _____

3) Name the four basic taste sensations detected by the four types of taste receptors _____

4. Ear Structure

a. Label the figure by placing the number of the structure in the space by the correct label.

_____ Auditory tube   _____ Round window

_____ Auricle   _____ Semicircular canals

_____ Cochlea   _____ Stapes

_____ External auditory canal   _____ Tympanic cavity

_____ Incus   _____ Tympanic membrane

_____ Malleus   _____ Vestibulocochlear nerve

_____ Oval window

b. Write the terms that match the statements in the spaces at the right.

1) Part of the bony labyrinth that contains receptors for

   a) hearing.   _____

   b) static balance.   _____

   c) dynamic balance.   _____

2) Fills membranous labyrinth.   _____

3) Fills bony labyrinth.   _____

4) Fills tympanic cavity.   _____

c.   Label the figure by placing the number of the structure in the space by the correct label.

_____ Basilar membrane

_____ Cochlear duct

_____ Cochlear portion of the vestibu-

locochlear nerve

_____ Hair cells

_____ Scala tympani

_____ Scala vestibuli

_____ Spiral organ

_____ Tectorial membrane

_____ Vestibular membrane

5. Hearing

a.   Write the terms that match the statements in the spaces at the right.

1) Receptor organ for hearing.

2) Receptor cells for hearing.

3) Carry vibrations from eardrum to perilymph.

4) Directs sound waves to tympanic membrane.

5) Contains fibers of increasing length.

6) Membrane-covered opening into scala tympani.

7) Membrane struck by sound waves.

8) Membrane that determines pitch of sound.

9) Membrane contacting hairs of receptor cells.

10) Allows air to enter tympanic cavity.

b.   Write the terms that complete the sentences in the spaces at the right.

Sound waves enter the __1__ and strike the __2__,   1) _____

causing it to vibrate. This vibration is transmitted   2) _____

by the __3__ to the __4__ that fills the scala vestibuli 3) _____

and scala tympani. Oscillating movements of this   4) _____

fluid cause comparable vibrations of portions of   5) _____

the __5__ membrane and the __6__ that rests upon   6) _____

it. This causes the hair cells to contact the __7__,   7) _____

which stimulates them to form __8__ that are car-   8) _____

ried to the brain by the __9__ nerve. The hearing   9) _____

centers in the __10__ lobes interpret these impulses 10) _____

as sound sensations.

6. Equilibrium

Write the terms that match the statements in the spaces at the right.

1) Receptor organ for static equilibrium.   _____

2) Chambers containing receptors for static
   equilibrium.   _____

3) Force stimulating hair cells of macula.   _____

4) Receptor organ for dynamic equilibrium.   _____

5) Locations of receptor organs for dynamic
   equilibrium.   _____

6) Fluid moving cupula when head is turned.   _____

7) Part of brain controlling equilibrium.   _____

7. Accessory Structures of the Eye

Write the terms that match the statements in the spaces at the right.

1) Lines eyelids and covers anterior sclera.   _____

2) Group of muscles that move the eye.   _____

3) Secretes tears.   _____

4) Collect tears at inner corner of eye.   _____

5) Carries collected tears into nasal cavity.   _____

8. Eye Structure

a. Write the terms that match the statements in the spaces at the right.

1) Fills anterior cavity.   _____

2) Pigmented layer of the eyeball.   _____

3) Substance holding retina against choroid.   _____

4) Opening in center of iris.   _____

5) Fluid mostly responsible for internal pressure
   in eye.   _____

6) Protective outer fibrous coat of eye.   _____

b.   Label the figure by placing the number of the structure in the space by the correct label.

_____ Aqueous humor in anterior cavity   _____ Optic disk

_____ Choroid coat   _____ Optic nerve

_____ Ciliary body   _____ Pupil

_____ Conjunctiva   _____ Retina

_____ Cornea   _____ Sclera

_____ Fovea centralis   _____ Suspensory ligaments

_____ Iris   _____ Vitreous humor in posterior cavity

_____ Lens

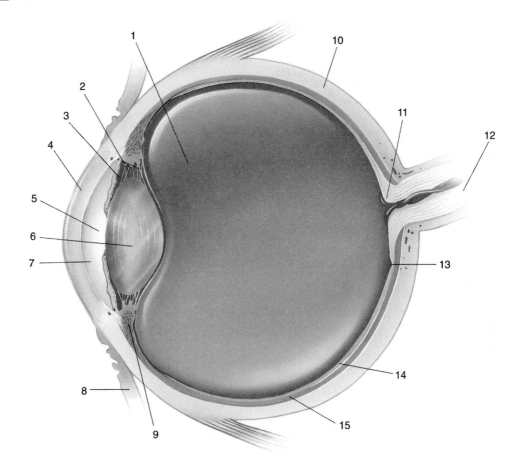

9. Vision

Write the terms that match the statements in the spaces at the right.

1) Contains photoreceptors.   _____

2) Site of direct vision.   _____

3) Clear window through which light enters eye.   _____

4) Controls amount of light entering eye.   _____

5) Focuses light rays on retina.   _____

6) Layer containing blood vessels.   _____

7) Changes shape of the lens.   _____

8) Retinal area lacking photoreceptors.   _____

9) Causes greatest bending of light rays.   _____

10) Absorbs excessive light in eye.   _____

11) Receptors for dim light vision.   _____

12) Receptors for color vision.   _____

13) Receptors absent in fovea.   _____

14) Carries impulses from retina to brain.   _____

15) Where medial nerve fibers cross over.   _____

16) Light-sensitive pigment in rods.   _____

17) Colors of light absorbed by three types of cones.   _____
_____
_____

18) Vitamin required for rhodopsin synthesis.   _____

10. Disorders of Hearing and Vision

Write the disorders described in the spaces at the right.

1) An infection called "pink eye."   _____

2) Cloudiness of the lens.   _____

3) Acute infection of the middle ear.   _____

4) Deafness due to exposure to loud noises.   _____

5) Deafness correctible by hearing aids.   _____

6) Results from unequal curvatures of lens or cornea.   _____

7) Corrected by convex lenses.   _____

8) Corrected by concave lenses.   _____

9) Decreased elasticity of the lens.   _____

10) Nausea due to repeated stimulation of equilibrium receptors.   _____

11) Group of disorders producing nausea, dizziness, and tinnitis.   _____

12) Cancer of immature retinal cells.   _____

13) Caused by excessive intraocular pressure.   _____

14) Crossed eyes.   _____

11. Clinical Insights

a.   An older patient calls the office and complains of pain at the base of the neck, left shoulder, and left arm. What is the probable cause of the pain? _____ Why was the pain localized in these areas?

_____

_____

What would you advise the patient to do? _____

b.   An audiometry test verifies that a college student has a decreased sense of hearing. Discussion brings out that he has been working as an audio engineer at a local disco for three years. What relationship probably exists between his job and his hearing loss? _____

_____

_____

1. Endocrine Glands

a. Label the endocrine glands in the figure by placing the number of the gland in the space beside the correct label.

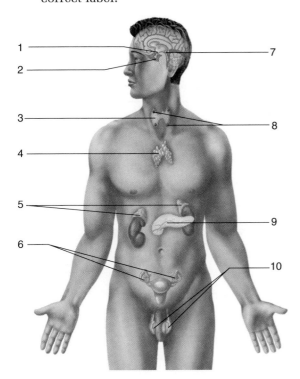

_____ Adrenal

_____ Hypothalamus

_____ Ovary

_____ Pancreas

_____ Parathyroid

_____ Pineal

_____ Pituitary

_____ Testis

_____ Thymus

_____ Thyroid

b. Contrast exocrine and endocrine glands.

1) Secretions of exocrine glands are carried by _____.

2) Secretions of endocrine glands are carried by _____.

2. The Nature of Hormones

a. Match the hormone with the correct statement.

1) Steroid hormone

_____ Binds to a plasma membrane receptor.

_____ Requires a second messenger.

_____ Fat-soluble hormone.

2) Nonsteroid hormone

_____ Receptor-hormone complex causes DNA to initiate synthesis of new proteins (enzymes).

_____ Binds to receptor within the target cells.

b.   Write the terms that match the statements in the spaces at the right.

1) Chemical messengers.   _____

2) Carries hormones throughout the body.   _____

3) Glands producing hormones.   _____

4) Cells containing hormone receptors.   _____

5) Excessive production of a hormone.   _____

6) Deficient production of a hormone.   _____

7) Usual regulatory mechanism for hormone
    production.   _____

8) Local "hormones" produced by nonendocrine
    cells.   _____

3. Pituitary Gland

a.   Secretes releasing hormones that activate the anterior pituitary gland. _____

b.   Produces oxytocin and ADH that are released within the posterior pituitary gland. _____

c.   Write the names of the pituitary hormones that match the statements in the spaces at the right.

1) Stimulates secretion of thyroid hormone.   _____

2) Stimulates cell growth and division.   _____

3) Stimulates secretion of estrogens.   _____

4) Stimulates secretion of testosterone.   _____

5) Stimulates secretion of cortisol.   _____

6) Stimulates sperm production.   _____

7) Stimulates water retention by kidneys.   _____

8) Stimulates contraction of uterus.   _____

9) Stimulates secretion of progesterone.   _____

10) Causes the onset of puberty.   _____

d.   Match the lobe with the hormone it produces.

1) Anterior lobe   2) Posterior lobe

1) _____ ACTH   _____ 3) Prolactin   _____ 5) TSH   _____ 7) Growth hormone

2) _____ Oxytocin   _____ 4) FSH and LH   _____ 6) ADH

4. Thyroid and Parathyroid Glands

Write the terms that match the statements in the spaces at the right.

1) Element essential for activity of thyroxine.   _____

2) Hormone that increases metabolic rate.   _____

3) Hormone that increases blood calcium.   _____

4) Hormone whose secretion is controlled by TSH.   _____

5) Hormone that decreases blood calcium.   _____

6) Gland that secretes calcitonin.   _____

7) Controls secretion of parathyroid hormone.   _____

5. Adrenal Glands

Write the terms that match the statements in the spaces at the right.

1) Converts glycogen into glucose. _____

2) Controls secretion of adrenal medulla. _____

3) Two related hormones secreted by the adrenal medulla. _____

4) Three groups of hormones secreted by adrenal cortex. _____

_____

_____

5) Controls levels of electrolytes in blood. _____

6) Inhibits inflammation; depresses immunity. _____

7) Secretion controlled by blood levels of sodium and potassium. _____

8) Prepares body to meet emergencies. _____

9) Increases blood levels of sodium and water. _____

10) Converts noncarbohydrates into glucose. _____

11) Increases heart rate and blood pressure. _____

12) Secretion controlled by ACTH. _____

6. Pancreas

Write the terms that match the statements in the spaces at the right.

1) Portion of gland secreting hormones. _____

2) Hormone decreasing blood glucose. _____

3) Hormone aiding movement of glucose into cells. _____

4) Hormone increasing blood glucose. _____

5) Controls secretion of pancreatic hormones. _____

6) Secretion stimulated by high glucose levels. _____

7. Gonads, Pineal Gland, and Thymus

Write the terms that match the statements in the spaces at the right.

1) Hormones formed by ovaries. _____

_____

2) Hormone secreted by testes. _____

3) Hormone of the pineal gland. _____

4) Hormone of the thymus. _____

5) Seems to influence biorhythms. _____

6) Stimulates development of male sex organs and secondary sexual characteristics. _____

7) Stimulates development of female sex organs and secondary sexual characteristics. _____

8) Involved in maturation of T lymphocytes. _____

8. Disorders of the Endocrine System

Write the names of the disorders described below in the spaces at the right.

1) Hypersecretion of GH in adults.   _____

2) Production of large amounts of dilute urine.   _____

3) Enlarged thyroid due to lack of iodine.   _____

4) Excessive metabolic rate and bulging eyes.   _____

5) Hyposecretion of thyroid hormone in adults.   _____

6) Hyposecretion of GH in growing years.   _____

7) Hyposecretion of aldosterone and cortisol.   _____

8) Hypersecretion of glucocorticoids.   _____

9) Hyposecretion of ADH.   _____

10) Continued growth of bones of face and hands.   _____

11) Inability of glucose to enter body cells.   _____

12) Hypersecretion of thyroxine.   _____

13) Mental retardation, sluggishness, and stunted
growth in an infant.   _____

14) Coarse, dry skin and hair; edema; and sluggishness
in adults.   _____

15) Round, full face; high blood pressure; high blood
glucose; and decreased immunity.   _____

9. Clinical Insights

a.   A patient is taken to the emergency room by her husband. She is sweating and breathing rapidly. A
blood test reveals acidosis and hyperglycemia. What hormone should be administered immediately?
_____ Explain. _____
_____
_____

b.   A new mother is informed that her baby has severe hypothyroidism. How would you explain the
importance of thyroxine medication for her infant? _____
_____
_____
_____

c.   A patient with high blood pressure and edema (water-logged tissues) is given a drug that counteracts
the action of ADH. Explain why this drug was administered and how it will work. _____
_____

1. General Characteristics of Blood

Write the answers that match the statements in the spaces at the right.

1) pH range of the blood.   _____

2) Liquid portion of blood.   _____

3) Blood cells and platelets.   _____

4) Percentage of blood formed by liquid portion.   _____

5) Percentage of blood formed by RBCs, WBCs
   and platelets.   _____

6) Average range of blood volume in males.   _____

7) Average range of blood volume in females.   _____

8) Basic function of blood.   _____

2. Red Blood Cells

Write the answers that match the statements in the spaces at the right.

1) Shape of erythrocytes.   _____

2) Red pigment in erythrocytes.   _____

3) Primary function of RBCs is transport of ____.   _____

4) Iron-containing portion of hemoglobin.   _____

5) Normal range of RBCs/mm³ in males.   _____

6) Normal range of RBCs/mm³ in females.   _____

7) Tissue-forming RBCs in children and adults.   _____

8) Hormone-stimulating RBC production.   _____

9) Organs releasing the hormone that stimulates
   RBC production.   _____

10) Organ producing intrinsic factor.   _____

11) Vitamins required for RBC production.   _____

12) Intrinsic factor enables absorption of ____.   _____

13) Cells from which RBCs originate.   _____

14) Average life span of RBCs.   _____

15) Organs where old RBCs are destroyed.   _____

16) Phagocytic cells destroying RBCs.   _____

17) Portion of heme that is recycled.   _____

18) Portion of heme that is excreted.   _____

19) Organ where heme breakdown occurs.   _____

3. White Blood Cells

a. Write the answers that match the statements in the spaces at the right.

1) Cell from which WBCs originate.

2) Normal range of WBCs/mm^3 of blood.

3) Basic function of WBCs is defense against _____.

4) Where most functions of WBCs occur.

5) Group of WBCs with cytoplasmic granules.

6) Group of WBCs lacking these granules.

7) WBCs with lavender-staining granules.

8) WBCs with blue-staining granules.

9) Largest leukocytes.

10) Smallest leukocytes.

11) WBCs with red-staining granules.

12) Form 20% to 25% of WBCs.

13) Migrate into tissues to become macrophages.

14) First WBCs attracted from blood into
damaged tissues.

15) WBCs that move into tissues to complete cleanup
of tissue damage.

16) Form 60% to 70% of leukocytes.

17) Release histamine in allergic reactions.

18) WBCs that neutralize histamine.

19) Become mast cells after entering tissues.

20) Destroy parasitic worms.

21) Produce antibodies.

22) Compose 3% to 8% of leukocytes.

23) Compose 0.5% to 1.0% of leukocytes.

24) Compose 2% to 4% of leukocytes.

25) Two major phagocytic WBCs.

b. Use colored pencils to draw these white blood cells as they appear after staining.

Neutrophil   **Eosinophil**   **Basophil**

Monocyte   **Lymphocyte**

4. Platelets

Write the answers that match the statements in the spaces at the right.

1) Alternate name for platelets. _____

2) Size compared to size of RBCs. _____

3) Number of platelets per mm³ of blood. _____

4) Cells that fragment to form platelets. _____

5) Two functions of platelets. _____

5. Plasma

Write the answers that match the statements in the spaces at the right.

1) Constitutes over 90% of plasma. _____

2) General term for dissolved substances. _____

3) Most abundant plasma proteins. _____

4) Plasma proteins that are antibodies. _____

5) Plasma protein converted into fibrin. _____

6) Plasma proteins transporting lipids. _____

7) Plasma proteins helping to regulate pH and osmotic
   pressure of the blood. _____

8) Organ forming most plasma proteins. _____

9) Nitrogenous wastes of protein breakdown. _____

10) Collective term for inorganic ions in the
    blood plasma. _____

6. Hemostasis

Write the answers that match the statements in the spaces at the right.

1) Three processes of hemostasis in order of occurrence. _____

_____

_____

2) Constriction of damaged blood vessel. _____

3) Formed elements that temporarily plug break in
   damaged blood vessel. _____

4) Substance released by platelets and damaged
   tissues that starts clotting process. _____

5) Electrolyte required for clotting to occur. _____

6) Threadlike strands forming a blood clot. _____

7) Cells that enter clot to form new connective tissue
   and repair damage. _____

8) Enzyme converting fibrinogen into fibrin. _____

7. Human Blood Types

Write the answers that match the statements in the spaces at the right.

1) Location of antigens used in blood typing.   _____

2) Location of antibodies against blood-typing antigens.   _____

3) Antigen(s) in type A blood.   _____

4) Antigen(s) in type AB blood.   _____

5) Antigen(s) in type O blood.   _____

6) Antibodies in type B blood.   _____

7) Antibodies in type AB blood.   _____

8) Antibodies in type O blood.   _____

9) Antibodies in Rh-blood of person sensitized to
the Rh antigen.   _____

10) Caused by maternal anti-Rh antibodies binding with
Rh antigens on fetal RBCs.   _____

8. Disorders of the Blood

Write the answers that match the statements in the spaces at the right.

1) Reduced ability to form blood clots.   _____

2) Reduced capacity to carry oxygen.   _____

3) An excessive concentration of erythrocytes.   _____

4) Infection of lymphocytes by Epstein–Barr virus.   _____

5) Anemia due to a deficiency of iron.   _____

6) Cancer producing excess of leukocytes.   _____

7) Anemia due to inability to absorb vitamin B_{12}.   _____

8) Anemia due to excessive bleeding.   _____

9) Anemia due to sickling of erythrocytes.   _____

10) Anemia due to premature rupture of RBCs.   _____

11) Anemia due to loss of red bone marrow.   _____

12) Fetal blood contains erythroblasts.   _____

9. Clinical Insights

a.   What ABO and Rh blood type could a person with type O Rh⁺ blood safely receive? _____
Explain._____

_____

b.   Mary's blood type is A, Rh⁻. She is at the hospital for delivery of her second child, and her first child
is Rh⁺. The attending physician wants blood available in case the baby exhibits erythroblastosis fetalis upon delivery. What blood type should he order? _____
Explain. _____

_____

c.   Chemotherapy destroys cancer cells because it disrupts cell division in rapidly dividing cells. What
impact would chemotherapy have on the production of blood cells? _____
Explain. _____

_____

1. Structure of the Heart

a. Write the correct labels in the spaces at the right.

1) _____

2) _____

3) _____

4) _____

5) _____

6) _____

7) _____

8) _____

9) _____

10) _____

11) _____

12) _____

13) _____

14) _____

15) _____

16) _____

17) _____

18) _____

b. Write the answers that match the statements in the spaces at the right.

1) Receives blood from venae cavae.

2) Receives blood from pulmonary veins.

3) Separates ventricles.

4) Prevents backflow of blood from right ventricle into right atrium.

5) Prevents backflow of blood from left ventricle into left atrium.

6) Prevents backflow of blood from aorta into left ventricle.

7) Prevents backflow of blood from pulmonary trunk into right ventricle.

8) Restrain cusps of A-V valves.

9) Pumps blood into pulmonary trunk.

10) Pumps blood into aorta.

2. Cardiac Cycle

Write the answers that match the statements in the spaces at the right.

1) Contraction phase of the ventricles. _____

2) Relaxation phase of the ventricles. _____

3) Valves closing to produce first heart sound. _____

4) Valves closing to produce second heart sound. _____

5) Valves open during ventricular systole. _____

6) Valves closed during ventricular systole. _____

7) Valves open during ventricular diastole. _____

8) Valves closed during ventricular diastole. _____

3. Heart Conduction System and Electrocardiogram

Write the answers that match the statements in the spaces at the right.

1) Small fibers carrying impulses to myocardium. _____

2) Pacemaker of the heart. _____

3) Thick fibers extending from A-V node. _____

4) Transmits impulses to atria and A-V node. _____

5) Transmits impulses to A-V bundle. _____

6) Wave caused by depolarization of ventricles. _____

7) Wave caused by repolarization of ventricles. _____

8) Wave caused by depolarization of atria. _____

4. Regulation of Heart Function

a. Write the answers that match the statements in the spaces at the right.

1) Term for the volume of blood pumped from the heart in 1 min. _____

2) Term for the volume of blood pumped from the heart in one contraction. _____

3) If the heart rate is 65 beats/min and the stroke volume is 70 ml/beat, what is the cardiac output? _____

4) Autonomic center controlling heart rate. _____

5) ANS division whose impulses increase heart rate. _____

6) ANS division whose impulses decrease heart rate. _____

7) Gender with faster heart rate. _____

8) Nerve carrying parasympathetic fibers to the heart. _____

b. Match the effect on heart rate with the factors listed.

1) Increases   2) Decreases   3) No effect

_____ Epinephrine   _____ Excess K⁺   _____ Insufficient Ca⁺⁺

_____ Old age   _____ Acetylcholine   _____ Excitement

_____ Fever   _____ Anxiety   _____ Thyroxine

_____ Physical conditioning   _____ Increase in blood pressure   _____ Norepinephrine

5. Types of Blood Vessels

Write the answers that match the statements in the spaces at the right.

1) Composed of endothelium only. _____

2) Vessels with thickest walls. _____

3) Vessels with valves. _____

4) Carry blood from capillaries to heart. _____

5) Carry blood from heart to capillaries. _____

6) Vessels exchanging materials with tissues. _____

7) Smallest and most numerous vessels. _____

8) Force moving fluid from blood to interstitial fluid. _____

9) Force returning fluid from interstitial fluid to blood. _____

10) Process moving dissolved molecules between
    capillaries and tissue cells. _____

6. Blood Flow and Blood Pressure

a.   Write the answers that match the statements in the spaces at the right.

1) Systemic vessel with fastest blood flow. _____

2) Vessels with slowest blood flow. _____

3) Systemic vessel with greatest blood pressure. _____

4) Primary force moving blood. _____

5) Two additional forces that help return venous
   blood to the heart. _____

   _____

6) Normal systolic blood pressure. _____

7) Normal diastolic blood pressure. _____

8) Autonomic center controlling diameter of
   blood vessels. _____

9) Systolic pressure minus diastolic pressure. _____

10) Effect on precapillary sphincters by a local decrease
    in oxygen and pH. _____

11) Effect on precapillary sphincters by sympathetic
    impulses. _____

b.   Indicate whether the following conditions cause an *increase* (+) or *decrease* (−) in blood pressure.

_____ An increase in peripheral resistance.

_____ A marked decrease in blood volume.

_____ A decrease in cardiac output.

_____ Dilation of a great many arterioles.

_____ A significant increase in plasma proteins.

_____ Sympathetic impulses to arterioles.

_____ Constriction of most arterioles.

_____ An increase in heart rate.

7. Circulation Pathways

Trace the pathway of blood from a ventricle of the heart to the organ indicated and back to an atrium of the heart. Write the names of the correct heart chambers, arteries, and veins in the blanks.

1) Right little finger.

Left ventricle → _____ → _____ →

_____ → _____ →

_____ → _____ → right little finger

→ _____ → _____ →

_____ → _____ → _____

→ _____ atrium.

2) Small intestine.

_____ ventricle → _____ → _____

→ small intestine → _____ →

_____ → liver → _____ →

_____ → right atrium.

8. Systemic Arteries

Label the figure by writing the names
of the numbered arteries in the spaces.

1) _____

2) _____

3) _____

4) _____

5) _____

6) _____

7) _____

8) _____

9) _____

10) _____

11) _____

12) _____

13) _____

14) _____

15) _____

16) _____

17) _____

18) _____

19) _____

20) _____

21) _____

22) _____

23) _____

24) _____

25) _____

26) _____

27) _____

28) _____

29) _____

30) _____

Arteries of the head
and trunk

Arteries of the upper limb

Arteries of
the lower limb

9. Systemic Veins

Label the figure by writing the names of the numbered veins in the spaces.

1) _____

2) _____

3) _____

4) _____

5) _____

6) _____

7) _____

8) _____

9) _____

10) _____

11) _____

12) _____

13) _____

14) _____

15) _____

16) _____

17) _____

18) _____

19) _____

20) _____

21) _____

22) _____

23) _____

24) _____

25) _____

26) _____

27) _____

28) _____

29) _____

30) _____

Veins of the upper limb

Veins of the head and trunk

Veins of the lower limb

10. Disorders of the Heart and Blood Vessels

Write the disorders described by the statements in the spaces at the right.

1) Unusual heart sounds. _____

2) Hardening of the arteries. _____

3) Death of a portion of the myocardium. _____

4) Abnormal heart rhythm. _____

5) Inflammation of a vein. _____

6) Chronic high blood pressure. _____

7) Swollen veins due to defective valves. _____

8) Balloonlike enlargement of blood vessel. _____

9) Fatty deposits in walls of arteries. _____

10) Edema of lungs, viscera, legs, and feet. _____

11. Clinical Insights

a. A 60-year-old man complains of chest pain during moderate exercise. The pain goes away after he rests for a while. What is the likely cause of the pain? _____
Without treatment, what complications may arise? _____
_____

b. An accident victim has lost considerable blood. His blood pressure is only slightly below normal, and his pulse rate is elevated. How is the body compensating for the loss of blood? _____
_____

c. A patient has a blood clot in the right femoral vein. If a part of the clot should break loose, where is it likely to lodge? _____
Would this be a serious complication? _____ Explain. _____
_____
_____
_____

1. Lymph and Lymphatic Vessels

a. Write the answers that match the statements in the spaces at the right.

1) Fluid within tissue spaces. _____

2) Fluid within lymphatic vessels. _____

3) Smallest lymphatic vessels. _____

4) Lymphatic vessels draining large body regions. _____

5) Forms wall of lymphatic capillaries. _____

6) Lymphatic duct draining upper right portion of the body. _____

7) Lymphatic duct draining rest of the body. _____

8) Prevent backflow of lymph. _____

9) Provide forces that move lymph. _____

_____

10) Receives lymph from thoracic duct. _____

11) Empties into right subclavian vein. _____

12) Vessels collecting interstitial fluid. _____

13) Source of interstitial fluid. _____

b. Explain the value of the lymphatic system collecting interstitial fluid and returning it to the blood.

_____

_____

_____

_____

2. Lymphatic Organs

Write the answers that match the statements in the spaces at the right.

1) Grouped along larger lymphatic vessels. _____

2) Bilobed gland located above the heart. _____

3) Large lymphatic organ located near stomach. _____

4) Clustered at entrance to pharynx. _____

5) Organs that filter lymph. _____

6) Lymphatic organ that filters blood. _____

7) Site of T cell differentiation. _____

8) Vessels carrying lymph to lymph node. _____

9) Vessels carrying lymph from lymph node. _____

10) Intercept pathogens entering pharynx. _____

11) Contains a reserve supply of blood. _____

12) Hormone that promotes T cell maturation. _____

3. Nonspecific Resistance Against Disease

Match the type of nonspecific resistance with the statements.

1) Mechanical barriers   3) Phagocytosis   5) Fever

2) Chemicals   4) Inflammation

_____ Skin   _____ Release of histamine

_____ Mucus   _____ Abnormally high body temperature

_____ Lysozyme   _____ Attracts neutrophils and monocytes

_____ Mucous membranes   _____ Tissue macrophage system

_____ Low pH   _____ Flow of saliva

_____ Gastric juice   _____ Granulocytes and macrophages

_____ Interferon   _____ Increases local blood supply

_____ Produces edema   _____ Clot seals off pathogens

_____ Pus formation   _____ Speeds up body processes

_____ Flow of tears   _____ Pathogens are engulfed and digested

4. Immunity

a.   Indicate whether the following statements are true (T) or false (F).

1) Immunity is resistance against specific pathogens.   _____

2) Toxins are neutralized by cell-mediated immunity.   _____

3) Diseased body cells are destroyed by antibody-mediated
immunity.   _____

4) Immunity requires lymphocytes to distinguish between self
and nonself molecules.   _____

5) Antigens are foreign molecules that cause an immune response.   _____

6) Undifferentiated lymphocytes are produced in the spleen.   _____

7) All lymphocytes differentiate in the thymus.   _____

8) The majority of lymphocytes in the blood are T cells.   _____

9) Differentiation of lymphocytes occurs throughout life.   _____

10) T cells provide cell-mediated immunity.   _____

11) B cells provide antibody-mediated immunity.   _____

12) Lymphocyte receptors for specific antigens are inherited.   _____

13) Lymphocyte receptors are formed by contact with specific antigens.   _____

14) There are thousands of different types of B and T cells, and
each type responds to a different specific antigen.   _____

15) Immunity depends upon lymphocytes whose receptors fit
with a specific antigen.   _____

16) Immunity involves the interaction of lymphocytes, antigens,
and antigen-presenting cells.   _____

17) At any one time, either cell-mediated immunity or antibody-
mediated immunity is at work—never both at the same time.   _____

18) Reproduction of differentiated lymphocytes occurs in
lymphatic organs.   _____

b. Write the words that complete the sentences describing cell-mediated immunity in the spaces at the right.

Cell-mediated immunity begins when a/an __1__ engulfs a foreign antigen and displays part of the __2__, in combination with its own self __3__, on its plasma membrane. A T cell, which recognizes this __4__, binds to the antigen and the APC self proteins and becomes __5__. The activated T cell undergoes repeated mitotic divisions to form a __6__ of identical T cells. An activated helper T cell yields a clone of active helper T cells and __7__ T cells. An activated cytotoxic T cell yields a clone of active __8__ T cells and memory T cells.

Active helper T cells secrete __9__ that stimulate phagocytosis and activity of B and T cells. __10__ T cells are essential in starting an immune response by T cells and B cells. Active __11__ T cells bind to cells with the targeted antigen and inject a lethal dose of chemicals to kill the cell. After the pathogen has been destroyed, the dormant __12__ T cells remain to launch a quicker and stronger attack if the same antigen reappears in the body.

1) _____
2) _____
3) _____
4) _____
5) _____
6) _____
7) _____
8) _____
9) _____
10) _____
11) _____
12) _____

c. Write the words that complete the sentences describing antibody-related immunity in the spaces at the right.

Antibody-mediated immunity begins when a foreign antigen binds to __1__ of a B cell. The B cell engulfs and digests the antigens and displays part of the antigens on its __2__ along with its own self antigens. When a __3__ T cell binds to this antigen and self protein complex, it secretes __4__ that activate the B cell. The activated B cell divides repeatedly producing a __4__ of identical B cells. Most of the B cells in the clone become __5__, but some become __6__ B cells.

Plasma cells rapidly produce and release __7__, which circulate in blood and other body fluids binding to the targeted antigens so they are more easily destroyed by __8__ and by other means. After the pathogen has been destroyed, __9__ B cells remain to launch an even quicker and stronger attack if the same antigen reenters the body.

1) _____
2) _____
3) _____
4) _____
5) _____
6) _____
7) _____
8) _____
9) _____

d. Match the antibodies with the statements. More than one answer may apply.

IgA   IgD   IgE   IgG   IgM

1) Most abundant antibody in the blood.   _____

2) Fixes complement to antigens.   _____

3) Serves as receptors on B cells.   _____

4) Involved in allergic reactions.   _____

5) Transferred to child via mother's milk.   _____

6) Transferred to fetus via placenta.   _____

7) Binds with antigens.   _____

8) Protects mucous membranes.   _____

9) Neutralizes toxins.   _____

5. Immune Responses

a. Match the immune responses with the statements.

1) Primary immune response   2) Secondary immune response

_____ Occurs when an antigen is encountered for the first time.

_____ Occurs in subsequent encounters with same antigen.

_____ Results from activation of memory cells.

_____ The more rapid and intense response.

b. Match the types of immunity with the statements.

1) Naturally acquired active   3) Naturally acquired passive

2) Artificially acquired active   4) Artificially acquired passive

_____ Immunity from antibodies received in mother's milk.

_____ Immunity from a vaccine of dead pathogens.

_____ Immunity after having the disease and recovering.

_____ Immunity from injected antibodies.

_____ Immunity from DPT injections.

_____ Immunity from monoclonal antibodies.

6. Disorders of the Lymphatic and Immune Systems

Write the answers that match the statements in the spaces at the right.

1) Microscopic worms plug lymphatic vessels.   _____

2) An abnormally intense immune reaction.   _____

3) HIV destroys helper T cells.   _____

4) A tumor of lymphatic tissue.   _____

5) Inflammation of the tonsils.   _____

6) Lymphocytes attack own body tissues.   _____

7) Allergy attack that involves entire body.   _____

8) Transmitted via blood exchanges and sexual
   intercourse.   _____

7. Clinical Insights

a. Mary is a grocery checker with no evidence of heart disease. She complains that when she comes home from work, her feet and legs are swollen and sometimes painful. In the morning, the swelling is gone. How do you explain this? _____

_____

_____

b. The AIDS virus attacks helper T cells. Explain how this, in time, causes immunodeficiency. _____

_____

_____

c. Infants typically receive a series of three DPT injections (vaccinations) followed by a booster shot at four to six years of age. Explain the value of the booster shot. _____

_____

_____

1. Organs of the Respiratory System

a. Label the parts of the upper respiratory tract by placing the numbers of the structures by the correct labels.

_____ Conchae

_____ Epiglottis

_____ Laryngopharynx

_____ Larynx

_____ Lingual tonsil

_____ Nasal cavity

_____ Nasopharynx

_____ Nostril

_____ Oral cavity

_____ Oropharynx

_____ Palate, hard

_____ Palate, soft

_____ Palatine tonsil

_____ Pharyngeal tonsil

_____ Sinus, frontal

_____ Sinus, sphenoidal

_____ Tongue

_____ Trachea

b. Label the parts of the lower respiratory tract by placing the numbers of the structures by the correct labels.

_____ Bronchiole   _____ Bronchus, tertiary   _____ Pleural cavity

_____ Bronchus, primary   _____ Larynx   _____ Trachea

_____ Bronchus, secondary   _____ Parietal pleura   _____ Visceral pleura

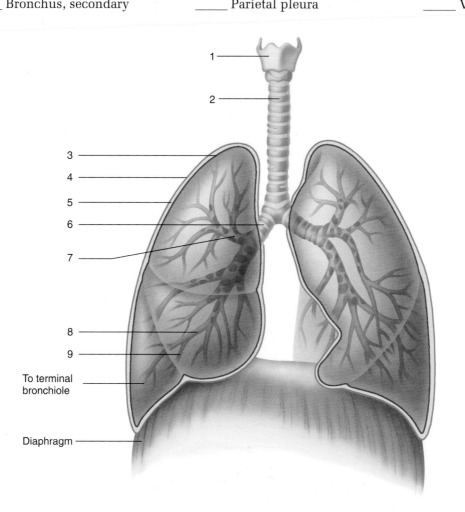

To terminal bronchiole

Diaphragm

c. Write the words that complete the sentences in the spaces at the right.

Air enters the nasal cavity via the __1__,   1) _____

and it is __2__, __3__, and __4__ as it flows   2) _____

over the nasal mucous membranes. Mucus   3) _____

and entrapped particles are moved by   4) _____

__5__ to the __6__ and are swallowed.   5) _____

                                                    6) _____

d. Write the names of the structures that match the statements in the spaces at the right.

1) Openings allowing air to enter nose.   _____

2) Interior chamber of nose.   _____

3) Separates oral and nasal cavities.   _____

4) Increase surface area of nasal cavity.   _____

5) Connects nasal cavity with larynx.   _____

6) Air-filled cavities in skull bones.

7) Lymphoid tissue in upper pharynx.

8) Lymphoid tissue at junction of pharynx and oral cavity.

9) Cartilaginous boxlike structure containing vocal folds.

10) Opening between vocal folds.

11) Cartilage forming Adam's apple.

12) Flops over larynx opening in swallowing.

13) Windpipe extending from larynx to bronchi.

14) Bronchi that enter lungs.

15) Support walls of bronchial tree passageways larger than bronchioles.

16) Lines air passageways larger than bronchioles.

17) Tiny air sacs at ends of alveolar ducts.

18) Membrane covering outer surface of lung.

19) Membrane lining inner wall of thorax.

20) Potential space between pleurae.

2. Breathing

a. Write the words that complete the sentences in the spaces at the right.

Air flows into the lungs during __1__ and out of the lungs during __2__. During breathing, air flows from an area of __3__ pressure to an area of __4__ pressure. Contraction of the __5__ and the __6__ muscles causes an increase in the __7__ of the lungs, which decreases the air __8__ within the lungs. Air flows into the lungs because of the __9__ atmospheric pressure. When the muscles of inspiration relax, the __10__ of the lungs is decreased, which increases the air __11__ within the lungs. Air flows out of the lungs because of the __12__ air pressure within the lungs.

1) _____
2) _____
3) _____
4) _____
5) _____
6) _____
7) _____
8) _____
9) _____
10) _____
11) _____
12) _____

b. Indicate whether each statement is true (T) or false (F).

_____ Negative pressure in the pleural cavity is necessary for inspiration.

_____ Surfactant prevents collapse of alveoli.

_____ Forceful expiration involves contraction of abdominal and internal intercostal muscles.

_____ Pneumothorax causes collapse of a lung.

_____ Breathing exchanges air between the atmosphere and the alveoli of the lungs.

3. Respiratory Volumes

Match the respiratory volumes with the statements.

1) Expiratory reserve volume   4) Tidal volume

2) Inspiratory reserve volume   5) Total lung capacity

3) Residual volume   6) Vital capacity

_____ Volume of air exhaled in quiet expiration.

_____ Air that always remains in the lungs.

_____ Volume forcefully exhaled after quiet expiration.

_____ Volume forcefully inhaled after quiet inspiration.

_____ Maximum volume forcefully exhaled after maximum forceful inspiration.

_____ Averages about 500 ml.

_____ Averages about 5,800 ml.

4. Control of Breathing

Write the terms that match the statements in the spaces at the right.

1) Name the two respiratory control groups located in
   the medulla oblongata.

   _____

   _____

2) Name the respiratory control group in the pons.

   _____

3) Controls rhythmic, quiet breathing.

   _____

4) Integrates sensory inputs and sends impulses to
   the VRG to modify breathing cycles.

   _____

5) Receives input from higher brain areas and relays
   impulses to the DRG to modify breathing cycles.

   _____

6) Controls voluntary changes in the breathing cycle.

   _____

7) Occurs when the VRG sends impulses to the muscles
   of breathing.

   _____

5. Factors Influencing Breathing

Indicate whether each statement is true (T) or false (F).

_____ A fever increases the breathing rate.

_____ The respiratory center detects blood levels of carbon dioxide and oxygen.

_____ An increase in the blood H^+ concentration increases the breathing rate.

_____ A mild increase in blood oxygen concentration decreases the breathing rate.

_____ An increase in blood CO_2 concentration increases the breathing rate.

_____ Higher brain centers can permanently override the action of the respiratory center.

_____ Chemoreceptors for blood oxygen are located in the carotid and aortic bodies.

_____ A very low blood oxygen concentration increases the breathing rate.

6. Gas Exchange

Write the words that complete the sentences in the spaces at the right.

The exchange of respiratory gases occurs by __1__. In comparison to the air in the alveoli, blood returning to the lungs has a lower concentration of __2__ and a higher concentration of __3__. Therefore, oxygen diffuses from the __4__ into the __5__, and carbon dioxide diffuses from the __6__ into the __7__. Blood leaving the lungs is __8__-rich and __9__-poor.

In comparison to concentrations in tissue cells, blood entering tissue capillaries has a lower concentration of __10__ and a higher concentration of __11__. Therefore, oxygen diffuses from the __12__ into the __13__, and carbon dioxide diffuses from the __14__ into the __15__. Blood leaving tissue capillaries is __16__-rich and __17__-poor.

1) _____

2) _____

3) _____

4) _____

5) _____

6) _____

7) _____

8) _____

9) _____

10) _____

11) _____

12) _____

13) _____

14) _____

15) _____

16) _____

17) _____

7. Transport of Respiratory Gases

a. Use symbols (O_2 and CO_2) and arrows to show the direction of diffusion for respiratory gases between blood in capillaries and body (not lung) cells.

Body cells

Blood flow in capillary

b. Write the terms that match the statements in the spaces at the right.

1) Compound in which most oxygen is transported.   _____

2) Cell in which most oxygen is transported.   _____

3) Compound in which most CO_2 is carried.   _____

4) Combination of hemoglobin and CO_2.   _____

5) Enzyme speeding up reaction of CO_2 and H_2O
   to form carbonic acid.   _____

6) Cell in which most carbonic acid is formed.   _____

c. Indicate whether each statement is true (T) or false (F).

_____ Hemoglobin can carry both O_2 and CO_2 at the same time.

_____ Oxygenated blood carries some carbon dioxide.

_____ Deoxygenated blood carries some oxygen.

_____ Hemoglobin loads or unloads oxygen, depending on the surrounding oxygen concentration.

_____ Oxygen and carbon dioxide compete for the same binding site on the hemoglobin molecule.

_____ Blood loads or unloads CO_2 depending upon the surrounding carbon dioxide concentration.

8. Disorders of the Respiratory System

Write the disorders that match the statements in the spaces at the right.

1) Accumulation of fluid in the lungs.   _____

2) Inflammation of the bronchi.   _____

3) Rupture of alveoli due to exposure to airborne
   irritants.   _____

4) Acute inflammation of alveoli due to viral or
   bacterial infection.   _____

5) Collapse of alveoli in infants due to an insufficient
   amount of surfactant.   _____

6) Wheezing, labored breathing due to constriction of
   bronchioles.   _____

7) Viral disease characterized by fever, chills, aches,
   and coldlike symptoms.   _____

8) Disorder characterized by a reduction of the
   respiratory surface area and decrease in the
   expiratory reserve volume.   _____

9) Inflammation of nasal membranes.   _____

10) Blockage of artery in lung by a transported
    blood clot.   _____

9. Clinical Insights

a. One treatment for hyperventilation is having the patient breathe into a paper bag. How does this
    reestablish normal breathing? _____

    _____

b. A newborn infant, born a month early, is having difficulty breathing and is placed under an O_2 hood.
    What is the probable problem? _____
    Should the infant receive pure oxygen or an oxygen–carbon dioxide mixture? _____
    Explain. _____

    _____

1. Digestion: An Overview

Indicate the substances that perform these roles in chemical digestion.

1) Combines with food molecules and splits them
   into smaller molecules.

_____

2) Speed up hydrolysis of food molecules.

_____

2. Alimentary Canal: General Characteristics

a. Label the parts of the digestive system by placing the numbers of the structures in the spaces by the correct labels.

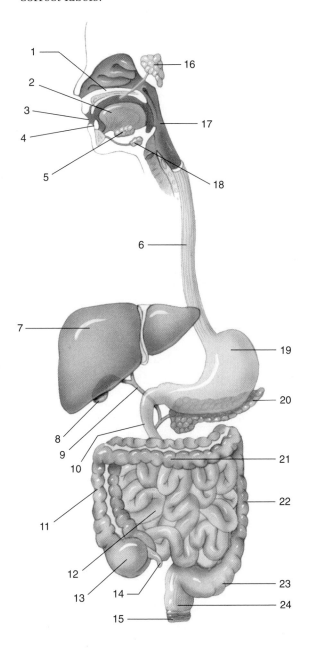

_____ Anus

_____ Appendix

_____ Cecum

_____ Colon, ascending

_____ Colon, descending

_____ Colon, sigmoid

_____ Colon, transverse

_____ Common bile duct

_____ Duodenum

_____ Esophagus

_____ Gallbladder

_____ Liver

_____ Mouth

_____ Palate

_____ Pancreas

_____ Parotid gland

_____ Pharynx

_____ Rectum

_____ Small intestine

_____ Stomach

_____ Sublingual gland

_____ Submandibular gland

_____ Tongue

_____ Tooth

b. List the layers of the wall of the alimentary canal from inside out.

1) _____   3) _____

2) _____   4) _____

c. What contractions propel food through the canal? _____

3. Mouth

a. Label the figure by placing the numbers of the structures in the spaces by the correct labels.

_____ Alveolar bone

_____ Cementum

_____ Crown

_____ Dentin

_____ Enamel

_____ Gingiva

_____ Periodontal ligament

_____ Pulp cavity

_____ Root

_____ Root canal

b. Write the terms that match the statements in the spaces at the right.

1) Form lateral walls of the mouth.   _____

2) Separates oral and nasal cavities.   _____

3) Manipulates food during chewing.   _____

4) Tiny projections containing taste buds.   _____

5) Number of deciduous and permanent teeth.   _____

6) Teeth used to bite off pieces of food.   _____

7) Teeth used to grasp and tear food.   _____

8) Teeth used to crush and grind food.   _____

9) Three pairs of salivary glands.   _____

_____

_____

10) Cleanses and lubricates mouth.   _____

11) Salivary enzyme acting on starch.   _____

12) End product of digestion in mouth.   _____

13) Saliva secretion is regulated by   _____
    (neural or hormonal) means.   _____

4. Pharynx and Esophagus

Write the terms that match the statements in the spaces at the right.

1) Tube carrying food to the stomach. _____

2) Relaxes to let food enter stomach. _____

3) Carries food from mouth to esophagus. _____

4) Covers laryngeal opening in swallowing. _____

5. Stomach

Write the terms that match the statements in the spaces at the right.

1) Region of stomach joining esophagus. _____

2) Region of stomach joining duodenum. _____

3) Glands of mucosa secreting gastric juice. _____

4) Hormone stimulating gastric secretion. _____

5) Hormones inhibiting gastric secretion. _____

6) Autonomic impulses stimulating gastric secretion. _____

7) Hormone secreted by gastric mucosa. _____

8) Acid in gastric juice. _____

9) Gastric enzyme acting on proteins. _____

10) Gastric enzyme curdling milk. _____

11) Products of gastric protein digestion. _____

12) Gastric substance enabling absorption of
    vitamin B$_{12}$ by small intestine. _____

6. Pancreas

Write the terms that match the statements in the spaces at the right.

1) Carries pancreatic juice from pancreas to duodenum. _____

2) Two hormones stimulating secretion of
    pancreatic juice. _____

3) Source of these hormones. _____

4) Pancreatic enzyme acting on starch. _____

5) Product of pancreatic starch digestion. _____

6) Pancreatic enzyme acting on fats. _____

7) Products of pancreatic fat digestion. _____

8) Pancreatic enzyme acting on proteins. _____

9) Products of pancreatic protein digestion. _____

7. Liver

a.   Label the figure by placing the numbers of the structures in the spaces by the correct labels.

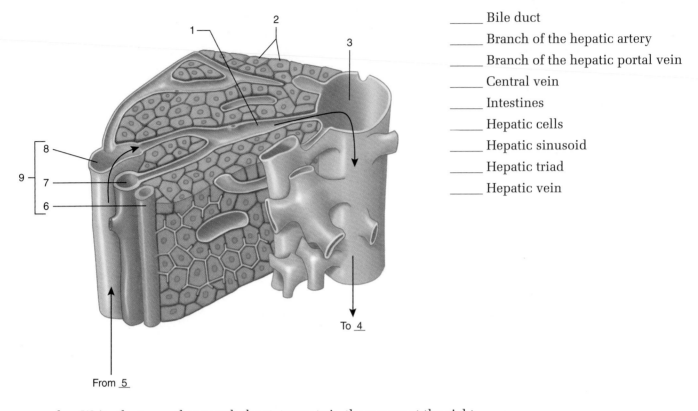

_____ Bile duct

_____ Branch of the hepatic artery

_____ Branch of the hepatic portal vein

_____ Central vein

_____ Intestines

_____ Hepatic cells

_____ Hepatic sinusoid

_____ Hepatic triad

_____ Hepatic vein

b.   Write the terms that match the statements in the spaces at the right.

1) Removed from amino acids and converted to urea.

2) Vessels carrying blood to liver:

   a) carries oxygen-rich blood.

   b) carries nutrient-rich blood.

3) Vessel carrying blood from liver.

4) Structural and functional units of the liver.

5) Spaces in a hepatic lobule receiving blood from branches of the hepatic artery and hepatic portal vein.

6) Vessels in hepatic lobules that merge to form the hepatic vein.

7) Carbohydrate stored in liver.

8) Secretion formed by liver.

9) Stores excess bile.

10) Carries bile to duodenum.

11) Hormone contracting gallbladder.

12) Bile component emulsifying lipids.

13) Bile component from hemoglobin breakdown.

8. Small Intestine

a.   Label the figure by placing the numbers of the structures in the spaces by the correct labels.

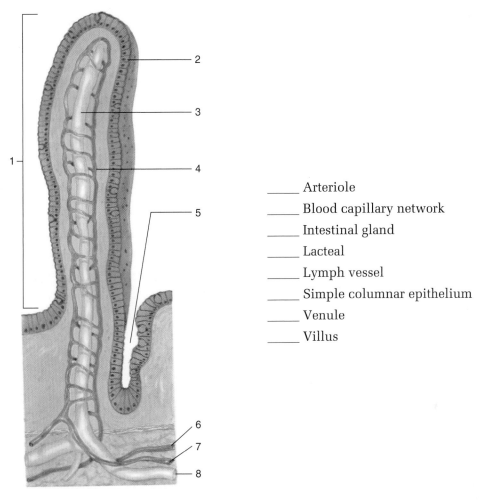

_____ Arteriole

_____ Blood capillary network

_____ Intestinal gland

_____ Lacteal

_____ Lymph vessel

_____ Simple columnar epithelium

_____ Venule

_____ Villus

b.   Write the terms that match the statements in the spaces at the right.

1) Segment continuous with the stomach.   _____

2) Segment continuous with the cecum.   _____

3) Membranes supporting small intestine.   _____

4) Relaxes to allow chyme to enter the small intestine.   _____

5) Secretion of intestinal glands.   _____

6) Fingerlike projections of the mucosa.   _____

7) Microscopic folds of exposed epithelial cell
   membranes.   _____

8) Hormone released by mucosa due to presence
   of fat-laden chyme.   _____

9) Hormone released by mucosa due to presence
   of acid chyme.   _____

10) Mechanism (neural or hormonal) that
    stimulates secretion of intestinal juice.   _____

11) Enzyme acting on sucrose.
_____

12) End products of sucrose digestion.
_____

13) Enzyme acting on lactose.
_____

14) Enzyme acting on maltose.
_____

15) End product of maltose digestion.
_____

16) End products of lactose digestion.
_____

17) Enzyme acting on fats.
_____

18) End products of fat digestion.
_____
_____

19) Enzyme acting on peptides.
_____

20) End products of peptide digestion.
_____

c.   Write the terms that complete the sentences in the spaces at the right.

Monosaccharides and amino acids are
absorbed into the __1__ networks of __2__ .
Monoglycerides and fatty acids are absorbed
into __3__ cells, where they reunite to form
__4__ . Clusters of triglycerides are coated
with protein, forming __5__ that enter the
__6__ of the __7__ .

1) _____

2) _____

3) _____

4) _____

5) _____

6) _____

7) _____

9. Large Intestine

Write the terms that match the statements in the spaces at the right.

1) Pouchlike first part of large intestine.
_____

2) External opening of large intestine.
_____

3) Colon segment along left side of abdomen.
_____

4) Colon segment along right side of abdomen.
_____

5) Colon segment continuous with rectum.
_____

6) Wormlike extension of cecum.
_____

7) Involuntarily controlled anal sphincter.
_____

8) Voluntarily controlled anal sphincter.
_____

9) Decompose undigested materials.
_____

10) Fluid absorbed by large intestine.
_____

11) Relaxes, allowing chyme to enter cecum.
_____

12) Reflex activated by filling of rectum with feces.
_____

10. Nutrients: Sources and Uses

Write the terms that match the statements in the spaces at the right.

1) Process producing ATP from energy foods.
_____

2) Plant polysaccharide providing fiber.
_____

3) Preferred energy source for body cells.
_____

4) Organs regulating blood glucose levels.
_____

5) Most common lipids in the diet.   _____

6) Type of fats common in animal foods.   _____

7) Type of fats common in plant foods.   _____

8) Lipid abundant in egg yolks.   _____

9) Lipid used to form steroid hormones.   _____

10) Lipid forming much of plasma membranes.   _____

11) Molecules transporting lipids in blood.   _____

12) Organ helping to regulate blood levels of
triglycerides and cholesterol.   _____

13) Amino acids that cannot be made by liver.   _____

11. Disorders of the Digestive System

Write the names of the disorders that match the statements.

1) Inflammation of the large intestine.   _____

2) Self-induced starvation due to an abnormal concern
about weight control.   _____

3) Decay of the teeth due to acids formed by certain
oral microorganisms.   _____

4) Dry, hard feces making defecation difficult.   _____

5) Crystallization of cholesterol in bile within the
gallbladder.   _____

6) Replacement of destroyed liver cells by connective
tissue.   _____

7) Repeated overeating and purging.   _____

8) Inflammation of the liver.   _____

9) Digestion of stomach mucosa by gastric juice.   _____

10) Inflammation, bleeding, and degeneration of the
gingivae and alveolar bone.   _____

11) Watery feces due to excessive peristalsis.   _____

12) Enlarged and inflamed veins in anal canal.   _____

13) Inflammation of the appendix.   _____

14) Inflammation of the peritoneum.   _____

15) Inflammation of colon diverticula.   _____

12. Clinical Insights

a. Severe diarrhea in infants or small children can be a life-threatening event. Explain why. _____

_____

_____

b. A patient is found to have a gastric ulcer. Antibiotics and a drug to reduce the secretion of gastric
juice are prescribed. Explain the basis for the prescriptions. _____

_____

_____

_____

What serious results may occur with an untreated ulcer? _____

_____

c. A patient is admitted to the emergency room complaining of severe and spasmodic pain in the epigastric region, and the whites of his eyes are yellowish. He informs the physician that he has had
similar but milder pains after meals for four to six weeks. What is the likely problem and the likely

solution? _____

_____

1. Urinary System, General

a. Label the figure by placing the numbers of the structures in the spaces by the correct labels.

_____ Aorta   _____ Kidney   _____ Ureter

_____ Inferior vena cava   _____ Renal artery   _____ Urethra

_____ Hilum   _____ Renal vein   _____ Urinary bladder

b. Write the names of the organs that match the functions in the spaces at the right.

1) Stores urine temporarily.   _____

2) Produces urine.   _____

3) Carries urine from the body.   _____

4) Carries urine from the kidneys.   _____

5) Maintains composition and volume of
    body fluids.   _____

2. Kidneys

a. Write the names of the structures that match the statements in the spaces at the right.

1) Outer layer containing renal corpuscles.   _____

2) Region containing renal pyramids.   _____

3) Flattened cavity continuous with ureter.   _____

4) Receptacles surrounding renal papillae.   _____

5) Thin layer of connective tissue enveloping
   kidney.   _____

6) Arterial capillaries in renal corpuscle.   _____

7) Functional units of the kidneys.   _____

8) U-shaped portion of renal tubule.   _____

9) Part of renal tubule joined to glomerular
   capsule.   _____

10) Part of renal tubule joined to a collecting duct.   _____

11) Formed of modified cells at point of contact
    of distal tubule and afferent arteriole.   _____

b. Label the figure by placing the numbers of the structures in the spaces by the correct labels.

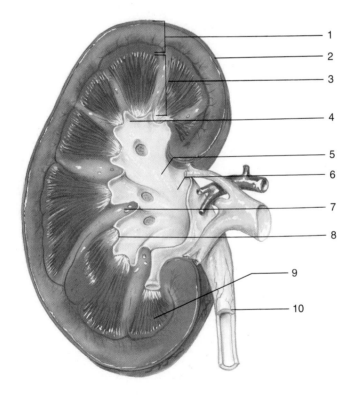

_____ Major calyx

_____ Minor calyx

_____ Renal capsule

_____ Renal column

_____ Renal cortex

_____ Renal medulla

_____ Renal papilla

_____ Renal pelvis

_____ Renal pyramid

_____ Ureter

c. Label the figure by placing the numbers of the structures in the spaces by the correct labels.

_____ Afferent arteriole

_____ Collecting duct

_____ Distal convoluted tubule

_____ Efferent arteriole

_____ Glomerular capsule

_____ Glomerulus

_____ Nephron loop

_____ Peritubular capillary

_____ Proximal convoluted tubule

3. Urine Formation

a. Write the words that complete the sentences in the spaces at the right.

Urine formation begins with __1__, which forces water and diffusible solutes from blood plasma into the glomerular __2__. As the filtrate moves along the renal tubule, useful solutes are moved back into blood in the __3__ by __4__ and certain solutes are moved from blood in the peritubular capillary into the filtrate by __5__. Hypertonic urine is formed by the reabsorption of __6__ from the collecting duct.

1) _____

2) _____

3) _____

4) _____

5) _____

6) _____

b. Write the words that complete the sentences in the spaces at the right.

A decrease in the glomerular filtration rate causes the __1__ apparatus to secrete __2__, which triggers the __3__ __4__ mechanism. The end product of these reactions is __5__, which increases systemic blood pressure by __6__ arterioles, stimulating __7__ secretion by the posterior pituitary, and stimulating __8__ secretion by the adrenal cortex.

1) _____

2) _____

3) _____

4) _____

5) _____

6) _____

7) _____

8) _____

c. Write the terms that match the statements in the spaces at the right.
    1) Three homeostatic processes that maintain the
       glomerular filtration rate.   _____

    2) Plasma component that cannot pass through
       glomerular pores.   _____

    3) Force producing filtration.   _____

    4) Fluid in glomerular capsule.   _____

    5) Recovery of needed materials from filtrate
       into the blood.   _____

    6) Volume of filtrate formed per day.   _____

    7) Method of transport of sodium ions.   _____

    8) Method of transport of water.   _____

    9) Method of transport of glucose.   _____

    10) Method of transport of chloride ions.   _____

    11) Process moving substances from blood in the
        peritubular capillary into the filtrate.   _____

d. Indicate whether each statement is true (T) or false (F).

    _____ Urine contains waste and excessive materials removed from the blood.

    _____ Urine formation depends upon maintenance of the blood pressure within the glomeruli.

    _____ Most of the filtrate volume is reabsorbed.

    _____ Negatively charged ions and positively charged ions are electrochemically attracted to each
            other.

    _____ The active reabsorption of sodium ions increases the rate of water reabsorption by osmosis.

4. Maintenance of Blood Plasma Composition

a. Write the terms that match the statements in the spaces at the right.
    1) Hormone promoting water reabsorption.   _____

    2) Hormone promoting reabsorption of Na^+.   _____

    3) Hormone promoting secretion of K^+.   _____

    4) Hormone decreasing blood level of Ca^{++}.   _____

    5) Hormone increasing blood level of Ca^{++}.   _____

    6) Hormone inhibiting sodium and water
       reabsorption.   _____

    7) Three nitrogenous wastes in urine.   _____

                                                                     _____

                                                                     _____

b. Indicate whether each statement is true (T) or false (F).

    _____ Cellular metabolism does not affect plasma composition.

    _____ Plasma composition is changed by the work of kidneys.

    _____ Electrolytes are totally reabsorbed into the blood.

    _____ About 99% of water in the filtrate is reabsorbed.

_____ Water is lost from the body only in urine.

_____ Urine volume is reduced when water intake is curtailed.

_____ Perspiring heavily may reduce the volume of urine.

_____ Electrolyte balance is largely maintained by the active reabsorption of positively charged ions.

_____ Nephrons remove all nitrogenous wastes from the blood.

_____ Urea is the most abundant nitrogenous waste in urine.

_____ Urea is formed by the kidneys from amine groups.

_____ Buffers are chemicals in body fluids that either combine with or release hydrogen ions.

_____ The production of carbon dioxide by metabolizing cells tends to make the blood more alkaline.

_____ Kidneys help to regulate the pH of body fluids by secreting excess hydrogen ions into the filtrate.

_____ Water and electrolyte balance in body fluids is essential for normal cell functioning.

_____ ADH is released by the posterior pituitary gland when the water concentration of the blood is reduced.

_____ Aldosterone is secreted by the adrenal cortex when the concentration of K^+ in the blood is reduced.

_____ ADH increases the permeability of the distal tubules and collecting ducts to water.

_____ Electrolyte concentrations in the blood affect the movement of water into cells by osmosis.

_____ Atrial natriuretic hormone promotes the reabsorption of sodium ions and the excretion of water to decrease blood volume.

5. Excretion of Urine

a.   Write the terms that match the statements in the spaces at the right.

1) Carry urine to urinary bladder.   _____

2) Provides temporary storage of urine.   _____

3) Muscle in wall of urinary bladder.   _____

4) Carries urine from urinary bladder.   _____

5) Method of urine transport by ureters.   _____

6) Type of muscle composing the internal urethral
   sphincter.   _____

7) Type of muscle composing the external urethral
   sphincter.   _____

8) Type of muscle in walls of ureters.   _____

b.   Write the words that complete the sentences in the spaces at the right.

The accumulation of __1__ stretches the   1) _____

urinary bladder wall, which triggers the __2__   2) _____

reflex. This reflex causes rhythmic involuntary   3) _____

contractions of the __3__ muscle and opens   4) _____

the involuntarily controlled __4__ urethral   5) _____

sphincter. If the voluntarily controlled __5__   6) _____

urethral sphincter is relaxed, __6__ occurs.

6. Characteristics of Urine

Indicate whether each statement is true (T) or false (F).

_____ The color of urine is due to the presence of urochrome.

_____ The pH of urine is usually slightly acidic.

_____ Normal urine is never alkaline.

_____ Urine has a specific gravity greater than 1.000.

_____ Normal urine does not contain proteins or hemoglobin.

7. Disorders of the Urinary System

Write the names of the disorders matching the statements in the spaces at the right.

1) Inflammation of the glomeruli.   _____

2) Inflammation of the urinary bladder.   _____

3) Inflammation of nephrons and renal pelvis.   _____

4) Excessive urine production.   _____

5) Kidney stones.   _____

6) Inflammation of the urethra.   _____

7) Deposits of uric acid in the renal pelvis.   _____

8) Characterized by uremia.   _____

9) Characterized by protein in the urine.   _____

8. Clinical Insights

a. A 60-year-old woman comes to the clinic with severe edema of her lower legs and feet. A diuretic is prescribed, and she is placed on a salt-free diet. She is also advised to take a 30-minute walk each morning and afternoon and to elevate her feet higher than her head for 20-minute periods morning and afternoon. Explain how the diuretic will reduce her edema. _____

_____

_____

Explain how the salt-free diet will help reduce her edema. _____

_____

_____

_____

_____

_____

Explain how elevating her feet and walking will help reduce her edema. _____

_____

b. Explain why women develop cystitis more frequently than men. _____

_____

1. Male Reproductive System

a. Label the figure by placing the numbers of the structures by the correct labels.

_____ Bulbourethral gland

_____ Corpus cavernosum

_____ Corpus spongiosum

_____ Ejaculatory duct

_____ Epididymis

_____ Glans penis

_____ Penis

_____ Prepuce

_____ Prostate gland

_____ Scrotum

_____ Seminal vesicle

_____ Testis

_____ Urethra

_____ Urinary bladder

_____ Vas deferens

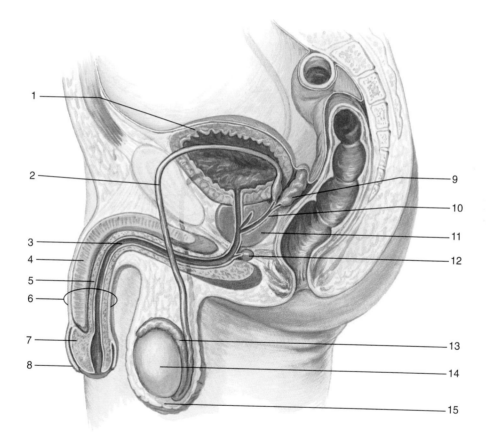

b. Trace the path of sperm cells from a testis to the outside by placing the numbers of the ducts in the spaces below.

1) Ejaculatory duct

2) Epididymis

3) Urethra

4) Vas deferens

Testis → _____ → _____ → _____ → _____ → outside.

c.   Write the terms that match the statements in the spaces at the right.

1) Male gonads, or sex glands.

2) Tubules producing sperm cells.

3) Cells producing testosterone.

4) Process of sperm formation.

5) Number of chromosomes in spermatogonia
   and primary spermatocytes.

6) Type of cell division forming primary
   spermatocytes.

7) Type of cell division forming spermatids from
   primary spermatocytes.

8) Number of chromosomes in each spermatid.

9) Cell formed from each spermatid.

10) Location of nucleus in a sperm cell.

11) Provides motility for a sperm cell.

12) Tubule where sperm cells mature.

13) Secrete fluid, neutralizing acidity of urethra
    prior to ejaculation.

14) Secrete fluid containing fructose.

15) Secretes fluid, activating swimming movements
    of sperm cells.

16) Mixture of glandular secretions and sperm cells.

17) Contains testes outside the body.

18) Approximate temperature of testes required for
    production of viable sperm.

19) Male copulatory organ inserted into vagina
    during sexual intercourse.

20) Erectile tissue in penis surrounding urethra.

21) Two dorsal columns of erectile tissue in penis.

22) Sheath of skin covering the glans penis.

2. Male Sexual Response

Write the words that complete the sentences in the spaces at the right.

Sexual stimulation causes ___1___ nerve
impulses to ___2___ the arterioles and ___3___ the
venules serving the erectile tissue in the penis.
Engorgement of the erectile tissue results in
___4___ of the penis. At the same time, the ___5___
glands secrete an alkaline fluid that neutralizes
the ___6___ of the urethra. Continued sexual
stimulation results in ___7___, which is
characterized by a sensation of sexual pleasure
and ___8___, the forcing of ___9___ out the urethra.

1) _____
2) _____
3) _____
4) _____
5) _____
6) _____
7) _____
8) _____
9) _____

3. Hormonal Control of Reproduction in Males

a. Write the terms that match the statements in the spaces at the right.

1) The male sex hormone.

2) Secretes gonadotropin-releasing hormone.

3) Releases FSH and LH.

4) Hormone stimulating testosterone secretion by testes.

5) Two hormones that act together to stimulate spermatogenesis.

6) Stimulates maturation of male sex organs.

7) Stimulates development and maintenance of secondary sexual characteristics.

8) Produces androgens in male fetus.

9) Hormone whose first secretion triggers onset of puberty.

10) Hormone preventing excess sperm production by inhibiting FSH secretion.

b. Record the numbers of the male secondary sexual characteristics listed in the space provided.

1) Maturation of the testes.

2) Enlargement of the larynx.

3) Broad shoulders.

4) Growth of body hair.

5) Production of sperm cells.

6) Increased metabolic rate.

7) Increased muscle development.

8) Increased RBC production.

9) Maturation of the penis.

10) Deepening of the voice.

c. Write the words that complete the sentences in the spaces at the right.

The production of testosterone by __1__ in the testes is regulated by a __2__ feedback system. When the level of testosterone in the blood declines, secretion of __3__ by the hypothalamus is __4__, causing an __5__ in the release of __6__ from the anterior pituitary, which, in turn, __7__ testosterone production. As the level of testosterone increases, it inhibits __8__ production, which decreases the release of __9__, resulting in a __10__ in testosterone production.

1) _____

2) _____

3) _____

4) _____

5) _____

6) _____

7) _____

8) _____

9) _____

10) _____

4. Female Reproductive System

a. Label the figure by placing the numbers of the structures by the correct labels.

_____ Anus

_____ Cervix

_____ Clitoris

_____ Fimbriae

_____ Labium majus

_____ Labium minus

_____ Ovary

_____ Urethra

_____ Urinary bladder

_____ Uterine tube

_____ Uterus

_____ Vagina

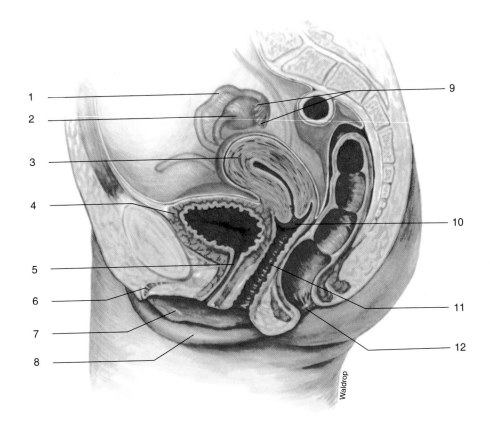

Waldrop

b. Write the terms that match the statements in the spaces at the right.

1) Produces female sex cells.

2) Receives penis in sexual intercourse.

3) Holds embryo/fetus during pregnancy.

4) Carries secondary oocyte toward uterus.

5) Narrow space between labia minora.

6) Birth canal during childbirth.

_____

_____

_____

_____

_____

_____

c.   Write the words that complete the sentences in the spaces at the right.

During fetal development, __1__ cell
division of germinal epithelial cells forms
millions of __2__, but most of them
degenerate. Survivors become __3__
oocytes containing __4__ chromosomes.
Single layers of follicular cells envelop
each oocyte forming __5__ follicles, but
most of them degenerate; the survivors
become __6__ follicles. After puberty,
usually __7__ dominant follicle develops
each month, and its oocyte undergoes
the first __8__ division, producing a
__9__ oocyte and a first __10__. Both of
these cells contain __11__ chromosomes.
Continued growth results in rupture of
the follicle at __12__, and the released
oocyte enters a __13__ tube. If the secondary
oocyte is penetrated by a __14__, the
second __15__ division forms an __16__
and a second __17__, each with __18__
chromosomes.

1) _____
2) _____
3) _____
4) _____
5) _____
6) _____
7) _____
8) _____
9) _____
10) _____
11) _____
12) _____
13) _____
14) _____
15) _____
16) _____
17) _____
18) _____

d.   Write the terms that match the statements in the spaces at the right.
1) Inner lining of the uterus.
2) Moves oocyte through uterine tube.
3) Type of muscle in uterine wall.
4) Collective term for the external female
   reproductive organs.
5) Nodule of erectile tissue corresponding to the
   penis in males.
6) Portion of uterus projecting into vagina.

_____
_____
_____

_____

_____

_____

e.   Female Sexual Response
Write the words that complete the sentences in the spaces at the right.

Sexual stimulation results in enlargement of the
__1__ and erection of the __2__ and nipples due
to increased blood flow. Increased secretion of
the __3__ glands lubricates the vestibule. Sexual
response culminates in __4__, which produces
rhythmic contractions of the pelvic floor, __5__,
and __6__ tubes plus intense pleasure.

1) _____
2) _____
3) _____
4) _____
5) _____
6) _____

5. Hormonal Control of Reproduction in Females

a. Match the hormones listed with the following statements.

Estrogen   GnRH   Progesterone

FSH   LH

1) Secreted by the follicular cells.   _____

2) Stimulates maturation of female sex organs.   _____

3) Maintains uterine lining in pregnancy.   _____

4) Develops female secondary sexual characteristics.   _____

5) Secreted by corpus luteum.   _____

6) Secreted by the hypothalamus.   _____

7) Stimulates development and function of
   corpus luteum.   _____

8) First secretion starts onset of puberty.   _____

9) Stimulates development of ovarian follicles.   _____

10) Prepare endometrium for pregnancy.   _____

11) High concentrations inhibit GnRH secretion.   _____

12) Promotes thickening of endometrium.   _____

13) Promotes formation of blood vessels in
    endometrium.   _____

b. Write the words that complete the sentences in the spaces at the right.

Between puberty and __1__, a woman experiences
one reproductive cycle per month consisting of
an ovarian cycle and a __2__ cycle. These cycles
are controlled by __3__ and average about __4__
days in length. A cycle is started by the secretion
of __5__ by the hypothalamus, which activates the
release of __6__ and __7__ by the anterior pituitary.
FSH stimulates the development of a primary
__8__ and the secretion of __9__ by the follicular
cells. __10__ promotes the thickening of the
endometrium. The increasing estrogen production
triggers a sharp increase in __11__ secretion and a
lesser increase in FSH production, leading to __12__
on day 14. Under stimulation by LH, the follicle
remnants become a __13__ that secretes a high level
of __14__ and estrogen, which together prepare the
__15__ of the uterus to receive an early embryo. The
high level of __16__ inhibits secretion of GnRH,
preventing development of additional ovarian
follicles. If pregnancy does not occur, the corpus
luteum degenerates and the levels of estrogen and
__17__ rapidly decline, resulting in breakdown of
the endometrium leading to __18__ and secretion of
GnRH starting a new reproductive cycle.

1) _____

2) _____

3) _____

4) _____

5) _____

6) _____

7) _____

8) _____

9) _____

10) _____

11) _____

12) _____

13) _____

14) _____

15) _____

16) _____

17) _____

18) _____

6. Mammary Glands

Indicate whether each statement is true (T) or false (F).

_____ Mammary glands are specialized for milk production.

_____ Breasts contain connective tissue but little fat.

_____ Alveolar glands occur in lobes of mammary glands.

_____ Estrogen stimulates the development of mammary glands.

_____ A pigmented areola surrounds a protruding nipple.

_____ Mammary glands are present but nonfunctional in males.

_____ Breasts are formed internal to the pectoralis muscles.

7. Birth Control

Indicate whether each statement is true (T) or false (F).

_____ Contraceptives are designed to prevent union of sperm and egg.

_____ Contraception and birth control are synonymous.

_____ Spermicides act by killing the sperm cells.

_____ Progesterone in the "pill" inhibits GnRH secretion.

_____ Spermicides are usually used with barrier methods.

_____ It is impossible to catch STDs when using a condom.

_____ Diaphragms and cervical caps are about equally effective.

_____ The rhythm method relies on knowing when ovulation occurs.

_____ A condom is a barrier contraceptive.

_____ Pregnancy is not possible when using a condom.

_____ The "pill" is the most effective contraceptive.

_____ There are no undesirable side effects of hormonal birth control.

_____ An IUD prevents implantation of an embryo.

_____ Induced abortion is a contraceptive procedure.

_____ A tubal ligation prevents ovulation.

_____ Diaphragms and cervical caps are barrier contraceptives.

_____ A vasectomy prevents the ejaculation of sperm.

_____ Use of an IUD may cause pelvic inflammatory disease.

_____ Withdrawal is less effective than a condom.

_____ Undesirable side effects may result from induced abortion.

8. Disorders of the Reproductive Systems

Write the disorders that match the statements in the spaces provided.

Male Disorders

1) Inability to maintain an erection.   _____

2) Common reproductive cancer in males.   _____

3) Inflammation of the prostate glands.   _____

4) Inability to produce sufficient viable sperm.   _____

5) Causes constriction of urethra in about
   one-third of older males.   _____

Female Disorders

1) Physical pain during menstruation. _____

2) Growth of endometrial tissue outside the uterus. _____

3) Absence of menstruation without pregnancy. _____

4) Associated with highly absorbent tampons. _____

5) Inability to become pregnant. _____

6) Infection in reproductive organs and/or
   pelvic cavity. _____

7) Physical and emotional distress just prior to
   menstruation. _____

8) Caused by toxin formed by *S. aureus*. _____

Sexually Transmitted Diseases

1) Results from infection with herpes simplex
   virus type 2. _____

2) Fatal disease resulting from HIV infection. _____

3) Two bacterial diseases that may lead to sterility
   in females. _____
   _____

4) Characterized by chancre in first stage. _____

5) Caused by human papillomavirus (HPV). _____

6) Bacterial diseases curable with antibiotics. _____
   _____

7) Viral diseases for which there are no cures. _____
   _____

9. Clinical Insights

a. Failure of the testes to descend into the scrotum (cryptochordism) causes sterility in males. Explain why. _____

_____

b. Secondary amenorrhea in female athletes results from strenuous activity, which blocks the hypothalamic regulation of reproduction. How does this stop the reproductive cycles? _____

_____

Women with amenorrhea produce little, if any, estrogen, which causes osteoporosis (bone loss). Why are such women deficient in estrogen? _____

_____

c. Without effective treatment, a bacterial sexually transmitted disease usually leads to pelvic inflammatory disease (PID) in females. How does this happen? _____

_____

1. Fertilization and Early Development

a. Write the terms that complete the sentences in the spaces at the right.

A __1__ oocyte containing __2__ chromosomes is released at ovulation, and it is enveloped by several layers of __3__ cells. After entering a __4__ tube, it is slowly carried toward the __5__ by beating __6__ of cells lining the tube. The oocyte remains viable for about __7__ hours after ovulation. Sperm deposited in the __8__ swim into the uterus and up the __9__ tubes. They usually encounter the secondary oocyte in the upper __10__ of a uterine tube. Sperm remain viable in the female reproductive tract for about __11__ hours.

Many sperm are required to separate the __12__ cells enveloping the secondary oocyte. Once a __13__ enters the secondary oocyte, chemical changes in the __14__ prevent other sperm from entering. The secondary oocyte immediately completes the __15__ meiotic division, forming an __16__ and another polar body, each containing __17__ chromosomes. Union of __18__ and __19__ nuclei complete fertilization, forming a __20__ containing __21__ chromosomes.

1) _____

2) _____

3) _____

4) _____

5) _____

6) _____

7) _____

8) _____

9) _____

10) _____

11) _____

12) _____

13) _____

14) _____

15) _____

16) _____

17) _____

18) _____

19) _____

20) _____

21) _____

b. Write the terms that match the statements in the spaces at the right.

1) Type of cell division in the zygote.   _____

2) Solid ball of cells formed by cleavage.   _____

3) Hollow ball of cells.   _____

4) Mass of cells within the blastocyst.   _____

5) Outer wall of the blastocyst.   _____

6) Embedding of blastocyst in endometrium.   _____

7) Length of preembryonic stage.   _____

8) Length of full-term pregnancy.   _____

2. Hormonal Control of Pregnancy

Write the terms that match the statements in the spaces at the right.

1) Hormone secreted by trophoblast.

2) Maintains corpus luteum for two to three months.

3) Hormone maintaining the uterine lining.

4) Hormone detected by pregnancy tests.

5) Takes over secretion of estrogen and progesterone from second or third month to birth.

6) Prevents GnRH secretion by hypothalamus during pregnancy.

7) Secretes estrogen and progesterone for the first two to three months of pregnancy.

8) Two hormones that prepare mammary glands for milk secretion after birth.

3. Embryonic Development

a. Matching (more than one answer may apply).

1) Ectoderm   2) Mesoderm   3) Endoderm

_____ Primary germ layers   _____ Liver and pancreas

_____ Connective tissue   _____ Epidermis

_____ Nervous system   _____ Dermis

_____ Muscles   _____ Kidneys and gonads

_____ Lining of digestive tract   _____ Lining of respiratory passages

b. Write the terms that match the statements in the spaces at the right.

1) Becomes the chorion.

2) Connects embryo to placenta.

3) Form early embryonic blood cells.

4) Serves as shock absorber for fetus.

5) Membrane surrounding embryo/fetus.

6) Fingerlike projections from chorion that penetrate endometrium.

7) Source of oxygen and nutrients for embryo or fetus.

8) Site of exchange of materials between embryonic and maternal bloods.

9) Name given embryo after eighth week.

10) Attaches embryo to the uterine wall.

11) Fluid in which the embryo develops.

12) Developmental stage between second and eighth weeks.

c.   Label the figure by placing the numbers of the structures in the spaces by the correct labels.

_____ Allantois

_____ Amnion

_____ Amniotic cavity

_____ Chorion

_____ Developing placenta

_____ Umbilical cord

_____ Uterine wall

_____ Yolk sac

4. Birth

a.   Label the figure by placing the numbers of the structures in the spaces by the correct labels.

_____ Amniochorion

_____ Cervix of uterus

_____ Placenta

_____ Umbilical cord

_____ Uterine wall

_____ Vagina

b.   Write the terms that match the statements in the spaces at the right.

   1) Relaxes symphysis pubis as birth nears.   _____

   2) Softens cervix as birth nears.   _____

   3) Hormone that inhibits uterine contractions
      during pregnancy.   _____

   4) Hormone that sensitizes uterine muscles for
      starting contractions as birth nears.   _____

   5) Term for physical and physiological processes
      associated with birth.   _____

   6) Hormone starting and maintaining uterine
      contractions.   _____

   7) Receives neural impulses formed by stretching
      of the cervix.   _____

   8) Secretes oxytocin.   _____

   9) Longest stage of labor.   _____

   10) Stage of labor when baby is born.   _____

   11) Stage when the afterbirth is expelled.   _____

   12) Name for the birth process.   _____

c.   Write the words that complete the sentences in the spaces at the right.

As the time of birth approaches, the high   1) _____

concentration of __1__ overrides the inhibitory   2) _____

effect of __2__ on uterine contractions so that   3) _____

such contractions are possible. The __3__   4) _____

feedback mechanism controlling labor seems to   5) _____

be started by pressure of the fetus on the __4__, 6) _____

which forms __5__ that are carried to the   7) _____

hypothalamus. The __6__ stimulates the posterior   8) _____

pituitary to secrete __7__ that stimulates   9) _____

uterine __8__. Dilation of the __9__ increases the 10) _____

frequency of __10__ sent to the hypothalamus,   11) _____

which, in turn, stimulates the posterior pituitary 12) _____

to release more __11__, which increases the   13) _____

strength and frequency of uterine __12__. This   14) _____

pattern of positive feedback produces increasingly 15) _____

stronger contractions until the baby is __13__.   16) _____

Shortly after birth, uterine contractions cause the 17) _____

detachment and expulsion of the __14__.   18) _____

   When the __15__ is cut, the level of __16__   19) _____

increases in the infant's blood, stimulating the

__17__ control center to trigger the first breath.

After the first breath, breathing becomes easier

because __18__ in the alveolar fluid keeps the

__19__ open.

5. Circulatory Adaptations

a.   Write the terms that match the statements relating to fetal circulation in the spaces at the right.

    1) Opening between left and right atria.   _____

    2) Return blood from fetus to placenta.   _____

    3) Carries blood from umbilical vein to inferior
       vena cava, bypassing the liver.   _____

    4) Carries blood from pulmonary trunk to
       aortic arch.   _____

    5) Vein carrying oxygen-rich blood from the
       placenta to the fetus.   _____

b.   Write the words that complete the sentences regarding fetal circulation in the spaces at the right.

The fetal blood receives oxygen and nutrients from __1__ blood in the placenta. Oxygen-rich blood is carried from the placenta by the __2__ vein that enters the fetus at the __3__. This vessel divides near the liver, and about half of the oxygenated blood passes through the __4__, bypassing the liver, to mix with deoxygenated blood in the inferior __5__. When this mixed blood enters the __6__ atrium, most of it passes through the __7__ into the __8__ atrium and flows into the __9__ ventricle. Contraction of the ventricle pumps blood into the __10__ to the body cells. Blood entering the __11__ ventricle is pumped into the pulmonary trunk, but some of it bypasses the lungs by flowing through the __12__ into the aorta, increasing the blood supply to body cells. A small amount of blood is carried by __13__ arteries to the nonfunctional lungs and returned to the left __14__. Blood is returned to the placenta by two __15__ arteries.

1) _____

2) _____

3) _____

4) _____

5) _____

6) _____

7) _____

8) _____

9) _____

10) _____

11) _____

12) _____

13) _____

14) _____

15) _____

c.   Write the terms that match the statements relating to postnatal circulatory changes in the spaces at the right.

    1) Remnant of the umbilical vein.   _____

    2) Remnants of the umbilical arteries.   _____

    3) Remnant of the ductus venosus.   _____

    4) Remnant of the ductus arteriosus.   _____

6. Lactation

a.   Write the terms that match the statements in the spaces at the right.

1) Two hormones preparing mammary glands
   for lactation.   _____

2) Hormone stimulating lactation.   _____

3) Secretes prolactin-releasing hormone.   _____

4) Secretes prolactin.   _____

5) First secretion of mammary glands.   _____

6) Two hormones whose high levels inhibit
   secretion of PRH.   _____

7) Hormone stimulating milk ejection.   _____

b.   Write the words that complete the sentences in the spaces at the right.

After birth, the drop in __1__ and __2__ levels   1) _____

allows the hypothalamus to secrete __3__,   2) _____

which stimulates release of __4__ by the anterior   3) _____

pituitary, promoting lactation. __5__, the first   4) _____

secretion of the mammary glands, is rich in   5) _____

__6__ and contains no __7__. True __8__ secretion   6) _____

starts within two to three days.   7) _____

   Suckling stimulates formation of __9__ that   8) _____

are carried to the hypothalamus, causing it to   9) _____

secrete __10__, which continues production of   10) _____

prolactin, which maintains __11__, and   11) _____

stimulates the posterior pituitary to secrete   12) _____

__12__, which stimulates contraction of   13) _____

lactiferous ducts, causing milk __13__.

7. Disorders of Pregnancy and Prenatal Development

Write the terms that match the statements in the spaces at the right.

1) Implantation of embryo at a site other than the uterus. _____

2) Spontaneous abortion.   _____

3) Increased blood pressure, edema, and convulsions
   or coma in late pregnancy.   _____

4) Nausea and vomiting in early pregnancy.   _____

5) Major cause of death in newborn infants.   _____

6) Substances or influences causing birth defects.   _____

7) Results from too rapid destruction of fetal red blood
   cells after birth.   _____

8) Caused by insufficient surfactant in alveoli.   _____

9) May result from fetal exposure to X-rays, alcohol,
   and illegal or legal drugs.   _____

10) Most common teratogen causing birth defects.   _____

8. Genetics

a.   Write the terms that match the statements in the spaces at the right.

1) Number of chromosomes in human body cells. _____

2) Number of chromosomes in human gametes. _____

3) Sex chromosomes in a female. _____

4) Sex chromosomes in a male. _____

5) A unit of inheritance. _____

6) Alternate forms of a gene. _____

7) Condition in which both alleles for a trait are identical. _____

8) Condition in which the alleles for a trait are different. _____

9) An allele that is always expressed. _____

10) An allele that is expressed only when a dominant allele is absent. _____

11) A type of gene expression in which unlike alleles are both expressed. _____

12) A type of inheritance involving more than two dominant or recessive alleles. _____

13) A type of inheritance involving many genes that produce a gradation of expression in the human population. _____

14) The observable characteristics of a trait. _____

15) All of the alleles controlling the expression of a trait. _____

16) Traits whose alleles occur on the X chromosome. _____

17) Type of cell division that separates chromosome pairs into gametes. _____

b.   Indicate the genotypes for the following traits.

1) Heterozygous freckled. _____

2) Homozygous freckled. _____

3) Homozygous nonfreckled. _____

4) Color-blind male. _____

5) Normal female carrying allele for color blindness. _____

6) Color-blind female. _____

7) Homozygous type A blood. _____

8) Type AB blood. _____

9) Type O blood. _____

10) Heterozygous type B blood. _____

1

c. Indicate the possible genotypes of gametes that can be formed by parents with these genotypes.

1) Homozygous freckled. _____

2) Heterozygous freckled. _____

3) Homozygous nonfreckled. _____

4) Color-blind male. _____

5) Normal vision, carrier female. _____

6) Color-blind female. _____

7) Heterozygous type A blood. _____

8) Type AB blood. _____

d. Indicate the predicted phenotype ratios for the following matings.

1) Homozygous freckled × homozygous nonfreckled. _____

2) Heterozygous freckled × homozygous nonfreckled. _____

3) Type AB blood × type O blood. _____

4) Heterozygous type A blood × type O blood. _____

5) Normal vision, color-blind carrier mother ×
   normal vision father. _____

9. Inherited Diseases

Indicate whether each statement is true (T) or false (F).

_____ Genetic disease may be caused by the presence of an extra chromosome.

_____ Recessive sex-linked traits appear more frequently in females since they have two X chromosomes.

_____ Traits that show a gradation of expression in the population are determined by polygenes.

_____ It is possible to examine fetal cells for chromosome abnormalities.

_____ Some genetic diseases caused by specific alleles do not show up until adulthood.

_____ Down syndrome is caused by trisomy 21.

_____ Amniocentesis is used to obtain a sample of amniotic fluid for examination.

_____ Genetic counseling may be helpful for prospective parents with genetic disease in their family histories.

10. Clinical Insights

a. When the sperm count in semen falls below 20 million/ml, male infertility results. How do you

explain this? _____

_____

b. Physicians advise women to avoid all drugs (legal and illegal) during pregnancy. What is the basis for

this advice? _____

_____

c. What problems would occur if a newborn infant's foramen ovale failed to close? _____

_____

_____

d. Why can monozygotic twins receive blood transfusions from each other without difficulty, but dizy-

gotic twins often cannot? _____

_____

e. Mary and Joe have discovered that they are both heterozygous for sickle-cell anemia. They want to know

what the chance is that their children will inherit sickle-cell anemia. What would you advise them? ____

_____

_____

APPENDIX A

Keys to Medical Terminology

Medical terms may consist of three basic parts: a prefix, a root word, and a suffix. All terms have a root word, but some terms may lack either a prefix or a suffix. A **prefix** is the first portion of a term and comes before the root word. A **suffix** comes after the root word and is the last portion of a term. Both the prefix and suffix modify the meaning of a root word, and they may be used with many different root words. The **root word** is the main portion of the term. Root words often occur at the beginning of a term, but they also may end a term or may be sandwiched between a prefix and suffix. When determining the meaning of a term, you start with the suffix, then move to the prefix, and finally consider the root word. Consider these examples.

1. **Laryngitis** becomes **laryng/itis** when broken into its component parts.

   laryng- = the root word meaning *larynx*
   -itis = the suffix meaning *inflammation*

   Thus, the meaning of laryngitis is *inflammation of the larynx*.

2. **Endogastric** becomes **endo/gastr/ic** when broken into its component parts.

   endo- = the prefix meaning *within*
   gastr- = the root word meaning *stomach*
   -ic = the suffix meaning *pertaining to*

   Thus, the meaning of endogastric is *pertaining to within the stomach*.

The parts of a term are linked together in a way that aids pronunciation. This often requires the use of *combining vowels*. For example, when linking *gastr-* and *-pathy* to form a term meaning disease of the stomach, the vowel *o* is inserted to form *gastropathy*.

Some terms consist of more than one root word. For example, *gastr/o/enter/o/col/itis* means inflammation of the stomach, intestine, and colon.

You can see that once you know the meaning of common prefixes, root words, and suffixes, understanding medical terminology becomes much easier.

In the sections that follow, some common prefixes, suffixes, and root words are listed along with examples to help you understand medical terminology.

Singular and Plural Endings

Most medical terms are derived from Greek and Latin words. Therefore, changing from singular to plural is done by changing the ending of the term rather than by adding an *s* or *es* or changing a *y* to *ies* as in English terms. Examples of singular and plural endings are

Singular Ending	Plural Ending	Example
-a	-ae	pleura; pleurae
-en	-ena	lumen; lumena
-is	-es	testis; testes
-ma	-mata	carcinoma; carcinomata
-um	-a	epicardium; epicardia
-ur	-ora	femur; femora
-us	-i	glomerulus; glomeruli
-x	-ces	appendix; appendices

Common Prefixes

Prefix	Meaning	Example
a-	without, not	a/sepsis: sterile; without germs
ab-	away from, from	ab/duct: carry away from
ad-	to, toward	ad/duct: carry toward
an-	without, not	an/ergia: without energy
ante-	before	ante/cibum: before meals
anti-	against	anti/histamine: against histamine
bi-	two	bi/lobed: having two lobes
bio-	life	bio/logy: study of life
brachy-	short	brachy/gnathia: shortness of the lower jaw
brady-	slow	brady/cardia: slow heart rate
cent-	hundred	centi/meter: 1/100 of a meter
circum-	around	circum/oral: around the mouth
co-, com-, con-	with, together	com/press: squeeze together
de-	from, down	de/congest: reduce congestion
dia-	through	dia/rrhea: flow through
dis-	apart	dis/infect: free from infection
dys-	bad, difficult	dys/pepsia: difficult digestion
ect-	external, outer	ecto/derm: outer skin
en-	in, on	en/cranial: in the cranium
end-	within	endo/crine: secrete within
epi-	upon	epi/dermis: upon the skin
ex-	out, away from	ex/halation: to breathe out
extra-	outside of, in addition to	extra/ocular: outside the eye
hemi-	half	hemi/plegia: paralysis of one-half of the body
hyper-	above, over	hyper/trophy: excessive growth
hypo-	below, under	hypo/dermic: under the skin
infra-	below, beneath	infra/orbital: below the orbit
inter-	between	inter/cellular: between cells

Prefix	Meaning	Example
intra-	within	intra/cellular: within cells
kil-	thousand	kilo/gram: 1,000 grams
macr-	large	macro/cyst: large cyst
mal-	bad, ill, poor	mal/ady: disease, disorder
mes-	middle	meso/nasal: middle of the nose
meta-	after, beyond	meta/tarsals: beyond the tarsals
micr-	small	micro/colon: abnormally small colon
milli-	one-thousandth	milli/gram: 1/1,000 of a gram
multi-	many	multi/cellular: having many cells
neo-	new	neo/plasm: new growth
ob-	against, in the way of	ob/scure: indistinct, hidden
olig-	few	oligo/spermia: few sperm
onc-	tumor	onco/genic: tumor-causing
per-	through	per/forate: to make holes
peri-	around	peri/osteum: around a bone
poly-	many	poly/morphous: many forms
post-	after	post/ocular: behind the eye
pre-	before, in front of	pre/mature: before maturation
presby-	old	presby/cardia: old heart
pro-	before, in front of	pro/chondrial: before cartilage
re-	again, back	re/flex: bend back
retr-	backward, behind	retro/nasal: back part of nose
semi-	half	semi/lunar: half moon
sub-	under	sub/cutaneous: under the skin
super-	above, superior	super/acute: strongly acute
supra-	above, superior	supra/nasal: above the nose
sym-	together, with	sym/physis: growing together
syn-	together, with	syn/dactyly: fusion of fingers
tachy-	fast	tachy/cardia: rapid heart rate

Common Suffixes

Suffix	Meaning	Example
-algia	pain	neur/algia: pain in a nerve
-centesis	puncture to aspirate fluid	amnio/centesis: puncture amnion to obtain a sample of amniotic fluid
-cide	kill	bacterio/cide: substance killing bacteria
-cis	cut	in/cision: a cut into
-cyte	cell	erythro/cyte: red blood cell

Suffix	Meaning	Example
-dynia	pain	entero/dynia: intestinal pain
-ectomy	cut out	append/ectomy: procedure to cut out the appendix
-emesis	vomiting	poly/emesis: much vomiting
-emia	blood	an/emia: without blood
-gnosis	knowledge	pro/gnosis: foreknowledge
-gram	record	myo/gram: muscle record

Common Suffixes *continued*

Suffix	Meaning	Example
-graphy	making a record	myo/graphy: making a record of muscle action
-iasis	abnormal condition	candid/iasis: *Candida* infection
-itis	inflammation	sinus/itis: inflammation of sinuses
-lepsy	seizures	narco/lepsy: seizures of numbness
-logy	study of	bio/logy: study of life
-lysis, -lytic	breakdown, dissolve	myo/lysis: breakdown of muscles
-megaly	enlargement	nephro/megaly: kidney enlargement
-oid	resembling	ov/oid: resembling an egg
-oma	tumor	carcin/oma: cancerous tumor
-osis	abnormal condition	nephr/osis: abnormal kidney condition
-ostomy	make an opening	ile/ostomy: opening into the small intestine
-pathy	disease	neuro/pathy: disease of nerves

Suffix	Meaning	Example
-penia	deficiency, poor	leuko/penia: deficiency of white blood cells
-pepsia	digestion	dys/pepsia: poor digestion
-philia	attraction, love	acido/philic: attracted to acid
-phobia	abnormal fear	acro/phobia: fear of heights
-plasia	formation	hypo/plasia: deficient formation
-plasty	make, shape	angio/plasty: shaping a blood vessel
-plegia	paralysis	para/plegia: paralysis of lower body and both legs
-pnea	breath	brady/pnea: slow breathing
-rrhea	discharge, flow	pyo/rrhea: pus discharge
-soma, -some	body	chromo/some: colored body
-stasis	control, stop	hemo/stasis: stop bleeding
-therapy	treatment	thermo/therapy: heat therapy
-tomy	to cut	laparo/tomy: to cut into the abdomen
-trophy	development	hyper/trophy: excessive development
-uria	urine	glucos/uria: glucose in the urine

Common Root Words

Root Word	Meaning	Example
acr-	extremity, peak	acro/phobia: fear of heights
aden-	gland	aden/oma: tumor of a gland
angi-	blood vessel	angio/pathy: diseased vessel
arthr-	joint	arthr/itis: inflammation of joints
brachi-	arm	brachi/al: pertaining to the arm
carcin-	cancer	carcin/oma: cancerous tumor
card-	heart	cardio/logy: study of the heart
carp-	wrist	carp/al: pertaining to the wrist
cephal-	head	cephal/ic: pertaining to the head
cervic-	neck	cervic/al: pertaining to the neck
chole-	bile	chole/cyst/itis: inflammation of the gallbladder
chondr-	cartilage	chondro/cyte: cartilage cell
colp-	vagina	colpo/dynia: vaginal pain
cost-	rib	cost/algia: rib pain
crani-	skull	cranio/malacia: softening of the skull
cutan-	skin	sub/cutan/eous: under the skin
cyan-	blue	cyan/osis: bluish skin color
cyst-	bladder	cyst/algia: pain in bladder
cyt-	cell	cyto/logy: study of cells

Root Word	Meaning	Example
dactyl-	fingers, toes	dactylo/megaly: abnormally large fingers or toes
dent-	tooth	denti/form: toothlike
derm-, dermato-	skin	hypo/derm/al: under the skin
dors-	back	dors/al: pertaining to the back
duct-	carry	ad/duct: carry toward
edema	swelling	edema/tous: swollen
encephal-	brain	encephal/itis: inflammation of the brain
enter-	intestine	enter/dynia: intestinal pain
erythr-	red	erythro/cyte: red blood cell
esthe-	sensation, feeling	an/esthe/tic: substance causing an absence of sensation
esthen-	weakness	my/esthenia: muscle weakness
febr-	fever	febr/ile: feverish
gastr-	stomach	gastro/spasm: stomach spasm
gen-	to produce	patho/gen: disease-causing agent
gingiv-	gum	gingiv/itis: inflammation of the gums
glu-, glyc-	sugar	hyper/glyc/emia: excessive blood sugar
gynec-, gyno-	female	gyneco/logy: study of female disorders

Common Root Words *continued*

Root Word	Meaning	Example
hem-, hemato-	blood	hemo/genesis: blood formation
hepat-	liver	hepat/ectomy: removal of the liver
hist-	tissue	histo/logy: study of tissues
hom-, home-	same	homo/sexual: attracted to the same sex
hydr-, hydra-	water	hydra/tion: gaining water
kerat-	horny, cornea	kerat/osis: condition of abnormal horny growths
lacrim-	tear	lacrim/al: pertaining to tears
lact-	milk	lacta/tion: producing milk
lapar-	abdomen	laparo/tomy: to cut into the abdomen
laryng-	larynx	laryngo/pathy: disease of the larynx
later-	side	uni/lateral: one-sided
leuc-, leuk-	white	leuko/cyte: white blood cell
lingu-	tongue	lingu/iform: tongue-shaped
lip-	lipids, fat	lip/oid: similar to fat
lith-	stone	oto/lith: ear stone
mamm-	breast	mammo/gram: X-ray of breast
melan-	black	melan/in: black skin pigment
men-	monthly, mensis	meno/pause: cessation of menses
metr-	uterus	myo/metr/ium: muscle layer of uterus
morph-	shape, form	morpho/logy: study of shape
my-	muscle	myo/card/itis: inflammation of the heart muscle
myel-	marrow, spinal cord	myel/algia: pain of the spinal cord or its membranes
nas-	nose	nas/al: pertaining to the nose
nephr-	kidney	nephr/itis: inflammation of a kidney
neur-	nerve	neur/ectomy: excision of a nerve
odont-	tooth	odonto/pathy: disease of the teeth
oo-	egg, ovum	oo/genesis: formation of ova
orchid-	testis	orchid/itis: inflammation of a testis
oss-, oste-	bone	osteo/malacia: softening of bones
ot-, aur-	ear	oto/lith: ear stone aur/icular: pertaining to the ear

Root Word	Meaning	Example
path-	disease	patho/logy: study of disease
pect-	chest	pecto/ral: pertaining to the chest
ped-	child	ped/iatrics: medical specialty dealing with children's disorders
pep-, peps-	digest	pep/tic: pertaining to digestion
phag-	eat	phago/cyt/osis: engulfment of particles by cells
pharyng-	throat, pharynx	pharnygo/rrhea: discharge from the pharynx
phleb-	vein	phleb/itis: inflammation of a vein
pneum-	air	pneumo/thorax: air in the chest
pneumon-	lung	pneumono/pathy: disease of a lung
proct-	rectum	procto/col/itis: inflammation of the rectum and colon
pseud-	false	pseudo/hernia: false rupture
psych-	mind	psycho/genic: originating in the mind
pulmo-, pulmon-	lung	pulmon/ary: pertaining to a lung
py-	pus	pyo/cele: cavity containing pus
pyel-	kidney pelvis	pyelo/gram: X-ray of kidney pelvis
quadr-	four	quadri/plegia: paralysis of both arms and both legs
rhin-	nose	rhin/itis: inflammation of the nose
salping-	uterine tube	salping/ectomy: removal of a uterine tube
scler-	hard	scler/osis: hardening
sect-	cut	sect/ion: process of cutting
sept-	presence of microbes	septic/emia: infection of blood
sten-	narrow	sten/osis: narrowed condition
strict-	draw tight	con/strict/ion: draw tightly together
therm-	heat	hypo/thermia: low body temperature
thorac-	chest, thorax	thoraco/dynia: chest pain
thromb-	clot	thromb/us: a blood clot
tox-	poison	tox/in: poisonous substance
vas-	vessel	vaso/dilation: expansion of a vessel
viscer-	internal organ	viscero/genic: originating in the internal organs
vita-	life	vita/l: essential for life

APPENDIX B
Answers to Self-Review Questions

Chapter 1
1. physiology
2. cardiovascular
3. nervous
4. distal
5. appendicular
6. popliteal
7. femoral
8. dorsal; vertebral
9. right upper; epigastric
10. mediastinum
11. peritoneum
12. homeostasis

Chapter 2
1. protons
2. ion
3. molecule
4. covalent
5. water
6. less
7. synthesis
8. monosaccharides
9. amino acids
10. nucleotides
11. fat
12. ATP

Chapter 3
1. plasma membrane
2. DNA
3. mitochondria
4. ribosomes
5. nucleolus
6. endoplasmic reticulum
7. diffusion
8. filtration
9. active transport
10. cellular respiration
11. messenger RNA
12. mitosis

Chapter 4
1. one
2. little
3. pseudostratified ciliated columnar
4. simple columnar
5. epithelial
6. matrix
7. loose (areolar)
8. fibrocartilage
9. cardiac
10. smooth
11. neuroglia
12. mucous

Chapter 5
1. basale
2. keratin
3. dermis
4. subcutaneous
5. papillae
6. hypodermis
7. eccrine
8. arrector pili
9. reduces
10. wrinkles and sagging skin
11. athlete's foot
12. calluses; corns

Chapter 6
1. support; protection
2. epiphyses; spongy
3. foramen
4. intramembranous
5. periosteum
6. axial
7. mandible; temporal
8. atlas; occipital
9. costal cartilages
10. pectoral girdle
11. humerus; ulna; radius
12. ilium; ischium; pubis
13. femur; tibia
14. hinge; ball-and-socket
15. osteoporosis

Chapter 7
1. fibers (muscle cells)
2. tendons
3. sarcomere
4. acetylcholine
5. thin actin
6. lactic acid
7. insertion
8. masseter
9. rectus abdominis
10. latissimus dorsi
11. deltoid
12. triceps brachii
13. gluteus maximus
14. quadriceps femoris
15. gastrocnemius

Chapter 8
1. axon
2. interneurons
3. sodium
4. neurotransmitter
5. corpus callosum
6. frontal
7. cerebrum
8. hypothalamus
9. medulla oblongata
10. cerebellum
11. subarachnoid
12. spinal cord
13. anterior
14. autonomic
15. sympathetic

Chapter 9
1. Meissner's corpuscles; free nerve endings
2. referred pain
3. taste buds
4. olfactory
5. accommodation
6. hearing; equilibrium
7. endolymph
8. spiral organ; basilar
9. ear ossicles
10. saccule; utricle
11. cornea; lens
12. cones; color
13. ciliary body
14. vitreous humor
15. optic chiasma

Chapter 10
1. endocrine; hormones
2. receptors
3. nonsteroid
4. negative feedback
5. hypothalamus
6. TSH; adrenal cortex; FSH; LH
7. thyroxine; thyroid
8. calcitonin; parathyroid hormone
9. medulla
10. aldosterone
11. glucagon
12. estrogen; testosterone

Chapter 11
1. 45
2. hemoglobin; erythrocytes
3. hemacytoblasts
4. oxygen; erythropoietin
5. liver
6. leukocytes
7. neutrophils; monocytes
8. basophils
9. eosinophils
10. lymphocytes
11. plasma
12. thrombocytes (platelets)
13. fibrinogen; fibrin
14. antigen(s)
15. AB

Chapter 12
1. pericardium
2. left atrium
3. tricuspid; right atrium
4. atrial; systole
5. S-A; A-V
6. sympathetic; parasympathetic
7. arteries; veins
8. arteries; capillaries
9. diffusion; filtration
10. right; trunk; arteries; veins; left
11. brachiocephalic; internal carotid
12. thoracic; celiac; hepatic
13. hepatic-portal; hepatic; inferior
14. popliteal; external iliac; common iliac; inferior
15. axillary; subclavian; brachiocephalic; superior

Chapter 13
1. interstitial fluid
2. lymph; subclavian

3. lymph nodes; lymphocyte
4. spleen; red blood
5. nonspecific
6. neutrophils; macrophages (monocytes)
7. inflammation
8. thymus
9. antigen-presenting; helper T
10. helper, memory helper, cytotoxic, memory cytotoxic
11. antibody; cell
12. helper T; B; T
13. plasma; antibodies
14. active natural
15. vaccination; secondary

Chapter 14
1. filtered; mucous membrane
2. larynx; glottis
3. cartilaginous rings; bronchioles
4. alveoli
5. pleural cavity
6. surfactant
7. atmospheric; intrapulmonary
8. tidal; 500
9. medulla oblongata; DRG; PRG
10. carbon dioxide; hydrogen ions
11. oxygen; carbon dioxide
12. oxyhemoglobin; bicarbonate ions

Chapter 15
1. digestive enzymes; nutrient molecules
2. mucosa
3. peristalsis
4. dentin; enamel
5. salivary amylase; maltose
6. peristalsis; lower esophageal sphincter
7. pepsin; proteins
8. parasympathetic; gastrin
9. secretin; cholecystokinin; cholecystokinin
10. amylase; lipase; trypsin
11. small intestine; monosaccharides; amino acids
12. villi; capillaries; lacteal
13. large intestine
14. liver
15. vitamins

Chapter 16
1. nephrons
2. cortex

3. medulla; collecting ducts and nephron loops
4. glomerular; systemic
5. glomerular capsule; filtrate
6. filtrate; peritubular capillaries
7. actively; passively; osmosis
8. renin
9. antidiuretic; collecting ducts
10. aldosterone; potassium
11. urine
12. ureters; peristalsis
13. urethra
14. internal; external
15. 60

Chapter 17
1. testes; scrotum
2. seminiferous tubules; spermatogenesis
3. epididymis; ejaculatory duct; urethra
4. blood
5. FSH; testosterone
6. ovaries; oogenesis
7. secondary oocyte; uterine tube
8. secondary oocyte; polar body
9. vagina
10. GnRH; LH
11. estrogen
12. corpus luteum; endometrium
13. decrease; menstruation
14. ovulation; implantation
15. estrogen; testosterone

Chapter 18
1. uterine tube
2. fertilization
3. blastocyst; seventh day
4. human chorionic gonadotropin; progesterone
5. germ layers
6. amnion; placenta
7. eighth; fetus
8. labor; oxytocin
9. foramen ovale; ductus arteriosus
10. prolactin-releasing hormone; prolactin
11. genes; DNA
12. 46; female
13. males
14. homozygous
15. probability

GLOSSARY

abdomen The anterior portion of the trunk located between the diaphragm and pelvis.

abdominal cavity The portion of the abdominopelvic cavity between the diaphragm and the pelvis.

abdominopelvic cavity The portion of the anterior body cavity inferior to the diaphragm.

abdominopelvic quadrants The four divisions of the abdominopelvic surface formed by perpendicular longitudinal and transverse lines through the umbilicus.

abdominopelvic regions The nine divisions of the abdominopelvic surface formed by two equidistant longitudinal lines and two equidistant transverse lines.

abduction The movement of a body part away from the midline.

abortion The removal of an embryo or fetus from the uterus prior to birth.

absorption The taking up of substances by cells.

accessory organs Organs that assist the functions of primary organs.

accommodation Adjustment by the lens to focus an image on the retina of the eye.

acetylcholine A neurotransmitter secreted from the axon tip of many neurons.

acid A substance that ionizes in water, releasing hydrogen ions.

acne Inflammation of a hair follicle.

acquired immunodeficiency syndrome (AIDS) A progressive decrease in immune capability caused by infection of T lymphocytes and macrophages with HIV.

acromegaly A disorder caused by excessive secretion of growth hormone after epiphyseal lines have fused.

ACTH Adrenocorticotropic hormone.

actin myofilament A thin protein filament that interacts with myosin to produce contraction of a myofilament.

action potential A nerve impulse; depolarization of a neuron membrane.

active immunity Immunity derived from activation of B cells and T cells by an invasion of a pathogen.

active transport A process that requires the use of energy to move substances across plasma membranes.

Addison's disease An endocrine disorder caused by a deficient secretion of hormones by the adrenal cortex.

adduction The movement of a body part toward the midline.

adenine A nitrogen base of nucleic acids that pairs with thymine in DNA and uracil in RNA.

adenosine diphosphate (ADP) A molecule used to form adenosine triphosphate.

adenosine triphosphate (ATP) A molecule that temporarily holds energy in its high-energy phosphate bonds and releases it to power cellular processes.

adipose tissue Loose connective tissue containing large numbers of fat-storing cells.

adrenal cortex The outer portion of an adrenal gland.

adrenal gland An endocrine gland located on the top of each kidney.

adrenal medulla The inner portion of an adrenal gland.

adrenocorticotropic hormone (ACTH) A hormone secreted by the anterior pituitary that stimulates the adrenal cortex to secrete hormones.

adult stem cells Partially specialized cells capable of producing several types of specialized cells.

aerobic respiration The part of cellular respiration that requires oxygen.

afferent arteriole The arteriole carrying blood to the glomerulus of a nephron.

agglutination The clumping of red blood cells in an antigen–antibody reaction.

agonist A muscle whose contraction moves a body part.

agranulocyte A type of white blood cell that lacks cytoplasmic granules.

albumin An abundant plasma protein that helps maintain the osmotic pressure of blood.

aldosterone A mineralocorticoid hormone produced by the adrenal cortex that regulates potassium and sodium concentrations in the blood.

alimentary canal The digestive tube through which food passes from the mouth to anus.

alkaline Pertaining to a base.

allantois An extraembryonic membrane that branches from the yolk sac.

allele An alternate form of a gene.

allergen A foreign substance capable of stimulating an allergic reaction.

allergy An abnormally intense immune reaction.

all-or-none response The type of response by muscle and nerve cells to simulation; total response or no response.

alopecia Excessive hair loss.

alveolar ducts Tiny air passages that open into alveoli.

alveolus An air sac in a lung.

Alzheimer's disease A disorder caused by a loss of cholinergic neurons in the brain and characterized by loss of memory.

amenorrhea The absence of menstrual cycles.

amino acid The structural unit of proteins.

amnion The extraembryonic membrane that envelops the embryo and fetus.

amphiarthrosis A slightly movable joint.

ampulla The expanded portion of a semicircular canal.

amylase An enzyme that catalyzes the digestion of starch.

anabolism Metabolic processes forming more complex molecules from simpler molecules.

anaerobic respiration The portion of cellular respiration that does not require oxygen.

anaphase The stage of mitosis in which chromatids of replicated chromosomes separate and move to opposite poles of the cell.

anatomy The study of body organization and structure.

androgen Collective term for male sex hormones.

anemia The decreased ability of the blood to carry oxygen.

aneurysm A bulging, weakened portion of a blood vessel.

antagonist A muscle whose contraction opposes that of the agonist or prime mover.

antebrachium The forearm.

antecubital The anterior surface of the elbow.

anterior Pertaining to the front of the body.

anterior cavity The body cavity composed of thoracic and abdominopelvic cavities; the ventral cavity.

anterior root The anterior attachment of a spinal nerve to the spinal cord that carries motor nerve fibers.

antibody A substance produced by B lymphocytes in response to the presence of an antigen.

antibody-mediated immunity Immunity resulting from the production of antibodies.

anticodon A group of three nucleotides of a transfer RNA molecule that pairs with a codon of a messenger RNA molecule.

antidiuretic hormone The hormone secreted by the posterior lobe of the pituitary that promotes the reabsorption of water by the kidneys.

antigen A substance that stimulates production of antibodies.

antigen-presenting cell (APC) A phagocytic cell that engulfs a foreign antigen and displays the antigen on its plasma membrane.

anus The terminal opening of the alimentary canal.

aorta The systemic artery receiving blood directly from the left ventricle.

aortic semilunar valve A valve at the base of the aorta preventing the backflow of blood into the left ventricle.

apocrine gland A sweat gland that opens into a hair follicle.

aponeurosis A sheet of fibrous connective tissue that attaches a muscle to a bone or other connective tissues.

appendicitis Inflammation of the appendix.

appendicular Pertaining to the upper and lower extremities.

appendicular skeleton The bones of the pectoral girdle, pelvic girdle, and upper and lower extremities.

appendix A functionless tubular extension of the cecum.

aqueous humor A watery fluid filling the anterior cavity of the eye.

arachnoid mater Middle membrane of the meninges enveloping the brain and spinal cord.

arrhythmia An abnormal heartbeat such as bradycardia or fibrillation.

arteriole A small artery that leads to a capillary network.

arteriosclerosis Hardening of an arterial wall due to the deposition of calcium salts.

artery A blood vessel that carries blood away from the heart and to body tissues.

arthritis An autoimmune disorder of joints.

articular cartilage The cartilage that covers the ends of bones in freely movable joints.

articulation A joint; the joining of bones to form a joint.

association area A region of the cerebrum involved in memory and reasoning.

asthma Chronic inflammation and constriction of the respiratory passages.

astigmatism A visual disorder caused by an unequal curvature of the cornea or lens.

astrocyte A type of neuroglial cell joining blood vessels to neurons.

atherosclerosis A decrease in the lumen of an artery caused by fatty deposits in the vessel wall.

athlete's foot A fungal infection of the skin.

atmospheric pressure The pressure produced by the weight of the atmosphere.

atom The smallest unit of an element.

atomic number The number of protons in an atom of an element.

atomic weight The sum of the neutrons and protons in an atom of an element.

atrial natriuretic hormone Hormone secreted by atria of the heart that promotes excretion of water to reduce blood volume.

atrioventricular bundle (A-V bundle) Specialized muscle fibers carrying impulses from the A-V node to the Purkinje fibers; the bundle of His.

atrioventricular node (A-V node) A node of specialized tissue that receives impulses from the S-A node and transmits them to the A-V bundle.

atrioventricular valve (A-V valve) A valve that prevents a backflow of blood from a ventricle into an atrium.

atrium A heart chamber that receives blood returned to the heart by veins.

auditory Pertaining to the ear.

auditory tube A tube connecting the middle ear to the pharynx; the eustachian tube.

autoimmune disease A variety of diseases caused by the immune system attacking the body's own tissues.

autonomic ganglion A cluster of autonomic neuron cell bodies outside the central nervous system.

autonomic nervous system (ANS) The portion of the nervous system that functions involuntarily in the control of internal organs.

axial Pertaining to the longitudinal axis of the body.

axial skeleton The portion of the skeleton that supports and protects the head, neck, and trunk.

axon A neuron process that carries impulses away from the cell body or dendrites.

B lymphocyte A lymphocyte that produces antibodies; a B cell.

base A substance that ionizes in water, releasing hydroxyl ions (OH–).

basement membrane A thin layer of noncellular material attaching epithelial tissue to underlying connective tissue.

basilar membrane The membrane supporting the spiral organ.

basophil A granulocytic leukocyte with large blue cytoplasmic granules.

bedsores Skin ulcers caused by a deficient blood supply to localized areas.

benign tumor A tumor that does not spread to another site.

bicuspid (mitral) valve The atrioventricular valve between the left atrium and left ventricle; the mitral valve.

bile Fluid secreted by the liver and stored in the gallbladder.

bilirubin A bile pigment formed by the breakdown of hemoglobin.

bipolar neuron A neuron with only one dendrite and one axon.

blastocyst A preembryonic stage of development consisting of a hollow ball of cells.

blood The specialized connective tissue that transports substances to and from cells.

boil A bacterial infection of a hair follicle and its sebaceous gland.

bone The hardest and most rigid connective tissue whose matrix consists of calcium salts.

botulism Food poisoning caused by the bacterium *Clostridium botulinum.*

brachial Pertaining to the arm.

brain stem The portion of the brain including the midbrain, pons, and medulla oblongata.

Broca's area The portion of the frontal lobe of the cerebrum that coordinates muscles involved in speech.

bronchial tree The bronchi and their branches.

bronchiole A small branch of a bronchus.

bronchitis Inflammation of the bronchi.

bronchus A large branch from the trachea that carries air to and from a lung.

buffer A substance that stabilizes the pH of body fluids by combining with or releasing hydrogen ions.

bulbourethral glands Male accessory reproductive glands that secrete an alkaline secretion into the urethra.

bursa A fluid-filled sac in or near a joint that reduces friction during movement.

bursitis Inflammation of a bursa.

calcitonin The thyroid hormone that helps regulate the calcium level of the blood.

callus Thickened layers of epidermis caused by chronic friction.

calyx A funnel-like receptacle receiving urine from a renal pyramid's papilla.

canaliculi Microscopic canals between lacunae in bone.

cancellous bone Spongy bone; bone formed of a network of bony plates leaving numerous spaces between them.

cancer A malignant tumor; a tumor that can spread to other sites.

capillary A microscopic blood vessel extending between an arteriole and a venule.

carbaminohemoglobin (HbCo$_2$) A compound formed by the combination of carbon dioxide and hemoglobin.

carbohydrate An organic compound composed of carbon, hydrogen, and oxygen with a 2:1 ratio of hydrogen atoms to oxygen atoms.

carbonic anhydrase An enzyme in RBCs that catalyzes the combination of carbon dioxide and water to form carbonic acid.

cardiac Pertaining to the heart.

cardiac conduction system Specialized fibers that transmit impulses from the S-A node to the myocardium.

cardiac control center The center in the medulla oblongata controlling the heart rate.

cardiac cycle A single heartbeat composed of systole and diastole.

cardiac muscle tissue The muscle in the wall of the heart.

cardiac output The quantity of blood pumped from the heart in one minute.

carotene A yellowish pigment that occurs in the skin; a precursor of vitamin A in plant foods.

carpus The wrist; collective term for the wrist bones.

carrier protein A protein that carries a specific molecule through a plasma membrane in active transport.

cartilage A type of connective tissue characterized by a semisolid matrix and cartilage cells located within lacunae.

catabolism A metabolic process that breaks down large molecules into smaller ones.

cataract A vision disorder in which the lens of the eye becomes clouded.

cecum The pouchlike first portion of the large intestine.

cell The primary structural and functional unit of the body.

cell body The portion of a neuron that contains the nucleus.

cell cycle The stages through which a cell passes from formation through cell division.

cell division The division of a parent cell to form new daughter cells.

cell-mediated immunity Immunity that is characterized by a direct attack on pathogens by T lymphocytes.

cellular respiration The process that releases energy from nutrients to form ATP.

cementum The hard substance that attaches a tooth to the periodontal membrane.

central nervous system (CNS) The portion of the nervous system formed of the brain and spinal cord.

centriole A cytoplasmic organelle involved in the formation of the spindle during cell division.

centromere The portion of a chromosome that is attached to a spindle fiber during cell division.

cephalic Pertaining to the head.

cerebellum The part of the brain that coordinates body movements.

cerebral cortex The outer layer of the cerebrum that is composed of gray matter.

cerebral hemispheres The two major parts of the cerebrum that are separated by the longitudinal fissure.

cerebral palsy A motor disorder caused by brain damage, resulting in uncontrolled muscular contractions.

cerebrospinal fluid The fluid filling the ventricles of the brain and the subarachnoid space of the meninges.

cerebrovascular accident (CVA) A stroke; brain impairment caused by aneurysm, hemorrhage, embolism, or thrombus.

cerebrum The portion of the brain involved in conscious action, sensory perception, memory, and intelligence.

ceruminous gland A gland that produces cerumen (wax).

cervical Pertaining to the neck or to the cervix of the uterus.

cervix The narrow end of the uterus that opens into the vagina.

chemical bond A bond that joins two atoms together.

chemical compound A substance composed of two or more elements chemically combined.

chemical element A substance that cannot be broken down into a simpler substance by chemical means.

chemical formula A shorthand designation of the kinds and numbers of atoms in a molecule.

chemoreceptor A receptor that forms impulses when stimulated by certain substances.

chief cell A cell of a gastric gland that secretes digestive enzymes.

cholecystokinin A hormone secreted by the mucosa of the small intestine that stimulates secretion of pancreatic juice and contraction of the gallbladder.

cholinergic fiber A neuron axon that releases the acetylcholine at its tip.

cholinesterase An enzyme promoting the breakdown of acetylcholine in synapses.

chondrocyte A cartilage cell.

chordae tendineae Cords of connective tissue that anchor A-V valve cusps to papillary muscles.

chorion The outermost extraembryonic membrane derived from the blastocyst wall and forming part of the placenta.

chorionic gonadotropin The placental hormone that maintains the secretion of estrogen and progesterone during pregnancy.

chorionic villi Fingerlike projections of the chorion that penetrate into the endometrium.

choroid coat The middle, pigmented vascular layer of the eyeball.

choroid plexus A specialized mass of capillaries in the ventricles of the brain that secrete cerebrospinal fluid.

chromatid One-half of a replicated chromosome.

chromatin granules Portions of extended, uncoiled chromosomes appearing as dark granules in a cell nucleus.

chromosome A rodlike, dark body appearing in the nucleus during cell division; composed of DNA and protein.

chronic obstructive pulmonary disease (COPD) A group of disorders in which the airflow to the lungs is obstructed.

chylomicron A microscopic droplet of fat coated with protein.

chyme The semiliquid mass that exits the stomach into the small intestine.

cilia Microscopic, hairlike projections from the free surface of ciliated epithelial cells.

ciliary body An enlarged ring of the choroid coat containing the ciliary muscles in the eye.

circumduction The movement of a body part in a circular path.

cirrhosis The destruction of liver tissue and its replacement with connective tissue.

citric acid cycle A series of chemical reactions in the aerobic phase of cellular respiration.

cleavage The early divisions of a zygote leading to the formation of a morula.

clitoris A small nodule of erectile tissue at the anterior junction of the labia minora.

clone A population of identical cells derived from a common ancestral cell.

coagulation The formation of a blood clot.

cochlea The coiled portion of the inner ear containing the receptors for hearing.

codon Three nucleotides of messenger RNA that code for a specific amino acid and that are complementary to both the three nucleotides of DNA and an anticodon of transfer RNA.

colitis Inflammation of the colon mucosa.

collagen A fibrous protein that provides strength to fibrous connective tissues.

collagenous fibers Fibers formed of collagen.

collecting ducts Microscopic tubules composing renal pyramids.

colon The major portion of the large intestine.

color blindness The inability to see certain colors or all colors.

coma A state of unconsciousness.

common bile duct A small tube that carries bile from the cystic duct into the duodenum.

common cold A virus-caused inflammation of air passages and associated structures.

compact bone Bone tissue formed of tightly packed osteons.

complement A group of plasma proteins that works with antibodies to destroy cells of pathogens.

concentration gradient The difference in the concentration of a substance at two different locations.

concussion A jarring of the brain caused by a blow to the head.

conductivity The ability of neurons to conduct impulses.

condyle A rounded process of a bone.

cones Receptors for color vision that are located in the retina.

congestive heart failure A disorder in which the heart is unable to pump out all of the blood it receives.

conjunctiva The mucous membrane lining the eyelids and covering the anterior surface of the eye.

conjunctivitis Inflammation of the conjunctiva.

connective tissue One of a group of supporting and protective tissues that includes cartilage, bone, fibrous tissues, and blood.

constipation Difficult defecation of hard, dry feces.

contraception Devices or procedures that prevent contact of sperm and egg in sexual intercourse.

contraction The shortening of a muscle in response to stimulation.

cornea The anterior transparent window in the outer layer of the eyeball.

coronary Pertaining to the heart.

corpus callosum A mass of neuron processes connecting the two cerebral hemispheres.

corpus luteum A ruptured ovarian follicle after ovulation.

cortex The outer layer of an organ.

cortisol A glucocorticoid hormone secreted by the adrenal cortex.

costal Pertaining to the ribs.

costal cartilages Cartilages attaching the ribs to the sternum or to other costal cartilages.

covalent bond A chemical bond between two atoms that is formed by the sharing of valence electrons.

coxal Pertaining to the hip.

cramp A sudden, continuous tetanic contraction.

cranial Pertaining to the cranium.

cranial cavity The cavity in which the brain resides.

cranial nerve A nerve that originates from the brain.

cranium The skull bones forming the cranial cavity and enveloping the brain.

creatine phosphate A compound in muscle tissue that temporarily holds additional energy for forming ATP.

creatinine A nitrogenous waste produced by muscle metabolism.

cretinism A congenital disorder due to a lack of thyroid hormone.

crista ampullaris A sense organ in the ampullae of semicircular canals that contains receptors for dynamic equilibrium.

crural Pertaining to the anterior surface of the leg.

cubital Pertaining to the elbow.

Cushing's syndrome A disorder due to the hypersecretion of glucocorticoids by the adrenal cortex.

cutaneous Pertaining to the skin.

cutaneous membrane The skin.

cystic duct The duct leading from the gallbladder to the common bile duct.

cyclic adenosine monophosphate (cAMP) The second messenger involved with most nonsteroid hormones.

cystitis Inflammation of the urinary bladder.

cytokinesis The division of the cytoplasm during telophase of cell division.

cytoplasm The semiliquid material located between the nucleus and plasma membrane of a cell.

cytosine A nitrogen base of nucleic acids that pairs with guanine.

cytotoxic T cell (Tc) A T lymphocyte that binds to cells with foreign antigens and injects chemicals to kill the cells.

deamination The removal of amine groups ($-NH_2$) from amino acids.

deciduous teeth The first set of teeth, which are lost and replaced by permanent teeth.

decomposition reaction The breakdown of complex molecules into simpler molecules.

defecation The expulsion of feces through the anus.

dehydration synthesis The combining of two molecules by the removal of a water molecule.

dendrite A neuron process that receives impulses from other neurons and sensory receptors.

dendritic (Langerhans) cell A type of white blood cell located within the epidermis.

dental caries Tooth decay.

dentin The hard substance that forms most of a tooth.

deoxyhemoglobin The molecule remaining after oxyhemoglobin has given up its oxygen.

deoxyribonucleic acid (DNA) The double-stranded nucleic acid forming the hereditary component of chromosomes.

depolarization The loss of unlike charges on each side of a membrane.

dermal papillae Conelike projections of the dermis at the dermis–epidermis border.

dermis The true skin located under the epidermis.

detrusor muscle The muscle in the wall of the urinary bladder.

diabetes insipidus A disorder caused by a deficiency of antidiuretic hormone.

diabetes mellitus A disorder caused by a deficiency of insulin.

diaphragm The sheetlike skeletal muscle separating the thoracic and abdominopelvic cavities.

diaphysis The shaft of a long bone.

diarrhea Production of watery feces.

diarthrosis A type of joint that is freely movable.

diastole The relaxation phase of the cardiac cycle.

diastolic blood pressure The blood pressure in systemic arteries during heart diastole.

diencephalon The portion of the brain containing the thalamus, hypothalamus, and pineal gland.

differentiation The process by which cells become specialized for various functions.

diffusion The passive movement of molecules from an area of higher concentration to an area of lower concentration.

digestion The mechanical and chemical process that breaks down food molecules into absorbable nutrient molecules.

dipeptide A molecule composed of two amino acids chemically combined.

disaccharide A molecule composed of two monosaccharides chemically combined.

dislocation Displacement of a bone forming a joint.

distal Farther from the origin of an extremity.

diuresis The excessive production of urine.

diverticulitis Inflammation of diverticula of the colon mucosa.

dopamine A neurotransmitter secreted by certain neurons in the brain.

dorsal cavity The body cavity composed of the cranial and spinal cavities.

dorsum Pertaining to the back; the posterior surface of the thorax.

ductus arteriosus A short artery that carries blood from the pulmonary trunk to the aorta in a fetal heart.

ductus venosus A short vein that carries blood from the umbilical vein to the inferior vena cava during fetal development.

duodenum The first portion of the small intestine.

dura mater The outermost membrane of the meninges.

dynamic equilibrium The maintenance of balance when the head and body are in motion.

dyslexia A reading disorder in which letters and words are reversed.

dysmenorrhea Painful menstrual periods.

ear ossicles Three tiny bones in the middle ear that transmit vibrations from the tympanic membrane to the inner ear.

eccrine glands Sweat glands that open on the surface of the epidermis.

eclampsia A disorder of pregnancy characterized by high blood pressure, edema, and possibly convulsions and coma.

ectoderm The outermost tissue of the blastodisk.

ectopic pregnancy A condition in which the embryo is implanted at a site other than the uterus.

eczema A skin disorder characterized by red, dry, scaling skin.

edema The swelling of tissues due to the excessive accumulation of interstitial fluid.

effector A muscle or gland that responds to neural stimulation.

efferent arteriole An arteriole carrying blood from a glomerulus.

eicosanoids A group of chemicals secreted by nonendocrine cells that function as intercellular messengers affecting the activity of nearby cells.

ejaculation The discharge of semen from the male urethra.

ejaculatory duct A short duct formed by the merger of the duct from a seminal vesicle and a vas deferens.

elastic fibers Protein fibers providing elasticity in certain connective tissues.

electrocardiogram A record of the electrical activity of the heart during a cardiac cycle.

electrolyte A substance that ionizes when dissolved in water.

electron A negatively charged particle that revolves around an atomic nucleus.

elephantiasis A disorder in which lymphatic vessels are plugged by an infestation of microscopic worms.

embolism The blockage of a blood vessel by a clot or gas bubble formed elsewhere and carried by blood to the site.

embryo The developmental stage from weeks 2 through 8 after fertilization.

embryonic stem cells Unspecialized cells capable of producing all types of specialized human cells.

emphysema A lung disorder in which alveolar walls rupture, reducing the respiratory surface.

enamel The hard outer layer of a tooth crown.

endocardium The inner lining of the heart chambers.

endochondral bone Bone that is first formed of hyaline cartilage, which is replaced by bone.

endochondral ossification The formation of bone tissue within a cartilage.

endocrine gland A gland that secretes hormones.

endocytosis The process by which a cell engulfs particles and liquids.

endoderm The innermost embryonic tissue of the blastodisk.

endolymph The fluid in the membranous labyrinth of the inner ear.

endometriosis The growth of endometrial tissue at sites other than in the uterus.

endometrium The inner lining of the uterus.

endoplasmic reticulum (ER) A network of membranous channels used to transport substances within a cell.

endosteum The epithelial lining of a medullary cavity.

endothelium The inner lining of the heart chambers and blood vessels.

enzyme A protein that aids and speeds up (catalyzes) a specific chemical reaction.

eosinophil A granulocytic leukocyte with red cytoplasmic granules.

ependymal cell A type of neuroglial cell that lines the ventricles of the brain.

epicardium Innermost pericardial membrane that adheres to the surface of the heart.

epicondyle A bony projection located above a condyle.

epidermis The stratified squamous epithelium covering the dermis; the outer layer of the skin.

epididymis The highly coiled tube that carries sperm from the seminiferous tubules to the vas deferens.

epigastric region The upper middle portion of the abdomen.

epiglottis A cartilaginous flap that closes over the larynx during swallowing.

epilepsy A neural disorder characterized by sudden lapses of consciousness and possible convulsions.

epinephrine A hormone secreted by the adrenal medulla in response to stress.

epiphyseal line The line of fusion between an epiphysis and diaphysis when bone growth in length is complete.

epiphyseal plate The plate or disk of hyaline cartilage located between an epiphysis and the diaphysis of a long bone.

epiphysis The enlarged end of a long bone.

epithelial tissue The body tissue that covers the free surfaces of organs and the body, and forms secretory portions of glands; epithelium.

erection The process by which erectile tissue engorges with blood.

erythroblastosis fetalis A fetal disorder caused by maternal antibodies attacking fetal Rh+ erythrocytes.

erythrocyte A red blood cell; RBC.

erythropoietin The hormone that stimulates erythrocyte production.

esophagus The portion of the alimentary canal carrying food from the pharynx to the stomach.

essential amino acids Amino acids that must be obtained in food because they cannot be synthesized by the body.

estrogen A female hormone secreted by the ovaries that promotes the development of primary and secondary sexual characteristics.

eversion The movement that turns the sole of the foot outward.

exchange reaction A reaction in which two reactants exchange components to form two different products.

excretion The removal of metabolic wastes and excessive substances from the body.

exocrine gland A gland whose secretion is carried to a specific site by a duct.

exocytosis The process by which a cell rids itself of unwanted particles and liquids.

exophthalmic goiter An endocrine disorder caused by an excessive secretion of thyroid hormone.

expiration The exhalation of air from the lungs.

extension A movement that increases the angle between two body parts forming the joint.

external Pertaining to the surface of the body.

external auditory canal A canal in the temporal bone that leads from the exterior to the middle ear.

external respiration The exchange of oxygen and carbon dioxide between air in the lungs and the blood.

extracellular Pertaining to regions external to cells.

extremity An arm or leg.

extrinsic eye muscles Muscles that move the eyeball.

facet A small, flat surface of a bone that is an articulation site for another bone.

farsightedness A visual disorder in which the image is focused posterior to the retina.

fascia Fibrous connective tissue supporting, covering, and separating muscles.

fat A triglyceride; adipose tissue.

fatigue The lack of response to stimulation by muscle or nerve cells.

fatty acid An organic molecule that forms part of a triglyceride.

feces Material discharged from the anus in defecation.

fertilization Union of sperm and egg nuclei.

fetus The human developmental stage from the ninth week to birth.

fever A higher-than-normal body temperature.

fever blister A cold sore; small vesicles on the lips caused by a *Herpes* virus infection.

fibril A microscopic filament.

fibrin The insoluble protein filaments that form a blood clot.

fibrinogen A soluble plasma protein converted into insoluble fibrin during blood clot formation.

fibroblast A connective tissue cell that forms intercellular protein fibers.

fibrosis The replacement of muscle tissue with fibrous connective tissue.

fibrositis Inflammation of connective tissue.

filtrate The substances removed by filtration.

filtration The forcing of water and solutes through a plasma membrane by hydrostatic pressure.

fissure A long, narrow cleft separating two parts.

flagellum A long, hairlike extension from a cell.

flexion Movement at a joint causing the angle of the bones forming the joint to be decreased.

follicle A cavity or saclike depression.

follicle-stimulating hormone (FSH) A hormone secreted by the anterior pituitary gland that stimulates development of ovarian follicles in females and sperm production in males.

follicular cells Cells that surround a developing oocyte.

fontanel Membranous regions between cranial bones of an infant.

foramen A small canal or passageway in a bone or membrane.

foramen ovale The opening between the atria in a fetal heart.

formed elements The cellular components of blood; blood cells and platelets.

fossa A depression in a bone or organ.

fovea centralis A small depression in the retina that contains only densely packed cones.

fracture A broken bone.

free nerve endings Unattached axon tips that serve as pain receptors.

frontal plane A plane dividing the body or organ into anterior and posterior portions; a coronal plane.

gallbladder A small sac that temporarily stores bile.

gallstones Concretions of cholesterol and salts in the gallbladder.

gamete A sex cell; a sperm or ovum.

ganglion A mass of neuron cell bodies outside the central nervous system.

gastric gland A gland of the stomach mucosa that secretes gastric juice.

gastric juice The secretion of gastric glands containing HCl and digestive enzymes.

gastrin A hormone secreted by the stomach mucosa that stimulates the secretion of gastric juice.

gene A determiner of a hereditary trait.

genotype The genetic composition of an individual.

germinal epithelium Specialized epithelium in ovaries and testes that produces sex cells.

germ layers Three cell layers of the blastodisk that form all tissues during embryonic development.

gigantism An endocrine disorder caused by excessive secretion of growth hormone prior to the formation of epiphyseal lines.

gland A cell or group of cells that produces a secretion.

glaucoma An eye disorder caused by excessive intraocular pressure that damages the retina.

globulin A type of plasma protein.

glomerular (Bowman's) capsule A glomerular capsule enclosing a glomerulus.

glomerular filtration The forcing of water and small solutes from the blood in a glomerulus into a glomerular capsule.

glomerulonephritis Inflammation of the kidney involving the glomeruli.

glomerulus A ball-like mass of capillaries located within a glomerular capsule of a nephron.

glottis The narrow opening between the true vocal cords.

glucagon The pancreatic hormone that promotes the formation of glucose from glycogen.

glucocorticoid A group of hormones secreted by the adrenal medulla that influences glucose metabolism.

glucose The monosaccharide that is the primary energy source for cells.

glycerol An organic compound that is the backbone of triglyceride and phospholipid molecules.

glycogen The polysaccharide that is the storage form for carbohydrates in the body.

goblet cell A mucus-producing epithelial cell.

Golgi complex A cellular organelle that packages substances for secretion from the cell.

gonad A primary sex gland; an ovary or testis.

gonadotropin A hormone from the anterior pituitary that stimulates activity of the gonads.

gonadotropin-releasing hormone (GnRH) Hormone secreted by the hypothalamus that activates the release of gonadotropic hormones from the anterior pituitary gland.

granulocyte A leukocyte containing cytoplasmic granules.

gray matter The portion of the central nervous system lacking myelin.

groin The anterior body region at the junction of a thigh and pelvis.

growth The enlargement of the body or a body part.

growth hormone (GH) The hormone of the anterior pituitary that promotes cell division and cell enlargement.

guanine A nitrogen base of nucleic acids that pairs with cytosine.

hair cells Sensory receptors for hearing and equilibrium.

hair follicle The tubelike structure in which a hair develops.

head An enlargement on the end of a bone.

heart murmur An abnormal heart sound usually caused by a leaking valve.

heart rate The number of heart contractions (beats) per minute.

helper T cell (T_H) A T lymphocyte that initiates immune responses after binding to a foreign antigen on an APC.

hematopoiesis The formation of blood cells.

hemocytoblasts Stem cells in red bone marrow from which erythrocytes, leukocytes, and platelets develop.

hemoglobin The red pigment of erythrocytes that transports oxygen.

hemophilia A disorder in which clot formation is impaired.

hemopoiesis The formation of new blood cells.

hemorrhage Bleeding; excessive blood loss.

hemorrhoids Swollen, inflamed veins of the anal canal.

hemostasis The stoppage of bleeding.

hepatic Pertaining to the liver.

hepatic lobules The structural and functional units of the liver.

hepatitis Inflammation of the liver.

herniated disk A bulging intervertebral disk.

heterozygous A condition in which the paired alleles controlling a trait are different.

hives An itching rash resulting from an allergic reaction.

homeostasis The maintenance of a dynamically stable internal environment.

homozygous A condition in which the paired alleles controlling a trait are identical.

hormone A chemical secreted by an endocrine gland that affects the functions of target tissues.

human chorionic gonadotropin (HCG) An LH-like hormone secreted by the trophoblast of the blastocyst that maintains the corpus luteum.

hydrogen bond A weak bond between a positively charged hydrogen atom and a negatively charged atom in the same or different molecule.

hydrogen ion H^+; a single proton.

hydrolysis The breakdown of complex molecules into simpler molecules by the addition of water molecules.

hydroxide ion OH^-.

hymen A membrane that partially covers the vaginal opening.

hyperglycemia An excessive concentration of glucose in the blood.

hypersecretion Production of an excessive amount of a secretion.

hypertension Chronic high blood pressure.

hypertonic solution A solution with a greater concentration of solutes than the solution with which it is compared.

hypochondriac region Either the left or right upper lateral portion of the abdomen lying lateral to the epigastric region.

hypodermis The loose connective tissue located just under the skin.

hypogastric The lower middle region of the abdomen.

hypoglycemia A deficient concentration of glucose in the blood.

hypophysis The pituitary gland.

hypopituitary dwarfism Abnormal growth caused by a deficiency of growth hormone from the anterior pituitary.

hyposecretion Production of an insufficient amount of secretion.

hypothalamus The part of the brain lying below the thalamus and to which the hypophysis (pituitary) is attached.

hypotonic solution A solution with a lesser concentration of solutes than the solution with which it is compared.

iliac region Either the left or right lower abdominal portion lying lateral to the hypogastric region.

immunity Resistance to specific disease-producing antigens.

immunoglobulin Plasma proteins consisting of antibodies.

impetigo A highly contagious bacterial infection of the skin characterized by pustules that rupture and become crusted.

implantation The embedding of an embryo in the endometrium.

impotence The inability of a male to obtain and maintain an erection for sexual intercourse.

impulse A depolarization wave passing along a neuron process.

infectious mononucleosis A viral infection of lymphocytes that causes them to resemble monocytes.

inferior vena cava Large vein that returns blood to the right atrium from regions inferior to the heart.

infertility In females, the inability to conceive; in males, the inability to produce sperm to achieve fertilization of the ovum.

inflammation A tissue response characterized by increased blood flow, redness, and fluid accumulation.

inflammatory bowel disease (IBD) A group of chronic disorders characterized by inflamed intestines and intestinal cramps resulting from an overactive immune system.

influenza A virus-caused disorder with coldlike symptoms.

inhibin A hormone produced by ovaries and testes that inhibits secretion of FSH.

inorganic compounds Compounds whose molecules do not contain both carbon and hydrogen.

insertion The movable attachment of a muscle.

inspiration Inhalation; breathing air into the lungs.

insulin The pancreatic hormone that helps glucose to enter body cells.

integument The skin.

interatrial septum Septum separating the left and right atria of the heart.

intercalated disk A dark-staining membrane at the junction of adjoining cardiac muscle cells.

intercellular Pertaining to the spaces between cells.

internal Pertaining to the interior of the body or organ.

internal respiration The exchange of oxygen and carbon dioxide between the blood and tissue cells.

interneuron A neuron of a neural pathway that is located between sensory and motor neurons.

interphase The nondividing phase between two cell divisions.

interstitial cell A cell located between seminiferous tubules that secretes testosterone.

interstitial fluid Intercellular fluid; tissue fluid.

interventricular septum Septum separating the left and right ventricles of the heart.

intervertebral disk The fibrocartilaginous pad separating two adjacent vertebrae.

intestinal gland A gland of the mucosa of the small intestine that secretes intestinal juice.

intestinal juice The secretion of intestinal glands.

intracellular Pertaining to within cells.

intramembranous bone Bone that develops within layers of membranes.

intramembranous ossification The formation of bone tissue within a fibrous membrane.

intrinsic factor A substance secreted by gastric glands that is essential for adequate absorption of vitamin B_{12}.

inversion The movement that turns the sole of the foot inward.

involuntary Without conscious control.

ion An atom or group of atoms with an electrical charge.

ionic bond A chemical bond formed between two ions with opposing electrical charges.

ionization The dissociation of molecules forming ions.

iris The colored circular muscle that controls the amount of light entering the lens of the eye.

irritability The ability of a neuron to respond to a stimulus by forming an impulse.

isotonic solution A solution with the same concentration of solutes as a solution with which it is compared.

isotope An atom with a different number of neutrons than most atoms of the element.

joint An articulation; the junction of two or more bones.

juxtaglomerular apparatus Specialized cells of the afferent arteriole and distal tubule that are involved in controlling glomerular blood pressure.

keratin A waterproofing protein formed in the epidermis, nails, and hair.

keratinization The process by which cells form large amounts of keratin.

labia majora The outer folds of the vulva.

labia minora The inner folds of the vulva.

labor The series of events associated with childbirth.

labyrinth The interconnecting tubes and chambers of the inner ear.

labyrinthine disease A group of inner ear disorders that produce symptoms of dizziness and nausea.

lacrimal apparatus Structures involved in the production and removal of tears.

lacrimal gland A gland that secretes tears.

lactase The enzyme that catalyzes the digestion of lactose into glucose and galactose.

lactation Milk secretion.

lacteal A lymphatic capillary within a villus of the small intestine.

lactic acid An organic by-product formed from pyruvic acid during anaerobic cellular respiration.

lacuna A cavity in bone or cartilage.

lamellae Layers of solid bone matrix in compact bone.

laryngitis Inflammation of the larynx.

larynx The cartilaginous boxlike structure located between the pharynx and trachea that contains the vocal folds.

lateral Pertaining to the side.

lens The structure that focuses images on the retina of the eye.

leukemia A cancerous blood disorder characterized by an excess production of certain leukocytes.

leukocyte A white blood cell; WBC.

leukotrienes Secretions by cells that promote inflammation in nearby cells.

ligament A fibrous cord or sheet attaching bones to each other.

limbic system The portion of the cerebrum and diencephalon involved in emotions and moods.

lingual Pertaining to the tongue.

lipase The enzyme that catalyzes the digestion of lipids.

lipid A class of organic compounds that includes steroids, triglycerides, and phospholipids.

liver The digestive gland that secretes bile and processes absorbed nutrients prior to their entrance into the general circulation.

longitudinal fissure The deep fissure that separates the left and right cerebral hemispheres.

lumbar Pertaining to the posterior trunk region between the ribs and hips.

lumen The space within a tubular structure.

lungs The respiratory organs for gas exchange.

luteinizing hormone The anterior pituitary hormone that controls the functions of the corpus luteum in females and testosterone secretion in males.

lymph Interstitial fluid that has entered a lymphatic vessel.

lymph node A small mass of lymphoid tissue along a lymphatic vessel that filters lymph as it passes through.

lymphatic vessel A vessel transporting lymph.

lymphocyte A type of white blood cell that is involved in immune reactions.

lymphokine A chemical secreted by helper T cells that stimulates the division of B cells to form a clone.

lymphoma A cancer of lymphatic tissue.

lysis Rupture of a cell due to a rapid uptake of water.

lysosome A cellular organelle consisting of a sac of digestive enzymes.

macrophage A modified monocyte that has entered tissue spaces and is involved in phagocytosis and immune reactions.

macula Sense organs of the inner ear that contain receptors for static equilibrium.

macula lutea The yellow spot on the retina containing the fovea centralis.

malignant tumor A tumor with the capability of spreading (metastasizing) to other sites; a cancer.

maltase The enzyme that catalyzes the digestion of maltose into glucose and fructose.

mammary gland A milk-producing gland located within a female breast.

marrow Connective tissue filling spaces in bone.

mast cell A modified basophil in tissue spaces that releases histamine and serotonin in allergic reactions.

mastication The chewing of food.

matrix The intercellular substance in connective tissues.

matter Anything that has weight (mass) and occupies space.

maximal stimulus A stimulus producing a maximum response by a muscle.

mechanoreceptor A sensory receptor that is sensitive to mechanical stimuli.

medial Toward the midline.

medial plane A plane that divides the body or an organ into equal left and right halves.

mediastinum Connective tissue separating the thoracic cavity into left and right portions.

medulla The inner or central portion of an organ.

medulla oblongata The part of the brain stem that is continuous with the spinal cord.

medullary cavity The central cavity in the shaft of a long bone.

meiosis The process in meiotic cell division that reduces the number of chromosomes in daughter cells to one-half that of the parent cell.

meiotic cell division The type of cell division involved in the formation of sperm and eggs.

Meissner's corpuscle A sensory receptor for light touch located in the skin.

melanin The brown-black pigment found in the epidermis.

melanocyte A cell of the epidermis that produces melanin.

melatonin A hormone secreted by the pineal gland that influences reproductive cycles.

memory cell A dormant B or T lymphocyte produced in an initial immune response that can respond quickly if the same antigen reappears.

meninges A group of three membranes that envelops the brain and spinal cord.

meningitis Inflammation of the meninges.

menopause The cessation of menstrual cycles.

menstrual cycle The monthly female reproductive cycle characterized by the buildup, breakdown, and discharge of the uterine lining.

menstruation The breakdown and discharge of the uterine lining.

mental illness A group of disorders characterized by abnormal behaviors.

mesentery A fold of the peritoneum that supports internal abdominal organs.

mesoderm The middle embryonic tissue of the blastodisk.

messenger RNA (mRNA) The type of RNA that carries information for protein synthesis from DNA to the ribosomes.

metabolism The sum of the chemical reactions of life.

metaphase The phase of cell division characterized by the chromosomes arranged along the equator of the cell.

microfilament A microscopic protein strand within cells that is part of the cytoskeleton.

microglial cell A type of neuroglial cell that supports neurons and is involved in phagocytosis.

microtubule A microscopic tubule of protein within cells that is part of the cytoskeleton.

microvilli Microscopic projections of the plasma membrane on the free surfaces of certain epithelial cells.

micturition Urination.

midbrain The small region of the brain that is located between the thalamus and pons.

mineralocorticoids A group of hormones secreted by the adrenal cortex that influence the concentration of electrolytes in body fluids.

miscarriage A spontaneous abortion.

mitochondrion A cellular organelle that is the site of aerobic cellular respiration.

mitosis The process in mitotic cell division that distributes replicated chromosomes so that daughter cells receive the same number of chromosomes as the parent cell.

mitotic cell division The process of cell division that produces daughter cells identical to the parent cell; is involved in growth and repair of the body tissues.

mixed nerve A nerve consisting of both sensory and motor fibers.

mole A slow-growing, pigmented skin tumor.

molecule Two or more atoms chemically combined; the smallest unit of a compound.

monocyte A large agranulocytic leukocyte that functions in phagocytosis.

monosaccharide A simple sugar; a structural unit of carbohydrates.

morning sickness A temporary disorder of pregnancy characterized by nausea upon arising.

motor area The region of the cerebrum that initiates actions of muscles and glands.

motor division Portion of the nervous system carrying impulses from the CNS to muscles and glands.

motor nerve A nerve that consists only of axons of motor neurons.

motor neuron A neuron that activates a muscle or gland.

motor unit A single motor neuron and the muscle fibers that it controls.

mucosa A mucous membrane such as the lining of the alimentary canal.

mucous membrane A membrane lining tubes or cavities that open outside of the body.

mucus Thick fluid produced by goblet cells.

multiple sclerosis A disorder characterized by the degeneration of the myelin sheath surrounding neurons in the central nervous system.

multipolar neuron A neuron with several dendrites and one axon.

muscle fiber A muscle cell.

muscle tissue The type of body tissue that is specialized for contraction.

muscle tone A state of partial contraction.

muscular dystrophy A disorder characterized by the atrophy of muscles.

mutation A spontaneous change in a gene.

myasthenia gravis A disorder characterized by severe muscular weakness.

myelin sheath The fatty, insulating sheath formed around some nerve fibers.

myocardial infarction Death of a portion of the myocardium due to blockage of a coronary artery; a heart attack.

myocardium The muscle layer of the heart wall.

myofibril A thin contractile element within a muscle cell.

myofilament Contractile filament within a myofibril; composed of either actin or myosin.

myoglobin A compound in muscles that temporarily stores a small amount of oxygen.

myosin myofilament A protein that interacts with actin to produce contraction of a myofibril.

myositis Inflammation of a muscle.

myxedema An adult disorder caused by a lack of thyroid hormone.

nasal cavity The interior cavity of the nose.

nasal septum The partition of bone separating the nasal cavity into left and right portions.

nearsightedness A vision disorder in which the image is focused in front of the retina.

negative-feedback mechanism A control mechanism in which an increase in the concentration of a substance inhibits the production of that substance.

neonatal Pertaining to a newborn infant; the period from birth to the end of the first month.

nephron The functional unit of a kidney; composed of a renal corpuscle and tubule.

nerve A bundle of nerve fibers (neuron processes).

nerve impulse A depolarization wave passing along a nerve fiber.

nerve tissue Tissue specialized for the formation and conduction of nerve impulses.

nerve tract Myelinated ascending and descending bundles of nerve fibers in the central nervous system.

neuralgia Pain in a nerve.

neurilemma The outer sheath of a Schwann cell enveloping a nerve fiber.

neuritis Inflammation of a nerve.

neuroglia Tissue in the central nervous system that supports the neurons.

neuroglial cells Supportive and protective cells within the nervous system.

neuromuscular junction The junction of the axon tip of a motor neuron with a muscle fiber.

neuron A nerve cell.

neuropeptide A naturally occurring substance in the brain that modifies neural responses to neurotransmitters; enkephalins and endorphins.

neurotransmitter A chemical secreted by an axon tip that stimulates action of a muscle or gland, or the formation of an impulse in an adjoining neuron.

neutron A noncharged particle in an atomic nucleus.

neutrophil A phagocytic leukocyte with pale lavender cytoplasmic granules.

Nissl bodies Dark-staining membranous sacs in the cytoplasm of neurons comparable to the endoplasmic reticulum.

node of Ranvier A space between adjacent Schwann cells wrapped around a neuron process.

nonspecific resistance Resistance mechanisms that act against all types of pathogens.

norepinephrine A neurotransmitter released by axon tips of sympathetic neurons and secreted by the adrenal medulla.

nuclear envelope The double membrane surrounding the nucleus of a cell.

nucleic acid A compound whose molecules are composed of a series of nucleotides; either DNA or RNA.

nucleolus A dark-staining spherical structure within a cell nucleus that is composed of protein and rRNA.

nucleotide The building unit of nucleic acids; consists of a simple sugar, a phosphate group, and a nitrogen base.

nucleus The spherical cellular organelle containing the chromosomes; the core of an atom; or a mass of neuron cell bodies in the brain.

nutrient A substance in foods that is required for the normal nutrition of the body.

olfactory Pertaining to the sense of smell.

oligodendrocyte A type of neuroglial cell that supports neurons and forms myelin around some nerve fibers within the central nervous system.

oocyte An immature ovum (egg cell).

oogenesis The process of ovum formation.

oogonia The diploid stem cells in an ovary that become primary oocytes.

ophthalmic Pertaining to the eye.

optic Pertaining to the eye.

optic chiasma The X-shaped site on the interior surface of the brain formed by optic nerve fibers that partially cross over to the opposite side.

optic disk The blind spot; the site of retinal nerve fibers exiting the eye to form the optic nerve.

oral Pertaining to the mouth.

organ A structure formed of two or more tissues that performs specific functions.

organ system A group of organs that work in a coordinated fashion to carry out specialized functions.

organelle A distinct structure within a cell that performs specific functions.

organic compound Compounds containing both carbon and hydrogen in their molecules.

orgasm The culmination of sexual stimulation.

origin The nonmovable attachment of a muscle.

osmosis The diffusion of water through a selectively permeable membrane.

osseous tissue A hard connective tissue with a rigid matrix of calcium salts, bone.

ossification The process of bone formation.

osteoblast A cell that deposits bone matrix.

osteoclast A cell that removes bone matrix.

osteocyte A bone cell.

osteon The structural unit of compact bone consisting of lamellae and osteocytes around an osteonic canal.

osteonic (central) canal A microscopic canal in bone that contains blood vessels and nerves, and that is encompassed by lamellae.

osteoporosis A disorder in which bone matrix is reabsorbed, producing weakened bones.

otitis media A middle ear infection.

otolith A granule of calcium carbonate associated with receptors for equilibrium.

oval window The opening in the labyrinth of the inner ear into which the stapes is inserted.

ovarian Pertaining to an ovary.

ovarian cycle From puberty to menopause, the monthly formation and release of a secondary oocyte.

ovary The female gonad producing ova and female reproductive hormones.

ovulation The rupture of a mature ovarian follicle, releasing a secondary oocyte.

ovum A female reproductive cell; a female gamete.

oxygen debt The amount of oxygen necessary to metabolize lactic acid accumulated during anaerobic respiration.

oxyhemoglobin (HbO_2) The compound carrying oxygen to body cells.

oxytocin The posterior pituitary hormone that stimulates uterine contractions and milk ejection.

pain receptor A free nerve ending.

palate The roof of the mouth formed of the hard and soft palates.

palmar Pertaining to the palm of the hand.

pancreas An abdominal organ secreting both digestive secretions and hormones.

pancreatic duct The tube carrying pancreatic juice to the common bile duct.

pancreatic islets Clumps of pancreatic cells that secrete insulin.

papilla A small, nipplelike projection.

papillary muscle A projection of the myocardium to which chordae tendineae are attached.

paralysis A disorder in which a muscle is unable to contract.

paranasal sinus An air-filled cavity in a bone located near the nasal cavity.

parasympathetic division The part of the autonomic nervous system arising from the brain and sacral region of the spinal cord.

parathyroid glands Small endocrine glands embedded in the posterior surface of the thyroid gland.

parathyroid hormone The secretion of the parathyroid glands that helps regulate the concentrations of calcium and phosphate in the blood.

parietal Pertaining to the wall of a cavity.

parietal cell A type of cell in gastric glands that secretes hydrochloric acid and intrinsic factor.

parietal pericardium A membranous sac enclosing the heart.

parietal peritoneum The membrane lining the wall of the abdominal cavity.

parietal pleura A pleural membrane lining the interior of the thoracic cavity.

Parkinson's disease A neural disorder characterized by muscular weakness, tremor, and rigidity.

parotid glands The largest salivary glands located just anterior and inferior to the ears.

parturition The birth process.

passive immunity Immunity provided by an injection of antibodies that have been formed in another organism.

passive transport Movement of substances through plasma membranes without the expenditure of energy.

pathogen A disease-causing virus or organism.

pectoral Pertaining to the chest.

pectoral girdle The bones that attach the upper extremities to the trunk at the shoulder.

pelvic Pertaining to the pelvis.

pelvic cavity The inferior portion of the abdominopelvic cavity.

pelvic girdle The bones that attach the lower extremities to the trunk at the hips.

pelvic inflammatory disease Inflammation of the female reproductive organs and pelvic tissues.

pelvis The ring of bones formed by the os coxae and sacrum.

penis The external male reproductive organ containing the urethra.

pepsin An enzyme secreted by gastric glands that catalyzes the splitting of proteins.

peptic ulcers Digestion of part of the stomach mucosa.

peptidase The enzyme that catalyzes the digestion of peptides into amino acids.

peptide A compound composed of two or more amino acids.

peptide bond A bond that joins two amino acids.

pericardial Pertaining to the pericardium.

pericardial cavity The potential space between the epicardium and parietal pericardium.

pericarditis Inflammation of the pericardium.

pericardium Collective term for the three membranes enveloping the heart.

perichondrium The fibrous membrane surrounding a cartilage.

perilymph The fluid in the bony labyrinth of the inner ear.

perineum In males, the region between the anus and the scrotum; in females, the region between the anus and the vulva.

periodontal disease A disorder in which gums are inflamed and associated periodontal ligaments and bone degenerate.

periodontal ligament The fibrous membrane attaching a tooth to alveolar bone.

periosteum The fibrous membrane covering the surface of a bone.

peripheral nervous system (PNS) The part of the nervous system outside the central nervous system; the cranial and spinal nerves.

peripheral resistance Resistance of the flow of blood; friction between the blood and the walls of blood vessels.

peristalsis The wavelike contractions that move materials through tubular organs.

peritoneal cavity The potential space between the visceral and parietal peritoneal membranes.

peritoneum The serous membrane lining the abdominal cavity and covering internal abdominal organs.

peritonitis Inflammation of the peritoneum.

peritubular capillary The capillary network that surrounds a nephron tubule.

permeable Allowing the passage of materials.

pH A measure of the hydrogen ion concentration of a solution.

pH scale A scale that establishes the values of pH from 0 to 14.

phagocytosis The process by which cells engulf particles.

pharynx The throat; the cavity between the mouth and the esophagus or larynx.

phenotype The observable characteristics of an inherited trait.

phlebitis Inflammation of a vein.

phospholipid A molecule containing two fatty acids and a phosphate group attached to glycerol.

photoreceptor A receptor sensitive to light stimuli; a rod or cone.

physiological jaundice A disorder of newborn infants caused by the rapid destruction of fetal erythrocytes.

physiology The study of body functions.

pia mater The delicate, innermost membrane of the meninges.

pineal gland A small endocrine gland within the brain that is involved in biorhythms.

pinocytosis The process by which cells engulf liquids.

pituitary gland The endocrine gland attached to the hypothalamus; the hypophysis.

placenta The temporary organ attaching an embryo or fetus to the uterine wall.

plantar Pertaining to the sole of the foot.

plasma The liquid portion of the blood.

plasma cell An activated B lymphocyte that produces antibodies.

plasma membrane The membrane that separates a cell from its environment.

plasma protein One of several proteins dissolved in the plasma.

platelet A thrombocyte; a cell fragment formed in red bone marrow that contains enzymes initiating blood clot formation.

pleura The membrane lining the thoracic cavity and covering the lungs.

pleural Pertaining to the pleural membranes.

pleural cavity The potential space between the visceral and parietal pleurae.

pleural membranes The serous membranes that line the thoracic cavity and cover the surfaces of the lungs.

pleurisy Inflammation of the pleural membranes.

plexus A network of nerves or blood vessels.

pneumonia An acute inflammation of the alveoli caused by bacterial or viral infection.

polar body A small, nonfunctional cell formed during oogenesis.

polar molecule A molecule with positive or negative charges on its surface.

polarization The formation of an electrical charge on a plasma membrane due to unequal concentrations of ions on either side of the membrane.

poliomyelitis A viral disease in which motor neurons are destroyed, causing paralysis.

polycythemia A disorder in which there is an excessive number of erythrocytes.

polypeptide An organic compound formed of many amino acids.

polysaccharide An organic compound formed of many monosaccharide units.

pons The part of the brain stem located between the midbrain and the medulla oblongata.

popliteal The body region composed of the posterior portion of the knee.

positive-feedback mechanism A control mechanism in which an increase in the concentration of a substance stimulates an increase in the production of that substance.

posterior Toward the back; dorsal.

posterior cavity The cavity composed of cranial and spinal cavities; the dorsal cavity.

posterior root The posterior attachment of a spinal nerve to the spinal cord that contains sensory nerve fibers; a dorsal root.

postganglionic fiber Autonomic nerve fibers leading from an autonomic ganglion.

postnatal The period after birth; opposite, *prenatal*.

preganglionic fiber An autonomic nerve fiber leading to an autonomic ganglion.

pregnancy The female condition in which a developing baby is in the uterus.

premenstrual syndrome (PMS) A female disorder occurring just prior to menstruation characterized by pain and emotional stress.

prenatal The period from conception to birth; opposite, *postnatal*.

presbyopia The visual condition in which the near-point distance becomes greater with age.

pressure receptor A sensory receptor that is sensitive to pressure changes.

prime mover A muscle whose contraction is primarily responsible for a particular movement.

process A projection on a bone.

progesterone A female reproductive hormone secreted by the corpus luteum and the placenta that maintains the uterine lining.

projection The brain mechanism that makes a sensation seem to come from the body part being stimulated.

prolactin The anterior pituitary hormone that stimulates the production of milk by mammary glands.

pronation Turning the hand so the palm faces downward.

prophase The phase of mitosis in which the chromosomes coil, appearing as rodlike structures.

proprioceptor A sensory receptor in skeletal muscles and tendons sensitive to stretching and contraction.

prostaglandins A class of eicosanoids that promote a variety of effects in nearby cells.

prostate gland An accessory male reproductive gland that surrounds the base of the urethra.

protein A complex, nitrogen-containing organic compound whose molecules consist of many amino acids.

prothrombin An inactive plasma protein that is converted to thrombin in blood-clot formation.

prothrombin activator Substance released by platelets that converts prothrombin into thrombin.

proton A positively charged particle in an atomic nucleus.

protraction The movement of a body part anteriorly.

proximal Pertaining to nearer the origin of an extremity.

pseudostratified An arrangement of cells that appears layered but is not.

psoriasis A chronic skin disorder characterized by redness, itching, and excessive scaling.

puberty The developmental stage in which the reproductive organs mature and become functional.

pulmonary Pertaining to the lungs.

pulmonary circuit Blood vessels that carry blood from the heart to the lungs and back to the heart.

pulmonary semilunar valve The valve preventing a backflow of blood from the pulmonary trunk into the right ventricle.

pulmonary trunk Large artery that carries blood from the right ventricle and divides to form the pulmonary arteries.

pulse The expansion of an artery resulting from a surge of blood generated by ventricular contraction.

pupil The opening in the iris that allows light to pass through the lens to the retina.

Purkinje fibers Specialized cardiac muscle fibers that transmit the cardiac impulse from the A-V bundle to the myocardium.

pus A thick fluid composed of leukocytes and bacteria.

pyelonephritis Inflammation of the kidney involving the renal pelvis.

pyruvic acid An organic molecule formed by the breakdown of glucose in the anaerobic phase of cellular respiration.

receptor Portion of the peripheral nervous system that responds to certain stimuli by forming impulses.

receptor molecule A specialized protein on a plasma membrane to which a specific chemical attaches.

rectum The terminal portion of the large intestine.

red marrow Blood-forming tissue in the spaces of spongy bone.

referred pain Pain that seems to originate from a site that is different from the site being stimulated.

reflex A rapid response to a stimulus that occurs without voluntary action; an automatic response.

reflex arc The neuron pathway of a reflex; usually involves sensory neuron, interneuron, and motor neuron.

refraction The bending of light rays.

relaxin The hormone secreted by the placenta that softens the cervix and loosens the pubic symphysis.

renal Pertaining to a kidney.

renal calculi Kidney stones.

renal corpuscle The first portion of a nephron consisting of a glomerulus and a glomerular capsule.

renal cortex The outer layer of a kidney.

renal failure Reduction or cessation of urine formation by the kidneys.

renal medulla The interior portion of a kidney.

renal pelvis A cavity within a kidney that is continuous with a ureter.

renal tubule The tubular portion of a nephron.

renin The enzyme released by the juxtaglomerular apparatus that converts a plasma protein into angiotensin II.

renin–angiotensin mechanism A chemical control mechanism that regulates the blood pressure in glomeruli.

rennin A gastric enzyme that curdles milk proteins.

reproduction The process leading to the formation of offspring.

respiratory control center The areas in the pons and medulla oblongata that control breathing.

respiratory distress syndrome A disorder of newborn infants whose alveoli produce insufficient surfactant.

respiratory membrane Membrane formed of alveolar and capillary cells through which gas exchange occurs between air in lungs and blood in capillaries.

resting potential The polarized state of a muscle or neuron membrane.

reticular formation A neural network in the diencephalon, brain stem, and spinal cord that is connected to higher brain centers and arouses the cerebrum to wakefulness.

retina The inner layer of the eyeball that contains the photoreceptors.

retinoblastoma A cancer of immature retinal cells.

retraction The movement of a body part posteriorly.

rhinitis Inflammation of the nasal cavity.

ribonucleic acid (RNA) A single-stranded nucleic acid whose nucleotides contain ribose sugar.

ribosomal RNA (rRNA) The RNA composing ribosomes.

ribosome A tiny cellular organelle composed of protein and rRNA and serving as the site of protein synthesis.

rickets A disorder caused by a deficiency of vitamin D resulting in weakened bones due to insufficient deposition of calcium salts.

rod A photoreceptor associated with black-and-white vision.

rotation The turning of a body part on its longitudinal axis.

round window A membrane-covered opening between the middle ear and the labyrinth of the inner ear.

saccule A portion of the vestibule of the inner ear containing sensory receptors for static equilibrium.

sacral Pertaining to the sacrum.

sagittal plane A plane dividing the body or an organ into left and right portions.

saliva The secretion of salivary glands.

salivary glands Glands secreting saliva into the mouth.

sarcolemma The plasma membrane of a muscle cell.

sarcomere The contractional unit of a myofibril.

sarcoplasm The cytoplasm of a muscle cell.

sarcoplasmic reticulum The smooth endoplasmic reticulum of a muscle cell.

saturated fats Fat molecules whose fatty acids do not have double carbon–carbon bonds.

Schwann cell A neuroglial cell that forms the myelin sheath and neurilemma around fibers of peripheral nerves.

sciatica Neuralgia of a sciatic nerve.

sclera The fibrous outer layer of the eyeball; the white of the eye.

scrotum The external pouch containing the testes in males.

sebaceous gland An epithelial gland secreting sebum into a hair follicle.

sebum The oily secretion of a sebaceous gland.

second messenger An intracellular messenger activated by a nonsteroid hormone.

secretin A hormone secreted by the intestinal mucosa that stimulates the pancreas to secrete pancreatic juice.

selectively permeable membrane A membrane that allows some substances to pass through it while keeping out others.

semen The seminal fluid consisting of secretions from accessory reproductive glands and sperm.

semicircular canal A loop of the membranous labyrinth of the inner ear that contains receptors for dynamic equilibrium.

semilunar valve A valve located at the base of the aorta or pulmonary trunk.

seminal vesicles Accessory male reproductive organs whose secretions contribute to semen.

seminiferous tubule A tubule within which sperm are formed in a testis.

sensation Awareness as a result of the brain interpreting sensory impulses.

sensory adaptation The decrease in impulse formation as a receptor is subjected to continuous stimulation.

sensory area The portion of the cerebrum that interprets sensory impulses.

sensory division Portion of the nervous system carrying impulses from sensory receptors to the central nervous system.

sensory nerve A nerve composed of sensory neuron processes.

sensory neuron A neuron that carries sensory impulses from a receptor to the central nervous system.

septum A partition such as the interventricular septum.

serotonin A substance released by thrombocytes that constricts blood vessels.

serous fluid Fluid secreted by serous membranes.

serous membrane A membrane that lines enclosed body cavities.

serum The fluid remaining after blood has clotted.

sesamoid bone A small bone embedded in a tendon.

severe combined immunodeficiency (SCID) A group of disorders that result from a deficit or absence of both B and T lymphocytes.

sex hormones Estrogen and testosterone.

sexually transmitted diseases Various infections caused by bacteria or viruses transmitted via sexual intercourse.

shingles Inflammation of a peripheral nerve due to reactivation of the chickenpox virus.

simple epithelium Epithelium composed of a single layer of cells.

simple goiter Enlargement of the thyroid gland caused by a deficiency of iodine in the diet.

simple sugar A monosaccharide.

sinoatrial node (S-A node) Specialized tissue in the right atrium that initiates heart contractions; the pacemaker of the heart.

sinus An air-filled cavity in a bone.

sinusitis Inflammation of a sinus.

skeletal muscle tissue The type of muscle tissue that is attached to bones.

skull Bones of the cranium and face.

smooth muscle tissue The type of muscle tissue in the walls of hollow organs except the heart.

solute A substance dissolved in a solvent.

solution A fluid composed of solutes dissolved in a solvent.

solvent A fluid that can dissolve solutes.

somatic nervous system (SNS) The portion of the nervous system involved in voluntary responses.

spasm A sudden, involuntary contraction of a muscle.

sperm A male reproductive cell; a male gamete.

spermatid A haploid cell formed in spermatogenesis that matures to become a sperm cell.

spermatocyte A cell that is involved in the meiotic cell divisions of spermatogenesis.

spermatogenesis The process of sperm production.

spermatogonium A diploid cell that divides by mitosis to form primary spermatocytes.

sphincter A circular muscle that closes an opening of a tubular structure.

spinal Pertaining to the spinal cord.

spinal cord The portion of the central nervous system that occupies the vertebral canal.

spinal ganglion A small mass of sensory neuron cell bodies in the posterior root of a spinal nerve.

spinal nerve A nerve that branches from the spinal cord.

spinal plexus A network of spinal nerves in which nerve fibers are resorted before continuing on.

spindle A spool-shaped arrangement of spindle fibers formed during prophase of cell division.

spiral organ The sense organ in the inner ear that contains receptors for hearing.

spleen A large lymphatic organ located in the upper left quadrant of the abdomen.

spongy bone Cancellous bone; bone formed of thin interconnected plates with numerous spaces between them.

sprain An injury caused by the tearing of a ligament.

starch A common polysaccharide in foods derived from plants.

static equilibrium Maintenance of balance when the head and body are motionless.

steroid A group of lipids that includes sex hormones and cholesterol.

stimulus A change in the environment.

stomach The expanded portion of the alimentary canal that receives food from the esophagus.

strabismus The inability to focus both eyes simultaneously on the same object.

strain An injury caused by overuse or overstretching of a muscle.

stratified Layered.

stratum basale The innermost layer of the epidermis whose cells are involved in cell division.

stratum corneum The outermost layer of the epidermis composed of keratinized cells.

stroke volume The quantity of blood pumped from each ventricle of the heart during one contraction.

subarachnoid space The space under the arachnoid mater that is filled with cerebrospinal fluid.

subcutaneous Pertaining to under the skin.

submucosa Connective tissue under a mucous membrane.

substrate A substance acted upon by an enzyme.

sucrase The enzyme that catalyzes the digestion of sucrose into glucose and fructose.

sudoriferous gland A sweat gland.

superficial Near the surface of the body or organ.

superior Toward the head.

superior vena cava Large vein that returns blood to the right atrium from regions superior to the heart.

supination Turning the hand so the palm faces upward.

suppressor cell A type of T lymphocyte that inhibits the formation of antibodies.

surfactant A substance formed by alveoli that decreases the attraction between water molecules and makes it easier for alveoli to fill with air.

suture An immovable joint joining skull bones.

sympathetic division The portion of the autonomic nervous system arising from the thoracic and lumbar regions of the spinal cord.

symphysis A slightly movable joint formed by bones joined by fibrocartilage.

synapse The junction between an axon tip of one neuron and a dendrite or cell body of another neuron.

synaptic cleft The space between an axon tip and another neuron within a synapse.

synaptic knob The enlarged portion of an axon tip.

synaptic transmission The passage of an impulse from one neuron to another across a synapse.

synarthrosis An immovable joint.

synergist A muscle whose contraction helps the prime mover perform its action.

synovial fluid Fluid secreted by synovial membranes within a joint.

synovial membrane The membrane that lines the interior of freely movable joints.

synthesis reaction The combining of smaller molecules to form more complex molecules.

systemic circuit The blood vessels that carry blood from the heart to all parts of the body except the lungs and back to the heart.

systole The contraction phase of the cardiac cycle.

systolic blood pressure Arterial blood pressure during ventricular systole.

T lymphocyte A type of lymphocyte involved in cell-mediated immunity; a T cell.

target cell A specific tissue on which a hormone acts.

tarsus The ankle; bones forming the ankle.

taste bud An organ on the tongue containing receptors for taste.

telophase The final phase of cell division in which daughter nuclei and cells are formed.

tendon A band or cord of fibrous connective tissue that attaches a muscle to a bone.

testis A male gonad; the primary male reproductive gland that produces sperm and testosterone.

testosterone The male sex hormone.

tetanic contraction A sustained muscle contraction.

tetanus A potentially fatal disorder caused by a bacterial toxin; lockjaw.

tetany A continuous, maximal muscle contraction.

thalamus The portion of the brain forming the walls of the third ventricle inferior to the cerebrum.

thermoreceptor A sensory receptor sensitive to temperature changes.

thoracic Pertaining to the thorax.

thoracic cavity The portion of the anterior cavity located superior to the diaphragm.

threshold stimulus The minimal stimulus that produces formation of a nerve impulse.

thrombin The enzyme that converts fibrinogen into fibrin.

thrombocyte A cell fragment containing an enzyme that starts the formation of a blood clot; a platelet.

thrombosis A condition in which a blood clot blocks a blood vessel.

thrombus A blood clot.

thymine A nitrogen base found only in DNA that pairs with adenine.

thymosin The hormone secreted by the thymus.

thymus An endocrine gland located in the mediastinum above the heart.

thyroid gland A bilobed endocrine gland located just inferior to the larynx and anterior to the trachea.

thyroid hormone A hormone secreted by the thyroid that increases the rate of cellular metabolism.

thyroid-stimulating hormone (TSH) The anterior pituitary hormone that stimulates the secretion of thyroid hormone.

thyroxine (T_4) The primary thyroid hormone.

tissue A group of similar cells performing a similar function.

tissue macrophage system Wandering and fixed macrophages; formerly called the reticuloendothelial system.

tonsillitis Inflammation of the tonsils.

tonsils Masses of lymphoid tissue located around the opening to the pharynx.

toxic shock syndrome A female disorder caused by toxins released by bacteria growing in a tampon.

trachea The air passageway leading from the larynx to the bronchi; the windpipe.

transcription The rewriting of the DNA code into the codon sequence of messenger RNA.

transfer RNA (tRNA) A type of RNA that carries amino acids to a ribosome during protein synthesis.

translation The process in which the codons of mRNA place amino acids of a forming protein in a specific sequence.

transverse plane A plane that divides the body or organ into superior and inferior portions.

transverse (T) tubule system Invaginations of the sarcolemma into a muscle cell.

tremor Involuntary, repetitive weak contractions.

tricuspid valve The atrioventricular valve between the right atrium and right ventricle.

triglyceride A lipid molecule composed of three fatty acids attached to glycerol; a fat molecule.

triiodothyronine (T_3) The secondary thyroid hormone.

trochanter A large, broad process of a bone.

tropic hormone A hormone that stimulates an endocrine gland.

trypsin A pancreatic enzyme that catalyzes the breakdown of protein molecules.

tubal ligation A sterilization procedure in which the uterine tubes are cut and tied.

tubercle A small, rounded process of a bone.

tuberculosis Inflammation of the lungs caused by the bacterium *Mycobacterium tuberculosis*.

tuberosity A raised portion of a bone.

tubular reabsorption The movement of substances from the filtrate in a renal tubule into blood in the peritubular capillaries.

tubular secretion The movement of substances from blood in peritubular capillaries into the filtrate in a renal tubule.

tympanic membrane The thin membrane between the outer and inner ear; the eardrum.

umbilical cord The connecting link between the placenta and the developing embryo or fetus.

umbilical region The central abdominopelvic region surrounding the umbilicus.

unipolar neuron A neuron with a single process that divides into two branches extending in opposite directions.

unsaturated fats Fat molecule whose fatty acids have one or more double carbon–carbon bonds.

uracil A nitrogen base in RNA that pairs with adenine.

urea The nitrogenous waste formed by the liver as a result of protein metabolism.

ureter A narrow tube that carries urine from a kidney to the urinary bladder.

urethra A tube carrying urine from the urinary bladder to outside the body.

urethritis Inflammation of the urethra.

uric acid A nitrogenous waste produced from nucleic acid metabolism.

urinary bladder The hollow, muscular-walled organ that temporarily stores urine.

urine Waste and excessive substances removed from the blood by the kidneys and excreted from the body.

uterine Pertaining to the uterus.

uterine tube A tube extending from the uterus to an ovary; it carries female sex cells toward the uterus.

uterus The female organ that contains the embryo and fetus until birth; the womb.

utricle An enlarged portion of the membranous labyrinth of the inner ear containing receptors associated with static balance.

uvula The fleshy appendage that hangs down from the posterior margin of the soft palate.

vagina A tubular organ that extends from the vestibule of the vulva to the uterus.

valence shell An atom's outermost shell of electrons.

varicose veins Dilated, swollen veins whose valves are nonfunctional.

vas deferens A slender tube leading from an epididymis to the urethra in males.

vascular Pertaining to blood vessels.

vasectomy A sterilization procedure in which the vasa deferentia are cut and tied.

vasoconstriction The narrowing of a blood vessel.

vasodilation Expansion of the lumen of a blood vessel.

vasomotor center The portion of the medulla oblongata that controls the diameter of blood vessels.

vein A blood vessel that carries blood toward the heart.

ventral cavity The body cavity composed of the thoracic and abdominopelvic cavities.

ventricle A cavity, such as a pumping chamber of the heart or a fluid-filled space in the brain.

venule A small blood vessel that carries blood from a capillary to a vein.

vertebral canal The portion of the dorsal cavity that contains the spinal cord.

vesicle A fluid-filled, membranous sac in the cytoplasm of a cell.

vestibule The space between the labia minora.

villus A small, fingerlike projection of the intestinal mucosa.

visceral Pertaining to organs in the abdominal cavity.

visceral peritoneum The portion of the peritoneum that covers the surfaces of organs in the abdominal cavity.

visceral pleura The portion of a pleural membrane that covers the surface of a lung.

viscosity The resistance of a fluid to flow.

vitamin An organic nutrient other than a protein, lipid, or carbohydrate that is needed in small amounts from food for normal metabolism.

vitreous humor The gel-like substance filling the posterior cavity of an eye.

vocal cords Folds of tissue within the larynx that vibrate to produce sounds as air passes over them.

voluntary Consciously controlled.

vulva The external female reproductive structures surrounding the vaginal opening.

wart A skin tumor caused by a localized virus infection.

water balance The state of equilibrium between water intake and water output.

X-linked traits Traits determined by genes on the X chromosome.

yellow marrow Marrow filling the medullary cavity of a long bone.

yolk sac An extraembryonic membrane that forms embryonic blood cells.

zygote The cell formed by the union of sperm and ovum; a fertilized egg.

CREDITS

Chapter 1

Opener: © Fancy Photography/Veer RF; 1.3: © Terry Cockerham/Cynthia Alexander/Synapse Media Productions; 1.5: © McGraw-Hill Company, Inc., Joe DeGrandis, photographer; p. 10 (left): © Scott Camazine; p. 10 (right): © Photodisc RF

Chapter 2

Opener: © Fancy Photography/Veer RF; p. 29: © McGill University/CNRI/Phototake.com

Chapter 3

Opener: © Fancy Photography/Veer RF; 3.3b: © Stephen L. Wolfe; 3.4a: © Don Fawcett/Photo Researchers; 3.6a: © Bill Longcore/Photo Researchers; 3.7: © G. Murti/Photo Researchers; 3.8b: Courtesy American Lung Association; 3.9: © Manfred Kage/Peter Arnold/Photolibrary; 3.22b, 3.23b, 3.24b and 3.25b: © Ed Reschke

Chapter 4

Opener: © Fancy Photography/ Veer RF; 4.1 and 4.2: © Ed Reschke; 4.3: © Manfred Kage/Peter Arnold/ Photolibrary; 4.4: © Ed Reschke; 4.5: © Fred Hossler/Visuals Unlimited; 4.6, 4.7, 4.8, 4.9, 4.10, and 4.11: © Ed Reschke; 4.12: © McGraw-Hill Higher Education/Carol D. Jacobson, Ph.D., Dept. of Veterinary Anatomy, Iowa State University; 4.13b: © Victor B. Eichler, Ph.D.; 4.14: © Ed Reschke/ Peter Arnold/Photolibrary; 4.15: © Ed Reschke; 4.16: © Manfred Kage/Peter Arnold/Photolibrary; 4.17 and 4.18: © Ed Reschke

Chapter 5

Opener: © The McGraw-Hill Companies; 5.2: © Herve Conge/ISM/ Phototake.com; p. 87: © SPL/Photo Researchers

Chapter 6

Opener: © The McGraw-Hill Companies; 6.3: © BioPhoto Associates/Photo Researchers

Chapter 7

Opener: © The McGraw-Hill Companies

Chapter 8

Opener: © Image DJ/Alamy RF; 8.3: © Ed Reschke; 8.12: Courtesy Branislav Vidic; 8.16b: © Per H. Kjeldsen, University of Michigan

Chapter 9

Opener: © Image DJ/Alamy RF; 9.17a: © Brand X Pictures/Getty RF

Chapter 10

Opener: © Image DJ/Alamy RF

Chapter 11

Opener 11a: © Steve Cole/Getty RF; Opener 11b&c: © iStockphoto; Opener 11d © Science Photo Library/ Getty RF; 11.2: © Bill Longcore/Photo Researchers; p. 228: © Meckes/Ottawa/ Photo Researchers; 11.5, 11.6, 11.7, 11.8, and 11.9: © Victor Eroschenko; 11.12: © David M. Phillips/Visuals Unlimited

Chapter 12

Opener 12a: © Steve Cole/Getty RF; Opener 12b&c: © iStockphoto; Opener 12d: © Science Photo Library/ Getty RF; 12.25a: © Chuck Brown/ Photo Researchers; 12.25b: © Visuals Unlimited/Corbis

Chapter 13

Opener 13a: © Steve Cole/Getty RF; Opener 13b&c: © iStockphoto; Opener 13d: © Science Photo Library/Getty RF; 13.4: © McGraw-Hill Higher Education, Inc./Kent Van de Graaf, photographer; 13.7b: © The McGraw-Hill Companies, Inc./Al Telser, photographer

Chapter 14

Opener 14a: © Steve Cole/Getty RF; Opener 14b&c: © iStockphoto; Opener 14d: © Science Photo Library/ Getty RF; 14.5c: © Collection CNRI/ Phototake.com

Chapter 15

Opener 15a: © Steve Cole/Getty RF; Opener 15b&c: © iStockphoto; Opener 15d: © Science Photo Library/Getty RF

Chapter 16

Opener 16a: © Steve Cole/Getty RF; Opener 16b&c: © iStockphoto; Opener 16d: © Science Photo Library/ Getty RF

Chapter 17

Opener: © Brand X Pictures RF; 17.3a: © Biophoto Associates/ Photo Researchers; 17.5b: © David M. Phillips/Photo Researchers; 17.10: © Ed Reschke/Peter Arnold/ Photolibrary; 17.15a: © The McGraw-Hill Companies, Inc./Jill Braaten, photographer; 17.15b–d: © McGraw-Hill Companies, Inc., Bob Coyle photographer; 17.15e: © The McGraw-Hill Companies, Inc./Jill Braaten, photographer

Chapter 18

Opener: © Brand X Pictures RF; 18.1: Reprinted with permission from T. Tegner and D. Epel, "Sea Urchin Sperm: Eggs Interaction Studied with Scanning Electron Microscopie" in *Science*, 179 (16 Feb 1973) pp. 685–88. Copyright 1973 AAAS.; 18.9: © Scott Camazine/Phototake. com; 18.14: © Biophoto Associates/ Photo Researchers; 18.17: Courtesy Integrated Genetics; 18.18: Courtesy Colleen Weisz

Study Guide

p. 449: Courtesy Branislav Vidic

INDEX